Rock & Roll

An Introduction

Rock & Roll
An Introduction

3rd edition

Michael Campbell

 CENGAGE

Australia • Brazil • Mexico • Singapore • United Kingdom • United States

Rock and Roll: An Introduction, 3e
Michael Campbell

Product Director: Marta Lee-Perriard

Product Manager: Colin Grover

Product Assistant: Cindy Liu

Marketing Manager: Laura Kuhlman

Content Manager: Mary Ann Lidrbauch

Manager, Content Delivery: Andrea Wagner

IP Analyst: Ann Hoffman

IP Project Manager: Betsy Hathaway

Production Service: MPS Limited

Compositor: MPS Limited

Senior Designer: Sarah Cole

Text and Cover Designer: Sarah Cole

Cover Image: Alexander Rieber/EyeEm/Getty Images

For product information and technology assistance, contact us at Cengage Customer & Sales Support, 1-800-354-9706 or support.cengage.com.

For permission to use material from this text or product, submit all requests online at **www.cengage.com/permissions.**

Library of Congress Control Number: 2018944481

Book Only:
ISBN: 978-0-357-04274-8

Cengage
20 Channel Center Street
Boston, MA 02210
USA

Cengage is a leading provider of customized learning solutions with employees residing in nearly 40 different countries and sales in more than 125 countries around the world. Find your local representative at **www.cengage.com.**

Cengage products are represented in Canada by Nelson Education, Ltd.

To learn more about Cengage platforms and services, register or access your online learning solution, or purchase materials for your course, visit **www.cengage.com.**

Printed at CLDPC, USA, 10-19

TABLE OF CONTENTS

CHAPTER 11

Words, Melody, and Rock in the Early Seventies............................179

CHAPTER 12

Black Popular Music in the Early Seventies.....................................193

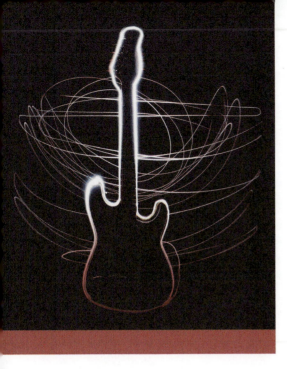

PREFACE

Hello! I'm Michael Campbell, the author of *Rock and Roll: An Introduction*. I'm an emeritus professor of music at Western Illinois University (I retired in 2003), and also the author of two other college texts, *Popular Music in America* and *MUSIC*. Since 2009, I have been an adjunct faculty member at Arizona State University, where I've been teaching a two-semester rock music survey from my home in Rhode Island. I'd like to take this opportunity to introduce myself to you, thank you for using my text, and tell you a little bit about what's in store for you.

What you're holding in your hands is a print companion to the MindTap version of *Rock and Roll: An Introduction 3e*. It's useful for those occasions when you simply want to read from a book rather than a mobile device or computer screen. However, for just about everything else, you may well prefer to use MindTap. For me as a user, it has been a big step up, and it should be for you as well. Here are some of the reasons:

- *It's convenient.* Everything is in one place: text, music, video, resources (including an aural glossary), organization—including your calendar, and assignments. Having almost everything to do with the course a click or two away really streamlines your workflow.
- *It's customized for your class.* Your instructor can modify MindTap so that it shows only what you need to see. The days of "read pages 15–22 in Chapter 2" are over.
- *It integrates multimedia.* For me—and I hope for you as well—this is the real breakthrough. It's made connecting the sounds—and at times, the look—of the music with the words that describe them easier and more meaningful.

My overarching objective as a teacher and author is to help students become more aware as listeners—for life. I've worked to create materials that hone your listening skills—not only in the music presented here, but also with any rock-related music that you listen to. This should in turn enable you to gain a better understanding of style and history in rock-era music.

I hope that you enjoy the book and encourage to discover these and other resources in MindTap.

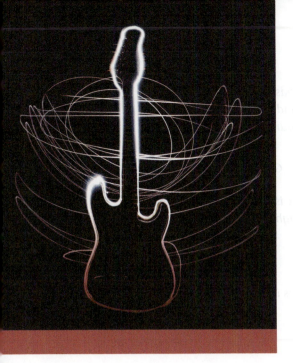

CHAPTER 1

INTRODUCTION: ROCK IS . . .

Learning Objectives:

1) Discuss the various definitions of the musical term "rock."

2) Explain the relationship between **beat**, **rhythm**, **measure**, and **tempo**.

3) Audibly identify an **eight-beat rhythm** in a musical example.

4) Compare and contrast **beat**, **backbeat**, and **syncopation**.

5) Describe the musical roles of the core instruments in a rock band.

6) List the musical form used in a core rock song.

Chapter Introduction

The 963rd issue of *Rolling Stone*, published December 9, 2004, features a list of the "500 Greatest Songs of All Time." "All Time" apparently refers to the rock era, as only one song on the list—by Hank Williams—predates 1950. And it also refers mainly to rock and rock-related music: no Barbra Streisand or Miles Davis. The number one song on the list was—almost inevitably—Bob Dylan's **"Like a Rolling Stone."** The order of the remaining 499 songs seems almost arbitrary, as if the distinguished group that assembled the list dumped all but Dylan's song into a tumbler and pulled the titles out without looking. Certainly, other critics have questioned the choice and ranking of songs on the list. And the list has the definite bias of rock's first generation; over three quarters of the tracks—and 44 out of the top 50—predate 1975. (See MINDTAP)

Despite what seem, in retrospect, serious lapses in judgment—no James Brown, for example—the top 50 songs on the list are a useful tool for addressing the question, "What is rock?" It can help us bring its center—the core features that most readily and emphatically define it—into focus and convey some sense of its range.

1–1 Rock Is . . .

The most brutal, ugly, desperate, vicious form of expression it has been my misfortune to hear.

Frank Sinatra

A type of sensuous music unfit for impressionable minds.

Tip O'neill, former Speaker of the House

A combination of good ideas dried up by fads, terrible junk, hideous failings in taste and judgment, gullibility and manipulation, moments of unbelievable clarity and invention, pleasure, fun, vulgarity, excess, novelty, and utter enervation.

Greil Marcus, noted rock critic

Dead. The attitude isn't dead, but the music is no longer vital. It doesn't have the same meaning. The attitude, though, is still very much alive—and it still informs other kinds of music.

David Byrne

Not so much a question of electric guitars as it is [of] striped pants.

David Lee Roth

To dress up to.

Frank Zappa

[A music that] can change things. I know that it changed our lives.

Bono

"a style of popular music that derives in part from blues and folk music and is marked by a heavily accented beat and a simple, repetitive phrase structure."

Before it is anything else, rock is music. Everything else that is part of its world—the attitudes it communicates, its cultural impact, the musicians from around the world who continue to produce it, and the comparably broad audiences who listen to it—grows out of this inescapable fact. From our twenty-first-century perspective, rock is a rich musical tradition over half a century old. In the deeply interwoven relationships among its numerous and disparate forms, it resembles an extended family that spans several generations and includes all of the in-laws. Rock can be vocal or instrumental, soft or loud, acoustic or electric, cobbled together in a garage or generated on a computer. It can stimulate your brain, touch your heart, and move your hips and feet.

Defining "rock" musically is a challenge because the term has several distinct, if interrelated, connotations. Four are briefly described below; each identifies an increasingly specific body of music.

1. **The music of the rock era.** This includes virtually all music from the fifties to the present that has some element of rock style. Early in the rock era, this included rock elements trickling in to established styles: pop rock, rock musicals, country rock, jazz rock. It has also included styles that were offshoots of it (e.g., reggae, disco, eighties pop).

2. **Music created or performed by rock musicians.** This includes not only rock but also music that may lack some or even all of the more prominent features of the core rock style: the Beatles' **"Michelle"** is a familiar example.

3. **Music by (mostly) white musicians.** Although Chuck Berry's music decisively differentiated rock and roll from rhythm and blues, and Jimi Hendrix set the bar for rock guitar playing, rock has been largely music performed by white musicians. Most of the rock-era music of black musicians, from fifties R&B to rap, is related to rock but discernibly different. Without question, there has been considerable intermingling between the two rock-era musical streams, but in the sixties, it was rock vs. soul, and now it's alternative or classic rock vs. hip hop.

4. **"Dictionary definition" rock:** the core rock style, undiluted and unfiltered.

We begin on our path to a broad understanding of what rock is with a discussion of the core rock style and how we describe it.

1-2 Talking About Rock: The Core Rock Style

In 2008, the Australian band AC/DC released *Black Ice*, their first since 2000. It fulfilled a pent-up demand for their music, as the album quickly went to the top of the charts in 29 countries. Among the tracks on the album was "**Rock 'n' Roll Train.**"

Please watch this video of AC/DC's "Rock 'n' Roll Train", then read this description of the introduction to the song: (See MINDTAP)

> AC/DC's "Rock 'n' Roll Train" begins with guitarist Angus Young playing a **syncopated** five-note **riff**. The sound of his guitar is loud and distorted. Each note of the riff is **harmonized** with a power chord. After a short pause, Young resumes with a longer statement that ends on a syncopation. As he repeats the riff and response, the rest of the band—Angus's brother Malcolm (guitar), bassist Cliff Williams, and drummer Phil Rudd—joins in. Malcolm and Williams reinforce the riff and response with lines that use the same rhythm, while Rudd lays down a **rock beat** with a loud bass drum thump on the first and third beats, a strong **backbeat**, and light marking of the 8-beat rhythm on a cymbal. With the rest of band playing, it's easier to determine the **tempo**, which is 119 beats per minute (bpm). All four repeat the riff and response two more times. As they do, they move in time to the beat. So does the crowd; for them, the song has a great beat.

Then watch the breakdown of the instrumental introduction and try to connect the words in bold with what you're hearing. (See MINDTAP)

The main objective of this exercise is to help you connect the sounds you hear to words that can describe them well enough that when you read a term that describes a musical feature, you can call to mind instances of the sounds that it represents. The materials that follow define these terms and highlight their use in "Rock 'n' Roll Train." We begin with the beat.

1-3 The Rhythms of Rock

By the mid-fifties, Jimmie Rodgers Snow, the son of country legend Hank Snow, seemed well on his way to country music stardom. He'd released a few singles on RCA, and he moved in the same circles as Elvis, Buddy Holly, and other legendary rock and roll stars. However, in a search for "lasting peace," he answered a calling to the ministry.

In one of his early sermons he preached with great fervor about the evils of rock and roll. Speaking directly from his personal experience, he tells the congregation that he knows how it feels to be drawn into the music. Then he asks rhetorically what it is about rock and roll that makes it so seductive to young people, and immediately answers his own question by shouting "The BEAT! The BEAT! The BEAT!" while pounding the pulpit in time to his words. Of course, he was right. It *was* the beat that drew teens to rock and roll during the fifties, and it has continued to draw listeners to rock ever since. The beat is at the heart of our experience not only of rock rhythm but also of rock music. It is the music's most compelling feature, as Snow so vigorously pointed out. Chances are that it would take a conscious

riff A short (two to seven pitches), rhythmically interesting melodic idea.

rock beat Eight evenly spaced sounds per measure (or two per beat) over a strong backbeat.

backbeat A percussive accent occurring regularly on the second beat of beat pairs: 1 2 1 2 or 1 2 3 4.

tempo The speed of the beat.

decision for you to resist tapping your foot, bobbing your head, or otherwise moving your body to "Rock 'n' Roll Train," as the audience did in the band's official video.

In this most meaningful way, we all know what the **beat** is—it is that aspect of the music that makes you want to move. This meaning of *beat* is much the same as that used by teens on the "Rate-a-Record" segment of Dick Clark's *American Bandstand*, as in "I give it an 85 (out of 98) . . . it has a nice beat to it."

This qualitative meaning of beat is one of three common meanings of "beat" in popular music. The other two meanings are more quantitative. The differences among them are implicit in these three sentences:

- The tempo of "Rock 'n' Roll Train" is about 119 bpm.
- "Rock 'n' Roll Train" has an eight-beat rhythm or, alternatively, a rock beat.
- "Rock 'n' Roll Train" has a great beat; it makes you want to move to the groove.

The meaning of *beat* in each of these sentences is distinct from the other two. The first refers to the regular measure of time, the second refers to the rhythmic foundation of the style, and the third refers to the interaction of other rhythms with the regular measure of time and the rock beat. We consider each in turn. (See MINDTAP)

1-3a "Timekeeping" Beat

Listen to the beginning of "Rock 'n' Roll Train" and start tapping your foot as soon as you find the beat. Once you find it, you will probably notice that you are marking off time at regular intervals, in time with the music. In other words, the time between foot taps is the same from one beat to the next. This rhythm moves at a steady pace, rather than speeding up or slowing down.

Beat and Rhythm

In this context, beat refers to a regular rhythm that moves at a speed to which you can comfortably respond with physical movement. A regular **rhythm** is a rhythm that measures time in equal increments. The tapping of your foot is a regular rhythm because the time that elapses between one tap and the next is always the same. In "Rock 'n' Roll Train" there are other regular rhythms, both faster and slower than the beat, but we identify this particular regular rhythm as the beat because it lies in our physical comfort zone. It is the rhythm to which we time our movements when we dance, exercise, or simply tap our foot or bob our head in time with the song.

Tempo

We use the word **tempo** to refer to the *speed* of the beat. We generally measure tempo in bpm: the tempo of "Rock 'n' Roll Train" is 119 bpm. In rock songs, tempos generally range between 110 and 140 bpm. Tempos outside this range may connect powerfully to the musical message: the frenetic tempos of punk (often around 160 to 170 bpm) reinforce the confrontational nature of the style; by contrast, the languid tempos (often between 60 and 70 bpm) of so many doo-wop songs (such as **"I Only Have Eyes for You"**) encourage the slow dancing that is often the prelude to the romance expressed in the lyrics.

The Measure

In rock, beats almost always coalesce into groups of four, although other groups—2, 3, or even 5—are also possible. We call a consistent grouping of beats a **measure**, or **bar**. The measure represents a slower regular rhythm. And because it is slower, it is a more convenient form of rhythmic reference for longer timespans: we refer to a 12-bar blues, for instance, rather than a 48-beat blues.

In "Rock 'n' Roll Train," we can hear the relationship between beat and measure when drummer Phil Rudd enters. The most prominent element in his playing is the

---

beat (1) The rhythmic quality of a piece of music that invites a physical response ("that song has a good beat"). (2) The (usually) regular marking of time at walking/dancing/moving speed (usually between 72 and 144 beats per minute). (3) The rhythmic foundation of a style or substyle, distinguished by the consistent use of regular rhythms and rhythmic patterns: a two-beat, a rock beat, a shuffle beat.

rhythm The time dimension of music. The cumulative result of musical events as they happen over time.

measure A consistent grouping of beats. A waltz has measures containing three beats; a march has measures with two beats. Also called bar.

alternation between the bass drum thump and the sharp rap on the snare drum. The bass drum thump sounds on the first and third beat, the rap on the second and fourth.

So far we have identified the most generic meaning of *beat*, which could be applied to a wide range of music—rock, pop, jazz, classical, and any other music with a steady pulse. (So do the terms *tempo, measure,* and *bar*.) We consider next a more specific meaning of *beat*.

1–3b "Number" Beat

"Rock 'n' Roll Train" begins with a guitar riff that seems to float in time. The continuation creates a more consistent rhythmic flow, but not until the rest of the band joins in, as Young repeats the pattern, do we hear Rudd's persistent tap on the hi-hat. As the band joins in as Young repeats the riff and response, we can notice three features of the rhythm:

1. The cymbal tap marks a regular rhythm moving twice as fast as the beat, or eight times per measure.
2. This regular rhythm is the fastest regular rhythm heard in the song
3. The rhythms in the other parts—guitars, bass—align with this fast-moving regular rhythm.

In effect, the beat, backbeat (more on that shortly), and faster rhythm serve as a template for the rhythmic organization of the song. This template has two widely used names: eight-beat rhythm or rock beat/rock rhythm. It is called an eight-beat rhythm because the rhythm that divides the measure into eight equal segments is the fastest regular rhythm and because most of the rhythmic activity and interest map onto this layer of the template, rather than the beat. It is called a rock beat, because it is—more than any other musical element—the defining feature of rock. Most rock songs have a rock beat; popular music before rock did not.

Frequency of rhythmic templates in the top 50 of *Rolling Stone's* 500 greatest songs of all time.

The Backbeat

There is one other regular rhythm in "Rock 'n' Roll Train": the backbeat. The **backbeat** is a sharp, percussive sound on the second of each pair of beats. After Young's riff and response, Rudd brings the band in on the backbeat with a strong rap on his snare drum. It's the loudest sound that he produces.

In rock-era music, the backbeat is typically even more pervasive than the rock-defining rhythmic layer. Virtually every rock song has a backbeat. As Chuck Berry sang in **"Rock 'n' Roll Music"**, "It's got a backbeat, you can't lose it." The backbeat is all but universal, even in those songs that do not use a rock beat. Together, the backbeat and the rock rhythmic layer (which moves twice as fast as the beat) form the foundation of rock rhythm. (See MINDTAP)

1–3c "Good" Beat

Among the most popular segments on *American Bandstand*, the television show that brought rock and roll into millions of homes from 1957 (when ABC began to broadcast the show nationally) to 1990 (when it finally went off the air), was "Rate-a-Record." In this segment, three participants would listen to a new song while the others danced, then give the song a numerical rating somewhere between 35 and 98. Ratings were often based on the perceived quality of the beat: when asked why a song received a high rating, one of the participants might answer something like "It has a good beat, and you can dance to it." "Rock 'n' Roll Train" has a good beat, and you can dance to it. Indeed, it makes you—and the crowds that flock to AC/DC concerts—want to dance or at least move to the beat. Why? What is it about the rhythm of the song that invites us to respond physically? To address that question, we introduce another common feature of rock rhythm: syncopation.

Syncopation: "It Has a Good Beat, and You Can Dance to It"

A **syncopation** is a rhythm or accent that does not line up in an expected way with the beat or other regular rhythm. We hear two syncopations in Young's opening riff, and another at the very end of the response. They are even more prominent in the chorus: "train," "-ning," "-ight" (when it slides down), and "track." All of this activity conflicts with the regular rock rhythm in the rhythm guitar and drums. The tension created by the interplay between the regular rhythms and the rhythms that fall off the beat, creates much of the rhythmic interest in the song. More than any other aspect of the rhythm, it is what gives the song a "good beat." (See MINDTAP)

This meaning of *beat* is more subjective and less precise than either of the other two meanings. Those we can quantify easily enough, and they will be the same to every listener: the tempo is 119 bpm, and the drummer is marking off a rock beat. However, listeners may differ regarding what defines a good beat. Still, just about any consensus opinion regarding the quality of the beat in a group of rock songs will favor more syncopated rhythms.

Rock is about rhythm, and rhythm in rock starts with the beat, in all three of its meanings. The time-measuring beat is at the center of our rhythmic experience, in mind and body. The number beat is the rhythmic template of the music and the source of much of its power, as we will discover again and again during our survey of rock-era music. And a good beat is one of the elements that can draw us to the music. "Rock 'n' Roll Train" offers clear illustrations of all three meanings of *beat*. Its rhythms serve as an ideal starting point for further explorations of rock and roll.

1-4 The Sounds of the Core Rock Style

Since the days of Buddy Holly and the Crickets, the instrumentation of the core rock band has been two electric guitars (lead and rhythm), bass, and drums. By the time of the British Invasion of the early sixties, the electric bass had replaced the acoustic bass, and by the time the Rolling Stones became the "world's greatest rock 'n' roll band," this instrumentation was firmly established as the norm. There were a few important "power trios" (e.g., Jimi Hendrix Experience, Cream, Led Zeppelin), but even these groups occasionally overdubbed rhythm guitar parts underneath guitar solos. Some bands augmented this nucleus: pianist Ian Stewart regularly contributed to Rolling Stones recordings. Other instruments, such as saxophones, extra percussion, or even a third guitar, were optional; the sound of unfiltered rock was complete with just a vocalist and the four core instruments.

The instruments play loudly in live performance—so loudly that what ex-AC/DC singer Brian Johnson called "industrial noise" contributed significantly to the hearing loss that ended his career with the band.

The song, like many AC/DC hits, projects a dense, dark sound mainly for three reasons:

1. Both pitched (guitars, bass) and unpitched (drums) instruments generally operate in a low and midrange—Johnson's vocal line is often among the highest sounds, and harmonizing the riff adds more low tones.

2. The distortion thickens the sound considerably.

3. Harmonizing the accompanying guitar lines with power chords adds more low-register sound.

And of course the high volume level (heard live or with the sound up) augments the already dense sound. The dark sound of the core dates back to the mid-sixties, just as rock and roll was morphing into rock. Songs like "**(I Can't Get No) Satisfaction**" and the Kinks "**You Really Got Me**" are the antecedents of the music of groups like AC/DC. (See MINDTAP)

1–5 Riffs and Chords: Melody and Harmony in the Core Rock Style

When AC/DC reaches the chorus of "Rock 'n' Roll Train," the rest of the band and many in the audience join Johnson in singing: "Runaway train, running right off the track." When simply spoken, the lyric has no particular cadence or rhythm. But when sung in this song, the phrase is broken up into four short segments, containing from one to four syllables. All end with a syncopation, and are separated from the next segment by the length of the last note or silence.

1–5a Riffs

These segments are straightforward examples of **riffs**. A riff is a melodic idea that is:

1. *Short*—typically no more than six or seven notes
2. *Separated*—either by silence or by a long note
3. *Syncopated*—syncopation isn't essential to a riff in rock-era music, but it is customary.

All three characteristics are heard in the chorus of "Rock 'n' Roll Train." The first phrase has four notes: it's essentially the sung version of the opening guitar riff, minus the last note. As you have heard (and can see below), it's short, separated from the next part with silence, and syncopated. The second phrase has the other three segments, which together add up to seven notes. ("Right" is sung to two different pitches.) There are good reasons that riffs typically have these qualities. Their brevity makes them easy to remember, the silence (or long note) defines their boundaries, and the syncopation adds musical interest. And to make sure that listeners remember it, riffs are almost always repeated many times during the course of the song—that's certainly the case in "Rock 'n' Roll Train."

In rock-era music, riffs are often building blocks for melody. In this song, we hear three common strategies for developing a riff into longer melodic units. The guitar introduction shows one: expand the riff into a longer statement by varying some feature of the riff. In this case, what's varied is the pattern of rise and fall. The verse shows another: answer the riff with a different riff. Here, that's personified by the exchanges between Young and Johnson during the verse of the song. The third option is to repeat the riff several times, which is what happens in the chorus. (See MINDTAP)

1–5b Chords

In their most obvious form, **chords** are groups of notes that sound together. Most of the chords in "Rock 'n' Roll Train" are "power chords": Power chords are not chords as they had been understood in pre-rock music, and they don't function like these more traditional chords. Instead, their primary purpose seems to be thickening the sound by supporting riffs and accompanying patterns from below. The extra notes, distortion, and high volume make power chords powerful indeed.

Chords of all kinds typically perform at least two functions. First, they provide a point of departure and return: a harmonic round trip. The very first chord of

chords A group of pitches considered as a single unit. The notes of a chord may be played simultaneously, or they may be played in a series as an arpeggio.

Young's introductory riff is also the first chord of the verse and the first chord of the chorus, as well as the last chord of his response, the last chord of the chorus—which lasts for a while—and the last chord of the song. Second, they outline a slower-moving rhythm as they change every few beats. In "Rock 'n' Roll Train," the opening riff and the chorus have the same basic chords in the same rhythm. These slower and more predictable patterns help outline the form of a song.

Listening to chords is the opposite of listening to melody. More often than not, melody is either the highest part, or among the highest parts. That's the case in "Rock 'n' Roll Train" during the vocal sections and the guitar solo. By contrast, when we listen to chords, we want to first seek out the lowest note—the bass—because chords are built from the bottom up.

1–6 The Form of a Core Rock Song

"Rock 'n' Roll Train" lasts four minutes and twenty seconds. In that time span, there are three statements of the form of the song, plus an introduction, a guitar solo, and other shorter interpolations.

Each statement of the form contains three sections: **verse**, **bridge**, and **chorus**.

1. **The verse** is the opening section. Its primary function is to relate a chunk of the story. The focus is generally on the words, which are different in each statement of the form. As a result, this section tends to be the most low-key section of the form.
2. **The bridge** is the transition from the verse to the chorus. Its purpose is build up from the more low-key verse to the chorus, which is the high point of the song. Typically, the music becomes more active and goal-oriented—the goal being the arrival at the chorus.
3. **The chorus** typically features a melodic hook repeated several times, and sung to the same lyric each time. The lyric of the chorus embodies the main point in the story, and the riff to which it's sung is the melodic hook that listeners remember.

This sequence of musical events is not only the template for "Rock 'n' Roll Train," but also the structure of an almost uncountable and ever-expanding number of rock-era songs.

The beauty of this template is its ability to combine familiarity with flexibility. The broad outline of the form is well established, but there is no set length for any of the sections, and no limitation on the kinds of musical materials that are included beyond the general prescription outlined above—and even that can be altered. To cite just one of several examples in "Rock 'n' Roll Train," AC/DC extends the chord just before the chorus to build up suspense. Both the sequence and likely musical features of the three sections are predictable enough on a general level that even first-time listeners can navigate through a song, yet they can be potentially different and distinctive on a more detailed level. (See MINDTAP)

1–6a It's Only Rock 'n' Roll

AC/DC bills themselves as a "rock and roll" band. Judging by this and dozens of other songs—they have been mining a mother lode of riffs and rhythms for decades—playing what they consider rock and roll involves these key features:

- Including two electric guitars (with some but not excessive distortion), bass, and drums backing a lead singer who sings in a high range
- Having the sound way up
- Laying down a strong rock beat with the entire band

- Creating a foundation for the vocal line from a syncopated riff, which they repeat several times
- Supporting the riff with a series of three power chords, which run through the entire song
- Marking off large sections with an exchange of simple but syncopated vocal riffs, in which both words and music are repeated several times

Collectively, these features describe prominent musical attributes of AC/DC's songs and, by extension, the "old time rock and roll" that is the core rock style. This sound is our central reference point for a broader discussion of rock-era music. We continue by examining the diverse roots of this core rock style.

1-7 Talking About Rock: The Roots of Rock; Routes to Rock

Among the briefest and best known accounts of the provenance of rock is Muddy Waters's line: "The blues had a baby and they called it rock and roll." It's a great-sounding line, and it does highlight the central role of the blues in the shaping of rock and roll (and rock). But it oversimplifies the connection between blues and rock. It was not the straightforward lineage that Waters's remark suggested, but rather many blues styles shaping multiple generations and styles of early rock-era music. And it doesn't account for the other genres—for example, country, gospel, pop, folk, Afro-Cuban music, jazz—that also contributed to the sounds of rock. We present a more comprehensive take on the roots of rock, and the route by which popular music evolved into rock.

1-7a The Roots of Rock

Like almost all twentieth-century popular music, rock's deepest roots are in two musical traditions so unlike each other that there is virtually no common ground, musical or otherwise. One tradition was a product of the white upper class and the middle class that emulated them; they based their music on European models or imported it directly from Europe, usually by way of England. The other tradition was the music of sub-Saharan Africa that the slaves brought with them. They reconstructed what they could of their music; they were limited to a great extent because slave owners banned drums throughout the South. Rock is one family of styles that resulted from the interaction of the two traditions.

If we contrast secular song in the United States during the early nineteenth century with music from Africa and the African diaspora that demonstrates no influence of European music, we can grasp how dissimilar the traditions are. (See MINDTAP)

Despite these pronounced differences, musical exchanges between white and black musicians did occur. Anecdotal evidence suggests that both whites and blacks interpreted the music of the other in terms of their own tradition. Slaves learned the Christian hymns of their masters, but accounts of early nineteenth-century religious revivals indicate they had very different ways of singing them. The banjo is associated with traditional country music, but scholars believe that it is an adaptation of a west African plucked instrument. Early on, the white takes on black music were certainly more superficial than the black takes on white music. To cite just one example, T. D. Rice's "Jump Jim Crow" (1828), his wildly popular mimicking of a black stevedore's song and dance, shows no evidence of traditional African musical features. That would change—slowly but surely—over the next several decades. The creative friction between the two traditions would drive the evolution of popular music to, and through, rock.

1-7b Routes to Rock

Our brief account of the long route to rock begins early in the nineteenth century, a time when the music industry in the United States was beginning to take shape, and before there was a distinctively American popular music. Our starting point is the European-derived music outlined above, as exemplified in the parlor songs that remained popular in genteel households for much of the century.

As we compare songs like "Jeanie with the Light Brown Hair" to "Rock 'n' Roll Train," we can wonder whether there's any common ground between the two. However, there are two features of AC/DC's song not found in the African tradition that trace back in popular music to songs like these. (See MINDTAP)

1-7c Minstrelsy

Minstrelsy, introduced by the Virginia Minstrels in 1843 and a sensation almost overnight, was an all-around entertainment: singing, playing instruments, dancing, acting out skits, telling jokes, and more. Before the Civil War, it was presented only by white performers in blackface; after the Civil War, blacks also performed as minstrels—also in blackface.

The music for the early minstrel show was the first American popular music—it was a sound without precedent in European music. Although the minstrels purported to be black and adopted a clumsy imitation of black speech (if song lyrics are any indication), music for the minstrel show owes more to folk music from the British Isles than black music. Still, there are three features that moved popular music closer to rock.

1-7d Ragtime

Ragtime began as music for piano: essentially, rags are syncopated marches for piano. Ragtime caught on around the turn of the twentieth century, despite fierce opposition from society's self-appointed moral guardians. Ragtime was the first authentic African-American music that could be conveyed in musical notation, so it gave those who could read music the opportunity to experience a core element of African music. (See MINDTAP)

1-7e The Early Fox-Trot Song

The syncopated rhythms of ragtime helped transform popular song: as the 1910s began, popular song began to feature melodies built around riffs. These more conversational melodies were supported by the rhythms of the most popular social dance of the early twentieth century, the fox-trot. The syncopated melodies over a march-influenced rhythmic foundation were clear signals that a shift toward a more modern style was underway.

1-7f Jazz and "Jazz," Blues and "Blues"

The first published blues songs hit the market in the early teens; the all-white Original Dixieland Jazz Band made the first recordings of jazz in 1917. Both were sensations that filtered down into more mainstream music. During the twenties, musicians and more adventurous listeners heard black jazz and blues musicians live in ballrooms, theaters, and speakeasies; they and others also heard them on record. This music brought revolutionary new sounds and rhythms to mainstream popular music.

1-7g Swing

Swing crossed over to the mainstream in the latter half of the thirties and continued through World War II. It was swing vs. sweet for the decade, bringing popular music a big step closer to rock. For a brief period, jazz was a popular music, and the influence of the blues deepened.

1–7h Fast Blues, Deep Blues

Two sharply contrasting blues styles that profoundly influenced rock left a recorded legacy. Fast boogie-woogie is the direct antecedent of Chuck Berry's rock-defining rhythm guitar patterns, and the "deep" blues of Delta bluesmen inspired a generation of rock guitarists.

1–8 The Route to Rock and the Transmutation of Popular Music

We pause our tour along the route to rock in 1945, about the time that the new sounds that became rhythm and blues began to take shape. The reshaping of mainstream popular music from parlor songs to big band swing was comprehensive, and so radical that it's difficult to hear the connection between the two without the intervening steps. These steps outline the process that transmuted parlor songs into swing: an ongoing cycle of African-American interpretation of existing European practice, the reinterpretation of African-American versions by whites, and the subsequent reinterpretation of the white versions by black musicians. It's a process that continued throughout the twentieth century. The arrival at the core rock style was a milestone along this evolutionary path, but not an endpoint.

To return to Waters's statement about the lineage of rock and roll: it's clear that the blues—not one but several styles (including some discussed later)—played a key role in birthing both rock and roll and, a decade later, the core rock style. However, rock-era music encompasses much more than just this sound. We preview our account of this music by sketching the outline of rock's multiple genres and generations.

1–9 Talking about Rock: The Rock Era, 1945–

"Old Time Rock and Roll"—the core rock style—has become a timeless sound. It remains much the same today as it was in the mid-sixties, when it took shape in the music of the Rolling Stones and other like-minded bands. In this respect, it is unlike rock-era music, which has been evolving for more than seven decades and is far more diverse and inclusive.

The gestation of rock began after World War II, principally through two bodies of black music: more rhythmic and/or bluesy versions of swing, and gospel-influenced versions of pop songs, both old and new. By the mid-fifties, rock-era music had achieved a distinctive identity as (real) rock and roll through a new approach to rhythm and sound. By the mid-sixties, rock-era music was a mature music; its stylistic conventions were established and widely understood. And even as its core coalesced into what would become its timeless form, it simultaneously became a far more diverse music. Its range extended from an array of hybrid styles created through the interplay with other kinds of music (e.g., folk rock, pop rock, southern rock, art rock, jazz rock/fusion), to innovative new directions (Motown, heavy metal, soul, late Beatles). During this same period, rock-related music became commercially and culturally dominant. It replaced pre-rock pop at the top of both the singles and album charts and on radio, and it forced established styles—pop, musical theater, country, jazz—to embrace rock, at least to some extent, or be perceived as out of step with the times.

Punk/new wave, and disco and funk, two important new directions in the latter half of the seventies, signaled the emergence of a new generation of rock-era music. The two new styles represent contrary directions. In its purest form, punk was a reactionary trend. It was the Everclear of rock, a distillation and intensification of its sounds and rhythms. By contrast, disco continued the evolution of rock-era music: it brought an array of synthesized sounds and the more active 16-beat rhythms into the mainstream. Along with funk, a related but less commercially important style, it provided a foundation for new directions in post-eighties rock, pop, and R&B. The new sounds of the early eighties included music that continued a single approach (e.g., early alternative, techno) and music that synthesized the two trends in myriad, often inventive ways (e.g., the music of Michael Jackson). In the latter part of the decade, these new syntheses moved beyond the dance floor, most notably in significant music by U2 and Prince. The other significant development of the latter part of the 1980 was the growing commercial and cultural impact of rap. Meanwhile, new acts working in the rock and R&B styles of the previous generation found fresh approaches (e.g., the music of Nirvana).

By the mid-nineties, it was clear that the rock era, and more broadly, twentieth-century popular music, had reached the end point of a long evolutionary cycle that had begun with ragtime. The ongoing interaction of European and African music had swung the stylistic pendulum from melody to rhythm. Songs with flowing melodies were dominant in popular music at the beginning of the twentieth century. By the end, the voice had become a percussion instrument and a further doubling of the number of beats would have rendered the rhythm unintelligible and unplayable at dance tempos.

Those searching for melody frequently turned to country music or tuneful classic rock—the re-release of The Beatles' No. 1 hits was the best-selling album of both 2000 and the first decade of the twenty-first century. Many rock-era acts continued to work in first- and second-generation styles. Most evidenced mastery of the conventions, and some found imaginative new sounds, but the change from earlier rock-era music was incremental, not revolutionary.

For most seeking a new direction, sound became the dominant element. This approach involved two complementary strategies: finding and exploiting new sounds and sound combinations, especially those made possible by digital technology, and minimizing interest in other musical elements: melody, harmony, and rhythm. Critically acclaimed acts, most notably Radiohead, led the way in this regard. Not surprisingly, there was a trickle-down effect from the music of these sound explorers. Less radical versions of these strategies have played a key role in creating a distinctive twenty-first-century popular music, and at the same time creating an extraordinarily diverse musical landscape, one that easily accommodates both Adele and Drake.

We remain in the rock era almost by default, because there has been no similarly disruptive sequel to the rock revolution of the sixtie—no new style that takes over the mind and the market and renders rock-era music out of date. Instead, music of many genres and several generations divvy up the market for popular music, with older music, and music in older styles, outselling even much critically acclaimed new music. We have unprecedented access to music in multiple genres and from several generations. There's something for everyone, and it's available almost any time at the tap of a finger.

Our outline of the rock era complements our closer examination of its core style: the latter defines its heart, the former sketches its temporal boundaries and hints at the range of the music over several generations. In the chapters ahead, we chart the evolution, revolution, and even devolution of rock-era music and explore its remarkable diversity. (See MINDTAP)

PART I

Becoming Rock: The Rock Era, 1945–1965

Part Introduction

Among the favorite pastimes of rock critics has been making a case for the first rock and roll record. In their book, *What Was the First Rock 'N' Roll Record*, Jim Dawson and Steve Propes nominate 50 recordings, making a case for each one. If one defines "rock 'n' roll" as the music that led directly to rock, then only Little Richard's 1955 recording "Tutti Frutti" (No. 48 on their list) would seem to qualify. The first song on their list, Illiois Jacquet's 1944 live performance of "Blues 2," belongs to the swing era, despite Jacquet's impassioned playing. However, most of the tracks from the latter half of the forties are a new sound: more rhythmic than pre-war blues, and more bluesy than swing. Before 1949, this music had no name and little popular presence, and those who performed it recorded their music on small independent labels rather than Columbia or RCA. "Rock and roll" referred to activity between the sheets rather than on the bandstand. Still, this new black music was the beginning of rock-era music, even if it wasn't yet rock 'n' roll.

The first part of our survey of rock-era music begins just after the end of World War II and ends about two decades later, just before the rock revolution began in earnest. The development of this music from early rhythm and blues to the black pop and rock of the early sixties unfolded in four stages, each lasting about five years, and each characterized by increased musical diversity and commercial presence. The black music that would become rhythm and blues by the mid-fifties included not two but three distinct, if often, intermingling streams. The most rhythmic was a more bluesy form of swing, performed by small groups instead of big bands. The most bluesy was a more powerful version of Delta blues through the use of an amplified guitar and other rhythm instruments. However, there was also a new kind of pop singing by black groups influenced by earlier black vocal groups (e.g., the Mills Brothers, the Ink Spots) and gospel. All three made clear that what was now called rhythm and blues was different from the pop and jazz of other black artists. And all three marked starting points for trends that would produce soul, hard rock, and Motown in the sixties.

All three streams continued into the fifties, and were slightly augmented by Latin/blues fusions. Two major developments in rhythm and blues involved the response to this music, rather than new musical developments. One was the greater awareness of this music, first by those in the music business (e.g., musicians, DJs, those involved with record companies), followed by expansion of the audience for rhythm and blues among both blacks and whites. The other was a series of white takes on black music, from rockabilly to cover versions of early doo-wop. This laid the groundwork for the performer who made "rock and roll" a household expression.

In 1955, rock and roll began its commercial ascent and started to separate from rhythm and blues musically as well as racially. Almost overnight, Elvis took over all three singles charts—pop, country and western, and rhythm and blues—then took on Hollywood before his induction into the Army. He was early rock and roll's singular commercial presence; no one else came close to his impact. Even as Elvis fascinated teenagers and horrified their parents, Little Richard and Chuck Berry were working out the rhythmic foundation for rock and roll—the new beat that would distinguish it from R&B and lead to rock. During this brief five-year period, rock and roll went from a white take on rhythm and blues to a new dance music and ultimately a new rhythmic template for a wide range of music—fast and slow, loud and soft. The major musical innovations in rhythm and blues were the fusion of blues, gospel, and pop elements into a new, more soulful sound. By the end of the decade, there was a clear musical difference between R&B and rock and roll.

The first half of the sixties was the adolescence of both rock and roll and rhythm and blues. By mid-decade, rock and roll had become rock, as a new generation of rock and rollers adapted Chuck Berry's approach to rhythm and sound on the guitar to the rest of the band. The British Invasion by the Beatles and a host of other acts from the United Kingdom made rock an international music as they conquered the US charts. Doo-wop morphed into distinctive new—and popular—black pop styles: girl groups, Motown, and more. Rhythm and blues got a rock beat, and funneled the passion and grittiness of the blues into soul. A folk revival that began in the late fifties as a sincere attempt to bring old songs to life turned topical in the early sixties, as Bob Dylan and others set powerful, even confrontational, lyrics to simple melodies and accompaniments. Collectively, these developments fomented a revolution—musical, commercial, and cultural. It was well under way by 1965.

Pop before the Rock Revolution

The conventional wisdom about winners writing history certainly seems to apply to popular music. Ask the proverbial person on the street to name the top acts in popular music during the fifties, and you're likely to get a list that reads like the maiden class of inductees into the Rock and Roll Hall of Fame: Chuck Berry, Ray Charles, Sam Cooke, Fats Domino, the Everly Brothers, Buddy Holly, Jerry Lee Lewis, Elvis Presley, Little Richard. Mention Perry Como, Frankie Laine, Patti Page, or Eddie Fisher, and you may elicit only a quizzical glance or a fleeting memory—Perry Como, didn't he have a TV show? Eddie Fisher, wasn't he married to Liz Taylor?

The actual state of affairs was quite different. Of these first-generation rock stars, only Elvis topped the singles charts on a regular basis. Albums were largely the province of classical music, musical theater, jazz, and what we now call "easy listening." For much of the fifties, radio stations that programmed the new music were few and far between; Buddy Holly and his friends drove around Lubbock late at night to find a spot where they could pick up a clear-channel radio station that played rhythm and blues. Television occasionally featured rock-and-roll acts. Carl Perkins appeared on Perry Como's popular television show, but Como—a smooth-voiced pop singer-turned-television personality—*had* the show; audiences tuned in to him every week. Even among teenagers, enthusiasm for real rock and roll was far from unanimous. Pat Boone, a contemporary of Elvis who sang mostly pre-rock pop (although his disastrous cover of Little Richard's "Tutti Frutti," still reached No. 12 on the pop charts), was more successful than any rock-and-roll act besides Elvis. Most rhythm-and-blues artists were even less known; only Fats Domino charted on a regular basis.

Early on, rock and roll aroused hostile reactions from the majority of Americans: a sizeable percentage of teens, and most of their parents and grandparents. (Many of the older generations had apparently forgotten the hostility that the new music of their youth had aroused.) To appease censors, Elvis was shown only from the waist up on his last appearance on *The Ed Sullivan Show* in 1956. By the end of the decade, the federal government had gotten into the roll-over-rock-and-roll act; the moral degradation caused by rock and roll was an unspoken subtext to the payola hearings at the end of the decade.

The Musical Hierarchy in 1950s America

In the first two post–World War II decades, there was a clear cultural hierarchy in American musical life. At the top was classical music. Directly under it was musical theater, best exemplified by the musicals of Rodgers and Hammerstein. Modern jazz was for hipsters: it was the sound track for the counterculture of the fifties. It was heard mainly in small nightclubs frequented by Bohemian types. Although admired by esteemed musicians both classical and popular (among them the conductor/composer Leonard Bernstein), modern jazz was not as prestigious as musical theater in part because so many of the important musicians were black. Pop crooning was a rung below musicals in prestige, and well above rock and roll, R&B, country, blues, and other outsider genres.

Before the rock revolution, the musical measuring stick of cultural prestige in popular music was the degree of its alignment with classical music, frequently evidenced in such features as prominent strings and little or no percussion, the absence of syncopation and other forms of rhythmic play, flowing melodies and rich harmonic cushions supporting them, supple rhythms and languid tempos, and pleasant—even operatic—vocal styles. "Some Enchanted Evening," the love song from Rodgers and Hammerstein's 1949 musical *South Pacific* (released on film in 1958) is a stellar example of the "classicization" of popular music.

The Broadway musicals and their film counterparts, from Rodgers and Hammerstein's *Oklahoma!* (1943) through Walt Disney's *Mary Poppins* (the soundtrack from this film topped the album charts for fourteen weeks in 1965!) represented the most extreme form of a devolutionary trend that began in the thirties. In the late thirties, musical antonym to swing was sweet: melodious fox-trots in a slow tempo, rather than syncopated riffs over a driving swing rhythm. After the end of the war, much mainstream pop retreated even more from the energy of the twenties, not only on Broadway but also in bland white-bread songs like Perry Como's "Hot Diggity," a No.1 pop hit in 1956. That this music remained popular among a large segment of the American public (and among those who controlled the distribution of popular music) through the first half of the sixties made rock's usurping of the market even more revolutionary. This would be the music that rock rebelled against, even as rock-era musicians co-opted elements of it when it served their purposes.

The revolution was over quickly—a matter of a couple of years. The prelude to the revolution took the better part of two decades. We jumpstart our journey from early rhythm and blues to the eve of the revolution with music from Louis Jordan. (See MINDTAP)

CHAPTER 2

RHYTHM AND BLUES, 1945–1955

Learning Objectives:

1) Describe the social climate surrounding the **rhythm and blues** genre following World War II.

2) Give examples of some of the musical developments in the **rhythm and blues** genre.

3) Ascertain the various musical roles of the instruments within a **jump band**.

4) Contrast the differences between early 1950s **rhythm and blues**, **electric blues**, and **doo-wop**.

5) Illustrate the sequence of musical events within the **twelve-bar blues form**.

6) Discuss the various ways Latin music influenced **rhythm and blues**.

race records A term that came into use in the early 1920s to describe recordings by African American artists intended for sale primarily in the African American community.

classic blues The popular blues style of the 1920s, which typically featured a woman singing the blues (e.g., Bessie Smith) accompanied by one or more jazz musicians.

Chapter Introduction

In January 1922, Okeh Records placed an advertisement in the *Chicago Defender*, a black newspaper, that announced "All the greatest race phonograph stars can be heard on Okeh Records . . . Ask your neighborhood dealer for a complete list of Okeh **race records**." Okeh had recorded Mamie Smith's "**Crazy Blues**" at the end of 1920. Its success opened the door for other **classic blues** singers, most notably Bessie Smith. "**Down Hearted Blues**," Smith's first recording for Columbia Records (now Sony), in 1923, reputedly sold over 1 million copies.

During the twenties, recordings by black musicians, mainly for a black audience, occupied a small but important niche within the recording industry. Other major companies, most notably Victor and Columbia (which would ultimately merge into Sony BMG), created branches of their catalog to serve the "race" market. Joining them in catering to the black community were small labels like Paramount and W. C. Handy's Black Swan, which was bought by Paramount in 1924. However, the race record part of the music industry almost went under during the first years of the Depression. Sales of race records, which had been as high as 5 percent of total sales at the end of the twenties, dropped to only 1 percent in the early thirties, and several record companies went out of business or stopped recording black musicians.

Business began to pick up toward the end of the thirties. By 1942, *Billboard*, then and now the bible of the entertainment industry, began charting "race record" hits.

Experience an interactive version of this era in ✦ MINDTAP

The magazine dubbed the chart the "Harlem Hit Parade" (reportedly chart position was determined by an informal poll of a handful of record stores in Harlem). After World War II, *Billboard* reverted to "race records" as the chart label. In 1949, Jerry Wexler, then a staff writer at the magazine, suggested the more politically correct and musically appropriate term **rhythm and blues**.

2-1 The Emergence of Rhythm and Blues

By the time the renamed chart made its first appearance on June 25, 1949, rhythm and blues (R&B) had become a small but significant part of the record industry. During World War II, what we now call rhythm and blues was just an occasional blip on the radar screen of **popular music**. After the war ended, rhythm and blues took off—maybe not as fast as Jackie Brenston's "**Rocket 88**"—but quickly enough to get the attention of *Billboard*'s staff. However, it was in the fifties that rhythm and blues began to expand its niche in the pop marketplace, even as it carved out its distinctive sound identity. Within a decade, rhythm and blues became part of what would soon be a new kind of popular music.

The commercial growth of rhythm and blues during the first postwar decade was mainly a product of four factors: the economic and social empowerment of blacks, a media revolution that introduced new recording formats and redefined the role of radio, the growing interest of whites in black music, and the crossover appeal of the music itself.

2-1a Black Social and Economic Issues in Postwar America

The central issue for blacks after World War II was equality: racial, economic, and social. Black and white soldiers had fought for the United States during World War II, sometimes side by side, but more often in segregated units. The irony of blacks fighting to defend freedom in a country that did not treat them as free men was not lost on President Truman. In 1948, he signed an executive order demanding an end to discrimination in the armed services. This was one of numerous postwar developments that moved the United States—however painfully—closer to an integrated society.

If World War II brought the equality issues to the fore, the postwar economic boom, the massive emigration of blacks from the rural South, and the Cold War gave the United States the reasons to respond to it. The flourishing postwar economy meant more and better-paying jobs. It put more money in the pockets of blacks, although not at the same rate as whites, and it reduced competition for jobs, which was one reason for trying to maintain the status quo, especially in the South. The migration of blacks to the North and West, which had begun in earnest after the turn of the century, accelerated during and especially after World War II. There they had the right to vote, which enabled them to exert pressure on politicians.

Another factor was the evident hypocrisy of the United States during this time: presenting itself to other nations as a defender of freedom, and denying it to some of its citizens at home. During the Cold War, schoolchildren recited the Pledge of Allegiance every day, reiterating that the Republic was "one nation under God, indivisible with liberty and justice for all." Observers outside of the South, as well as those in other countries, were increasingly reminded that so long as all Americans were not equal under the law, this pledge—what the nation professed to believe and practice—was in fact a lie.

The two events that catalyzed the civil rights movement occurred within a year of each other. The first was the Supreme Court's 1954 decision, *Brown v. Board of*

rhythm and blues A term used since the mid forties to describe African American popular styles, especially those influenced by blues and/or dance music.

popular music Music that appeals to a mass audience, is intended to have wide appeal, and has a sound and a style distinct from classical or folk music.

Education of Topeka, which rescinded the "separate but equal" policy sanctioned by the Court's 1896 decision in *Plessy v. Ferguson*. In *Plessy*, the Court had held that blacks could be educated in separate (or segregated) schools as long as they were "equal" in quality to the schools whites attended. Now, the Court said that there could be no equality unless blacks and whites had equal access to all schools.

Following this decision, the civil rights movement gained momentum in the courts and on the streets. In 1955, Montgomery, Alabama, native Rosa Parks refused to give up her bus seat to a white person. When she was arrested and sent to jail, blacks in Montgomery boycotted the municipal bus service for a year. Two years later, Dr. Martin Luther King Jr. organized the Southern Christian Leadership Conference, which advocated nonviolent protest modeled after that used by Mahatma Gandhi in India. All of this laid the foundation for the major advances in civil rights during the sixties.

Rhythm-and-blues artists did not lift their voice in support of the civil rights movement during the postwar years. Their contribution was indirect: the appeal of their music helped heighten awareness of black culture. At the same time, rhythm and blues benefited from the increased attention given to race relations in the media; it was a two-way street.

2–1b The Media Revolution

Two major developments—the emergence of commercial television and the development of new record formats—triggered a media revolution during the fifties. The ripple effect from their impact helped open the door for rhythm and blues.

Television and Radio

The television industry mushroomed after the war. In 1946, the industry was in its infancy; only 6,000 television sets were sold that year. Three years later, sales topped 2 million sets. By the mid-fifties, television was a household staple, and the first color sets were on the market. Television quickly took over radio's role as the primary source of all-purpose entertainment. Soap operas, situation comedies, variety shows, mystery shows—all of these and more moved from radio to television.

As a result, radio redefined itself as a medium. To fill the void left by the migration of these shows to television, radio stations began programming recorded music—most prominently, pop. Some stations, however, began to offer programs that provided an alternative to the bland pop fare. Not surprisingly, these programs were broadcast at odd times—late at night, early in the morning. Still, many attracted a small but fervent following.

Disc jockeys (DJs), a new breed of radio personality created by the more extensive use of prerecorded material, hosted these shows. Listeners tuned in for the DJ as well as the music. During these early years of radio programming, DJs chose their own music. As rhythm and blues and rock and roll caught on, their ability to choose the music that they played gave them enormous clout, which they abused on occasion. (We discuss Alan Freed's rise and fall, the most familiar instance of this abuse, in **Chapter 3**.)

Record Formats

After World War II, the major record companies fought a format war. For decades, shellac 78 rpm (revolutions per minute) recordings had delivered about three minutes of popular music on 10-inch discs and about four minutes of classical music on 12-inch discs. In 1948, Columbia Records began issuing long-playing (LP) records, that revolved at 33 rpm. These were vinyl discs that held over half an hour of music and didn't break when you dropped them. The next year, RCA brought out

style The set of those common features found in the music of a time, place, culture, or individual.

ska The dominant Jamaican popular music through the first part of the 1960s. The most distinctive feature of ska is a strong after-beat: a strong, crisp chunk on the latter part of each beat.

the 7-inch 45 rpm single. This disc was also vinyl and, despite its much smaller size, also held about three minutes of music.

It took a while for these new formats to catch on because they required new record players. However, by the mid-fifties, the new 45 rpm format had largely replaced the 78. Record companies used the 45 for singles targeted at teens, who liked the convenience and durability of the new format and had enough money to buy them. Rhythm-and-blues and rock-and-roll 45s found their way into more and more teenage bedrooms; they also turned up on jukeboxes and radio stations more frequently.

Indies

The music market was there, thanks to the postwar economic boom. The way to make money was there, thanks to radio, jukeboxes, and record stores. The way to bring the money in was there, thanks to Broadcast Music Incorporated—a music licensing agency formed in 1939 to collect fees on behalf of those clients (blues and country musicians) not represented by ASCAP, the licensing organization for pop songwriters and performers. All that was needed was someone to record the music.

The growth of indie (independent) music in the last few decades, as opposed to the major recording companies, relives the rise of independent labels in the late forties and early fifties. Today's technology is different: it is more sophisticated and less expensive than the primitive but costly tape recorders of the postwar era. The distribution is different: bands and their companies can stream their music online, instead of selling records from the trunk of a car (as forties indie pioneer Leonard Chess did). And the music is different. Many of today's indie bands, mostly white, explore peripheral retro styles and **style** fusions, like **ska** and punk. More than half a century ago, legendary independent labels recorded blacks whose music was the cutting edge of popular music.

What the indies of yesterday and today have in common is an entrepreneurial spirit and a desire to bring the music, to which they are passionately devoted, to a larger audience—and make some money in the process. For Leonard Chess, a Polish immigrant, it was another potential source of income. Chess and his brother Phil owned several nightclubs on Chicago's South Side, including the Macomba, a club that featured some of the best black performers in the city. In 1947, sensing that the recording industry offered another good business opportunity, the Chess brothers bought into a newly formed independent label, Aristocrat Records. Like most other independents, Aristocrat concentrated on music outside of the pop **mainstream**. The first releases on the new label featured **jazz** and **jump band** performers. Over the next several years, they added such key figures as Muddy Waters and Chuck Berry to their roster.

The story of Chess Records was replicated with some variation in cities around the country. Ahmet Ertegun, a Turkish immigrant living in New York, founded Atlantic Records in 1947; Jerry Wexler bought in six years later. Art Rupe's Specialty Records based in New Orleans, Lew Chudd's Imperial Records based in Los Angeles, and Syd Nathan's King Records based in Cincinnati, all helped preserve and disseminate the sound of rhythm and blues (and country and western). So did Sam Phillips's Sun Records. His recording studio, the only place that blacks could record in Memphis, also recorded top **rockabilly** acts, beginning with Elvis Presley. Starting and running an independent label was a risky business. Some folded. Labels like Imperial, Chess, and King carved a niche in the market on the strength of a few good acts. Only Ertegun's Atlantic grew into a major label. Still, all the independent labels left an impressive legacy.

mainstream
Prevailing styles.

jazz A group of popular related styles primarily for listening. Jazz is usually distinguished from the other popular music of an era by greater rhythmic freedom (more syncopation and/or less insistent beat keeping), extensive improvisation, and more adventurous harmony. There are two families of jazz styles: those based on a four-beat rhythm and those based on a rock or 16-beat rhythm.

jump band In the late 1940s, a small band—rhythm section plus a few horns that played a rhythm-and-blues style influenced by big-band swing and electric blues. Saxophonist/ vocalist Louis Jordan was a key performer in this style.

rockabilly According to Carl Perkins, a country take on rhythm and blues, performed mainly by white Southerners, that combined elements of country music with rock and roll. Rockabilly was most popular in the mid fifties.

2-2 The Range of Rhythm and Blues

Like "race records," "rhythm and blues" came into use as a marketing term: it identified music made by black musicians mainly for a black audience. Jerry Wexler's label implied that this new black music was a family of styles. Indeed, "rhythm and blues" embraced far more than basic blues and music with a big beat. Among the most important developments in rhythm and blues during the decade that followed World War II were:

- Up-tempo good-time blues styles with a strong beat and/or backbeat
- Electric blues, a transformation of country blues through the use of amplified guitar and the addition of a rhythm section
- The incorporation of Latin rhythms and instruments
- A new black pop style, shaped by a long history of pop and gospel vocal groups

These trends were like colors on an artist's palette; they could be mixed together in countless ways. For example, Latin-tinged rhythm and blues included such diverse examples as Professor Longhair's **"Tipitina,"** Ruth Brown's **"Mambo Baby"** (a No. 1 R&B hit for her in 1954), and **Bo Diddley**'s "Bo Diddley." We sample music from all of these sources, beginning with music that put a lot of rhythm in rhythm and blues.

2-3 Jump Bands

Jump bands stripped down and souped up the sound of big-band swing. They kept the rhythm section but reduced the horn sections drastically, paring down three full sections to a couple of saxophones and a trumpet. Often, they strengthened the beat by converting the four-beat swing rhythm to a shuffle. They built songs on repeated **riffs**, usually over a blues or blues-based form. The songs typically took a medium **tempo** because shuffle rhythm put the more frenetic swing tempos out of reach. Jump bands also emphasized singing more than swing had. The vocalist was the key figure in the group, and the lyrics typically told a funny story or allowed the singer to brag a little, or both. A blend of hokum, boogie-woogie, and big-band swing, jump band music was different from all of them.

"**Choo Choo Ch'Boogie**" was a big hit in 1946 for Louis Jordan and His Tympany Five. Louis Jordan (1908–1975) first made his mark as a saxophonist in Chick Webb's fine swing band. He played for Webb from 1936 through 1938, then formed his own smaller group a year later. Unlike many later rhythm-and-blues artists, Jordan got a record deal with a major label, Decca, with whom he signed a contract in 1939. This undoubtedly helped build his audience.

The song begins with the pianist laying down a boogie-woogie bass while the horns play a simple riff. The first part of Jordan's vocal is a series of six short phrases, all of which rhyme and all of which develop from a simple repeated riff. Although the words happen over a blues harmonic progression, they do not follow the standard **form** of the blues lyric. Instead, they serve as a storytelling verse to the catchy chorus that follows. The theme, of course, is life on the railroad—certainly a common topic for songs of that era. (Note the reference to "ballin' the jack," that is, getting the train moving.) As with "Maybellene" (**Chapter 1**), "Choo Choo Ch'Boogie" adapts the conventional blues form to a verse/chorus pattern; the hook of the chorus provides an easy point of entry into the song.

---

country blues A family of African American folk blues styles that flourished in the rural South. Country blues differs from commercial blues mainly in its accompanying instrument-usually acoustic guitar-and its tendency toward less regular forms.

rhythm section The part of a musical group that supplies the rhythmic and harmonic foundation of a performance. Usually includes at least one chord instrument (guitar, piano, or key-board), a bass instrument, and a percussion instrument (typically the drum set).

gospel A family of religious music styles: there is white and black gospel music. Black gospel music has had the more profound influence on popular music by far. Created around 1930 by Thomas Dorsey and others, gospel has influenced popular singing, especially rhythm and blues, since the early 1950s.

swing Rhythmic play over a four-beat rhythm

In a jump band like Louis Jordan and His Tympany Five, the roles of the musicians are clearly defined: the bass walks; the drummer plays a shuffle beat; the guitar and/or the piano also helps keep the beat—the pianist may also play fills and solo; the saxophone honks riffs, either behind the vocalist, in response to him, or in a solo; and the other horns join the sax in creating harmonized response riffs. There is a clear hierarchy.

The tone of the lyric is humorous and self-deprecating; we sense that the "I" in the song is a happy-go-lucky kind of fellow. (The wanderer has pretty much disappeared from our twenty-first-century lives, but even in the decade after World War II, hoboes—men who "rode the rails" from place to place [stowed away on trains], working odd jobs in exchange for food, a roof, and maybe a little cash, or simply begging—were more common. Their mystique, a holdover from the Great Depression, was still powerful.) The music—with its bouncy shuffle beat, catchy riffs (not only in the vocal parts but also in both the piano and the sax solos), and pleasant vocal style—helps capture the mood of the lyric.

This became the formula for Jordan and many of the jump bands that followed him. One reason for the increasing appeal of these songs, to black Americans and gradually to whites as well, was the easy points of entry: upbeat lyrics; repeated riffs, either sung or played on a honking saxophone; a clear beat, usually in a shuffle rhythm; and a chorus-based form.

2-4 Big-Beat Rhythm and Blues

During the early fifties, rhythm and blues became more rhythmic. Three widespread changes often coordinated to make the rhythm more prominent and impactful:

- Use of an amplified guitar
- More rhythmic activity moving faster than the beat
- A stronger backbeat

Each expressed in a different way the drive to shift the balance toward rhythm. The use of amplified guitar was key, even though other instruments weren't amplified. Guitarists typically conveyed both rhythm and **harmony** by playing repeated patterns that outline **chords** and reinforce the distinctive rhythm of the underlying template, which was usually a shuffle rhythm. In addition, the increased volume level of the guitar effectively compelled the other rhythm instruments—especially drums and piano—to play more loudly.

Pianists often responded by playing rapid repeated chords in a **triplet** rhythm. As used in R&B, triplets divide each **beat** into three equal parts. Triplets align with the shuffle rhythm: the first two notes of the triplet in each beat sound with the "long" part of the long/short shuffle pattern, while the third triplet sounds with the "short" part of the shuffle rhythm. We hear examples of all three rhythmic features in two enduring songs from the early fifties, Jackie Brenston's "Rocket 88" and Joe Turner's "**Shake, Rattle and Roll**."

Jackie Brenston's "Rocket 88" (1951) was a big rhythm-and-blues hit with a big beat. Although Brenston (1930–1979) was the singer on this date, it was the band of pianist Ike Turner (1931–2007) that Brenston fronted, and the most distinctive sound on this recording is Willie Kizart's distorted guitar, not Brenston's singing. The story of how it found its way onto a record is the stuff of rock-and-roll legend.

According to most accounts of the making of this record, the band was driving from Mississippi to Memphis, with their instruments strapped on top of the car.

hokum An upbeat blues style that emerged between the first and second world wars.

form The organization of a musical work in time.

chorus (1) A large singing group. (2) In verse/chorus and rock songs, that part of a song in which both melody and lyrics are repeated. (3) In blues and Tin Pan Alley songs, one statement of the melody.

verse/chorus The most popular song form of the late nineteenth century. The verse tells a story in several stages (this section is strophic, i.e., different words are set to the same melody), whereas the chorus, which comes at the end of each verse, repeats both words and melody to reinforce the main message of the song. In early verse/chorus songs, the chorus was often sung by a small group, usually a quartet.

harmony Chords and the study of chord progressions.

triplet Rhythmic pattern that divides each beat into three equal parts

At some point, the guitar amp fell off, or was dropped, and the speaker cone was torn. As a result, the guitar produced a heavily distorted sound, even after Kizart had stuffed it with paper. When recording engineer Sam Phillips heard it, he decided to make an asset out of a perceived liability, so he made the guitar line, which simply adapts a shuffle-style boogie-woogie left hand on the guitar, stand out.

Both the distortion and the relative prominence of the guitar were novel features of this recording—these are the elements that have earned "Rocket 88" so many nominations as "the first" rock-and-roll record. From our perspective, "Rocket 88" wasn't the first rock-and-roll record, because the beat is a shuffle rhythm, not the distinctive rock rhythm heard first in the songs of Chuck Berry and Little Richard. Still, the distortion and the central place of the guitar in the overall sound certainly anticipate key features of rock style.

So does the prominence of the rhythm: Kizart's relentless pattern outlines the shuffle rhythm at a medium fast tempo, and Turner's occasional triplets inject a jolt of energy. The sax riffs also reinforce the driving rhythm.

Joe Turner (1911–1985), commonly identified as "Big" Joe Turner because of his girth, grew up in Kansas City, Missouri, which was a wide-open city and a major center for jazz and blues during the thirties. During the forties, Turner's career gathered momentum; he became a popular R&B recording artist, hopping from one independent label to the next. His career peaked in the mid-fifties: "Shake, Rattle and Roll" topped the R&B charts in 1954. Perhaps because of its lyrics, Turner's version never crossed over to the pop charts; a **cover version** by Bill Haley with some less suggestive lyrics reached No. 7 that same year.

> **cover version**
> Recording of a song by an act other than the first to record it

Among the most distinctive musical features of "Shake, Rattle and Roll" is the heavy backbeat. The drummer's sharp rap on the snare drum, reinforced periodically by Turner's clapping, make it the most prominent rhythmic feature of the recording: Upbeat rhythm-and-blues songs like "Shake, Rattle and Roll" were the direct source of the heavy backbeat that is such an important component of rock rhythm. The two songs also exemplify two common musical features of swing-derived rhythm and blues: blues form and honking saxophone solos.

2-4a Blues Progression

Blues can be a *feeling*: music to convey sadness, or music to chase the blues away, like the two examples here. Blues can be a *style* of singing and playing, as we heard in these two songs, the next two, and several earlier examples.

Blues can also be a *form*, a consistent way of organizing music in time. The key musical element in blues form is a blues progression, a series of chords in a well-established sequence. The three chords are generally referred to as the I, IV, and V chords. (The Roman numerals indicate chords built on the first, fourth and fifth notes of a major scale.)

12-bar blues form (so called because one statement of the form lasts twelve **measures**) consists of three four-measure phrases, in this sequence:

- The first phrase begins on the I chord and typically stays on it through the phrase
- The second phrase begins on the IV chord and returns to the I chord halfway through
- The third phrase begins on the V chord; it also arrives back on the I chord halfway through

Thus, each phrase *begins* on a different chord and *returns* to the I chord halfway through. Within this harmonic framework, there is ample opportunity for variation, as we will discover. But the six chords, each falling on odd-numbered bars, serve as milestones through each statement of the form.

Both "Rocket 88" and "Shake, Rattle, and Roll" use blues form. In "Rocket 88," Kizart's guitar pattern clearly outlines the three chords in the conventional sequence. This is the blues progression in its most basic form, clearly stated. "Shake, Rattle, and Roll" uses the same basic version, but the chords are not as prominent.

2–4b Honking Saxophones

Rhythmic rhythm-and-blues bands were as consistent in their approach to **instrumentation** as they were in their approach to rhythm and harmony. "Rocket 88" is typical: the band behind Jackie Brenston consists of a full early-fifties-style rhythm section—electric guitar, piano, bass, and drums—plus two saxophones, one of which takes an extended solo. Turner's backup band is similar: a complete rhythm section, but without a guitar, plus a pair of saxophones. In a fifties rhythm-and-blues song we expect to hear bands with a rhythm section and at least one saxophone; the saxophone will usually be a solo instrument as well as an accompanying instrument; and both accompaniments and solo passages will feature repeated riffs. This instrumental arrangement would morph into the **soul** bands of the sixties and the **funk** bands of the seventies and early eighties.

2–4c Blues Themes: Cars and Sex

Postwar rhythm and blues positioned itself against mainstream pop in words as well as music. Even as many fifties pop songs gravitated toward the sanitized lyrics reminiscent of contemporary sit-coms (who would say in everyday speech, "Hot-diggity, Dog-diggity, what you do to me?"), R&B lyrics spoke about everyday topics in everyday language—albeit metaphorically if necessary. "Rocket 88" focuses on a favorite subject during the postwar years: cars. "Rocket 88" was inspired by Joe Liggins's 1947 recording, "**Cadillac Boogie**," and it is one link in a chain that passes through Chuck Berry's "**Maybellene**" to the Beach Boys' "**Little Deuce Coupe**." By contrast, Joe Turner's song explores a subject with a long history in the blues: what "rock and roll" referred to before it was a musical **genre**.

The blues has always been a personal music, and there is no more personal subject in secular culture than man–woman relationships. In "Shake, Rattle and Roll," Turner talks about a woman in his life, and it's not pretty: she's lazy, trashy, loose with money and her favors, and diabolical.

The most physically intimate aspect of a relationship is sexual intercourse. In our time, lyrics can and do discuss this explicitly. By contrast, blues lyrics have usually talked about sexual relations indirectly, typically through metaphor. We heard this in Bessie Smith's song: her partner is a "coffee grinder" who's got a brand new grind. In Blind Lemon Jefferson's "**Black Snake Moan**," one of the very early country blues recordings, it's easy to imagine what the black snake is, especially when he sings "black snake crawling in my room/and some pretty mama better come and get this black snake soon." Hokum was a blues genre dedicated to the double entendre; songs like "**It's Tight Like That**" are laced with "wink-wink" lyrics. It was the exceptional bluesman who did not deal with sexual relations in at least one of his songs. In Robert Johnson's "**Terraplane Blues**," the woman is a car; he continues the metaphor when describing intercourse: "when I mash down on your little starter/then your spark plug would give me fire."

The lyrics of many postwar rhythm-and-blues songs continued to explore all aspects of man–woman relationships. On some blues recordings the lyrics were so raunchy that they were not issued commercially (a few circulated as bootleg

instrumentation Literally, the instruments chosen to perform a particular score; broadly, the instrumental and vocal accompaniment for a recording.

soul A term used widely in the 1960s by both white and black Americans to describe popular music by African Americans, particularly music, like that of James Brown, marginally influenced by pop or white rock styles.

funk An R&B-derived style that developed in the 1970s, primarily under the guidance of George Clinton. It is character-ized mainly by dense textures (bands may include eight or more musicians) and complex, often sixteen-beat rhythms.

genre Stylistic category.

recordings). Others approached the matter implicitly, as in Roy Brown's 1947 classic **"Good Rockin' Tonight,"** when he says "I'm gonna hold my baby as tight as I can/ Tonight she'll know I'm a mighty mighty man." Here, the "rockin'" in the title refers to sex, not music. In "Shake, Rattle and Roll," Turner describes foreplay in this line: "I'm like a one-eyed cat peeping in a seafood store." It was a metaphor that eluded not only the censors but apparently the musicians who redid the song: in his cover version, Bill Haley changed some of the lyrics in an effort to clean them up but left that line in.

What the blues started, rap has finished. Rap lyrics can talk about sex in the most explicit terms; some leave nothing to the imagination. It is now possible to discuss sexual matters openly, although recordings must wear the record industry's scarlet letter. But perhaps this freedom has come at a price: the music has lost some of the fun that goes along with describing sexual matters elliptically or metaphorically. The good humor that seems to accompany indirect references to sex is a thread that runs from the earliest blues recordings through rhythm and blues and into rock. It seems to have disappeared in recent years.

> **rap** A musical style of the 1980s and beyond characterized by a rhymed text spoken in a heightened voice over a repetitive, mostly rhythmic accompaniment.

2–4d Rhythm and Blues, Rock and Roll, and the Beat

Much of this big-beat music was considered rock and roll, especially when it crossed over to the pop charts and/or was covered by white bands. And many critics and commentators have claimed that "Rocket 88" was the first rock-and-roll record, largely because of the prominent distorted guitar sound. In 1956, these songs and others like them, such as Fats Domino's **"Ain't That a Shame,"** would have been labeled "rock and roll." As Domino told an interviewer, "What you call rock and roll is what we've been playing in New Orleans for 15 years." However, if we understand rock and roll as the music that led directly to rock, and agree that the most fundamental and pervasive feature of rock music is its beat, then this strain of rhythm and blues is not rock and roll: these songs and others like them have the wrong beat.

The fascinating aspect regarding the emergence of rock rhythm is that white bands adopted it before black bands. What makes this fascinating is that the impetus for denser and more active rhythms in popular music has come from Afro-centric musical cultures, especially those in the United States, Cuba, and Brazil, and that the beat that would soon distinguish rock and roll from rhythm and blues would come from Little Richard and Chuck Berry. Despite this, the vast majority of black acts retained the four-beat rhythms—either the standard swing beat or the more active shuffle rhythm—of earlier rhythm and blues through the end of the decade, even as white rock-and-roll bands jumped on the rock-beat bandwagon.

2–5 Electric Blues

Attend any of the many blues festivals throughout North America and you will hear band after band take the stage. Most will feature a full rhythm section with one or more electric guitars; horns are optional. For most contemporary listeners, this is the sound of the blues: the classic blues style that has remained largely unchanged for over half a century. The sounds of these bands are unlike the blues of the twenties and thirties, and it is different from the rhythm and blues that we have just heard. It came together in the early fifties, when deep blues moved north from Mississippi to Chicago and went electric.

> **deep blues** Early acoustic blues originating from the Missis-sippi and surrounding areas.

2–5a Electrifying the Blues

The electric guitar, already a staple in country music and jazz by the early forties, soon began to find its way into the blues. Muddy Waters began playing electric guitar in 1944, so that he could be heard over the crowd noise in the bars where he performed; others followed suit. At the same time, bluesmen like Waters surrounded themselves with other instrumentalists—another guitarist, a drummer, a bass player, and in Waters's case, Little Walter, the soulful master of the harmonica. This new sound has been called electric blues; now it is just the blues.

Electric blues came of age in the fifties. It completed its transformation from a rural to an urban music and its migration from the juke joints and street corners of Mississippi to the bars of Chicago's South Side. Blues kept its soul through the journey, in the music of bluesmen like Muddy Waters and Elmore James.

> **country music** A music genre which emerged out of the commercialization, broadcasting, and recording of southern folk music.

Muddy Waters

Muddy Waters (born McKinley Morganfield, 1915–1983), grew up in Clarksdale, Mississippi, the northwest part of the state in the heart of what is called the Delta region. The population was mostly black, and for the vast majority, life was brutal. Both males and females worked as sharecroppers, often from childhood; Waters was a farm laborer as a boy. Some men made a little more money working as stevedores loading riverboats along the Mississippi, but there too, the days were long, the work hard, and the pay meager. Most lived at subsistence level, trapped in an unending cycle of economic dependence. From this harsh and isolated environment came what Robert Palmer called deep blues, a powerful music that gave expression to, and release from, the brutal conditions of the Delta.

Waters heard this music while he was growing up and began to play it in his teens. He started on the harmonica, then took up the guitar, because, "You see, I was digging Son House and Robert Johnson." By his late 20s, Waters had become a popular performer in the region.

Like many other southern blacks, Waters moved north during World War II, settling on Chicago's South Side. He continued to play, first at house parties, then in small bars, and recorded for Columbia in 1946. (The recordings were not released until many years later.) Still, it was not enough to pay the rent, and Waters was working as a truck driver when he approached Aristocrat Records about recording for them.

Muddy Waters's singing and playing retained its earthiness and passion after he moved north; however, he added the power of amplification and a full rhythm section during his first years in Chicago. Both voice and guitar gained a presence not possible with the "man and his guitar" setup of country blues.

"(I'm Your) Hoochie Coochie Man," the 1954 recording that was Muddy Waters's biggest hit, epitomizes the fully transformed electric blues style. It retains the essence of country blues in Waters's singing and playing yet creates a far richer and more powerful sound than we heard in Robert Johnson's blues. Blues singer Big Bill Broonzy described Waters's appeal in this way:

> It's real. Muddy's real. See the way he plays guitar? Mississippi style, not the city way. He don't play chords, he don't follow what's written down in the book. He plays notes, all blue notes. Making what he's thinking.

And certainly it is all of a piece: Waters's singing brings Willie Dixon's lyrics to life. It makes the references to love potions and voodoo charms, sexual prowess and special status seem believable. It is easy to conjure up such a world and him as the hoochie coochie man. That much remained virtually unchanged from the rawest country blues of the twenties and thirties.

The great achievement of electric blues, however, is that everything else that goes on amplifies Waters's message. Instrumental support includes what amounted to Chess Records' house blues band—bassist (and blues songwriter) Willie Dixon, pianist Otis Spann, and drummer Fred Below—plus guitarist Jimmy Rogers and harmonica player Little Walter, Waters's musical alter ego. Together they weave a dense musical fabric out of riffs and repeated rhythms.

The song alternates between two **textures**: the stoptime of the opening (an enormous expansion of the first four bars of the standard 12-bar blues form), where an instrumental riff periodically punctuates Waters's vocal line, and the free-for-all of the refrain-like finish of each chorus. The stop-time opening contains two competing riffs—one played by the harmonica, the other by the electric guitar. In the refrain, everybody plays—harmonica trills; guitar riffs; piano chords, either lazy Fats Domino–style triplets or on speed; thumping bass; shuffle pattern on the drums—all are woven together with Muddy's singing.

These different melodic and rhythmic strands are an important part of the mix, but none is capable of standing alone. This kind of dense texture, with independent but interdependent lines, was almost unprecedented in small-group music before rock. The closest parallel would be early **New Orleans jazz** band recordings, such as those by King Oliver. And it works. No one gets in anyone else's way. There is no stylistic inconsistency, as is so often the case when country blues singing is mixed with horns or strings.

The electric blues of the fifties also brought nastier guitar sounds into popular music. The distorted guitar in "Rocket 88" may have been an accident, but the overdriven guitar sounds that jumped off numerous blues records were intentional. Almost as soon as they went electric, blues guitarists began to experiment with distortion in order to get a guitar sound that paralleled the rawness of singers like Muddy Waters and Howlin' Wolf. Among the leaders in this direction were Buddy Guy and Elmore James, both based in Chicago through much of the fifties.

Like Waters, Elmore James (1918–1963) came from the Mississippi Delta, but at the southern fringe—closer to Jackson than Clarksdale. Also like Waters, he connected with established Delta bluesmen like Robert Johnson; while in his teens, he began touring with Sonny Boy Williamson. After a three-year tour of duty with the Navy in World War II, he returned to Mississippi and worked during the day as a radio repairman and in the evenings as a musician. He would leave for Chicago in 1951, shortly after recording his top-ten R&B hit song, **"Dust My Broom."**

"Dust My Broom" is a remake of Robert Johnson's 1936 recording "**I Believe I'll Dust My Broom.**" A comparison of the two versions shows how amplification of the guitar and its reverberation through the rest of the band transformed the deep blues of the thirties into the classic electric blues sound of the fifties. James preserves the two key elements of Johnson's guitar playing, the familiar shuffle-style accompanying pattern and the triplet chords that he uses to respond to the vocal phrases. Still, he is just a man with one (acoustic) guitar: skilled but constrained by having to handle both accompaniment and responses.

That's not a problem for James, who is backed by a band with a full rhythm section, including another guitarist playing the shuffle pattern and a drummer rapping out the backbeat along with the rhythm. James opens the song with his signature slide guitar triplets. James apparently used his electronics skills to tweak the sound of his **amplifier** to give his guitar a nastier, more distorted sound. His solo playing is the seminal slide guitar style on an amplified instrument. Electric guitarists playing slide style trace the roots of their approach back to this recording.

textures The relationship of the parts in a musical performance.

New Orleans jazz Style of jazz performance based on the early bands that performed in and around New Orleans; revived in the late 1940s, it is based on collective improvisa-tion and quick tempos. The front-line instruments usually include cornet or trumpet, clarinet, and trombone, with a rhythm section usually including banjo, tuba, and sometimes piano. Also called Dixieland jazz.

amplifier A piece of equipment that can increase the strength of an electric signal.

Early electric blues is a crucially important stage in the transformation of Delta blues into rock guitar playing. Both Johnson and James sing and play in a gritty, deeply felt style, but by amplifying the guitar and supporting it with strong, more active rhythms, the sound is far more forceful.

In the music of Waters and other like-minded Chicago bluesmen, electric blues found its groove during the fifties. By the end of the decade, it had evolved into its classic sound, which it has retained to this day. Its most consistent features include:

- Regular blues form (or an easily recognized variant of it)
- Rough-edged vocals
- Vocal-like responses and solos from the lead guitar or harmonica
- A dense texture, with several instruments playing melody-like lines behind the singer
- A rhythm section laying down a strong beat, usually some form of the shuffle rhythm popularized in forties rhythm and blues

During this time, its stars attracted a loyal following, mostly in the black community. Records by Muddy Waters, B. B. King, Howlin' Wolf, Lowell Fulson, Elmore James, and Bobby Bland consistently found their way onto the R&B charts. They were not as well-known as the pop-oriented groups, but far better known—within and outside the black community—than their country kin from previous generations.

2–5b From Electric Blues to Rock

What electric blues gave to rock came in two installments. The first arrived in the mid-fifties, when Chuck Berry adapted the basic blues band instrumentation—prominent lead guitar, second chord instrument, piano, bass, and drums—to his influential brand of rock and roll.

The second arrived a decade later, when rock musicians dipped deeply into the blues. The Rolling Stones took their name from a 1950 Muddy Waters recording. Rock musicians adapted the blues attitude, as expressed in words and music. The Stones covered Muddy Waters's "**I Can't Be Satisfied**," then reworked it into "(I Can't Get No) Satisfaction" (even though the story behind the title came out differently). Bluesmen like Howlin' Wolf inspired the onstage persona and singing of Jagger and countless others.

Rock also took its dense texture most directly from electric blues and found inspiration in the sounds of blues guitarists. The sounds of the Rolling Stones, the Who, Jimi Hendrix, Eric Clapton, and other major sixties acts have deep blues roots.

Although it was innovative and influential in many other ways, electric blues was certainly in the R&B rhythmic mainstream. The tempos were slower, but the shuffle rhythm heard in so many jump band recordings was also the mainstay of electric blues.

2–6 The Latin Tinge

During the first half of the twentieth century, what was called Latin music infiltrated popular music in America in three waves. The first was the tango, an Argentine dance that was enormously popular during the 1910s. In 1930, Don Azpiazú, a white Cuban bandleader leading black musicians, had a surprise hit with a song entitled "El Manisero" ("**The Peanut Vendor**"). The song introduced Afro-Cuban rhythm and instruments to American audiences and sparked a new dance craze, the rumba, prompting many **Tin Pan Alley** songwriters to write Latin songs.

Tin Pan Alley A nickname for a section of East 28th Street in New York City, where many music publishers had their offices. Also, the styles of the songs created in the first half of the century for these publishers: a Tin Pan Alley song refers to songs by Irving Berlin, George Gershwin, and their contemporaries.

mambo First twentieth-century Latin dance fads to develop on American soil; it merged authentic Afro-Cuban *son* with big-band horns and riffs

The final pre-rock Afro-Cuban dance fad was the **mambo**. Unlike earlier Latin dance fads, the mambo was homegrown, not imported; it was developed during the early forties in uptown New York. Latin musicians, some of whom had worked in the swing bands, cross-bred big-band swing with Latin rhythms and percussion instruments and came up with a hot new dance music. By the late forties, non-Latins were filling up ballrooms. The mambo craze peaked in the fifties. By the end of the decade, the much simpler cha-cha-chá had become the Latin dance of choice.

2–6a Clave Rhythm

The most characteristic feature of Afro-Cuban rhythm is the clave pattern. Clave is to Afro-Cuban rhythm what the backbeat is to American dance rhythms: its most elemental feature and main point of reference. Playing in clave is to Afro-Cuban music what rocking is to rock or swinging is to swing. In stylistically authentic Cuban music, other rhythms conform to clave or react against it in a specific way.

clave rhythm The characteristic rhythm of Afro-Cuban music. It can be represented as: //X x x X x x X x // x x X x X x x x //. The x's indicate an eight-beat rhythm; X's are accented notes. To create a reverse clave rhythm, switch the two measures.

The asymmetrical nature of **clave rhythm** highlights the fundamental difference between Afro-Cuban rhythm and the black rhythms heard in jazz, blues, and popular song. In American black rhythms the beat is typically marked with an instrument such as a walking bass or a strummed guitar. In Afro-Cuban music, the attention is on the faster rhythms and the clave pattern; the beat is felt but not kept by any particular instrument.

However, American musicians, black and white, most often reinterpreted Afro-Cuban rhythm in terms of their own experience. Almost always, they preserved the even division of the beat into two equal parts and typically added elements of the clave pattern and extra percussion instruments to give their music a Latin flavor.

Some of the Latin-influenced music of the early rock era came from New Orleans, where it was blended with the blues. However, much of the more familiar Latin-tinged R&B derived from the Americanized Latin music popular during the fifties: Ruth Brown's "Mambo Baby" was a No. 1 R&B hit in 1954 and other rhythm-and-blues acts, most notably Ray Charles, featured at least one Latin number in their sets. However, the most overt and distinctive merging of Afro-Cuban rhythm and rhythm and blues during the fifties seems to come out of nowhere.

2–6b The Bo Diddley Beat

The nature of the connection between clave rhythm and Bo Diddley's famous beat is just one of several unanswered questions about one of the most fascinating musicians of the rock era. The questions begin with his name. He was born in McComb, Mississippi, in 1928. His father's name was Bates, but he was adopted by a relative, Gussie McDaniel; by most accounts, his real name is Elias McDaniel. In the mid-thirties, the McDaniels family moved to Chicago and settled on the South Side. Like many other black performers (such as the bluesmen Muddy Waters and Howlin' Wolf) he acquired a stage persona, but he claims it came from his schoolmates. As he tells it, students started calling him "Bo Diddley" during his teens and it stuck. (Given McDaniel's Mississippi roots, the name would seem to connect to the diddley bow, a homemade instrument popular in the deep South. However, there is no evidence of such a connection.)

There are musical questions as well. How do we reconcile the extent of his influence with his lack of commercial success? In his fifty-year career, he has had only a few R&B hits and only one Top 40 hit—"Say Man," which reached 20 in 1959. Yet he is, without question, a rock icon; among his many distinctions, he was a second-year inductee into the Rock and Roll Hall of Fame (1987). And he is a celebrity: he returned to the spotlight in the nineties in a famous commercial with Bo Jackson.

There is one aspect of his music about which there is no question: his interest in rhythm. Bo Diddley was fascinated by rhythms and percussion. (The story goes that he added maracas to his street-corner band because he wanted a percussive sound but didn't want to lug a drum set around town. Still, he kept the maracas when he added drums.) Not surprisingly, then, his most important and memorable contribution to popular music is not a song but a beat—the Bo Diddley beat—which appears in the aptly titled 1955 song "Bo Diddley," the first of his R&B hits.

The source of the Bo Diddley beat is the biggest question of all. Although the Bo Diddley beat is virtually identical to the clave pattern, there is no clear connection between the two. We can infer that his famous beat may well have come from a long-standing African American tradition. The practice of beating out rhythms on one's body dates back to slavery; slaves could not make or play percussion instruments, so they used their body. The practice was called patting juba; one such rhythm was apparently the hambone rhythm. Whether there is a link between the rhythm as it was heard in the American South and Cuban rhythm is an open question: keep in mind that New Orleans is close to the Delta and also the original gateway for Cuban music into the United States.

Provenance of the Bo Diddley beat aside, the song "Bo Diddley" focuses on rhythm. It consists mainly of riff-like vocal fragments alternating with the Bo Diddley rhythm, played on guitar and drums. All of this happens over one chord. The lyric is true stream of consciousness: diamond rings, private eyes, animals slaughtered for Sunday clothes, now-you-see-them-now-you-don't people; there is no story. In this respect, it is a grown-up version of a child's song, and it is Bo Diddley's rhythmic take on the one-chord Delta blues style. Rhythms and chords provide a continuing undercurrent to a repetitious, sing-song melody. Even in an era of genuine novelty, Bo Diddley's music stands apart.

2–6c Latin Music and R&B

Recall that Afro-Cuban rhythms and rock rhythm both divide the beat into two equal parts. However, the rhythmic foundation of Afro-Cuban rhythm is more complex than the rhythmic foundation of rock. Its basic texture is richer, yet more open, and the beat is marked less explicitly than in rock and roll. When black music eventually assimilated rock rhythm around 1960, it often gravitated to more Latin rhythmic textures, instead of simply aping the prevailing rock style. Afro-Cuban influence is apparent in both the more "open" sound of the **Motown** songs and the new rhythmic approach that James Brown announced in **"Papa's Got a Brand New Bag"** (1965). Indeed, both occasionally used the clave pattern (for instance, the Miracles' **"Mickey's Monkey"** and Brown's **"Get It Together"**).

The frequent use of Latin percussion instruments (conga, bongos, and others), especially in Motown recordings, provides additional evidence of Afro-Cuban influence. The rhythms of black music from the mid-sixties on are generally more intricate, complex, and active than those heard in the music of white rock bands. Afro-Cuban music was not the sole source of these new rhythms, but its influence—however indirect—was certainly significant, even though it is generally not acknowledged.

2–7 Doo-Wop: R&B Pop

"Life could be a dream, life could be a dream"; "doo, doo, doo, doo, sh-boom." The first part of the lyric is typical of the romantic pop of the era, the second is the signature of **doo-wop**, the most popular kind of fifties rhythm and blues. As the song unfolds, the lyric alternates between explaining why life could be a dream and

Motown A set of stylistic features heard in sixties Motown recordings: melodic saturation, a good mellow beat, a broad spectrum of sound and a predictable format.

doo-wop A pop-oriented R&B genre that typically featured remakes of popular standards or pop-style originals sung by black vocal groups. Doo-wop died out in the early 1960s with the rise of the girl groups and Motown.

nonsense syllables like "hey, nonny ding dong, shalang alang alang." "Sh-boom" returns regularly between phrases of the lyric; it is like a gentle prod that keeps the rhythmic momentum going. Periodically, an entire phrase of nonverbal sounds interrupts the romantic scene unfolding in the rest of the lyric, and the nonverbal sounds from the introduction also serve as the vocal part behind the saxophone solo. Significantly, the title of the song comes from one of these nonsense syllables, not from the first phrase of the lyric.

The function of the nonsense syllables is to inject rhythmic energy into the song. The syllables are typically rich in consonant sounds that explode ("*b*") or sustain ("*sh*" or "*m*"). In the "sh-boom" type parts of the song, the voices become instruments. They are not percussive instruments per se, because they have **pitch**, but the vocal sounds have a percussive quality, like the plucking of a string bass or the slapping of an electric bass.

> **pitch** The relative highness or lowness of a musical sound, determined by the frequency with which it vibrates.

The practice of using the voice to imitate instruments, especially percussive-sounding instruments, is a distinctively black practice. In jazz, the practice is called scat singing. The first familiar examples come from Louis Armstrong's late-twenties recordings; there is no difference in conception between Armstrong the trumpeter and Armstrong the vocalist. Armstrong's vocalizations influenced black performers like Cab Calloway, famous as the "hi-de-ho" man. ("Hi-de-ho" were nonsense syllables woven into his account of "**Minnie the Moocher**," a big hit for him in 1931; the parallel with "Sh-boom" should be clear!) Scat singing gave be-bop (later shortened to **bop**), the new jazz sound of the forties, its name ("be-bop" are the syllables that end a scatted stream of notes). Male gospel quartets were a more direct influence. Most sang *a cappella* (that is, without instrumental accompaniment), so backup vocal parts often assumed a rhythmic as well as a harmonic role.

> **bop** A jazz style that developed in the 1940s, characterized by fast tempos, irregular streams of notes, and considerable rhythmic conflict.

The practice became part of the sound of rhythm and blues in the forties, in such hit songs as Lionel Hampton's "**Hey! Ba-Ba-Re-Bop**" and "Stick" McGhee's "**Drinking Wine Spo-Dee-O-Dee**." With doo-wop the practice became so integral to the music that it gave the style its name. The term doo-wop—borrowed from songs that used the phrase—was applied retrospectively to this music to acknowledge its most salient feature.

2–7a Doo-Wop and Black Singing Groups

Group singing by blacks has a history in sound that extends back to the nineteenth century: there are recordings by vocal groups such the Unique Quartet, the Oriole Quartette, and the Standard Quartette from as early as 1893. These are among the earliest recordings by black performers. Such groups sang a little of everything, from **minstrel-show** routines to sacred songs.

> **minstrel-show** A form of stage entertainment distinguished by cruel parodies of African Americans. Minstrelsy was popular from the early 1840s to the end of the nineteenth century.

The first black vocal group to enjoy widespread popular success was the Mills Brothers, who charted regularly from the mid-thirties. Other black vocal groups followed in their wake, most notably the Ink Spots. These groups sang in a smooth pop style quite different from the gospel male quartets active around the same time.

2–7b Early Doo-Wop

After World War II, pop, gospel, and rhythm and blues came together in a new family of styles that featured male or mostly male singing groups. The styles ranged from gospel-tinged pop ideally suited for slow dancing, to up-tempo numbers and novelty songs. The common threads seem to be the gospel and pop influences (the male gospel quartets and pop vocal groups like the Mills Brothers) and the names, which identify the groups as a unit: the Platters, the Penguins, the Cadillacs, the

Drifters, and countless others. The first recordings of these new sounds appeared in the late forties, many by "bird" groups such as the Ravens and the Orioles.

The Orioles' 1953 hit, "**Crying in the Chapel**," blazed the trail. Its history highlights the blurred genre boundaries in the early rock era: "Crying in the Chapel" was a country song that crossed over to the pop charts, which was then covered by an R&B group whose version also made the pop charts!

2–7c "Sh-Boom," the First Crossover Hit

The breakthrough hit "**Sh-Boom**" came the following year. The original R&B version by the Chords hit both pop and rhythm-and-blues charts the same week: July 3, 1954. The Chords' eye toward the pop charts is clearly evident in "Sh-Boom": it's a blend of "jump band lite" and pre-rock pop. From the jump band it took the shuffle rhythm and instrumentation: rhythm section plus saxophone. But the beat is discreet—very much in the background—and the good saxophone solo straddles the boundary between jazz and honking R&B. Moreover, the song is not a blues, but a pop song in form, if not style.

The song focuses on the voices; the instrumental accompaniment is very much in the background. The Chords' sound is typical: a lead singer (Carl Feaster) with a pleasant but untrained voice, plus four backup singers, including the requisite bass voice (William "Ricky" Edwards), who steps into the spotlight briefly. When singing behind Feaster, the backup singers alternate between sustained chords and the occasional rhythmic interjection—"Sh-boom." And during the saxophone solo, the singers' nonverbal sounds from the introduction mimic the backup riffs behind a soloist in a swing-era **big band**.

The Chords' song exemplified another phenomenon of the early rock era: the one-hit wonder. The Chords recorded on Cat Records, an obscure subsidiary of Atlantic Records; the company released only eighteen discs. This is undoubtedly one reason the group never reached either the pop or R&B charts again. Another factor was their frequent name-changing. After "Sh-Boom" hit, they discovered that another group already owned the name, so they became the Chordcats, then the Sh-Booms. Neither name worked for them, although they remained active as the Sh-Booms through the mid-sixties.

> **big band** Swing-era or swing-style music performed by a big band.

2–7d "Heart and Soul" Songs

Most of the songs sung and recorded by doo-wop groups were either pre-rock pop "standards" (a **standard** is a pop song that has retained its popularity) or newly composed songs that used modern-era popular songs—and one song in particular—as a model. The song most associated with doo-wop is "**Heart and Soul**," a 1938 song written by Frank Loesser and Hoagy Carmichael. The song was important to doo-wop not because it was recorded frequently—the first doo-wop style recording of the song, by the Cleftones, wasn't released until 1961—but because so many songs copied its harmony. It's heard not only in "Sh-Boom" but also "Earth Angel," another big crossover hit in 1954, and numerous other songs, including "You Send Me," discussed in **Chapter 4**.

> **standard** A song that remains popular well after its initial appearance; songs that live on in recordings, films, and live performances.

A sizable majority of the pop songs written between 1925 and 1945 used what was called AABA form. A is an eight-measure section that ends with a musical punctuation of some kind. The other two A phrases are always at least quite similar and occasionally identical. The B section is contrasting, and open-ended, because it leads back to the final statement. This form, and the harmony that helps define it, served as a template for numerous doo-wop songs during the fifties.

Underpinning each A section in "Sh-Boom" is a four-chord progression that repeats four times. Three of the four chords are the same as those used in the blues progression, but the rate of chord change is faster and more regular. This sequence of chords dates back centuries: for Mozart and his contemporaries, it was the grammar of the musical language that they used. However, as used in doo-wop songs, these same progressions represent a transition to a different understanding of the role of harmony. By cycling through a series of chords several with an unvarying rhythm, the progressions anticipate harmonic practice later rock-era rock and pop, and especially twenty-first century pop. It has been common practice in much recent popular music to support the **melody** with cycling chords that remain virtually unchanged for an entire section, or even the complete track. And the "Heart and Soul" progression lives on, in songs like Justin Bieber's 2010 hit "**Baby**."

"Earth Angel" and the Doo-wop Pop Ballad

"**Earth Angel**," another enduring crossover hit from 1954, blended old (Tin Pan Alley–style melody, harmony, and form plus a slow four-beat rhythm in bass and drums) and new (triplet rhythm overlay and the refreshingly untutored singing of Cleveland Duncan and the rest of the Penguins). This distinctive mix transformed "Earth Angel" into one of the most recognizable sounds of the fifties.

Although the song as written is a pre-rock pop song in the style of "Heart and Soul," it clearly belongs to the early rock era, for several reasons. Most obvious is the singing style, which is far removed from the pop crooners who dominated the charts during the fifties. Another is the prominent triplet chords in the piano part, which keep the rhythm afloat at the unusually slow tempo. A third is the more melodic role of the backup singers. Unlike the backup singers in "Sh-Boom," whose main responsibilities were to sing the occasion "Sh-Boom" response and harmonize the melody, the backup singers in the Penguins are singing a melody-like line.

This second layer of melody is an early instance of what would become a common feature in much rock-era music: melodic diffusion. Many rock-era genres spread interesting and appealing melodic material over several vocal and instrumental parts, rather than concentrating melodic interest in the lead vocal part. The Marcels' version of "Blue Moon," recorded in 1961 as doo-wop was in decline, is arguably the ultimate example of this practice in doo-wop: the backup vocal line all but overpowers the melody.

2–7e Cover Versions and Commercial Success

Like "Sh-Boom," "**Earth Angel**" was covered by the Crew-Cuts, whose version charted higher than the original. (A cover is a recording of a song by an act other than the first act to record the song.) The notion of a cover version is a rock-era concept; it depends on a recording being understood as the definitive version of a song, and not simply one of many versions of the song.

Many doo-wop songs were, in effect, cover versions—that is, remakes of existing songs—before the idea of covers surfaced. Many of the songs reconceived by the early doo-wop groups were standards that had been around for a while. However, "**Cross Over the Bridge**," like "Crying in the Chapel," was a current hit. In doo-wop at least, song covering was a two-way street. The repertoire that doo-wop groups recorded clearly suggests that they were trying to locate the pop middle ground.

White covers of black songs occurred frequently in the early years of rock and roll. These early cover versions have acquired racial baggage because commentators have viewed them as white acts riding on the coattails of black acts, and enjoying the success that should have gone to the black act. The injustice of covers is not so much a musical issue: the black acts who sang doo-wop were borrowing liberally

---

melody The most musically interesting part of a musical texture. The melody is typically distinguished from other parts by the interest and individuality of its contour and rhythm.

from white pop. Instead, it's mainly a financial and racial issue: that blacks did not have easy access to the pop market, that many were naive about the music business and never saw the money that their records made, that the labels that signed and recorded them could not compete with the **majors**, and that white versions sold better than the black originals.

The greatest *musical* injustice evident in white covers of black recordings is bad taste: the pop music establishment superimposing their conception of a sound with mass appeal without any real understanding of what was innovative and meaningful about R&B. Pat Boone's covers of Little Richard's **"Tutti Frutti"** and Fats Domino's "Ain't That a Shame," both of which outsold the originals, are particularly egregious examples of this practice. The musical result was more satisfactory when the white musicians studied and understood the music that they were covering. The recording of "Shake, Rattle and Roll" by Bill Haley is more satisfactory musically because of his stylistic affinity with R&B. And covers were occasionally a springboard to creativity: Buddy Holly's cover of "Bo Diddley" was a precursor to "Not Fade Away."

> **majors** Major record labels.

2–8 Rhythm and Blues, 1945–1955

The rhythm and blues that took shape after the end of the war was a group of vigorous and vital new sounds in popular music. The rhythms were more active and aggressive, the sounds louder and often grittier, the riffs more frequent, and the lyrics in blues songs often more direct and down to earth. The contrast with the dominant popular music was striking and substantial. So it was not surprising that doo-wop was the music that helped R&B cross over to the pop market. For whites, doo-wop put a fresh coat of paint on familiar-sounding material. For the majority of white teens who had heard their parents' pop growing up, the familiar elements must have made the music more accessible.

The first decade of rhythm and blues is a body of music whose influence far exceeds its commercial success during the decade it was released. Market presence came only at the end, and then more so in cover versions by white acts than the original versions. Although some of the songs occasionally resurface in cover versions—Death Cab for Cutie released their reconception of "Earth Angel" in 2005!—the legacy has more to do with the styles and their role in shaping the next half-century of popular music. This music did not use rock rhythm, but the strong, active rhythms in so much of it—shuffle rhythm, triplets, prominent backbeat— were an important precursor to rock's most defining feature. Electric blues quickly evolved into its classic style, which numerous blues and boogie bands emulated. Doo-wop was the bridge between pre-rock pop and the new black pop of the sixties. By the time rhythm and blues began to cross over to the pop charts, it had a new name: rock and roll.

CHAPTER 3

ROCK AND ROLL

Learning Objectives:

1) Discuss the difficulty of pinpointing the origin of rock and roll.

2) Compare the musical differences between **rockabilly** and **rhythm and blues**.

3) Audibly identify a **walking** bass line in a musical example.

4) Comment on some of the key musical contributions of Chuck Berry.

5) Contrast the styles of Little Richard and Jerry Lee Lewis.

6) Summarize the developments of early rock and roll through key performers.

Chapter Introduction

In 1986, the Rock and Roll Hall of Fame Museum in Cleveland, Ohio, admitted its first class of inductees: Chuck Berry, James Brown, Ray Charles, Sam Cooke, Fats Domino, the Everly Brothers, Buddy Holly, Jerry Lee Lewis, Elvis Presley, and Little Richard. Performers become eligible for induction 25 years after the release of their first record. Selection criteria include "the influence and significance of the artist's contributions to the development and perpetuation of rock and roll."

If the complete list of inductees can be used as a reliable guide, rock and roll is, for the Rock and Roll Hall of Fame, more or less equivalent to our rock era as an umbrella term for the rock-related music of the last several decades. In this chapter, we describe another more specific understanding of "rock and roll." Our central point of reference will be those artists who will not have been discussed in **chapters 2** and **4**, or—in the case of James Brown—whose most important work would come in the sixties. We look to the music of Chuck Berry, the Everly Brothers, Buddy Holly, Jerry Lee Lewis, Elvis Presley, and Little Richard to lead us to a musical understanding of rock and roll.

The music of these six musicians is the heart and soul of this more time-limited understanding of rock and roll. Although their music represents only a small fraction of the new music of the late fifties, it defines the core and the boundaries of rock and roll, as a style distinct from both pop and rhythm and blues in the fifties, and the rock of the sixties. Rock and roll grew out of rhythm and blues; in the latter part of the fifties, it acquired an increasingly distinct identity. Our primary objective in this chapter is to trace the evolution of rock and roll from its first use as a "cover" label for rhythm and blues to its premature "death" in 1959, by which time it had laid the foundation for sixties rock. We begin in 1951.

Experience an interactive version of this era in MINDTAP

3–1 The Beginnings of Rock and Roll

When did rock and roll begin? The answer depends a great deal on the context in which the question is asked. Does it have to do with the term itself? Did rock and roll begin when people labeled rhythm and blues "rock and roll"? Or did it begin when young white singers began covering rhythm-and-blues songs? Or when the media acknowledged a new kind of music and its new stars? Or when what was called "rock and roll" brought new sounds to the pop charts? The answers to all of these questions shed light on the emergence of rock and roll.

3–1a Alan Freed

"Rockin' and rollin'" was originally a euphemism for the sexual act, as we have noted. The expression had been in use on recordings for almost 30 years by the time disc jockey Alan Freed attached "rock and roll" to a musical style. Freed was an early and influential advocate of rhythm and blues. Unlike most of the disc jockeys of the era, he refused to play white cover versions of R&B hits, a practice that gained him respect among black musicians but made him enemies in the business. While broadcasting over WJW in Cleveland in 1951, he began using "rock and roll" as a euphemism of a different kind: through him, the term became a code word among whites for "rhythm and blues."

Freed's "Moondog's Rock and Roll Party" developed a large audience among both whites and blacks, so he took his advocacy of rhythm and blues one step further, into promotion. He put together touring stage shows of rhythm-and-blues artists, which played to integrated audiences. His first big event, the Moondog Coronation Ball, took place in 1952; 25,000 people, the majority of them white, showed up at a facility that could accommodate only a small fraction of that number. The ensuing pandemonium was the first of many "incidents" in Freed's career as a promoter.

Freed linked the term *rock and roll* to rhythm and blues, so it's no wonder that Fats Domino and producer Dave Bartholomew, the mastermind of so many New Orleans R&B hits, commented that rock and roll *was* rhythm and blues. Bartholomew said, undoubtedly with some bitterness, "We had rhythm and blues for many, many a year, and here come in a couple of white people and they call it rock and roll, and it was rhythm and blues all the time!"

In 1954, Freed moved to New York in order to offer his rock-and-roll radio show on WINS. By that year, rock and roll took its first steps toward an identity distinct from rhythm and blues, with white takes on rhythm and blues. In 1954, the best-known example of this was the Crew Cuts' cover of "**Sh-Boom**." However, in Memphis and in small towns in Pennsylvania and neighboring states, rockabilly, a more significant white reinterpretation of R&B, was taking shape.

3–2 Rockabilly

Carl Perkins, perhaps the truest of the rockabilly stars, once explained his music this way: "To begin with . . . rockabilly music, or rock and roll . . . was a country man's song with a black man's rhythm. I just put a little speed into some of the slow blues licks." As Perkins described it, rockabilly was the latest take in a long line of country takes on black music. It continues a trend that began with Jimmie Rodgers's blue yodels, and ran through Bob Wills's **western swing**, and Hank Williams's "moanin' the blues."

> **western swing** A swing style of country music which emerged in the Southwest in the 1930s.

Rockabilly was a state of mind—and body. It was the music of liberation for southern white males: what they danced to on Saturday nights when they wanted to "get real, real gone." As Glenn Gass observed, "Rockabilly was distinctly and proudly southern." Its capital was Memphis, and its capitol building a small storefront located at 706 Union Avenue, where Sam Phillips operated Sun Records. A legion of Johnny B. Goodes, many of whom sang and played with the abandon of black rhythm-and-blues musicians, beat a path to Phillips's door. However, even as southern rockabilly was taking shape in Memphis, other musicians outside the South were following a similar path.

The first big rockabilly hit came from an unlikely source, by way of an unlikely place, and took an unlikely path. Bill Haley (1925–1981), who recorded it, grew up in Pennsylvania listening to the Grand Ole Opry and dreaming of country music stardom. By the late forties he had begun fronting small bands—one was called the Four Aces of Western Swing—and enjoyed some local success. Over the next few years, he began to give his music a bluesier sound and chose—or wrote—songs with teen appeal. "**Crazy, Man, Crazy**" (1953) was his first hit. In 1954, he had some success with a song called "**Rock Around the Clock**"; it reached No. 23 on the pop charts.

A year later, "Rock Around the Clock" resurfaced in the film *The Blackboard Jungle*. The connections among film, song, and performer were tenuous. The film portrays juvenile delinquents in a slum high school, but "Rock Around the Clock" is exuberant rather than angry, and Haley, at almost 30, looks nothing like a rebel. But it was music for and about teens (parents weren't likely to rock around the clock); that was enough for the producers. With the release of the film, the song returned to the charts and skyrocketed to No. 1. It was Haley's big moment. He had a few other minor hits but never repeated his chart-topping success.

"Rock Around the Clock" might be characterized as a lite version of rhythmic R&B: it has the shuffle beat that we associate with so much fifties rhythm and blues, but the tempo is faster, and the beat-keeping is more subtle. The sound is also less aggressive: the vocal style is not as rough, and the instruments play in a higher register; the saxophonist doesn't honk a solo—the electric guitar is the featured instrument. Overall, it's a brighter sound.

"Rock Around the Clock" also takes its form and harmony from rhythm and blues. Like so many songs of the era, it is a 12-bar blues. As in songs like "**It's Tight Like That**," the first four bars function as the verse, and the last eight as the refrain.

While Haley nibbled at the charts, a grittier form of rockabilly was taking shape in Memphis. We encounter it in the music of the performer who would eventually become rock and roll's biggest star.

3-2a Elvis, Sam Phillips, and Rockabilly

In the summer of 1953, a young truck driver named Elvis Presley (1935–1977) walked into the Sam Phillips Recording Service to make a demo record. Phillips wasn't in, so his assistant, Marion Keisker, handled the session. Perhaps to make him feel at ease, she asked him about himself. The conversation went something like this:

Marion: What kind of singer are you?

Elvis: I sing all kinds.

Marion: Who do you sound like?

Elvis: I don't sound like nobody.

Marion: Hillbilly?

Elvis: Yeah, I sing hillbilly.

Marion: Who do you sound like in hillbilly?

Elvis: I don't sound like nobody.

This now-legendary encounter gives us some insight into Elvis's success. Imagine yourself—barely out of high school and with no professional experience—having such a clear sense of who you are and what you can do. Elvis truly didn't sound like anyone else; he was the "white man with the negro feel" that Sam Phillips had been seeking for several years.

Presley recorded his first local hit for Phillips's Sun Records in 1954. The record, a cover of bluesman Arthur Crudup's **"That's All Right,"** sparked interest on country-western radio (although some stations wouldn't play it because Elvis sounded too black). Within a year he had reached No. 1 nationally on the country-and-western charts with **"Mystery Train"**—one of Elvis's most enduring early hits. Elvis's Sun sessions are quintessential rockabilly. In Junior Parker's 1953 version—the one Presley covered—**"Mystery Train"** is a boogie-based rhythm-and-blues song; it chugs along at a slow pace underneath Parker's bluesy vocal and the occasional saxophone train whistle. Elvis's version is brighter and more upbeat (recall Perkins's remark), and it uses a more country-style beat. The rhythm section sets a honky-tonk, **two-beat** bass alternating with a heavy backbeat on the electric guitar. But the backbeat is modified with a quick rebound that begins alternately on, then off, the beat. In form, the song is a modified blues; it has the poetic and melodic form of a blues song, but its harmony and phrase length are slightly irregular.

Elvis's singing is the magical element. In both its basic **timbre** and its variety, his sound is utterly unique—the purest Elvis. It ranges from a plaintive wail on the opening high notes to the often-imitated guttural singing at the end of each chorus. Elvis positions himself not only between country and rhythm and blues, but beyond them. We don't hear the nasal twang so common in country music, nor do we hear the rough-edged sound of a blues singer. Elvis draws on both but sounds like neither ("I don't sound like nobody").

The distinctive sound of Elvis's voice is only part of the magic. Just as remarkable is his ability to adapt his sound to suit the material. He can emulate the "high lonesome" sound of **bluegrass** singers like Bill Monroe, or croon when he sings pop songs like **"Harbor Lights"** and **"Blue Moon."** Elvis could evoke almost any style and still sound like himself. Although he didn't play much guitar, he played the radio really well. He was an equal opportunity listener with an insatiable appetite for music, and what he heard he used.

Sam Phillips, Sun Records, and Rockabilly

Elvis was not the only rockabilly artist to get his start at Sam Phillips's Sun Studio. In 1950, while still working as a DJ, Phillips (1923–2003) started his Memphis Recording Service. Initially, he recorded rhythm-and-blues artists like Jackie Brenston and Ike Turner, as well as important Memphis-based bluesmen like B. B. King and Howlin' Wolf. Phillips's studio was by far the best place in the region for black musicians to record. Phillips treated the musicians with respect and approached his work with them imaginatively, as we heard in **"Rocket 88."** Phillips saw the growing market for rhythm and blues from the inside and formed Sun Records after problems with other record companies. He stayed on the lookout for the "white man with the negro feel" until Elvis walked in his door in 1953. In the wake of Elvis's regional success, other top rockabilly acts soon showed up at his studio: Carl Perkins, Jerry Lee Lewis, and somewhat later, Roy Orbison. He also recorded some of the top hard-country acts of the era, including Johnny Cash.

---

two-beat The division of the measure into two primary beats or accents; the rhythmic basis of the fox trot and other early syncopated instrumental styles.

timbre The distinctive tone quality of a voice or an instrument.

bluegrass An updated version of country's old-time string band music. Bluegrass developed in the late 1940s under the guidance of mandolinist Bill Monroe.

Like so many other men behind the scenes during the early years of rock, Phillips wore many hats. As he built up the Memphis Recording Service into Sun Records, he became not only the engineer but also the producer and promoter of the recordings on his label. In recognition of his seminal role in shaping rock and roll and rhythm and blues, Phillips was, with Alan Freed, the first nonperformer inducted into the Rock and Roll Hall of Fame.

3–2b Rockabilly and Rock and Roll

In rockabilly songs like "Rock Around the Clock" and "Mystery Train," we hear the first stage in the separation of rhythm and blues and rock and roll. Unlike the pop-oriented covers of rhythm-and-blues (and country-and-western) songs (such as the Crew Cuts' version of "Sh-Boom," a dated-sounding cover of the original), rockabilly was a genuinely new sound. It drew on rhythm and blues, but it was distinctly different. In 1955 "Rock Around the Clock" was rock and roll: the first No. 1 hit that was neither pop nor a white cover of a rhythm-and-blues song. But it lacked crucial features that would soon distinguish rock and roll not only from pop but also from rhythm and blues, and that would ultimately define rock.

Bill Haley would never really go beyond rockabilly; for the rest of his career he essentially relived his early hits. His star faded about the time Elvis's soared. For Elvis, the defining moment in his career came late in 1955 when, with the help of his manager-to-be Colonel Tom Parker, Elvis moved from Sun Records to RCA. Although Elvis's records were selling well, Phillips was in a financial bind, so he was willing to sell Elvis's contract to the highest bidder, because he was sure that Carl Perkins, another one of his up-and-coming acts, would be just as popular. RCA paid Phillips $35,000 for the contract, $10,000 more than Atlantic Records had offered. Almost overnight, Elvis became a national celebrity.

3–3 Elvis Presley: The First Rock-and-Roll Star

RCA quickly got Elvis in the studio. "**Heartbreak Hotel**," his first No. 1, topped the charts in March 1956. Later that year, he made his first Hollywood film, *Love Me Tender*; he would make three more, including *Jailhouse Rock*, before his induction into the army. Within a few months, Elvis had become a national phenomenon. Within two years, he had recorded several No. 1 hits and appeared on numerous television programs, including *The Ed Sullivan Show*, the Sunday night staple for so many Americans during the fifties.

Elvis's sound caught the attention of radio listeners, but it was his looks and his moves that propelled him to stardom. He became the symbol of rock and roll for millions—both those who idolized him and those who despised him. With his totally uninhibited stage manner, teen-tough dress, greased pompadour, and energetic singing style, Elvis projected a rebellious attitude that many teens found overwhelmingly attractive. By contemporary standards, Elvis seems tame—almost wholesome. But in his day, this was bold stuff, and he took a lot of heat for it. On this account, we can admire Elvis's courage. He was rock and roll's lightning rod. For teens, he was all that was right with this new music; for their parents, he symbolized all that was wrong with it. And, for all intents and purposes, he stood alone.

The *Billboard* charts reflect his singular status. Except for Elvis's hits, rock and roll represented only a modest segment of the popular-music market. The top-selling albums during this time were mostly soundtracks from Broadway shows and film musicals. Even sales of singles, which teens bought, show that rock and roll did not enjoy the unconditional support of America's youth. The top singles artists during the same period were either pre-rock stars (Frank Sinatra and Perry Como), younger artists singing in a pre-rock style (Andy Williams or Johnny Mathis), teen stars like Pat Boone, who covered early rock-and-roll songs, or vocal groups like the Platters, whose repertoire included a large number of reworked Tin Pan Alley standards. Among the lesser figures—from a commercial perspective— were such important and influential artists as Buddy Holly, Chuck Berry, Little Richard, and Ray Charles. Elvis was, by far, the most important commercial presence in rock and roll; no one else came close.

3-3a The King of Rock and Roll?

Here's a heretical thought: Elvis Presley, the king of rock and roll, sang very little rock and roll. Such a statement would have been literally incredible to teenagers living in 1956 or 1957; for them, and their parents, Elvis embodied rock and roll. In his discussion of Elvis in *The Story of Rock*, Carl Belz writes:

> Elvis Presley is the most important individual rock artist to emerge during the music's early development between 1954 and 1956. His extraordinary popularity surpassed that of any artist who appeared in those years, and it remained as a standard for almost a decade. . . .. For the music industry, Presley was "king" for almost ten years. He was the first rock artist to establish a continuing and independent motion picture career, the first to have a whole series of million-selling single records— before 1960 he had eighteen—and the first to dominate consistently the tastes of the foreign record market, especially in England, where popularity polls listed him among the top favorites for each year until the arrival of the Beatles.

Belz equates importance almost exclusively with popularity. His list of Elvis's firsts contains no musical innovations; importance is strictly numbers and visibility. However, Elvis's contributions to rock and roll (and rock) extend beyond his remarkable commercial success. He brought a fresh look, a fresh attitude, and a fresh sound to popular music. All three proved to be enormously influential.

Elvis gave rock and roll its most memorable visual images. His looks sent girls into hysteria and guys to the mirror, where they greased their hair and combed it into Elvis-like pompadours. His uninhibited, sexually charged stage persona scandalized adults even as it sent teen pulses racing. These images endure, as the legion of Elvis imitators reminds us. There had been flamboyant black performers, like T-Bone Walker, whose stage antics included playing his guitar behind his head while doing the splits, but no popular white entertainer had ever moved like Elvis did, and no one had ever looked like he enjoyed it as much. Even now, when we watch clips of Elvis performing, we sense that he is having fun. This was an extraordinarily liberating presence for a new generation of pop stars.

We get some sense of his presence and his appeal in the scene from his 1957 film *Jailhouse Rock* where he sings the title song. In staging the scene, choreographer Alex Romero wisely asked Elvis to perform some of his songs, then choreographed the movements of the other dancers to mesh with Elvis's moves. In the scene, we see that for Elvis, all of this is fun. He moves freely, spontaneously; the other dancers seem routine by comparison. Elvis's uninhibited movement, evident in film and television clips, contrasts sharply with pop singers—white and black—who simply stand in front of **microphones** and croon their songs.

microphones A device that converts sound waves into an electric signal. The microphone has been in use in popular music since the 1920s.

"Jailhouse Rock," which was released as a single in conjunction with the film, highlights the qualities that made Elvis so appealing, evidences the craft of Leiber and Stoller, who wrote the song, and shows rock and roll on the road to musical differentiation from rhythm and blues.

"Jailhouse Rock" begins with guitar and drums marking off a stop-time rhythm, which continues as Elvis begins to sing. The beginning of the song is, practically speaking, all Elvis, and he makes the most of it. There is an exuberance and a lack of inhibition in his singing that jumps out of the speakers. In this song, Elvis communicates fun—the exhilaration of moving to the beat (even when it can only be felt)—in a way that was unprecedented in pop. Especially when compared to songs like Perry Como's "Hot Diggity," there is an emotional honesty to Elvis's singing that transcends the staginess of the scene in the film. The story may be fake, but Elvis's enthusiasm is real. Elvis found this kind of realness in the blues, and in songs like "Jailhouse Rock" he brought it into the mainstream.

When viewed in the context of the music that he recorded before his induction into the army, Elvis's performance is even more remarkable, because it is only one of many dimensions to his musical personality. In slow songs like "Love Me Tender" and "Don't," he becomes rock's first crooner; his voice is lower, sweeter, and more intimate. Even a quick sampling of his early hits and Sun recordings shows his almost chameleon-like ability to adjust his vocal style to the musical and lyrical context. Few rock-era singers have matched either the innate quality or the expressive range of his voice.

"Jailhouse Rock" was the work of Jerry Leiber and Mike Stoller. Leiber and Stoller were a white songwriting and (later) producing team, also from Los Angeles, who had grown up listening to rhythm and blues. Active from 1950, they had scored big in 1953 with "Hound Dog," recorded initially by Big Mama Thornton and later covered by Elvis. They later wrote several other songs for Elvis, most notably "Jailhouse Rock."

"Jailhouse Rock" is a verse/chorus blues form in which the first phrase is doubled in length. To make the verse (and Elvis) stand out and highlight the verse/chorus distinction, Leiber and Stoller provide minimal accompaniment—just enough to sustain the momentum under Elvis's singing. In the chorus part of the form, when the rhythm instruments play continuously, the guitar pumps out the boogie-based pattern that is almost identical in pitch to that used in "Rocket 88." It operates just above the electric bass—still a new instrument in 1957. By contrast, the piano is in a very high register. The wide separation leaves the midrange completely to Elvis; the prominence of guitar and bass gives the texture a dark sound that helps project the message of the song: we're in jail (dark), but we're still going to have a good time (Elvis).

Rhythmically, "Jailhouse Rock" shows rock and roll in transition. The most rocklike feature is the guitar pattern, which divides the beat into two equal parts. The difference between this version and the same pattern in a shuffle rhythm (as heard in "Rocket 88") is striking; it shows rock and roll moving away from the shuffle rhythm heard in so much rhythm and blues. But Elvis is not fully committed to this new rhythmic approach. By accenting and slightly lengthening the first note of each pair, Elvis creates a rhythmic feel (evident especially in the stop-time verse sections) that is somewhere between a standard rock rhythm and a shuffle rhythm. And even though the bass player is playing an electric bass, he is still walking—one note on each beat, like a swing-era or jazz bassist. Most strikingly, the band switches to a swing rhythm in the instrumental interlude; we can almost hear a sigh of relief from the guitarist and drummer as they let go in a rhythm that they know how to feel. Because of the rhythmic inconsistencies, "Jailhouse Rock" is rock and roll commercially but not quite rock and roll rhythmically.

The most influential and musically significant part of Elvis's career lasted only three years. It ended in 1958, when he was inducted into the army. Although still a major public figure in the sixties and seventies, he seldom recaptured the freshness of his earlier years. His fans still call him the king of rock and roll, but is that a reflection of his enduring popularity or his contribution to the development of rock and roll? We consider this question in our discussion of Chuck Berry.

3–4 Chuck Berry: The Architect of Rock and Roll

Sometime early in 1955, well before Elvis's fateful meeting with Colonel Parker, Chuck Berry (1926–2017) "motorvated" (to use a Chuck Berry word) from St. Louis to Chicago to hear Muddy Waters perform at the Palladium Theater. Waters had been Berry's idol for years, although when Berry performed with the Johnny Johnson Trio, they played many different kinds of music. After the concert, Berry went backstage to meet his idol. When he asked Waters how to find a record deal, Waters suggested that he get in touch with Leonard Chess. Two weeks later, Berry was back in Chicago, to give Leonard Chess a demo tape containing four songs. Among them was Berry's remake of a song called "**Ida Red**." Chess liked the song, Berry recorded it, retitled it "**Maybellene**," and Chess released it on August 20, 1955.

"Maybellene" caught the ear of Alan Freed, who promoted the song by playing it frequently on his radio show after negotiating a share of the songwriting credits—and the royalties that went with them. With Freed's considerable help—legend has it that Freed played the song for two hours straight on one broadcast—"Maybellene" quickly jumped to No. 5 on the *Billboard* "Best Seller" chart.

It would take Berry almost a year to get another song on the pop charts. "Roll Over, Beethoven" reached the charts in the fall of 1956. However, over the next two years, Berry had four Top 10 singles, from "**School Days**" to "**Johnny B. Goode**." In the hits from "Roll Over, Beethoven" to "Johnny B. Goode," Berry assembled the distinctive sound of rock and roll, step by step. When he was done, rock and roll was well along the road to rock: bands like the Beach Boys, the Beatles, the Rolling Stones, and the Dave Clark Five covered far more Chuck Berry songs than any other rock-and-roll artist.

3–4a "Maybellene," His First Hit

Berry's musical innovations were a synthesis of the music that he liked and played. Waters's music was a big influence, although Berry took his music in a quite different direction. Berry's musical apprenticeship also included singing and playing not only blues, but also rhythm and blues, pop, and what he called hillbilly—his take on country music. These numbers were especially popular with the patrons at the Cosmopolitan Club in East St. Louis, where Berry fronted a trio. Another key element was his long-time association with Johnny Johnson, a fine blues pianist who was a master of boogie-woogie. Johnson originally hired Berry to join his trio, but Berry, the more flamboyant entertainer by far, soon took over as leader.

Because Chess's featured artist was Waters, Berry included tapes of blues numbers to his meeting with Chess. But Chess thought that "Ida May," Berry's reworking of the old-time country song "Ida Red," had a much better shot at crossing over to the pop market. Berry claimed that he had learned the song from Bob Wills's recording of "Ida Red." (Some years later Wills provided his own sequel: "Ida Red Likes the Boogie"). Berry's version, which became "Maybellene" (allegedly after the cosmetic company) at the recording session, was a transformation of the original so drastic that the connection between the two songs is not at all clear.

Chess was right: "Maybellene" was an immediate success, and Berry was on his way to rock-and-roll fame. In "Maybellene" we can hear several of the features that distinguished Berry's music throughout the latter part of the fifties. Here they are, in order of appearance:

An Aggressive Guitar Sound

The song begins with an unaccompanied guitar riff. There are two features of the riff that stand out. One is the edge to the sound—not as distorted as Kizart's guitar in "Rocket 88" but far from mellow. It is a much more aggressive sound than that heard in pop, country, or even most rhythm and blues. The exception, of course, is electric blues; Berry's sound is closer to the guitar style of electric blues guitarists like T-Bone Walker and Muddy Waters than any other guitar style of the era. This is one important area of influence.

The other is a Berry trademark: the use of double notes. When Berry plays two notes simultaneously, it makes the sound thicker, which in turn gives it more impact. His way of bending the notes (heard here mainly in the guitar solo) is reminiscent of the slide (or bottleneck) guitar style of blues guitarists.

A Full Rhythm Section

Almost immediately, the other instruments enter: piano, string bass, drums, and maracas (played by Jerome Green, who also played them with Bo Diddley). Maracas aside, this is, with Berry, the instrumentation of the fifties electric blues band: full rhythm section but with no saxophone. And as in the electric blues band, the electric guitar is the most prominent instrument. That the recording would feature blues-band instrumentation is not surprising: Berry brought pianist Johnny Johnson, his long-time associate, with him from St. Louis. Bassist Willie Dixon, who wrote Waters's **"(I'm Your) Hoochie Coochie Man,"** and drummer Fred Below were Chess house musicians during the fifties.

A Souped-Up Honky-Tonk Beat

"Maybellene" features Berry's take on the two-beat rhythm used in honky-tonk. Except for the guitar solo, where the band shifts into a four-beat swing rhythm, the song features a two-beat rhythm. The difference between Berry's version of a two-beat rhythm and the one in general use is mainly in the backbeat, which is far stronger than in a pop or country two-beat. With both Berry and the drummer emphasizing it, it is more prominent than the beat. It stands out more in the two-beat sections than it does in the swing beat sections because it is in opposition to the beat, rather than in addition to a beat. The heavy backbeat would be one component of Berry's revolutionary rock beat.

Verse/Chorus Blues Form

The title-phrase refrain frames several episodes in Berry's humorous account of a car chase. The refrain is a straightforward 12-bar blues. The verses are also twelve bars in length, but the accompaniment stays on one chord throughout. Almost all of Berry's fifties hits use some kind of blues form.

Teen-Themed Lyrics

The refrain of "Maybellene" seems to set up a story about lost love. However, the verses are strictly car talk. We learn much more about the two cars—a Coupe de Ville Cadillac and a V8 Ford—than we do about their drivers, and we never do find out what happens when Berry finally catches Maybellene.

The lyrics are key to the success of Berry's song. They tapped into the fifties teen enthusiasm for cars—this was the age of the so-called hot rod (think *Grease*).

And the idea of a working-class car overtaking the far more expensive car of the era made the story even more appealing. (Ironically, Chuck Berry went on to have a garage filled with vintage Cadillacs in pristine condition.)

What is absent from "Maybellene" is the most critical component of Berry's conception of rock and roll. He would add and perfect it in a series of hits, beginning with "**Roll Over, Beethoven**."

3–4b Rock Rhythm and Rock Style

Berry's hit recordings between "Roll Over, Beethoven" (1956) and "Johnny B. Goode" document the synthesis that eventually produced rock and roll's beat and texture. Berry's instrumental contribution was twofold: he provided both the first important model for lead guitar playing and the first definitive rock rhythm guitar style.

The lead guitar style came first. In "Roll Over, Beethoven," the guitar introduction builds on the thick double-note style that Berry used in "Maybellene." It becomes even more insistent because it is now based on rock rhythm. Berry was not a virtuoso guitarist, like many of those who followed him, such as Jimi Hendrix or Eric Clapton. But his playing was perfectly suited to broadcast the new rhythm that would define rock and roll: the repeated notes made the rhythm insistent; the double notes gave it density.

In the long nights at the Cosmopolitan Club, Berry must have heard hours and hours of Johnny Johnson's boogie-woogie. What Berry did was transfer boogie-woogie left-hand patterns, similar to the ones heard on "**Roll 'Em, Pete**," to the guitar. The repetitive boogie-woogie patterns became, in Berry's adaptation, the first authentic rock-based rhythm guitar style; even in medium-tempo songs, he typically divides the beat into two equal parts. In "Roll Over, Beethoven," this pattern is very much in the background. In "**Rock and Roll Music**," it is more prominent, but there is no lead guitar.

Finally, in "Johnny B. Goode" (1958), Berry—presumably through the miracle of **overdubbing**; there is no other guitar player credited on the recording date— puts the whole package together: great solo breaks, plus the boogie pattern prominent under both lead guitar and vocal lines. This recording brings together some of the essential features of rock style: backbeat; the **eight-beat rhythm**, completely purged of any swing influence; strong rhythm guitar; and assertive lead guitar. It was this sound, above all, that would inspire the next generation of rockers.

What is fascinating and somewhat surprising is that neither the drummer nor bass player seemed to grasp Berry's new conception and adapt it to their instruments. Below, the drummer, continues to pound out the backbeat but does not try to match up with Berry's rock rhythm. Throughout most of "Johnny B. Goode," bassist Willie Dixon plays a walking bass line, more appropriate for swing or rhythm and blues. Occasionally he interjects a fast-moving line, but the overall feel is still the walking bass. This may have been due in part to his instrument: it is hard to play loud and play fast on an unamplified string bass. Musically, "Johnny B. Goode" is rock and roll and not rock because the bass is acoustic, not electric, and because both bass and drums are playing a swing rhythm with a strong backbeat, similar to that heard in "**Shake, Rattle and Roll**." Berry was sending the message in his vocal and in his guitar playing, but the rest of the band wasn't receiving it. Rhythmically, rock and roll became rock only when the entire band bought into a rock rhythmic conception. That would not happen until the early sixties—at times in covers of Berry's songs.

Like most of Berry's fifties hits, "Johnny B. Goode" is a verse/chorus blues. Here, the song begins with a storytelling verse, which consists of six two-measure

overdubbing The process of recording an additional part onto an existing recording.

eight-beat rhythm A rhythmic template in which the fastest rhythmic layer moves twice the speed of the beat: two times per beat! four beats = 8-beat rhythm. Also called a "rock beat" because it is the most common rhythmic foundation in early rock and punk.

phrases set to the blues progression. By contrast, the chorus repeats the refrain "Go, go Johnny go" five times before concluding with "Johnny B. Goode."

Berry was remarkably inventive in his approach to blues form: there are subtle differences from song to song, yet all clearly build on the basic blues progression. His use of refrain-type blues form offers additional takes on this now-venerable practice. Still, his seemingly limitless variations kept both his sound and the form fresh.

3-4c Berry and His Audience

In "Johnny B. Goode," Berry might be describing a rockabilly, or a bluesman—we don't know the race. What is clear is that the hero of the song comes from the outside. As with "Maybellene," the subject resonated with teens. Like so many songs of the mid-fifties, Berry's hits have teen themes: cars, school, rebellion, rock and roll. But that's where the similarity ends. Unlike "Earth Angel" and its countless clones, Berry's lyrics were not sentimental pop watered down for teens. Nor were they the barely articulate sentiments of Gene Vincent ("Be-Bop-A-Lula, she's my baby . . . don't mean maybe") or the personal reflections of Buddy Holly.

His lyrics are accessible, yet sophisticated: "Roll Over, Beethoven, and tell Tchaikovsky the news." They have catchy new words, like "motorvatin'." They talk about relationships but not love: "Maybellene" is a good example. They're instructive: the lyric to "Rock and Roll Music" not only lays out a key ingredient of the style "got a backbeat, you can't lose it" but also distinguishes rock and roll from all the other music in the air.

How did a black man speak so easily to white teens without either compromising his dignity or threatening the establishment during a period of real racial tension? (1957, the year that Berry recorded "Rock and Roll Music," was also the year that President Eisenhower forcibly integrated the Little Rock schools.) Perhaps it's because the lyrics speak with such detachment and humor about their subjects. Berry is usually an impersonal commentator. Even when he is (presumably) the subject of the song, he deflects attention away from himself toward events (the car chase in **"Maybellene"**) or activities (going dancing in **"Carol"**). Even in **"Brown-Eyed Handsome Man,"** possibly his most autobiographical song, he writes in the third person.

There are no real precedents for Berry's lyrics. They are as clever in their own way as the most sophisticated Cole Porter lyrics, but they speak to a different audience with a different language. Their most direct antecedents are, of course, the lyrics of blues and rhythm and blues. But there is none of the self-deprecation so common in jump band lyrics: no one is out of work, getting arrested, or getting drunk. And they contain none of the posturing ("tonight you'll know I'm a mighty man") or the personal passion ("the sky is cryin'") heard in so much blues and rhythm and blues.

Berry's lyrics talked about new ideas in a new way to a new audience. As such, they were both a model for sixties rock musicians and a standard to be measured against. Yet, as influential as his lyrics were, Berry's music was even more innovative.

Berry's groundbreaking work was done by 1958. Most of his subsequent recordings—"Carol," **"Sweet Little Rock and Roller,"** and **"Back in the USA"**—mine this same rhythmic and textural vein. They are great songs but add nothing significant. **"Memphis,"** which features a more delicate texture and subtle presentation of rock rhythm, is an intriguing exception.

Still, in his early hits, Chuck Berry was the architect of rock and roll and the musician who laid the foundation for rock. He assembled rock and roll out of blues, boogie-woogie, rhythm and blues, and country, blending them into the sound that most distinctively defines rock and roll as the music that leads to rock. He gave rock and roll its two most distinctive features: its beat and its most prominent instrumental sound: an assertive guitar.

For the last several decades of his life, Berry toured with only his guitar, and contented himself with replaying his hits for the umpteenth time. He would stop in the middle of a performance if necessary to correct his pickup band. Even Keith Richards was not exempt from his criticism: an episode in the documentary *Hail, Hail, Rock and Roll* shows Berry scornfully correcting Richards's rendition of a guitar lick in "Carol." His attitude makes clear that he knows his place in the history of rock and roll: at the top. No other musician contributed more.

3-5 Rock and Roll's Wild Men

Little Richard and Jerry Lee Lewis were among the few true kindred spirits of rock and roll. Both

- grew up poor in the South
- were manic performers: if Elvis stretched the boundaries of acceptable performance, Jerry Lee Lewis and Little Richard broke through them and kept on running
- played the piano, not the guitar
- found a narrow groove and stayed in it during their brief moment in the sun

Their most obvious differences were their race and their sexual orientation. Little Richard was black, Jerry Lee Lewis was white. Little Richard was flamboyantly homosexual; Jerry Lee Lewis decidedly heterosexual. In this matter, both strayed well outside the sexual norms of the time. Little Richard was overtly gay during a time when few men, and even fewer black men, were out of the closet. Lewis went through a string of wives—three before he reached 24! It was his third marriage, to his 13-year-old cousin Myra Gale Brown, that caused the scandal that torpedoed his career. Not only was she underage, but he had neglected to divorce his previous wife. Little Richard was the first to hit nationally: "**Tutti Frutti**," released in late 1955, reached No. 17 on the pop charts in early 1956 and caused enough of a sensation to merit a Pat Boone cover. Lewis's first hit, "**Whole Lot of Shakin' Going On**," appeared on the charts about a year and a half later—not much time in the larger view of things but half a lifetime in the brief flourishing of rock and roll.

3-5a Little Richard

Little Richard (born Richard Penniman, 1932) was the first and the loudest of the early rock and rollers. His flamboyant personality, outrageous appearance (wearing eyeliner decades before Michael Jackson), dynamic stage presence, and jet-propelled energy established a standard for rock-and-roll performance that only Elvis and Jerry Lee Lewis approached. He took the stage, literally throwing himself into his work; at one moment casting a leg up onto the top of the piano, then leaping to the ground in a leg split. Little Richard embodied the new style: wild, uninhibited, and sexually charged. From the moment he sang "Womp-bomp-a-loo-bomp, a-lomp-bomp-bomp!" to start "**Tutti Frutti**," popular music would never be the same.

Little Richard brought substance as well as style to rock and roll. He introduced several of its most characteristic musical features: its volume, a vocal style that valued power over prettiness, and its beat. His music started loud and stayed that way. It was a conscious decision, as he acknowledged:

> I came from a family where my people didn't like R&B. Bing Crosby and Ella Fitzgerald was all I heard. And I knew that there was something that could be louder [sic] than that, but I didn't know where to find it. And I found it was me.

He sang with a voice as abrasive as sandpaper. He hurled his lyrics at the microphone, periodically interrupting them with his trademark falsetto howls and whoops. His singing, like his piano playing, is more percussive than anything else: we are more aware of rhythm than melody, which in most cases is minimal.

Rhythm is where Little Richard made his greatest contribution. He brought the new **rock beat**—the one that Chuck Berry would consolidate—into rock and roll. Listen to a group of mid-fifties rhythm-and-blues songs and interpolate a Little Richard hit: it immediately stands out because of its beat. Rock and roll had a name before Little Richard; after "Tutti Frutti," however, it also had its beat.

Little Richard has acknowledged the source of the beat: boogie-woogie. His two major contributions were:

- To keep the beat division even at all tempos (recall that medium-tempo boogie-woogie typically features a shuffle rhythm)
- To take a two-handed approach to the rhythm; Little Richard often played patterns with his right hand that also reinforce this new rock rhythm, which typically pop out in the piano's high register

His gospel roots are evident in every one of the melismatic flourishes. But his combination of boogie, gospel, blues—and his own personality—gave the mix an unprecedented aggressiveness. His music was loud, fast, and in the face of everyone who listened to it.

Little Richard made his mark in a series of songs released between late 1955 and early 1958. Many of them were about girls: **"Long Tall Sally," "The Girl Can't Help It"** (the girl in this case was blonde bombshell Jayne Mansfield, the star of the film for which the song was written; Little Richard also appeared on screen), **"Lucille," "Good Golly, Miss Molly,"** and **"Jenny, Jenny"** stand out.

He found his sound right away in "Tutti Frutti" and kept it pretty much the same throughout his three years in the limelight. His songs seem to offer little variation, mainly because his vocal style is so consistent but also because they are fast and loud and rely so heavily on standard blues form. "Long Tall Sally" could be grafted onto "Tutti Frutti" without dropping a beat—they are that much alike.

"Lucille" and a New Orleans Conception of Rock and Roll

The changes in Little Richard's music are due mainly to the musicians behind him. Unlike Chuck Berry's backup band, they quickly adapted to Little Richard's new rhythm. In his first hits, such as "Tutti Frutti," the band plays in a rhythm-and-blues style: walking bass, heavy backbeat on the drums, and so on. However, in some of his later hits, such as "Lucille" (1957), the entire band is thinking and playing rock rhythm. Bass, guitar, and sax play a repetitive riff in a low register, while Little Richard hammers away, and the drummer taps out a rock beat and a strong backbeat. The contrast with Berry's songs from the same year is clear: Berry is single-handedly trying to establish the new beat; in songs like "Lucille," the entire band is on the same page as Little Richard.

The low-register riffs and the interplay between them and a strong, active, and steady beat are among the most distinctive elements in the music coming from New Orleans during the fifties, whether heard in rhythm and blues or Little Richard's rock and roll. In particular, the heavy bass line and slower tempo forecast the rhythmic feel of sixties rock.

Like so many early rock-and-roll songs, "Lucille" is a verse/chorus blues. The scene-setting sections feature stop-time breaks (when the band stops playing underneath Little Richard) and no change in harmony. The lyric tells the tale of the wayward "Lucille," but the song is really about Little Richard's voice and the beat. We don't listen to Little Richard songs for the lyrics, as we do with Chuck Berry. It would seem that they're there simply because he has to sing *something*.

There is no questioning Little Richard's importance to rock and roll. He embodied its spirit more outrageously and flamboyantly than any other performer of the era. He gave it one of its most identifiable and influential vocal sounds. And he blazed its rhythmic trail. If he had been a good-looking white heterosexual guitar player, he would have been the undisputed king of rock and roll. His music found a slim groove and stayed there, but what a groove it was! And is!

3–5b Jerry Lee Lewis

Of the ten rock-era acts inducted into the Rock and Roll Hall of Fame in 1986, the first year of induction, no one had a shorter career, fewer hits, or less influence than Jerry Lee Lewis (b. 1935). So why was he a member of the inaugural class?

For all intents and purposes, Lewis's rock-and-roll career lasted just over a year. He began recording late in 1956 with a country song, "**Crazy Arms**." He recorded his first rock-and-roll song, "Whole Lot of Shakin' Going On," in March 1957 and scored big. It went to the top of the R&B and C&W charts and reached No. 3 on the pop chart. He had three more big hits—"**Great Balls of Fire**," "**Breathless**," and "**High School Confidential**"—within a year. Then he watched his career go down in flames after he married his underage cousin.

Still, if any performer ever deserved rock immortality for a single song, it would be Lewis for "Great Balls of Fire." It was rock and roll's first recorded orgasm, or as close to it as anyone could get in the fifties: "kiss me, baby . . . HOOOOOO . . . feels good!" The recording was overtly sexual to a degree that surpassed even Elvis and Little Richard; it anticipated Ray Charles's comparably orgasmic "**What'd I Say**" by more than a year.

"Great Balls of Fire"

The song is one minute and forty-eight seconds of ecstasy, from the opening words of the lyric to the last four chords. Unlike most of the impersonal, teen-themed songs of the period, this song shouts its message loud and clear. And the music, with its pulsing beat, sends the same message, just as loudly and just as clearly.

"Great Balls of Fire" was the aural counterpart to Elvis's gyrations. It made the link between the original and musical meanings of rock and roll explicit. Songs with strong sexual overtones were common in blues and rhythm and blues, but most were different from Lewis's song. The lyrics often talk about what will happen: for example, in "**Good Rockin' Tonight**," Elvis (and others) sing "Tonight you'll know . . ." By contrast, Lewis's lyric is of the moment; he's right in the middle of the experience he's describing. Moreover, his singing and playing imply that he's experienced—that he knows what he's talking about. Lewis was a white man singing blatantly about lust and using rock and roll as a subtext. It was a moment of liberation for rock and roll: a prelude to the sixties.

Among the first great rock and rollers, only Lewis matched Little Richard's musical frenzy. His voice was not as assertive as Little Richard's, whose sound cut through a band like a buzz saw, but he made up for it by attacking the piano, pounding out rock-and-roll chords and swooping up and down the keyboard with his trademark glissandos. For that alone, he's worth remembering.

Both Little Richard and Jerry Lee Lewis were so outside the mainstream that they could not have Elvis's impact. Girls could develop crushes on Elvis because he was enough like their schoolmates (many of whom tried to copy Elvis's looks and mannerisms). Little Richard and Lewis were far less likely to attract adoring fans: Richard because of race and sexual preference, Lewis because of his well-documented marital issues. More fundamentally, however, it was because the world was not ready for them: Little Richard's overt homosexuality (gays were "queers" in the fifties) and Lewis's overt sexuality. Still, their music and their stage personas were crucial in liberating rock—and American culture.

3-6 Rock and Roll, Rhythm and Blues, and Race: Chuck Berry and Little Richard

The most apparent distinction between rock and roll and rhythm and blues during the fifties is racial: rhythm and blues is black music; rock and roll is, for the most part, white music. The most prominent of the early rock-and-roll stars were white, and through the latter part of the decade, the rock-oriented hits on the pop charts came mainly from white acts.

The success of white rock and roll acts vis-à-vis black rhythm-and-blues acts, especially with respect to cover versions of R&B hits, may suggest that the difference between rock-and-roll and rhythm-and-blues was a matter of race. In the middle of the fifties, this may have been true to some extent. However, by the end of the decade, there was also a musical difference. The most compelling evidence of this is the music of Little Richard and Chuck Berry. Both are black, and—as we have heard—they were the musicians most responsible for formulating rock rhythm. Berry played the more important role because he not only presented the new beat but also showed how it should be played on the most important rock instrument, the electric guitar.

Their music demonstrates that the *musical* difference between rhythm and blues and rock and roll has to do mainly with rhythm, not race. A simple exercise bears this out: mix "Lucille" and "Johnny B. Goode" into a playlist of fifties rhythm-and-blues songs, such as those discussed in **chapters 2** and **4**. The two songs should clearly stand apart from the rhythm-and-blues songs because of their beat. And because of this difference, we consider their composers to be rock-and-roll musicians, rather than rhythm-and-blues musicians.

3-7 Beyond the Dance Floor: The Everly Brothers and Buddy Holly

It's hard to imagine two rock-and-roll acts more different in temperament from Jerry Lee Lewis and Little Richard than the Everly Brothers and Buddy Holly. They were shy where Jerry Lee and Little Richard were flamboyant. Their music was different, too—Holly's was more varied and innovative, the Everly Brothers' more melodic. Together, they showed that rock and roll also had a gentler and more introspective side.

3–7a The Everly Brothers

The Everly Brothers—Don (b. 1937) and his younger brother Phil (1939–2014)—stand out in the history of rock and roll for two related reasons: they continued rock and roll's country connection, and they popularized melodious song with a rock beat. The brothers had begun their career as country entertainers not long after they started school. Their parents, Ike and Margaret Everly, had featured the boys on their radio show, broadcast from Iowa, during the mid-forties. After their parents retired, the brothers went to Nashville, where they wrote songs and tried to secure a recording contract. They finally did, with Cadence Records, a small label that recorded mostly pop and jazz. Their first hits were teen-themed country songs that crossed over to the pop charts. **"Bye, Bye, Love"** and **"Wake Up, Little Susie"** were among the biggest hits of 1957. These songs relate to rock and roll mainly in their subject matter. Musically, they relate much more to country music—especially their sweet-voiced close harmony.

Quickly, their music moved closer to rock and roll. As it did, they created—with the help of Felice and Boudleaux Bryant, who wrote most of their early hits—a new sound: the rock ballad. As we have heard in the music of Chuck Berry, Little Richard, and Jerry Lee Lewis, early rock-and-roll songs—real rock and roll—were set over a driving, up-tempo rock rhythm. Slower songs were usually "Earth Angel"-type songs, with muted triplets in the background.

With their 1958 hit **"All I Have to Do Is Dream,"** the Everly Brothers changed that. There is much about the song that links it to pre-rock pop. The theme of the lyrics is romantic love—commonplace in pop but increasingly on the wane in rock-era music. The form of the song is the venerable pop-song form of the twenties, thirties, and forties, not a blues-based form or even the verse/chorus form used in so many country songs. The song has a flowing melody (the melody is the dominant strand in the texture), and the tempo is slow—all like "Earth Angel."

The modern elements include the gentle rock beat, kept mainly by an acoustic rhythm guitar and subtle drums. The singing of the brothers is the perfect complement to the melody—sweet but not saccharine. The key element in integrating old and new into this brand-new rock ballad style is the lyric.

Lyrics, Speech Rhythm, and the Melodious Rock Song

In the discussion of the modern popular song we noted that one of the important new developments was the creation of lyrics that spoke everyday language and melodies that captured, then amplified, the **inflection** of speech.

By contrast, the phrase "All I Have to Do Is Dream" has minimal inflection and accentuation when spoken. It is much more natural to say the words over a gentle rock rhythm than it is to say them in the loud-long/soft-short rhythm of pre-rock pop. As a result, the song works as a melodious *rock* song because the rhythm and inflection of the lyrics are much better suited to a rock rhythm than a **fox-trot** or swing rhythm.

This was a major innovation—one that added an important new dimension to rock-and-roll music. Out of this subtle adjustment came songs like the Beatles' **"Yesterday,"** arguably the most popular song of the rock era, and Carole King's **"You've Got a Friend."** The gentler inflection helped the music create a more intimate and personal atmosphere. The mood is miles away from "Lucille" and "Great Balls of Fire," but the song marks the beginning of the path that will lead through the Beatles and Bob Dylan to the **singer-songwriters** of the early seventies.

The Everly Brothers' music represented the quietest side of rock and roll, but its impact was nevertheless almost as revolutionary as the louder music. Songs such as "All I Have to Do Is Dream" marked the real beginning of the end for pre-rock pop. Prior to these songs, pop traditionalists could dismiss rock and roll as crude, noisy,

inflection Moment-to-moment changes in dynamic level. Aretha Franklin sings in a highly inflected style.

fox-trot A popular social dance of the 1920s and 30s that introduced a clearly black beat into mainstream culture.

singer-songwriters A term that came into use around 1970 to describe songwriters who performed their own music. The music of singer-songwriters was generally characterized by an emphasis on melody, a folk-like accompaniment, and a relatively low dynamic level.

vulgar dance music for tasteless teens. But these songs signal the emergence of a new, rock-beat-based pop: rock and roll was meeting pop on its own terms—and holding its own. By the early seventies, songwriters like Lennon and McCartney, Burt Bacharach, Paul Simon, Joni Mitchell, and others had created a body of melody-first songs that certainly rival, even surpass, the best songs of earlier generations.

The hard rockers may have represented rock and roll's cutting edge, but it was groups such as the Everly Brothers that would ensure rock's complete domination of popular music within a decade. Their music guaranteed that there was something for almost everyone.

3-7b Buddy Holly

Buddy Holly (born Charles Holley, 1936–1959) occupies a unique position in the history of rock: he is the musical bridge between fifties rock and roll and sixties rock. In the music of Chuck Berry, Elvis, Little Richard, and Jerry Lee Lewis, rock and roll coalesced out of several diverse styles, as we have seen. Their achievement was to form a new style out of existing sources. Buddy Holly's achievement was just the opposite. Using this newly formed style as his point of departure, he opened up rock and roll to new sounds, forms, harmonies, and rhythms. All would resurface in the sixties, especially in the music of the Beatles and Bob Dylan, and would become the main inspiration for the eclecticism that characterized so much sixties rock.

What makes Holly's achievement even more remarkable is that it happened in such a short time. He began rock and roll's second generation less than two years after the style had begun to come together. By the time he began recording, he had assimilated the music of his heroes and was using it as a springboard for rock-based innovations. Moreover, his career as a major rock-era artist lasted only a year and a half, from August 1957, when **"That'll Be the Day"** topped the charts, to February 1959, when he died at age 22. No one got more done in less time.

Holly was an unlikely rock star. With his horn-rimmed glasses, he looked more like a nerd than a sex symbol. His singing voice was high, somewhat thin and reedy—the most ordinary sound of the rock-and-roll greats. Saturated with hiccups, stutters, and other Elvis-isms, Holly's sound could have been Elvis-lite: a gifted teen who wanted to sound like Elvis but lacked Elvis's vocal presence or expressive range. (Of course, that was true of many other early rock stars.) Curiously, all this seemed to work in his favor. His looks, voice, and reserved stage manner gave him an everyman quality. Seeing him perform, the implicit message was that one didn't need super looks, a great voice, and a total lack of inhibition to be a rock star.

This image resonated beautifully with the images portrayed in the lyrics. From "That'll Be the Day" to **"Think It Over,"** so many of the songs deal with the insecurities of teen relationships. Male teens may have wanted to be another Elvis, but they could put themselves in Buddy Holly's shoes much more easily. Many did, in garages around the United States and in England.

Holly hid a curious, open, and imaginative mind beneath his shy, rather gawky exterior. It was fueled by the diverse musical influences that he encountered growing up. The first was country music. Lubbock, Holly's hometown, is in west Texas, just below the panhandle and close to the New Mexico border. Texas had been home to Jimmie Rodgers toward the end of his life and the home base of western swing king Bob Wills, so progressive country music was definitely in the air.

Holly also listened to rhythm and blues intently. A friend recalls sitting with him in his car late on Saturday nights so that they could hear an R&B show on a station out of Shreveport, Louisiana. Not surprisingly, then, numerous R&B elements pop up in his songs: the Bo Diddley beat of **"Not Fade Away"** is an obvious example. Elvis was a more powerful and immediate influence.

He performed in Lubbock twice during 1955, in the spring and fall, and both times Holly and his friend Bob Montgomery opened the show. This direct contact not only influenced his singing but also strengthened his resolve to pursue a career in music. By the time Elvis returned for his second engagement, Holly was pumping him about how to get a recording contract.

In 1956, Holly went to Nashville to record for Decca Records, with indifferent results. After returning home, he headed west, to Clovis, New Mexico, where Norman Petty operated a well-equipped studio—the best in the region. In Petty, Holly found a soul mate, someone interested in record production and in expanding the sound world of rock and roll. Although their relationship ended badly, their work together helped lay the groundwork for the recording innovations of the Beatles and other major sixties artists.

Country, Elvis-isms, rock and roll, and rhythm and blues all figure in Holly's music, but it was more than just a synthesis of these styles. His hit recordings are a catalog of innovations and adaptations, but perhaps the most daring was a song that did not chart, "Not Fade Away."

Its rhythmic point of departure was not rock rhythm, but was the Bo Diddley beat—itself firmly rooted in the clave rhythm of Afro-Cuban music. In this song, the rhythm is a slight alteration of the typical clave pattern. The persistent call-and-response exchanges between Holly and the backup singers also recall Bo Diddley's self-titled hit. (Holly recorded "**Bo Diddley**" in 1956, but it was not released until 1963.)

However, despite this connection to rhythm and blues, "Not Fade Away" is *philosophically* different from the rock and roll of Berry, Little Richard, and the others. Their rock and roll is dance music—loud, assertive dance music. This song is not. A typical rock-and-roll song reinforces three regular rhythms: the eight-beat rock rhythm (for instance, Berry's guitar), the beat (usually kept by the bass), and the backbeat. Here, none of these rhythms is consistently present.

Jerry Allison's drumming is especially unconventional here. He marks the clave rhythm on the hi-hat and keeps time intermittently on a deadened drum, a sound that suggests the conga drum much more than the standard drum set.

Throughout the song, almost all of the accents play against the beat and measure instead of confirming it. The backup vocalists don't sing on the first note of the clave pattern, so they never mark the beginning of the measure. And Holly gives a strong accent on the last beat of the second measure of the pattern. Moreover, there is no bass or rhythm guitar. No one marks time, so we don't get our rhythmic bearings until Holly sings the lead vocal line. This kind of rhythmic ambiguity was unprecedented in rock and roll.

"Not Fade Away" introduces into rock and roll the idea that a song can be more than dance music. It can tell a story—here, at something less than full volume. It's an about-face from the music's original message and a door opening to a new sound world.

In its approach to rhythm and percussive sounds, "Not Fade Away" is arguably Holly's most experimental song. Interestingly, Holly's more conventional songs, from "That'll Be the Day" on, were key in establishing the standard rock band instrumentation: two guitars, bass, and drums. This instrumentation was another of Holly's important contributions.

Buddy Holly stands apart among the early rock and rollers. If the others showed the world what rock and roll was, he showed them what it could—and would—become. His songs were an obvious inspiration for the innovative music of the Beatles, Dylan, Simon & Garfunkel, and many others. Add to his impressive musical achievement the sense of loss that his death created, and it's easy to understand the veneration that he has enjoyed.

call-and-response
A rapid exchange, usually of riffs, between two different timbres: solo voice and guitar; solo voice and choir; or saxophones and trumpets.

accents A musical event that stands out from its neighbors because of a change in one or more musical elements. The most common sources of accent are intensity (the event is louder), duration (longer), density (the event contains more parts), or pitch (higher or lower).

3-8 The Birth, Death, and Resurrection of Rock and Roll

In this chapter, we have charted the rise and fall of rock and roll during the fifties. To summarize the emergence and evolution of rock and roll, we offer the following timeline.

Rock and Roll, 1951–1959	
Pre-1951	*Rock* and *roll* are black euphemisms for sex.
1951–1954	*Rock and roll* is Alan Freed's code phrase for rhythm and blues. The term does not represent a new kind of music.
1954–1956	Rock and roll begins to develop an identity: an image, in the appearance and movements of Elvis, Little Richard, Chuck Berry, and others; a sound, beginning with rockabillies like Bill Haley, Carl Perkins, and Elvis; white cover acts like the Crew Cuts and (yes) Pat Boone; black crossover acts like the many doo-wop groups and Fats Domino; and in the initial rock-defining songs of Little Richard and Chuck Berry; a fresh, impudent attitude expressed in image, lyrics, and sound that teens find appealing; and a commercial presence, most prominent in the overwhelming success of Elvis Presley.
1957–1959	Rock and roll solidifies its distinct musical identity, most significantly in the music of Chuck Berry, and begins to grow beyond teen dance music, most notably in the music of Buddy Holly.

3-8a Rock and Roll's Hall of Fame Acts

We have chosen to focus in this chapter mainly on five solo acts and one duo who were among the first class of inductees to enter the Rock and Roll Hall of Fame. Collectively, they did more than any other acts to give rock and roll an image, an attitude, and a musical identity, and they played the most decisive roles in defining both its essence and its range:

- Elvis Presley personified rock and roll: he gave the music its most memorable voice, its most indelible image, and its strongest commercial presence.
- Little Richard brought in the beat and performed with an outrageousness that inspired generations of rockers.
- Chuck Berry put together its key musical elements: the beat and the sound and style of lead and rhythm guitar. He contributed more than anyone else to the distinct musical identity of rock and roll.
- Jerry Lee Lewis reinforced the beat and brought unrestrained abandon into rock and roll.
- The Everly Brothers introduced the melodious rock song.

- Buddy Holly was the most important bridge between rock and roll and rock: he gave rock its basic instrumentation, new forms and harmonies, and its primary way of creating the future out of the past. He also led the way in showing that rock and roll could be more than teen dance music.

Five of them seemed to share a common karma, finding success very quickly and then suffering death or a career-damaging experience almost as quickly. In 1955, Berry had his first hit, "Maybellene." His rock-and-roll-defining records, such as "Roll Over, Beethoven," would begin to appear in the following year. Little Richard gave 1956 a wake-up call with "Tutti Frutti." Elvis became a national celebrity with "Heartbreak Hotel" a few months later. Lewis and Holly would score with No. 1 hits the following year.

Their decline was just as sudden. Little Richard traded the stage for the pulpit in the middle of a 1957 Australian tour. It was the first of several vacillations between secular and sacred careers. The next year, Lewis married his 13-year-old cousin and saw his career go into a tailspin. Elvis's induction into the army that same year put a huge two-year hole in his career. In 1959, Holly died in a plane crash, while Berry had a scrape with the law that eventually put him in jail for two years. Only the Everly Brothers escaped the fifties more or less unscathed; their career remained strong until the **British invasion**. In that brief window of time, however, the six acts defined rock and roll, put it on the map, and set it on its course.

3–8b The Death and Resurrection of Rock and Roll

The silencing of rock and roll's most important acts seemed to be one sign that rock and roll was just a fad that had run its course. (Hindsight is the great clarifier: it may be hard to believe that in 1959 many Americans thought that rock and roll was ready to disappear from the pop music scene.) Another indicator that rock and roll would not survive was a multipronged attack on the music and those responsible for it. Leading figures denigrated it: Steve Allen, host of a popular late-night television show, mockingly read the lyrics to Gene Vincent's "**Be-Bop-A-Lula**" with tinkly music in the background; Frank Sinatra spoke for the pop music establishment when he derided rock and roll as "the most brutal, ugly, desperate, vicious form of expression it has been my misfortune to hear." At the same time, as soon as the music industry saw that there was money to be made, the major labels began churning out their versions of rock and roll, none of which had any lasting impact. After the British invasion, popular music would belong to a new generation.

3–8c Payola

The pop establishment, in conjunction with the government, launched their heaviest attack on the men who played the records: the disc jockeys. **Payola** is the practice of paying disc jockeys for playing records. Rewarding people for promoting songs is almost as old as the popular-music business. Indeed, two bribes—money and the promise of a good review for the singer who introduced it—greased the wheel that made "After the Ball" (1893) Tin Pan Alley's first big hit.

In the fifties, disc jockeys were the people to bribe, because they controlled airplay. Representatives of the small independent labels often resorted to bribes of one kind or another in order to get their records on the air. Sometimes it was money, but there were other favors. Alan Freed got partial songwriting credit—and royalties—for Chuck Berry's "Maybellene" and many other rock-and-roll songs in return for promoting them on his shows. In many cases, payola was the only leverage that the indies had, because the big labels were firmly entrenched.

British invasion An influx of British bands in the early 60s whose styles borrowed from American pop, rock and roll, rhythm and blues, and early blues and who, in turn, were to have a profound influence in the emergence of rock.

Payola The practice of record companies' bribing disk jokeys to secure airplay for their records.

In 1958, the pop music establishment, and in particular the members of ASCAP, the licensing agency that represented traditional pop songwriters and publishers, pressured Congress to study abuses within the pop music industry, particularly among purveyors of rock and roll. Payola was part of the investigation. The results from the congressional report released in 1960 were less than satisfactory, as far as the pop establishment was concerned; teens were still listening to the new music. The most publicized casualty was Alan Freed, whose career was ruined. He died in 1965. By contrast, Dick Clark, whose *American Bandstand* was the cornerstone of his growing publishing/production empire, came out of the hearings with reputation and power intact.

ASCAP members had an ulterior motive for seeking an investigation: they felt threatened by the growing market share of BMI, the licensing agency that represented virtually all of the rock-and-roll and rhythm-and-blues songwriters, and had convinced themselves that rock and roll was being kept afloat by payola. The payola hearings had no discernible impact on BMI.

Ultimately, condemnation, co-opting, and the congressional investigation had no effect on the rise of rock and roll. What seemed like the death of rock and roll was in fact the beginning of the last stage of its transformation into rock. We trace that leg of the journey in the next chapter.

3–8d Rock and Roll: A New Attitude

In spite of the death or decline of its first heroes, rock and roll helped engineer a major cultural shift—first in the generation that listened to it and ultimately in the English-speaking world. Like the civil rights movement, rock and roll entered mainstream consciousness slowly, often through disruptive events. In the latter part of the fifties, the majority of Americans were more concerned with the Cold War and the threat of nuclear annihilation than they were with civil rights, despite television coverage of such troublesome issues as the integration of the Little Rock public schools, when President Eisenhower had to send in federal troops to maintain order and enforce the law.

Some Americans chose to escape through film and stage musicals, many of which depicted different times and places; or through television, which offered situation comedies like *Father Knows Best*, in which problems were solved on a weekly basis in 30 minutes—minus a few minutes for commercials—or westerns, which distorted life in the nineteenth-century West as severely as situation comedies distorted reality in America during the fifties.

Most of the parents and grandparents of fifties teens had lived through the Great Depression and two major wars. With the specter of the Cold War and the chance to make good money after decades of deprivation, many did not want to concern themselves with unresolved issues, like segregation. They sought comfort, not challenge, in their entertainment. They wanted their listening easy, gentle, and smooth, not hard, loud, and rocking. But their children, most of whom had not endured their parents' trials, were ready for music that was more vigorous, more challenging, and more "real."

It is against this background that we can understand rock and roll as the soundtrack for the first steps in a seismic shift in western culture. This environment planted the seeds of the rock revolution—and the social and cultural revolution of which rock was such an integral part. Rock and roll was not overtly political, like the music that would soon emerge from the folk revival. It did not champion social causes, criticize segments of society, or comment on controversial events, as Bob Dylan, Marvin Gaye, Neil Young, and so many others would. Still, implicit in the images, words, and above all in the sounds of the music were values that confronted and challenged the status quo.

The images remain vivid: Elvis's gyrating pelvis, Little Richard in full makeup with one leg up on the piano, Chuck Berry's duck walk. There were certainly plenty of bad lyrics in early rock and roll (as there have been in any generation of popular music), but there were also lyrics that set the tone for the next generation: Berry's good-humored defiance; the unabashed directness of Jerry Lee Lewis's feeling good; Buddy Holly's honest portrayals of teen angst. All of these foreshadowed the "realness" of rock.

Ultimately, however, it was the music that delivered the heart of the message. It was often loud; listeners couldn't avoid it. It was aggressive—Berry's guitar sound, from "Maybellene" on, Little Richard's abrasive voice, Jerry Lee Lewis's piano pounding. It blurred racial boundaries: Elvis was the white man with the Negro feel. And most of all, it was the new beat: the first 5 seconds of "Johnny B. Goode," where Berry pumps out two strings of two-note chords, distill the essence of this new, more insistent beat. Here is where the impact of this new music is felt most powerfully. As the decade came to an end, more and more acts were harnessing this power. We follow this path into the sixties, in the next several chapters.

CHAPTER 4

RHYTHM AND BLUES, 1955–1960

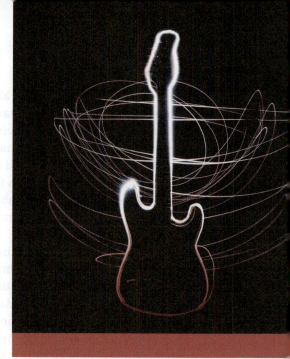

Learning Objectives:

1) Summarize how rhythm evolved within the late 1950s R&B genre.

2) Discuss Fats Domino's approach to rhythm.

3) Describe the key musical characteristics found within the works of the Platters.

4) Define the **New Orleans sound**.

5) Compare the musical characteristics of the Coasters to the second incarnation of the Drifters.

6) Give examples of the various genres performed by Ray Charles.

Chapter Introduction

In a 1965 interview, Fats Domino (b. February 1928) said, "What they call rock 'n' roll is rhythm and blues. I've been playing it for fifteen years in New Orleans." His assessment might have been true for his own music, but not for the new music of the late fifties. What it did reflect accurately was the deepening interest of whites in rhythm and blues.

4–1 Crossing Over

The arc of Domino's career provides a timeline for the broadening appeal of rhythm and blues. Before 1950, he was all but unknown outside New Orleans. Beginning with his 1950 hit, **"The Fat Man,"** he began to develop a nationwide following, mainly among blacks. Still, between 1950 and 1955, only two of his long string of R&B hits crossed over to the pop charts. After 1955, however, almost all of his R&B hits also charted on pop, with ten songs released in the late fifties reaching the top 10.

Domino's commercial success—he sold over 65 million records in his career and was the most popular black recording artist during the early years of the rock era—is evidence of the changing taste of whites, or at least young whites. Domino's songs and style remained remarkably consistent throughout his career. He made little effort to modify any aspect of his music in order to attract a wider audience. Domino let the white audience come to him, rather than catering to their taste.

Domino was an exception to the rule. Much of the popular rhythm-oriented music after 1955 was rock and roll, with its faster beat, rather than rhythm and blues. Rhythm-and-blues performers were slow to abandon the shuffle-based rhythmic conventions of the previous decade. Moreover, the crossover success of **"Sh-Boom"** and **"Earth Angel"** motivated other black acts to follow much the same pop-oriented path up the pop charts. In the latter part of the decade, white covers were less frequent and less successful because consumers increasingly favored the original versions. In much pop-derived group and solo singing, melody and harmony are in the forefront; rhythm is in the background.

Rhythm and blues incorporated rock rhythm reluctantly. We identify Chuck Berry and Little Richard as seminal figures in rock and roll, not rhythm and blues, because of their essential role in shaping the new rhythm of rock. White acts— Eddie Cochran, Jerry Lee Lewis, Danny and the Juniors—embraced this new beat more enthusiastically than their black counterparts. Only toward the very end of the decade did R&B songs begin to feature a rock beat. Instead, there was more focus on elaborate production, which often involved incorporating pop trappings, such as violins and white choral singers. Ray Charles's singular and eclectic approach and mastery of multiple styles him apart from his contemporaries. We sample a wide range of late fifties rhythm and blues next.

4-1a Fats Domino's Timeless Triplets: Rhythmic R&B in the Late Fifties

Fats Domino's first hit, "The Fat Man," (1950) is right in step with the rhythmic rhythm and blues of the new decade: it features a strong boogie-based shuffle rhythm. But from this point on, the rhythm in his hit songs becomes more aggressive. The songs make use of two rhythmic options. One is a gospel-like two-beat rhythm with a strong backbeat. The other, which was his go-to approach in so many of his hits, features loud repeated-chord triplets and a strong beat over a loping bass line.

The aggressiveness of the rhythm sets it apart from most of the R&B of the period, even some of the doo-wop that featured triplets. In his 1955 crossover hit, "Ain't That a Shame," Domino's piano triplets, a strong backbeat, and the distinctive bassline pattern doubled by saxophone and guitar compete with the vocal line. The resulting texture is thick and busy. It's not Chuck Berry-style rock and roll, but it's more active and insistent than a shuffle rhythm.

Domino's signature sound was a distinctive blend of active rhythms, dense textures, with saxophone riffs or sustained chords in addition to a full rhythm section featuring Domino's playing, mixing with his common-man singing. There's nothing exceptional about his voice, as there was with Sam Cooke, Ray Charles, or Ben E. King. And in this context, it was probably an asset, because the focus in his music went to the total sound package: the loud, full sound and busy rhythms.

Domino performed seated at the piano. Unlike other rock-and-roll royalty— Elvis, Chuck Berry, Little Richard, Jerry Lee Lewis—he projected a nonthreatening image, yet his music had a powerful sound. Given the racial attitudes of the time, this may have contributed to his consistent success during the fifties. Teens didn't swoon over him, but they certainly enjoyed the beat.

Domino's music was not the only rhythmic R&B that was commercially successful: the Coasters had two novelty hits with an upbeat two-beat: **"Yakety Yak"** and "Charlie Brown." Two "old-school" R&B recordings reached the top of the pop charts in 1959: Lloyd Price's **"Stagger Lee"** and Wilbert Harrison's **"Kansas City."** Other music from New Orleans, most notably that of Huey "Piano" Smith featured a more collaborative and less driving rock beat. Still, the more popular music of the time was more melodious vocal music. The Platters epitomized this trend.

4-1b Sophisticated Doo-Wop: The Platters

Early doo-wop hits like "Sh-Boom" and "Earth Angel" were more commercially successful in their cover versions. When white listeners began to turn more to black singing groups, it was The Platters, the most popular of the fifties doo-wop groups, who scored first, with two No. 1 hits, **"The Great Pretender"** at the very end of 1955 and **"My Prayer"** a year later. They led the way into the sixties with a string of hits, including two more No. 1 records.

The Platters were not only the most successful of the doo-wop groups but also the slickest. Guided by their vocal coach Buck Ram, who wrote or adapted most of their material, they found commercial success with a real middle-of-the-road style. What stands out in their early hits is the fullness of their sound. Their distinctive sound is achieved with limited resources: lead singer, vocal harmony, saxophone, and rhythm section. Lead singer Tony Williams has a warm tenor voice of extraordinary range. The sustained background harmonies give rich support. Modest, unobtrusive instrumental accompaniment underpins the voices: drums playing brushes, bass playing every other beat, piano triplet chords or **arpeggios**. It's clear that their "big" sound comes from the voices, not the instruments—and with plenty of help from the recording engineer.

In "My Prayer," the Platters position themselves more toward pre-rock pop than any other major doo-wop group of the era. Instrumentally, common features of doo-wop are present, but attenuated and subdued. The triplets are broken chords (arpeggios) in the opening part of the song, rather than the block chords of "Earth Angel" (or their previous No. 1 hit, "The Great Pretender"). The drummer taps out the triplet rhythm and backbeat using brushes instead of drumsticks. The climactic sections are supported by repeated riff-like patterns in the saxophone. The tempo is much slower than Glenn Miller's version, which was a hit in 1939. What's missing is the signature feature of the style: the "doo-wops." Rhythmically energizing vocal riffs on nonsense syllables are not part of the Platters sound in their early hits. Instead, the four backup vocalists sing sustained harmonies throughout to create the central element of their full sound.

Almost all of the Platters hit songs were pop standards; they recorded relatively little new material. In their approach to these songs, doo-wop elements are present—especially the slow tempos, triplets, and rich vocal harmonies. Their distinctive vocal sound—more forceful than crooners, but smoother than most other R&B vocal groups—helps the Platters straddle the boundary between pre-rock pop and doo-wop remakes. That combination was their "Magic Touch." It captured the ears of millions of listeners.

The Platters were not the only group to rework pop standards. One of the most enduring recordings of the era is a thorough reworking of "I Only Have Eyes For You" by the Flamingos.

arpeggios A chord whose pitches are performed one after the other instead of simultaneously. Also called broken chord.

4-1c The Sound of Slow Doo-Wop

Like the Penguins, the Flamingos were one of the numerous "bird" groups of the era. The group, made up of two pairs of cousins and lead singer Sollie McElroy, came together in 1952. They enjoyed modest success in the middle of the decade, but their biggest hit came only in 1959: **"I Only Have Eyes for You"** was the only one of their recordings that would cross over to the pop charts during the fifties.

"I Only Have Eyes for You" dates from the thirties: it was a hit in 1934 and became a favorite of Frank Sinatra and many other singers over the years. However, the Flamingos' recording reworks it so extensively that it becomes virtually a new song.

Their remake of the song has numerous features that make their approach to doo-wop pop distinctive. The vocal sound of the group finds a midway point between slickness of the Platters—McElroy's voice is not as extroverted as Tony Williams's—and the rougher sound of the Penguins. The tempo is slower than that of "My Prayer," and about twice as slow as Sinatra's famous recording of the song. In this respect, it is reminiscent of the slow tempos in black gospel: black gospel choirs typically sing a hymn like "Amazing Grace" at a much slower tempo than their white counterparts. And in this recording, as in so much black gospel and slow doo-wop, dividing the beat into triplets activates the rhythm. Here, the pianist plays soft repeated triplet chords in a high register.

However, the most exceptional feature of this version of the song is what happens underneath the melody. The harmony at the beginning of the song is static; the Flamingos swapped out the conventional pop chords for a three-chord sequence that's cycled through four times. That cycle becomes the basis of a low-register riff. Above that is the signature "doo-wop-chi-bop" riff, which stands in counterpoint to both the lead vocal and low riff during the opening. By adding the signature riff, dropping the tempo to a snail's pace, and changing the harmony so drastically, the Flamingos give the song a completely new identity.

The Flamingos' recording is classic doo-wop: slow, well sung, beautifully har-monized, and with "doo-wop" always in the background. It is an especially good example of the mainstream black vocal group style. By contrast, the most distinc-tive style of the era belonged to the Coasters, a group produced by Jerry Leiber and Mike Stoller during their peak years. We consider the rise of music production, as exemplified in two Leiber-Stoller produced songs, by the Coasters and the second incarnation of the Drifters.

4–2 Songwriting and Production in Fifties Rhythm and Blues

Sam Phillips's inspired decision to record Willie Kizart's distorted guitar was an early hint of what would soon become an important creative dynamic in popular music: the interplay between artist and producer. This in turn reflected a reconcep-tion of what a song was and where it existed. Recall that in pre-rock popular music, songs existed independently of any particular version of the song. For example, "I Only Have Eyes for You" was sung by Dick Powell, a popular singer and actor during the thirties, in the film *Dames*. In short order, several other recordings of the song appeared on the market; at least three were hits. The song continued to be recorded over the next several decades; the Flamingos' distinctive rendition was still only one of many versions of the song.

By contrast, in the new music of the fifties—rhythm and blues and rock and roll—the song was often what was on the recording; it was not *independent* of the recording. A remark by Leiber and Stoller sums up this new approach: "We don't write songs, we write records." In many fifties recordings, the sound on the record-ing owes as much to the producer as the featured artists.

The first producers wore several hats—artist and repertoire man, song-writer, arranger, contractor—as well as recording engineer, in several cases. Because pro-ducers controlled so many elements, they often put their own stamp on the sound of a recording. For example, the New Orleans sound was the product of a distinc-tive arranging style played by the same nucleus of musicians. Dave Bartholomew at Imperial Records (who produced Fats Domino's sessions) and "Bumps" Blackwell at Specialty Records (who produced so many of Little Richard's hits) favored a heavy sound. To achieve this, they would have saxes, guitar, and bass all play a low-register riff: Little Richard's **"Lucille"** (discussed in **Chapter 3**) is a clear example. It could be part of the sound, regardless of the featured artist. Indeed, behind virtually all of the major fifties stars was an important producer, who often doubled as recording engineer. Sam Phillips oversaw Elvis's early career and Jerry Lee Lewis's rock-and-roll records, while Leonard Chess produced Chuck Berry's hits and Norman Petty most of Buddy Holly's.

In their work with the Coasters, Leiber and Stoller were among the first to elevate record production to an art. They were meticulous in both planning and production, often recording up to 60 takes to obtain the result they sought. Their most distinctive early songs were what Leiber called "playlets"—songs that told a funny story with serious overtones; Stoller called them "cartoons." As with print cartoons, the primary audience was young people—of all races—who identified with the main characters in the story. These were humorous stories, but with an edge.

4–2a The Coasters

The Coasters—so named because they came from the west coast, unlike most of the other doo-wop groups—were really doo-wop in name only, because their music was so different from almost all the other groups of the time. They had formed as the Four Bluebirds in 1947 and became the Robins in 1950, singing backup behind Little Esther. They reformed in late 1955, renaming themselves the Coasters.

The group's fortunes changed when they met Jerry Leiber and Mike Stoller in 1953. By the time the Coasters recorded **"Young Blood"** in 1957, Leiber and Stoller were independent producers for Atlantic Records, often writing the songs and supervising all aspects of the recording, all the while working with Elvis on songs like **"Jailhouse Rock."**

Through the mid-fifties, the Robins/Coasters were the vehicle for Leiber and Stoller's playlets. Their list of hits includes not only "Young Blood," which topped the R&B charts and reached the Top 10 in the pop charts in 1957, but also "Smokey Joe's Cafe," **"Charlie Brown,"** and "Yakety Yak."

The story told in "Young Blood" deals with youthful infatuation, but it is a far cry from the starry-eyed romance found in songs like "Earth Angel"—and with no happy ending. As "Young Blood" shows, the Coasters' songs were the opposite of most doo-wop: steely-eyed, not sentimental, and darkly humorous. The Coasters' singing sounds slick, but not sweet. Although the Coasters have a black sound, the theme of the song is universal: teens of all races could relate to it, and did.

The musical setting is a distinctive take on fifties rhythm and blues. The core instrumentation is typical: full rhythm section plus saxophone behind the vocal group. However, there are other instruments in the background. A shuffle rhythm with a heavy backbeat provide the underlying rhythmic framework. But the most prominent rhythm is the repeated guitar riff, which has a distinct rhythmic profile, and there are numerous shifts in the rhythmic flow—breaks that showcase the Coasters' trademark humorous asides that drop down the vocal ladder, with bass singer Bobby Nunn getting in the last word, and sections where the rhythm players sustain long chords instead of marking the beat. These and other features separate "Young Blood" musically from more straightforward R&B songs (like "Shake, Rattle and Roll"), just as the lyrics separate the song from both blues-oriented lyrics and romantic doo-wop.

Leiber and Stoller spent the latter half of the fifties dividing their time and energy between Elvis (prior to his induction into the army), the Coasters, and the second incarnation of the Drifters.

4–2b The Drifters

The Drifters were a vocal group formed in 1953 as a showcase for Clyde McPhatter. McPhatter had been the lead singer for the Dominos for three years but left because he felt underappreciated and underpaid. He stayed with the Drifters for only two years before being inducted into the army. The group continued to perform without him despite a contentious relationship with their manager, George Treadwell. Treadwell fired the group after an incident in 1958 and promptly hired another vocal group, the Crowns, and renamed them the Drifters, to fulfill the bookings he'd negotiated for the original group. The lead singer in this second version of the Drifters was Ben E. King.

The Drifters were under contract to Atlantic Records. Ahmet Ertegün and Jerry Wexler, who ran Atlantic and produced many of their recordings, hired Leiber and Stoller to work with the Drifters. Their work together produced a string of Top 40 hits from 1959 through the early sixties, including the No. 1 pop hit, **"Save the Last Dance for Me."**

"Save the Dance for Me" shows R&B—and Leiber and Stoller—exploring a new approach to Latin sounds and rhythms. They combine these three elements with more background parts in support of the vocal parts:

- a syncopated three-note bass pattern adapted from the first part of the clave pattern by way of Elvis's **"Don't Be Cruel,"** **"Hound Dog,"** and numerous other 50s rock-and-roll hits
- strummed Spanish-style acoustic guitars moving mainly in a steady 8-beat rhythm
- a triangle, also tapped at 8-beat speed

The space in the bass line, the subtle, fast-moving rhythms in middle and high ranges, and high string parts—alternately sustained and busy—create a smoothly flowing rhythmic cushion for the voices. It is more transparent than rhythm and blues because of the spacing between parts and the subtlety of the fast-moving rhythms. And the texture is lighter than most pop because the rhythms are active without being obtrusive. The melody drifts on this instrumental background; it's a showcase for Ben E. King's warm voice. This was a new kind of pop—a rock-era mix of pop, rhythm and blues, and Latin music combined creatively and imaginatively.

Leiber and Stoller's work with the Coasters and the new Drifters evidences the growing role of the producer and the shift in perception of the relationship between song and recording: the recording *is* the song, not just a performance of the song that happened to be recorded. The role of the producer would continue to grow, to the point where in some cases the most identifiable feature of the music would be the background sounds, rather than the featured artists.

4–3 Gospel-Influenced Solo Singing

Ray Charles (born Ray Charles Robinson, 1930–2004) lost his sight at age 7 to an undiagnosed case of glaucoma. The onset of blindness may well have stimulated what was already a voracious appetite for music. Charles grew up listening to and playing everything: blues, gospel, country, jazz, classical, pop. He launched his professional career in the late forties; in his first recordings he emulated the style of Nat Cole, the most popular black vocalist of the era and a fine jazz pianist. In 1952, Atlantic Records bought his contract from Swingtime, the label that had released his first recordings. For about two years, he recorded rhythm-and-blues songs distinguished mainly by the unique quality of his voice. However, late in 1954, Charles made one of those abrupt shifts in musical direction that characterized his career.

The song that signaled this sudden shift was "**I Got a Woman.**" Charles did not write the song; rather, he gave the gospel hymn "**Jesus Is All the World to Me**" new words and a new beat. His transformation of the sacred into the profane scandalized members of the black community. The blues singer Big Bill Broonzy summed up what Charles had done and why it outraged so many when he said, "He's crying, sanctified. He's mixing the blues with the spirituals. He should be singing in a church."

Charles had mixed rhythmic rhythm and blues with the most fervent kind of gospel singing, the kind one might hear in black Pentecostal churches. It was a defining moment in the assimilation of gospel music into rhythm and blues, for at least two reasons: first, it transformed a hymn into a pop song, and second, it introduced the vocal style that would define soul music. However, by the time "I Got a Woman" charted in early 1955, the influence of gospel on solo singing was evident in a wide range of music, from Charles's proto-soul to gospel-flavored pop.

Gospel's influence on rhythm and blues went far beyond doo-wop's gospel/ pop/ R&B blends. The full range of its influence becomes apparent only in the work of gospel-influenced solo singers. Three performers whose careers took off in the mid-fifties demarcated innovative paths. Each blended gospel with another style. Cooke and Charles are discussed following; the profile of Little Richard more properly belongs in the discussion of rock and roll (see **Chapter 3**).

Pop/gospel—Sam Cooke blended smooth-voiced gospel singing with pop, defining a new black pop solo-singing style in the process.

Gospel/rock and roll—Little Richard combined gospel's ecstatic side with the old/new beat of boogie-woogie/rock and roll.

Gospel/blues—Ray Charles secularized the uninhibited passion of the sanctified church and mixed it with the deep feeling of the blues.

The careers of Sam Cooke and Ray Charles run parallel in several important respects and opposite in others. Both were commercially successful, especially within the black community. They were also the best at what they did. In the late fifties, their music epitomized the possibilities within black pop solo singing and the blues/gospel merger that would soon become soul.

However, the paths of their careers ran in opposite directions. Cooke started on the outside (with gospel, a noncommercial style), and came "inside" in search of pop success. Charles, on the other hand, started out on the inside by emulating the popular style of Nat "King" Cole, then made his mark by creating a new "outside" style.

They also differed in the amount of adversity they had overcome. Cooke, whose looks matched his talent, seemed to be sailing through life, as much as any black man could in the fifties and sixties—signing with a major label, headlining at the Copacabana—until his sudden, shocking death. By contrast, Charles had to battle through numerous problems—most obviously his blindness, but also a well-publicized drug problem. He overcame both to become one of the icons of the rock era.

4-3a Sam Cooke

The son of a minister, Sam Cooke (born Sam Cook, 1931–1964) grew up singing in church. His family moved from Mississippi to Chicago in 1933, and in 1950 he joined one of the top gospel groups of the era, the Soul Stirrers, as the lead singer. In 1956, he began recording secular material under the direction of Bumps Blackwell, the producer at Specialty Records who also recorded Little Richard. Blackwell determined the course of Cooke's career early on by packaging him in a purely pop setting. This hybrid sound bothered Art Rupe, the owner of Specialty Records, enough that he agreed to let Cooke and Blackwell keep the record masters in exchange for a release from their contract.

"You Send Me"

Among the recordings they took to Keen Records was a Cooke original, "**You Send Me**" (1957). The song is yet another take on the "heart and soul" ballad style so popular in rhythm and blues, and the setting includes an understated rhythm section accompaniment and a choir of white pop singers, which adult listeners of the time would typically hear in easy-listening recordings.

The distinctive element in "You Send Me" was Cooke's singing, which was admired throughout the music industry. Jerry Wexler, who by this time was a partner in Atlantic Records—the label that had Charles, the Coasters, and several other top R&B acts on their roster—commented on Cooke's singing:

> Sam was the best singer who ever lived, no contest... He had control, he could play with his voice like an instrument, his melisma, which was his personal brand—I mean, nobody else could do it—everything about him was perfection.

In "You Send Me," two features of Cooke's singing stand out. First and foremost, there is his beautiful, effortless sound, a rock-era analog to Nat Cole. Second, there are the elements he brought from gospel, most notably the melisma that Wexler found so distinctive and the rhythmic freedom that allows him to soar over the beat. Aside from Cooke's singing, however, "You Send Me" is pop. Both the song and the setting—discreet backup, white chorus—are closer to Patti Page or Perry Como material than to rhythm and blues.

Cooke seemed to have it all: looks, charm, and one of the truly superb voices in popular music history. Recognizing this in 1960, RCA brought him to their label, where he produced a stream of hits. But his career ended abruptly one night in 1964 when he was shot and killed by a woman in a Los Angeles hotel room. Everyone connected with the event seems to have a different story, and his death remains a mystery.

Cooke's tragically short career followed a mainstream, pop path. The disparity between the expressiveness of his singing and the treacly pop settings widens. Cooke's voice never finds a perfectly complementary accompaniment on his commercial pop recordings. For most of this material there is only one reason to listen: Cooke's singing. For every "**Bring It on Home to Me**" there seem to be ten trite songs, like "**Sad Mood**" and "**Ain't That Good News**." Even on his most soulful studio recordings, the background never measures up to the quality of his singing. If it had, Cooke's legacy as a pop singer would have been far more substantial. Still, we are grateful for what we have.

Because his voice was all but inimitable and because his music usually looked to the past, rather than the future, Cooke had almost no influence on the course of rock-era music. Just the opposite is true in the case of Ray Charles, whose music we consider next.

4–3b Ray Charles

The music of Ray Charles presents a puzzle of a different kind: why did a man who had created such an important new musical direction suddenly turn his back on it? Unlike Cooke, who simply brought his voice, Charles brought the whole gospel package to rhythm and blues: the songs, his uninhibited singing, the open-ended "getting happy" exchanges, the beat, the feel of the music.

"I Got a Woman," the 1955 recording that integrated this full gospel sound into rhythm and blues, marked an abrupt change from his earlier recordings. For him, and for the world of popular music, it was a brand-new sound, as new in its own way as rock and roll. It brought him a measure of success, especially within the black community—much more than he had enjoyed previously. For about five years, he refined and expanded this new concept, producing some of the definitive music of the decade.

Charles's two live recordings from the fifties, from performances at the 1958 Newport Jazz Festival and in Atlanta a year later, show how he filtered a broad array of music through his gospel experience—and vice versa—to come up with a range of new sounds. There is blues, rhythm and blues, Latin dance music, jazz, secularized gospel, even minstrel songs (Stephen Foster's **"Old Folks at Home"** becomes "Swanee River Rock").

These recordings also document the range and power of his blues/gospel synthesis. In effect, he infuses all the blues strains in rhythm and blues with a gospel tinge and updates their sound. It is not that Charles's blues become more powerful than Bessie Smith's or Robert Johnson's; rather, it is that they are powerful in a different way. The sad blues find a new way to communicate their melancholy, while the happy blues convey a heaven-on-earth ecstasy that could arrive only by way of gospel.

Some of his most emotionally charged music comes out at a slow tempo. Perhaps the best example is **"A Fool for You."** In this song, he sings with the deep feeling of the blues, enriched with the most expressive devices of gospel singing—the melismas, the soaring phrases, the high-pitched wails—all set to the stately swing of slow gospel. Charles's fusion of blues feeling with gospel style in slow songs was a unique synthesis and an expressive milestone in the history of popular music. Few popular performers have communicated with such emotional intensity, and only Aretha Franklin followed in Charles's footsteps with comparable artistic success.

"What'd I Say"

Perhaps the song that best summarizes the many facets of Charles's musical personality during the fifties was his only Top 10 hit from that decade: **"What'd I Say."** There are two recordings of the song from 1959—a live performance in Atlanta and a studio recording that lasts about 6½ minutes—both sides of a 45. It combines not only blues and gospel—musically, verbally, and in spirit—but also draws on Latin music and jazz. The extended length of the studio recording allows Charles to let the song unfold slowly. It begins with a comprehensive instrumental introduction and adds musical layers one by one—Charles's singing, the horn section, and then the Raelettes, his backup vocal group—as it builds to an orgasmic climax.

In the instrumental section we hear Charles's take on Latin rhythm. The opening piano figure evokes the piano parts of Afro-Cuban music, and the drum part is much closer to Americanized Latin drumming than standard rock drumming, circa 1959. Charles was not the first to blend Latin rhythms into rhythm and blues—recall the New Orleans songs—but his Americanized Latin rhythm was certainly a catalyst in pointing rhythm and blues toward the more rhythmically free approach to the rock rhythm heard in black music during the sixties.

The solo vocal section alternates between stop-time and a more continuous flow in which the vocal line soars over the instrumental riffs. Although the solo vocal section uses the by-now venerable verse/chorus blues form, it does not tell a story. Instead, it alternates between images of a dancing woman with all the right moves and Charles's need for sexual satisfaction. His need is fulfilled in the final section, in which Charles's exchanges with the Raelettes depict sexual ecstasy about as graphically as one can in music.

"What'd I Say" defined a crucial juncture in the relationship between gospel and blues, and in black music during the rock era. The song revisits a blues tradition—in subject matter (the pleasures of sex), narrative style (pictures, not a story), upbeat mood, and form (verse/chorus blues)—that began with songs like Thomas A. Dorsey's **"It's Tight Like That."** Soon after Dorsey recorded "It's Tight Like That," he brought the blues into black sacred music. Charles closes that particular circle by bringing gospel music into a "It's Tight Like That"-type blues song. The use of the fervent gospel style is functional; it adds a dimension to the blues that was not there before. Sexual relations (or the lack of them) have been the most recurrent theme in blues, as we have noted. The infusion of ecstatic gospel style communicates the experience of sex more powerfully than is possible in traditional blues. Songs like this are the bridge between blues and soul.

Shortly after "What'd I Say" charted, Charles's contract with Atlantic expired. At that time, Atlantic was still a relatively small label, and so Charles and his agent sought a record deal with a major label. They eventually negotiated a lucrative contract with ABC-Paramount that guaranteed Charles a hefty annual advance and a clause that stipulated that the rights to his recordings would revert back to Charles after five years.

Charles used the move as an opportunity to explore genres that he'd put on the shelf, or at least the back-burner, while he was churning out his blues/gospel hits for Atlantic. In rapid succession, there were excursions into pop (1960), jazz (1961), and country music (1962). These detours brought him unprecedented success: while his gospel/blues fusions made him a top artist among blacks, his gospel/blues/jazz/pop/country fusions made him one of the most successful and influential artists in all of popular music during the early sixties—and indeed, for the rest of the century.

Georgia On My Mind

The song that established him as an artist for all audiences was his 1960 recording of **"Georgia On My Mind."** The decision to record the song—and the album from which it was taken—mixed professional savvy with personal inclination. In choosing to record pop standards, he was simply continuing on the well-trodden path followed by pop-oriented R&B acts seeking crossover success, as we have heard. And he had started his career emulating the style of Nat Cole's trio, before Cole went on to one of the great careers in pre-rock pop, so on a more immediate level, this was a return to his professional starting point. However, when Charles revisited this repertoire, he infused his performance of the songs with much the same passion and pacing that he had brought to his R&B work in the previous decade.

The musical backdrop for the recording was standard suave pop fare: lush strings, bland, rather stiff white choral singing, a jazz/pop rhythm section laying down a discreet two-beat. The contrast between the setting and his singing and piano playing was striking. Perhaps because it was so polished, it heightened the expressive impact of Charles's performance by setting it in relief.

There have been very few singers of pre-rock pop who have been able to strip away the layers of prettiness and idealized romanticism to uncover the more deeply felt emotions expressed so frankly in the blues: Louis Armstrong in the thirties, Billie Holiday, Frank Sinatra in the fifties and sixties were among the best. In his sixties pop recordings, Charles not only joins this select company but demonstrates a heartfelt, gospel-tinged approach that influenced several generations of singers:

rock, country, R&B, and pop. As he said in an interview shortly before his death, "To be honest with you, I sing what I feel, what I genuinely feel. That's it. No airs."

For Charles, there were no boundaries or limits. He was equally at home singing and playing with soul partner Aretha Franklin, country great Willie Nelson, pop-rocker Billy Joel, jazz vibraphonist Milt Jackson, or gospel legend Andrae Crouch. By his own account, Charles listened to, and absorbed, all kinds of music when he was growing up, and it all came out in his music over the course of his career. He brought to popular music one of the most unusual dualities in its history: one of the most personal, immediately identifiable voices in all of popular music, paired with an eclecticism that embraces almost every popular style of his generation.

Charles's influence has come in two installments. The first grew out of his work in the late fifties, when he mapped out new directions in the gospel/rhythm-and-blues synthesis that was already well underway. It was his musical example, more than anyone else's, that led black music to soul and inspired numerous white musicians along the way. The second resulted from his recordings of popular song and country music. In particular, the country recordings opened up expressive possibilities to a new generation of country performers. It is an impressive legacy.

4-4 Rhythm and Blues, 1955–1960

In 1955 began, rhythm and blues was on the cusp of a commercial breakthrough. The Crew Cuts' cover version of "Sh-Boom" had reached No. 1 the year before, other cover versions did well, and Chuck Berry, Fats Domino and the Platters reached the top ten on the pop singles charts. These three acts exemplify the three main trends in rock-era music during the latter half of the fifties. Berry would chart the course of rock and roll. Although he assembled his distinctive conception from three blues styles, his music had far less influence on black musicians than whites. Domino represented the status quo—strong rhythm and some of the blues. It did not change much until later in the decade, when several of his fellow New Orleans musicians led the way in the shift to rock rhythm. The Platters' continued success highlighted the growing commercial impact of pop-oriented rhythm and blues.

The key roles of producers like Buck Ram (for the Platters) and Jerry Leiber and Mike Stoller (for the Coasters and Drifters) in shaping the musical result of their acts' recordings provided evidence of their growing importance. Producers would play an even larger role in the fifties.

By 1960, a generational shift was underway. Ray Charles showed the way toward a music that blended active rhythms with a vocal style that harnessed the expressive power of blues and gospel. That would soon become soul. Doo-wop was the forerunner of new black pop styles of the sixties. It would die out during the early sixties; the girl groups and Motown acts that built on the foundation that doo-wop acts established would be even more successful. We encounter samples of this music, and more, in the next chapter.

CHAPTER 5

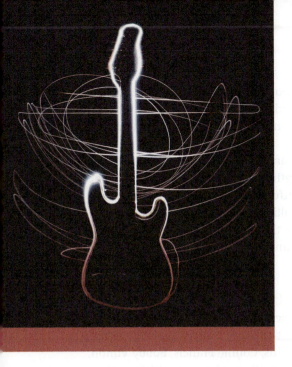

ON THE ROADS TO ROCK: FROM GIRL GROUPS AND GARAGE BANDS TO FOLK AND SURF MUSIC

Learning Objectives:

1) Discuss the social impact of the **twist**.

2) Comment on how **girl groups** influenced the early 1960s perceptions of gender, race, and sex.

3) Define the musical term: **wall of sound**.

4) Compare and contrast how music was produced and popularized between the 1920s and the 1960s.

5) Ascertain the two different branches within the 1960s folk revival.

6) Identify the common musical characteristics found within music of the early 1960s.

Chapter Introduction

If Buddy Holly's death on February 3, 1959, symbolized the death of rock and roll, then the appearance of the Beatles on *The Ed Sullivan Show* on February 9, 1964, signaled the birth of rock. Certainly it was perceived that way in the years that followed. Robert Christgau, one of the most authoritative and outspoken critics of the rock era, wrote in 1973 that rock—as distinguished from rock and roll—"signifies something like 'all music deriving primarily from the energy and influence of the Beatles . . . .'" The transformation of rock and roll into rock was one product of an ongoing musical evolution that lasted half a decade. Our focus in this chapter is charting the development of rock-era music between these two milestones.

5–1 Pop, Rock, and Rhythm and Blues in the Early Sixties

In the early sixties, rock did not rule. Compared to the previous five years, when rock and roll exploded on the national consciousness, and the subsequent five years, when rock came of age, the early sixties seem to be a time of transition.

Experience an interactive version of this era in ✦ MINDTAP

There were no new acts that were supremely popular or influential, like Elvis was or the Beatles would be, nor were there the kinds of wholesale changes in the pop music landscape that accompanied the emergence of rock and roll and the coming together of rock.

Still, the five years between Holly's death and the Beatles' American debut were an eventful time in the history of rock and rhythm and blues, in much the same way that the years of adolescence are an eventful time in the development of a person. There were occasional moments of brilliance—and moments of silliness. Above all, there was the gradual maturation of the music: rock and roll became rock, and rhythm and blues became Motown and soul.

5–1a Pop Versus Rock and Rhythm and Blues

A new generation of rock and R&B musicians scrambled to find room at the top of the singles charts. They competed with the post-military Hollywood Elvis; a group of young pop singers that included Johnny Mathis, Connie Francis, Bobby Vinton, and Bobby Darin; sedate bandleaders like Percy Faith and Lawrence Welk; and the occasional one-hit wonder. The album charts were foreign territory for rock musicians, except for two giants who defected: albums by Elvis and Ray Charles did very well. Everyone bought the soundtrack to *West Side Story*—or so it seemed. In general, soundtracks from films and Broadway shows did well. The two most commercially successful new styles were the pop-oriented **folk music** of acts like the Kingston Trio and Peter, Paul, and Mary and the Brazilian **bossa nova**. Both would filter into rock-era music, but through circuitous paths.

Many of the developments that would reshape popular music were occasional blips on the radar screen, or seemed to slip under the radar entirely. They took place in Liverpool and London and Hamburg, Germany; near the beaches of southern California; at 2845 West Grand Boulevard in Detroit; in the Brill Building and Greenwich Village cafes in New York; and countless garages throughout the United States—most notably in Portland, Oregon.

5–1b The Integration of Popular Music

On November 30, 1963, *Billboard* suspended its R&B singles chart. Their decision was a sensible reaction to the enormous crossover between the R&B and pop charts; for the previous few years, they had become so similar that the R&B chart had become redundant. The brief merging of the two charts—they would separate again just over a year later—was one aspect of a wholesale shift toward a more integrated musical world and the drive toward a more integrated society. It was apparent not only on the charts but also in the recording studio, in the sound of the music, and in the lyrics of folk-inspired protest songs.

Rock and R&B also opened the door to women a little wider. Rock and roll was music for "guys": all its early stars were male. So was rhythm and blues, for the most part. Doo-wop groups were, with few exceptions, male, and so were most of the top solo acts. However, the early sixties saw the emergence of girl groups such as the Shirelles and Ronettes, as well as Motown stars such as Mary Wells and Martha and the Vandellas. Behind the scenes, Carole King, Cynthia Weil, and other female songwriters turned out hit after hit, while Deborah Chessler trailblazed the path for women producers.

There was a kind of generational coming together as well. One catalyst was a new dance made popular not once, but twice, by a Fats Domino fan. It helped bring parents and their children together, at least on the dance floor.

folk music Music made by a group of people (e.g., Cajuns, Navahos, or whites from rural Appalachia), mostly without formal musical training, primarily for their own amusement or for the amusement of others in the group. Within the group, folk music is transmitted orally. Within the popular tradition, folk music has also referred to folksongs sung by commercial musicians (e.g., the Kingston Trio) or music with elements of folk style (e.g., the folk rock of the late 1960s).

bossa nova A samba-based, jazz-influenced Brazilian popular-song style that became popular in the United States in the early 1960s.

5–2 Twisting the Night Away

In the fifties, rock and roll was dance music for teens. Most adults were still fox-trotting and cha-cha-chá-ing. The song that would change all that was "The Twist," a two-time hit for Chubby Checker.

Checker (born Ernest Evans in 1941) was part of pop promoter Dick Clark's stable of artists. Clark was always on the lookout for new dance sensations, because he hosted the popular *American Bandstand*, a dance-oriented television program for teens. "The Twist" first appeared on the rhythm-and-blues charts in 1959 as a minor hit for Hank Ballard and the Midnighters, a Detroit-based doo-wop group that had had several R&B hits during the fifties. When Clark discovered Ballard's song, he had Checker record it for a local Philadelphia label. Clark, who had a financial interest in the label, then promoted the song vigorously on his show. The song was an immediate sensation, and it had staying power as well: it was the only rock-era song to reach the top of the charts twice—first in 1960/1961, then again in 1962.

"The Twist" got everybody dancing to rock and roll. It was easy to learn, even for adults—and they did. Suddenly, dancing the twist (and the frug, watusi, and subsequent dance sensations) was the "in" thing to do. John F. Kennedy watched dancers twist the night away in the East Room of the White House; his bad back kept him on the sidelines. Christopher Lawford, Kennedy's nephew, recalls dancing the twist with Marilyn Monroe.

5–2a "The Twist"

"The Twist" shows its rhythm-and-blues provenance in most of its features. We hear the standard fifties R&B instrumentation: lead and backup vocals, plus rhythm section and honking saxophone. The song is a straightforward blues, in lyrics and form. It has a bright tempo, set by a walking bass. There is one significant difference: the persistent rock rhythm pounded out on the drums and the piano. It's as if Fats Domino's piano triplets were reset to create a rock beat. This energizes the accompaniment underneath Checker's vocal. There is nothing subtle about the rock beat; it is as simple and straightforward as the dance itself.

"The Twist" is one of those right-time/right-place moments that are so much a part of rock history. Neither the song nor Checker's performance were exceptional, but its timing was impeccable. It also provides another demonstration of the enormous power wielded by DJs during the early years of the rock era. Just as Alan Freed helped make "Maybellene" a hit by playing it over and over, Clark (who, like Freed, had a financial interest in the song) pumped up "The Twist" by featuring it on his show. Clark's impact was more far-reaching because the medium was television, not radio. For so many teens, *American Bandstand* was obligatory after-school viewing; they couldn't miss it.

The twist was the most popular (and least athletic) of the dance fads of the early sixties. It was the signature dance of the early rock era, much as the Charleston (the most popular of the black-inspired dances of the early twenties) was the signature dance of the early modern era. And like the Charleston, but unlike the fox-trot, the twist was a "do-it-alone" dance. Interestingly, none of the popular dances of the sixties ever evolved into a real partner dance, where a couple could enjoy the "lingering close contact" that had scandalized bluenoses during the first decades of the twentieth century.

The dance also shows the complex way in which black and white drew together. The roots of the song and the dance are black. But the new rhythm, while also of black origin, had become prominent mainly through white performers. The song went from a relatively obscure R&B hit to the only two-time No. 1 pop song

Charleston The most popular of the vigorous new dances of the early 1920s.

in the early rock era, largely through the influence of a white powerbroker. Chubby Checker's role in making the song a hit is relatively inconsequential; others could have easily filled the role. It was all but inevitable that a new dance would signal the mainstreaming of a new kind of popular music. The twist fulfilled that role.

5-3 Girl Groups, Young Songwriters, and Celebrity Producers

In the early sixties, the best evidence of musical integration came from the songs of the girl groups. We can understand girl groups like the Shirelles, the Crystals, and the Ronettes as a continuation of doo-wop, but there are several differences, the most noteworthy being:

- The vocal group is exclusively female, not completely or mostly male.
- Race is not really a factor in the message of the words or the music.
- The songs, written mainly by young white songwriters, belong to the rock era. They are not remakes of Tin Pan Alley songs or new songs in an older style.
- The musical weight is more in the production than in the vocals. Although they are in the forefront, the singers are virtually interchangeable; the song and—even more—the sounds behind the vocals are often the more distinctive characteristics of the style.

The girl groups are a true musical fusion of white and black, not simply a black take on white music (like most doo-wop hits) or a white take on black music (such as Pat Boone covering Little Richard). This fusion marked the first time that a black-sounding *style*—not just a black artist—was competing on equal terms with white music.

We consider these points in more detail.

5-3a Gender and Race

All-female vocal groups were a novelty in rock-era music but not in popular music. They first appeared on recordings in the late twenties, when bands began to record with vocalists. Groups like the Boswell Sisters and the Andrews Sisters were very popular in the thirties and forties; so were the Chordettes and the McGuire Sisters in the fifties. Three things made the Shirelles and the other girl groups different: they sang rock-era songs, they were not family, and they were black.

Girl groups broke through the gender barrier—in black music and in rock. Black female groups were rare in all genres. In gospel, there were countless male quartets; women typically appeared as soloists, although they often had backup vocalists in performance. In pre-rock pop, the most popular black vocal groups were also male: the Mills Brothers, the Ink Spots. Doo-wop, which emerged from the merger of gospel and pop, also remained almost exclusively male.

The same held true in rock and roll and rhythm and blues. There were no white female rock-and-roll stars in the fifties, and only a few successful female R&B singers: for example, LaVern Baker, Ruth Brown, Etta James. Both genres were largely a man's world.

The breakthrough of the girl groups evidences a shift in consciousness, yet resounds with the echoes of longstanding racial and sexual attitudes. The songs of the girl groups are typically about love: both of the songs discussed below feature young ladies talking to their peers. Up until 1960, it was rare in any branch of the entertainment industry—popular song, stage musicals, films, or television—for black women to talk or sing about love in the first person, and when they did, they directed their attention to black males. Far more common were the stereotypical roles, like Butterfly McQueen in *Gone with the Wind*. Any suggestion of an interracial relationship was taboo. Lena Horne, a wonderful singer/actress and an ideal candidate for the role of Julie, a light-skinned black in the landmark musical *Show Boat*, was passed over in the thirties and again in the fifties. It is against this background that we can understand the girl groups as a sign that the times were "a changin'."

The girl groups represent a chink in the armor of racism. One sees them with the beehive hairdos fashionable in the early sixties among white women, wearing matching prom dresses. The look is designed to break down the barrier between white and black, not build it up. The stories that they tell in their songs and the questions that they ask—"Will you still love me tomorrow?"—are universal; they are not delimited by race. Their voices sound black, but not Muddy Waters or Ray Charles black. In image, words, and sound, they met their intended audience—teens of all races—more than halfway.

All of this opened the door for white males to imagine black partners and for white females to see their black counterparts as kindred spirits. At least one white male walked through the door: Phil Spector courted Ronnie Bennett of the Ronettes, one of the girl groups that he produced, and married her in 1968. That the marriage ended disastrously should not obscure the fact that American society was gradually growing more receptive to the idea of interracial relationships, although miscegenation was still illegal in the South for most of the sixties.

Of the two possible interracial relationships—white male/black female versus black male/white female—the white male/black female was less controversial by far, unless it involved marriage. White male/black female relationships were part of the fabric of life in the South; most looked the other way, even when such a relationship produced offspring. By contrast, a black man caught with a white woman too often ended up at the end of a rope, a victim of a lynching. The popularity of the girl groups, and the Motown acts that featured female performers such as the Supremes, owe something to this imbalanced dynamic.

The girl groups were both a sign and a catalyst for the social change well underway during the early sixties. It was—and is—a slow process, although those who have grown up seeing Denzel Washington romance women of many races may not understand the mindset of the couple portrayed by Spencer Tracy and Katharine Hepburn in the 1967 film *Guess Who's Coming to Dinner*, which featured Sidney Poitier as the black fiancé of the couple's white daughter.

5-3b Songs and Production

The music of the girl groups represents a pivotal moment in the history of rock, for two reasons. First, a new kind of song emerges: in attitude, form, and approach. Second, a new definition of what a song is emerges. The two songs discussed following illustrate these developments.

A New Kind of Song

Many of the girl-group hits came from young songwriters working for publishers in New York's Brill Building. In the sense that they were songwriters writing songs for others to sing, they connect back to Tin Pan Alley. However, the songs that they created represent a decisive break with pre-rock song, in words and music. Many of the songs, like "Da Doo Ron Ron," make use of verse/chorus form, and even those that do not still adapt older forms: "Will You Love Me Tomorrow?" unfolds slowly, with the main phrase building to the title riff at the end.

"Will You Love Me Tomorrow?" cowritten by Carole King and Gerry Goffin, her husband at the time, continues the kind of intimate, personal, and real feelings hinted at in the music of Buddy Holly. Even more significant, it expresses these feelings from a woman's perspective. Its message—the emotional uncertainty of a new relationship: is this love at first sight or a one-night stand?—is presented in plain, direct language. This kind of candor presages the realism of sixties rock.

By contrast, "Da Doo Ron Ron" is mindless. With its nonsense syllables and dumbed-down lyric, it recalls songs like Gene Vincent's "Be-Bop-A-Lula." We explore the implications.

The Producers

Here are the lyrics for the first verse and chorus of the Crystals' "Da Doo Ron Ron," a huge hit for them in 1963:

> Met him on a Monday and my heart stood still
>
> Da Doo Ron Ron Ron, Da Doo Ron Ron
>
> Somebody told me that his name was Bill
>
> Da Doo Ron Ron Ron, Da Doo Ron Ron
>
> Yes, my heart stood still
>
> Yes, his name was Bill
>
> Yes, when he walked me home
>
> Da Doo Ron Ron Ron, Da Doo Ron Ron

Compared to the cleverness of Chuck Berry's lyrics, or the honesty and emotional commitment of "Will You Love Me Tomorrow?" these lyrics seem the work of an uninspired third-grader. One can argue that sophisticated, interesting, or even emotionally honest lyrics would have worked at cross purposes to the message of the song. Instead, the lyrics seem to be there simply because songs have lyrics. The song is not about the message of the words, or even the Crystals' singing of it. Rather, it is about the wall of sound behind the vocals. That wall of sound was the work of Phil Spector, the first celebrity producer.

From the start, producers played an integral role in shaping the sound of records. In previous chapters, we heard the impact of seminal rock producers like Sam Phillips (Jackie Brenston, early Elvis), Dave Bartholomew (Fats Domino and Little Richard), and Norman Petty (Buddy Holly). We encountered the work of Jerry Leiber and Mike Stoller, who wrote songs for specific acts, then produced them: not only several of Elvis's hits, but also virtually all of the Coasters' hits. Recall their remark: "We don't write songs; we write records."

Among the musicians who worked briefly with Leiber and Stoller in New York was Phil Spector. Spector soon formed his own record company, Philles (for Phil and Les [Sill], his partner at the time), and began churning out a string of hits in the early sixties, mainly with two girl groups: the Crystals and the Ronettes.

Although the songs appeared on the charts, in record stores, and on radio as the music of the Crystals or Ronettes, they were really about Spector and his radically new conception of what a rock-and-roll record could be. Spector crafted what he called a "Wagnerian approach to rock and roll." "Wagnerian" refers to the mid-nineteenth-century German opera composer Richard Wagner, whose music was noted for, among other things, bombastic orchestral writing, and—more important—embedding more of the *musical* meaning in the orchestral background than the vocal lines.

Spector was on target with his self-assessment. His songs were not about the words, the melody, or even the singers—the Crystals and the Ronettes were as interchangeable as the anonymous session musicians behind them. Spector would gather several of the finest available freelance musicians in a small room with hard walls and record them with extensive echo and reverb to create an almost tangible mass of sound. It is this feature, which was ideal for AM radio, with its relatively low fidelity, that gave the songs that Spector produced their distinctive character. Indeed, in songs like "Da Doo Ron Ron," there would seem to be a kind of arrogance in the use of simpleminded lyrics and melodies. It is as if Spector is saying, "I can transform even the most mundane material into a hit that everyone will want to hear." Even though he never sang on his recordings and seldom played an instrument, the records that he produced captured *his* sound.

During his run in the first half of the sixties, Spector raised the status of the producer. People knew that the "wall of sound" recordings were by Spector, in a way that they didn't know that Dave Bartholomew was behind the New Orleans sound or that, somewhat later, George Martin was behind the sound of the Beatles' music. More important, Spector's work added a symphonic dimension to rock music. He showed that the final result and the musical message could be far more powerful than that predicted by the most obvious elements—words, melodies, singers.

5–3c Style and Commerce

The result of this activity—white songwriters and producers creating songs sung by young black women, backed by musicians of both races—was a unique moment in pop music history. The girl-group recordings represent a style in which black and white elements are evident, yet all of a piece: it is a sound in which everything blends together seamlessly. In this respect, it goes further than Elvis's singing and further than the rock and rollers who built on the foundation laid down by Chuck Berry and Little Richard.

The listening audience for this music seemed as integrated as the music itself. The many girl-group hits played a major role in collapsing pop and rhythm and blues into a single chart. Whites and blacks seemed to buy them in comparable numbers. Indeed, the girl-groups' recordings often did as well or better on the pop charts than they did on the R&B charts before they were merged. Musically, it was a fresh new sound, with something for everyone.

5–3d Girl-group Songs

We contrast two girl-group recordings: the Shirelles' "Will You Love Me Tomorrow?" and the Crystals' "Da Doo Ron Ron." In one, the song is important; in the other, the wall of sound is preeminent.

The Shirelles

The Shirelles were a female vocal quartet—Shirley Owens (b. 1941), Micki Harris (1940–1982), Beverly Lee (b. 1941), and Doris Coley (1941–2000)—who first came together as the Poquellos in 1957 while still in high school. Their rise to the top of the charts is another of the happy accidents of the rock era. The group had won over the crowd at a high school talent show with a song they wrote themselves: "**I Met Him on a Sunday**." A classmate, Mary Jane Greenberg, introduced them to her mother Florence, who after some haggling, signed them to record the song for her fledgling label—Tiara Records. It was a local hit—big enough to be picked up by Decca Records. When released by Decca, the song charted nationally; it became the Shirelles' first hit.

After a few more Decca-released recordings that went nowhere, Greenberg reformed Tiara as Scepter Records and brought in Luther Dixon to produce the group. From 1960 to 1963, the group was almost always on the charts. Their biggest hit came in 1960, in a song written by Carole King and Gerry Goffin: "**Will You Love Me Tomorrow?**"

The song and its creation give us a wonderful preview of the tumultuous changes to come in the sixties. It was written and performed by women; the lyric gives us a woman's perspective on the fragility of new love.

Before rock, there had been few women songwriters (Kay Swift, who wrote the 1930 hit "Fine and Dandy," stands out). Moreover, most of the songs that they and their male counterparts wrote were gender-neutral; there is no obvious clue in words or music that a song is written by a woman for women. Even songs written for a female role in a musical—such as "My Funny Valentine," written by Richard Rodgers and Lorenz Hart for the 1937 musical *Babes in Arms*—would be performed by male singers, with a little tweaking of the lyrics. Before rock, we get the woman's perspective mainly from female blues singers (Bessie Smith's "Empty Bed Blues") and country songs like Kitty Wells's "It Wasn't God Who Made Honky Tonk Angels" (1952), her famous retort to Hank Thompson's "The Wild Side of Life."

Carole King's song gives us the other side of boastful, male, R&B songs ("Good Rockin' Tonight"). The man thinks only of tonight; the woman worries about tomorrow. There is no mistaking the message of the song; the lyrics are simple and clear. This kind of frankness became possible in mainstream popular music only when society, or at least the audience for this kind of song, could accept this straight talk. That change in attitude was underway by 1960. We hear this song as a transitional step between the Donna Reed–ish façade of fifties pop and the confessional songs of early seventies female singer/songwriters such as Joni Mitchell.

The music reinforces the message of the lyrics, not because it presents a coherent setting, but because its main components send such different messages. There are three groups of sounds: the rhythm section, the string section, and the Shirelles. The rhythm section lays down a rather mundane rock beat, one that was fashionable during these years in rock-influenced pop. It remains constant throughout the song; there is almost no variation. But the string writing is bold and demanding—the most sophisticated part of the sound. The intricate string lines stand in stark contrast to the Shirelles' vocals, especially Shirley Owens's straightforward lead.

And therein lies the charm. The instrumental backup, and especially the skillful string parts, contrast with the naive schoolgirl sound of the Shirelles (none of them was 20 years old when the song was released). All this meshes perfectly with King's lyrics, the song's simple melody, and the look of the group. Owens sounds courageous enough to ask the question—and vulnerable enough to be deeply hurt by the wrong answer. She, like the lyric, sounds neither worldly nor cynical.

The song and the singers were both a product and an agent of change—helping to close the gap between black and white. As a product, the song reflected the changes in rock-era music. As an agent of change, the song was written by a white woman, produced by a black man, supported with white-sounding string writing, and sung by young black women. The message of the song is colorblind. Teens of all races could relate to its theme. The Shirelles crossed over more consistently and successfully than any of the black acts of the fifties in part because of the changing racial climate (the civil rights movement was gathering steam) and in part because they were teens like their audience. In "Will You Love Me Tomorrow?" they sing peer-to-peer about a meaningful issue.

Phil Spector and the Crystals

Like the Shirelles, the Crystals were a female vocal group made up of black teens. At the time they recorded "**Da Doo Ron Ron**," the five members of the group were Barbara Alston, Dee Dee Kennibrew, Mary Thomas, Patricia Wright, and La La Brooks, who sang lead on the recording.

The Crystals had caught the ear of Spector while they were rehearsing in the Brill Building. Spector signed them up, then proceeded to jerk them around. After he and the group scored hits with "There's No Other (Like My Baby)" and "Uptown," Spector, who was at odds with the group about who should sing lead, took matters into his own hands and recorded Darlene Love as "the Crystals." In 1963, the actual group was back in the studio with Spector to record two of their biggest hits: "Da Doo Ron Ron" and "**Then He Kissed Me**."

Perhaps "Da Doo Ron Ron" was the product of a war of wills. Spector had shown the group how dispensable they were by recording another singer under their name, which he owned. It galled them to have to sing songs that they didn't record during their constant touring in 1963. Given Spector's volatile personality—he was convicted in 2009 for the murder of Lana Clarkson—it was certainly possible that he would find another way to show the group how small a part they were in the equation for success. Certainly, their relationship grew more strained when Spector became enamored with the Ronettes and their lead singer, Ronnie Bennett. In 1965, the group bought out their contract and moved to Imperial Records, a move that ended in failure. The group disbanded in 1966.

In any event, the most striking feature of "Da Doo Ron Ron" is the sound behind the singers. Spector's wall of sound is tall: it extends from the strong bass line, low-pitched drums, and sustained low saxophone chords to the high-register piano part—an oscillation between a single note and a chord that at once confirms and conflicts with the triplet rhythm that energizes the song.

Much of its impact comes from the fact that the rhythm, like the instrumentation, is clearly stratified. At the center is the beat, marked firmly by the bass instruments, the bass drum, and handclaps. There is a slower rhythm created from the sustained chords in the saxophones. On top, there is the triplet rhythm heard throughout in the piano part and occasionally reinforced in the drum part. This triplet rhythm obviously derives from the Fats Domino–style triplets heard in many of his medium- and slow-tempo hits. Here, the tempo is so fast that the pianist must play an oscillating pattern instead of simply repeating the chords. The oscillation, because it groups the notes of the triplets in pairs, creates a constant rhythmic conflict. It is one of the signature elements of the sound of this recording.

The vocal line is heavily syncopated. In particular, the title phrase is almost completely off-beat. The syncopated accents highlight the fact that the phrase is about rhythmic excitement—**syncopations** literally in the middle of several layers of rhythm. The title-phrase syllables sung by the Crystals are meaningless as words; they are used simply to make the rhythm of the vocal line more emphatic.

> **syncopations**
> Accents that come between the beats of a regular rhythm, rather than with them.

5–3e Redefining Song in the Early Rock Era

"Da Doo Ron Ron" offers an ideal illustration of one of the most significant changes of the rock era: a radically new conception of song. Every crucial element of a song—what it is, how it is created, and how it reaches its audience—underwent major revision. To appreciate the magnitude of this reconception, we need to examine how popular music reached its audience before the rock era.

The popular songs of the twenties, thirties, and forties generally went from inspiration to hit in several stages:

1. A songwriter or songwriting team (composer and lyricist) wrote the song.
2. An arranger scored the song for the group that would perform it: the orchestra, for a Broadway or Hollywood musical, a dance band or a studio orchestra supporting a singer such as Frank Sinatra.
3. Once a song caught on, it was "out there," for anyone to perform. Typically, several bands would record different versions of the song, all at about the same time. Live performances—in a nightclub, at a dance, over the radio—would be even more varied.
4. At the same time, the song's publisher would print a piano/vocal setting of the song. This would offer a simplified version of the melody and harmony of the song, appropriate for home use.

As a result, the song would exist simultaneously in several forms. For instance, listeners in 1935 could hear Irving Berlin's hit song "Cheek to Cheek," featured in the film *Top Hat*, on records by Fred Astaire, Ginger Rogers, and several others, performed live on radio broadcasts and in night clubs and restaurants, or they could buy the sheet music and play it themselves.

Two aspects of this process stand out. First, there was no one person who controlled the sound of the song. Second, there was no authoritative version. The songwriter and the lyricist wrote the words, melody, harmony, and basic rhythms of the song. However, their published version of the song did not specify the instruments to be used in an ideal performance, the vocal style of the singer, the overall form of the performance, and many other features. Moreover, the songwriter effectively lost artistic control of the song when he or she finished it. Arrangers and performers could change almost any aspect of the song—and usually did.

By the early sixties, however, every aspect of this process had changed. Increasingly, the progress of a song from idea to finished product typically went like this:

1. Songwriters—either professional songwriters like Carole King and Gerry Goffin, producers like Spector, or musicians like Roy Orbison—would write a song, either for a band in which they played or (in the case of the girl groups) for a specific act. They would then flesh out the basic features of the song with the rest of the band in rehearsal or prepare an arrangement that added distinctive features that would become part of the song's identity, like the string lines in "Will You Love Me Tomorrow?" or the piano oscillation in "Da Doo Ron Ron."
2. They would bring it into the recording studio, where a producer would oversee the entire recording process: the basic recording, overdubbing, mixing, and so forth.
3. A record company would release the song as a single.
4. If the song became a hit, it would be played on the radio and bought in record stores throughout the country. Any other version of the song would be identified as a cover.
5. A simplified sheet music version might appear. However, most people learned the sound and style of a song from the recording. If they used the sheet music at all, it was only as a bare-bones guide.

This new process produced two far-reaching changes. First, the creators of the song generally retained some control of the end result throughout the entire creative process. Second, there was, as a result, a *definitive* version of a song: the original recording by the group or team that conceived it. The song became the sound captured on record: not just the melody and chords, but the complete sound experience. Unlike earlier popular songs, *the recording was the document.*

Everything about the recording—its beat, the choice of instruments, the sound of the singer(s), signature riffs, accompaniments—helped define the song. Any other version of the song, whether a cover recording or a sheet music reduction, lacked the authority of the original.

Moreover, songs often represented a more unified conception. It could be the musical vision of one individual or a collaboration among songwriter, performer, and producer, with one person often filling two of the roles. In either circumstance, the song represented a collectively conceived viewpoint, worked out mainly in one place (a recording studio) within a narrow timeframe (over the course of a recording session).

Steady improvement in recording technology made this new creative process possible. The most far-reaching innovation was **multitrack recording**, which enabled producers to assemble a song layer by layer. Experimentation through trial and error was possible on a much broader scale at every stage of the process, from initial idea to final mix. This more-or-less continuous evolution of a song was a far cry from the severely segmented assembly of a recorded performance in pre-rock pop.

Spector was not the first producer to craft a record. From Sam Phillips's inspired use of a broken speaker cone through Leiber and Stoller's hits for the Coasters and Luther Dixon's work with the Shirelles, producers had come to play an increasingly important role in the creative process. However, Spector turned the traditional relationship between song and sound on its head. Before the sixties, a song was mainly the words, the melody, and the person singing it—Elvis's numerous hits exemplify this perfectly. Everything else is in the service of the song and the singing of it. However, with Spector, the song and the singers are in the service of the sound. The most important element in his girl-group hits is the wall of sound.

That was what teens heard when they listened to the songs on their car radios or on the tinny transistor radios that were flooding the market in the early sixties. These first-generation transistor radios—the predecessors of the Walkman—could receive only AM radio stations, and they had a limited frequency range. Spector designed his wall of sound to maximize the impact of the song *as it would be heard on a transistor or car radio*. (If your playback device has an equalizer, try reducing the very lowest and highest frequencies to replicate this experience as you listen to the song.) It was a revolutionary, and extremely influential, strategy.

Songs like "Da Doo Ron Ron" represent an extreme position in the relationship between song and sound. We might surmise that Spector's ego—his need to show the world who was the most important player in the song-creating game—clouded his judgment. As fascinating as his wall of sound is in songs like this, it doesn't make up for the lack of substance in other areas. Still, Spector's symphonic conception of rock offered subsequent producers a roadmap for expanding rock's sound world. It was a major contribution.

multitrack recording The process of recording each part of a performance separately, then mixing them into a complete performance. The Beatles, along with their producer George Martin, were among the first to take full advantage of multitrack recording techniques.

5-4 From Folk to Rock

The folk revival that began in the late fifties had a short lifespan, even by pop standards. As a movement with mass appeal, it began in 1958, when the Kingston Trio's recording of "**Tom Dooley**" topped the pop charts. It ended seven years later, when Dylan went electric at the Newport Folk Festival, and Alan Lomax and Pete Seeger went ballistic.

In its revived form, folk music was an urban music. The earlier folk revival of the 1940s and early fifties, sparked by the work of the Lomaxes, Woody Guthrie, and—most popularly—the Weavers, had brought folk music into the city. The second revival, which began in the late fifties, made the separation between country roots and contemporary urban performance even wider. By 1960, this old/new folk music was flourishing in coffeehouses, often located in the more bohemian parts of major cities (Greenwich Village in New York, North Beach in San Francisco) or near college campuses.

The folk revival was apolitical at first. Its audience liked the tuneful melodies, pleasantly sung. That soon changed, as this new folk revival quickly rediscovered its past. Historic preservation and social commentary, the two main directions of the folk movement of the thirties and forties, resurfaced within a year.

5–4a Restoring the Past

The restoration of traditional music during this folk revival had two branches. One was the rediscovery of folk musicians, white and black. The other was the re-creation of folk music by contemporary performers. The blues revival of the early sixties was one dimension of the folk revival. Delta bluesmen who hadn't sung professionally in 25 years were suddenly touring college campuses and appearing at folk festivals. Equally important was the reissue of early recordings. This helped folk traditionalists try to replicate the country and blues styles that they heard on folk recordings. Their search for authenticity went far beyond learning a song out of a songbook.

The most notable and popular of these traditionalists was Joan Baez. Her covers of traditional songs, such as those recorded by the Carter Family, show a conscientious attempt to re-create not only the songs but also the sound of traditional folk music. It is most evident in the accompaniment: Baez's guitar playing closely resembles that of Maybelle Carter. However, her pure-toned singing has none of the Carters' nasal quality or country twang. It is as far from their style as New York is from the southern Appalachians. Still, it is far more connected stylistically to the Carters than it is to the rock and popular music of the early sixties.

5–4b Social Commentary: The Legacy of Woody Guthrie

The folk revival also gave voice to the protest movement. The drive for racial equality had been gathering momentum since the end of World War II. The gradual dismantling of the "separate but equal" policy and the confrontations that ensued brought the issue into the national spotlight. In the early sixties, both performers and audiences embraced this and other social issues of the day. The image of ex-Weaver Pete Seeger, the strongest link between the folk revivals of the forties and the sixties, leading the masses in singing **"We Shall Overcome"** is still vivid. He became godfather to a new generation of activists. Other folk performers, like Bob Dylan (born Robert Zimmerman, 1941) and Phil Ochs, were even more outspoken. Their songs would prod a generation of young people into thinking, then acting: massive rallies, marches on Washington, sit-ins.

In effect, this new folk revival relived the history of the music that inspired it. That is, it began by re-creating folksongs and classic "folk" performances (such as those by the Carters). However, just as Woody Guthrie gave the folk sound a contemporary focus, so did folksingers like Dylan begin to write topical songs. These were social commentaries with more sting, such as Dylan's

"**Talkin' John Birch Paranoid Blues**." Indeed, Guthrie was the patron saint of the folk revival; a momentous event in Bob Dylan's life was his visiting Guthrie who lay dying in a New York hospital.

Social commentary, presented in folk-style songs, gushed forth from the coffeehouses of New York's Greenwich Village and college towns around the United States. The audience was young and idealistic. They turned to these songs, despite their musical simplicity, because no other music was comparably relevant.

5–4c Bob Dylan and the Folk Revival

Dylan's music from the early sixties epitomizes the substance and spirit of this activist branch of the folk movement. The repertoire on his first few recordings includes mostly original songs as well as the occasional folk or blues cover—for instance, "**House of the Rising Sun**," popularized by the Almanac singers (Guthrie, Seeger, and others) in 1941, or "**See That My Grave Is Kept Clean**," a blues by Blind Lemon Jefferson. The original material ranged from songs like the aforementioned "Talkin' John Birch Paranoid Blues," which he delivered in his distinctive folk/rap style—resonant speaking over a strummed guitar accompaniment, with an occasional harmonica interlude—to anthemic songs like "**Blowin' in the Wind**." In either case, the words were preeminent; the guitar accompaniment typically consisted of simple strumming of the I, IV, and V chords, the three basic chords of common practice tonality. The main musical variable was the melody—including whether there was one.

Bob Dylan's first big hit—although it would be a hit for someone else, not him—was "Blowin' in the Wind," the first track on his 1963 album *The Freewheelin' Bob Dylan*. (The album rose as high as No. 22 and eventually went gold.) It is hard to imagine a more striking contrast between "Blowin' in the Wind" and "Da Doo Ron Ron," although, ironically, they were released only a few months apart. Dylan's song is all about the words. The melody is simple, repetitive, and catchy, an ideal backdrop for important lyrics. The guitar strumming supports the melody unobtrusively, sustaining the flow when Dylan is not singing or playing the harmonica. In an indirect way, Dylan's voice also draws attention to the words. It is a grating sound, not a pretty one; listeners are not likely to be so seduced by its beauty that they would ignore the words. At the same time, his voice has an urgency that amplifies the message of the lyrics.

The lyrics of "Blowin in the Wind" challenge listeners, both in their message and in the way Dylan presents the message. The song is strophic: three stanzas set to the same melody, with the title phrase as a short refrain. Dylan begins generally: he alludes to the long road to maturity, the dove of peace, and an archaic armament in the first stanza. In the second stanza, he juxtaposes the glacial pace of erosion with the lingering effects of racism; by implication, change comes much too slowly. In the third stanza, he focuses on the terrible cost of racism, for the victims and the perpetrators. Dylan avoids specifics in the images and—even more—in the refrain. By simply stating that the answer is there for everyone to see, rather than stating the theme of the song specifically, Dylan demands that his listeners respond actively.

We can hear the importance of Dylan's acerbic singing and harmonica playing to the message of the song if we compare Dylan's version to the cover version by Peter, Paul, and Mary. Peter, Paul, and Mary (Peter Yarrow, Noel Paul Stookey, and Mary Travers) were the Kingston Trio of the early sixties: commercial, but with a conscience. They rode the crest of the protest movement: "Blowin' in the Wind" was a No. 2 hit for them in 1963. Their straightforward presentation of the melody made the words easily comprehensible; their pleasant voices and subdued guitar accompaniment made it palatable to a broad audience. However, their sound related to the message of the song far less than Dylan's, and only in a generic way. Their other No. 2 hit, "**Puff (The Magic Dragon)**," sounds virtually identical, although the lyric is ostensibly a children's story (some have interpreted it as an invitation to smoke marijuana) rather than a call to action. Still, the clean, careful, sweet-voiced singing seems out of sync with the message of Dylan's song.

We accept this music as part of rock history mainly because of its message and the way in which it invited rock to matter, and—more important—because of Dylan's subsequent gravitation toward rock. Dylan's song has virtually no musical connection with the other music of this chapter, or—for that matter—with the music of the two previous chapters. Dylan would address precisely this issue by going electric.

5–5 From Rockabilly to Rock: The Music of Roy Orbison

Roy Orbison (1936–1988), a shy Texan, was the last rockabilly, the first country rocker, and one of the architects of the symphonic pop-rock sound of the early sixties. After recording his first songs at Norman Petty's studio in Clovis, New Mexico, Orbison migrated to Tennessee in 1956. During stops in Memphis and Nashville, he rubbed shoulders with all of the important figures in white rock and roll by the end of the decade: Elvis, Buddy Holly, Jerry Lee Lewis, Sam Phillips, Norman Petty, the Everly Brothers.

His music—especially that produced at the peak of his career—would blend all these influences. Indeed, Orbison's major hits from the early sixties summarize and update the country elements of rock and roll and provide a fascinating early glimpse of the transformative changes that distinguish the rock of the sixties from rock and roll. Orbison's partner in these significant developments was producer Fred Foster, who worked with him at Monument Records.

Their summarizing work took two forms. In songs such as "**Only the Lonely**" (1960), they cultivated a more melodramatic version of the rock ballad introduced by the Everly Brothers. In "**Meanwoman Blues**" (1963), Orbison simultaneously updates rockabilly—the song is a country take on rock and roll, not rhythm and blues—and lays the foundation for **country rock**. The song is a musical stew: Orbison's singing with gentle overtones of Jerry Lee Lewis, backup vocals and saxophone borrowed from rhythm and blues, a bluesy guitar solo over the riff from the Surfari's "Wipeout," played on a saxophone. These were part of the sound world of the early sixties. Underpinning this is a rhythmic conception that would become the rhythmic foundation of country rock: a honky-tonk two-beat rhythm—electric bass alternating with heavy drum backbeat—with a clean rock beat layered on top. Along with the dense texture, this driving rhythm amplifies the swagger of the lyric. All of this happened several years before the idea of country rock surfaced, and almost a decade before the release of the Eagles' "**Take It Easy**," the song that clearly defined the genre.

Orbison's masterpiece was "**Oh, Pretty Woman**" (more commonly known as "Pretty Woman"). Although the song was released after the onset of the British invasion, we include it in this chapter because the early sixties were the most successful stretch of Orbison's career.

The song evidences several features that would become trademarks of sixties rock. Among the most significant are:

- A straightforward rock rhythm
- A signature guitar riff to open the song and serve as an instrumental refrain
- A bass line that moves in a free rhythm, rather than a walking pattern or other narrowly defined role

country rock Music combining a strong honky-tonk two-beat with a clear, simple rock rhythm.

Among the most distinctive features of the song is its form. More than any other song discussed to this point, "Pretty Woman" illustrates the more flexible approach to form that characterizes rock music. More than that, the memorable musical events in the song seem to respond almost cinematically to the images described in the lyric. Like a good soundtrack, they capture the basic mood of the story and highlight the constantly shifting emotions.

The story is a cliché of romantic comedies, music videos, and television commercials: boy sees beautiful girl, boy makes some kind of contact with girl, boy is apparently rebuffed, but gets the girl in the end. Here are the musical events that help tell the story:

The opening guitar riff is assertive, yet the chord that it outlines, and the silence that follows, asks a question that is not answered conclusively until the final notes of the song. The periodic return of the guitar riff not only outlines the form of the song but keeps us focused on the main issue in the song: will the pretty woman like the hero?

The first two sections of the vocal line begin by setting the scene. But both end by dangling on the V chord. The second time, the suspenseful ending highlights the crucial question: "Are you lonely, just like me?"

In the section that follows, the hero of the song hits on the pretty woman. A new melody, with short, pleading phrases in a higher register, underscores the intensity of his interest. Orbison extends the pleading section by dropping down into a lower register as he attempts to persuade her more intimately, in both words and music. This extension is the first clear signal that Orbison is molding the form to fit the pacing of his story: a more conventional song would have returned to the opening section before the extension.

He continues to press his case as the opening vocal section returns. However, the suspenseful ending is expanded enormously as the hero seems to lose the pretty woman, then discovers that she's returning. The sudden ending after the big buildup is, in effect, a quick fade to black as the hero and the pretty woman come together.

In "Pretty Woman," Orbison molded the form to the story, not the other way around. He underscored the feelings of his protagonist musically, in both the guitar riff and the melody. His hero's success with the pretty woman owes much to the persuasiveness of the music. Orbison's flexible approach to form and musical reinforcement of the story line would become increasingly common in rock. However, few would connect the music with the story as closely and powerfully as Orbison did here.

With songs such as "Pretty Woman," Orbison survived the first wave of the British invasion. But the arrival of the second wave, a switch to MGM records, and personal tragedy (the death of his first wife and son in a fire at his Nashville home in the late sixties) sent his career into a tailspin.

In the early sixties, folk music and country music seemed worlds apart: one flourished in Greenwich Village and other urban areas, the other mainly in the South. Orbison and Dylan would play key roles in bringing country and folk into rock: Orbison first with his recordings, and Dylan soon after, when he went electric. In 1988, just before Orbison's death, there was a symbolic celebration of both men's roles in bringing together folk, country, and rock in the almost accidental formation of the Traveling Wilburys: this famous supergroup included not only Orbison and Dylan, but also George Harrison, Jeff Lynne, and Tom Petty.

Orbison's "Pretty Woman" is among the memorable songs from 1963 and 1964 that line up on the rock side of the rock and rock-and-roll boundary. We encounter two more from the same period next.

5-6 Garages and Cars, and Surf and Sun

Rock and roll came from the center of the United States: New Orleans, Memphis, Texas, Chicago. However, it quickly spread to both coasts and beyond. While Dick Clark was filling the airwaves with teen idols and Philadelphia teens were twisting the night away, rock and roll was taking root elsewhere, most notably on the west coast of the United States and in England. We consider two locales in the United States in this chapter and England in the next.

The two songs considered here are the Kingsmen's version of "**Louie Louie**" and the Beach Boys' "**I'll Get Around**." The Beach Boys are forever linked to southern California, while the Kingsmen were based several hundred miles up the coast, in Portland, Oregon. In the sense that both bands were based on the west coast, away from the geographical center of rock, there is some geographic connection. There is also a clear musical affinity; in such basic features as instrumentation and rhythm, the songs are more like each other (and Orbison's "Oh, Pretty Woman") than they are like other songs discussed in the chapter.

However, there is a striking contrast in the way that they prepared for the recording sessions and the quality of the recording. The Kingsmen were the first big-time garage band; their recording of "Louie Louie" was one of only three songs by the band that charted; the other two rode its coattails. By contrast, the Beach Boys' song is carefully worked out and recorded with comparable care. Under the "fun in the sun" surface is a well-crafted song.

Together, however, the two songs show the two main facets of a revolutionary change in the creative process that took place during the early years of the rock era. One was the increased use of recordings as a tool for the transmission of music, the other was multitrack recording.

5-6a Rock and Recordings: A New Mode of Musical Transmission

All music is an aural art. However, before the twentieth century, there were only two ways to create music and transmit it from one person to another. One way was by ear. A musician could invent a song or dance. When he or she performed it, others could listen to the musician's music and learn it. This is how folksongs and dances were passed around and passed down through generations. There were two limitations on this process. One involves location: the listener had to be in the same place at the same time as the person performing the music in order to learn it. The other has to do with difficulty. Musical notation (a set of visual symbols that represent musical sounds with varying degrees of precision) becomes a necessary tool when the music is too complex to work out strictly by ear—because the piece is too long, too difficult to execute, too complex, and/or involves too many musicians. Beethoven could have composed the melody we know as the "Ode to Joy" without notation, and we can learn it without reading music, but the symphony of which it is a part, his *Ninth Symphony*, absolutely demands notation. The work is about seventy minutes long (it was this piece that determined the storage capacity of the compact disc; the people responsible for the development of the CD wanted to be able to include the entire symphony on a single disc!) and requires four vocal soloists, a large choir, and an orchestra of about a hundred musicians.

Recording, radio, and talking films offered another way to pass music on. People could learn music via these new technologies. Recordings in particular offered the possibility of repeated scrutiny during the learning process. Folksingers like Bob Dylan and Joan Baez could learn songs by the Carter Family, Blind Lemon

Jefferson, and dozens of other folk and blues performers. Jazz, rhythm and blues, and rock-and-roll musicians could steal licks from recordings and work them into their own performances.

During the early years of the rock era, the recording gained in authority. Aspiring rock-and-roll musicians understood that the record was the song. One can imagine the Wilson brothers listening to Chuck Berry's **"Sweet Little Sixteen"** countless times, then reworking it into **"Surfin' USA."** Implicit in their recording is the idea that the song is more than the melody; among its most distinctive features is a band-wide realization of Berry's conception of rock rhythm.

In the case of the Kingsmen's "Louie Louie," the path is more circuitous. The original version of the song was by Richard Berry, a Los Angeles–based R&B singer; he recorded the song in 1956 with his band the Pharaohs. By Berry's account, he drew on several sources for the song: Chuck Berry's **"Havana Moon"** was a principal source for the pseudo-Jamaican style of the lyric, while the repeated riff that is the song's signature came from a Latin song—Berry had been working with an R&B band that also played a lot of Latin music. Over the next several years, several bands covered Berry's song. One of them was Rockin' Robin Roberts and the Fabulous Wailers, a small-time band based in the Pacific Northwest; the group recorded their version in 1961. This is the version from which the Kingsmen crafted their memorable version.

This is the rock-era analog to the folksong-style creation, re-creation, and dissemination. One can easily imagine newly formed rock-and-roll bands setting up in garages across the country working out three-chord songs like "Louie Louie." As each band works through it, it assumes a different form. The Kingsmen's version is noticeably different from Berry's original; the Wailers' version is somewhere in between. And there are numerous other versions of the song, enough to warrant two "Best of 'Louie Louie'" anthologies—just as there are multiple versions of folksongs. The main difference, of course, is the recording, which eliminates the need for personal contact and which provides a more reliable reference. But a simple song like "Louie Louie" quickly spawned many different renditions, including the one that made the Kingsmen famous.

5–6b Multitrack Recording

"I Get Around," by contrast, is a sophisticated song supporting teen-themed lyrics. Brian Wilson, the mastermind of the Beach Boys' sound, took considerable care in shaping the harmony, rhythm, instrumentation, and texture of the song. His main tool in this enterprise was a multitrack tape recorder. According to his personal website, **www.brianwilson.com**, Wilson worked out the Beach Boys' distinctive sound before their first recording:

> It was a unique fusion that Wilson had been tinkering with in the family garage where, inspired by The Four Freshman and their complex vocal blends, and armed with a multi-track tape recorder, he'd spent hours exploring the intricacies of harmony and melody. By overlapping his own dynamic voice (which peaked in a soaring falsetto) and various instruments, he could create the effect of a full group.

Wilson's early exercises in multitrack recording show a new creative process at work. Before multitrack tape recorders, musicians had to imagine the sound that they wanted in their head, perhaps try it out on an instrument, such as the piano, then write out what they heard and assemble a group of musicians to hear the actual sound of the musical mental image. If the final result was not to their liking, they rewrote the composition or arrangement and reassembled the musicians. In most stages of the process, the musicians had to convert sounds—real or imagined—into notation, which is necessarily an imperfect rendering of the musical sound. Then they had to rely on the musicians to not only play what was written but also supply those elements of the performance that could not be notated. However, in multitrack recording, musicians like Wilson are working with actual sounds throughout the entire creative process. Further, they are able to experiment with their work at every stage of the process: they can add a part, and if it is not the desired result, they can remove it.

Today, creating music in a sound-only environment is commonplace. Buy an Apple computer; open up Garage Band (the audio workstation software that comes with the computer), drag and drop a few times: you have an instant dance track. Wilson's work is among the most noteworthy early examples of this process; it would soon become the *modus operandi* in rock music, as we discover in the next chapter. It is a process that belongs to the rock era; it is the result of technology responding to musical needs, much as the technology of the twenties responded to the musical needs of that time. It is a revolutionary change in the creative process, one that is as far-reaching as the invention of musical notation and one whose possibilities are still being expanded. For those who have come of age in the twenty-first century, it may be hard to imagine a musical world without this technology. But 50 years ago, Wilson was on the cutting edge.

5–6c A Garage-Band Triumph: "Louie Louie"

The success of "Louie Louie" is due largely to incompetence. The great attraction of the song seems to have been the incomprehensibility of the lyrics. The original lyrics are innocuous enough, although by today's standards, the pseudo-Jamaican dialect would probably be deemed politically incorrect. However, it has been impossible to reconstruct the lyrics of the song as sung by lead singer Jack Ely on this recording. The absence of a definite text led teens to imagine their own lyrics, led parents to wonder what their sons and daughter were listening to, and led the FBI to investigate the song; 31 months later the FBI could only conclude that the song was "unintelligible at any speed." Of course, in the absence of intelligible lyrics, randy teens supplied their own, some of which were documentably raunchy.

The recording took place late at night. It was supposed to have been a demo to help the band land a gig on a cruise ship; the session cost the band $36. Why were the lyrics unintelligible? The two most likely culprits are Robert Lindahl, the engineer for the session at Northwestern Inc., a recording studio in Portland, and the lead singer Jack Ely. The record sounds like it was recorded live at a fraternity party, rather than in a studio. The quality is so bad, especially when compared with the version recorded by Paul Revere and the Raiders at the same studio not long after, that some have speculated that the band thought that they were simply playing through the song to warm up rather than recording the final take. Some responsibility has to fall on Lindahl. However, most of the blame must fall on Ely—various accounts have him hung over or simply drunk, wearing braces, or hoarse from singing; the actual reason remains a mystery.

Whatever the reason, a rumor spread from Portland throughout the country that the song contained obscene lyrics; this seems to be the main reason for the popularity of the Kingsmen's version of the song. (Recall that this song foreshadows the era when fans believed that there were subliminal messages hidden in song lyrics that only became audible when the record was played backward. Both the Beatles and Led Zeppelin were accused of this practice.)

In 1963, the Kingsmen were a more-or-less basic garage band. The members of the band at the time of the recording were Ely, who played guitar as well as sang, drummer Lynn Easton, keyboardist Don Gallucci, guitarist Mike Mitchell, and bassist Bob Nordby. This is the standard rock band lineup—two guitars, electric bass, and drums—augmented by Gallucci's keyboard.

The most easily remembered parts of the song are Ely's vocal and the high-register riff, played on keyboard and guitar. However, the more interesting aspects of the song, at least from an evolutionary perspective, are the bass and drum parts. The bass part stands out because the other instruments are in a high register; the drums stand out because of the informal recording technique. Both Nordby and Easton, the bassist and drummer, break away from the rather mechanical roles typically assigned to them in rock-and-roll and rhythm-and-blues songs through the early sixties: compare the bass and drum parts here with their counterparts on "Will You Love Me Tomorrow?" Similarly, the guitar solo ("Let's give it to 'em right now!"), built exclusively on the pentatonic scale heard so often in Delta blues recordings, helped usher in a more blues-oriented solo guitar style. The greater freedom of the rhythm section and a blues-influenced guitar solo style were among the features that distinguish rock from the music that came before it. Their use by the Kingsmen shows that they were becoming common practice.

Rock critic Dave Marsh claimed that "Louie Louie" was the "world's most famous rock and roll song" and argued his case in a book that examined both the history and (as he put it) the mythology of the song. Most famous or not, "Louie Louie" was one of the first real rock songs, in style and attitude. It brought back the edge of early rock and roll even as it updated its conception. In the process, it assured the Kingsmen a small slice of immortality. Ironically, Ely, whose garbled vocals were the main reason for the success of the song, left the group shortly after they recorded the song.

5–6d Surf Music: A Regional Rock Style

When I arrived at college in Massachusetts in the fall of 1963, two dorm mates from the east coast asked me these three questions: What's your name? (Mike) Where are you from? (California) Do you surf? (No—I'm from northern California.)

For teens who had grown up with snowy winters and dreary, late-arriving springs, the beaches of southern California seemed like a hedonist's dream: sun, surf, cars, babes—the endless summer. Although *Beach Party*, the first in a series of films celebrating the surfing lifestyle, had been released just a month earlier, most teens, including my dorm mates, learned about the southern California lifestyle from the lyrics of songs by the Surfaris, the Ventures, Jan and Dean, and—above all—the Beach Boys. These bands created the soundtrack for the "fun in the sun" lifestyle.

Surf music was responsible for two important firsts in rock history. It was the first post-1959 rock style to add significantly to rock's sound world. Perhaps the most distinctive new sound was the high-register close harmony vocals of the Beach Boys and, to a lesser extent, Jan and Dean. More influential, however, were the array of new guitar sounds—intense reverb, single line solos in a low register (most famously in the Ventures' "**Walk, Don't Run**"), and above-the-rapid, down-the-escalator tremolos and other virtuosic effects popularized by Dick Dale (the "king of the surf guitarists" and one of rock's first cult figures) and those who imitated him. Indeed, Dale is arguably rock's first virtuoso guitarist—Hendrix, who like Dale was left-handed, copied Dale's guitar setup.

Surf music A regional rock from California notable for high-register close harmony vocals and innovative guitar effects.

In large part because of these distinctive sounds—high vocals, "surf guitar"—surf music acquired an indelible regional identity. A single vocal harmony or descending tremolo was all that was needed to put a listener on a Malibu beach watching the waves or cruising along the strip in a little deuce coupe or a station wagon with real wood paneling.

This was the first time in the short history of rock where the music evoked a strong sense of place. Rock and roll developed first in the center of the country, from Chicago through Memphis to New Orleans. There was a New Orleans sound, but the songs of Little Richard don't call to mind gumbo or wrought-iron railings the way early jazz does. The music coming from Sam Phillips's studio had a distinct sound identity, but our images are of the performers, not the place; the same is true with Chuck Berry. By contrast, the name says it all: surf music is a sound about a place and a lifestyle. It would not be the last. A few years later, a street corner in San Francisco would become the geographic center of another rock-driven lifestyle; others would follow.

More generally, the new sounds coming out of California were the first clear signal of the geographic diffusion of rock. The British invasion would be a far more potent sign, because it made an American music international. It is in this early sixties development that we see the first stages in what would become the global reach of contemporary rock-era music.

5–6e The Beach Boys

The most important and innovative of the surf music bands was the Beach Boys. Their band was a family affair. The original group consisted of three brothers, Carl (1946–1988), Dennis (1944–1983), and Brian Wilson (b. 1942); their cousin, Mike Love (b. 1941); and a friend, Al Jardine (b. 1942).

The Beach Boys' first recordings point out their debt to rock's first generation. They feature Chuck Berry riffs—even entire songs—borrowed almost note-for-note. (However, they combined Berry's riffs with a completely new vocal sound.) In their recordings released between 1963 and 1965, they glorified the surfer lifestyle in songs that subtly varied their innovative, immediately recognizable sound.

"I Get Around," a song that reached the top of the charts in June 1964, shows key elements of their style and the variety possible within it. The song begins with just voices, presenting the essence of the Beach Boys' vocal sound. In order, we hear **unison** singing, tight harmonies, and a soaring single line melody juxtaposed with harmonized riffs: all sung with no **vibrato**.

The refrain follows, its split melody supported by a driving rock rhythm played by the entire band. Unlike this rhythm, the distinctive vocal sound of the Beach Boys came from outside rock: its source was the Four Freshmen, a slick, skilled, jazz-flavored vocal group who navigated complex harmonies as nimbly as Count Basie's saxophone section. Wilson, who admired the group and acknowledged them as a source of inspiration, used their sound as a point of departure. The song is harmonically richer than any other song that we have heard to this point; Wilson charts a distinctly new path in the fresh new chord progressions underneath the vocal.

The scene-painting verse sections are set off from the chorus by the substitution of an open-sounding, loping rhythm for the straightforward rock rhythm of the refrain. Even the instrumental solos have a characteristic, clearly defined sound. The short interlude in the verse combines a doubled organ and bass line with double-time drums, while the guitar solo is supported with sustained vocal harmonies.

unison Two performers playing the same pitch.

vibrato Subtle alteration of the pitch of a note.

The "fun in the sun" lyrics of the song suggest a mindless hedonism—enormously appealing not only to southern Californians but to teens everywhere. They belie the considerable sophistication of the music: not only the harmonies and key changes that range well beyond the three-chord rock progressions of so many bands, but also the beautifully interwoven vocal parts, sharp contrasts in texture that outline the form of the song, varied timekeeping, and other subtle features. This sophistication was mainly the work of Brian Wilson, who wrote the song, sang and played in the band, and produced the recording. In their peak years, the sound of the Beach Boys was Brian Wilson's conception.

5-7 Coming Together: From Rock and Roll to Rock and Soul

Brian Wilson might be the poster boy for the rock of the early sixties. He was nineteen when he and his brothers recorded their first Beach Boys song. The songs that they recorded exemplify rock in late adolescence. The teen-themed lyrics sound innocent when compared to those of Dylan, the Beatles, the Who, the Rolling Stones, and so many other bands just a few years later. The music is clearly rock, not rock and roll, but it is not as muscular as the rock of the late sixties and early seventies. Like the basketball stars who jump from high school to the NBA, it took a little while for the bodies to fill out. Wilson's influences are obvious: "Surfin' USA" is naive in its aping of Berry's song. Yet there is also significant innovation: Wilson's use of the multitrack recorder as a dynamic new creative tool and the musical new directions in harmony, instrumentation, and production.

In differing ways, all of the music surveyed in this chapter suggests the late adolescence of rock-era music. The twist becomes a dance for adults as well as teens. The two girl-group (not woman-group) songs mix naiveté and immaturity (what does "Da Doo Ron Ron" mean?) with sophistication and innovation. Dylan's "Blowin' in the Wind" captures the high-mindedness and idealism of his peers. The songs of Orbison, the Kingsmen, and the Beach Boys show rock on the verge of maturity and significance.

In most cases, we hear the transformative impact of the new recording technology. Indeed, in Spector's recording, we hear the beginning of the divorce between live and recorded performance: it would have been difficult to emulate the sound of the Crystals' song in live performance with early sixties technology. Dylan's minimalist song is the striking exception to this trend.

5–7a Common Musical Features of Early Sixties Music

Despite the significant differences in style, there are some common musical features that stamp virtually all of this music as from the early sixties, not the fifties. Among the most prominent and pervasive are these:

1. *The use of electric bass and the liberation of the bass line.* The switch from acoustic to electric bass boosted the low register of the rock band. The use of an amplifier made it much easier to play loudly. This in turn freed the bass player from working hard simply to produce a walking bass line. Rock bass players could now take a more flexible approach to the bass line—active or laid back, on the beat or rhythmically independent. We get hints of this in the majority of the songs.

2. *A collective conception of rock rhythm.* Musically, the clearest indication that rock and roll had become rock could be heard in the rhythm section. Guitarists like

Chuck Berry had shown how rock rhythm should sound. When drummers and especially bass players (now playing electric bass exclusively) also think in terms of this faster rhythm, then rock and roll became rock—and rhythm and blues became a new kind of black pop. We hear this on the Shirelles' song and on the recordings by Chubby Checker, Orbison, the Kingsmen, and the Beach Boys.

3. *Diffusion of melodic interest.* Dylan's "Blowin' in the Wind" is the exception that proves the rule. That song is a simple melody with a simple, straightforward accompaniment. In so many other songs, and especially the last three, melodic interest is diffused throughout the band, rather than concentrated in the vocal lines. "Pretty Woman" and "Louie Louie" begin with distinctive and memorable instrumental riffs; the one used in "Louie Louie" continues with virtually no change. In "I Get Around," Wilson distributes melodic material to both vocal lines and the instruments. The piano tremolo in "Da Doo Ron Ron" is an even more basic expression of this principle.

These were the most pervasive musical innovations of the early sixties. A new generation of rock and R&B acts would build on them during the mid-sixties. We meet them in the next several chapters.

PART II

The Rock Era, 1965–1975: The Rock Revolution

Part Introduction

To this day the rock revolution still seems like the most momentous change in the history of popular music. Nothing since has transformed popular music to such a degree, and only the modern-era revolution of the twenties has had a comparable impact. There are several reasons for this perception:

- It happened quickly. The revolution was effectively over in just a few years.
- Much of the music came from "outside." In fact, the music that made the biggest splash came from abroad. The British invasion marked the first time that music from beyond the United States became the commercially important music of a generation.
- The memory of the music is still vivid. The generation that grew up with it is still around, still working, still writing books about popular music. Oldies stations continue to feature this music, much of which now sounds comfortable rather than challenging. The music continues to sell well, several of the top acts of the era continue to tour, and the songs are used in films and commercials.
- The music grew up very quickly, and we have it all down on record. By 1965 a new Beatles album was an event; a year later, their album releases were an even bigger deal because the group had stopped touring. Their transformation over an eight-year period from the "Fab Four" to the creators of some of the most inspired and intriguing music of the century mirrored the maturation of rock from music for teenyboppers into a substantial musical language.
- Seemingly everyone knew this new music. In the sixties, a sizable majority of the audience knew—and liked—the top songs.

- The music was the soundtrack for a decade of extraordinary social change. Civil rights, the Vietnam War, free love, the gradual empowerment of women, the environmental movement, a huge generation gap—all of this was a brutal challenge to the established social order. And it seemed even more revolutionary compared with the fifties, when the bland façade portrayed in the media promoted the American dream even as it covered up the abuses of McCarthyism, bigotry, big business, and the like.

A Revolutionary Music

Finally, though, it comes down to the music itself. Rock and roll and rhythm and blues promised a new musical direction; rock, Motown, and soul fulfilled that promise, and changed musical life in the process.

The rock revolution was comprehensive, not cosmetic. It affected every aspect of the music: its influences, its creative process, its authorship, its sound, its musical message, and its end product. The music took advantage of brand-new and still-evolving technology in both performance and production. It reflected significant social shifts in both words and music. And despite the range of styles, it represented a coming together musically, the most important since the twenties. Among the most significant new developments were these:

A Fully Integrated Music

Rock is an integrated music. It isn't just that the music of the sixties was more profoundly influenced by black music than any earlier mainstream style. It's also that the influence went both ways—we hear black influences in music by white bands and white influences in music by black performers. And, most important, these various influences are assimilated into a new sensibility and a new sound. Integration is about not only being together but also blending together.

Song Ownership and the Creative Process

From the outset rock changed the relationship between composer and performer. Most of the early rock stars, such as Chuck Berry, Buddy Holly, and Little Richard, performed original material—Elvis was an interesting exception to this trend. In their music the song existed as it was recorded and performed, not as it was written, if indeed it was written down at all. A song was no longer just the melody and the harmony but the total sound as presented on the record: not only the main vocal line but also guitar riffs, bass lines, drum rhythms, and backup vocals.

Increasingly, rock musicians took advantage of multitrack recording, an emerging new technology, to shape the final result even more precisely. Multitrack recording made it possible to record a project in stages instead of all at once. Strands of the musical fabric could be added one at a time and kept or discarded at the discretion of the artist or the producer.

This ability to assemble a recording project in layers fostered a fundamental change in the creative process. It was possible to experiment at every stage of a project, and it was normal for one person or group to stay in creative control of the project from beginning to end.

Rock Attitudes and the Musical Message

Rock expressed a wholesale shift in attitude that was at the core of the revolution. Three qualities of this new attitude stand out: sixties rock was egalitarian, it was eclectic, and it was real. Until 1960 most groups had a leader, who fronted the band, or a featured performer. In the thirties it was Benny Goodman with his orchestra. After the war it was Muddy Waters, or Louis Jordan and His Tympany Five.

Even Buddy Holly fronted the Crickets. Vocal groups, like the Mills Brothers and the girl groups, were the almost singular exception.

By contrast, most sixties rock bands took group names: the Beatles, the Beach Boys, the Who, Jefferson Airplane. In so doing they projected a collective identity. There was nothing in their name that said one member was more important than the others. The interplay among voices and instruments was another key: in hooking the listener with a catchy riff or in laying down the beat, no one person was consistently in the spotlight.

The sources of the new rock style, and the way in which they made their way into rock and soul, also evidenced this new attitude. Rock took a pragmatic approach to musical borrowing: musicians took what they needed, no matter what its source, and transformed it into something new.

Contrast that with music before 1960. Pop artists gave country songs a shower and a shave before putting them on record, as a pop cover of any Hank Williams song will attest. If the recordings are any indication, neither the singers nor the arrangers made much of an effort to understand either the sound or the sensibility of country music. Similarly, rhythm and blues usually got a bleach job: the Chords' cover of "Sh-Boom" is one example among too many. Even many of the teen idols, from Pat Boone to Fabian to Frankie Avalon, dressed the part, but neglected the sound and the style of rock and roll.

In the sixties, sounds came from everywhere: Delta blues, East Indian music, symphonic strings, the classical avant-garde, jazz, music hall, folk, country—if it was out there, it was available for adoption. More important, rock musicians didn't necessarily privilege any particular style or family of styles. There is no sense of connection between the social standing of a style and its use in rock, unless it's an inverted one: the grittier the source, the more it was admired, as in the case of Delta blues. The Beatles' music epitomizes this egalitarian, eclectic approach: one track can be sublime, the next can sound like a children's song.

There was a hierarchy of importance within rock, especially in the wake of the Beach Boys' *Pet Sounds* and the Beatles' *Sgt. Pepper's Lonely Hearts Club Band*. The possibility of making an artistic statement in rock has been part of its collective understanding since the mid-sixties. But artistic statements were typically crafted out of seemingly ordinary materials. Even when rock emulated classical music and other established traditions, it did so on its own terms: the Who's *Tommy* was a rock opera but a far cry from conventional opera. For the best rock bands, the sound world of the sixties was like a well-stocked kitchen; bands simply took what they needed to create the feast.

Finally, rock was real in a way that earlier generations of pop had not been. Rock formed a bond with its audience that was different from the connection between Tin Pan Alley popular song and its audience. Tin Pan Alley songs typically offered listeners an escape from reality, whereas rock songs often intensified the reality of life in the present. Moreover, the message of the song was often more personal because rock-era songwriters usually performed their own songs. Songs were not written so much for something—such as a musical or a film—as to say something.

Rock's concern with the present, combined with its direct and often personal communication between song, singer, and audience, elevated the role of the music for many members of that audience from simple entertainment to, in the words of noted rock critic Geoffrey Stokes, "a way of life."

The rock revolution was comprehensive. Rock became the commercially dominant music: ruling the charts, flooding the airwaves, and attracting huge crowds: over 400,000 people attended Woodstock in August, 1969. Rock was culturally ascendant. It upended the prevailing ideas of artistic worth, and it compelled established styles to absorb rock elements or go out of fashion. Pop rock, country rock, jazz/rock fusion, rock musicals, even minimalism, an important new direction in classical music: all were new sounds shaped by their interaction with rock.

By the early seventies, the revolution was over. Rock was the newly established style—or, more accurately, family of styles. It was now at the center of the music business, which had taken over and expanded considerably in every domain: recordings, media, and live performance. The music lost some of its daring, but gained in craft. We sample the substantial legacy of this decade in rock history in the next several chapters. (See MINDTAP)

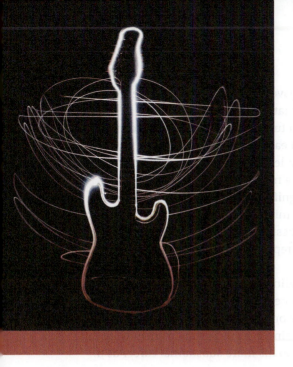

CHAPTER 6

BOB DYLAN AND THE BEATLES

Learning Objectives:

1) Summarize the key elements found in the music of Bob Dylan.

2) Identify characteristics of other genres that directly contribute to the musical works of both Bob Dylan and the Beatles.

3) Discuss the unique characteristics that define each of the four phases of the Beatles' music.

4) Define the term: **concept album**.

5) Describe how the Beatles influenced the recording industry.

6) Explain how **overdubbing** can be utilized in a recording.

Chapter Introduction

Making Rock Matter

On August 28, 1964, Bob Dylan and the Beatles met face-to-face for the first time. The Beatles were on tour in the United States and staying at the Delmonico Hotel in New York. They had acquired *The Freewheelin' Bob Dylan* while in Paris in January 1964; according to George Harrison, they wore the record out, listening to it over and over. John Lennon, in particular, seemed drawn to Dylan's gritty sound and rebellious attitude. Somewhat later during that same year, Dylan was driving through Colorado when he heard the Beatles for the first time over the radio. Later he would say, "I knew they were pointing the direction where music had to go." Each had something that the other wanted and perhaps found intimidating: the Beatles, and especially Lennon, wanted Dylan's forthrightness; Dylan responded to the power of their kind of rock and envied the Beatles' commercial success. It was Lennon who requested the meeting, through Al Aronowitz, a columnist for the *New York Post*, who brought Dylan down from Woodstock.

Whatever initial uneasiness Dylan and the Beatles may have felt with each other soon went up in smoke. Upon learning that none of the Beatles had tried marijuana, Dylan promptly rolled a couple of joints and passed them around. As Paul McCartney later recalled, "Till then, we'd been hard Scotch and Coke men. It sort of changed that evening."

The Beatles' encounter with cannabis is credited with helping to change the course of their music. Ian MacDonald, author of *Revolution in the Head*, a track-by-track account of the Beatles' recordings, observed: "From now on, the superficial states of mind induced by drink and 'speed' gave way to the introspective and sensual moods associated with cannabis and later LSD."

Still, there was more to this meeting than turning the Beatles on. It seemed to further motivate both parties to learn from each other. For the Beatles, Dylan raised the bar—the standard to which the Beatles would hold their music. More specifically, his music occasionally served as a model for their songs, especially those in which Lennon provided the more significant creative input. Later, in explaining their musical breakthrough in the mid-sixties, McCartney said, "We were only trying to please Dylan." Without question, the music they created after the meeting, especially from *Rubber Soul* on, represents a far more substantial legacy than their earlier work.

As for Dylan, the experience gave him additional motivation to go electric. His next album, *Bringing It All Back Home*, which he recorded in January 1965, featured acoustic tracks on one side and electric tracks on the other. After that, he never looked back. In retrospect, his years as a folk singer, as important as they were to his career and to rock, were simply a prelude to his more substantial career as a rock musician.

There are obvious differences between Dylan and the Beatles: solo performer versus group; private versus public persona; seat-of-the-pants versus state-of-the-art record production; talking, barely melodic songs versus tuneful melodies.

However, they were alike in at least two crucial ways: they came to rock from the outside, and they stretched rock to its outer limits. Outside for Dylan meant starting his professional career as a folk singer. Outside for the Beatles meant, more than anything else, Liverpool, England. The idea of foreigners redefining American popular music—and thereby internationalizing it—was without significant precedent.

We focus on the most significant period in the careers of both acts—from the date of the meeting through the release of *Sgt. Pepper's Lonely Hearts Club Band*. We begin with Dylan.

6-1 Dylan Goes Electric

Unlike CDs, vinyl albums contain content on both sides of the disc. So it was convenient, and perhaps expedient, for Dylan to dedicate one side of an LP to where he was coming from and the other side to where he was going. In *Bringing It All Back Home*, his first album of 1965, Dylan moves forward by returning to his roots: his first musical experiences were with a rock-and-roll band. To Alan Lomax, Pete Seeger, and the folkies who thought he'd committed musical blasphemy, this was the beginning of the end. But looked at in relation to the rest of his career, it was the end of the beginning. From that point on, Dylan was a rock musician, not a folk singer.

6-1a From Folk to Rock

If Dylan needed any additional incentive to put his folk phase behind him, he received it from the Byrds' cover of "**Mr. Tambourine Man**," one of the acoustic songs on *Bringing It All Back Home*. Having obtained a pre-released version of the song in August, 1964, The Byrds converted Dylan's elusive and elliptical ramble into a tight pop song and released it as their first single in April, 1965, a month after Dylan released his version. The success of the single—it topped the charts in June—inspired Dylan to seek out a more commercially promising path.

Dylan's version of "Mr. Tambourine Man" features just his singing, harmonica and guitar accompaniment, plus another guitar playing an obbligato line. The song combines a catchy melody and memorable refrain ("Hey Mr. Tambourine Man, play a song for me") with impressionistic lyrics ("evening's empire," "magic swirlin' ship," "skippin' reels of rhyme," "twisted reach of crazy sorrow," "circled by the circus sands"), and the perfect sixties symbol: a pied piper leading a group of hip individuals to a new level of consciousness. "Mr. Tambourine Man" opened popular music up to a radically new kind of lyric. Country, folk, and blues lyrics were direct, as we have seen and heard. Pop-song lyrics could be sophisticated; rock-and-roll lyrics could talk nonsense ("Da Doo Ron Ron") or capture the essence of teenage angst ("Not Fade Away"). But none had been surreal.

However, surrealism did not spark success. For all his critical acclaim, Dylan was still on the outside looking in, at least on the singles charts. (The albums fared far better.) "**Subterranean Homesick Blues**," a track from the electric side, was the first of his recordings to chart as a single—it reached No. 39. For all its easy appeal, Dylan's version of "Mr. Tambourine Man" did not chart. As with "Blowin' in the Wind," it was another group that would bring his song to the top of the charts. This time it was the Byrds, whose version hit No. 1 in June 1965.

6-1b The Byrds

The Byrds came together in the summer of 1964 to form what would become the first folk-rock band. The original lineup included guitarists Jim (later Roger) McGuinn, Gene Clark, and David Crosby; bassist Chris Hillman; and drummer Mike Clarke. McGuinn, Clark, and Crosby had formed a folk trio in Los Angeles in late 1963, which went nowhere. Adding Hillman and Clarke changed their sound and put them on the cutting edge of the mix between folk and rock.

A comparison of the two versions of "Mr. Tambourine Man" is instructive. Dylan's version is acoustic. The Byrds' cover uses a full band, including McGuinn's electric 12-string guitar. Dylan's version lasts five minutes and thirty seconds; the Byrds' version lasts only two minutes and twenty-nine seconds. And even that difference is deceptive, because the Byrds' recording has a slower tempo and includes McGuinn's introductory riff, which also serves as an extended tag.

The Byrds' version is also much more like a rock song in form. Two statements of the refrain frame just one of the four verses. This truncated version cut out over half of the lyrics—precisely the element that had made the song so special for Dylan fans. But the expanded instrumentation, simpler form, and slower tempo gave the song much wider appeal. McGuinn's famous opening riff, played on a 12-string guitar, seemed to evoke the "jingle-jangle" of the refrain.

6-1c Dylan Rocks

Judging by his next record, the connection between accessibility and commercial success was not lost on Dylan. He officially entered the rock era with his next album, *Highway 61 Revisited*. Recorded in the summer of 1965, the album brought into full flower the rock-fueled power latent in the electric side of *Bringing It All Back Home*. The songs mix blues, country, rock, and even pop—in "**Ballad of a Thin Man**"—into a new Dylan sound. The title of the album suggests this roots remix. US Highway 61 begins in Minnesota and runs through the heart of the Mississippi Delta. The title track is a hard shuffle with strong echoes of deep blues.

"**Like a Rolling Stone**," the first track to be recorded, shows how he channeled his verbal virtuosity into an accessible rock song. The words still have sting: the song paints an "I told you so" portrait of a young girl who's gone from top to bottom. But they tell a story that we can follow, even on the first hearing.

obbligato A second melody playing under the main melody.

trio One of the two main sections of a march, in a different key.

The song sounds like rock from the outset: it begins with a free-for-all of riffs that overlay Dylan's vigorous electrified strumming and a straightforward rock beat on the drums. This sound is maintained throughout the song, with Dylan's harmonica competing with Mike Bloomfield's guitar in the instrumental interludes.

The body of the song consists of four long sections. Within each section, verse and refrain alternate, as they do in many rock songs. However, Dylan immediately puts his own spin on this rock convention: each section has, in effect, two verses and two hooks. The first verse of each section consists of two rapid-fire word streams, saturated with internal rhymes—typical Dylan. But each word stream paints only one picture, and each phrase ends with a short, riff-like idea (such as "Didn't you, babe?"), followed by a long pause. The slower pacing of the images and the break between phrases help the listener stay abreast of Dylan's lyric.

The second verse serves as a long introduction for the first of two melodic hooks: Dylan's voice drips scorn as he sings "How does it feel?" followed by a memorable organ riff; this is repeated, the question left hanging in the air. Dylan then gives a series of equally scornful responses that fill out our picture of the girl's plight. These culminate in the title phrase. By expanding each section internally, Dylan also expands the dimensions of the song: it lasts over six minutes, twice the length of a typical song.

"Like a Rolling Stone" established Dylan's rock credentials and his originality as well as any one song could. No one else could have written a song like this: a cinematic portrayal of a privileged princess who's strung out and trying to survive on the streets. Despite its length, the song would become one of Dylan's most successful singles, briefly reaching No. 2 in the summer of 1965.

However, it was the album, taken as a whole, that would fully reveal what Dylan would bring to rock. The next five songs on the album are extraordinarily diverse:

- **"Tombstone Blues,"** an up-tempo song with a hard honky-tonk beat
- **"It Takes a Lot to Laugh, It Takes a Train to Cry,"** a Dylanesque transformation of the blues, set to a medium groove shuffle rhythm
- **"From a Buick 6,"** a blues-form song with piles of riffs and a honky-tonk beat
- **"Ballad of a Thin Man,"** a ballad with slithery pop-ish harmony and a light shuffle beat
- **"Queen Jane Approximately,"** an early sixties-style rock ballad

There are no recurrent stylistic conventions, such as a basic beat, harmonic approach, or formal plan. Instead, Dylan used these and the other songs on the album to invest rock with a freewheelin', anything-goes attitude. In the album, Dylan thumbed his nose at the conventions of pop music and at the pop music business. Songs ranged in length from just over three minutes to well over eleven minutes; most were five minutes or more. The song titles could be descriptive and evocative—or not: the title of one song, "From a Buick 6," has no apparent connection to the song itself. These are outward signs that the songs themselves are unconventional—shockingly original, despite their deep roots in rock and roll, blues, folk, country, and Beat poetry.

The songs seem to have come about almost by spontaneous combustion; they would take shape in the recording studio with seemingly arbitrary decisions—such as Al Kooper playing organ for the first time on "Like a Rolling Stone"—crucially shaping the final result. The songs juxtapose the sublime and the ridiculous and package elusive ideas in images that brand themselves on your brain. Above all, they democratize popular music while elevating its message in a way that had never been done before: with Dylan, high art did not have to be high class.

The music was comparably original, particularly in the evocative use of musical style. He used beats, instruments, harmonies, forms, and the like to create an atmosphere. In the title track, "Highway 61 Revisited," for example, the rough-and-tumble ensemble sound recalls Delta blues, which contextualizes the title. Earlier generations of pop artists had used style evocatively, but no one before Dylan had let it penetrate so deeply into the fabric of the music. *Highway 61 Revisited* became one of the most influential rock albums of all time.

Blonde on Blonde, his next album, offers an even more spectacular example of his eclectic electric style. Dylan recorded it in Nashville during early 1966, at the suggestion of his producer, Bob Johnston. Several of his collaborators were veteran Nashville session men, most of whom knew nothing about Dylan's music. After an awkward adjustment period, they worked splendidly together, in large part because Dylan brought them into the creative process. He gave very little guidance before they started taping, preferring to let the songs take shape as they recorded.

It worked. *Blonde on Blonde* expands Dylan's range in every way: verbally, musically, and—most important—emotionally. The contrasts are even more pronounced. In **"Visions of Johanna,"** he follows doggerel-like quick rhymes—gall/all/small/wall/hall—with the thought-provoking "Infinity goes up on trial" and the searing "Mona Lisa had the highway blues, you can tell by the way she smiles."

Each song on the album has a distinct musical identity. Dylan's eclecticism embraces an even broader range of mood and style: a funky Salvation Army—type band (**"Rainy Day Women #12 & 35"**), the delicate rock ballad ("Visions of Johanna"), a gritty electric blues/R&B mix in "Obviously 5 Believers."

The constant element throughout all of this music is Dylan's voice, his most personal innovation. When he sings, it is not pretty, by conventional pop standards, and much of the time he talks/shouts/rants instead of singing. But his singing serves to remind rock that expressive power and personality counts for far more than prettiness. His blues and blues-influenced songs on *Highway 61 Revisited* and *Blonde on Blonde* show this better than any comparable group of songs. In them, Dylan sings with the spirit and feel of the blues. His sound is completely original yet perfectly appropriate: he sounds like himself, not a white guy trying to sound black.

After a serious motorcycle accident in the summer of 1966, an event that prompted him to retire briefly, he resumed recording in 1967 with *John Wesley Harding*. Since 1967, his work has taken many twists and turns and shaped important trends in rock-era music. For example, his late-sixties albums strongly influenced country rock. But none of his later work has had the pervasive impact of the first three electric albums, and the electric half of *Bringing It All Back Home*, if only because these albums were available as a standard of comparison.

It is in these albums that we can best gauge the fact and the nature of Dylan's importance. His lyrics raised the level of discourse in rock in a completely original way. Drawing on blues and folk, the topical songs of Woody Guthrie, and the Beat poets—after hearing Dylan, Beat poet Allen Ginsberg said, "The world is in good hands"—Dylan synthesized all of this into something radically new. The contrast between Dylan's lyrics and those in the previous chapters is so pronounced that it is hard to conceive of them as part of the same musical tradition.

Similarly, Dylan's musical settings opened up new sound worlds, and—more important—new possibilities for the integration of words and music. Precisely because the lyrics were often so provocative and challenging, Dylan used musical settings to evoke mood—to convey the general character of the song without overpowering the words.

In both words and music, it was not just that Dylan made rock a music that mattered almost overnight. His songs were significant in a way that popular song had never been: they were profound, not clever, and they were without compromise. They approached the standards typically reserved for music considered art—for example, classical art songs, bop, and post-bop jazz. Just as significant, Dylan made his music important completely on its own terms, rather than by emulating an established style.

Dylan challenged his audience to meet him at his level, rather than playing down to them as, for example, Phil Spector did. As a result, he never enjoyed the kind of broad commercial success of so many other top acts: "Like a Rolling Stone" and "Rainy Day Women #12 and 35" reached No. 2 on the singles charts; "**Lay Lady Lay**," released in 1969, was his only other song to reach the Top 10. However, his music profoundly influenced many of the important acts of the 1960s and beyond. Nowhere is Dylan's influence more evident than in the music of the Beatles.

6-2 The Beatles

The Beatles are rock's classic act, in the fullest sense of the term. Their music has spoken not only to its own time but to every generation since. Their songs are still in the air; they remain more widely known than any other music of the rock era. The Beatles' music is a cultural artifact of unsurpassed importance. No single source—of any kind—tells us more about the sixties than the music of the Beatles.

Not surprisingly, no rock-era act has received more attention—from fans, fellow musicians, and scholars. The brief span of their career together encourages this. Their recordings represent a largely finite legacy, like Beethoven's symphonies and sonatas. And like Beethoven's compositions, their recordings document a musical evolution that continued until death—in the Beatles' case, the death of the group.

We can trace the beginning of the Beatles back to the summer of 1957, when John Lennon (1940–1980) met Paul McCartney (b. 1942) and soon asked him to join his band, the Quarrymen. George Harrison (1943–2001) joined them at the end of year; the group was then known as Johnny and the Moondogs. They went through one more name change, the Silver Beetles, and one more drummer, Pete Best, before settling on the Beatles and Ringo Starr (born Richard Starkey, 1940), who joined the group after they had signed a recording contract.

The major phase of the Beatles' career lasted just under eight years. For all intents and purposes, it began on June 6, 1962, when they auditioned for George Martin, the man who would produce most of their records. It ended on April 10, 1970, when Paul McCartney announced that the Beatles had disbanded. After their breakup, all continued their careers as solo performers. But we remember the Beatles mainly through their recordings, and those were made between 1962 and 1970.

6-3 The Music of the Beatles

Our discussion of the Beatles begins and ends with two musical questions: what made their music unique; and how did their music change over the course of their career? Other inquiries about their music—for example, who were their major influences, and what was the nature and extent of their influence—come out of these questions.

It is difficult to gauge the impact and importance of the Beatles' music in a small sampling of songs. There are two reasons for this difficulty: the rapid evolution of their music, and its unparalleled emotional and musical range. If we didn't know their history so well, it would be hard to believe that the band that recorded **"Love Me Do"** in 1962 and **"I Want to Hold Your Hand"** in 1963 had become the retro band of "Back in the USSR," the groove merchants of "Get Back," or the soul-, gospel-, and folk-influenced creators of "Don't Let Me Down," "Let It Be," and "Here Comes the Sun"—all recorded between 1969 and 1970. No group changed so much in so short a time. More than any artists of the rock era, the Beatles elude one-dimensional description, even though their career lasted less than eight years.

The five late recordings also hint at the Beatles' range. What other group could shift moods and styles so drastically—from the parody of **"Back in the USSR"** and the pathos of **"Don't Let Me Down"** to the (yes) sunniness of **"Here Comes the Sun,"** the spaciness of **"Get Back,"** and the soulfulness and universality of **"Let It Be"**—and still sound like themselves? And this is just a sample.

As a point of departure, we can make the following observations about their music:

1. The Beatles had their own sound, right from the start.
2. Their uniqueness grew out of their collaborative approach to music making; they were a *group*, in the fullest sense of the word.
3. Their music is both simple and sophisticated. Their songs always provide easy points of entry that hook us, yet they also contain subtle details that set them apart from the mundane. This blend of simplicity and sophistication is one key to their commercial and artistic success.
4. They had the uncanny ability to absorb outside influences—sometimes almost overnight—and integrate them seamlessly into their music.
5. The Beatles' music went through four phases, each lasting about two years:
   - Beatlemania: from 1962 to the end of 1964
   - Dylan-inspired seriousness: 1965–1966
   - Psychedelia: late 1966–1967
   - Return to roots: 1968–1970

Not surprisingly, transitions from one phase to the next were gradual. Still, the differences between representative examples are easily heard. Our discussion of the Beatles' music describes each of these phases. We mention several songs in passing and discuss two songs in greater detail: **"Eleanor Rigby"** and **"A Day in the Life."** These two songs highlight how the Beatles' innovations expanded the range of rock music and invested it with the kind of significance associated with high art. Both qualities were among the most important musical contributions of the Beatles to rock and popular music.

The Beatles and Drugs

Drugs were an inescapable fact of musical life in the sixties. Again, the Beatles were not the first. Dylan turned the Beatles on to marijuana, and a friend sent Lennon on his first acid trip by spiking a drink, well after Dylan and others had been tripping regularly. However, the Beatles were among the most prominent drug users of the sixties.

(Continued)

While we can never know all the details of the Beatles' drug use, it's clear that drugs actively shaped their music. Indeed, it's not too much to say that the Beatles' shifts in style are a direct consequence of the drug they were taking: alcohol and speed until 1964; marijuana until 1966, acid during the *Sgt. Pepper* and *Magical Mystery Tour* years, and a cutting down or, in Lennon's case, a switch from acid to heroin in the last few years.

Moreover, the Beatles essentially advertised drug use, at least indirectly. For example, one of the most persistent rumors of the sixties was that **"Lucy in the Sky with Diamonds"** was a coded reference to LSD. Lennon's adamant denial only helped strengthen everyone's conviction that it was so. In any case, the group's use of drugs made them "cool"—if far from legal or beneficial.

6–3a Beatlemania

The first phase of the Beatles' Martin-produced recording career spanned a little more than two years. It began in September 1962, when they recorded their first song, "Love Me Do," and ended early in 1965, with songs like **"Ticket to Ride"** clearly indicating that their music was exploring new territory.

During this first phase, the Beatles could be characterized as a rock band with a difference. Their instrumentation was conventional. Like so many bands of the early sixties, they were a Holly-esque quartet: two guitars, bass, and drums, with most of the band singing as well as playing. However, their singing was rougher than that of most other bands, especially the pop pap that was standard fare on British radio.

The Beatles' Voices

The Beatles' singing gives us one clue to their popularity. In rock and roll's first decade (1955–1965), there were three overwhelmingly popular singles sources: Elvis, the Beatles, and the various Motown groups. All sang tuneful songs with voices that were not as sweet as those of pop singers, but not so rough that mainstream youth would find them unpleasant.

The difference also shows up in the songs. It seems that even their first hits had at least one feature that was special to that song and specific to the Beatles. It might be an element that carried through the entire song, or a little detail—or both. In "Love Me Do," for example, the opening phrase of the vocal melody is harmonized mainly with raw-sounding open fifths. **"Please, Please Me,"** their first song with a rock beat, features McCartney's active bass line, a novelty for the time.

6–3b Dylan-Inspired Seriousness (and Humor)

Rubber Soul (released in December 1965), *Yesterday . . . and Today* (released June 1966), and *Revolver* (released in August 1966) are the three American albums from this second phase of their career. Dylan's influence is evident in the lyrics, which were more meaningful, less teen-oriented, and more wide-ranging in subject matter and tone. It is also evident in the music; although, it takes a quite different form. Like Dylan, the Beatles were expanding their sound world but in a more adventurous and more encompassing way. Dylan drew mainly on existing popular styles and used them evocatively. By contrast, the Beatles reached farther afield, into musical traditions far removed from rock and its roots, such as classical Indian music (for instance, the sitar and finger cymbals heard in "**Norwegian Wood**") and string playing reminiscent of classical music. Moreover, they synthesized these extraneous sounds seamlessly into their music; they became part of the fabric of sound behind the vocals.

As their music matured, it became bolder and more individual. The songs are more clearly the work of the (new) Beatles—no one else could have made them— and less like each other. The contrast from song to song had clearly deepened. One can almost reach into a bag filled with song titles, pull out any five, and marvel at the distinctive identity in meaning and sound of each song and the pronounced differences from song to song. A representative sample: the soul-influenced and sharply tongued "**Drive My Car**"; the alternately positive and philosophical "**We Can Work It Out**," colored nicely with harmonium and a brief shift into a heavy-footed waltz; "Norwegian Wood," the one-night stand that wasn't, in which Harrison's East Indian sitar saturates the track like the smell of incense in the bird's apartment; "**Yesterday**," which simultaneously evokes and updates the popular songs of "yesterday" (that is, pre-rock popular song), and the somber "Eleanor Rigby." We discuss "Eleanor Rigby" in more detail next.

"Eleanor Rigby"

A song about the unlamented death of a relationship is unusual enough in popular music. A song about an unlamented death was unprecedented. "Eleanor Rigby," recorded in June 1966, for the album *Revolver*, broke sharply with pop-song conventions in both words and music. McCartney relates the story of Eleanor Rigby with a detachment rare in popular music. There is no "you" or "I," even of the generic kind. The story is told strictly in the third person. Her tale is as gloomy as a cold, damp, gray day. Even the refrain is as impersonal as a Greek chorus. They simply ask: "Ah, look at all the lonely people." There's no particular empathy for either Eleanor Rigby or Father McKenzie.

The musical setting is as bleak as the words. A string octet (four violins, two violas, and two cellos), scored by George Martin from McCartney's instructions, replaces the rock band; there are no other instruments. The string sound is spare, not lush—the chords used throughout emulate a rock accompaniment, not the dense cushions of sound heard in traditional pop. Like Eleanor Rigby herself, the melody of both chorus and verse don't go anywhere. Set over alternating chords, the chorus is just a sigh. The melody of the verse contains longer phrases, but they too mostly progress from higher to lower notes. The harmony shifts between chords; there is no strong sense of movement toward a goal. Lyric, melody, harmony, and the repetitive rhythm of the accompaniment convey the same message: time passes, without apparent purpose.

With "Eleanor Rigby," the Beatles announced that their music—and, by extension, rock—was, or could aspire to be, art. The most obvious clue was the classical-style string accompaniment. However, the subject of the song and the detachment with which it is presented have more in common with classical art songs than pop or rock songs. Having recorded rock's answer to the art song, the Beatles soon created rock's answer to the art song cycle: the **concept album**.

concept album A rock-era album which represented a unified artistic vision rather than a compilation of a group or individual's songs.

> ### "Good Vibrations"
>
> Although *Sgt. Pepper* seems a logical next step in the Beatles' musical evolution, it can also be understood as a response to the Beach Boys' album *Pet Sounds*. The album, and especially the song "Good Vibrations," represented a major step forward in the use of multitrack recording technology. Wilson recorded "Good Vibrations" in four studios over a period of six months. The song, his wonderfully imaginative setting of it, the novel instrumentation, and—above all—the superb production (a remarkable achievement in the days before 24-track boards) made "Good Vibrations" unique, and a challenge to the Beatles and all who aspired to a higher standard of production.

6-3c Psychedelia

The cover to *Sgt. Pepper's Lonely Hearts Club Band* tells the story. In a "group portrait," the Beatles appear twice—"live" and dressed in band uniforms and in wax museum–style likenesses. Icons of high and popular culture, mainly from earlier generations, surround them: Karl Marx, Laurel and Hardy, and Marilyn Monroe are but a few; Dylan is their only contemporary. That they represent themselves as wax figures or in costume suggests that the Beatles no longer see themselves publicly as they had been in *A Hard Day's Night*. Instead, they are playing a role.

> Although the costumes and wax effigies connect most directly to the conceit of the album, the decision by the Beatles to mask their identity might also symbolize their retirement from live performance. On August 25, 1966, shortly after the release of *Revolver*, the Beatles gave their last performance as a touring band.

Further, by placing themselves among several generations of cultural icons, they seem to imply that their music is culturally significant—that it connects to the past even as it promises a new postmodern future, and that the division between high and low art is not divinely ordained. Indeed, the message seems to be that gaps—both generational and cultural—implode, leaving artistic significance in the eye and ear of the beholder.

LSD helped fuel this relativistic vision of reality. Indeed, this vision is part of the underlying concept of the album. Throughout the album, there are contrasts between the everyday world and the heightened sensibility experienced while tripping on acid.

This contrast is most sharply drawn in "Lucy in the Sky with Diamonds." In this song, Lennon and McCartney put a truly original spin on verse/chorus form. The verse evokes a dreamy state. The lyric contains numerous psychedelic images ("marmalade skies"), and the music floats along in waltz time. It gives the impression of a person in the middle of an acid trip. By contrast, the chorus is straight-ahead rock and roll, which conveys a sense of normalcy. The repetition of the title phrase suggests a second persona in the song: a detached outsider who is watching the "verse" person while he's tripping.

However, the song that best sums up the *Sgt. Pepper* worldview is "A Day in the Life." Here, the contrast between the mundane everyday world and the elevated consciousness of acid tripping is made even more dramatic. It is projected by the most fundamental opposition in music itself, other than sound and silence: music with words versus music without words. The texted parts of the song are everyday life, while the strictly instrumental sections depict tripping—they follow "I'd love to turn you on" or a reference to a dream.

This contrast is made even more striking by the nature of the words and music. The text of the song, and the music that supports it, paints four scenes. The first scene is Lennon's response to a newspaper account of a man who dies in a horrible automobile accident while (Lennon suspects) he was tripping. The second pictures Lennon attending a film—perhaps an allusion to the film *How We Won the War*, in which he'd acted a few months prior to recording the song. The third depicts Lennon in the rat race of the workaday world. The last one is a commentary on another even more mundane news article. In Lennon's view, it is news reporting—and, by extension, daily life—at its most trivial: who would bother counting potholes?

The music that underscores this text is, in its most obvious features, as everyday as the text. It begins with just a man and his guitar. The other instruments layer in, but none of them makes a spectacular contribution. This everyday background is opposed to the massive orchestral blob of sound that depicts, in its gradual ascent, the elevation of consciousness. The dense sound, masterfully scored by George Martin, belongs to the world of avant-garde classical music— it recalls the Polish composer Krzysztof Penderecki's *Threnody to the Victims of Hiroshima* (1960) and other works of that type, works familiar to classical music insiders but not well-known generally. This creates another strong opposition: well-known versus obscure, and by implication, the unenlightened masses (that is, those not turned on) versus those few who are enlightened.

The apparent simplicity of the vocal sections obscures numerous subtle touches. Starr's tasteful drumming and McCartney's inventive bass lines are noteworthy. So is the doubling of the tempo in the "Woke up" section. What had previously been the rock beat layer is now the beat. This expresses in music the narrator's frantic preparation for work without disturbing the underlying rhythmic fabric of the song. Perhaps the nicest touches, however, are found in the vocal line: the trill heard first on "laugh" and "photograph," then expanded on "nobody was really sure" before floating up to its peak on "lords." It is precisely this melodic gesture—the trill, now set to "turn you on"—that presages the move from the vocal section to the orchestral section and by extension the beginning of an acid trip. When the trill/leap material returns in the film-viewing vignette, this connection becomes explicit: the melodic leap is followed by the trill, which blends seamlessly into the orchestral texture. As a melodic gesture, the trill/leap sequence is also a beautiful surprise, strictly on its own terms—a sequel of sorts to the leap to "hand" in "I Want to Hold Your Hand."

The final chord is an instrumental "om," suggesting the clarity of enlightenment after the transition, via the orchestral section, from mundane life in the "normal" world. It is a striking ending to a beautifully conceived and exquisitely crafted song, a song that is one of the most powerful metaphors for the acid experience ever created.

6-3d Return to Roots

The Beatles reached a pinnacle with *Sgt. Pepper's Lonely Hearts Club Band*. Their subsequent efforts, most significantly *Magical Mystery Tour*, were not as successful, either artistically or commercially. By 1968, they had begun to retreat from the grandiose. Instead of attempting to make yet another major artistic statement, they created music that responded to the music around them. From one perspective, the songs from this period are their unique reinterpretations of the styles that were "out there." Gone, for the most part, are the big orchestras, electronic collages, crowd noises. In their place, more often than not, is some straight-ahead, high-class rock and roll.

But there are two crucial differences. First, they brought to their task what seems like a lifetime of experience and exposure. Second, the music around them had also grown up. Rock—in all its manifestations, black and white—was now an established family of styles, in a way it hadn't been five years previously, so they had much more to draw on. Their maturity, and the maturation of rock, gave their music a depth and breadth that it could not have had at the beginning of the decade.

Yet, despite the more modest scale of their efforts (although *The Beatles* was a double album), the songs of their last period continued to expand the emotional range of their music. Influences come from everywhere. Here's a sampling:

- "Back in the USSR" is twice-fried rock and roll: it recalls both Chuck Berry and the Beach Boys (the pseudo–Beach Boys harmonies and allusions to "Moscow girls" ironically recall the sunny surf music that the Beach Boys popularized).
- **"Ob-La-Di, Ob-La-Da"** is the Beatles' take on West Indian music. The song is touched by calypso and ska, the Jamaican precursor of **reggae**, which was known in England all through the sixties.
- **"The Ballad of John and Yoko"** owes part of its sound to country rock— appropriately enough, since ballads (long storytelling songs) have deep country roots.
- "Something" is a pop ballad: "the greatest love song of the past fifty years," according to Frank Sinatra—who should know.
- "Let It Be" comes straight out of black gospel.

The fact of the Beatles' familiarity with—and comfort in—so many different kinds of music is remarkable enough. However, it is their ability to personalize any style they absorb into their music—to make it work for a particular song—that sets their music apart from everyone else's.

Ironically, one reason for the greater range of these songs was the growing divisions within the Beatles. Their increasingly fractious relationship meant that they did as little as possible together. Typically, they would come together to record the basic tracks, and the person who wrote the song would supervise its production. That they created so much high-quality music in the midst of this turmoil is remarkable.

6-4 The Beatles: Impact and Influence

In the documentable history of music, there has been one composer and one composing/performing group who have enjoyed widespread popularity and critical acclaim during their career, and whose music has never gone out of favor. The composer was Ludwig van Beethoven; the group was the Beatles. Beethoven and the Beatles have more in common than commercial and critical success. The music of Beethoven and the Beatles is remarkable for its range; both were able to create music of widely varying moods without forsaking their

> **reggae** The most widely known Jamaican popular music, it has a distinctive, intoxicating rhythm. It emerged around 1970 in the music of Jimmy Cliff, Bob Marley, and others.

musical identity, significantly more than was the case with their predecessors or contemporaries. Both are remarkable for their substantial evolution during the course of their careers. Both elevated the social status of the creator: Beethoven was the man most responsible for the perception of the composer as artist, with the commensurate upgrade in social standing; the Beatles invested rock with artistic stature. And both had a profound impact on the music of subsequent generations: Beethoven's influence was evident throughout the nineteenth century and well into the twentieth century; the Beatles' music continues to influence rock-era music, through its continuing popularity—every generation discovers it anew, demonstrating what is possible in rock by example.

The impact and influence of the Beatles reshaped every aspect of rock music: what it was and what it could be, how it was created, what it stood for, its place in the music business. The early Beatles recordings helped draw the boundary between rock and roll and rock. However, from 1965 on, Beatles songs really begin to sound different from one another, yet they all sound like Beatles songs. Furthermore, they stretched the boundaries of rock: rock became whatever the Beatles produced, simply because it was by the Beatles.

6–4a The Musical Breadth of the Beatles

How do we account for their extraordinary boundary-stretching growth as a group? Here are three important ways.

1. *Knowledge of styles.* They had firsthand familiarity with a broad range of styles. In their dues-paying years, the band performed not only rock-and-roll covers and original songs but also pop hits of all kinds. Unlike the vast majority of contemporary groups, they had a thorough knowledge of pop before rock, and they clearly absorbed styles along with songs.

2. *Melodic skill.* Along with the Motown songwriting teams, the Beatles were the first important rock-era musicians to write melody-oriented songs that were in step with the changes in rhythm, form, and other elements that took place during this time. No one since has written so many memorable melodies.

3. *Sound imagination.* Aided by the development of multitrack recording and the consummate craftsmanship of George Martin, their producer, the Beatles enriched their songs by startling, often unprecedented, combinations of instruments and—occasionally—extraneous elements, such as the crowd noises and trumpet flourishes of *Sgt. Pepper.*

6–4b Creating a Record

The Beatles were *the* major players in the transformation of the recording industry. They influenced several developments that made popular music recording in 1970 substantially different from what it had been in 1960. Among the most significant were:

1. *The record becomes the document.* This process was well underway by 1965. The Beatles confirmed this trend by divorcing recorded performance from live performance.

2. *The first studio band.* Beginning with *Rubber Soul*, Beatles' records explored a sound world built on cutting-edge recording technology—including more than an orchestra's worth of instruments, everyday sounds such as crowd noises, and special effects such as tapes run in reverse. The result was a stream of recordings that would be difficult, if not impossible, to replicate in live performance.

3. *Multitrack recording.* The Beatles were not the first band to make use of this technology; overdubbing had been around for over a decade. However, they achieved the most spectacular results with it, especially on albums such as *Sgt. Pepper's Lonely Hearts Club Band*, and they inspired legions of imitators. Just as important, they used this still-new technology to help redefine the creative process: musicians could create a song in stages, through trial and error, rather than conceiving of it completely before entering the studio or improvising it in the moment.

Because of their work, rock records—by the Beatles and others—sounded a lot different in 1970 than they did in 1962. They were better produced, and they offered a broader palette of sounds.

6–4c Popularity

Elvis put rock and roll on the cultural map with his unprecedented success on the singles charts. The commercial breakthrough, for the Beatles and for rock, was their *total* domination of the album charts, in addition to their success on the singles charts. Although Dylan introduced the idea that the album was the appropriate medium for significant rock, it was the Beatles who made it the more meaningful medium for all of rock. Before the Beatles, rock records were promoted mainly as singles; albums were compilations of singles. However, with the Beatles, from *Rubber Soul* on, the process was reversed: the singles now typically came from the album. Part of the message in this reversal of form was that this music was important (that is, adult) enough to be released in album format. Indeed, Beatles' albums became rock milestones.

Record sales were only one dimension of their popularity. When their career took off, Beatlemania gripped the Western world. At concerts, their fans would drown out the group with their screaming. Beatle sightings would inevitably produce a crush of fans. Their first film, *A Hard Day's Night*, shows the intensity of fan adulation. The film, acclaimed as innovative in its "day in the life" portrayal of the group and refreshing in its lack of pretense, only fanned the flames of their popularity. All this audience attention eventually backfired; the incessant pressure was a major factor in their decision to stop touring.

The mere fact of the Beatles' popularity gave weight to everything they did. Their work was both inspiration and model to a generation of rock musicians. It is likely that even without the Beatles, rock would have eventually become the dominant language of popular music. Because of the Beatles, however, it happened almost overnight. By the end of the decade, rock ruled—in the record stores, on the radio, and on stage.

6–5 Rock That Matters

Nineteen sixty-five was the year that rock matured, the year that it went well beyond a good-time music, as well as becoming an even better good-time music than before. The two acts most responsible for elevating its level of discourse and expanding its horizons were Bob Dylan and the Beatles. Dylan did it mainly with words. The musical backdrop might suggest a mood or call to mind an association, but it was always subordinate to the lyrics. The Beatles did it with both words and music; there is typically a beautiful and precise coordination between the lyrics and the significant musical features—for example, the shape of the melody (for example, the verse and chorus of "Eleanor Rigby" or the slow oscillation that serves as the bridge between everyday and heightened reality in "A Day in the Life"), the rhythms (the double-time third verse in "A Day in the Life"), the imaginative sound choices (such as the string group in "Eleanor Rigby"). This was music that could challenge listeners as well as entertain them, that could ask them to stretch their minds as well as shake their hips.

The music of Dylan and the Beatles in the mid-sixties was part of an explosion of innovation that created a new sound world and took over the popular music marketplace. There were other significant developments during that same period—among them the emergence of an important new black pop, soul music, the consolidation of rock style, the proliferation of numerous rock substyles. And there were other groups working along the same path, or at least in somewhat the same direction: for instance, Brian Wilson, the Who, and Frank Zappa and the Mothers of Invention. But no one did more to legitimize rock as a compelling form of expression than Dylan and the Beatles.

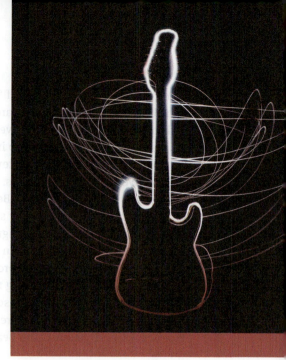

CHAPTER 7

BLACK MUSIC IN THE SIXTIES

Learning Objectives:

1) List the key contributions of black performers/performing groups of the 1960s.

2) Illustrate Berry Gordy Jr.'s **Motown** pyramid formula.

3) Define the **Motown sound**.

4) Compare the differences and similarities between black **soul** and white rock genres.

5) Describe the two different types of **southern soul**.

6) Discuss the rhythmic language found in 1960s Memphis **soul**.

Chapter Introduction

Motown and Soul

"Ain't No Mountain High Enough." For black music in the sixties, this was finally true. By 1960, the influence of black culture had been evident in popular music for more than a century. The sounds of black music had been in the air for more than a half century. Black performers had begun to achieve stardom in the twenties. Black styles had become increasingly prominent during the next several decades. But it was not until the sixties that the obstacles that had kept black music on the lower rungs of the pop music ladder seemed to disappear. By mid decade, the Supremes, the Temptations, and other Motown acts routinely kept pace with the British bands at the top of the charts. Aretha Franklin, James Brown, and the Stax soul stars also found a large, integrated audience. It was a glorious period in American music.

Black music reached this artistic and commercial peak just as the civil rights movement crested. The sixties began full of promise as much of the nation—from President John F. Kennedy on down—finally joined civil rights crusaders in the march toward racial equality. Many Americans were inspired by the words and deeds of Martin Luther King Jr., and other civil rights leaders. When racial equality became the law, racial harmony seemed possible.

However, the afterglow from these legislative successes was short lived. In 1968, everything went sour. The pivotal event was the assassination of Dr. King, which left many wondering whether "the dream died with the dreamer," as Stax producer Al Bell put it. Race riots in Detroit and Watts and the confrontation between liberals and radicals during the 1968 Democratic Convention replaced the idealism of the

Experience an interactive version of this era in **MINDTAP** civil rights movement with disillusionment. The nation quickly discovered that laws do not change attitudes overnight. Nevertheless, the civil rights movement and the legislation it prompted profoundly redefined race relations in the United States.

The new black music of the sixties reshaped the popular music landscape just as profoundly. Even as it carved its new identity, it penetrated deeply into the fabric of popular music. The sounds of soul would resonate through much of the music of the late sixties and seventies—black and white—and they have continued to shape popular music into the present.

Moreover, black popular music had just about shed the racial stigma that it had carried for generations. The first black popular styles—for example, coon songs and **ragtime**—had been considered by many to be low-class, wrong-side-of-the-tracks music, capable of corrupting the morals of whites who came in contact with it. With the emergence of jazz, and crossover black performers such as Lena Horne and Nat Cole, this attitude was neither as prevalent nor as hostile. Still, fifties rhythm and blues carried heavy racial baggage: recall that Alan Freed used "rock and roll" as code for "rhythm and blues." However, by the sixties, black music, and especially Motown, had lost any negative connotation, at least among the younger generation. In theory, at least, the playing field had become level.

In the seventies, the popular music audience would realign along racial lines to some degree. Nevertheless, popular music did not retreat to a pre-soul past, just as the nation could not return to the federally sanctioned injustices of segregation.

The great black music of the sixties came mainly from two cities, Detroit and Memphis. Detroit was the home of Berry Gordy's Motown empire. Memphis was "soul city" in the sixties, just as it had been the mecca for rockabillies in the fifties. As before, it was a single recording studio that was the magnet: in the sixties, Jim Stewart and Estelle Axton's Stax Records eclipsed Sam Phillips's Sun Records as the source of cutting-edge sounds from Memphis.

Two stars transcended these geographical boundaries. Aretha Franklin, a Detroit native whose career took off with the support of the Stax house band, linked the two, symbolically and musically. James Brown followed his own path, geographically (from Georgia to the world via Cincinnati's King Records) and musically.

All of this music was called "soul" at the time. In fact, however, there were two distinct, if related, style families: the black pop of Motown and the real soul music of Aretha, James Brown, and the Stax artists.

> **ragtime** A popular style at the turn of the twentieth century that mixed European forms, harmony, and textures with African-inspired syncopation. Ragtime began as a piano music, but soon the term was applied to any music—song and dance as well as piano music—that had some syncopation.

7-1 Motown

When Berry Gordy Jr. (b. 1929) got out of the army in 1953, he returned to Detroit, his home town, and opened a record store. He stocked it with jazz, a music he loved, but refused to carry rhythm-and-blues records, in spite of a steady stream of customers coming in to ask for them. Two years later, he was out of business. He would learn a crucial lesson from that experience: there was much more money to be made from pop.

After a couple of years working on an assembly line at the Ford plant, Gordy returned to the music business. In 1957, Gordy began writing songs for Jackie Wilson, at the beginning of Wilson's solo career; several of his songs were hits. Although encouraged by his songwriting success, Gordy realized that the only way he could gain complete artistic control of his music was to form his own record company.

Gordy started Motown in 1959 with little more than his dream and his drive. He knew that storytelling songs sold, and he soon learned how to sell them: Motown's first No. 1 R&B hit (the Miracles' "**Shop Around**") came in 1961; the label had a No. 1 pop hit the following year (the Marvelettes' "**Mr. Postman**"). By 1964, the roster of Motown performers included Mary Wells, Martha and the Vandellas, the Supremes, Stevie Wonder, Marvin Gaye, the Miracles, the Temptations, and the Four Tops. By mid decade, three out of every four Motown releases charted—unprecedented success for a record label.

Motown was a unique phenomenon in popular music. Gordy was the first black to create and manage a major record label, and the empire that he created was like no other. The Motown sound was a collective effort. It was hundreds of people— Gordy, his singers, songwriters, producers, musicians, plus all the business and clerical staff—all working together to produce a reliable product.

7-1a The Motown Formula

Gordy's Motown empire blended careful planning and tight control over every aspect of the operation, with inspiration and spur-of-the-moment decisions. As it developed during the early sixties, Motown's organizational structure was a pyramid. At the top of the pyramid was Gordy. Underneath him were those who wrote and produced the songs, like Smokey Robinson and the Holland/ Dozier/Holland team. Underneath them were the arrangers and house musicians. Berry recruited his core players from Detroit's jazz clubs. He relied on the skill and inventiveness of musicians such as bassist James Jamerson (the man most responsible for the freer bass lines of sixties rhythm and blues and rock), keyboardist Earl Van Dyke, drummer Benny Benjamin, and guitarists Robert White and Joe Messina. They brought to life the songs sent down to the garage–turned– recording studio by the arrangers. The fourth level were the acts themselves: Stevie Wonder, Smokey Robinson and the Miracles, the Supremes, the Four Tops, Martha Reeves and the Vandellas, Mary Wells, and the two we consider here: the Temptations and Marvin Gaye.

There is no question that the acts were the most visible part of Motown. Gordy, who ran what amounted to a finishing school for his groups, made sure they were well dressed, well rehearsed, and presentable in every way. And there is no question that they were essential to the artistic and commercial success of the label. However, in terms of defining the Motown sound—the qualities that often identified the style before a note was sung—they were among the most interchangeable parts. Indeed, one act would often cover another act's hit. The essence of the sound was in the songwriting, the production, the conception of the studio musicians, and—above all—in Gordy's overriding vision.

7-1b The Motown Sound

In many respects, the Motown sound was predictable; fans knew pretty much what to expect from a Motown record. Yet the individual songs were usually different enough, and imaginative enough, to avoid becoming predictable in every respect. Within the general design, there was room for variation, as we hear following in comparing two enduring Motown hits: the Temptations' "**My Girl**" (1964) and Marvin Gaye's version of "**I Heard It Through the Grapevine**" (1967).

The Temptations

The Temptations were the premier Motown male group act. In sound and image, they embodied the Motown esthetic: five elegantly dressed men moving smoothly in skillfully choreographed steps, and singing with the grit and soulfulness of street-corner singers but with perfectly polished harmonies. It was the Motown blend of soul and class.

The group was a vocal quintet that originally came together in 1960 from members of two aspiring vocal groups, the Primes and the Distants, to audition for Gordy. Their career took off when David Ruffin replaced original member Eldridge Bryant as the lead singer. Ruffin would stay for four years, from 1964 to 1968. This now-classic version of the quintet included—from high to low, Eddie Kendricks, David Ruffin, Otis Williams, Paul Williams, and Melvin Franklin, the deep bass voice of the group.

Their first No. 1 hit on both the pop and R&B charts was the 1964 song "My Girl." It is one of the best early examples of the assembly-line process of hit-making that served Motown so well in the sixties. The first stage in the process was the writing of the song itself. "My Girl" was one of several hits that Smokey Robinson (b. 1940), the lead singer in the Miracles and one of the top Motown songwriters, wrote for the Temptations. Robinson, a long-time associate of Gordy, recalled that Berry Gordy told him very early in their association that a song must tell a story. Motown songs do that—or at least paint pictures. The simple lyric of "My Girl" offers a succession of images that give us a character portrait of his "girl."

The song begins with a simple bass riff that is distinctive enough to be memorable: if you are familiar with the song, it's likely that you'll recognize it just from this riff. The guitar enters with another more elaborate—and even more memorable—riff; like the bass riff, it is repeated several times. Lead vocalist David Ruffin enters, singing the two short phrases of the verse. On the second phrase, the other Temptations discreetly support his vocal with gentle background harmonies. The chorus begins with a short, simple transition that builds to the title phrase, which is repeated several times. Horns reinforce the vocal harmonies, although they stay in the background. Lush string parts soar over the several statements of "my girl."

The second verse is virtually identical to the first melodically. However, the background is much richer, with strings and horns present throughout. In most of the background parts there are little snippets of melody—trumpet flourishes, string countermelodies. After the second set of "my girls," the violins play an elaborate interlude that moves the melody to a higher key. Like the second verse/chorus statement, the melody remains the same, and the instrumental background remains rich and active. The song ends with an extended tag that hammers home the main point of the song. In this song, we hear key components of the Motown sound.

These features work together to provide multiple points of entry for a widely varied audience. The instrumentation dissolves class and racial boundaries—all of the sounds, from the fingersnap (the easiest homemade percussion sound of all) to the symphonic strings (members of the Detroit Symphony moonlighted on these recordings) mix together easily. There are abundant melodic hooks—the bass and guitar riffs, the many iterations of "my girl," and more. The rhythm is catchy but not overpowering; the tune remains the dominant element. The form is easy to navigate, not only because of the lyrics and melody but also because of the texture, which helps shine the spotlight on the title phrase.

This is the Motown sound template. It is predictable enough that listeners would find new songs familiar, yet customizable enough to give each song a distinct identity, not only in melody but other features as well. The flexibility of the Motown template is evident when we compare "My Girl" with Marvin Gaye's "I Heard It Through the Grapevine."

Marvin Gaye

Of all the Motown artists, none sang with more emotional intensity than Marvin Gaye (1939–1984). His turbulent life—stormy relationships with his wife and other women, drug and alcohol abuse, and his death by his father's hand—seemed to find expression in his music. Whether singing about love, as in "I Heard It Through the Grapevine," or contemporary life, as in several songs from his groundbreaking 1971 album *What's Going On*, he communicated an almost tangible range of feeling: pain, hope, joy, frustration.

"I Heard It Through the Grapevine" (1967) is one of the great recorded performances in the history of popular music. It is beautifully integrated: every element blends seamlessly to convey the sense of the text, which gradually unfolds the story of love gone wrong. The opening keyboard riff, harmonized with open intervals, immediately establishes a dark mood. Other instruments enter in stages, leading to the entrance of the voice. Each statement of the melody of the song contains four sections. The first two are blueslike, in that they generally stay within a narrow range and go down more than up. The third builds to the final section for the hook of the song: "I heard it through the grapevine." It is the emotional center of each statement. A Greek-chorus commentary by the backup singers ends each section.

We hear all of the key elements of the Motown sound in this recording as well. The song begins with a memorable instrumental hook. It has a muted rock rhythm. There are lots of melodic ideas woven into the texture. The rich instrumental accompaniment includes rhythm instruments, horns, and strings. "I Heard It Through the Grapevine" also has a verse/chorus form that builds to a title-phrase hook. As in "My Girl," these features provide easy entry into the song and provide enough interest to keep our attention.

Within these general parameters, we hear the variation in detail that keeps the Motown formula from being formulaic. The mood of the song is the mirror image of "My Girl": the bitter end of love, rather than the anticipation of it. This is conveyed most directly in the melody of the song, written by Norman Whitfield, another of the many fine songwriters on the Motown staff, and in Gaye's singing. The instrument choices and instrumental roles also help convey the mood. The opening electric piano riff is ominous, portending the bad news that's sure to follow. The low-pitched percussion sounds reinforce the initial darkness. The form is extended by the commentary of the backup singers at the end of each chorus.

As before, the appeal of the song comes from an exquisite balance between melody and rhythm; a form that is not rigid but still easy to track; a rich vocal and instrumental backdrop; and, most prominently, Gaye's singing. The gospel-inflected yet pop-oriented singing style of Motown acts like the Temptations and Gaye was a new black pop sound, one that struck a balance between novelty and familiarity. Together, the two songs demonstrate that both emotional and musical variety were possible within a consistent overall plan.

7-1c Motown and Black Pop

Motown updated black pop. From Armstrong and Ethel Waters, through Nat Cole and the Mills Brothers, into doo-wop and the girl groups, one direction in black music had been a distinctly black take on popular song. Motown offered not just a new take on pop, but a new, black popular style—and a new kind of romantic music.

In this sense, Motown was heading in the opposite direction from rock. Rock tended to look at love cynically (the Beatles' **"Norwegian Wood"** comes to mind), lustfully (such as the Rolling Stones' **"Satisfaction"**), or not at all. Motown songs preserved the romance present in the popular songs of the thirties and forties, even as they brought both lyrics and music into the present. It's evident not only in the sound—the rich string writing, the understated playing of the rhythm section—but also in the look. The groups wore tuxedos and gowns, like Las Vegas acts, not tie-dyed shirts and jeans, like the Woodstock crowd.

Motown was one of the remarkable success stories of the sixties. A black entrepreneur with fine musical instincts and an equally fine business sense created an empire. For the first time in history, a black style was on equal footing with white music. Motown's success was no accident. Rather, it was the result of Berry Gordy's carefully calculated strategy: he created a style positioned to appeal to as broad an audience as possible. He was lucky to be in the right place at the right time. But in his case, luck was largely the residue of design.

Gordy billed the music coming from his Motown studio as "the sound of young America." He was right. During the mid-sixties, the Motown sound spoke to young Americans of all races and backgrounds. Two generations later, many of the songs are classics, known not only to those who grew up with them, but also to their children and grandchildren.

7-2 Soul

In 1969, almost after the fact, *Billboard* changed the name of its R&B chart from "Hot Rhythm and Blues Singles" to "Best Selling Soul Singles." "Soul" had replaced "rhythm and blues" as the umbrella term for the new black music that had emerged during the mid-sixties; the change in chart name belatedly acknowledged this. Much of this music was popular, by any measure. The Motown success story was the most spectacular evidence of the ascendancy of black music, but Motown artists shared the charts with other black performers, as well as whites: twelve of the top 25 singles acts during the decade were black. It was a diverse group that included James Brown, Aretha Franklin, Ray Charles, Dionne Warwick, and the Supremes; they represented not one style but several.

7-2a Black and White Music in the Sixties

Black music charted musical paths that were different from (mostly) white rock. The Motown examples follow one route; the diverse examples of soul music discussed following highlight another. Although much black music crossed over to the pop charts and influenced musicians of all races (Paul McCartney claims Motown bassist James Jamerson as a primary influence), black performers created music distinctly different from that of most of their white counterparts.

There are three main reasons for this. The first and most significant is the strong gospel tradition. Most of the major black performers of the sixties had grown up singing in church. There is no better example than Aretha Franklin, the queen of soul: Aretha's father was pastor of one of the largest churches in Detroit, and she sang at his services from early childhood.

Another was the increasing musical distinction between rock and roll and rhythm and blues. As we heard in the previous chapters, the differences between the two styles increased toward the end of the fifties, not only because of the gospel influence in the singing, but also because of differences in rhythm, instrumentation (for example, horn sections were the rule in black music; they were rare in white music), and texture (the bass was in the foreground in black music, the guitar typically more in the background; the reverse was true in white rock). The trend continued with black artists whose careers began in the sixties.

A third reason for the array of distinctly black styles in the sixties was the artistic control of a few key producers. Berry Gordy, the emperor of Motown, was one. Another was Jerry Wexler, who had helped build Atlantic Records into a major pop label. Memphis-based Stax Records relied more on the musical intuition of its house musicians—which included Booker T. and the MGs, and the Memphis horns—to create a "house" sound.

7-2b Soul Power

Soul was more than a musical term. It came into use as an expression of the positive sense of racial identity that emerged during the decade: "black is beautiful" was the slogan of many politically active members of the black community. This shift in attitude, among both blacks and some whites, was the social dimension of the relentless pursuit of racial equality. It went hand in hand with the enfranchisement of so many blacks through the Civil Rights Act of 1964 and the Voting Rights Act of 1965.

7-2c Black Music and Civil Rights

Black music was both an agent and a product of the enormous social changes that grew out of the civil rights movement. For whites, it opened the window into the black community a little bit wider: now it was not so much a matter of individual performers, like Louis Armstrong or Nat Cole, as it was styles: the girl groups, Motown, Stax/Volt (Volt was a subsidiary label of Stax Records). The cultural penetration of black music during the sixties was unprecedented.

As the drive for racial equality peaked, then deflated in the wake of the assassination of Martin Luther King Jr., black music occasionally became a vehicle for social commentary. James Brown released a series of exhortations, beginning with the 1968 song "Say It Loud—I'm Black and I'm Proud." Marvin Gaye's landmark album *What's Going On* appeared in 1971. But most of the music did not contain overt references to social conditions or racial issues. More often, it dealt with the subjects that so often transcended race: love won and lost, and the good and bad times that resulted.

Black music benefited from white America's increased awareness of and sensitivity to racial issues. Open-mindedness toward black cultural expression paralleled open-mindedness toward political and social concerns. It didn't hurt that the music provided such accessible points of entry.

Another important factor in the popularity of black music in the sixties was the deepening influence of black music on mainstream pop. Fifties rock and roll represented a major infusion of both the rhythm and the blues elements of rhythm and blues. Because of this, black music—even music without a strong pop orientation—sounded less different to sixties ears than Muddy Waters would have sounded to fifties ears. It is hard to imagine James Brown finding his new bag or finding a substantial white audience in the mid-fifties. A decade later, both happened.

With the passage of time, our view of soul has changed. In retrospect, *soul* refers to the emotionally charged black music of the sixties, music that draws deeply on the blues and on gospel. It is best exemplified by the music that came from two southern cities, Memphis and Muscle Shoals, Alabama, and two performers, Aretha Franklin and James Brown. This was music of real commitment: Percy Sledge bares his soul when he sings "**When a Man Loves a Woman**," and James Brown was, among other things, "the hardest working man in show business." The music expressed deep feelings, with little or no pop sugar coating: when Aretha asks for respect, she spells it out.

7-2d Soul Music

Like most of the music from the mid-sixties, soul music was a synthesis, a new sound created from several sources. What makes it virtually unique is the fact that the sources were almost exclusively black. Soul combined the emotional depth and range of the blues, the fervor of gospel, and the energy of rhythm and blues and rock. The result was one of the most memorable and influential styles of the rock era.

Southern Soul Music

If Gordy's Motown operation was as sleek and well-oiled as a Cadillac, the southern soul scene was more like a souped-up, beat-up Chevy pickup that, despite appearances, ran exceedingly well. Owners and musicians learned the music business as they went, usually the hard way. Yet, despite all the internal bickering, late-night partying, session-skipping, and other unprofessionalisms, some great music was made and recorded.

Southern soul generally came in two speeds: fast and slow. Up-tempo songs built on the groove found in the rock-influenced rhythm and blues of the early sixties. Some are upbeat as well as up-tempo, while others sermonize or upbraid. The slow songs almost always deal with the pain of love. We introduce soul with one example of each: Otis Redding's **"I Can't Turn You Loose,"** recorded for Stax Records, and Percy Sledge's "When a Man Loves a Woman," recorded in Muscle Shoals at the Fame Recording Studio for Atlantic Records.

Stax Records

Memphis, Tennessee, rockabilly's home base in the fifties, became soul's spiritual center in the sixties, mainly through Jim Stewart and Estelle Axton's Stax Records (Stax is an acronym for Stewart and Axton). In many respects, Stax Records was set up like Motown: it had owners, producers, staff songwriters, a house band, and interchangeable singers. (This organizational arrangement distinguished their operations from most of the rock produced by white bands, such as the Beatles and Rolling Stones. These groups wrote their own material; there was no such thing as a "house sound" for their record label.)

Nevertheless, there were key differences from Motown. The Stax sound seemed more a collective effort than a decision from above. Instead of playing from written arrangements, the Stax musicians would listen to a song a few times and construct what amounted to a head arrangement (that is, created on the spot—off the top of their heads). They would play the song through and briefly discuss among themselves who should do what. Then, often within minutes, they would be ready to record.

Moreover, the operation was thoroughly integrated. Stewart and Axton (who were brother and sister) were white. Producer Al Bell, songwriters Isaac Hayes and David Porter—who penned "Soul Man" and many other Stax hits—and the headliners—Otis Redding, Rufus and Carla Thomas, Sam and Dave, and others—were black. The house rhythm section, which recorded under its own name as Booker T. and the MGs, included two blacks, keyboardist Booker T. Jones and drummer Al Jackson, and two whites, guitarist Steve Cropper and bassist Donald "Duck" Dunn. The horn players—who became famous on their own as the Memphis Horns—were all white. In the cocoon that was the Stax recording studio, race didn't seem to matter, even if it mattered a great deal as soon as they stepped out onto the street.

Otis Redding

The king of southern soul singers was Otis Redding (1941–1967). Redding, who grew up in Georgia, first tried to break into the music business in Macon; he eventually ended up singing behind Little Richard. After he secured an Atlantic recording contract, he turned out a string of R&B hits at Stax. He broke through to the pop market with a scintillating performance at the 1967 Monterey Pop Festival, where he won over a new, largely white audience for his music. Tragedy struck soon after: he died in a plane crash later that year. The posthumously released **"(Sittin' on the) Dock of the Bay**," written with Steve Cropper in Monterey, was his biggest hit. (Ironically, it was one of his least soulful recordings.)

Redding's singing calls to mind a fervent black preacher. Especially in up-tempo numbers, his singing is more than impassioned speech but less than singing with precise pitch. It is as if the emotion of the moment is too strong to be constrained by "correct" notes. "I Can't Turn You Loose," one of his classic soul recordings, showcases his unique delivery, sandwiched between the Memphis Horns and the MGs.

The song is the quintessential illustration of the southern soul sound. The song begins with not one, but two, memorable melodic hooks, both of them instrumental. The first is the bass/guitar riff; the second is played by the horn section. There is a wide-open space between the low range guitar/bass riff and the horn riff: that's the range in which Redding sings. This is the typical instrumental backdrop for an up-tempo soul song: heavy on the bottom and top and basically empty in the middle (except, of course, for Redding's singing). The only chord sounds come from the piano, heard faintly in a high register.

The rhythm is also typical of sixties Memphis soul:

- Marking of the rock rhythm layer by the bass and guitar
- Strong beat keeping from the drums
- Frequent syncopations in both riffs that fight against the beat (the famous offbeat horn riff at the end of each big section is the classic example of this)
- Redding darting in and out of a steady rhythm with the kind of rhythmic freedom that all the great soul singers had

This performance has a harder edge than many soul recordings, not only because of Redding's gritty singing but also because the guitar is so prominent and has a little distortion. Perhaps the edge comes from rock: one of Redding's big hits was a cover of the Rolling Stones' "Satisfaction."

If we think of the sound world of Motown as comparable to an artist's palette, then the sound world of Memphis soul would be an 8-pack box of thick crayons. Up-tempo soul emphasizes power and impact over subtlety and refinement.

Bittersweet Soul Music

In soul music, tempo usually sends a direct message. Fast tempos signal an upbeat mood, or at least something to get excited about. By contrast, slow tempos typically reinforce a down mood; usually these tempos help convey a story involving love lost. One of the classic examples of this branch of sixties soul music is Percy Sledge's "When a Man Loves a Woman," a lament of love gone wrong.

Sledge (1940–2015) was born in Leighton, Alabama, a small town not far from Muscle Shoals, where he recorded "When a Man Loves a Woman" in 1966. Quin Ivy, a local disc jockey and all-around entrepreneur, had discovered Sledge singing in a local group called the Esquires. Ivy engineered a solo artist contract with Atlantic and arranged the recording date that produced Sledge's first and biggest hit.

Sledge's rapid rise to stardom proved once again that the black church was a very fertile training ground for soul. It seemed that many blacks (and not a few whites) sang gospel—not just the suave stylings of groups like Sam Cooke's Soul Stirrers but the raw, impassioned singing first secularized by Ray Charles. During the early rock era, gospel choirs provided a seemingly endless stream of talent.

Like the Motown acts who were lucky enough to live in Detroit, stardom for a soul singer seemed to be as much a matter of timing as talent. While there was no question that Otis Redding, Percy Sledge, and Wilson Pickett deserved their fame, there were certainly other talented southern blacks who could have achieved stardom if they had found themselves around people in the music business who could nurture their talent.

Soul ballads, of which "When a Man Loves a Woman" is perhaps *the* classic example, have an entirely different dynamic from up-tempo songs. Here the band is accompanist rather than partner, more like a frame to a painting than an indivisible part of the mix. The opening is about as unobtrusive as it can be in the rock era: walking bass, slow triplets and **backbeat** on the drums, sustained chords on a Farfisa organ (one of the wave of electronic keyboards that came on the market during the sixties). Other layers accumulate during the course of the song: guitar noodles, backup vocals, then horns on the final chorus. Their accompanying role is defined not so much by their volume—eventually the band all but overpowers Sledge—as by the complete lack of rhythmic or melodic interest in their parts. Only the guitarist is doing anything other than sustaining a chord or marking time, and his part remains pretty much in the background. As a result, the sound spotlight shines straight on Sledge.

Although this was Sledge's first recording, he "let it all hang out." He held nothing back; there is no emotional reserve in his singing. What you hear is what he feels, with no buffer in between. Previously, such naked emotion had been heard almost exclusively in the blues—and Ray Charles's blues/gospel synthesis. Here, as in Charles's best work, it is amplified through gospel style. Like the blues, the phrases start high and finish low, but the strain from singing so high in his range projects the pain that is inherent in the song.

The powerful emotion captured in this song touched a lot of hearts, black and white, here and abroad. The song was No. 1 on both the R&B and pop charts in 1966 and remains one of the great soul anthems.

The heyday of southern soul was brief—about four years, from 1965 through 1968. The bullet that killed Dr. King—ironically in Memphis—also seemed to pass through the heart of soul. The major southern soul studios were integrated operations: the Stax rhythm section was half black/half white, and the house musicians at Rick Hall's Fame studio were almost all white. In the wake of the racial tensions triggered by Dr. King's assassination, business ground to a halt at Fame and slowed down at Stax.

Audience attitudes seemed to change as well. Most of the southern soul stars saw their careers nosedive. Only vocalist Al Green had a major career after the glory years, although Isaac Hayes had a brief moment in the sun as a performer. Nevertheless, soul left an indelible imprint on the music of the rock era.

7-3 Aretha Franklin

Sam and Dave, Percy Sledge, Otis Redding, and almost all the other soul acts were southern men. The greatest of the sixties soul singers, however, was Aretha Franklin—neither a man nor a southerner. She was—and is—the queen of soul and one of the great artists in the history of popular music.

If any performer grew up with a destiny to fulfill, it was Aretha (b. 1942). Her father, C. L. Franklin, was one of the most charismatic preachers in the country. Although his home base was in Detroit (Berry Gordy recorded his sermons and released them on a Motown subsidiary), he toured the nation, attracting throngs to the black churches where he preached. Reverend Franklin was also a lavish and gracious host. The cream of the black entertainment world, both sacred and secular, passed through his house. Growing up, Aretha heard everyone from gospel star Mahalia Jackson to the virtuosic and elegant jazz pianist Art Tatum.

Although shy as a child (throughout her career, only her singing has been extroverted) and the daughter of a wealthy man, Aretha was anything but sheltered. As a teenager, she went on the road with her father and his entourage; her mother had left when she was six. She crammed a lifetime of experience into those few years. Before she set off for New York at eighteen to begin her secular career, she had repeatedly experienced the discrimination that went with being black in the fifties, endured endless bus rides from town to town, and given birth to two children. So when she sang about love and respect, her feelings came directly from her own experience.

Aretha Franklin's career in secular music began in 1960, when she signed a contract with Columbia Records. Her producer was John Hammond, perhaps the most knowledgeable and sensitive advocate of black music in the music business during the middle of the century. As a pioneering jazz critic, he had signed many top acts for Columbia over several decades. Although he recruited her for the label, the company didn't know how to tap her talent. Some of her recordings show her as a bluesy pop singer, à la Dinah Washington, who was very hot around 1960; others capture her singing pop treacle accompanied by syrupy strings. Jerry Leiber suggested that Aretha was "suffering from upward mobility." Although she produced some good work, her career went nowhere.

In 1966, Atlantic Records' producer Jerry Wexler bought her contract. He took her to Muscle Shoals in January 1967 for what in retrospect proved to be one of the most famous recording sessions of all time. Within seconds after she sat down at the piano to play through **"I Never Loved a Man,"** everyone in the studio knew they were in the presence of someone special. Although put together on the fly—the horns were in the studio's office working out the riffs while Aretha was rehearsing with the rhythm section—the song was recorded in a couple of takes. Its obvious success sparked camaraderie among those present at the session, which was fueled by liberal amounts of alcohol. Unfortunately, that proved too rich a mixture: a fight between studio owner Rick Hall and Ted White, Aretha's husband and manager at the time, broke out sometime in the wee hours. With that, the session was called off, Aretha headed back to Detroit, where she all but disappeared for weeks, and Wexler went back to New York with one-and-a-half songs. He finally got Aretha to return to finish the second song, and the rest is history.

Many of Aretha's first hits explored the heartbreak of love, like most soul ballads of the time. However, her first up-tempo hits, most notably her cover of Otis Redding's **"Respect"** and her own **"Think,"** emotionally redefined fast soul. What had frequently been a forum for men to boast about their sexual prowess became the backdrop to a demand for dignity in "Respect" and a tongue-lashing in "Think." In both songs, the groove is as good as it gets, but it assists a call to arms rather than an invitation to sensual pleasure. "Respect," in fact, took on a meaning beyond the intent of its lyric: it became an anthem for the women's movement, which was just gathering momentum.

The musical formula for "Respect" is much the same as for "I Can't Turn You Loose": interlocked rhythm section, with horns playing riffs or sustained chords. The two major differences are Aretha's singing and the backup vocals, which give the song a churchier sound. The most memorable and individual section of the song is the stop-time passage when Aretha spells out what she wants—"R-E-S-P-E-C-T"— so that there's absolutely no misunderstanding. What had been a straightforward verse/refrain song suddenly shifts up a gear. The remainder of the song features the dense texture previously heard in the refrain: a series of riffs from the backup vocalists—"sock it to me," "just a little bit," and finally the repeated "Re-re-re-re" (not only the first syllable of "respect" but also Aretha's nickname)—piled on top of the beat and horn riffs, with Aretha commenting on it all from above.

Having quickly established her credentials as the queen of soul, Aretha began to explore other musical territory. She has been one of the very few artists of the rock era who can cover songs convincingly. Her versions of Burt Bacharach's "**I Say a Little Prayer**," Sam Cooke's "**You Send Me**," Nina Simone's "**Young, Gifted, and Black**," and Paul Simon's gospel-influenced "**Bridge over Troubled Water**" are all standouts. Several of her own songs give further evidence of her expressive range: in "**Rock Steady**," she tips her hat to James Brown, while "**Daydreaming**" is as tender and romantic a song as any released in the early seventies.

Aretha's music is deeply personal and, at the same time, universal. The responsive listener feels her communicate one-on-one, yet her message transcends such a relationship. The best of Aretha's music seems to demand both empathy and ecstasy. We can give ourselves up to the groove even as we listen to her tough-time tales. No one in the rock era has fused both qualities more powerfully and seamlessly than she.

7-4 James Brown

James Brown (1933–2006) was the godfather of soul, the man who had nurtured it longer than anyone else and whose music had more influence than any other soul artist. Brown's career spanned almost the entire history of the rock era. His first hit recording, "**Please Please Please**," appeared on the R&B charts in 1956. We continue to hear his music today in multiple forms: not only the original recordings but also via **samples** woven into rap recordings.

It took Brown almost a decade to arrive at the original sound heard in "**Papa's Got a Brand New Bag**," his breakthrough 1965 hit. The majority of his hits in the fifties were typical slow R&B ballads. Other than Brown's singing, there is little in these recordings that anticipates the originality of his work in the sixties.

Brown came to his new sound by subtraction. He gradually eliminated anything not essential to maintaining the rhythmic flow of a song: repeated guitar riffs, repetitive bass lines, keyboard chords, busy drum parts, and the like. With "Papa's Got a Brand New Bag," the process is complete. Underneath Brown's short vocal riffs, the horns play short riffs, the baritone sax a single note, the guitar a chord on the backbeat (except for the double-time repeated chord at the end of each statement of the refrain—a brief moment in the spotlight), the bass short groups of notes separated by silence, while the drummer plays a rock rhythm on the hi-hat and bass drum kicks on the off-beat. The little timekeeping that's audible comes from the drummer.

The drummer's light timekeeping is like aural graph paper, onto which Brown and his band draw their rhythmic design. The open sound that results from this bare minimum texture was not only Brown's new "bag" (in sixties slang, a "bag" is a person's special skill; here, it refers to Brown's new conception of rhythm and texture), but also one of the most original conceptions of the rock era.

"Papa's Got a Brand New Bag" alternates blues-form refrains with sections that don't use blues form. The boundaries between sections are sharply drawn; so are the shifts within sections. Further, each section has its own well-defined character, which usually remains the same throughout. By sharply defining the character of

samples A small sound file. There are two basic kinds of samples in common use. One is the recorded sound of a voice or group of voices, an instrument (such as a grand piano) or group of instruments (a violin section), or some other sound. This sound can then be activated through another device. The other main kind of sampling involves lifting short excerpts from existing recordings to use in a new recording, much like a visual artist will use found objects to create a collage or assemblage. It has been a staple of rap background tracks since the technology became available in the mid eighties.

each section and the boundaries between sections, Brown creates forms that seem assembled from blocks. This differentiates them from the Motown songs, which proceed in waves of sound.

In "Papa's Got a Brand New Bag" and "**I Got You (I Feel Good)**," Brown emphasized rhythm, texture, and the soulfulness of his singing over melody and harmony. In "**Cold Sweat**" (1967), he goes a step further. The basic approach is the same: riffs layered over light timekeeping. However, there is virtually no harmonic movement: one chord lasts the entire opening section, and the bridge oscillates between two chords. At the same time, the texture is more active. The guitar part adds fast-moving rhythmic counterpoint. Of special interest is the new choked guitar sound: the guitarist strums across the strings while holding his hand across the neck, "choking" off the resonance to create a percussive scraping sound. The guitar becomes in effect, a percussion instrument, with more rhythm than pitch. Moreover, its pattern is active and highly syncopated, enriching the rhythmic texture more than any other line. Other strands—drums, bass, baritone sax, other horns—are also more consistently syncopated than in the previous songs. Because the texture is more active, Brown sings less, especially in the contrasting section. Here Brown seems to sing only when he feels like it. He is content to ride the band's rhythmic wave.

The combination of an active, syncopated rhythm texture and harmonic stasis creates a sense of open-ended time: we are immersed in an "eternal present." Because they create and maintain a groove, sections are infinitely extensible: they don't *go* anywhere, they just *are*. This was a huge conceptual breakthrough, anticipated only infrequently by such songs as Bo Diddley's "Bo Diddley." Brown goes well beyond these early efforts.

Brown's music, especially "Cold Sweat" and much of the work that followed it, bring popular music closer to its African roots than it had ever been before. Indeed, John Chernoff reported in his 1971 book, *African Rhythm and African Sensibility*, that African musicians felt more at home with James Brown's music than any other popular musician of the time.

Brown's music has been profoundly influential. With its emphasis on intricate rhythms and de-emphasis of melody and harmony, it would create the blueprint for funk and rap.

With deep roots in gospel, blues, rhythm and blues, and jazz, and its blending and modernizing of these styles, the music of James Brown represents a unique soul synthesis. In its originality and individuality, it stands apart from all the other music of the sixties. It remains one of the most influential styles from that decade.

7-5 The Impact of Black Music of the Sixties

In the film *Good Morning, Vietnam*, Robin Williams portrays Adrian Cronauer, an Air Force disc jockey brought in to improve morale among the troops. Cronauer junks the staff-approved tame white pre-rock pop, replacing it with an integrated playlist that includes James Brown, Motown, and the Beach Boys. While he's on the air, the film cuts away to scenes of the soldiers, on and off duty, listening to the music that he's playing. They are smiling, dancing, moving to the groove. In the film, music is the most powerful symbol of the huge generation gap between the old guard and the young troops.

More than any other aspect of American culture, music—and especially Motown and soul—brought home the arrival of a new generation and the profound changes taking place in American society. The new black music was fresh and it was good. And it was popular, among young people of all races. At least while they listened to it, race no longer mattered, except in a good way. This was no longer "wrong side of the tracks" music. Its broad acceptance was one important sign of the wholesale shift in attitude that would characterize the sixties.

For a brief time in the mid-sixties, it seemed that divisions of race, class, and culture were about to be eliminated. That didn't happen, but the changes that took place during that time were irreversible. The "one-color" world of mid century film and television was gone forever; the music that was its soundtrack is largely forgotten. The black music of the sixties helped bridge the gap between that world and the multicultural society we now see in both the media and real life. It lives on: the best of it sounds as good today as when it was released.

CHAPTER 8

ROCK

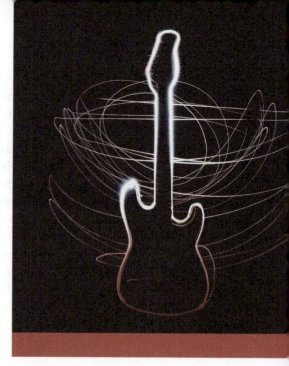

Learning Objectives:

1) Define the two British styles: **trad** and **skiffle**.

2) Discuss the necessary musical features found within **deep blues**.

3) Identify the different roles that form a **power trio**.

4) Recall the key musical characteristics of Eric Clapton's electric blues style.

5) Audibly identify a **double-time rhythm** in a musical example.

6) Compare the musical differences between heavy metal and 1960s rock.

Chapter Introduction

In our opening discussion of rock's core style, we began at the end, with a 2008 recording of AC/DC, performing in a distinctive style that had remained largely unchanged for more than a generation. We resume our discussion of the core rock style by tracking its development through the better part of a decade, to better understand how it arrived at its now-classic form.

When we think of timeless rock, we expect to hear bands with a core of electric guitar, electric bass, and drums playing songs with heavy riffs over a rock beat at a loud volume. Within these general parameters, there is considerable room for variation: in the music discussed here, we will hear solo- and group-oriented rock, other instruments added to the rhythm section nucleus, and different ways of assimilating the blues—the most profound outside influence on this music.

However, the most exciting aspect of this dynamic view of core-defining rock is hearing the maturation of rock rhythm—from the straightforward rock of the first two examples (released in 1964 and 1965) to the compelling and timeless rhythms of the examples from the early seventies. We will discover that in less than a decade, rock musicians learned to play with rock rhythm: adding other rhythmic layers, most of which conflict with the timekeeping layers; adding faster rhythms; varying the timekeeping, even to the point of completely omitting it for long stretches; and focusing particularly on the rock rhythmic layer. In the process, they transformed rock rhythm from the relatively straightforward rhythms heard in music from the early and mid-sixties into the irresistible groove that is the heart of rock and roll. Most fundamentally, rock is about rhythm; in these examples, we hear rock rhythm assume its mature first-generation form.

Experience an interactive version of this era in MINDTAP

All of this—rhythms, riffs, sounds, virtuosity—was in the service of the defiant, provocative, sexually charged attitude that is conveyed so powerfully in the music. This attitude, present in much of the music heard here but not heard as powerfully in earlier rock, was the result of a second infusion of blues.

8–1 From Blues to Rock

In the early sixties, while the Quarrymen were molting into the Beatles, other young British musicians were hanging out at Alexis Korner's London-based Blues and Barrelhouse Club. Korner, a trad and skiffle musician during the fifties, spearheaded the blues revival in Great Britain as the sixties began.

> During the forties and fifties, British popular music consisted mainly of pop stylings and "trad": British-style Dixieland jazz. In the late fifties, "skiffle" was the hot new sound in the United Kingdom. Skiffle mixed American and British folk music, rockabilly (in its use of the drum set), and other sources. It is often viewed as the first British take on US rock and roll.

Korner nurtured a generation of British musicians who had grown up listening to the blues. Their primary contact came from the recordings of Muddy Waters, John Lee Hooker, Howlin' Wolf, and other country and electric bluesmen—highly prized because they were so hard to obtain in Britain. Korner's club, a regular stop for American bluesmen touring England, was a mecca for British blues fans. It was also an outlet for the British blues musicians—a place where they could gain valuable performing experience.

The roster of musicians who played at Korner's club reads like a Who's Who of British rock in the sixties and early seventies. Both the Rolling Stones and Cream were made up of Korner alumni, while key members of Led Zeppelin, the Yardbirds, John Mayall's Bluesbreakers, and other notable bands also paid their dues there.

At first, British musicians were content to play a pale imitation of the real thing. However, when Sonny Boy Williamson visited England, he was accompanied by a very young, very green Eric Clapton. This encounter with a real bluesman transformed Clapton as a musician, as he related some years later to blues scholar Robert Palmer:

> It was a frightening experience, because this man was real and we weren't. We didn't know how to back him up, and he put us through some bloody hard paces. I was very young, and it was a real shock. I realized we weren't being true to the music; I had to almost relearn how to play. But it taught me a lot. It taught me the value of that music, which I still feel.

By the time Clapton and his peers "got real," they had transformed their blues experience into a completely new music: the most essential form of rock. This was music with a hard edge, music that confronted and challenged. Although often popular, it was *not* pop. Nor was it simply heavily amplified blues, although blues attitude and style saturates the music. It was something new.

Another musician who grew up on the American side of the Atlantic had a similar agenda. Jimi Hendrix, following his own path, transformed the blues into the most daring and influential instrumental style of the sixties. Hendrix was born and raised in Seattle, paid his dues touring with blues and rhythm-and-blues artists, got his solo career going in England, made his first big splash in the United States at the 1967 Monterey Pop Festival, and died in London. His powerful and imaginative playing linked like-minded musicians on both sides of the Atlantic.

8-2 Deep Blues and Rock

This rock was the second child of the blues, and it favored a different parent. The music of Blind Lemon Jefferson, Robert Johnson, John Lee Hooker, Muddy Waters, and other blues greats was at most an indirect influence on the rock-era music of the fifties. Electric blues, the most vital and authentic blues style of the postwar era, barely touched rock and roll; its main contribution was instrumentation. Throughout most of the fifties, electric bluesmen lived in their own world, and the old Delta bluesmen who were still alive were all but forgotten.

The blues revival that paralleled the folk revival of the late fifties and early sixties exposed young rock musicians to the power and emotional depth of what rock critic Robert Palmer called deep blues. The British musicians who immersed themselves in the blues took from it several of its most distinctive features: the attitude and posturing of the bluesmen, often obvious in its sexual challenge; lyrics that told their stories in plain, direct language, often with a nasty edge (Muddy Waters's "**I Can't Be Satisfied**" and the Rolling Stones' "**[I Can't Get No] Satisfaction**"); a rough, declamatory vocal style; heavy guitar riffs and string-bending blues-scale guitar solos; a strong beat; and a thick, riff-laden texture. This music is identified variously as hard rock, as a hard-rock substyle, such as **heavy metal** or southern rock, or simply as "rock." In this small but revealing sampling, we trace the persistence of the defiant and provocative attitude, and the musical features used to convey it, and the dramatic evolution of rock rhythm over an eight-year period.

heavy metal A hard rock style that developed in the early 1970s, featuring often ear-splitting volume; heavy use of distortion; simplified chord progressions and melodies; lyrics that reflect adolescent, often male preoccupations; and elaborate stage shows.

8-2a Hard Rock in the Mid-Sixties

Among the horde of British bands that invaded the United States in the mid-sixties were blues-influenced groups such as the Animals, the Kinks, and the Rolling Stones. They had a tougher sound than the Beatles: more prominent and more distorted guitar, a stronger beat, rougher vocals, and, behind it all, a more aggressive attitude.

The Animals' interest in the blues resonated with their working-class upbringing in Newcastle. They were the backup band of choice for the American bluesmen who visited there, and they were among the first British bands to score a US hit with "**The House of the Rising Sun**" (1964). Later that same year, the Kinks also had the first of several US hits: "**You Really Got Me**."

The Kinks

Like the Beach Boys, the Kinks were largely a family affair. Two brothers, Ray and Dave Davies, formed the band in 1963—Ray (b. 1944) was the lead vocalist and main songwriter; Dave (b. 1947) was the lead guitarist—by inviting bassist Pete Quaife (1943–2010) and drummer Mick Avory (b. 1944) to join them. The Kinks scored early: "You Really Got Me" and "**All Day and All of the Night**," the band's first and most influential hits, charted in late 1964. In them, they laid down a formula borrowed from the blues that would become a hallmark of hard rock styles.

The idea of building a song over a short, repetitive guitar riff came directly from electric blues: recall the riff that opens Muddy Waters's "**Hoochie Coochie Man**." In "You Really Got Me," the Kinks transform Waters's approach by harmonizing the riff with a power chord, adding distortion, speeding up the tempo, substituting a rock beat for a slow shuffle, and repeating the riff at successively higher pitches throughout the song. In these changes, we can hear both the connection with electric blues and the differences between blues and blues-drenched rock.

The guitar/bass riff is the dominant rhythmic feature of the song: it is louder than any other instrumental sound, and it runs continuously through the song. Regular rhythms are either implicit or in the background: The backbeat is a barely audible drum stroke, a tambourine marks the beat, and drums and occasional piano faintly mark the rock rhythmic layer. In the dominance of the riff rhythm and rhythmic freedom of the bass, the rhythmic texture is clearly rock. But there is not the kind of rhythmic variety or complex interplay that we will encounter in later examples.

The harmony of the song puts a new spin on blues-based harmonies. Recall that a common alternative to the conventional blues progression in Delta blues is a simple one-chord accompaniment. In this song, the Kinks adapt this one-chord approach to a verse/chorus form. They sustain one basic harmony through the first two phrases, then shift up to another chord, and then skip up to still another chord, which underpins the multiple statements of the hook containing the title phrase. This was a novel way to build momentum toward a goal without using standard progressions.

Heavy, distorted riffs set to power chords convey Ray Davies's unbridled lust more powerfully than the lyrics, which in retrospect seem pretty tame. Songs like this formed the bridge between electric blues and heavy metal. Using this sound as a point of departure, heavy metal bands increased the volume and the distortion, as Van Halen's 1978 cover of the song evidences.

However, the song seemed to represent a dead end for the Kinks. Their music went in several different directions (such as the proto-punk of "**You Do Something to Me**") but seldom returned to the simple but powerful formula of their two early hits. Nevertheless, the Davies brothers have maintained the Kinks in some form since 1963. The only rock band with a lengthier active career is the Rolling Stones.

The Rolling Stones

That the Rolling Stones' first major hit should be entitled "(I Can't Get No) Satisfaction" is a karmic acknowledgment of the enormous influence of the blues, and Muddy Waters in particular, on the group. Both the band's name and the song title trace back to early Waters's recordings: a 1950 recording entitled "Rolling Stone" and a 1948 recording entitled "I Can't Be Satisfied."

The Rolling Stones grew out of a chance encounter in 1960, when Mick Jagger (b. 1943) saw Keith Richards (b. 1943) standing in a train station with an armful of blues records. It was not their first meeting; both had grown up in Dartford, England, and had attended the same school for one year, when they were six. Their meeting eleven years later would be the beginning of their band.

Both spent a lot of time at Korner's club, where they met Brian Jones (1942–1969) and Charlie Watts (b. 1941). At the time, Watts was the drummer for Korner's Blues Incorporated, which would also include Jagger after 1961. The band came together in 1962 when they added bassist Bill Wyman (born William Perks, 1936) via an audition. Keyboardist Ian Stewart (1938–1985) was also a member of the band at the time. He stopped performing with the group soon after their career took off but retained a close connection with the Stones and performed on many of their recordings.

Like the other British bands, the Rolling Stones began by covering blues and rock-and-roll songs. Within a year, Jagger and Richards, inspired by the success of Lennon and McCartney, started writing original songs for the band. They had their first U.K. hit in 1963 and reached the top of the American charts for the first time in 1965 with "(I Can't Get No) Satisfaction." By the time they recorded the song, they had pretty well defined their sound, style, and image.

For the Stones, "(I Can't Get No) Satisfaction" was a musical and commercial milestone. No other major band so thoroughly distilled their essence into their first major hit. Every aspect of the song—the title, its lyric, its melody and form, Jagger's singing and Richards's guitar playing, the sound of the band, and the relentlessness of its beat—embodied the rebellious image the band wanted to project.

"Satisfaction" begins with one of the most memorable guitar riffs of all time. It sounds menacing, because Richards uses fuzztone (an effect he seldom used subsequently), situates the riff in the lowest register of the guitar, and places a strong, syncopated accent on the highest and longest note of the riff, which pushes against the beat established in the first two notes. If sound can sneer, then it does so in this riff.

The riff functions not only as an introduction, but also as a refrain. It clarifies both the sequence of events and the underlying meaning of the lyric. Recall that a rock-era song typically begins with a verse, then builds toward the chorus, which includes at least one vocal hook. Here, the sequence is reversed. The title phrase comes where the verse typically appears. The music builds toward a high point, which is sustained for several measures. In a song with a conventional form, this would be the chorus. However, after "I can't get no . . .," the lyric is verse-like: Jagger spews out a litany of complaints. Here, Jagger is dissembling; what is *really* bothering him is that he cannot get sexual satisfaction. Richards's guitar riff mimics the energy and rhythm of intercourse; that it never changes underscores the fact that Jagger never gains sexual release, at least during the song. Here, the music seems to convey directly what the lyrics do not.

The apparent sexual undercurrent of "Satisfaction" may have emerged originally from the group's subconscious. By Richards's own account, the riff came to him in the middle of a restless night: he woke up from a troubled sleep long enough to play it into a tape recorder, then went back to sleep. The words and the working out of the rest of the song came later.

"Satisfaction" presents a more complex form of rock rhythm than we heard in "You Really Got Me." Watts strongly marks both the beat and the rock beat layer; Jones's rhythm guitar part also reinforces the rock rhythm layer. These steady rhythms serve as a foil for other parts: Richards's guitar riffs, Jagger's vocal line and occasional tambourine rattles, and Wyman's free bass lines. Together they create a dense overlay of conflicting rhythms. The result is a thick, active rhythmic texture that balances heavy timekeeping with strong syncopations.

The songs by the Kinks and the Rolling Stones present a rock rhythmic conception that is purged of any transitional elements. However, in both cases, the beat is routinely marked, which inhibits the flow of the rhythm somewhat.

In the examples that follow, we will hear bands shift the emphasis away from beat-keeping to a stronger backbeat and greater emphasis on the rock rhythmic layer.

Neither "You Really Got Me" nor "(I Can't Get No) Satisfaction" is a blues song. Still, this group-oriented music by the Rolling Stones and the Kinks embraced essential aspects of blues style and sensibility. It's evident in the attitude conveyed in both words and music—and in gesture and movement, when seen in live performance. Musically, the strongest connections are found in the rough vocal quality of singers like Jagger, the heavy reliance on repeated riffs, and the dense, dark texture resulting from the interplay of instruments operating in middle and low registers.

Power Trios: Rock as a Soloist's Music

Among the most compelling new sounds of the late sixties were power trios such as Cream and the Jimi Hendrix Experience. These were bare bones bands—just guitar, bass, and drums—set up to showcase the skills of their exceptionally able guitarists: Eric Clapton and Jimi Hendrix. These and other like-minded guitarists, such as Jeff Beck and Jimmy Page, took one additional element from blues—the guitar as the bluesman's "second voice." They used it as a point of departure as they introduced a new element into rock: virtuosic soloing. We explore the blues connection and the new conception next.

8-2b Blues Guitar and Rock

Throughout the recorded history of deep blues, the guitar had been a melody instrument as well as a harmony and rhythm instrument in support of the voice. From Blind Lemon Jefferson on, bluesmen would answer sung phrases with vocal-like guitar lines, double the vocal line, or showcase the guitar's melodic capabilities in an instrumental solo. This melodic aspect of blues guitar—the guitar as expressive solo voice—resonated deeply with Hendrix, Clapton, and the others, who brought it into rock.

The guitar had been a solo instrument from the earliest days of rock and roll. It was featured in Chuck Berry and Buddy Holly recordings, as well as in instrumentals such as the Ventures' **"Walk, Don't Run"** and Dick Dale's early surf music. Chuck Berry's solos remain models of their kind, but they are riff-based. Dale's guitar lines contain novel effects, like the low-register scale that slithers and snakes down the fingerboard. However, none are vocally inspired. In retrospect, they seem somewhat limited in their exploration of the expressive potential of the electric guitar.

While Berry and others were creating rock guitar styles, electric bluesmen such as Guitar Slim, Buddy Guy, and Freddie King (one of Clapton's idols) were playing the guitar in a style that paralleled their raw, earthy singing, exploiting such novel effects as severe distortion in the process. Their style served as a direct inspiration for a new generation of rock guitarists.

Because they were the dominant soloists of their time, Clapton and Hendrix are inextricably linked. However, despite their strong connection in time, place, and purpose, they were two quite distinct musical personalities. Some of the differences between Hendrix and Clapton may have grown out of their early exposure to the blues. Hendrix grew up with the blues, hearing it as part of a broad spectrum of black music that also included jazz and rhythm and blues. Clapton approached the blues with the fervor of a convert, especially after his encounters with American bluesmen.

Although they used the blues as a point of departure, Hendrix and Clapton took these new-found capabilities several steps further. In so doing, they helped transform the electric guitar into the transcendental solo instrument of rock.

Eric Clapton and Cream

During the sixties, Eric Clapton (b. 1945) refined and purified his blues conception, especially during his short stint with John Mayall's Bluesbreakers in 1965 and 1966. The purity of this conception was important to him: he had left the Yardbirds just prior to joining Mayall when the band moved away from blues toward **psychedelic rock**.

By the time he formed Cream in 1966, with bassist Jack Bruce (1943–2014) and drummer Ginger Baker (born Peter Baker, 1939), Clapton had developed into rock's premier guitar virtuoso. He was the first major rock performer to play extended, improvised solos, especially in live performances. To accommodate his solo excursions, Cream dispensed with the rhythm guitar in live performance, although a second guitar was often added on recordings.

Cream was the first of the power trios: lead guitar, bass, and drums but no chord instrument. In live performance, the spotlight was on Clapton, although Bruce and Baker played active roles in support of his solos. They became a different band in the studio. The demands of AM radio airplay, with its three-minute target, constrained Clapton's solo excursions. Their material gravitated toward the then-fashionable psychedelic rock, although it still retained a strong blues connection. And, through the miracle of overdubbing, the band acquired additional instrumental voices without additional personnel—most notably, Clapton on rhythm guitar.

"Strange Brew," not a singles hit but one of their best-remembered studio recordings, shows the studio side of their musical personality. The lyric has psychedelic overtones—what *is* the "strange brew"?—but the real story is in the music. Here the blues influence runs deep, yet it's transformed into one of the most influential rock sounds of all time.

Blues influences begin with the form. The underlying harmony is a basic 12-bar blues; the lyric and melodic form use the verse/chorus blues form first heard in "It's Tight Like That." However, the deeper blues influence is in Clapton's guitar playing. Clapton fills three distinct roles in this song. One is the sharp chords that come on alternate backbeats. A second is the rapidly rising riff that runs throughout the song. Third are the solo episodes: during the introduction, answering the vocal, and the brief solo in the middle of the song. The deep blues influence is most evident in the solos, where Clapton adapts many trademark features of electric blues style: the fast vibrato, bent notes, free rhythms, extensive use of the pentatonic scale, and heavy inflection of individual notes. With his impressive command of the instrument, Clapton makes all of this sound easy; his guitar becomes a miraculous prosthetic device that creates vocally inspired musical gestures far surpassing what he could do with his voice.

Clapton's solo playing put him in the vanguard among the rock guitar soloists. Also innovative, however, are Clapton's riff-derived accompaniment, Bruce's syncopated bass lines, and the loose-jointed rhythm that they create. Clapton's repeated riff is a textural breakthrough for rock. From Chuck Berry on, rhythm guitarists had typically played chords. Usually they surfaced as some kind of boogie-woogie derived pattern (Berry, Holly), strummed (Beatles, Rolling Stones), or arpeggiated (Dylan, Beatles). Clapton's alternative, while certainly based on chords, breaks away from the rhythmic and melodic regularity that are customary in rhythm guitar parts. In this respect, it is more like a repeated riff in an electric blues than anything commonly found in rock and roll.

psychedelic rock A rock substyle defined not by a musical feature but simply by the music's ability to evoke or enhance the drug experience.

Similarly, the texture created by the riff, Clapton's lead guitar line, and Bruce's bass line resembles the intertwined melodic strands of the electric blues style heard in the Muddy Waters examples. (The connection shouldn't be surprising because Clapton claimed Waters to be his major influence.) At the same time, the concept is considerably updated, not only by the shift to rock rhythm, but also the emancipation of the bass line.

Cream helped loosen up rock rhythm. The basic beat is the eight-beat rhythm of rock, but all three instruments occasionally include patterns that move twice as fast as the basic rock beat. The most persistent and obvious is Clapton's riff, but there are also occasional double-time patterns in the drum part (a variant of the "fatback" beat so popular in soul music) and the double-time break toward the end. The double-time rhythms (that is, twice as fast as the rock beat layer) open up new paths toward greater rhythmic complexity.

Clapton's solo work demonstrates how he brought the essence of blues guitar style into rock. Jimi Hendrix would transform it into the most admired and emulated guitar style of the rock era.

Jimi Hendrix

Jimi Hendrix (1942–1970) grew up in Seattle, Washington, which is about as far away from the Mississippi Delta as one can get and still be inside the continental United States. However, the blues were as close as his father's record collection, which also included a fair amount of jazz. Both would be profound influences on his playing.

After a hitch in the army, cut short by a back injury suffered in a parachute jump, Hendrix began his musical apprenticeship by working in the backup bands of a wide variety of black performers: bluesman B. B. King, Little Richard, saxophone great King Curtis, the Isley Brothers, and Jackie Wilson.

In 1966, Hendrix formed his own band: Jimmy James and the Flames. They were heard in New York by ex-Animals' bassist turned talent scout Chas Chandler, who encouraged Hendrix to come to England. When he arrived, Chandler introduced him to bassist Noel Redding and drummer Mitch Mitchell, who began jamming with Hendrix. Soon, they were performing on the London club scene as the Jimi Hendrix Experience. Their first hit, **"Hey Joe,"** released in the fall of 1966, made Hendrix a star almost overnight. Their first album, *Are You Experienced?* released early in 1967, secured Hendrix's reputation in England. A spectacular performance at the 1967 Monterey Pop Festival spread his reputation in the United States. For the remainder of his too-short career, he cemented his place as rock's most influential and innovative soloist.

Hendrix was one of the most flamboyant performers of sixties rock. Like several of the bluesmen who inspired him, he developed unconventional ways of playing the guitar: between his legs, behind his neck, during a somersault. On stage, his guitar was an erotic instrument as well as a musical one. No rock musician before him had so graphically connected the guitar with male sexual potency.

However, his most memorable visual moment came at the Monterey Pop Festival, when he drenched his guitar in lighter fluid and set it on fire. His red guitar, flickering with flames, remains one of rock's most enduring visual images.

Of course, the most important part of Hendrix's legacy is his music. In his all-too-brief career, Hendrix set the standard for solo **improvisation** in rock. Hendrix's contribution to rock, and more particularly improvisation in rock, is so substantial because it is multifaceted. He brought to rock guitar playing unprecedented fluency, a new expressive vocabulary, and a dazzling array of new sounds. In all

improvisation The act of creating music spontaneously rather than performing a previously learned song the same way every time. Improvisation is one of the key elements in jazz. It gives musicians the opportunity to express inspirations and react to situations; requires virtuosity, melodic inventiveness, personal-ity, and the ability to swing.

three dimensions, we hear both Hendrix's deep indebtedness to the blues and his thorough transformation of this blues foundation into the most spectacular and influential rock guitar style of the early rock era. These qualities are evident in recordings such as "**Voodoo Child**," a track from his 1968 recording, *Electric Ladyland.*

"Voodoo Child" is a blues-inspired song, on several levels. The vocal sections of the song inflate and reshape 12-bar blues form. The lyric begins as if it is a conventional rhymed couplet with the first line repeated. But Hendrix adds a refrain-like fourth line to the lyric, which contains the title phrase of the song. Hendrix also modifies the musical features of blues form by extending the length of the phrases and by using a strikingly different harmonization: static in the first part of the song, then fresh-sounding chords in the latter part. The relationship between voice and guitar recalls the Delta blues of Robert Johnson and Muddy Waters in the heterophonic passages (the guitar version of the melody is usually far more elaborate) and the call-and-response between voice and guitar. The vocal sections serve as formal pillars, supporting what is in essence an unbroken five-minute improvisation. Hendrix ignores the harmony of the vocal section in his solos; they take place over one chord.

Hendrix's brilliant improvisations are the expressive focus of the performance. They are skilled to a degree matched only by jazz in the popular music tradition before rock. Indeed, toward the end of his life, Hendrix immersed himself in the music of John Coltrane, one of jazz's great virtuosos as well as its most progressive voice in the sixties, and collaborated with fusion guitarist John McLaughlin, who also recorded with Miles Davis at this time.

The quality that stands out above all is the astounding variety of Hendrix's playing. It is most apparent in his improvisatory strategies and range of sounds. Hendrix does not limit himself to any particular improvisatory style—for instance, a fast-moving single-line melody or variations on a riff. Instead, he roams over the entire range of the instrument, interweaving sustained bent notes, rapid running passages, riffs, and chords in a dizzying sequence.

Just as masterful is the dazzling array of sounds he draws from his guitar—an inventory of the sound possibilities of the instrument. They range from the pitchless strummings of the opening of "Voodoo Child" and the biting sound on the rapid repeated intervals on the bottom strings (at about two minutes into the song) to the sustained high-note wails, distorted chords, and hyper-vibrated notes in his solos. And he mixes them together in dazzling sequences that seem completely spontaneous in their unpredictability.

Hendrix plays in Technicolor—there are times when almost every note has a sound that's different from the ones around it. Both the degree and frequency of sound variety far exceed that heard in earlier improvisation-based styles—indeed, such variety was not possible before Hendrix began to exploit the potential of the electric guitar.

Hendrix's solos represent a new kind of genius, one that emerges from the particular demands of rock improvisation. In them, he elevated sound variety to a level of interest comparable to pitch and rhythm, and he enormously expanded the vocabulary of available sounds. In a Hendrix solo, *how* a note sounded became just as important as its pitch and rhythmic placement. In so doing, he built on the expressive sounds of the blues and the artistry and melodic inventiveness of jazz, merging and transforming them into a definitive improvisational style in rock.

Hendrix's legacy is his playing. It not only helped define rock-based improvisation more than the work of any other artist, but it also helped redefine the possibilities of improvisation within popular music. It echoes through much of the music of the seventies and eighties, especially heavy metal and hard rock. Others have built on it, a few have extended it, but none have surpassed it in imagination and originality.

A comparison of Hendrix's solo in "Voodoo Child" with Clapton's solo in "Strange Brew" contrasts two quite different approaches to blues-based improvisation within rock. Clapton's playing is more focused than flamboyant, whereas Hendrix's solo playing is like a fireworks display, with new sounds firing off in an almost random sequence.

The two recordings also highlight the creative tension in rock between individual brilliance and group impact. The instrumental sections in the Cream recording feature three layers of pitched sound: the bass line in the lowest register, the repeated guitar riff in the low middle register, and the solo guitar line in the high middle register. By contrast, there are only two layers of pitched sound in the Hendrix recording: the bass line and Hendrix's guitar, which roams from the lowest notes on the guitar to a high register. For long stretches, there is a void in the low middle register, where one typically hears a guitar playing riffs or chords. Much of rock's impact comes from the dense mass of sound and consistent rhythm produced by bass, rhythm guitar, and drums. It is not present in Hendrix's recording. Indeed, it is hard to imagine adding a rhythm guitar part to the recording that would satisfactorily complement Hendrix's flights of fancy. Nevertheless, there is an emptiness in the texture that is not present in the other three recordings that we have heard in this chapter. How to integrate solo brilliance into a group conception became an issue for rock bands in the wake of Hendrix's expansion of rock guitar resources. We discuss two remarkable solutions later in the chapter.

8-2c The Perfection of Rock Rhythm

What the Rolling Stones began with songs like **"Get off My Cloud"** and **"(I Can't Get No) Satisfaction"** was complete less than a decade later in songs like **"It's Only Rock 'n Roll (But I Like It)."** Although they would explore numerous musical directions in the late sixties (including *Their Satanic Majesties Request*, their "answer" album to the Beatles' *Sgt. Pepper*), their most significant achievement was the perfection of rock rhythm.

The breakthrough came in the late sixties, in songs like **"Jumping Jack Flash"** and **"Honky Tonk Women."** It involved two interrelated developments: a change in timekeeping and an enrichment of the rhythmic texture. The new approach to timekeeping involved two major changes:

1. increased emphasis on the rock rhythmic layer and the backbeat and
2. the virtual elimination of steady beat-keeping.

The enrichment of the rhythmic texture involved adding more layers of rhythm while maintaining an ideal balance between regular timekeeping and rhythms that conflict or play with the regular rhythms.

Consider the very beginning of "Jumping Jack Flash." The song begins with Richards's syncopated guitar riff. Rhythm guitarist Brian Jones enters on the second iteration of the riff, marking the rock rhythm; Wyman also enters playing a bass line that matches up rhythmically with the main guitar riff. On the third iteration of the riff, Watts enters, marking both the rock rhythm and the backbeat, in alternation with a bass drum sound on the first and third beats. At this point, rhythm guitar and drums are marking the regular rock rhythmic layer, while bass and lead guitar play against this regular rhythm. Nowhere in the rhythm do we hear any instrument marking off the beat; our sense of the beat emerges from the interaction of the other rhythms, rather than some kind of steady timekeeping. The absence of beat-keeping gives the rhythm a flow that is not present in "Satisfaction" and other songs that evidence a similar approach to rhythm.

The rhythmic texture is also richer, with several rhythmic layers in the drum part, a steady but occasionally syncopated bass line, plus riffs and insistent rhythms in the guitar parts. The chorus features not only vocal harmony but also a freer bass line and a high obbligato guitar part—all of which produce a rich, vibrant rhythmic texture.

The increased density of the texture and the guitar halo during the chorus are just two of several features that the Stones add to this otherwise straightforward verse/chorus rock song to give it an individual character. Also noteworthy are the addition of piano and maracas, the extended tag, and the alternation between static harmony in the instrumental sections and the verse and active harmony during the chorus. In any noteworthy Rolling Stones song, there are always features—some obvious, some more subtle—that lift the song well above the ordinary.

The Rolling Stones' sound was the result of teamwork. What they did best, they did as a group, even though at the time this song was recorded, there was considerable friction between Richards and Brian Jones. Their rock-defining groove grew out of the interaction among all the band members. So did the loose, somewhat unkempt texture. Although Jagger is the visual focus of the band, there is no one musician whose talent dominates the sound. Finally, there are the sounds—most notably Jagger's singing and Richards's guitar playing—that project the Stones' particular kind of insolence. Shortly after this recording was released, the Rolling Stones began billing themselves as "the World's Greatest Rock and Roll Band." It wasn't bragging because they could back it up.

8-3 Heavy Metal in the Seventies

No music of the rock era has been more misunderstood than heavy metal. It has been vilified as cretinous not only by those outside of rock but also by numerous rock critics and musicians. Until the nineties, surveys of any Top 40/50/100 list of major acts of the rock era generally gave metal groups short shrift. The only names likely to have appeared were Led Zeppelin, a group that quickly transcended the boundaries of the genre, and Van Halen, whose music crossed over to the pop charts fairly early in their career. Seminal metal bands, most notably Black Sabbath, are conspicuous by their absence.

For much of its history, heavy metal has existed with its audience in a largely self-contained world. The music's main outlets have been concert performances and recordings. Metal has received relatively little airplay, especially on mainstream recordings.

For many years, its audience was almost exclusively young males, typically disaffected and from middle- or lower-class environments. (More recently, the audience for heavy metal has broadened to include both older males—those who have grown up with it—and females.) Immersion in heavy metal has been a rite of passage for many teens around the world. Audience members formed powerful bonds with the acts whom they admired, as strong as any in rock.

Critics of metal have targeted what they perceive as its crudeness and cheapness—such as the ponderous riffs of some metal bands or the makeup worn by Kiss and Alice Cooper. Yet metal has been home to many of rock's great geniuses, from Ritchie Blackmore and Jimmy Page to Eddie Van Halen, Randy

Rhoads, and Yngwie Malmsteen. Perhaps more than any other rock style, heavy metal values and demands technical excellence.

There is some confusion regarding the source of the term *heavy metal*, as it applies to rock. Everyone agrees that the term appeared in rock as part of the lyric ("heavy metal thunder") in Steppenwolf's 1968 song, "**Born to Be Wild**." Its history prior to that is less clear. Rock mythology has the term coming most directly from William Burroughs's *Naked Lunch*. That source is myth: Burroughs does not use the phrase anywhere in the book. In any event, it was in common use by the early seventies.

8–3a Sounds and Influences

Metal's sound signature is distortion—*extreme* distortion. It has other widely used musical conventions: blues-derived pentatonic and modal scales, often unharmonized; power chords; extended, flamboyant solos; ear-splitting volume; screamed-out, often incomprehensible lyrics; and pounding rhythms, often performed at breakneck speed. Still, the feature that most immediately identifies heavy metal is distortion.

Heavy metal has clear roots in the blues, especially electric blues. Its diabolical overtones, half-sung, half-spoken high-register vocal style, lack of harmonic movement, and reliance on riffs easily reach back to Robert Johnson ("**Come on in My Kitchen**"). Power chords and endlessly repeated riffs trace back to John Lee Hooker ("**Boogie Chillen'**"), and heavy distortion to mid-fifties bluesmen ("Rocket 88"). Blues influence is also indirect. It comes into heavy metal through the early music of the Kinks (for example, "You Really Got Me"), as well as Hendrix, Clapton, and the other blues-based rock guitarists of the late sixties. In transmuting blues rhetoric into heavy metal, bands intensified and stylized these features.

Interestingly, classical music has been another source of inspiration for many metal artists. From it, they have not only borrowed the idea of virtuosity but have expropriated virtuosic patterns from classical works, as we'll hear following. This emphasis on transcendent instrumental skills shows up not only in the guitar solos but also in the tight ensemble (typically, not a feature of blues style) and pedal-to-the-metal tempos.

Modality has been another seminal influence. Modes are virtually universal in heavy metal; it is hard to imagine a metal song using conventional harmony. There are several good reasons why metal bands used modes. First, they formed the scales of much English folksong: most of the early metal bands were British, so modality was part of their musical heritage. Second, modes were the basis of a fresh new harmonic language within rock, as we heard in the music of the Rolling Stones, the Beatles, and others. Third, the African American pentatonic scale maps onto most modes. In fact, modes can be understood as an expansion of the melodic resources of the pentatonic scale. Fourth, precisely because it is the basis of so much folksong, as well as medieval and Renaissance classical music, it connotes archaic, even mythical, times. This meshes smoothly with the gothic element in much heavy metal: the beginning to "**Stairway to Heaven**" seems to turn the clock back about 800 years.

Heavy metal is all of these influences, yet something apart from them and in many cases more than the sum of them. From these influences, metal musicians forged one of the most distinctive styles of the rock era. We will study this style, as realized in the music of the three bands that, more than any others, defined early heavy metal.

Joe Elliot, lead vocalist for Def Leppard, was quoted as saying, "In 1971, there were only three bands that mattered. Led Zeppelin, Black Sabbath, and Deep Purple."

art rock A rock substyle that sought to elevate rock from teen entertainment to artistic statement, often by drawing on or reworking classical compositions (e.g., Emerson, Lake, and Palmer's version of Mussorgsky's Pictures at an Exhibition). Art rock was often distinguished by the use of electronic effects and mood music-like textures far removed from the propulsive rhythms of early rock.

His statement summarizes the prevailing consensus. Of the three, Black Sabbath stayed the closest to the musical features that defined early metal. Although they could lay down a riff with anyone ("**Smoke on the Water**"), Deep Purple strayed far enough from metal basics that some critics considered them an **art rock** band. From the start, Led Zeppelin was much more than "just" a heavy metal band. Their music covered a broad range of styles, even at times within a single song; indeed, we discuss their music in a different context. The differences among the three bands make clear that heavy metal was anything but a monolithic style.

8–3b Black Sabbath

Take a poll among serious metal fans. Ask them to name the first heavy metal band. Chances are that Black Sabbath will receive the most votes. They were not the first band to play in a heavy metal style. Some writers credit Blue Cheer, a very loud San Francisco band. Others cite Led Zeppelin or Iron Butterfly. But Black Sabbath was the first band whose music consistently laid out the most widely used conventions of the heavy metal world. When you hear Black Sabbath, you're generally hearing heavy metal.

The name Black Sabbath evokes the occult, as it was supposed to. So did almost everything else about them. Black Sabbath's shows would feature crosses burned on stage and other images of devil worship. The lyrics of their songs often sound like they come straight from a gothic horror film. And the music formed the ideal backdrop for the words and images.

Black Sabbath was the third incarnation of a blues band from Birmingham, England. Vocalist Ozzy Osbourne (b. 1948), guitarist Tommy Iommi (b. 1948), bassist Terry "Geezer" Butler (b. 1949), and drummer Bill Ward (b. 1948) first came together as Polka Tuck, then changed their name to Earth. By 1969, they had become Black Sabbath; their first album appeared a year later.

Through relentless touring, they developed an international audience. As a result, their second album, *Paranoid* (1971), sold over 4 million copies. They remained the top metal act for the first half of the decade. With the ascendancy of **punk** and **disco** in the late seventies, their popularity waned, and Osbourne left Black Sabbath in 1979 to front his own highly successful and notorious group.

punk A rock style that emerged in the late 1970s characterized musically by relatively simple instrumentation, rhythms, and production. The Ramones and the Sex Pistols were among the best-known punk bands.

disco A dance music that rose to popularity in the mid seventies. Disco songs typically had a relentless beat; a complex rhythmic texture, usually with a 16-beat rhythm; and rich orchestration, typically an augmented rhythm section with horns and strings.

Cultivation of the occult may have been new to popular music but not classical music. The early Romantics (around 1830) also flirted with the diabolical. With his breathtaking talent and cadaverlike appearance, the violinist Niccolo Paganini was thought by many to have made a pact with the devil (long before Robert Johnson). According to his program for the work, Hector Berlioz's *Symphonie Fantastique* depicts a wild opium dream, with goblins, an execution, and a musical citation from the Mass for the Dead.

"**Paranoid**," the title track of their second album, typifies the sound of Black Sabbath and, by extension, early heavy metal. In its original studio version (there are other recordings of the song), it defines the salient features of early heavy metal. They include:

- Power-trio instrumentation: lead vocal, guitar, bass, and drums
- Substantial distortion in both guitar and bass
- Riffs built from power chords, which are repeated throughout most of the song

- Chord progressions developed from modal scales
- A strong, aggressive, clearly marked rock beat at a fast tempo, with syncopation mainly in the vocal line and the occasional riff
- A dramatic vocal style, in which the boundary between speech and song is often blurred
- A very loud dynamic level

This song offers a reductive approach to rock rhythm. The timekeeping is more prominent—guitar, bass, and drums all mark the eight-beat rock rhythm layer through most of the song. Most of the rhythmic conflict occurs with Osbourne's singing; he is constantly off-beat. There is not the rich interplay that we just heard in "Jumping Jack Flash." Nevertheless, Black Sabbath's approach to rock rhythm in "Paranoid" generates tremendous momentum. It is an approach that grew out of the breakthroughs of the late sixties.

Sound and Space, Chords and Power in Heavy Metal

The interaction of distortion, power chords, and **modal harmony** has played a central role in defining the sound of heavy metal. There would seem to be a causal relationship among distortion, the absence of conventional harmony, and the heavy metal esthetic. Consider that rock, like most music, defines a sound space. Typically, the main melodic line and the bass line roughly define the upper and lower boundaries of that space; guitar parts (rhythm guitar in the instrumental sections; both guitars during vocals) lie between these boundaries. The extensive use of power chords and distortion fill this space sonically, giving the music enormous impact. We consider how and why this happens.

> **modal harmony**
> Chords built from modal scales, rather than major and minor scales. Modal scales are common in British folk music.

Power Chords, Distortion, and Sound Space

Power chords are more than melody and less than (conventional) chords. In one respect, they are chords, because they feature several sounds played simultaneously. However, they are not conventional chords because the extra notes do not complete the harmony or even imply a complete harmony. Instead they are essentially overtones: other tones that vibrate in simple ratios with the main note. Moreover, the relationship among notes of a power chord never changes. Harmonizing a melody or riff with a series of power chords has the effect of thickening it, as if someone had painted over a line drawn in pencil with a thick-tipped brush. Often, the bass doubles the guitar line, which makes the line sound even thicker.

When enhanced with extreme distortion, power chords—with or without the bass doubled—fill the sound space with overtones and undertones (from the power chords) and white noise (randomly vibrating sounds over a wide range of frequency). This creates a mass of sound that stretches from below the lowest notes of the bass to beyond the highest notes of the power chords.

Power Chords, Power, and the Blues

Power chords imply power on at least two levels. The more obvious is the thickening of a melodic line, which is delivered with extreme distortion at high volume. Its effect is similar to a sumo wrestler invading your space. The more subtle, but just as telling, level has to do with the typical sequences of power chords in heavy metal songs.

In songs like "Paranoid," heavy metal groups like Black Sabbath reject not only conventional chords but also conventional chord progressions. One reason for abandoning conventional chord progressions may have to do with the message of the style. Conventional chord progressions—like the "Heart and Soul" progression heard in pre-rock popular songs and in so much melody-oriented rock-era music—often support songs that talk about romance. Conventional harmony implies movement toward a goal—the return to the home chord—via a well-defined path. Because the path is so firmly entrenched, it is possible to create expressive musical moments by deviating from the path and to control patterns of tension (being away from the home chord) and release (arriving at the home chord). This parallels in certain respects the negotiation that is part of a romantic relationship: if arrival at the home chord is marriage, or at least togetherness, then the progression that precedes it is the courtship.

By contrast, harmony in heavy metal is about *power*. Metal songs seldom negotiate harmonically via adherence to conventional progressions; more often they slam from one chord to the next. Particular sequences of chords are more common than others, but they do not create the same kind of musical tension and release as "heart and soul"–type progressions. Indeed, use of conventional chords and chord progressions would undermine the harmonic impact of the style; it would sound like nerd metal.

The roots of this practice seem to grow out of a radical reinterpretation of blues harmony. (Recall that most early heavy metal bands, including Black Sabbath and Led Zeppelin, first incarnated as blues bands.) As practiced by Delta bluesmen, blues harmony was itself a radical reinterpretation of conventional harmony. Bluesmen adapted conventional chords—I, IV, V—to the blues. But instead of arranging them in typical progressions, they simply shifted from one chord to the next, much like heavy metal guitarists shifted from one power chord to the next. In a conventional setting, I, IV, and V are dynamic; they imply a specific kind of movement toward a goal. As used in the blues, however, they become essentially static objects. The sense of directionality all but disappears. As blues entered popular music and jazz, it reacquired more conventional harmonies, which were interpolated between or substituted for the chords that outline the blues progression. This dilutes the elemental power of the blues. One would be hard-pressed to locate a deep blues with conventional harmonies marbled into the progression. By contrast, the harmonic strategies used by heavy metal groups are much truer to the conception of those bluesmen whose music was largely untouched by mainstream popular music. Although the chords and chord progressions are different from the blues progression, they are conceptually more in tune with deep blues, because harmonies simply shift away from the home chord and return.

Black Sabbath songs like "Paranoid" are in essence an introductory course in heavy metal. From them, we can learn the basics of the style. However, when compared to other early heavy metal songs, such as the two discussed following, one element of the style is conspicuous by its absence: virtuosity. Tommy Iommi has neither the technical skill nor the musical imagination to match Ritchie Blackmore, Jimmy Page, and other early guitar geniuses. We explore this and other aspects of heavy metal next, in the music of Deep Purple.

8-3c Deep Purple

Like Black Sabbath and other British groups, Deep Purple went through several incarnations before finding their groove. Theirs involved not only changes in personnel but also radical style changes. Their lineup during their most successful period, from 1970 to 1973, included vocalist Ian Gillan (b. 1945), guitarist Ritchie Blackmore (b. 1945), keyboardist Jon Lord (1941–2012), bassist Roger Glover (b. 1945), and drummer Ian Paice (b. 1948). The inclusion of a keyboard in a metal group was unusual. However, Lord was an important creative voice within the group. Among the first recordings of the newly constituted group was Lord's *Concerto for Group and Orchestra*, which Deep Purple recorded with the Royal Philharmonic. At this point, they were marching in step with classically influenced art rockers like Yes, King Crimson, and Emerson, Lake & Palmer.

However, the band soon shifted direction, focusing more on volume (they were listed in the *Guinness Book of World Records* as the loudest rock band) and heavy guitar riffs. Nevertheless, the classical influence was still apparent in both Lord and Blackmore's playing. Both were expert musicians who borrowed as heavily from the classics as they did from the blues. "**Highway Star**," a song from the album *Machine Head* (1972), shows how they combined the two influences.

"Highway Star" clearly demonstrates the influence of classical music, and especially the music of the early eighteenth-century composers J. S. Bach and Antonio Vivaldi. Blackmore acknowledged his classical sources: "For example, the chord progression in the 'Highway Star' solo . . . is a Bach progression." And the solo is "just arpeggios based on Bach." Lord also adapts the melodic patterns and fast even rhythms of Bach and Vivaldi to rock. (Both solos are overdubbed with harmony parts, further evidence of the skill of both players. It's difficult enough to play such fast, intricate passages, but even harder to synchronize a second line perfectly with the first.)

Blackmore's solo shows one way in which classical and blues influences come together in heavy metal: side by side, rather than blended. Blackmore's solo begins with blues-based riffs. After gaining considerable momentum, it reaches a climactic point where more energy is required. It is at this point that Blackmore shifts into classical high gear. The type of figuration that Blackmore uses here, like its Bach and Vivaldi models, is high-energy music. Quite simply, Blackmore wanted speed, and he went to Bach and Vivaldi to get it, because they were excellent models for how to play fast and intelligibly at the same time. After about 30 seconds, the solo returns to less active but more emotionally charged blues-based riffs.

In "Highway Star," blues-based and Baroque-inspired musical ideas coexist happily. That's especially true in Blackmore's solo, because its pacing makes the transition seem perfectly natural. Lord's **interpolation** of classical figuration has more of a "ready, set, go" quality. In both cases, however, the consistency of sound—both in the guitar and keyboard timbres and in the rhythmic undercurrent—helps link them together smoothly.

Deep Purple's infusion of classical elements into heavy metal brought new dimensions to the music. The most emulated was virtuosity, especially among individual performers. A list of rock's most technically proficient guitarists includes a disproportionately high number of heavy metal players. Indeed, for a handful of top guitarists (and those who wished to play at that level), Baroque music became a primary source for musical ideas.

The infusion of Baroque musical elements also led to a more straightforward rhythmic approach: classical music is seldom as syncopated as good rock music. The rhythmic excitement comes primarily from the speed—the fast tempo of the song and the double-time solo lines. As in "Paranoid," the rock rhythm is in the forefront; the primary syncopations occur in the vocal line and the answering riffs. However, there is much more rhythmic variety in this song because of the many contrasts—between vocals and solos and in the periodic breaks between sections.

A final note about virtuosity: in heavy metal it is not just in the solos. As "Highway Star" evidences, heavy metal also places a premium on precise ensemble playing, often at breakneck speeds. This is a different kind of virtuosity, but no less challenging, and it occurs more frequently in heavy metal than in any other important rock substyle.

interpolation The insertion of a song into a musical comedy for which it was not written. Interpolation was common in the early years of musical comedy, when producers would insert a song into a show simply because it was a hit.

8-3d Heavy Metal and Early Seventies Rock

Heavy metal took the blues and transmuted them into music of unprecedented power. It was powerful in an absolute sonic sense: no music was louder. But there was also power in the mastery of craft. Like the alchemists of old, heavy metal performers diligently studied ancient formulas: in this case, the musical patterns of Bach and Vivaldi. These they adapted to rock, then juxtaposed them with elemental musical material. Heavy metal evoked supernatural, or at least paranormal, power, especially in the group personas of Black Sabbath and Led Zeppelin. At a time when the women's rights movement was in the ascendancy—bras being burned, NOW being formed—metal bands projected masculine power, to the point where performers could sport skillfully styled long hair, wear makeup, and sing higher than many women without fear of abandoning their sexual identity, à la David Bowie. And heavy metal wielded power over its audience, creating an extremely loyal fan base. Metalheads were not casual listeners or consumers; Black Sabbath's *Paranoid* went platinum on the strength of the group's tours, not airplay.

What heavy metal gained in power, it often sacrificed in subtlety. It was not typically a vehicle for expressing the pain of love lost or the joy of love found. It was not a music of nuance, except perhaps in the blues-inspired inflections in guitar solos. Even songs that talked about man–woman relationships did so in an almost impersonal manner.

Most of the conventions of heavy metal—distortion; massive amplification; use of modes, pentatonic scales, and power chords; basic rhythms; power-trio instrumental nucleus—were also part of the vocabulary of all hard rock music in the early seventies. What metal bands did was to take these features and streamline or amplify them to give them more impact. Metal bands used more distortion and played more loudly. They took rock's shift away from traditional harmony several steps further by using conventional chords sparingly or, in some cases, abandoning harmony altogether. Its guitarists played power chords with more "power"—that is, greater resonance—and used them almost exclusively, and they developed more flamboyantly virtuosic styles. Its riffs and rhythms were stronger and more pervasive: at times, vocal lines seemed to ride on the riffs, like a whitewater raft. Indeed, both examples discussed here feature an aggressive form of rock rhythm throughout most of the song, with the rock beat layer hammered out by several instruments.

Above all, the music is *there* more. One quality that distinguishes heavy metal from most other styles is the sheer amount of nonvocal music. Even more important, music is the primary source of heavy metal's overwhelming impact and expressive power. Words serve a largely explanatory role. Most of the audience at a metal concert will know the lyrics to songs, but they *feel* the music. Many writers have observed that rock is ritual. If so, then heavy metal quickly became rock's most ritualistic music.

8-4 The Liberation of Rock and Roll

By the early seventies, the rock revolution was over. It was evident on the charts and in corporate offices. It was evident in the flurry of hastily arranged musical marriages between rock and pre-rock styles: pop rock, rock musicals, jazz fusion. Most fundamentally, however, it was evident in the music itself. It took rock musicians about fifteen years to really get it—that is, to completely assimilate the numerous musical influences and transform them into the now-dominant style and to become comfortable with the conventions of this new style.

In this chapter, we have followed two aspects of this maturation process: the assimilation of deep blues and the evolution of rock rhythm. We have heard how deep blues permeated key aspects of rock, most notably the vocal style, the use of repeated riffs, and the dense, dark texture produced by instruments playing in a low register. And we have heard rock rhythm gain in flow and energy as the musicians purge it of the last remnants of rock and roll. These final two examples, recorded by Led Zeppelin and the Who, illustrate the ways in which musicians could play with rock rhythm when they reached a comfort zone with its essential elements. Unlike the previous heavy metal songs, in which rock rhythm is explicit and in the forefront, these songs feature much more varied textures, including long stretches where rock rhythm is implicit. We begin with the Who's **"Won't Get Fooled Again."**

8–4a The Who

In 1969, Alan R. Pearlman founded ARP Instruments in order to produce **synthesizers** capable of creating a variety of electronic sounds. His first synthesizer, released in 1970, was a fairly large machine. His second model, the ARP 2600, which was released in 1971, was portable and flexible enough to be used in live performances, although it was *monophonic*—that is, capable of playing only one sound at a time.

To promote his new instruments, Pearlman gave units to some of the top rock and R&B musicians of the era, in return for permission to use their names in promoting his product. Among his first clients was the Who's Pete Townshend. Judging by the almost immediate results, Townshend was fascinated by the synthesizer and the cutting-edge technology it represented. He featured it on several tracks of their 1971 album *Who's Next*, where it served as the best possible advertising for ARP and its instruments.

The Who had come together as a group in 1964. Vocalist Roger Daltrey (b. 1944), guitarist Pete Townshend (b. 1945), and bassist John Entwhistle (1944–2002) had been part of a group called the High Numbers; they became the Who when drummer Keith Moon (1947–1978) joined them. A year later, their music began to appear on the British charts. Their early hits, most notably **"My Generation"** (1965) and **"Substitute"** (both 1966), speak in an ironic tone: indeed, "My Generation" became the anthem for the "live hard, die young, and don't trust anyone over 30" crowd.

Musically, they were a powerhouse band with a heavy bass sound that betrayed the strong influence of sixties rhythm and blues. Townshend's power chords, Entwhistle's talented bass playing, and Moon's flamboyant drumming gave Daltrey's searing voice a rock-solid foundation. Still, it seemed that they were no more than a singles band, incapable of anything more than a series of good three-minute songs. That perception began to change with the release of the album *Happy Jack* (1967), which included an extended piece, **"A Quick One While He's Away,"** and it was dramatically altered with the release of the rock opera *Tommy* in 1969.

In 1970, Townshend conceived of a sequel to *Tommy*, which he called *Lifehouse*, that was to be even grander. He eventually put the project aside but incorporated some of the material into an album of singles, entitled *Who's Next*. Unlike *Tommy* and several subsequent efforts (such as *Quadrophenia*), *Who's Next* is not thematic. It is simply a collection of good songs, among them "Won't Get Fooled Again."

In "Won't Get Fooled Again," Townshend spotlights the synthesizer right from the start. A steady stream of kaleidoscopically changing chords marking the eight-beat rhythm emerges from the opening chord. The band returns about 30 seconds later, at first intermittently, then settling into a groove. As the song proper gets

synthesizers A family of electronic instruments in which sounds are produced electronically, either by generating a waveform within the machine or by digitally recording acoustic sounds (e.g., the tones of a piano). Most, but not all, synthesizers are operated by a keyboard.

underway, it's clear that the synthesizer chords serve a particular purpose: they are, in effect, a futuristic rhythm guitar, pitched in a high register instead of the more characteristic midrange, but providing steady reinforcement of the rock rhythmic layer throughout the song. Musically, there is a direct line between Chuck Berry's transformation of boogie-woogie patterns and the synthesizer chords; both serve the same purpose.

> Because the ARP 2600 could only play one note at a time, Townshend must have created the synthesizer chords by overdubbing. In performance, the Who used a tape of the synthesizer part rather than an actual performer.

In this song, the insistent rhythm of the synthesizer chords seems to liberate the rest of the band. Townshend's power chords and riffs, Entwhistle's active and free bass lines, and Moon's explosive drumming all play off of this steady rhythm. It is this interplay between the steady rhythm of the synthesizer and the rest of the group that gives the song its extraordinary rhythmic energy.

Townshend's use of the synthesizer is innovative on two levels. One is simply the use of it—the ARP was a brand-new machine, and the Minimoog with which it competed had only been available for about two years. The more compelling inventiveness is his integration of the synthesizer into the heart of the band—a real novelty at the time.

The synthesizer seems to expand not only the sound world created in "Won't Get Fooled Again" but also the size of the song. It is a sprawling song—over eight and a half minutes of music. The long synthesizer introduction and even longer interlude toward the end provide a dramatic contrast to the vocal sections, and its steady rhythm underpins the electrifying group jams in the extended instrumental passages.

Here innovative technology enhances the basic sound and rhythm of a rock band. In both its featured role (where it contrasts with the heart of the song) and in its supporting role, the synthesizer part adds a significant dimension to both sound and rhythm. The groove is so compelling that the lyrics almost seem incidental; we lose ourselves in the sounds and rhythms of the song. It makes clear that the Who never forgot how to rock and roll.

8-4b Led Zeppelin

Most of the important contributions to the development of rock-era music have come from two kinds of artists: those who help define or affirm its core values by doing one thing supremely well (for example, Chuck Berry, the Rolling Stones, James Brown, the Sex Pistols) and those whose curiosity compels them to explore a wide range of influences and bring them into their music, thereby expanding the boundaries of rock (for example, Buddy Holly, Frank Zappa, Stevie Wonder, the Talking Heads). Few rock-era acts have been capable of contributing in both areas. One that did achieve this was the Who; we will encounter the boundary-stretching side of their musical personality in **Chapter 10**. Another was Led Zeppelin.

Although often cited as a seminal heavy metal band, Led Zeppelin ultimately defies categorization. From *Led Zeppelin* (1969), their first album, it was clear that heavy metal was just one aspect of their musical personality. Their center is clearly the blues; their version of heavy metal evolved from it. At the same time, there seems to be nothing in their musical world that is not fair game for appropriation.

What's particularly interesting in their music, all through their career, is the way in which influences bleed into one another. Their music may cover a lot of stylistic territory, but it is not compartmentalized.

The range of their music came mainly from guitarist Jimmy Page (b. 1944), whose curiosity led him to not only immerse himself in the blues but to seek out exotic musical styles (for example, Flamenco and East Indian music). Led Zeppelin's front man was vocalist Robert Plant (b. 1948), who was Page's second choice as lead singer but who turned out to be an ideal voice for the group. Bassist John Paul Jones (b. 1946) was, with Page, part of the British music scene in the late sixties; drummer John Bonham (1948–1980) was a friend of Plant's from their Birmingham days. Page also produced their albums. His production skills were as important a component of their success as his guitar playing: he brought a wonderful ear for sonority and texture to their music.

Page and Plant shared a deep interest in the mystic, the mythical, and the occult. This interest would increasingly inform their work, from untitled albums to cryptic covers, sparse liner notes, nonreferential lyrics, and numerous archaic musical influences.

Another quality that sets their music apart from every other group of the era is their ability to establish, then reconcile, extremes. The extremes are evident in virtually every aspect of their music making. Plant sang higher than most other male vocalists (and many females, too). Their ensemble playing was more daring, their riffs more elaborate and beat-defying, the contrasts within and between songs deeper and more striking. In some of their most memorable music—such as **"Dazed and Confused"** and "Stairway to Heaven"—they reconcile many of the extremes that characterize their music *within* a single song. These songs cover an enormous emotional and musical range: they can be tender one moment and overpowering the next.

The music of Led Zeppelin evolved considerably from their first album to *Physical Graffiti* (1975). That, coupled with the wide range of their music, makes it difficult to represent their achievement adequately with a discussion of a single album, much less a single song. However, the album that best captures the salient qualities of their music is the untitled fourth album, known variously as *Led Zeppelin IV, Zoso,* or the Runes LP. The music on the tracks ranges from the unbridled power of **"Rock and Roll"** to the delicacy of the acoustic **"The Battle of Evermore,"** which provides clear evidence of the group's mystical/mythical bent. "Stairway to Heaven," perhaps the best-known song on the album, merges both.

"Black Dog," another track from the album, demonstrates Led Zeppelin's connection with heavy metal and their role in the continuing evolution of rock rhythm. From the very beginning of the song, it is clear that they have internalized the feel of rock rhythm. Consider how it begins.

- A noodle on the guitar
- Plant singing without accompaniment
- The band playing an extended, blues-based melodic line, without a vocal

This is a major step forward in rhythmic freedom from typical sixties hard rock songs. Typically, these songs start with a guitar riff that sets the tempo. Other instruments layer in, setting up the groove. That doesn't happen here. Early on, we feel the beat strictly from Plant's vocal line. The silence that follows and the strung-out instrumental line make it difficult to group the beats into measures.

As they demonstrate in "Black Dog," Led Zeppelin became so comfortable with the rock groove that they could play with it—boldly. Even the refrain-like riff under Plant's "Oh, yeah" is completely syncopated. Throughout, the song has a great beat, but the timekeeping that does take place happens very much in the background. Indeed, in much of the song, we do not sense the beat at all, or sense it only from the rhythm of the main melody; what timekeeping there is in this song is purposeful and specific, rather than routine. In terms of freeing rhythm while still retaining the groove, "Black Dog" goes about as far as possible.

The extended instrumental lines in "Black Dog" also point to another feature of Led Zeppelin's approach to rock—one that would profoundly influence heavy metal bands. In effect, they harness solo-like lines within a tight group conception. In rock, guitar solos can be spectacular displays, but they can also undermine the collective conception that is at the heart of a rock groove. Page's solution was to work out these lines and integrate them into a group conception. For future heavy metal bands, this aspect of the recording was key: one of the marvels of good heavy metal performances is the tight ensemble of a band as they negotiate challenging and intricate passages. We can hear its roots in this recording.

"Black Dog" is closer to "pure" heavy metal than any other song on the album. It incorporates many of the features we expect from a metal song: Plant's high vocals, a riff by heavily distorted guitar and bass, loud volume, and a strong beat (some of the time). However, there are several differences from prototypical metal. Plant begins singing without accompaniment. The guitar/bass riff that answers Plant is long, convoluted, and full of rhythmic surprises, instead of short and simple. These and other dramatic contrasts within the song confirm Led Zeppelin's emphasis on extremes.

Despite, or perhaps partly because of, the mystery with which they enveloped themselves, Led Zeppelin gained a large, loyal audience. Their tours sold out and broke attendance records, and all of their recordings went platinum. They are still popular, almost three decades after they disbanded. There is no ambiguity as to why: their music is a rare combination of almost unrestrained power and subtle artistry, of raw emotion and superbly calculated craft. For some, the mix was too heady: the band never attracted the broad-based audience of the Beatles or Elton John. But for a large core, it was just the right strength. Millions of loyal fans remain unsatiated.

"Won't Get Fooled Again" and "Black Dog" show in quite different ways the rhythmic independence achieved by elite rock musicians when they felt comfortable with the rhythmic foundation of rock. The Who use a novel instrument as a substitute for a rhythm guitar, while Led Zeppelin dispense with persistent timekeeping altogether. That they can use this minimal timekeeping as a springboard for great rock is not only a testament to the excellence of both groups but also to the rapid and dramatic evolution of rock rhythm from the mid-sixties through the early seventies.

8-5 The Essence of Rock

At this point, we are back where we began. If we were to include one more song in this chapter, to affirm rock's core values, the Rolling Stones' "It's Only Rock 'n Roll (But I Like It)" would be an ideal choice. As presented in the first chapter, these values were simply an assertion. The examples in this chapter have provided us with a dynamic view of rock style; we can now hear the classic sound of the Rolling Stones' rock and roll as a product of an evolutionary process that began well before *rock and roll* was a musical term. Our discussion has focused on two central aspects of this evolution: the maturation of rock rhythm (the most essential feature of the style) and the assimilation of deep blues (the dominant influence on hard rock).

8–5a Assimilating Deep Blues

Led Zeppelin's "Black Dog" simultaneously demonstrates rock's deep debt to deep blues and its distance from blues style. The blues connection is clear in the rough vocal sound, the dark texture in those passages where the band plays continuously, and the use of riffs—and the nasty attitude that these features help project. The distance is evident in the differences between this song and a conventional blues. Unlike blues singers, who sing in their natural range, Plant sings very high—like doo-wop lead vocalists but with a far more aggressive sound. The extended riff at the beginning, while based on the African American pentatonic scale, is far more elaborate than a typical blues riff. The dark texture is mainly a result of register: low and low middle. However, instead of the riff free-for-all commonly heard in a blues song, the lines are carefully worked out, with guitar and bass moving in tandem.

With regard to rhythm, not only is the basic beat different—a rock beat versus a shuffle beat—but there are long stretches where there is no timekeeping. These are much longer than the stop-time sections one might hear in a blues song. It is as if Led Zeppelin has taken characteristic elements of blues style and pushed them to an extreme: really high vocal, extended riffs, expanded stop-time breaks. In the process, they thoroughly transform the blues elements into something quite new. In this song, and in the other three examples from the early seventies, blues elements have been seamlessly integrated into the fabric of each song.

In the first four songs, the influence of deep blues is more distinct. Still, all four songs—even the two power-trio songs, which are based on blues form—are far removed stylistically from a conventional electric blues style. In "Jumping Jack Flash," the blues connection is apparent mainly in the lyric, Jagger's singing, the thick texture, and the attitude that these features project. And it is this attitude— realized far more forcefully in this music than in rock and roll and early rock—that gives hard rock and heavy metal such power. In these songs, we hear the deep blues influence and the evolution beyond blues style.

8–5b The Maturation of Rock Rhythm

The maturation of rock rhythm was largely a process of liberation. Rock rhythm eventually arrived at its now-classic realization primarily by eliminating timekeeping at beat speed and increasing the amount of syncopation and other forms of rhythmic play. We hear this as a point of arrival in a journey that began with Chuck Berry's rock and roll–defining songs. Recall the opening of Chuck Berry's "**Johnny B. Goode**": in it we hear the key elements of rock rhythm: the eight-beat rock rhythmic layer in his rhythm guitar part, the syncopations in the lead guitar line, and the backbeat in the drum part. However, in terms of rhythm, Berry is swimming upstream. The rest of the band, and especially the bass player, are playing in a swing rhythm. "Rock and roll" became "rock" when the rest of the band—the drummer and the bass player—began emphasizing rock rhythm over the beat. (We noted this in the discussion of Roy Orbison, the Kingsmen, and the Beach Boys.)

In this chapter, we pick up the trail in mid decade. In "You Really Got Me" and "Satisfaction," the most prominent regular rhythm is the beat, and the dominant rhythmic conflict is a syncopated riff that is repeated throughout. The marking of the beat disappears in the next three songs, but at the same time, there is a substantial increase in rhythmic play over the regular rhythms, especially in the songs by Cream and the Jimi Hendrix Experience. The final four songs illustrate contrasting extremes of mature rock rhythm. "Paranoid" and "Highway Star" oppose strong rock rhythm timekeeping with equally strong syncopations—like two rams butting heads. "Won't Get Fooled Again" and "Black Dog" represent the opposite extreme, where rock rhythm timekeeping is in the background or missing altogether, and the patterns that conflict with the regular rhythms are in the forefront.

8-5c A Timeless Music

The years around 1970 were defining for the history of rock; it is during this time that rock emerged as a fully developed style. Up to this point, we hear rock musicians restlessly seeking to discover the optimal approach to rock rhythm; they find it around 1970. As we become aware of this process, we can place songs in time by how far they have come from Chuck Berry's initial efforts to define rock rhythm. Similarly, we can hear the increasing influence of blues style, until the point at which it is completely absorbed into rock. This also occurs around 1970.

From this point on, what groups from the Stones to AC/DC have called "rock and roll" becomes a timeless music. Its conventions are clear and widely understood, and they remain substantially unchanged. The rhythms and sounds of rock-era music would continue to develop beyond this point, as we will discover in the chapters that follow. But the music in the latter part of this chapter defines the core values of rock in a way that neither the rock that preceded it nor the rock that evolved beyond it does. "Rock and roll" is the lodestar of rock-era music: its central reference point.

CHAPTER 9

SAN FRANCISCO AND THE DIVERSITY OF ROCK

Learning Objectives:

1) Identify the various regional dialects of rock that were present in the 1960s.

2) Discuss how the social and political climate of the 1960s influenced the various styles of rock.

3) Describe Janis Joplin's contribution to the San Francisco rock scene.

4) Compare the differences between British and North American rock.

5) List key musical elements found in **Latin rock** that are derived from Latin and rock genres.

6) Audibly identify a **16-beat rhythm** in a musical example.

Chapter Introduction

From the start, rock has not been a single style, but a heterogeneous mix of styles linked by common musical features and shared attitudes. This became even more apparent during the latter part of the sixties, when rock became the dominant popular music and simultaneously went in several different directions, musically and geographically.

We may perceive the diversity of rock through geography in two ways. One is to note the numerous regional dialects of rock that surfaced in the sixties: in the United States, there was surf music from southern California, soul music from Memphis, Motown from Detroit, and southern rock from the Southeast. More significantly, rock became the first truly international popular music with the rise of the British bands. Their music added several dialects to the musical language that was rock.

The other way is to observe the activity within a geographical region. During the latter part of the sixties, one good place to do this was the San Francisco Bay Area. The region was the home not only to several important acid rock bands, but also to such diverse styles as Santana's Latin rock, Sly and the Family Stone's proto-funk, Creedence Clearwater Revival's all-American rock, and much more. We sample this diversity after a brief discussion of the culture that supported it.

9-1 The Counterculture

Those who came of age during the latter half of the sixties grew up in a world far different from the world of their parents. A decided majority experienced neither the hardships of the Great Depression nor the traumas of the two mid century wars: World War II and the Korean War. They were in elementary school during the McCarthy witch-hunt; in most cases, it had far less impact on them than it did on their parents. A good number came from families that were comfortable financially, so that as teens they had money to spend and time to spend it.

A sizable and vocal segment of these young people rejected the values of the group they pejoratively called the "establishment." They saw the establishment as excessively conservative, bigoted, materialistic, resistant to social change, obsessed with communism and locked into a potentially deadly arms race, and clueless about sexuality. Fueled by new technologies and drugs—both old and new—they incited the most far-reaching social revolution since the twenties.

For college-age youth of the mid-sixties, there were four dominant issues: minority rights, sexual freedom, drug use, and war. A generation that had grown up listening to rock and roll, rhythm and blues, and jazz found it difficult to comprehend the widespread discrimination against blacks that they saw as legitimized in too many segments of American society. They joined the drive for civil rights—through demonstrations, sit-ins, marches, and, for some, more direct and potentially violent activities, such as voter registration in the South. The successes of the civil rights movement created momentum for other minority rights movements: women, Chicanos, gays, Native Americans.

Commercial production of an effective oral contraceptive—the Pill—began in the early sixties. For some women, this was the key to sexual freedom; it enabled them to be as sexually active as males with virtually no risk of pregnancy. It precipitated the most far-reaching revolution in sexual practice in the history of western culture. Moreover, it extended the drive for equal rights from the voting booth—in the United States, women were granted the right to vote only in 1920—into the bedroom and sparked a revival of feminism, which sought, among other things, to extend these rights into the workplace.

During this same period, the recreational use of mind-altering drugs spread to large segments of the middle class. Previously, drug use had been confined to small subcultures: for example, many jazz musicians in the post–World War II era were heroin addicts. Marijuana, always a popular drug among musicians and minorities, became the most popular drug of the sixties among young people, and especially the counterculture. However, the signature drug of the sixties was D-lysergic acid diethylamide, a semi-synthetic drug more commonly identified as LSD or acid. The drug was developed in 1938 by Albert Hoffman, a Swiss chemist; Hoffman discovered its psychedelic properties by accident about five years later. Originally, psychiatrists used it therapeutically, and during the Cold War, intelligence agencies in the United States and Great Britain apparently ran tests to determine whether the drug was useful for mind control. The key figures in moving LSD from the lab to the street were two Harvard psychology professors: Timothy Leary and Richard Alpert. They felt that the mind-expanding capabilities of the drug should be open to anyone; in reaction, Sandoz, Dr. Hofmann's chemical firm, stopped freely supplying scientists with the drug, and the US government banned its use in 1967. Underground use of the drug has continued despite this ban.

In the latter part of the sixties, the Vietnam War replaced civil rights as the hot-button issue for young people. In 1954, Vietnam, formerly French Indo-China, was divided—like Korea—into two regions: the north received support from the USSR and communist China, while the southern region received the support of western nations, especially the United States. A succession of presidents saw a military presence in South Vietnam as a necessary buffer against communist aggression.

As a result, US military involvement gradually escalated over the next decade. Finally, in 1965, the government began sending regular troops to Vietnam to augment the special forces already there. This provoked a hostile reaction, especially from those eligible to be drafted. Many recoiled at the prospect of fighting in a war that seemed pointless; a few fled to Canada or elsewhere to avoid the draft. Massive antiwar demonstrations became as much a part of the news during the late sixties as the civil rights demonstrations were in the first part of the decade. The lies and deceptions of the government and military, which among other things reassured the American people that the war was winnable and that the US forces were winning, coupled with news reports of horrific events such as the My Lai massacre, in which US soldiers killed close to 500 unarmed civilians in a small village, further eroded support for the war.

Civil rights, sex, drugs, and war were issues for many young Americans during the latter part of the sixties. On all of these issues, the gulf between the older establishment positions and attitudes of young Americans widened as the decade wore on. Still, there was a major shift in values. Civil rights legislation passed, the role of women in society underwent a liberating transformation, recreational drug use became more common and socially acceptable in certain circles (although it was still illegal), and the war eventually ended in failure. As a result of this revolution, ideas and practices that seemed radical at mid century—such as multiculturalism, and equal opportunity in the workplace—are accepted norms in contemporary society.

9–1a Hippies

A small but prominent minority of young people chose to reject mainstream society completely. They abandoned the conventional lifestyles of their parents and peers; some chose to live in communes. They followed Timothy Leary's advice to "turn on, tune in, drop out." They dressed differently, thought differently, and lived differently. They were the ideological heirs of the Bohemians of nineteenth-century Europe and the Beats of the late forties and fifties. Members of the group were known as hippies; collectively they formed the heart of the counterculture.

Throughout the sixties, the San Francisco Bay Area was a center for radical thought and action. The free speech movement led by Mario Savio got started at the Berkeley campus of the University of California in 1964; it led to confrontations between student protesters and university administrators over student rights and academic freedom. In 1966, in Oakland—next to Berkeley and across the bay from San Francisco—Huey Newton, Bobby Seale, and Richard Aoki formed the Black Panthers, a radical black organization dedicated to revolutionary social reform by any means necessary, including violence. Hippies generally followed a less confrontational path.

For hippies, mecca was San Francisco; their counterpart to the Kaaba, Islam's most sacred mosque, was Haight and Ashbury, an intersection in a heretofore ordinary neighborhood in San Francisco, near Golden Gate Park, the largest public park in the city. The area became a destination for those who wanted to "make love, not war" and travel the fast route to higher consciousness by tripping on psychedelic drugs. Migration to San Francisco peaked during the 1967 "summer of love," when an estimated 75,000 young people flocked to the city.

Rock music was the soundtrack for the counterculture. Music was everywhere—inside and outside—and especially at the Fillmore. Promoter Bill Graham turned the Fillmore Ballroom, a musty building in a rather seedy part of town, into the main venue for rock bands and their fans. Audiences flocked there for endless concerts; "live at the Fillmore" albums appeared regularly in record stores. The venue was so successful that Graham named its New York counterpart "Fillmore East."

Because of Haight-Ashbury, "flower power," LSD, and the other trappings of the hippie scene, the music most associated with the Bay Area during the late sixties was acid rock (or psychedelic rock)—a rock substyle defined not by a musical feature but simply by the music's ability to evoke or enhance the drug experience. However, a list of bands active in the San Francisco Bay Area during 1969 makes clear that the Bay Area music scene was far more varied. At the center of it was a trio of acid-rock bands: Jefferson Airplane, Quicksilver Messenger Service, and the Grateful Dead. Of course, the Dead soon ranged far beyond acid rock. But there were also such acts as:

- Janis Joplin, who sang the blues with power and passion, fronting her Kosmic Blues Band
- Creedence Clearwater Revival, one of the great singles bands of the era, playing down-to-earth rock and roll
- Santana, Carlos Santana's one-band foray into Latin rock
- Sly and the Family Stone, whose music provided the crucial link between soul and funk

We sample the music from this special time and place next.

9-2 Acid Rock

The British writer Aldous Huxley, whose book *The Doors of Perception* inspired Jim Morrison to name his band the Doors, described his first acid trip, which he took in 1955, in this way:

> What came through the closed door was the realization—not the knowledge, for this wasn't verbal or abstract—but the direct, total awareness, from the inside, so to say, of Love as the primary and fundamental cosmic fact. These words, of course, have a kind of indecency and must necessarily ring false, seem like twaddle. But the fact remains . . . I was this fact or perhaps it would be more accurate to say that this fact occupied the place where I had been.

In his thoughtful account, Huxley struggles to put into words the nature of the acid experience. It is clear that for him there was an enormous gulf between everyday reality and the enhanced reality of the acid experience. Words seem inadequate to the task; he all but apologizes for their limitations in the middle of his description. But they are all he has as he tries to translate his heightened experience into mundane, if elegant, language.

As tripping on acid became more widespread, words, images, and music were used to capture the psychedelic experience. Psychedelic art—rich in color, dense and distorted, and often suffused with religious and mystical images—became an important new direction in the visual arts. The images were not confined to canvas, or even album covers and posters. Perhaps the most famous and memorable visual image of the psychedelic sixties was a 1939 International Harvester school bus painted in a rainbow of colors; it was the vehicle for the cross-country tours of Ken Kesey, the patron saint of the psychedelic world, and his Merry Pranksters.

Music was even more integral to the psychedelic experience because it was used not only to evoke but also to enhance tripping on acid. Music could contribute to the experience (as we will discover below), depict the experience (as we heard in the Beatles' **"A Day in the Life"**), and be a product of it (as was the case of much of the music from the mid- and late sixties). Indeed, the common bond that linked the widely varied music identified as acid or psychedelic rock was the connection to LSD. There was no specific musical feature, or set of features, that identified acid rock. (By contrast, consider the role of distortion in defining the sound of heavy metal, or the combination of horns and heavy bass in defining the sound of soul music.) Examples of acid rock ranged from the sprawling, blues-based improvisations of Jerry Garcia and the Grateful Dead to Jefferson Airplane's tight, flamenco-tinged **"White Rabbit,"** discussed following. The musical products were seemingly as varied as the acid trips themselves. The connection could be in the music, in the words, or both.

9-2a Jefferson Airplane

The band that first directed the spotlight to San Francisco and to acid rock was Jefferson Airplane. Other bands had a more authentic provenance—the Grateful Dead were the house band for Ken Kesey's "Acid Tests"—but it was the Jefferson Airplane that brought national attention to psychedelic rock and to San Francisco as its home base.

Vocalist Marty Balin (b. 1942) and guitarist Paul Kantner (1941–2016) formed Jefferson Airplane in 1965; the next year, Grace Slick (born Grace Wing, 1939) replaced Signe Anderson as the female vocalist with the group and soon became the face as well as the dominant voice of the group. Her good looks and extroverted and uninhibited stage personality were key elements in the success of the group. The rest of the group during the late sixties included lead guitarist Jorma Kaukonen (b. 1940), bassist Jack Casady (b. 1944), and drummer Spencer Dryden (1938–2005).

Slick brought two songs with her from the Great Society, the band she had formed with Jerry Slick, her husband at the time. As reworked by Jefferson Airplane, they became the group's two Top 10 singles: "Somebody to Love" and "White Rabbit." Both songs appeared on *Surrealistic Pillow* (1967), the first album the group recorded with Slick.

Of the two, "White Rabbit" connects more directly to the drug experience. The title of the song refers to the white rabbit in Lewis Carroll's *Alice in Wonderland*. In Carroll's tale, the rabbit, dressed in a waistcoat, leads Alice into a hole and into a fantasy world where she has all manner of strange experiences. The lyric comments on a scene in the story where she meets a caterpillar that seems to be smoking opium. Slick would later remark that the song was an indictment of parents who read stories like *Alice in Wonderland* to their children and then wonder why the children do drugs. However, the connection with LSD was oblique enough that the song made it past the censors, although the drug references (such as "feed your head") seem quite clear in retrospect.

In "White Rabbit," the lyrics (and Slick's singing) are primary; the music plays a supporting role. Among the defining features of the song are the flamenco-inspired instrumental accompaniment (adapted for a rock band) and the sustained crescendo to the final "feed your head." Slick remarked that the inspiration for the accompaniment came from her repeated listening to *Sketches of Spain* while tripping on LSD. *Sketches of Spain* was an adventurous album by the jazz trumpeter Miles Davis; the most extended track was a drastic reworking of a guitar concerto by the Spanish composer Joaquin Rodrigo.

Another remarkable feature of the song is its slow, steady crescendo (a gradual increase in volume). The song begins quietly with an extended instrumental introduction in which the instruments enter one by one—bass, drums, then lead and rhythm guitars. Both the rhythm and the chord progression evoke Spanish music. Slick also enters quietly. The music gets louder as the song proceeds, reaching a climax on the line "feed your head." As Slick belts out the lyric, the band shifts from the Spanish-flavored rhythm with which the song began to a straightforward rock rhythm; it is as if music, like the mind and Slick's voice, has been set free from the restrictive Spanish rhythm.

"White Rabbit" has retained its strong association with LSD, and by extension, other mind-altering drugs. To cite just one instance: it has been used in several episodes of *The Simpsons*, especially when the characters have taken hallucinogenic drugs, and they are starting to kick in.

Jefferson Airplane remained one of the leading psychedelic rock bands into the early seventies, when the group reconstituted itself with Slick and Kantner as Jefferson Starship. Although their new name implied that they had become even more adventurous—starships fly higher than airplanes—the band actually became more mainstream and enjoyed even more commercial success during the seventies and eighties.

Both the psychedelic scene and psychedelic rock lost their potency around 1970. The 1967 "summer of love" devolved into a bad trip at the end of the decade. Haight-Ashbury went into decline; it would become gentrified a decade later. For many, LSD lost its status as the mind-expanding drug of choice. The absence of a distinct musical identity made it difficult to sustain acid rock as a vital rock substyle; the style neither evolved (like heavy metal or country rock) nor achieved a more or less permanent stasis (like hard rock). It was—and remains—very much a period piece, a sound of a particular time and place.

One important reason that acid rock lacked a distinct musical identity was the fact that the drug experience was an overlay; it was not an integral element of the style. Indeed, most of the major acid-rock acts rooted their style in folk and blues: the Grateful Dead began as a jug band; the members of Jefferson Airplane had prior experience in folk, blues, and R&B; and both Jimi Hendrix and Eric Clapton, who were also associated with acid rock, had deep blues roots. For many of the top San Francisco–based acts, this connection with American roots music was a stronger musical bond than the drugs. Perhaps the clearest example of this came in the music of Janis Joplin.

9-3 Down to Earth: Janis Joplin and the Blues

The only woman performer in the San Francisco rock scene with a more commanding presence than Grace Slick was Janis Joplin. Like Slick, Joplin fronted a band, had a let-it-all-hang-out stage personality, and wrestled with a severe substance abuse problem. Both looked the part of the counterculture diva—both dressed and undressed. But there were differences. Slick was beautiful and had come from a high-class background. Before joining Jefferson Airplane she had modeled for three years at a high-end San Francisco department store and had begun her undergraduate education at Finch College, a finishing school for young ladies. Joplin had grown up a social outcast in a Texas oil town; music was her escape. Joplin sipped while Slick tripped; Janis's taste for Southern Comfort was legendary. (Ironically, it was Slick who later developed an alcohol abuse problem, while Joplin died of a heroin overdose.) And while Slick took her listeners into a fantastic world in songs like "White Rabbit," Joplin got real by drenching herself in blues and soul.

Like many other young musicians of the time, Janis Joplin (1943–1970) migrated to San Francisco during the mid-sixties. Born in Port Arthur, Texas, Joplin began performing in coffeehouses in her native state before traveling to California in 1965. There, she began performing with a local blues band: Big Brother and the Holding Company. A rather motley crew, the group made an enormous impact at the 1967 Monterey Pop Festival, thanks mainly to Joplin's dynamic stage performance. Signed to Columbia Records, they cut one album that was widely praised for the quality of Joplin's vocals, while the band was criticized for its ragged playing. Joplin soon separated from the band and became an important solo act for the rest of her brief life.

Joplin was rock's original blues diva. Before Joplin, few women sang with anything approaching the supercharged passion and freedom that is inherent in her singing; all of them were black—from Bessie Smith to Aretha Franklin. Indeed, Joplin's singing seemingly owes more to Otis Redding and other male southern soul singers than to any woman, because what distinguishes Joplin's singing from other female singers is the rawness of her sound and the sheer exuberance of her performing style. She had a voice that often sounded like it had been raked over broken glass, although she could also sing as tenderly as any crooner. She combined that with a unique kind of vocal virtuosity. With its stutters, reiterations, rapid-fire streams of words, melismas, interpolations, and the like, it is almost operatic in its exhibitionism.

Although Joplin thought of herself as a blues singer, most of the songs that she recorded were not blues, at least in the formal sense. Unlike the classic female blues singers of the twenties, who recorded mainly conventional blues songs, Joplin recorded a wide range of material. However, she brought blues feeling and style into everything she recorded, blues or not.

"Piece of My Heart" (1968), which she recorded while singing with Big Brother and the Holding Company, was the only song of hers to reach the singles charts during her lifetime. It was a track on *Cheap Thrills*, the band's first album for Columbia and by far their biggest success; the album topped the charts for eight weeks in 1968. "Piece of My Heart" remains the song most closely associated with her, two biographies include it in the title.

"Piece of My Heart" had been a modest R&B hit the previous year for Erma Franklin, Aretha Franklin's younger sister. Her original version was a solid and straightforward slow soul song. Characteristically, the lyric tells the story of a troubled relationship, here from a woman's point of view: she is at once vulnerable and—as the lyric says—tough. Given Joplin's history and personality, it is easy to understand why she would be eager to cover it.

The thorough transformation of the song begins with the band: the instrumental accompaniment features the kind of blues-tinged rock that was characteristic of the San Francisco psychedelic scene, rather than a bass-heavy R&B sound. The instrumentation is standard: two guitars, with some distortion in the lead guitar, bass, and drums. The rhythms are more active and freer than in a straightforward rock song.

All of this is a foil for Joplin's soulful singing, which is considerably more passionate and virtuosic than Erma Franklin's. There is enormous contrast, in volume and vocal quality, from the almost screamed opening ("Come on") to the almost whispered verse ("Didn't I make you feel") to the half-spoken/half-sung

("Each time I tell myself") and the wailed refrain. As she delivers the song, she lays herself emotionally bare—as if she had stripped off all of her clothes. Few singers of any era were willing to throw themselves into a performance the way Joplin did, and fewer had the vocal agility and range to carry it off successfully.

Even more than Grace Slick, Janis Joplin redefined the role of women in rock. It was no longer simply being a pretty face in front of the band; Joplin matched men—black and white—in power and presence. In this respect, she paved the way for a larger role for women in rock: Patti Smith, Annie Lennox, Bonnie Raitt, Madonna, and many others benefited from her trailblazing efforts.

She paid a price for her passion. With her premature death, she joined the not-exclusive-enough club of rock icons who lived too hard and died too young. Ironically, she did not live long enough to enjoy her biggest hit; **"Me and Bobby McGee,"** written for her by Kris Kristofferson, one of her ex-lovers, appeared on *Pearl*, an album released after her death. She left the album incomplete; she was to have added vocals to a track entitled **"Buried Alive in the Blues"** on the day she died.

Joplin and her music embody the tensions of the new womanhood that emerged in the sixties. On stage and in the studio, she is the equal of men, yet vulnerable in a specifically feminine way; she is modern in her sensibility, yet deals with timeless issues in her songs. For a new generation of women, she showed both what they might aspire to and the dangers of getting it.

9-4 Toward an American Rock Sound

Rock, like English, was spoken on both sides of the Atlantic during the sixties; the British invasion simply made North American listeners aware of the British rock scene. British and North American musicians drew on many of the same sources; the influence of the blues was pervasive. They listened to and talked with one another, and at times they played together. To cite just two familiar examples, the Jimi Hendrix Experience included two British musicians, bassist Noel Redding and drummer Mitch Mitchell; and American keyboardist Billy Preston played on Beatles' recordings.

Despite the obvious common ground, there was an overall difference in attitude and musical result between North American and British rock. The difference grows out of the division between highbrow and lowbrow, a division that in American music extends back to **blackface** minstrelsy. During rock's coming of age, there was a strong impulse in British rock to aspire to highbrow status by assuming the trappings of high art. By contrast, Dylan demonstrated that it was possible to create art without being "arty." This difference seems to emerge from a fundamental cultural difference between Great Britain and its former colonies: Buckingham Palace versus blue jeans.

Musically, the biggest difference was the far stronger impact of American folk and country music. Again, Dylan led the way on both fronts—first by his excursion in folk music and then by his extended embrace of Nashville. But country music and, in some cases, folk music helped shape music from all over North America, including the San Francisco Bay Area. The country and folk influence gave this music a distinctly American sound, although it took widely different forms. It shows up particularly in the scales on which many of the songs are based, the spun-out melodies, and the guitar riffs. To experience this, we consider songs by two of the most important Bay Area-based bands: Creedence Clearwater Revival and the Grateful Dead.

blackface Minstrel show practice in which white and (later) black performers applied burnt cork to darken their complexion.

9–4a Creedence Clearwater Revival

Unlike many other San Francisco bands, Creedence Clearwater Revival was a Bay Area band because its members grew up there. The four band members—John Fogerty (b. 1945), lead guitar; Tom Fogerty (1941–1990, John's older brother), rhythm guitar; Stu Cook (b. 1945), bass; and Doug Clifford (b. 1945), drums—grew up in the East Bay, northeast of San Francisco. Beginning in junior high school as the Blue Velvets, they finally incarnated themselves as Creedence Clearwater Revival (CCR) in 1967 and released their first album a year later. They were immediately successful; for three years they were the hottest singles band in the country.

In his liner notes to *Chronicle*, an anthology of CCR's greatest hits, Greil Marcus wrote about "**Proud Mary**" and three other songs that "literally define rock and roll—as a musical form, as a recurring event, as a version of the American spirit." The values that Marcus—and millions of listeners—seemed to find appealing were the basic, down-to-earth quality of the words and music (nothing fancy and no gimmicks); its independent spirit (CCR stayed away from the "flower power" scene); and its lack of pretense. It was music with a good story, a good beat, and unmistakable riffs.

The opening riff of "Proud Mary," among rock's most memorable ten-second sound slices, perfectly illustrates the fusion of blues and country influences. Fogerty harmonizes each note of the African American pentatonic scale with the three-note chords typical of country music. This apparent country retention makes Fogerty's riff stand apart from many other pentatonic riffs of the period, especially those of British bands. These were typically harmonized with power chords or not harmonized at all, as we heard in **Chapter 8**.

Like the opening riff, the rest of the song is a seamless mix of black and white roots music. Most of the time, Fogerty's melody noodles around the first three notes of the Anglo-American pentatonic scale, much like the minstrel songs of Stephen Foster: "Oh, Susanna" and "Old Folks at Home" ("way down upon the Swanee River") are good examples. This choice of notes helps give the song an "American" sound. So do the country-ish guitar riffs.

At the same time, there are elements that are clearly black. The texture of the song is dense and highly syncopated: the rhythm guitar pattern plays a key role here. There's a nice bent note on the word "Proud"; it is most expressive note in the song, in part because it goes outside the Anglo-American scale. And then there's Fogerty's singing, which resonates with Little Richard's influence.

All of this is in the service of two of the enduring themes in American culture: the rambling man and life along the Mississippi. "Proud Mary" is, of course, a steamboat traveling up and down the river. Fogerty's lyric sketches out a vivid picture of the protagonist finding a comfortable niche in a community of outsiders. The race of its protagonist is unclear: Fogerty is, of course, white, but "the man" is black slang for a boss—and in 1971 the song became a huge hit for Tina Turner. The story connects back to Mark Twain; it brings the myth into the sixties.

From the beginning of "Proud Mary" to the end, Fogerty blends the two folk traditions seamlessly. It is their presence, especially the country elements, that helps CCR achieve their distinctive, hard-driving rock-and-roll sound.

CCR was not a typical San Francisco band. They offered tight singles instead of rambling drug-juiced jams. Their Bay Area base was an accident of birth, not a choice, and unlike the Beach Boys, for instance, they didn't regionalize their sound. Their unique style was all-American.

9-4b The Grateful Dead

Keeping CCR company in the Bay Area were the Grateful Dead. During their ascent to stardom, the band consisted of guitarists Jerry Garcia (1942–1995) and Bob Weir (b. 1947), harmonica player "Pigpen" McKernan (Ronald McKernan, 1945–1973), bassist Phil Lesh (b. 1940), and drummer Mickey Hart (b. 1943). Lyricist Robert Hunter (b. 1941), who didn't perform with the band, collaborated with Garcia, Lesh, and Weir on most of their memorable songs.

On the surface, it might seem that the Grateful Dead and CCR were as opposite as two American bands could be, despite their conjunction in time and place. Where CCR was best known for its short singles, the Grateful Dead made their reputation through long concerts—up to five hours—which featured extended solos, especially by Jerry Garcia. CCR was on the outside of the San Francisco music scene. By contrast, the Dead were the quintessential San Francisco hippie band: they lived communally for years, ingested copious quantities of trendy drugs, and played all the time, often for free, especially in their early years. CCR had a huge, largely anonymous fan base. The Grateful Dead, who didn't chart a single until 1987 (!), slowly built an extremely loyal cult following, the Deadheads, who would travel from concert to concert to hear the band, in part because each concert was likely to be different.

Nevertheless, there is also an American-ness about the Grateful Dead and their music. Like CCR, the Grateful Dead explored America's romantic myths and images in their most highly regarded music. Moreover, the Dead followed their own muse, instead of striving for mass popularity, which exemplified the iconoclastic individualism that is also part of the American character. Their route to success was unique in the history of rock.

Workingman's Dead (1970), widely regarded as the Grateful Dead's finest album, offers substantial evidence of the American qualities of the Dead's music. The basic approach is similar in both words and music. And like CCR, they also drew on black and white roots music. But within these overall parameters, the Grateful Dead is yin to CCR's yang. Their music is more exploratory and more diverse in influence and blend than CCR. If CCR were the heart of American rock and roll at the end of the sixties, the Grateful Dead represented multiple directions that American rock music could go. One song cannot give an adequate picture of their range. Still, "**Uncle John's Band**," one of the most memorable songs from the album, can give some sense of the way in which they combined diverse influences.

Like "Proud Mary," "Uncle John's Band" taps into an enduring American image: here, it is the country fiddler as pied piper. And like so many rock songs from the sixties, it conflates the timeless with the current, the universal with the particular. The lyrics are rich in allusions to America's past: for example, buck-and-wing dancing (a popular tap dance at the turn of the twentieth century), as well as a fiddle tune called "Buck Dancer's Choice"; "Don't Tread on Me," a popular motto from the American revolution. However, the lyric has autobiographical undertones—Uncle John's band could easily be the Dead.

"Uncle John's Band" tells a long, slowly unfolding story, à la Woody Guthrie—or the New Lost City Ramblers, a trio that included Mike Seeger and that was among the most conscientiously authentic of the major folk revival groups. Several members of the Grateful Dead, including Garcia and lyricist Robert Hunter, were great admirers of the group and jammed with them on at least one occasion. (Subsequently, Hunter alluded to a connection between the group and the lyrics.)

The old-time music influence of the New Lost City Ramblers is even more evident in the music, at least at the beginning. The acoustic guitars heard at the beginning of the song—two strummed and another almost mandolin-like—recall the Grateful Dead's earlier roots in jug band music. Similarly, the vocal harmonies evoke the early folk revival groups, although more direct precedents were the harmonies of Crosby, Stills, Nash, and Young. Bass and drums enter discreetly to enrich the sound; Lesh's bass line is the most complex strand of the texture. In addition, the song relies almost exclusively on the major scales and chords of country and folk music, rather than the modal sounds of hard rock. Extra percussion sounds join in as the song unfolds: the persistent scrape of a guiro, then low-pitched drums, claves. Suddenly, about three minutes into the song, the song changes character. The harmony grows darker, the drums become more prominent, a riff is repeated over and over, and the rhythm shifts to a pattern of four plus three beats. The original melody returns, without instrumental accompaniment, then the band comes back in. The dark interlude returns briefly as a tag.

The gradual evolution of the song—from simple folk beginning, through mantra-like interlude, to the final section, which combines the two—underscores its autobiographical nature. It is as if we hear the history of the band in less than five minutes: its folk roots, its gradual incorporation of other elements (for example, the additional percussion instruments), the psychedelic phase (the dark interlude), and the current (circa 1970) state of affairs, where the group is open to all influences and can blend them effortlessly.

Even a cursory comparison of "Proud Mary" and "Uncle John's Band" reveals significant differences in the two bands' approach to an American sound, as well as the underlying similarities. CCR is straightforward rock and roll: the song is memorable, predictable in its instrumentation, form, rhythm, and melodic approach, and well done. There are no frills. By contrast, "Uncle John's Band" is full of subtleties and surprises, such as the acoustic guitars, extra percussion instruments, and rhythmic tricks. They may share a similar heritage, but they rework it quite differently.

It should be noted that this recording is not "trademark Dead": the sprawling, largely improvisational performances that kept the Deadheads on the road with them. Among their many virtues, the Dead were a great boogie band, as they revealed on songs like **"Turn on Your Love Light**," from *Europe '72*. In their collective persona, the management of their career, and, most of all, in their songs, the Grateful Dead followed the less-traveled road. That it included their own blends of folk, country, and blues influences only makes it that much more American.

9-5 Santana and Latin Rock

If CCR and the Dead represent an almost seamless blend of American roots music, then the music of Santana represents a spectacular instance of the merging of rock with a music with deep roots outside of the United States. The Latin rock of Santana was not the first mixing of Latin music and rock: Latin influence has been present from the start, as we noted in **Chapter 2**. Nor is Latin rock the first instance of the integration of nonrock styles from outside the US–UK world into rock. During the latter half of the sixties, rock musicians incorporated elements of such styles as East Indian music, classical music, and French cabaret music. However, these outside influences were, in most cases, used evocatively for a particular song; they were not inherent components of a hybrid style.

In Santana's Latin rock, both the rock and the Latin elements are easily heard: Latin percussion versus electric guitar and bass—a rhythmic conception that draws on rock and Afro-Cuban music but is neither one nor the other. Again, there were styles that drew on rock and nonrock in more or less equal measure: jazz/rock fusion is an early and extensive example. However, Latin rock is the first important *style* to mix rock with an exotic style in balanced proportions. The musician most responsible for the style was Carlos Santana.

9–5a Carlos Santana

Carlos Santana (b. 1947) was born and raised in Mexico. He moved to San Francisco in 1962. He made his first impression as a blues-inspired rock guitarist; his first commercial recording came from a live 1969 performance with blues guitarist Mike Bloomfield. That same year, he acknowledged his Hispanic heritage by forming Santana. Latin music has its roots in Cuba, as we have noted. Most Latin musicians at the time came from Spanish-speaking Caribbean countries, or had roots there; New York was the American home of this music. The music of Mexico (and Santana's father, a mariachi musician) is quite different. Nevertheless, Santana connected with Afro-Cuban music and took a lead role in integrating it into rock.

A prime example of his synthesis of the two styles is his 1971 version of Tito Puente's "**Oye Como Va.**" Here, Santana blends the sounds and rhythmic feel of Latin music with rock-based solos by Santana and organist Greg Rolie (b. 1947). The song begins with an irregular rhythmic pattern, played on the organ (and supported in the bass). It is not the clave rhythm of Afro-Cuban music, but it is similar in that it creates an asymmetrical rhythm over eight beats and serves as the main rhythmic reference. The performance consists mainly of several statements of Puente's simple melodic riffs, wrapped around strong organ and guitar solos.

In **Chapter 5**, we emphasized that Latin music was the silent partner in the rock revolution. Especially for R&B bands, it became an alternative to rock rhythm. As we listen to the guitar and organ solos in this song, we can hear how seamlessly Latin and rock rhythms merge. Both are built on the division of the beat into two equal parts, so the rhythms align when played together. One could easily imagine the solos of Carlos Santana or Gregg Rolie taking place over a groove laid down by a rock bassist and drummer. They would not have to adjust the rhythmic feel of their playing to play the same music with a rock band.

Despite this comfortable correspondence between Latin and rock rhythms, those who wish to combine them must reconcile the two, because the beat and the clave pattern are mutually exclusive ways of organizing a steady rhythmic stream. Marking the beat grounds the rhythm, because beat-marking divides time into regular intervals. By contrast, organizing the rhythm mainly around the asymmetrical clave pattern helps the rhythm float, because it doesn't come to rest on the beat. Santana's effective compromise is to keep Puente's clave-like rhythm in the forefront throughout most of the song.

What distinguishes Latin rock from more conventional rock? In "Oye Como Va," it is, more than anything else, the sheer quantity of percussion instruments and the persistence of Puente's clave-like rhythm that betrays Latin influence. There is no mistaking the emphasis.

Santana was Latin rock's lone star. New York–based Latin musicians also attempted rock/Latin fusions: *bugalú* was a minor sensation in the Latin community during the sixties and early seventies. But none of this music had the crossover appeal of Santana's early music. In the mid-seventies, Santana gravitated toward jazz fusion; Latin rock faded away. However, the influence of Latin music—especially via Cuba and Brazil—would be even more pronounced, and more seamlessly integrated, in the seventies and eighties.

9–6 Proto-funk Protest: Sly and the Family Stone

Musicians speak admiringly of a "tight" band: when they do, they are referring to a band that plays with great precision. James Brown's band was tight; he would fine musicians who missed cues or cracked notes. By contrast, Sly and the Family Stone was a loose band. This too can be an admirable quality; it produces a quite different feel.

The band was the brainchild of Sly Stone (born Sylvester Stewart, 1944), a disc jockey turned producer and bandleader. More than any other band of the era, Sly and the Family Stone preached integration. The lineup included two of Stone's siblings (his brother Freddie and sister Rosie), Cynthia Martin on trumpet, and several others, including trend-setting bassist Larry Graham: there were blacks and whites, and women as well as men.

In a series of hits spanning a five-year period (1968–1972), Sly and the Family Stone created an exuberant new sound. We hear it in **"Thank You (Falettinme Be Mice Elf Agin),"** one of their three No. 1 hits. The music of James Brown is the direct antecedent of this song and this style: like Brown's music, there is a groove built up from multiple layers of riffs, played by rhythm and horns; there is no harmonic movement—instead of two chords, there is only one; and the vocal part is intermittent, with long pauses between phrases.

However, Sly and the Family Stone create a sound that is much denser and more active than that heard in "Papa's Got a Brand New Bag." Although the drummer marks off a rock beat along with the backbeat, the basic rhythmic feel of the song is twice as fast—a 16-beat rhythm. We sense this faster-moving layer in virtually all the other parts: the opening bass riff, the guitar and horn riffs, and—most explicitly—in the "chuck-a-puk-a" vocalization. The more active texture opens up many more rhythmic patterns that can conflict with the beat; Sly's band exploits several of them.

And instead of Brown's spare, open texture, there are plenty of riffs: bass, several guitars, voice, horns. Moreover, there is a spontaneous aspect to the sound, as if it grows out of a jam over the basic groove. It is this quality that gives the song (and Stone's music) its distinctive looseness—looseness that implores listeners to "dance to the music."

If we just listen to the music, it can hypnotize us with its contagious rhythm. However, when we consider the words—the opening lines are "Lookin' at the devil, grinnin' at his gun/Fingers start shakin', I begin to run"—we sense that the band is laughing to keep from crying, or burning down the house. As with many other Sly and the Family Stone songs, there is a strong political and social message: we sense that the music is the buffer between the band and society, a restraint against violent activism.

This is our first example of what would become a growing trend in Afro-centric music, from the United States and abroad: powerful lyrics over a powerful beat. There is an apparent contradiction between the sharp social commentary in the lyrics and the seduction of the beat. They seem to be operating at cross purposes: full attention and response versus surrender to the groove. Perhaps that's so. However, it is possible to interpret this apparent conflict in other ways. One is to view the music as a tool to draw in listeners, to expose them to the message of the words. Another is to understand the music as a means of removing the sting of the conditions described in the lyrics: lose yourself in the music, to avoid simply losing it.

Sly and the Family Stone became popular after the assassination of Martin Luther King and after the backlash from the civil rights movement had built up steam. Civil rights legislation removed much of the governmental support for the racial inequities in American life. It did not eliminate prejudice or racial hatred, as many had hoped it would. Nor have they disappeared in the decades that followed, here and elsewhere. The lyrics of this and other songs by Sly and the Family Stone speak to that.

We find this same combination of strong rhythm and sharp words in Jamaican reggae, seventies funk, calypso from Trinidad, and, from the late seventies on, rap. Increasingly, the musical mood has become darker: rap, for example, often strips away the bright sounds from the horns, guitars, and keyboards. In these styles, there is a hardness to the sound; the fun is over.

The music provided one way to escape the pain of prejudice. Drugs were another. Sly Stone used them to excess and torpedoed his career in the process. He became increasingly unreliable, often not showing up for engagements; promoters stopped booking his band. Once again, drugs had silenced a truly innovative voice.

9-6a Slapping: The Bass as a Percussion Instrument

Afro-centric musicians—in the United States and elsewhere—have had a longstanding love affair with percussive sounds. As they assimilate an instrument into their culture, they explore ways to make it sound more percussively. Nowhere is this more persistently evident than in the bass instruments of popular music. The first bass instrument in the modern era was the tuba, or brass bass. Although tuba players can sustain long notes, just as trumpeters and other brass players can, the standard tuba part in a dance orchestra was a short note on every beat, in alternation with the backbeat from the banjo. The introduction of four-beat rhythms spelled the end of the tuba as a viable bass instrument: they couldn't "walk" because they had to breathe. As a result, the string bass replaced the brass bass—a sacrifice of power for speed.

In symphony orchestras, bassists usually play their instrument with a bow. Plucking the string with a finger (called *pizzicato*) is a special effect. Plucking the string produces a percussive sound: a sharp attack, followed by a quick decay. This contrasts sharply with the most widely used bowed style, in which notes are sustained and connected smoothly. In jazz and dance orchestras, bass players routinely pluck their instruments; bowing is the special effect. In classical music, the bass instrument typically supplies the foundation note for a harmony. So it is in popular music. But the bass instrument also supplied the rhythmic foundation: it was the percussive sound of the plucked bass that typically provided the rhythmic anchor by clearly marking the beat, even as it outlined the harmony.

The first electric bass players developed a way of plucking the strings that was similar to that used by string bass players. Because of powerful amplification, they didn't have to work nearly as hard as their acoustic counterparts to produce a big sound. James Jamerson and other leading rock bass players liberated the bass from its traditional roles—at least to some extent. The next major step forward in playing style came from Larry Graham (b. 1946), the bass player with Sly and the Family Stone and later the leader of Graham Central Station.

Larry Graham

Graham created new sounds from the bass by slapping the strings with the side of his thumb or popping the string by pulling it away from the fretboard and suddenly releasing it. Popping, slapping, and other similar techniques made the bass sound even more percussive, as we hear in the opening riff of "Thank You (Falettinme Be Mice Elf Agin)." Others who followed him—most notably Bootsy Collins, a bass-ist for James Brown, then George Clinton's Parliament and Funkadelic bands—ex-tended this technique, to the point that the percussive dimension of the sound may overshadow the pitch.

This "percussionization" of the bass was part of a general trend toward more percussive sounds in the late sixties and early seventies. Another expression of this trend was the choked guitar sound—where a guitarist depresses the strings only part of the way—heard early on in Jimi Hendrix's "**Voodoo Child**" and persistently in the music for *Shaft* and other early seventies blaxploitation films, and later in disco. A third came from new keyboard instruments, like the clavinet heard on so many Stevie Wonder recordings. In turn, this trend toward more percussive sounds is one aspect of the growing emphasis on rhythm over melody as the century progressed. It would reach its logical end in rap.

9–6b Bridging Soul and Funk

The longest-running evolutionary thread of the rock era is black music with a strong beat. It began in the jump bands of the late forties, before rhythm and blues had become rock and roll. By the mid-sixties, it had acquired a new name and a new beat. It had become soul music. The complex and compelling rock rhythms heard in the music of up-tempo soul songs from Memphis and, more influentially, in the music of James Brown had replaced the strong shuffle beat of the fifties. During the seventies, it would continue to evolve, acquiring even more complex rhythm and gaining a new name: funk. The most constant elements in this evolution have been the use of a band made up of horns and rhythm, a rough-edged vocal style, and above all an emphasis on rhythm and riffs.

Sly and the Family Stone played the key role in the transition from soul to funk. By incorporating the more active 16-beat rhythms over a rock beat, they supplied the inevitable next step in the rhythmic evolution of rock rhythm. This rhythmic conception was an innovation in the late sixties; Sly and the Family Stone were among the first to make use of it. It would become far more common in the music of the seventies, not only in funk, but also in disco and a wide range of black music. And it has been the most popular rhythmic foundation in rock-era music since the eighties, most notably in rap but also in a wide range of music, black and white. Sly and the Family Stone increased the density of the musical texture, and they emphasized rhythm and texture over melody and harmony. They stressed more percussive sounds, not only in the rhythm instruments but also in the vocal style.

The influence of the band's style was not limited to funk. Its impact is evident in other music of the seventies and beyond—directly in styles like the art/funk jazz fusion of Herbie Hancock and the film music of Curtis Mayfield and indirectly in styles like disco and the post-disco pop of the eighties.

9–7 Diversity, a Rock-Era Innovation

Our sample of six songs—all from the late sixties and early seventies and all from bands active in the San Francisco Bay Area—highlights an important dimension of the rock revolution: its extraordinary musical diversification. The songs include Jefferson Airplane's heady, flamenco-tinged evocation of the acid experience; Janis Joplin's blues-drenched rock ballad; CCR's mainline rock-and-roll anthem; the Grateful Dead's cautionary tale, with its eclectic mix of diverse influences; Santana's synthesis of Afro-Cuban music and rock; and Sly and the Family Stone's good-time/dark-message proto-funk. This is only a small fraction of the music produced in this time and place; it is representative only of the fact that rock suddenly became much more diverse.

One remarkable aspect of this diversity is that it happened suddenly; the late sixties saw a veritable stylistic explosion. As late as 1964, even an astute observer of rock music would have needed superior foresight to predict the many directions that rock-era music took in the latter part of the decade. The differences among songs and styles touch every aspect of the music—what songs are trying to communicate and how they communicate their message in words and music.

Another remarkable aspect of this stylistic explosion is that it happened during the same time period that rock-era musicians reached a common understanding about the essential features of this new music. Rock reached maturity during the latter part of the sixties, consolidating its core musical values even as it stretched its boundaries and assumed the dominant position in the music industry. It was as if centrifugal and centripetal forces were applied to the music simultaneously. Especially when compared to the music of the late twenties and early thirties—the last period of stylistic consolidation—rock and black music are far more varied, as even our small sample evidences.

That rock music enormously expanded its stylistic boundaries during a period of consolidation clearly signals a fundamental shift in cultural attitudes and values. The openness of rock musicians to music and ideas of all kinds and their eagerness to blend them with impunity flew in the face of old notions of good and bad, and high and low class. Rock challenged the pecking order of the music world and the assumptions behind it. Before 1965, the music industry in the western world had clearly drawn class boundaries. Classical music represented the aristocracy. Musical theater was the highest form of popular music; jazz was moving up in status, although its dominant venue was still a night club rather than a concert hall or festival stage. *Legit*, a term used by popular and jazz musicians to refer to their classical counterparts—such as, he's a legit (short for "legitimate") trumpet player—underscores the assumption of second-class status of popular music within the larger musical world.

With rock, this changed. Rock embraced classical music and the idea of music as art even as it challenged the notion of the inherent superiority of the established classical tradition, as we discover in **Chapter 10**. By widening the domain of art and redefining it to some extent on its own terms, rock helped set in motion a thorough reevaluation of culture and class. More specifically, it cast into doubt the privileged status of Euro-centric culture.

It is stretching the point to say that rock was the cause of multiculturalism. There were enormous changes taking place in virtually every domain—from the work of intellectuals like the Algerian-born literary critic Jacques Derrida (a seminal figure in **deconstruction** and postmodern thought), and Vatican II, which helped modernize the Catholic Church, to the numerous minority rights movements in the United States. However, it can be argued that rock-era music was the most visible and audible sign of this huge cultural shift and that the kind of diversity—in intent, words, and music—apparent even in this small sample is not only a sign of this shift but also an agent of change.

deconstruction
Construction of a song out of several components, which can be digitally modified, added to, and otherwise manipulated to create other versions of the song.

CHAPTER 10

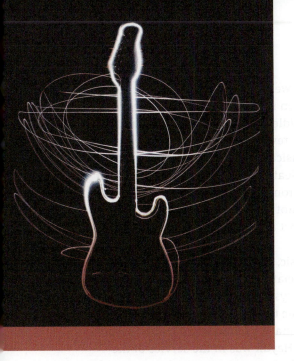

ROCK AS ART

Learning Objectives:

1) Discuss the tension that exists between "highbrow" music and rock.

2) Give examples of musical works that include classical/rock fusions.

3) Compare the similarities and differences between the Doors and the Velvet Underground.

4) Define the musical term: **proto-punk beat**.

5) Describe Frank Zappa's utilization of humor in his music.

6) Identify how **glam rock** challenged stereotypical gender roles.

Chapter Introduction

In 1962, *art rock* was an oxymoron. A decade later, art rock was an established rock substyle. As late as the early sixties, it was hard for many to imagine rock-era music as anything more than mindless, if occasionally clever, music for teens. That changed almost overnight in the music of Dylan and the Beatles, as we discussed in **Chapter 6**. By 1970, art rock and numerous other art-oriented styles were part of a new sound world, all of which contributed to a new understanding of art in music, and in culture.

10-1 Rock and Art

In its broadest meaning, *art* is the product of any human activity done skillfully and creatively. One can artfully manufacture an automobile, bake a soufflé, sew a quilt, or dunk a basketball. However, the artistic aspect of all of these activities is secondary to their function. A Ferrari may be beautiful to look at, but if it won't start, it is only an oversized ornament; a between-the-legs 360-degree dunk may garner style points, but in a game it is as unproductive as an air ball if it clanks off the rim.

10-1a Classical Music: Music as Art

We also use *art* more restrictively to refer to a product of a skilled and creative activity whose main purpose is to stimulate the mind, touch the heart, and delight the senses. This more specific connotation of art is most familiar in the visual arts, for example, the paintings of Rembrandt and the sculptures of Rodin. However, this meaning of *art* has also been used to describe music such as the symphonies of Beethoven and Brahms.

The most established art music is what we now call classical music. The idea of a "classical" music—that is, the re-creation in performance of the best music of earlier generations—took hold in the middle of the nineteenth century, after the death of Beethoven in 1827 and with the revival of the music of Bach around the same time. Prior to that, the musical world was closer to our own: concerts and opera performances typically featured a composer's most recent works, just as tours by rock bands tend to promote their current recordings. However, by the beginning of the rock era, not much more than a century later, classical music seemed timeless, almost as if it been ordained from the beginning of civilization.

Classical music was, and is, an elite music, not only because of its inherent quality and its purpose—simply to be appreciated and enjoyed as an esthetic experience—but also because of its support system. Through the eighteenth century, the musicians who created the music that we now call classical were able to practice their art because of the patronage of church and court: for most of his career, the Austrian composer Joseph Haydn was in the service of the Esterhazy family, perhaps the richest rulers in Europe during the latter part of the eighteenth century. As church patronage declined in the nineteenth century, other sources of patronage emerged. The wealthy joined the aristocracy in support of the arts. To cite just one example, New York's Carnegie Hall, the most famous North American venue for classical music, was built by the industrialist Andrew Carnegie. During the same time, the marketplace became another source of income for classical musicians, mainly through concert performances and music publishing.

Commerce altered the dynamic between musicians and their audience. With patronage, the relationship was specific: please the patron or look for work elsewhere. With a more diffused and impersonal audience, musicians often had to make a choice between following their muse—that is, creating the music that they felt impelled to create—or composing and performing music designed to attract a larger and more lucrative audience. Suffering for one's art—starving to compose for the ages rather than selling out to put food on the table—is a nineteenth-century idea, a product of this new environment. It too reinforced the idea of classical music as an elite music.

The prestige of classical music continued to grow during the first part of the twentieth century. Conservatories were founded to train classical musicians. Universities trained audiences through courses in music appreciation. So did the media: Leonard Bernstein's Young People's Concerts, in which Bernstein alternately talked about music and conducted the New York Philharmonic, ran for fifteen seasons, beginning in 1958. Universities also became patrons of a sort. Many important twentieth-century composers held teaching positions at universities; indeed, all major universities with serious graduate music programs offer advanced degrees in classical composition, although it has been virtually impossible for a classical composer to make a living wage strictly from the performance and sale of his or her music since World War II.

At the dawn of the rock era, classical music—the substantial and well-documented legacy of works created by generations of European composers, and the institutions that supported it—effectively defined what good music was. Classical music was "highbrow"; classical musicians were "legitimate." Those that did not "appreciate" it were regarded as unsophisticated by the self-proclaimed and well-entrenched cultural elite, in this country and even more in the British Commonwealth. Classical music and the world that had grown up around it was the clearest and most widely accepted measure of art in music.

10-1b Rock as an Art Music

For rock musicians and others who sought artistic status for their work, the existence of an established musical elite created several issues, all related to the notion of quality. The main issue was not whether the music of Bach, Beethoven, and Brahms was "good." It was—and is. This music has become "classic" as well as "classical" because it has qualities that have touched generations of performers and listeners. Rather, the issue was whether music that was not part of this legacy was somehow inferior and—more importantly—whether the standards by which commentators evaluated classical music were applicable to other kinds of music. For example, if a musical work was too short, did not use certain forms, or did not develop melodies in certain ways, was it somehow inferior? Complicating the issue was the fact that "good music"—that is, the classics—had accumulated the trappings of high culture: concerts took place in magnificent auditoriums and theaters; musicians dressed in formal wear; well-dressed audiences sat politely through a performance, then applauded enthusiastically at the end. The issue here was whether this concert decorum was the only "right" way to respond to music.

Rock both co-opted and challenged the prevailing view of musical art, often simultaneously. The Who's *Tommy* is identified as a rock opera: opera is among the most elaborate and prestigious classical genres. But *Tommy* is unlike any previous opera—in story, music, and staging. On the liner notes to *Freak Out*, his debut album, Frank Zappa offers a long list of influences. The list includes several important classical composers from the early part of the twentieth century as well as a few from the mid century avant-garde; they comprise a small fraction of the names on the list, which also includes familiar and obscure jazz, pop, blues, and rock musicians, as well as music industry people and others not directly involved in music. By combining his diverse influences noncategorically in a single long list, Zappa effectively blows away boundaries between musical traditions, as well as the class boundaries that accompany them.

10-1c Antecedents of Art-Oriented Rock

The practice in popular music of assuming the musical features and trappings of classical music emerged around the turn of the twentieth century, at about the same time that black music began to have a commercial presence. Scott Joplin and his publisher billed his rags as "classic"; in 1910, Joplin completed *Treemonisha*, an opera for which he received the Pulitzer Prize almost 60 years after his death. Irving Berlin's **"That Mesmerizing Mendelssohn Tune"** (1909) is a famous early example of a popular song based on a classical melody—in this case, Felix Mendelssohn's **"Spring Song."**

Both Joplin's opera and Berlin's tune evidence early instances of what would become a recurrent trend in popular music: an attempt to legitimize itself through an association with classical music. The two examples also illustrate the two basic strategies: transforming classical works into popular music (as Berlin did) or composing music using classical music as a model (as Joplin did). The most famous instance of this practice from the first part of the twentieth century is George Gershwin's *Rhapsody in Blue*; there are many others, including Gershwin's "folk opera" *Porgy and Bess*.

There are two main reasons that this has occurred—one social and cultural, the other musical. An association with classical music made musical social climbing possible. Its use, or at least its obvious influence, narrows or eliminates numerous gaps—racial (white/black), generational (old/young), cultural (traditional/novel), economic (rich/poor), class (highbrow/lowbrow)—that separate the new style from established ones. The musical reason is more mundane, yet more compelling.

Good musicians are creative. They are eager to explore possibilities or to reinterpret the past in terms of a vibrant new present. To cite only the most spectacular example, Gershwin's music represents an unmatched synthesis of classical and contemporary vernacular music.

As popular genres matured, more musically sophisticated styles and trends emerged. Both jazz and the Broadway musical had attained a kind of art music status by the late fifties: the orchestral albums of Miles Davis; third-stream music, which attempted to fuse jazz and classical music; and Leonard Bernstein's musical *West Side Story* are illustrative. This had the effect of blurring the musical and social boundary between classical and popular.

Classical music was also under siege from above: the most innovative practitioners were severely stretching its expressive boundaries during the years after World War II. Such developments as the chance music of John Cage, **musique concrète**, and the minimalist music of La Monte Young challenged the very definition of music. For many in the avant-garde, the function of art was simply to make a significant statement about something. It didn't necessarily require the conventions or materials of high art (such as a symphony orchestra). Instead, artists took a pragmatic approach to the means. In the case of Cage, for example, it could be no more than sitting quietly at a piano for 4 minutes 33 seconds. Several of Zappa's acknowledged influences came from this avant-garde.

Rock came of age in this turbulent artistic environment. As we noted in the discussion of Dylan and the Beatles, rock bought into the idea that art had more to do with *what* you said than with the *means* you used to say it, particularly in the wake of Dylan's electric music. There were no inherently privileged methods. In fact, one of rock's self-imposed challenges was to create new ways to make a statement. We will encounter this in the music of the Doors and the Velvet Underground.

Other art-like trends emerged in the late sixties and early seventies. One was art as spectacle—what was called **glam rock**. We experience this through the music of David Bowie. Glam rock also had classical precedents—especially the lavish operas of the Baroque era—if not direct classical models or sources.

Classical/rock fusions were another important direction. These were realized in diverse ways by progressive rock groups such as Emerson, Lake & Palmer, Pink Floyd, and Yes, and heavy metal bands such as Deep Purple. We sample all of these trends in the course of this chapter.

musique concrète
Music created by using prerecorded sounds.

glam rock A rock style of the early 1970s in which theatrical elements—makeup, outlandish dress—were prominent. David Bowie, in his various incarnations, is considered by many to be the major figure in glam rock.

10-2 Rock's Dark Side

While the Beatles were singing "**All You Need Is Love,**" other rock groups were exploring the dark side of the rock revolution. Two stand out: the Doors and the Velvet Underground. Each sought out different territory. The Doors visited (in their words) "the other side": nightmarish conflations of sex and death. The Velvet Underground's Lou Reed portrayed the underbelly of life in New York in his lyrics. For both groups, the words, and the way they were sung, were of primary importance. However, they were markedly different in the vocal and instrumental setting of the words.

10-2a The Doors: Rock, Sex, and Death

The Doors came together in 1965 through a meeting of two UCLA film students. After Jim Morrison (1943–1971) read one of his poems to keyboardist Ray Manzarek (1939–2013), they decided to form a band. They soon added drummer John Densmore (b. 1944) and guitarist Robby Krieger (b. 1946). Morrison named the group the Doors after Aldous Huxley's book, *The Doors of Perception*, a reference that was probably lost on much of their audience.

The Doors had a meteoric rise and a slow, painful fall. Their first album, *The Doors*, hit the charts in 1967, reaching No. 2 and establishing the group's reputation almost overnight. Less than five years later, it was over. Morrison, who had taken a leave of absence from the group and moved to Paris, was found dead in a bathtub in December 1971. Without Morrison, the group floundered, eventually disbanding two years later.

The band created a distinctive sound world, by late-sixties standards. The dominant sound is Manzarek's organ, for two reasons. First, his melodic parts are most often the most prominent instrumental strand of the texture; Krieger's guitar is mainly in the background, except during his solos. Second, Manzarek is also playing the bass line—at least on their first album. Because the organ effectively replaces both the lead guitar and the electric bass, the sound does not have the fullness that one might expect from a more conventional sixties rock band. Manzarek's playing is certainly skillful, but it is no match for the flamboyance of guitarists like Jimi Hendrix or Pete Townshend, even in his extended solos. Similarly, Krieger's playing is relatively restrained by the standards of guitarists of the late sixties.

This sets up an interesting tension between hot and cool. Morrison's words and singing are hot—that is, sexually charged. By contrast, the backgrounds crafted by Manzarek are cool. This tension is apparent in "**Light My Fire**," the biggest hit from their first album. The opening of the song, which features Manzarek's busy, classical-sounding organ introduction, creates an emotionally neutral backdrop for Morrison. In both the original studio version and subsequent live recordings, the instruments are subdued when Morrison is singing. Morrison's lyrics, which he sings in a throaty style, starts as a sexual come-on; the sex will be drug-enhanced ("fire"/"higher"). But in the second section of the song, Morrison rhymes "fire," which is patently sexual in this context, to "mire" and "pyre." In short order, then, Morrison manages to lump together four of the most powerful and enduring cultural taboos: illicit sex, drugs, filth, and death. For Morrison, life would too soon imitate art. Morrison's "accidental" falls into the audience, a routine feature of the Doors' stage show, would be revealed as a ploy; he would expose himself onstage, sometimes to urinate, other times simply "to see what it looked like in a spotlight"; and he died too young because of extreme substance abuse.

Morrison seemingly knew no limits. Apparently, there was no topic so taboo that he would avoid it, no act so outrageous that Morrison would refrain from doing it, no behavior so destructive that he would abstain from it. He poured this into the music of the Doors, in the studio and even more in live performance. Many in his audience must have viewed him with a mixture of admiration and horror. They could experience vicariously his flaunting of social norms and his self-destructive behavior, because he went where they wouldn't dare. They also may have viewed his actions as a cautionary tale, especially in light of his decline and premature death.

The recording that best exemplifies Morrison's willingness to explore theatrically the most difficult and personal issues is the psychodrama "**The End**," an eleven-minute excursion into oedipal conflict and its most violent resolution. With its East Indian overtones, the musical setting is even more low key than that heard on "Light My Fire." The beginning sounds like background music for an acid trip. The opening of Morrison's long, rambling discourse is histrionic—in the words, if not the music. The middle section offers an extended metaphor ("ride the snake"), abstruse images ("the blue bus is calling us"), and clichés ("the west is the best"). The juxtaposition of images and the musical drone underneath have an almost hypnotic effect. Morrison's switch to clear narrative is like waking up from a nightmare, except that the awakened state *is* the nightmare. The musical chaos of the fatal climax (about two minutes after Morrison the narrator announces that "I'm going to kill you") gives emotional credibility to the song's moment of truth.

Morrison's shock-provoking lyrics and his intense, often melodramatic vocal style convinced his audience that he spoke knowledgeably about the confluence of death, decadence, and sex. The emotional detachment of the rest of the band, especially Manzarek, only served to bring Morrison's words and singing into sharper relief. For popular music, songs such as "Light My Fire" and "The End" opened the door to life's underbelly.

From their first album, the Doors, and especially Morrison, were on the edge. In fact, Morrison lived out the dramas he wrote about in his songs: extreme alcohol and drug abuse, increasingly flagrant public obscenity, and finally death at 27, allegedly from a heart attack. Morrison's willingness to go to the limit—to immerse himself in a self-destructive lifestyle and publicize it in his music and behavior, to risk—even invite—spectacular failure and public humiliation (rock critic Lester Bangs once described Morrison as a "Bozo Dionysius")—put him in a category by himself. It made almost everyone else seem tepid by comparison. Morrison embodied contradictions: a curiosity about and commitment to big themes and deep thoughts, such as Jungian psychology and Native American shamanism, and a seeming failure to act upon these ideas honorably. He remains one of the most provocative figures of the rock era.

10-2b The Velvet Underground: Rock and Drugs

The Velvet Underground invites comparison with the Doors. Both took a long walk on the wild side. But the Doors were based in southern California, while the Velvet Underground were part of the New York scene. The Doors were popular; the Velvet Underground was known only to a few. The Doors, and especially Morrison, who fancied himself a major literary figure, aspired to high art. The Velvet Underground started with the support of the high priest of pop art, Andy Warhol, who created the famous peelable banana cover of their first album. Warhol's backing gave them instant "art" status.

Lou Reed (b. 1942) brought his literary sensibility to the group, as well as his low key vocal delivery and guitar playing. John Cale (b. 1940), a classically trained violist and composer who had worked with experimental minimalist La Monte Young in the early sixties, was the main architect of its original sound. Guitarist Sterling Morrison (1942–1995) and drummer Maureen "Moe" Tucker (b. 1944) rounded out the rhythm section.

Warhol produced their early records. To promote the group, he set up the "Exploding Plastic Inevitable"—a potent mixture of film, dance, and musical performance. Nico, a blond European-born actress who was part of Warhol's circle at the time, sang with the band for their tour and first album, *The Velvet Underground and Nico* (1967). Given her limited vocal ability, her function within the band would seem to have been visual ornament. In fact, the combination of her icy beauty and lispy, labored singing may have been a Warhol-esque artistic statement: a poor man's Marilyn Monroe for the rock era.

The Velvet Underground owed an obvious debt to Dylan. Both the primacy of words and Reed's flat, largely uninflected delivery recall Dylan. So does the mood-setting accompaniment, which harks back to Dylan's early electric days (just two years previously). However, it's clear that Reed and the Velvet Underground have found their own voice. Reed's lyrics are usually incisive where Dylan's are often elliptical. For example, in **"I'm Waiting for the Man,"** a track on their 1967 album *The Velvet Underground and Nico*, Reed needs only a few short phrases to portray a white guy so strung out that he ventures into Harlem to get his next fix. Each phrase comes to life, as if it were a scene from a film. Where Jim Morrison used a club, Reed used a needle to get his point across.

Reed can afford to be low key because the instrumental accompaniment plays such a powerful role in establishing and sustaining the character of the song. The four instrumental parts—the endlessly repeated guitar riff, the repeated bass notes, hammered drums, and the piano chords—are virtually faceless; they have little inherent musical interest. The piano part is the most distinctive, but that is relative; with the other three parts there is almost no change throughout the song. The minimal musical interest—for instance, no signature guitar riff in the forefront, no complex rhythmic interplay between bass and drums—renders the instrumental background faceless; it is a kind of aural scenery.

For Cale and the rest of the band, the use of rock rhythm—here distilled to its essence—is purposeful, not simply the default option for a late-sixties song. The propulsive proto-punk beat, a jangly conjunction of sound and rhythm driven by Cale's two-fisted piano playing, surrounds Reed's voice with the nervous energy of the dope-deprived addict. Its very simplicity and almost perverse insistence seems to convey in music the obsessive need of the man waiting for the man.

Even more spectacular is **"Heroin,"** where Cale's viola part mutates from a drone into an inspired frenzy to depict the drug coursing through the bloodstream of its user. In its own way, "Heroin" is just as powerful in its evocation of the drug experience as "The End" is in its evocation of the violent resolution of the oedipal conflict. Both songs use similar techniques—changing tempos, piling on textural layers—to depict a moment of terror, or, in the case of "Heroin," a moment of terrible ecstasy.

The Velvet Underground's tenure was even shorter than that of the Doors. Cale left after the second album, and the group dissolved soon after. Reed has enjoyed intermittent success as a solo artist and has built a cult following. So did the Velvet Underground, although most of the cult joined after the group's demise. Despite their modest commercial success, the group was a major influence on punk.

10-3 Rock as Serious Satire: Frank Zappa and the Mothers of Invention

We tend to think of art as serious. We sit quietly and respectfully during concerts of classical music; we talk in hushed tones as we stroll through a museum. Our demeanor in these environments suggests that we don't expect art to be humorous. The next guffaw you hear during the performance of Beethoven's *Eighth Symphony* will probably be the first, although it is arguably a cosmically humorous composition. The same is almost certainly true of Debussy's piano prelude **"The Interrupted Serenade,"** which depicts in music an ardent lover's comical misfortunes as he tries to serenade a señorita.

Serious can mean solemn; it can also mean important. *Serious music*, like *art music*, has been suggested as an alternative label to *classical music*, as the boundaries of traditional classical music stretch past the breaking point. It can also mean committed: when we say someone is "serious" about playing guitar, or bass, we mean that he or she is willing to work hard to develop mastery of the instrument.

During the heady sixties, the group that took humor most seriously was Frank Zappa and the Mothers of Invention. Their music was seldom solemn and then often mockingly so. However, in terms of importance and commitment, they were certainly dead serious. Zappa and his core group were far more serious about their humor than the album covers would suggest. They remain one of the most innovative and skilled bands of the rock era. Indeed, to identify them as a rock band is too limiting: they were an ensemble capable of shifting styles on the fly; rock and rock-related music was just part of their realm of expertise.

We get some insight into the nature of their humor and their sense of identity from their name. It is a double pun: necessity may have been the mother of invention, but "mother" was also street slang for a highly skilled performer—*and* something else.

Frank Zappa (1940–1993) was rock's great iconoclast. He was an equal opportunity satirist, taking potshots at almost everyone in and out of rock, including himself. At the same time, he was one of rock's cleverest and most knowledgeable minds and one of its great innovators. In addition to using rock as a vehicle for satire, he also pioneered multimedia extravaganzas, which he called "freak outs," concept-type albums (McCartney claimed that *Freak Out* [1966] influenced the Beatles' *Sgt. Pepper*), and wholesale eclecticism.

Zappa collected musical influences from everywhere. Among the most important was the French/American avant-garde composer Edgard Varèse. In a Zappa record, one might hear Varèse-influenced music juxtaposed with a fifties rock-and-roll parody. Such jarring contrasts were one of his innovations. He was also one of the pioneers of jazz/rock fusion, working with violinist Jean-Luc Ponty.

As with the Doors and the Velvet Underground, words are the main focus—when they are present. You have to listen to Zappa's lyrics; often the music seems to be strictly at the service of the words. Nevertheless, his compositions are in many ways the most sophisticated music of the rock era. They demand great technical proficiency and stylistic flexibility from the musicians who play them. Not surprisingly, his bands included some of the most accomplished and versatile musicians of the era.

Although his first album, *Freak Out*, immediately established him as a unique voice, it is his third album, *We're Only in It for the Money* (1967), that best represents his early work, in the judgment of many commentators. Zappa's tool was a sharp pin, which he used to pop lots of balloons. Deflation begins with the album cover, a send-up of the cover of the Beatles' *Sgt. Pepper*. On it, the group is wearing dresses, and the wax figures have become mannequins: one is "giving birth" to a baby doll. Their gallery includes Jimi Hendrix, Lyndon Johnson, and assorted cultural icons, many of whose eyes are covered with black rectangles, perhaps to suggest a kind of self-imposed censorship.

We are aware from the outset that *We're Only in It for the Money* is not a conventional album: not just a collection of songs. Although of course there are songs, there are also numerous spoken sections, accompanied by electronic noises (track 1), conventional instruments (**"Who Needs the Peace Corps"**), or no instruments at all (**"Telephone Conversation"**). In addition, there are extended instrumental sections.

There is a dazzling virtuosity in the variety. To cite just two examples: the instrumental opening of **"The Chrome Plated Megaphone of Destiny"** sounds more appropriate for an innovative classical music album than a rock disc, while the opening of "Who Needs the Peace Corps" sounds like a children's song. Zappa's lyrics can be devastating as well as devastatingly funny. The spoken section of "Who Needs the Peace Corps" parodies a definitely uncool guy mapping out his hippie lifestyle in San Francisco.

The biggest zinger, though, is probably **"What's the Ugliest Part of Your Body**?" The song begins with "Earth Angel"-style background vocals. Their pseudo-innocence only enhances the impact of the punch line. The next few minutes show Zappa's strategy: musical and verbal collage with jarring verbal and musical juxtapositions. He follows the revelation that your mind is the ugliest part of your body with some pompous sermonizing, accompanied by music in an irregular rhythmic pattern (2 + 2 + 3 quick beats, in place of the 2 + 2 + 2 + 2 pattern of rock). A question about "Annie" (who is she and what is she doing in this song, anyway?), accompanied by a slithering melody in waltz rhythm, interrupts the sermon. A piano solo that reaches back to Aaron Copland and ahead to new age music links the sermon with the next song, which begins with a snotty-toned definition of *discorporate*, but not before a woman mutters a snide aside about the limitations of her sexual activity.

It is a dizzying pace, because of the abrupt shifts between segments—the Mothers never miss a beat—and because of the extreme contrast between styles. If it were possible to get whiplash just listening to music, Zappa would be the one to cause it.

Zappa's lyrics were also often intentionally juvenile and scatological, as if to deflate his own high-art intentions. His often silly titles (such as **"Peaches en Regalia"**) for very sophisticated music, was another self-deflating strategy. Many critics missed the seriousness of the music and only focused on the often puerile lyrics—which for Zappa must have been part of the joke. It was if you had to pass through a series of tests to prove yourself a true Zappa fan and listener.

All of this renders Zappa's music, considered as a whole, less accessible than *Sgt. Pepper*. There are certainly straightforward moments: the parody songs and monologues stand out (perhaps this is why Zappa scored his only major hit with the silly parody song **"Valley Girl**," hardly his most innovative work). But this is not warm and fuzzy music or music that you can groove to. As his album cover makes clear, Zappa demands a commitment from his listeners.

That gives the title of the album a certain irony: it's quite clear that money is not a major motivation for Zappa. He and the Mothers were certainly skilled enough to have created music that would have kept them firmly entrenched in the Top 40 charts. But that would have required some selling out and the sacrifice of his unique vision. Zappa did neither during his lifetime. He took it upon himself to become rock's fiercest social critic as well as one of its most imaginative musicians and its greatest humorist; no one else was even close.

10-4 Rock Opera: The Who

No group of the sixties merged rock's essence with rock as art more effectively than the Who. Like so many of the important British groups of the sixties, the Who began as a blues-oriented band; their early stage shows mixed original songs with R&B covers, including Motown songs and even an early James Brown hit—Brown was Daltrey's idol. Moon's manic drumming, Entwhistle's inventive, soul-inspired bass lines, Townshend's windmilled power chords, and Daltrey's gritty vocals set the group apart from other British bands. So did the absence of a rhythm guitarist; they were among the first power trios, although Townshend was not a virtuosic guitarist. The group quickly gained an enthusiastic following, especially among

Mods, a British youth subculture drawn to trendy clothes, motor scooters, and soul—or at least soulful—music.

However, Townshend, the most intellectually adventurous member of the band, had been interested in expanding the Who's musical horizons. The group followed *Happy Jack* (released in the United Kingdom in late 1966 as *A Quick One*) with *The Who Sell Out* (1967), a concept album built around the idea of a radio broadcast, interspersed between a diverse group of songs are simulated commercials and public service announcements. The album cover features each band member grotesquely promoting a fake product.

Townshend's next big project would take the group in a dramatically different direction. The genesis of *Tommy* was a casual remark by Kit Lambert, the Who's producer and manager. When he suggested almost off-handedly that Townshend compose a rock opera, Townshend took the idea and ran with it.

Opera is the most spectacular and prestigious of classical music genres. Labeling *Tommy* a "rock opera" immediately implied its highbrow status, even if the label was misleading. As Richard Barnes points out, "Strictly speaking, [*Tommy*] isn't a rock opera at all. It has no staging, scenery, acting, or recitative." It doesn't have much of a plot, either, and what there is, is difficult to follow. Still, the story—of a deaf, mute, and blind child who becomes a messiah via pinball wizardry—unfolds in the songs, by fits and starts.

The songs don't pull any punches. The list of subjects addressed in *Tommy* includes (again, according to Barnes) "murder, trauma, bullying, child molestation, sex, drugs, illusion, delusion, altered consciousness, spiritual awakening, religion, charlatanism, success, superstardom, death, betrayal, rejection, and pinball." Not typical fare, even for the late sixties, but certainly a logical expansion of the Who's efforts in their previous albums.

Musically, what's remarkable about *Tommy* is not so much the fact that the Who make an artistic statement but *how* they make it. Unlike the Beatles and so many of those who followed in their footsteps, the Who didn't abandon their rock roots, or at least overlay them with classical music trappings. There are no strings, no synthesizers, and no other classical music features associated with so much of the art rock of the period.

Instead, the band remains pretty much self-contained. Rather than adding an orchestra's worth of instruments, they vary the sounds within the group. The most obvious nonrock sounds are Moon's tympani, Entwhistle's French horn, and Town-shend's various keyboard sounds. As he shifts from character to character, Daltrey displays extraordinary vocal flexibility, from the soul-drenched grittiness of **"Smash the Mirror"** to the tenderness of **"See Me, Feel Me."** Townshend and the rest of the band play classic hard rock in songs like **"Sparks,"** yet the instrumental **"Overture"** and **"Underture"** contain steely acoustic guitar playing—alternately gritty and sensitive, and always imaginative.

The other feature that immediately sets *Tommy* apart from standard rock fare is the pacing of the work. The tracks are as long as they need to be—no more, no less. There is no allegiance to the three-minute song, in either direction. The shortest "song" is **"Miracle Cure"**; it is twelve seconds long. And it is one of seven tracks well under two minutes. The longest track is the magnificent "Underture" (ten minutes and nine seconds), which divides the work in half—like the first and second acts of an opera. The irregular rhythm of the tracks is clear evidence that Townshend is responsive to the dramatic demands of his subject rather than the conventions of popular song.

In *Tommy*, the Who have the best of both worlds—in two ways. They make an artistic statement on a grand scale (seventy-five minutes long) without forsaking, or even downplaying, their rock roots. Moreover, they were able to perform *Tommy* live without hiring a symphony orchestra, because they stayed within the group's basic instrumentation. It was a unique achievement, for the Who, and for rock. Their subsequent operatic efforts, most notably *Quadrophenia*, did not enjoy similar success, and no other band produced anything comparable.

10-5 Glam Rock: Rock as Spectacle

Rock has had a strong visual element since Elvis first combed his hair into a pompadour, curled his lips into a sneer, and twitched his hips. By the late sixties, the visual dimension of rock had become, in its most extreme manifestations, far more flamboyant and outrageous: flaming or smashed guitars, provocative gestures and body movements, even public urination and vomiting. This outrageousness was in part a consequence of larger venues. With arena concerts now increasingly common, performers had to appear larger than life to have visual impact. Bands began touring with elaborate sets, special effects (lighting, smoke bombs, fireworks), and outlandish costuming.

In the first part of the rock era, the most spectacular form of theatrical rock was glam (or glitter) rock. It emerged in the early seventies, mainly in the work of David Bowie and T Rex, a group fronted by Marc Bolan.

10-5a Art as Artifice

As it took shape in the mid-sixties, rock prided itself on being real. It confronted difficult issues, dealt with real feelings, looked life squarely in the eye. The music of the Doors and the Velvet Underground are vivid examples of this dimension of rock. This realism provoked a reaction. The Beatles followed *A Hard Day's Night*, a documentary-style film of their life on the run, with *Sgt. Pepper*, in which they assumed personas, visually and musically. In rock, the mask became the yin to the yang of hyper-real rock.

Rock as artifice—rock behind the mask—found its fullest expression in glam rock, and especially in the music of David Bowie. In Ziggy Stardust, the first of his several incarnations, Bowie stripped identity down to the most basic question of all: gender. Was Ziggy male or female, or somewhere in between? With his lithe build, flamboyant costumes, and heavy makeup, Bowie as Ziggy seemed to be a hermaphrodite. Particularly because he was not well known prior to Ziggy—unlike Roger Daltrey before *Tommy*—there was no "real" Bowie to compare with his Ziggy persona. His sexual outrageousness was the mirror image of Morrison's: when Morrison exposed himself, he made explicit his gender. When Bowie pranced around onstage wearing a big feather boa, he put his gender—or at least his sexual preference—seriously in doubt. (With respect to confused sexual identity, Bowie was the rock-era counterpart to *castrati*, singers who were castrated as boys to keep their voices from changing; they sang male roles in a female vocal range in seventeenth- and early eighteenth-century opera.) Add to that a fantastical story, and—when performed live—a spectacular production, glam rock, as exemplified by Bowie, was the opposite of real.

10-5b David Bowie

Bowie (born David Jones, 1947–2016) began his career in the sixties as a British folksinger. Influenced by Iggy Pop, Marc Bolan, and the Velvet Underground, he began to reinvent his public persona. In 1972, he announced that he was gay.

(However, he commented in an interview over a decade later that he "was always a closet heterosexual.") Later that year, he put together an album and a stage show, *The Rise and Fall of Ziggy Stardust and the Spiders from Mars*. It featured Bowie, complete with orange hair, makeup, and futuristic costumes, as Ziggy, a rock star trying to save the world but doomed to fail.

Ziggy was Bowie's first and most outrageous persona. For the rest of his career, he continually reinvented himself in a variety of guises, all markedly different from the others: for example, "plastic soul" man, techno-pop avant-gardist. Bowie was rock's ultimate poseur. And that was his art: assuming so many different personas—not only in appearance and manner, but also in music—that he made a mystery of his real self. Given Bowie's constantly changing roles during the course of his career, it is small wonder that he was the most successful film actor among post-Elvis rock stars.

Bowie was intensely involved in all aspects of his roles, including the music. After recording at Philadelphia's Sigma Sound Studios (in the seventies, it was the home of "the Sound of Philadelphia"), he changed his stage show completely—from flair to bare—and incorporated sixties soul classics into his set. Despite his complete immersion in a role—or perhaps because of it—there was also detachment. Listening to his music and to the words of his songs, we hear both first and third person.

Ziggy Stardust

The songs from *Ziggy Stardust* provide the musical dimension of Bowie's role playing. Their effect is not as obvious as his appearance, but without them, his persona would be incomplete. The three components of the songs—the words, Bowie's singing, and the musical backdrop—all assume multiple roles, as we hear in "**Hang on to Yourself**," one of the tracks from the album.

The lyric is laced with vivid images: "funky-thigh collector," "tigers on Vaseline," "bitter comes out better on a stolen guitar." These arrest our ear, without question. But Bowie continually shifts from person to person as he delivers them. He "reports" in the verse, "She's a tongue-twisting storm," and entreats in the chorus, "Come on, come on, we've really got a good thing going." His voice changes dramatically from section to section. It's relatively impersonal in the verse and warm, almost whispered, in the chorus.

The music is more subtle in its role playing. Bowie embedded vocal and instrumental hooks into all his songs. The instrumental hook is the guitar riff; the vocal hook is the whispered chorus, a shock after the pile-driving verse. Both features make the song immediately accessible and memorable.

But there are also subtle clues woven into the song that seem to tell us that, for Bowie, the hooks are the dumbed-down parts of the music. With such features as the extra beats after the first line of the verse ". . . light machine" and elsewhere, Bowie seemed to be hinting that he was capable of a lot more sophistication than he was showing on the surface. Indeed, the spare style of the song was one of the freshest and most influential sounds of the seventies. Like Ziggy, he was descending down to the level of mass taste (even as he was reshaping it) because he wanted the effect it created, not because that's all he could do.

In *Ziggy Stardust*, Bowie created a persona that demanded attention but was shrouded in mystery. What made his persona so compelling, both in person and on record, was not only its boldness but its comprehensiveness. Precisely because accessibility and ambiguity were present in every aspect of the production—the subject of the show, Bowie's appearance, the lyrics, his singing, the music—Bowie raised role-playing from simple novelty to art. This quality made him one of the unique talents of the rock era.

Bowie was also one of the most influential musicians of the decade. The "lean, clean" sound of "Hang on to Yourself" was a model for punk and **new wave** musicians; indeed, Glen Matlock of the Sex Pistols remarked that "Hang on to Yourself" influenced "God Save the Queen."

10-6 Rock, Art, and Technology

Rock and music technology are connected symbiotically. Technology is integral to rock in every aspect, from the first steps in the creative process to the final result on recordings or in live performance, as we have noted. More significantly, technology made possible many of the innovations of rock-era music—from a new creative paradigm made possible by multitrack recording and a host of new instrumental sounds, to sound systems that filled stadiums.

Because of this dynamic relationship between rock and technology, a revolution in music-related technology occurred in tandem with, and in support of, the rock revolution. And because the new technologies helped make rock sound so different from earlier generations of popular music, it is easy to imagine that these technologies and their uses were exclusively the province of rock-related music, such as the wah-wah pedal popularized by Jimi Hendrix.

In addition to such rock-specific devices, rock musicians leveraged rapidly developing technology to explore and expand two sound families: real-world sounds and electronically generated sounds. Both of these sound families were used extensively in art-oriented rock. However, both emerged originally in the most esoteric music of the mid-twentieth-century—avant-garde classical music.

10-6a The Tools of Electronic Music

The practice of incorporating sounds from any source into a musical work took hold only after the tape recorder became commercially available. While it was possible to record sounds not produced by voices or musical instruments prior to the invention of the magnetic tape recorder, everything had to be done in real time. With magnetic tape, however, it was possible to collect sounds on tape, then splice them together. The pioneer in assembling musical works from a wide array of sounds, including those not traditionally associated with music, was the French composer and writer Pierre Schaeffer. Schaeffer called the sound collages that he recorded on tape musique concrète, because the composer worked directly (that is, concretely) with the sounds to be heard, rather than relying on notation to convey musical ideas to performers. Schaeffer created his first *musique concrète* work in 1948. Other innovative composers followed suit; by 1967, the year in which *Sgt. Pepper* and *We're Only in It for the Money* were released, it was a well-established if not widely accepted branch of the classical avant-garde.

In rock, it entered almost imperceptibly: crowd noises, alarm clocks, phone conversations, and other "nonmusical" sounds were incorporated into songs and compositions to make the atmosphere created in a particular track more vivid. Both avant-garde and rock composers took advantage of multitrack recording to mix real-world sounds with musical elements, rather than simply splice the sounds together in a predetermined sequence.

The first fully electronic instruments, most notably the theremin and Ondes Martenot, appeared just after World War I. With the theremin, the performer controlled sound by moving his or her hands; the Ondes Martenot used similar technology, but performers could control sound through a keyboard. The most popular and enduring of the pre–World War II electronic instruments was the

> **new wave** The "back to basics" movement within rock beginning in the late 1970s, featuring simplified instrumentation and basic chords and melodies. An early new wave band was the Talking Heads.

electronic organ, most notably the Hammond B-3. This instrument found its way into black churches, cocktail lounges, jazz clubs, basketball arenas, and rock bands, especially after 1945.

The first synthesizers appeared in the fifties. The most famous of these early machines was the RCA Electronic Music Synthesizer, introduced in 1955. This synthesizer was a huge machine—and cumbersome and time-consuming to program. The first commercial synthesizers appeared about a decade later; the one released by Robert Moog in 1964 was much smaller and was controlled in part by a keyboard. However, it was not suitable for live performance. The introduction of the Mini-moog, a portable instrument with preset sounds, appeared in 1970. Rock musicians quickly embraced the Minimoog and other performance-ready synthesizers that also appeared in the early seventies; those willing to master the new instruments gained a much-expanded palette of sounds.

10–6b Pink Floyd

Among the most familiar examples to mix real-world and synthesized sounds with more conventional rock was Pink Floyd's 1973 album *Dark Side of the Moon*. At the time of this recording, Pink Floyd consisted of guitarist David Gilmour (b. 1946), percussionist Nick Mason (b. 1944), keyboardist Richard Wright (1943–2008), and bassist Roger Waters (b. 1943); for this album, Waters wrote all of the lyrics and co-wrote most of the songs.

One can argue that the two applications of electrical technology—sounds from the real world and those produced on a synthesizer—used by Pink Floyd in *Dark Side of the Moon* were not only absolutely integral to the intent of the album but also essential to its impact and success. Waters's lyrics paint a bleak portrait of modern life. The tracks describe the stress of living in the modern world— stress that can be so overwhelming that it drives people to insanity. Moreover, he posed for himself the additional challenge of presenting his perceptions in easily understood language. On those tracks where the band plays, the musical setting is comparably direct and anything but cutting edge. Good straight-ahead rock alternates with sensitive rock ballads. There are no histrionics, à la Morrison; no immersion in sound, à la the Velvet Underground; none of the musical complexity heard in the music of Frank Zappa, or Yes (which we encounter later in this chapter). The most obvious deviation from basic rock by the band occurs in "Money": the meter groups beats by seven (4 + 3), rather than by four.

Instead, Pink Floyd relied on the array of "found" sounds—the cash register, the spoken asides (answers given in response to a set of questions prepared by Waters)—and the electronically generated musical ideas and effects—the "running" pattern on the second track, the heartbeat that opens the album—to give weight to the album as a whole. These "concrete" and electronically generated sounds are one dimension of a coordinated plan to support Waters's lyrics with significant-sounding music. Other aspects of this are the strong contrasts from track to track; the variation in pacing, from very slow to very fast; the inventive harmonies— familiar-sounding chords in fresh progressions; the rich reverb, especially in **"The Great Gig in the Sky,"** which features the soaring vocal line of Clare Torry; extended sections featuring instruments without vocals; and the continuous flow of the music from track to track.

Their formula worked: the album remained on the US Top 200 charts for 741 weeks—over fourteen years. No album has ever charted for a longer period of time. Periodic reissues have also sold well. *Dark Side of the Moon* was the first of Pink Floyd's several top-selling albums, almost all of which continued to explore difficult issues. The most acclaimed was the 1979 album *The Wall*. Live performances of the music from the album were spectacular; they ended with the crumbling of a wall constructed at the front of the stage, between the band and the audience.

10-7 Rock as Art and Art Rock

In the late sixties and early seventies, the most self-consciously arty branch of rock was the style known alternatively as art rock and progressive rock. Progressive rock musicians sought to elevate the status of rock by embracing a classical music esthetic and adapting it to rock. Most often, this meant applying concepts and features associated with classical music, and especially classical instrumental music, into their work: King Crimson's modernist uses of irregular meters and atonality is a notable example. Occasionally, and more specifically, it could involve wholesale borrowing of classical compositions: Procul Harum's **"A Whiter Shade of Pale"** mixed rock and Bach; Keith Emerson remade the Russian composer Modest Mussorgsky's *Pictures at an Exhibition*. Art rock/progressive rock became the mainly instrumental analog to concept albums and rock operas, which were typically more vocally oriented.

10-7a From Dance Floor to Concert Hall

In elevating rock from straightforward dance music to sophisticated music for listening, progressive rock musicians accomplished in about a decade what had taken classical music centuries to achieve. The earliest surviving examples of instrumental music are simple dances from the late thirteenth century. Until about 1600, most of the instrumental works published or preserved in manuscript were dances for the court. It wasn't until the early seventeenth century that composers regularly composed idiomatically for instruments—that is, composed in ways that took advantage of the particular capabilities of an instrument. Concertos and sonatas—instrumental compositions not used for dancing—joined dance and dance-inspired compositions as widely used genres.

Nevertheless, despite its growing complexity, instrumental music was considered inferior to vocal music: from the early seventeenth century through the end of the eighteenth century, opera was the most prestigious musical genre. Only in the early nineteenth century, in response to the symphonies and sonatas of Beethoven, did critics begin to regard instrumental music as equal to or even superior to vocal music. These works and others like them had moved far beyond dance music, although they often retained a dance connection: the third movement of a symphony was typically either a minuet or a scherzo—both dance-inspired.

Like classical instrumental music, rock began as music for social dancing. The first requirement of this kind of dance music is a good beat. As rock matured, musicians like Zappa, keyboardists Keith Emerson and Rick Wakeman, and guitarists Ritchie Blackmore (of Deep Purple) and Robert Fripp (of King Crimson) sought to elevate the level of discourse in rock by emulating certain aspects of classical instrumental music: complexity, virtuosity, rhythmic freedom, the grand gesture. This took rock out of the garage and into the concert hall, or at least to the arena. This shift in orientation from dance music to music for listening raised the esthetic bar. Rock had to have more than a good beat. It had to be inherently interesting on several levels, challenging to its audience, and rewarding to those who gave the music the attention that it demands.

Often, this is most evident in the approach to rhythm. A dance-oriented song (such as "The Twist") will typically establish and maintain a consistent, obvious, and danceable beat. By contrast, an art-oriented composition may well feature passages with a great dance beat. But it is also likely to contain rhythmic features that make it virtually unusable as dance music: for instance, tempo extremes and shifts in tempo; suspension of timekeeping; use of irregular meters (like the seven-beat measures in "Money"); active, syncopated rhythms that play off an unheard pulse.

Among the noteworthy progressive rock groups of the early seventies were Emerson, Lake & Palmer; Gentle Giant; Jethro Tull; King Crimson; and Yes. We listen to "**Roundabout**" by Yes as a commercially and artistically successful example of progressive rock.

Interestingly, almost all of the important progressive rock bands were British. Critic John Rockwell attributes this in part to the relatively greater prestige enjoyed by classical music in British society. In his view, rock musicians who wished to elevate their artistic status could do so by adapting classical values and procedures to rock. He feels that the impetus to do so was far stronger in the United Kingdom.

Another reason might well be the far greater importance of jazz in the United States. Jazz had already attained an art-like status by the late fifties. American musicians interested in following a similar path often turned to jazz/rock fusion. Guitarist John McLaughlin, a Scotsman who recorded with Miles Davis, straddled the two styles.

10-7b Yes

Singer Jon Anderson (b. 1944) and bassist Chris Squire (1948–2015) formed Yes in 1968. The band underwent two key personnel changes in 1971: keyboardist Rick Wakeman (b. 1949) replaced Tony Kaye, and guitarist Steve Howe (b. 1947) replaced Tony Banks. Drummer Bill Bruford (b. 1949) was an earlier recruit. *Fragile* and *Closer to the Edge* (both 1972), their first two albums with the new lineup, were their most successful; "Roundabout," from *Fragile*, was their most popular single of the decade.

While not mapped out on the broad scale of their later music, "Roundabout" nevertheless provides a helpful introduction to the qualities that defined progressive rock during this period. First, it's clear that the music is the most important dimension of the piece. There are extended instrumental sections throughout, and the lyric of the vocal sections is so vague and nonreferential as to be virtually meaningless. However, the words do provide milestones for listeners navigating their way through this lengthy song: "Roundabout" is only a third of the length of Yes' longer works (which often covered an entire album side); still, it is over eight minutes long, about three times the length of the average single.

Its sprawling form, the numerous contrasts, and the flashes of virtuosity also set the song apart from more mainstream rock. "Roundabout" is a big, multisectional piece. An extended slow introduction sets it in motion; its return with an organ obbligato marks the midpoint of the piece. There are several changes of texture and key, and occasionally it shifts away from the regular four-beat measures. The most striking of these shifts occurs in the "choral" section, which has measures with seven beats. Virtuosic ensemble passages, solos, and fills occur throughout: the doubled guitar/bass duet, Wakeman's fast fills, and Squire's well-grooved bass riff under the first vocal section are good examples.

Despite these departures from common practice, "Roundabout" never loses sight of the fact that it is rock. In fact, the gentler sections help the "groove" sections stand out because the contrast is so strong. Indeed, the second melodic idea, which sets "In and around the lake," uncannily anticipates Kool & the Gang's 1981 hit "**Celebration**"; they even share the same key.

Progressive rock took a good deal of criticism from some quarters as being pretentious, overproduced, and symptomatic of the decline of rock in the seventies. What this song shows, however, is some very capable and inventive musicians at play, stretching rock's boundaries.

10-8 Rock as Art Redux

As this small sample demonstrates, art-oriented rock encompassed an unusually diverse body of music: the dark-side excursions of the Doors and the Velvet Underground; the no-holds-barred/everyone's a target/extremely hip satire of Frank Zappa and the Mothers of Invention; the Who's reconception of opera; art as spectacle—David Bowie masking himself as Ziggy Stardust; Pink Floyd's mix of simplicity and significance, aided by a mix of conventional rock and cutting-edge technology; and Yes' virtuosic progressive rock. Despite their diverse conceptual and musical approaches, these musicians share attitudes and principles that provide a common ground and that distinguish their music from that of most other acts of the era. Most outstanding is a sense of importance: the music is supposed to be significant. This is conveyed in different ways:

- Tackling deep, difficult, or controversial subjects: the Doors, the Velvet Underground, Pink Floyd
- Elaborate artifice: Bowie/Ziggy; the Who/*Tommy*
- Superb musicianship: Zappa and Yes above all, but also the Who, Bowie and Spiders from Mars, and Pink Floyd
- Sophisticated satire: Zappa most obviously; the Who less directly
- Emulating, seeking inspiration from, or co-opting classical concepts, genres, and methods: the Who, Zappa, Yes, Pink Floyd
- Thinking big: concept albums by Zappa, the Who, Pink Floyd; long songs by the Doors, the Velvet Underground, and Yes
- Innovative sounds: Frank Zappa, the Who, Pink Floyd

In virtually all of this music, the divorce from popular song and dance is apparent. Of the examples considered here, only "Light My Fire" (the single version) and "Hang on to Yourself " are similar in length, form, and style to songs of the sixties and early seventies—and Bowie's song is typical because it is dramatically necessary at that point in the narrative to present a more-or-less typical rock song. The departure from late-sixties rock and roll is most apparent in rhythm and sound. Every song or album plays with time: extremes or extreme contrasts in track length (some very long; others very brief); extremes or extreme contrasts in tempo (very fast; very slow); and contrasts in beat-keeping and rhythmic play (strong beat marking versus no timekeeping versus highly syncopated rhythmic textures). And while "concrete" and synthesized sounds are not a requirement for art-oriented rock, they occur far more frequently in this music than they do in the music that we will hear in the next chapter.

10-8a The Impact of Rock as Art

The efflorescence of art-oriented rock was brief: its heyday was less than a decade. Among the reasons for its sudden decline were its own excesses, musical and otherwise; the demise of the Beatles; and the rise of a corporate mentality within rock—it seemed that the values of both musicians and audience shifted. Still, this

alternative A term to describe a family of rock-related, punk-inspired styles that began in the early eighties and continues into the twenty-first century.

grunge A style of rock music which emerged in the late 80s which fused punk disaffection with the power and distortion of heavy metal.

branch of rock demonstrated that it was possible to make significant statements in rock: its impact is evident in such diverse styles as the music of U2, early **alternative**, new wave, and **grunge**.

Interestingly, art-oriented rock seems to have had a more far-reaching impact on music from outside rock. We have already noted the emergence of jazz fusion, which combined rock and jazz. The rock musical emerged around 1970, most notably in the works of Andrew Lloyd Webber. Both jazz and musical theater had attained a quasi-art status at the beginning of the rock era. Art rock helped them retain their elite status as they merged with rock. And it is possible to view the interaction of classical music and rock as a two-way process: two of the most significant trends in classical music since 1965 have been minimalism and eclecticism. To cite just one noteworthy example, the music of the minimalist composer Philip Glass, the most commercially successful American composer of the latter part of the twentieth century, has more in common with rock than any classical tradition. This is not to claim any direct influence, although there have been instances of that. Rather, it is simply to point out that musical ideas and features expressed in various forms of art-oriented rock were in the air, where they could enter the consciousness of contemporary "classical" composers almost by osmosis.

More generally, art-oriented rock, because it was frequently commercially and artistically important, helped blur the boundaries between high and low culture. It can be seen as an important component of the move toward a more multicultural and democratic view of value in art—and through that, a more open-minded and multicultural society.

CHAPTER 11

WORDS, MELODY, AND ROCK IN THE EARLY SEVENTIES

Learning Objectives:

1) Give examples of **singer-songwriters** who were musically active in the late 1960s to early 1970s.

2) Articulate the musical components that contributed to the success of Don McLean's "American Pie."

3) Compare the vocal characteristics of Carole King and Joni Mitchell.

4) Illustrate James Taylor's role as a singer-songwriter.

5) Define key elements of countrified rock.

6) Discuss Elton John's varied instrumentation in his musical works.

Chapter Introduction

If there's one song that everyone knew in 1971—and for decades afterwards—it was Don McLean's "**American Pie**." Part of the song's appeal was a refrain that was easy to learn with just a few repetitions — maybe once through the long version of the song — coupled to a lyric that people are still trying to decode. Who is "Miss American Pie," and how does she connect to Chevys, dry levees, and good old boys drinking while awaiting death?

For over four decades, McLean turned down requests to explain his lyric—a verbal analog to the cover of The Beatles' *Sgt. Pepper*. Finally, he opened up in 2015, when he offered the manuscript of the lyric for sale at Christie's, the famous British auction house. In an interview for the auction catalog, McLean described the song as ". . . an indescribable photograph of America that I tried to capture in words and music." His "photograph" depicts an America where ". . . things are heading in the wrong direction. It is becoming less idyllic. I don't know whether you consider that wrong or right but it is a morality song in a sense."

For a detailed interpretation of the lyric, please visit **http:// understandingamericanpie.com**.

McLean's elegiac anthem was an especially noteworthy instance of a diverse body of rock-related music that focused on words and melody, and that relied on musical support that required as little as an instrument or two, and didn't require Marshall stacks. In the six tracks discussed below, the lyrics range from direct and plain spoken ("you've got a friend") to hedonistic ("come by, baby, don't say maybe/I gotta know if your sweet love is gonna save me") and high on life ("alive, alive, I wanna get up and jive/anna wreck my stockings in some jukebox dive").

The lyrics ride on melodies that flow more or less continuously and are the primary source of musical interest. The instrumental support was soft more than loud, instruments were acoustic more than electric, the rhythms engaging but not overpowering. The antecedents of this music came mainly from the folk revival and folk rock, country music, and the new rock-tinged pop of the sixties, but the sounds and the sensibility were new. The rock world dubbed them "singer-songwriters."

11-1 Singer-Songwriters

There is no more eclectic subcategory within rock music than singer-songwriter. Interpreted literally, *singer-songwriter* identifies those who perform the music they create—which covers most rock acts (but not as much R&B). However, the term came into use during the early seventies to identify a group of musicians whose music was in many ways the antithesis of the core rock style. The music of the singer-songwriters was often a music for small spaces and close, even personal connections between performer and audience. It was more at home in coffee houses than arenas.

But within these general boundaries, it was a diverse body of music. Some songs are intimate, first-person accounts, confessional in tone. Others are *cinéma vérité* portraits, or acerbic social commentary. Still others are cryptic accounts that leave the identity of the narrator in question. Most are songs in a restricted sense of the term: they have coherent melodies that help tell the story and make musical sense through an inner logic. They are seldom formulaic; formal and melodic imagination finds its greatest outlet in these songs.

There were old and new faces among the singer-songwriters presented here. Carole King was a Brill Building veteran; she had been a professional songwriter for over a decade before releasing her first album. Joining her was new generation of folk-inspired performers, most notably Joni Mitchell and James Taylor.

11-1a Meaning and Melody

The music of the singer-songwriters of the late sixties and early seventies represents the continuing evolution of the folk/country/pop fusions of the mid-sixties. Bob Dylan was the dominant influence on its development, through inspiration and example. In his acoustic phase he demonstrated, better than any of his contemporaries, the power of words set to music. In his electric phase, he showed how the impact of words and music could be amplified with the addition of other instruments. His songs set the tone. In them, he showed a new generation what they could say and how they could say it.

However, there were others within the rock tradition who helped shape its sound and sensibility. Buddy Holly, the Everly Brothers, Roy Orbison, and the Brill Building songwriters were important early sources. The Beatles and the Byrds were the most influential of Dylan's contemporaries. Other influences came from everywhere—folk and country especially, but also jazz, blues, pop, gospel, and Latin music.

11-1b From Ballads to *Blue*: The Deep Roots of the Singer-Songwriters

More fundamentally, the singer-songwriters who began their careers around 1970 can trace their lineage back to the folk music from the British Isles—in principle, if not often in actual practice. ("**Scarborough Fair,**" a British ballad recorded by Simon & Garfunkel, is a familiar, if rare, instance of direct reworking of a folksong.) In their music, as in this timeless folk music, the focus is more on words and melody than on rhythm. The intent is to touch the head and the heart more than the hips.

The impulse to tell a story in song is embedded in the cultures of the British Isles—English, Irish, and Scottish. It remained strong in those who emigrated to the colonies in North America. Storytelling songs remained part of popular music until the turn of the twentieth century. They resurfaced as a commercial music in the twenties with the emergence of country music, and as a modern folk music in the topical songs of Woody Guthrie and his disciples.

For Dylan and the singer-songwriters who followed him, this ancient folk tradition was the point of departure for a new, urban folk-inspired music. They assimilated it and transformed it into a new popular style, much as the rock bands discussed in **Chapter 8** assimilated the blues and transformed it into a new, and quite different, popular style. Indeed, they are complementary developments: one of the subtle ironies of the rock era was that North American musicians most fully embraced the musical tradition rooted in the folk music of the British Isles, while it was mainly the British bands that steeped themselves in the blues, the most distinctively American folk music. The songs presented here represent a new kind of popular song—melodious, like the folk music from which it ultimately derives, yet completely modern in its sound.

We sample six tracks linked in time—all were released in 1971 or 1972—that exemplify the core features and something of the range of the singer-songwriters of the early seventies.

11-2 "American Pie": The Singular Triumph of Don McLean

In 2001, the Record Industry Association of America (RIAA), the National Endowment of the Arts (NEA) polled "a broad cross-section of people who cared about music" to create a list of the "Songs of the Century." The 1,300 people surveyed by the RIAA started with a list of 1,100 songs/albums; the organization compiled a list of 365 songs from the 200 or so people who returned the survey.

The list spans a more than a century: the oldest recording, of banjoist Vess Ossman performing "Yankee Doodle," dates from 1894; among the most recent are Lauryn Hill's "Doo Wop (That Thing)" (1998) and Destiny Child's "Bills, Bills, Bills" (1999). It's not limited to American performers: Enrico Caruso, the Beatles, and the Police are on the list. Judging by the results, the original choices seem to be based on multiple criteria: enduring popularity, cultural significance, historical importance of the performer or composer, milestone recordings of style or substyle, and artistic significance are apparent. The results of the poll reflect the varied tastes of the "cross-section of people" asked to participate in the poll. The list is most useful as a document that reflects these tastes.

The first five songs on the list are, in order, Judy Garland's recording of "Over the Rainbow," with music composed by Harold Arlen, Bing Crosby's version of "White Christmas," written by Irving Berlin, Woody Guthrie performing his song "This Land Is Your Land," Aretha Franklin's recording of "Respect," written by Otis Redding, and McLean's "American Pie." Arlen and Berlin were major contributors to the "Great American Songbook," Garland and Crosby were among the top singers of their era. Guthrie was the voice of the working class during the Depression and a profound, if indirect, influence on rock-era music. Aretha remains the Queen of Soul, one of the great voices of popular music.

For all of these musicians, these recordings were highlights in important careers. However, for McLean, it was the defining moment of his career. No other song of his approached the success and recognition of "American Pie." Its unique place in his creative output was just one aspect of the uniqueness of the song.

McLean (b. 1945) grew up in Westchester County, NY, close to New York City. His dominant musical influence growing up was the Weavers' *Live at Carnegie Hall* album, and he also listened extensively to Buddy Holly and Frank Sinatra. He dropped out of college shortly after the assassination of John F. Kennedy, and started touring small clubs and campuses, where he worked with—and networked with—artists in several genres: folk, pop, blues, and rock. His commercial breakthrough came with the release of the *American Pie* album: both the single and the album did well, and sparked interest in McLean's other work. He has remained active, but has never matched the overwhelming success of the "American Pie" single.

"American Pie" stands apart from the vast majority of songs from the rock era not only because of its singular commercial success and iconic status (as the RIAA list evidence), but also because it's both familiar and distinctive—almost unique—musically. The refrain of the song embodies both elements. The melody of the refrain is immediately engaging: both words and melody are easy to remember. But it ends with a question about the lyric, what it is that he's talking about, and a musical question, because both melody and harmony end inconclusively. The mix of familiar and unusual extends to the rest of the song. It's a verse/chorus song, like so many other rock-era songs, but there are six verses, with the first and last framing the rest with striking shifts in tempo, and each verse is equivalent to a chorus of a pre-rock-style pop song. The overall length of the song is eight minutes and thirty-five seconds, about three times the length of an average single, and along with "Stairway to Heaven," is one of the few really long songs to receive frequent full-length radio airplay.

The song is all about the story. The musical setting is supportive: the mostly acoustic rhythm instruments set up a good groove in the heart of the song, especially during the refrain. It is also unobtrusive: there's nothing particularly evocative or mood-establishing in the music under McLean's voice. It is a memorable example of the fusion of folk, Dylanesque lyrics, and rock that represented one direction in the singer-songwriter movement of the early seventies. The next two involve women of exceptional reputation.

11-3 Elevating the Feminine

The rise of Carole King and Joni Mitchell to stardom at the end of the sixties symbolized a new role for women in rock, and in popular music. As we have noted, rock and roll was a male-dominated music: all of its major stars, and almost all of its acts, were men. This was due in large part to the sexual undercurrent running through rock and roll and the impact of the double standard in sexually charged behavior. Those who have grown up in the post-Madonna era are used to women performing as provocatively as their male counterparts. However, the movements encountered in music videos and in live performance would have been unthinkable in the early years of rock. Elvis was scandalous enough, by fifties standards; a woman moving like Elvis would have certainly been banned. Women who wanted to front a band like men had to wait for the sexual liberation of the sixties; even then, it required considerable courage.

Further, playing a rock-band instrument was a man's job, or so it seemed. Women rhythm-section musicians were almost unheard of during the early rock era. One can count the number of prominent women lead guitarists, bassists, and drummers on the fingers of one hand. The bassist Carol Kaye, who appeared on *Pet Sounds* and several other Beach Boys albums, was in demand throughout the fifties and sixties as a session musician; she had very little female company.

Black music, and particularly black pop, was more open to women, especially in the sixties. There were a few women stars in fifties rhythm and blues, but most of the acts were men. During the sixties, black women secured a more prominent place, first in the girl groups, then Motown and pop (Dionne Warwick had a string of hits written by Burt Bacharach and Hal David), then soul, most notably with Aretha Franklin. Aretha joined the short list of strong, soulful yet vulnerable black women that already included such notable singers as Bessie Smith, Billie Holiday, and Dinah Washington.

White female singers fared better in more pop-oriented yet rock-flavored music from the same period: Connie Francis, Brenda Lee, Petula Clark, and Dusty Springfield were among the top solo acts; the Mamas and the Papas were among the most prominent male-female groups.

However, it was the folk revival that provided women with the most accessible point of entry into rock. The urban folk music of the postwar era was far less macho than rock and roll, jazz, or blues. Indeed, young women folksingers were fixtures in coffeehouses throughout the fifties; Joan Baez was the most notable example of this group. Maybelle Carter, by far the most important member of the Carter Family, was a main inspiration. In the sixties, the repertoire of women performers who came out of the folk tradition, or were inspired by it, mutated from reworked folksongs to contemporary songs in a similar style. Judy Collins's work in the sixties embodies this transition; Janis Ian's "Society's Child" (1965–1967), her first hit, helped mark this new direction, which continued in the music of Joni Mitchell and Carole King.

Although the two women are linked in time, gender, and style, and share common musical collaborators (not only James Taylor but also several studio musicians), their careers are opposite in several respects. Where Mitchell grew up in the Canadian plains, about as far geographically and culturally as one could be from New York, King was born Carol Klein in Brooklyn. While Mitchell was singing in Canadian coffeehouses, King was at work in the Brill Building, cranking out a string of pop hits with her husband at the time, Gerry Goffin. We encounter music by both women next.

11-3a Joni Mitchell

Joni Mitchell's *Blue* is one of the most acclaimed albums of the rock era (e.g., No. 14 on VH1's 100 Greatest Albums of All Time, No. 30 on Rolling Stone's 500 Greatest Albums of All Time). Of the albums from the seventies on that list, it is arguably the least rock-like.

Mitchell recorded the album in the studios of A&M Records, the company founded by Jerry Moss and Herb Alpert (of Tijuana Brass fame), but could probably have recorded it almost as well in her living room. On six of the ten tracks, she accompanies herself on piano or guitar; it is the only instrument we hear. On the remaining four, she is joined by one or two other musicians; only one track, "**Carey**," features a complete rhythm section.

Joni Mitchell (b. 1943) was born Roberta Anderson in Fort Macleod, Alberta, Canada, and grew up in Saskatchewan, the neighboring province. As a young girl, she had equally strong interests in art and music. After high school, she enrolled in the Alberta College of Art and Design and played folk music in a local coffeehouse. Like many Canadians in search of a career, she gravitated to Toronto, where she met and married Chuck Mitchell, also a folksinger, in 1966. The couple moved to Detroit. After her divorce a year later, she moved to New York, where she connected into the folk scene, mainly as a songwriter. Tom Rush and Judy Collins recorded two of her early songs: "**The Circle Game**" and "**Both Sides Now**," respectively. Within a year, she had moved to southern California.

Mitchell began recording under her own name in 1968. She found her musical voice, and her audience, in a series of albums released between 1969 and 1974. In them, Mitchell uses the folk style of the early sixties as a point of departure, but she transforms every aspect of it—lyrics, melody, and accompaniment—into a highly personal idiom. We hear this in "**All I Want**," a track from her milestone 1971 album *Blue*.

Like so many of her early songs, "All I Want" has a romantic thread (or at least a relationship thread) woven through it. In this respect, she is right in step with so many other singer-songwriters, and—more generally—popular music, especially black pop. But there the similarity ends. Most love-related songs present their situation in a coherent narrative, through a series of images ("My Girl"), an outpouring of feeling (Buddy Holly's "Not Fade Away"), or a scene that unfolds ("I Heard It Through the Grapevine"), or a combination of these ("Natural Woman," encountered below). Typically, both words and music follow a predictable path toward a goal that serves as the expressive high point of the song.

By contrast, Mitchell's lyrics to "All I Want" seem to open the door to her subconscious. There are mercurial shifts in mood: one moment she's high on love ("Alive, alive, I want to get up and jive/I want to wreck my stockings in some juke box dive"), the next, she's licking her emotional wounds ("Do you see—do you see—do you see how you hurt me baby/So I hurt you too/Then we both get so blue"). The only consistent feature of the lyric is the emotional inconsistency of her relationship ("Oh I hate you some, I hate you some/I love you some"). It is as if we are inside Mitchell's head, with thoughts and images tumbling over each other in a stream of consciousness. There is no story; indeed, there is no sense even of time passing.

The music amplifies the temporal and emotional ambiguity of the lyric. The accompaniment begins with Mitchell playing a dulcimer and James Taylor playing guitar. Mitchell deliberately avoids establishing a key or even marking the beat clearly. The song itself is strophic: the same melody serves three stanzas of poetry. It begins tentatively, echoing the indecision of the lyric. The most intense point comes in the middle. Shorter phrases and a more active, wide-ranging melodic contour echo the more active and frequent images in the text. They in turn lead to the heart of the song: "do you want." Like smoke rising from one of Mitchell's ever-present cigarettes, the melody gradually drifts up, reaching its peak on the words "sweet romance," the real issue of the song. It drops down quickly, but not to rest; the final sustained note is not the keynote. The instrumental introduction returns as the outro; it ends limply, as if it is a musical question mark. All of this underscores the message of the lyrics. Mitchell describes a complex, difficult relationship and the emotional rollercoaster that it puts her through; there is no change in it during the course of the song, no resolution at the end.

As "All I Want" reveals, Mitchell's songs disdain the conventions of rock and pop. In her songs, ideas shape the forms, not vice versa. Melodies respond to the words, yet follow their own internal logic. Other aspects of the setting—most notably harmony, instrumentation, and rhythm—are individual to a particular song. They remain in a supporting role, the focus is squarely on the words and melody. One measure of Mitchell's genius is that words and melody are separable yet indivisible.

Her lyrics are studied as poetic texts; her songs are performed as instrumentals. Yet the sum is greater than the parts. Those searching for rock's counterpart to the art songs of classical music need look no further than the music of Joni Mitchell.

At the same time, they provide a postmodern perspective on love. In so doing, they bring the love song into the rock era. Scan the playlists of the last several chapters. Note how few of the songs by white artists mention any aspect of a man-woman relationship. And even in those that do, there is no real partner, just Orbison's pretty woman, or anonymous females that are not available to satisfy Jagger's lust. There is no emotional interaction. By contrast, Mitchell opens herself up, so that we can experience the turmoil in her troubled relationship with her. It is an emotional breakthrough—for her, for rock, and for popular music.

After 1974, Mitchell turned in other directions. Through the rest of the seventies, she connected with jazz and the avant-garde. This culminated in the collaboration with jazz great Charles Mingus, which was cut short by Mingus's death in 1979. Her seventies experiments anticipated the world music movement of the eighties. In the eighties, she continued to explore what some called "jazz/folk" fusion, as well as to develop her career in the visual arts as a photographer and painter.

11-3b Carole King

It took Carole King (b. 1942) the better part of a decade to move from behind the curtains to center stage. Although she had been a successful songwriter throughout the sixties, it wasn't until after her divorce from Gerry Goffin in 1968 that she began a solo career. She broke through in 1971 with *Tapestry*, which remained on the charts for almost six years.

Tapestry is, more than anything else, black pop written and sung by a white woman; King sings with real empathy for the sound and style of Motown and soul and speaks candidly about life and love from a woman's point of view. Two of the songs on the album were major hits for black female artists in the sixties. We discussed the seminal role of the Shirelles' **"Will You Love Me Tomorrow?"** in the creation of a black pop sound in **Chapter 5**. **"(You Make Me Feel Like A) Natural Woman,"** which came straight out of church, put Aretha Franklin in the Top 10 for the fourth time in 1967.

Most of the new songs on *Tapestry* are cut from similar cloth. **"You've Got a Friend"** projects the optimistic tone heard in so much black pop. There are also musical parallels: with a form that builds to the title-phrase hook, riff-based melody, and rich but mostly traditional harmony, it echoes hundreds of black pop hits. Not surprisingly, then, the song was almost as big a hit on the R&B charts for Roberta Flack and Donny Hathaway as it was for James Taylor on the pop charts. **"I Feel the Earth Move," "It's Too Late,"** and **"Where You Lead"**—with their solid grooves, instrumental and vocal hooks, rich harmony, Motown-style backup vocals, and end-weighted forms—could have been hits for the Temptations or the Supremes. Aretha or Percy Sledge could have covered **"Way over Yonder,"** and King's excellent gospel-style piano playing would have provided a first-rate accompaniment.

King's songs have an "everywoman" universality as they describe the ups and downs of love and life. There is ecstasy ("I Feel the Earth Move"), disillusionment ("It's Too Late"), loneliness (**"So Far Away"**), and the comfort of companionship ("You've Got a Friend"). They are "real," no-frills songs, sending their messages in plain language. There is no sugarcoating—just frank heart-to-heart talk. King's timing was perfect. Her songs found receptive ears, especially among women, just as the women's rights movement was gathering momentum. Aretha Franklin's

"Respect" had already been adopted as an anthem; Helen Reddy's **"I Am Woman"** would top the charts in 1972.

The straightforward lyrics were only part of the appeal. King's songs are skillfully crafted and make use of existing styles and conventions in an imaginative and individual way. "(You Make Me Feel Like A) Natural Woman," a song that King wrote in 1967 with the help of Goffin and Jerry Wexler, reworks two black musical styles: gospel and Motown. The gospel influence is most directly evident in the rhythm. The song features a slow triple meter (grouping of beats by three), which is widely used in black gospel (imagine a black congregation singing "Amazing Grace") and also is the underlying meter of "Lift Every Voice and Sing," the black national anthem. King sets the meter with the repeated piano chords; the piano was the most common accompanying instrument in traditional gospel.

The song unfolds like so many Motown songs: it begins simply with a short two-part verse, then slowly builds to the title-phrase refrain through a long transition. The refrain riff is repeated three times; the final statement completes the lyric and the melody. The second verse/transition/refrain section is identical melodically to the first. However, King substitutes a surprising new melody that sustains the intensity of the refrain before returning for the final time to the refrain. This too is a formal strategy in Motown songs: Smokey Robinson's **"Tracks of My Tears"** is a familiar example.

King's most individual touches come in the curve of the melody and the harmonies that support the melody. The song begins with two melodic drops, which amplify the depressed mood of the lyrics. The melody begins to move back up as the lyric describes the impact of her lover. The close relationship between words and music continues, especially in the new section between the last two refrains. King harmonizes the melody with fresh alternatives to standard chord progressions; they help give the song a distinctive character.

King's spare accompaniment—just two piano parts (both of which she plays via overdubbing), plus a bass for reinforcement in the refrain and overdubbed backup vocals—is much simpler than that used on Aretha Franklin's recording, which features full rhythm section, plus backup singers, strings, and horns. That King can offer a compelling version of the song with minimal instrumental resources points up the primacy of melody in the music of the singer-songwriters. In this song and others like it, the melody carries most of the expressive weight. It is a completely different orientation from the songs we heard in **Chapter 9**, for instance, that *depend* on the instruments to carry the flow of the song and convey the message.

Dylan has been regarded as the godfather of the singer-songwriter movement, and rightly so. But songs with melody and meaning had been part of rock since Buddy Holly's brief heyday and King's own "Will You Love Me Tomorrow?" in 1961. King's success made clear that the singer-songwriters had roots in pop as well as folk. And it was certainly gratifying to her to step out of the shadows and into the spotlight. She remained there a relatively short time. Her next two albums did well, but neither approached the colossal success of *Tapestry*.

11-4 They've Got Friends: James Taylor and the Intimate World of the Singer-Songwriters

The other performer on "All I Want" is James Taylor; Taylor also assists Carole King on several tracks on *Tapestry,* including "You've Got a Friend." For his recording of the song, the two women return the favor, King by supplying Taylor with one of his biggest hits and Mitchell by singing backup vocals. During the early seventies, the singer-songwriter movement seemed mainly the work of a few good friends: Taylor, King, Mitchell; other singer-songwriters like Jackson Browne and Carly Simon, whom Taylor married in 1972 (they divorced in 1983); and the studio musicians who appeared on so many of their recordings, including guitarist Danny Kortchmar (occasionally credited as Danny Kootch).

Taylor (b. 1942) seems at the center of these seemingly collegial partnerships, which is in keeping with the persona that he projects through his music. Taylor was rock's first great conversationalist; he sings as if he's talking with you one-on-one. He usually sings with emotional reserve, not excess, even when he talks about highly personal and obviously painful subjects—as in "**Fire and Rain**," an account of his reaction to the suicide of a fellow inmate at a mental asylum. In this respect, he is the polar opposite of those rockers who, like Little Richard, were looking for something loud and found it was them.

Taylor was able to project this public persona despite numerous personal problems that nearly cost him his career, and his life. He grew up in Chapel Hill, North Carolina. His childhood was privileged (his father was dean of the University of North Carolina Medical School, and the family was wealthy enough to summer on Martha's Vineyard) and problematic (Taylor committed himself to a psychiatric hospital while in his teens). Through his older brother Alex (all five Taylor siblings—James, Alex, Livingston, Hugh, and Kate—would have professional careers in music), he discovered folk and country music. After working in and around New York in the mid-sixties, he moved to England, where he recorded his self-titled debut album in 1968 for Apple Records. The album didn't do well, so Taylor returned to the United States, while singer-producer Peter Asher, who had produced his Apple recording, negotiated a contract with Warner Bros. Taylor's first two albums for Warner Bros. were enormously successful and established his career.

Taylor's songs are quintessential singer-songwriter material: autobiographical accounts that are nothing less than public confessions of his troubles and desires. These he delivers in a restrained, almost laconic manner—folksy, but also with a grit that comes from the blues (his 1976 hit "Steamroller" is an authentic-sounding, if tongue-in-cheek, take on electric blues). He sounds life-size, rather than larger than life: he could be your friend next door who sings and plays the guitar, except that he's really good at it. So it may not be surprising to discover that Taylor's biggest hit and most honored recording was his version of Carole King's "You've Got a Friend"; both the song and Taylor's recording won Grammys in 1971.

King's song follows much the same general plan that she used in "Natural Woman"—and sends much the same message. The verses, which describe the state of mind of "you," focus around a single note (sung at first to "down and troubled"): like the dark cloud hanging over "you," the melody can't seem to leave the note. Every move up quickly returns to this note; it is like a dead weight that can't be thrown off, until the friend enters the picture. In words and music, the mood becomes more upbeat; the melody rises, reaching a peak just before the title phrase. And, as in "Natural Woman," a more intense section replaces what would be the third statement of the verse. As with "Natural Woman," King tweaks a well-established form and shapes both melody and harmony so that they respond specifically to the message of the lyric.

The instrumental accompaniment, led by Taylor's imaginative take on Guthrie-style guitar figures, is an acoustic analog to a rock band: two acoustic guitars, string bass, plus congas and drums. The core instruments and their roles remain intact, but everything is understated. There is a clear rock rhythm, but it is presented gently; the emphasis is on the melody and the chords that support it. Its use here demonstrates two key points about rock-era music. The first is that the song evidences the ever-increasing diversity of rock-era music; this song, as well as the other songs discussed in this chapter, represents a clearly different direction from the music presented in the previous three chapters. The second and more significant point is the key role of rock rhythm in unifying rock-era music. The strongest connection between this song and more conventional rock songs is the use of a rock rhythm: Taylor's guitar line and the conga part move at twice beat speed, and the backbeat is subtly present, especially in the chorus. In rock, as in the music of previous and subsequent generations, it is the characteristic rhythm— the style beat—that connects a diverse body of music that differs in so many other ways.

Taylor's career peaked in the early seventies, as he scored a series of successes on both album and singles charts. He achieved further celebrity with his marriage to Carly Simon in 1972. He continues to please a sizable audience, and he remains a big attraction, especially on the summer circuit. He seems to have left his personal problems, including heroin addiction, in the past.

Taylor's best songs, and his singing of them, brought to rock an unprecedented intimacy and sense of personal connection with the artist. His music epitomized rock's gentler side. With its acoustic instrumentation, and restrained but expressive vocal sound, it added an important new dimension to the sound of rock.

11-5 From Country to City: Country and Rock

Southern California was the unlikely epicenter for the coming together of folk, country, and rock. The first strong evidence of this was the emergence of the Byrds, who pioneered folk rock. In 1967, Arkansas-born singer/guitarist Glen Campbell, who had recorded with such diverse acts as the Beach Boys, Elvis Presley, and the Monkees, graduated from session musician to star with a series of country-ish pop albums. That same year, Joni Mitchell also relocated there, where she played a seminal role in developing the singer-songwriter movement. In 1968, Gram Parsons, a singer and songwriter from the Southeast, moved to southern California, joined the Byrds, and led them into country music. The result was *Sweethearts of the Rodeo*. The music was miles away from "Eight Miles High"; more than anything else, it sounded like conscientious non-Southerners playing country. Still, it was significant because it represented a deep immersion in country music by an outsider, much as Eric Clapton and Jimmy Page drank in the blues.

In the early seventies, the fruits of the interchange between rock and its country music roots included not only Southern rock, the music of the singer-songwriters, and the "American" rock of bands like Creedence Clearwater Revival and the Grateful Dead, but also a true country/rock synthesis, as evidenced in the early music of the Eagles, another Los Angeles–based band.

11-5a The Eagles and the Rise of Country Rock

Formed in 1971 mainly from Linda Ronstadt's backup band, the Eagles became one of the most successful rock groups of the seventies. The original Eagles were Don Henley (b. 1947), drums; Glenn Frey (b. 1948), guitar; Bernie Leadon (b. 1947), country instruments—banjo, steel guitar, and others; and Randy Meisner (b. 1946), bass. Don Felder (b. 1947), who also played an assortment of country instruments, joined the group in 1974.

The song that helped put both the Eagles and country rock on the map was their first single, the 1972 hit, **"Take It Easy."** It demonstrates their wonderfully effective fusion of rock and country elements. The lyric is all country: women trouble, trucks, small towns (Winslow is east of Flagstaff), but the music smoothly blends rock and country elements. The song begins with a low-wattage power chord, after which it settles into a nice rock groove.

This countrified version of a rock beat has two distinct layers. One is a straightforward rock rhythm, played on the drums and acoustic guitar. The other is in essence a modified honky-tonk two-beat rhythm: bass and bass drum mark the first and third beats, in alternation with the backbeat on the second and fourth beats. This would soon become the most common form of rock rhythm in both country rock and rock-influenced country.

Almost everything else also has a country flavor: the guitar licks, the double-time banjo accompaniment, and the singing. The two exceptions are Meisner's occasionally roaming bass lines and the beautiful high-register close harmony, which seems to owe more to the Beach Boys than to the Everly Brothers or any country group.

As their career gained momentum, the Eagles moved toward the mainstream, often shedding country elements along the way. Still, songs such as **"Lyin' Eyes"** (1975) retain a strong country flavor. The band shifted direction rather abruptly in 1975, when guitarist Joe Walsh replaced Bernie Leadon. **"Hotel California"** (1977), their big hit from this later period, borrows from a southern sound of a quite different kind, as we discover in **Chapter 13**.

11-6 Elton John: From Singer-Songwriter to Rock Star

The Troubadour is a small West Hollywood club (300 seats) that has presented up-and-coming rock acts since 1957. During the sixties and early seventies, it was the launching pad for several important artists. Among the notable firsts: the Byrds' first performance of "Mr. Tambourine Man," Los Angeles debuts of Joni Mitchell, Neil Young, Kris Kristofferson, and James Taylor, and the US debut of Elton John.

John, his lyricist Bernie Taupin, and the members of his touring band arrived in August, 1970, to begin his first visit to the United States. By the time they arrived in Los Angeles, John had released his first successful album, the eponymous *Elton John*, and recorded his second, *Tumbleweed Connection*. His management packed the place with celebrities, fellow musicians, music business people, many of whom were intrigued by what they'd heard on *Elton John*. The show was a great success and a great start to his first visit to the United States.

The career of Elton John (born Reginald Dwight, 1947; his stage name came from the first names of fellow band members in his first band, Bluesology) documents one of the most fascinating professional metamorphoses in rock history. In his first albums, he established himself as a thoughtful singer-songwriter of exceptional talent.

John's early music brought new sounds to rock, not so much because of his songwriting or singing, but because of his piano playing. By the time he released *Elton John*, he had become a skilled and imaginative pianist. He was fluent in earlier piano-centric rock styles and developed his own distinctive and versatile approach to piano playing in rock, from active but relatively subdued accompaniments (**"Your Song," "Tiny Dancer"**) to extroverted playing (**"Take Me to the Pilot," "Bennie and the Jets"**).

During the sixties, the acoustic piano was almost exclusively a complementary instrument in rock. The core rock band featured two guitars; piano could serve as an alternative to one or both guitars ("Hey Jude") or as reinforcement (Ian Stewart on numerous Rolling Stones recordings). John (and Billy Joel) brought the piano to the forefront. As a lead instrument, it lacks the power and range of effects of a solid-body guitar, and it lacks the delicacy of the acoustic guitar used extensively in folk music and folk-influenced rock. However, these two radically different guitars present what is usually an either/or proposition—either power or delicacy—even when heard in the same song (e.g., Led Zeppelin's "Stairway to Heaven"). Pianists like John could do both: update Little Richard or the New Orleans piano professors or create a pianistic analog to complex acoustic guitar accompaniments. We hear elements of both in "Tiny Dancer," a memorable song from his 1971 album, *Madman across the Water.*

"Tiny Dancer" is a biographical song. The "L. A. lady" is Maxine Feibelman, whom Taupin and John met during their 1970 trip to Los Angeles. Feibelman and Taupin would marry the following year. Taupin's lyric begins as if it is going to tell a story. However, as it develops, it resolves into a collage of vivid images. It is as if we see short video clips, which quickly cut away to another scene.

John's setting of the lyric begins simply, with John playing nicely syncopated piano chords, first to get the song underway, then to accompany his singing of the melody. Through most of the opening statement of the verse, it is as if the song will be set simply and intimately. However, other instruments enter in stages: steel guitar at the end of the first large section, other rhythm instruments upon the repetition of the opening section, then a choir at the end of the repeated section. At that point, John shifts gears, using the piano to give a stronger, more marked rhythm and shifting the harmony into uncharted waters. This builds toward the chorus, which adds a string countermelody to the many instruments and voices already sounding. The range of John's music is evident in the gradual shift in mood and style, which are part of an organic whole; the craft is evident in such features as the skillfully paced growth in momentum over the full statement of the song and effective addition of instruments.

"Tiny Dancer" also illustrates John's approach to the expansion of rock style in the seventies. Here, it is most evident in its length, form, and resources. As recorded, it takes over six minutes to perform, and even at this length, there are less than two complete statements of the song. (In "Tiny Dancer," a complete statement consists of two verselike sections that are melodically identical, a transition and a chorus. This expands the verse/chorus template used, for example, in so many Motown songs.) We can gauge the degree of expansion by noting that one verselike *section* is equivalent to a complete "Heart and Soul" type song.

To realize this larger form, John uses a huge ensemble: his voice and piano, plus bass, drums, guitar, steel guitar, backup vocals, rich strings, and choir. The result is, when desired, a denser and fuller-sounding texture. Moreover, John adds and subtracts instruments to outline the form and accumulate musical momentum through the verse sections to the climax of the song in the chorus. "Tiny Dancer" begins quietly enough, with just voice and piano, but instruments gradually join in: steel guitar at the end of the first verse, drums and bass as the second verse section begins, then choir at the end of the second verse section. The song peaks on the words: "Hold me closer," the melodic high point and hook. The preceding material prepares this climax with a new, more agitated beat pattern, shorter phrases, and more active harmony. Only the interlude set to the text, "softly, slowly," momentarily arrests the momentum.

"Tiny Dancer" sheds light on the fact and nature of rock's continuing expansion in the seventies. The expansion is not one-dimensional: it is not just longer, louder, denser, or whatever. Instead, it is a comprehensive expansion: the supplementary instruments and voices—strings, choir, steel guitar—give shape to the expanded form of the song, articulating sections when they drop out, imparting a sense of movement toward a climax as they enter gradually. Here, the expansion of rock style is artfully managed.

The song illustrates John's musical approach just before his mainstream success. He has always been a gifted melodist, as he showed in this song. However, as the seventies unfolded, John transformed his music into true AOR material by inundating himself in Top 40 songs, swapping out the features that had given his music its identity for style elements adapted from currently popular styles (e.g., **"Philadelphia Freedom"** is a homage of sorts to the "Philadelphia sound" heard in the next chapter). Simultaneously, he adopted an outrageous stage persona; it was a visual complement to the masking of his original musical identity. His songs found the middle of the road and he found mega-stardom.

John's career is a testimony to the power of personality. Off stage, he is an unlikely looking rock star: short, chunky, balding, and bespectacled. On stage, his costumes and extroverted style made him larger than life; it rendered his natural appearance irrelevant. He was one of the top live acts of the seventies.

John remained active through the eighties and nineties, despite his short and difficult marriage to recording engineer Renate Blauel and his acknowledgment of his sexual preferences—after the divorce, he disclosed that he realized that he was gay before marrying; he also has had numerous substance abuse issues. In the early nineties, he cleaned up his life and directed his energy to film and stage. He won his first Grammy in 1994 for one of the songs from the Disney animated film *The Lion King*, written in collaboration with lyricist Tim Rice. Another of their successful projects was what one reviewer called a "camp" remake of Giuseppe Verdi's famous opera *Aida*.

Two of the most impressive and fascinating aspects of John's career are its longevity—he is still churning out hits—and the range of his collaborations. John Lennon's last public appearance came at an Elton John concert in 1974; about three decades later, John performed with Eminem at the Grammy awards ceremony. The list of those with whom he has performed and befriended reads like a rock-era Who's Who. This speaks to not only his musical flexibility but also his generous nature.

This same bighearted spirit extends beyond his musical career. He has been active in AIDS work since the mid-eighties, and he formed the Elton John AIDS Foundation in 1992 after the death of friend and fellow piano-playing rock star Freddie Mercury. The foundation has raised an enormous amount of money for treatment and research. He remains an active performer and the second highest-selling recording artist of all time, with sales of over 60 million units.

11-7 The Decline of Melody

John's gravitation toward new trends in pop reflected a larger shift away from melody-centric rock substyles. Both the singer-songwriters and country rock were short-lived trends; they began to fade away around middecade. John veered toward the mainstream. So did the Eagles, who also enjoyed greater commercial success after 1975. Joni Mitchell found jazz, James Taylor found continued success being James Taylor, Carole King remained active, although never quite repeating the success of *Tapestry*, and Don McLean found that people still loved to hear him sing "American Pie."

The decline of these two melody-centric styles was a key part of an overall shift away from melody in rock-era music. This shift was also evident in the declining market presence of soft rock and rock musicals, two other important melody-centric rock-related styles of the early seventies. The Carpenters, the royalty of soft rock, lived high on the charts in the early seventies, but were less successful in the latter half of the decade. Barbra Streisand, Neil Diamond, and Barry Manilow retained loyal followings, but their music was linked to the past, not the future. Rock musicals flourished in the years around 1970, then faded away. Andrew Lloyd Webber, who rose to prominence in 1970 with the rock opera *Jesus Christ, Superstar*, did not produce another successful production until the end of the decade (*Evita*, 1978). He would go on to be the most commercially successful music theater composer of the late twentieth century.

All of this activity came at the end of rock's first generation. The music of the singer-songwriters and country rock were progressive in their fusion of rock, folk, pop, and country elements, but retrospective in their focus on melody. Important new trends in the late seventies would continue to move rock-era music more toward rhythm and sound, and move the focus away from melody. Singer-songwriters would enjoy periodic revivals in the eighties and nineties: most of the important new acts were women. Country became a rock-era music by consistently incorporating important features of rock style, but remained largely apart from rock. It became increasingly popular in the last quarter of the century among those who wanted music that told stories through song.

CHAPTER 12

BLACK POPULAR MUSIC IN THE EARLY SEVENTIES

Learning Objectives:

1) Describe the three industry-related factors that reshaped black music in the early 1970s.

2) Illustrate how Marvin Gaye's music connects earlier blues to the future rap genre.

3) Comment on Stevie Wonder's use of rhythm and harmony.

4) Compare the differences between the **Philadelphia sound** and **Motown sound**.

5) Exemplify the varied vocal characteristics of Al Green.

6) Starting with the 1920s, summarize the transition from blues to rock.

Chapter Introduction

On May 13, 1971, Stevie Wonder (born Steveland Morris, 1950) turned 21. On that day, his contract with Motown Records expired. The arrangement had been good for both parties: Wonder was a child star, and Motown reaped the rewards. However, Wonder took the $1 million in royalties that Motown had been holding in trust for him, formed his own record and publishing companies (Taurus and Black Bull), and negotiated a new record deal with Motown. For Wonder, the crucial clause in the contract was "complete artistic control." In effect, he made his records and Motown sold them.

Wonder assumed artistic control in an unprecedented way. He immersed himself in electronics, learning how to use synthesizers and electronic keyboards (these were a new, rapidly evolving technology at the time). With these newly developed skills, he played most, sometimes all, of the parts on many of his recordings; a single artist with a lot of equipment replaced the multilevel Motown production pyramid. The string of albums that he produced in the early seventies did well enough that he was able to renegotiate his contract with Motown in 1975. The new deal gave him a $13 million advance and a 20 percent royalty rate.

Wonder's emancipation from Motown points up three key features of black music (as well as rock music in general) after 1970. One, this new music had become a big business. Two, important artists were determined to go their own way, no matter which direction it took them. Three, technology would play an increasingly important role. All of these factors reshaped black music during the early seventies. So did musicians' responses to the changing social climate.

Experience an interactive version of this era in ⚡ MINDTAP

12-1 Black Issues, Black Voices

The sixties, which had begun with such promise for blacks, ended dismally. The assassination of Martin Luther King Jr., the riots at the Democratic National Convention in 1968, the legal troubles of the Black Panthers, the election of Richard Nixon and the subsequent shift to more conservative attitudes: all these and more replaced hope with disillusion.

Black music of all kinds, from romantic pop to funk, generally reflected the shifting mood within the black community in response to the retreat from the social advances of the civil rights movement. It also reflected the maturation of its artists and, indirectly, their more secure position in the popular music world. With maturity, they had more to say, and they felt that they could speak more directly without losing their audience. Berry Gordy was extremely reluctant to release Marvin Gaye's landmark album *What's Going On* because of its dark mood and biting social commentary; as things turned out, it was a major success for Gaye, artistically and commercially.

This shift is most clearly evident in song lyrics. Granted, the six tracks discussed in this chapter are only a small sample, but still, only the Jackson 5's **"ABC"** continues the cheery mood heard in older Motown songs like "My Girl" or Phil Spector's "Da Doo Ron Ron." The other five take a harder look at everyday life: Gaye's **"Inner City Blues"** is a lament about tough times, misplaced priorities, and social inequities; Stevie Wonder's **"Superstition"** is a cautionary tale; the O'Jay's **"Back Stabbers"** rails against infidelity and treachery; Curtis Mayfield's **"Superfly"** portrays an antihero; Al Green's **"Tired of Being Alone"** tells the story of a relationship on the rocks.

12-1a Accentuating the Positive: Rhythm, Mood, and Message

In much of the memorable music created by white artists that we have heard (and will hear), there is a clear resonance between words and music: the Beatles' "Eleanor Rigby," Creedence Clearwater Revival's "Proud Mary," the Velvet Underground's "I'm Waiting for the Man," and the Rolling Stones' "Satisfaction" all project markedly different moods. In each case, the music and words work together to project the message of the song.

By contrast, such musical responsiveness to a full range of moods in the lyrics seems almost impossible in black music. Upbeat moods come across clearly, but there seems to be a dissonance in meaning between words and music in those songs with more downbeat lyrics. The reason is the rhythm. In all of the songs considered in this chapter, the rhythms are infectious. It is hard to project a dark mood when it is supported by a foot-tapping groove.

However, even though the impulse to create interesting and engaging rhythms seems to work at cross purposes with the specific message of a song, it sends a more fundamental message that is ultimately positive: where there's a groove, there's life and a reason to live. It can take various forms, as we will hear in the examples discussed in this chapter, and it is also present in funk and reggae, as we will discover in **Chapter 15**. Indeed, it is inherent in the black music of the last hundred-plus years, from ragtime to rap. In all of this music, we hear rhythm not only as an escape from the pain of the present but also as an affirmation of the spirit of a culture.

12-1b The Range of Black Music

Driven by the success of Motown and soul, black music gained a firm toehold in the popular music market during the sixties. During the seventies, it expanded its presence. Black pop became more diverse, with Motown artists moving beyond the restrictive vision of Berry Gordy, and other writer-producers taking the Motown idea in new directions. Black music found its way into film and television (for instance, Quincy Jones's music for the popular *Sanford and Son*). By contrast, soul, the most powerful expression of a black sensibility during the sixties, continued its late sixties decline. Al Green was the only major new voice of the seventies; as it turned out, he was the last of the great soul singers. His decision to leave the entertainment world for the ministry effectively closed the book on soul. Funk, the most African black music of the seventies, seldom crossed over to the pop charts. Its impact would occur late in the decade and into the eighties (we discuss it in **Chapter 15**).

All of this happened even though the largely integrated music scene of the sixties gave way to a more segregated and white-dominated industry. This was true at every level. The audience divided into black and white, to a greater extent than the decade before. The music industry, and especially AOR (album-oriented rock) radio, encouraged this. Entire genres—glam rock, art rock, soft rock—lost their connection to rock's roots. Nevertheless, the gains of black music, commercially and artistically, were not curtailed—just as civil rights legislation prevented conservatives from rolling back the progress toward racial equality. The most popular black music of the seventies talked about love, a theme universal enough to blur racial boundaries.

12-2 Motown in the Early Seventies: New Acts, New Attitudes

Perhaps the best way to understand Motown's evolution in the early seventies is generationally. The "Young America" that Gordy had targeted in the early sixties had grown up. At the same time, many of Motown's acts had also matured, and they were anxious to explore new directions. As a result, Motown's freshest sounds came mainly from two sources: new faces (most notably the Jackson 5) and Motown veterans going in new directions (Marvin Gaye, Stevie Wonder, and Diana Ross). The Jackson 5 attracted another generation of young fans, while many of the Motown veterans expanded their audience.

12-2a The Jackson 5

The Jackson 5 was both a Motown product and a product of Motown. Motown's success inspired scores of imitators. Among them was the family of Joseph and Katherine Jackson, living in the industrial city of Gary, Indiana. Joseph Jackson was a crane operator and frustrated musician; Katherine gave birth to nine children, all of whom would eventually have professional musical careers.

Their first successful incarnation was as the Jackson 5. It consisted of the five oldest boys in the Jackson family: Jackie (b. 1951), Tito (b. 1953), Jermaine (b. 1954), Marlon (b. 1957), and Michael (1958–2009). Their father had started them on their career as the Jackson 5 around 1964, when Michael was only six. Within a few years they were opening for major soul acts. In 1969, they came to the attention of Berry Gordy, most likely through Gladys Knight (although Diana Ross was given credit for "discovering" them). He signed them, they released their first single for Motown—the No. 1 hit **"I Want You Back"** (1969)—and they were on their way.

The Jackson 5 were an immediate sensation: they had three more No. 1 singles the following year. Among them was "ABC." The themes of the song are as old as rock and roll: school and teen love. However, even more than the teen idols of the late fifties or the Beatles, the Jackson 5, and especially Michael, were speaking *for* their age group rather than *to* it. Michael's pre-puberty sound gave their performance an innocence that it might not have had with a more mature voice. Certainly, when Michael asks the "girl" to "shake it, shake it, baby," there is none of the sexual innuendo heard in, let's say, Ray Charles's line from "What'd I Say," when he remarks that she sure knows how to "shake that thing."

If their lyrics and vocal style projected an air of childlike innocence (they voiced over their own Saturday morning cartoon beginning in 1971 and received a commendation from Congress in 1972 for their "contributions to American youth"), their music was sophisticated and current. Their father had drilled them relentlessly (Katherine's autobiography, released in the late eighties, detailed his abuses), and Motown, since relocated to Los Angeles, supplied topflight instrumental backing and production.

Like sixties Motown hits, "ABC" balanced accessibility and sophistication. The hook, "A, B, C," was simple enough to sink deeply, and the bass line underneath the chorus was a simple scale (the first three notes are A, B, C#!). What made the song current were the rhythm and the texture. An augmented rhythm section— drums, congas, tambourine—laid down an active, highly syncopated 16-beat rhythm that floated effortlessly under Michael during the verse. Partly because of these more active rhythms, the emphasis is more on rhythm than melody. The multiple percussion instruments—spotlighted in the middle of the song— join the Jacksons and electronic keyboards and bass to create a busy and vibrant texture.

Songs like "ABC" mark the beginning not only of a new kind of black pop, but also a new kind of pop. In the lyrics and how they are presented, the vocal style(s), and in the active, danceable rhythms, there is a direct link between the music of the Jackson 5 and the pop of Michael Jackson and Madonna in the eighties and on to Britney Spears, Mariah Carey, and Christina Aguilera around the turn of the century. We trace this connection in subsequent chapters.

The Jackson 5 was Gordy's last big act and Motown's only successful new act in the seventies. By the mid-seventies, Berry Gordy was no longer a major creative force in popular music. His reluctance to cede artistic control led to fractious relationships with many of his acts. From the beginning, he had butted heads with the Jacksons' father. By 1976, they had left Motown and re-formed themselves as the Jacksons, although Jermaine, who had married Gordy's daughter Hazel, remained at Motown. All of the remaining Jackson children had solo careers in addition to their on-again/off-again collaborations; Michael's and Janet's have been by far the most successful. Their collective and individual success have made the Jackson family pop music's most enduring family dynasty for the better part of three decades.

12–2b Beyond Motown: The Music of Marvin Gaye

From the beginning of their association, Marvin Gaye (1939–1984) had chafed at the tight control Berry Gordy exercised over his career. Gaye, who had a deep interest in jazz, wanted to branch out in that direction. Gordy, who rightfully viewed Gaye as Motown's sexiest male act, wanted him to mine the same vein that had brought him success with songs like **"How Sweet It Is (To Be Loved by You)"** and **"I Heard It Through the Grapevine."** After extensive wrangling, Gaye got Gordy's approval to create his own album.

The result was *What's Going On*. Released in 1971, it was a commercial and artistic success. It took a hard look at life in Motown—the city— with songs like

"Inner City Blues" and the title track. At the same time, the music behind the words and ideas developed in range and complexity, to support the deepened emotional weight of the songs. Both the album and three singles from it hit the Top 10.

Gaye's lyric in the title track is part lament, part exhortation. It alludes to Vietnam, race relations, and the generation gap—burning issues throughout the country at the time. In the title phrase **"What's going on,"** he simply shakes his head. At the same time, he urges us to find the answer to our problems in love, not hate. The music—with its lush texture, rich, jazz-inspired harmonies, and subtle and active rhythms—sends a similar message.

The darkest song on the album, in words and music, is "Inner City Blues." The song begins with percussion, a soft one-pitch riff on a keyboard, and sustained chords. Other instruments layer in: congas, bass drum, bass, and Gaye's wordless vocal that harks back to the scat singing of Louis Armstrong and Ella Fitzgerald. Despite the multiple instrumental strands and active rhythms, the sound is dark, bleak, and empty. The bass and conga drum are in the forefront; their low pitch helps darken the sound. The piano chords come at widely spaced but regular intervals, like a bell tolling. The static harmony—it shifts once to the IV chord, then returns—is not a blues progression, but it is blues-like in its slow shifts between harmonies. It seems to convey the despair of those trapped in an endless cycle of poverty. The active percussion sounds seem to emulate an urban soundscape: the ambient noises of the ghetto. Even in this context, they are a sign of life.

Gaye's vocal lines—he sings all the vocal parts—start high and finish low, as they typically do in a blues song. Mostly there are snippets of melody: two- or three-note riffs, until the key phrase of the lyric "make you wanna holler." When the strings—the other prominent strand in the texture—enter, they operate in a high register. The open space between violins and bass is filled mainly by Gaye's voices; this spacing reinforces the bleak mood of the song. Just past the middle of the track, Gaye gives up on words and simply scats; this leads to an out-of-tempo reprise of the first part of "What's Going On," which in turn reinforces the underlying unity of Gaye's album.

"Inner City Blues" clearly grows out of the Motown sound. It retains Motown's easy points of entry: straightforward lyrics, melodic hooks, distinctive sounds (the piano chords, especially), active rhythms. But it is richer in texture, more purposeful musically, and totally different in mood from most Motown songs—recall that Gordy had grave reservations about the marketability of this album. And it strips away the polish that we associate with Motown acts, just as the cover of the album shows Gaye wearing everyday clothes for a winter day, not the tuxedo that he and other male Motown singers typically wore in performance.

In its depiction of the hard life of inner-city residents in both words and music, "Inner City Blues" is exceptional. There are few examples of black pop that address social issues, and even fewer that succeed in enhancing the message musically as well as Gaye does here. In the previous discussion, we noted the musical influence of the blues on Gaye's song. In an important way, Gaye's song is a bridge between blues and rap, the two black styles that have tackled social issues more frequently than any other. It updates the blues as social commentary and lays the groundwork for rap; Gaye's wordless vocal and the dark, empty texture seem to anticipate early rap tracks.

Gaye's album, and its success, indicated major changes at Motown; so did the music of Stevie Wonder. Wonder, a popular member of the Motown stable since his early teens, assumed artistic control of his music shortly after Gaye did. He would enjoy his greatest success in the seventies.

12-2c Beyond Motown: The Music of Stevie Wonder

There's a certain irony that Motown's most powerful and original talent, and its longest-running success story, is in many ways the antithesis of the Motown image and sound. Stevie Wonder is a solo act; most Motown acts were groups. The visual element was crucial to Motown's success: its groups, dressed in gowns or tuxedos, moved through stylized, carefully choreographed routines as they sang their songs. Our enduring image of Stevie Wonder? A blind man with sunglasses and long braided and beaded hair, dressed in a dashiki, sitting behind a keyboard and rocking from side to side in a random rhythm. Motown recordings were collective enterprises; behind the groups were largely anonymous songwriters and studio musicians. Wonder created his own recordings from soup to nuts: not only singing and playing all the instruments at times, but also performing the technical tasks— recording, mixing, mastering, and so on.

There are also differences in subject and attitude. In the mid-sixties, Motown song lyrics talked mainly about young love, usually in racially neutral, often idealized language. Only reluctantly did they begin to address "real life" in songs like the Supremes' **"Love Child."** By contrast, Stevie Wonder took on social issues from his self-produced first album; the vignette of an innocent man's arrest in **"Living for the City"** is chilling. Where Berry Gordy waffled politically and socially, even at the height of the civil rights movement, Stevie Wonder has advocated a long list of causes, from his firm push for a national holiday for Martin Luther King Jr. to rights for the blind and disabled.

Stevie Wonder was born Steveland Morris (some accounts say Steveland Judkins) in 1950. A hospital error at birth left him blind. By age 10, he was a professional performer, singing and playing the harmonica (he also played piano and drums). Within two years, he had signed a Motown contract and was being billed as "Little Stevie Wonder, the 12-Year-Old Genius." (The "little" disappeared two years later, but the "Wonder" stuck.) He had a number of hits in the sixties, including **"Uptight"** (1966) and the beautiful love song, **"My Cherie Amour"** (1969), but emerged as a major force in popular music only in the early seventies

Wonder was the most popular black artist of the seventies. A series of albums, beginning with *Music of My Mind* (1972), established his unique sound and cemented his reputation as a major player in popular music. Each album release was a major event within the black community, and his recordings also enjoyed enormous crossover success.

The widespread popularity of Wonder's music grows out of a style that is broad in its range, highly personal in its sound, and universal in its appeal. His music is a compendium of current black musical styles: in his songs are the tuneful melodies and rich harmonies of black romantic music, the dense textures and highly syncopated riffs of funk, the improvisatory flights of jazz, and the subtle rhythms of reggae and Latin music. Yet, even though he absorbs influences from all quarters, his style is unique.

"Superstition," a No. 1 single from the 1972 album *Talking Book*, is a funky up-tempo song with a finger-wagging lyric; in it he chastises those who would let their lives be ruled by superstitious beliefs. The melody that carries the lyric grows slowly out of a simple riff. Like so many Motown (and rock-era) songs, it builds inexorably to the title phrase. The harmony shows the two sources of his style: the verse sits on a bed of riffs, all built from the African American pentatonic scale; there is no harmonic change. By contrast, the transition to the hook is supported by rich, jazzlike harmonies.

The most distinctive element of Stevie Wonder's sound, however, is the rich texture that flows underneath the vocal line. The song begins simply enough, with a rhythmically secure drum part. Onto this, Wonder layers multiple lines: the signature riff, a repeated-note bass line, plus several more riffs in the background, all highly syncopated. Stevie played all the lines on synthesizers, overdubbing until he produced the dense, funky texture that became one of his trademarks. (Wonder was one of the first musicians to develop a sound based almost completely on synthesizers.)

12–2d Stevie Wonder and Blacks' Embrace of Technology

Among the people of the African diaspora, the impulse to play with sound seems almost as strong as the impulse to play with rhythm. Two aspects of this impulse that seem especially persistent are the discovery of found sounds and the quest to make multiple sounds at the same time. Found sounds have taken many forms: making instruments out of everyday materials, like the cowbell in Cuban music, the steel drums of Calypsonians, or the turntables of rap DJs; using everyday objects—a toilet plunger, the neck of a beer bottle—to modify the sound of a conventional instrument; or simply inventing new ways of making sound from an instrument, like "patting juba" by tapping out rhythms on various parts of one's body or slapping an electric bass.

The most familiar instance of the tendency to play multiple instruments simultaneously is the drum kit. More complex expressions of this practice range from jazz multi-instrumentalist Rahsaan Roland Kirk's ability to play the saxophone and two other instruments simultaneously to one-man bands like the obscure Abner Jay, the self-styled "last great southern black minstrel show," who accompanied himself with an electric guitar, bass drum, and hi-hat when he sang or played harmonica.

With his emancipation from Gordy's tight control, Wonder was able to combine both of these practices and take them high-tech. Both the electronic instruments—especially keyboards—that Wonder used on recordings like "Superstition" and the 24-track mixing boards that made the recording possible were new, rapidly developing technologies. Wonder was the first major artist, black or white, to take them to their logical extreme: make a complete recording by not only assembling it track by track but recording each track himself.

Others followed his lead in using high-end technology in the production process, although few filled as many roles as he did—Prince stood out in this regard. But the skillful production of Quincy Jones for Michael Jackson; the house music scene in Chicago and techno in Detroit during the eighties; the sampling of rap producers from the mid-eighties on—all these and more are clear signs of the enthusiasm with which blacks have embraced cutting-edge technology. It is as if they are making up for the generations in which they had little or no access to new technology. From this perspective, we can understand Wonder as a pivotal figure: the person who modernized and combined the practices of playing multiple instruments and finding new sound by using the latest technology.

"Superstition" shows us the rhythmic side of Wonder's musical personality; there is also a romantic side, as evidenced in songs like **"You Are the Sunshine of My Life."** In either mode, Stevie Wonder is an optimist, a "the glass is half full" person. Even in his darkest songs, hope is implicit, if not in the lyric, then in the bounce of the beat. How can you be down if your hips are shaking and your foot is tapping the beat? Wonder's optimism is remarkable in light of numerous personal problems. Not only has he been blind from birth, but he suffered through a devastating automobile accident in 1973 that left him in a coma for several days. He followed this adversity with some of his best music. He remains one of the icons of rock-era music.

12-3 The Philadelphia Sound—and Beyond

In the early seventies, it seemed as if Motown had opened a branch office in Philadelphia. The most Motown-like records of the period appeared on Gamble and Huff 's Philadelphia International label, not Gordy's. The basic formula was the same: lush orchestrations, solid rhythms coming from a rhythm section that had played together for years, jazz-tinged instrumental lines—all supporting vocal groups singing about the ups and downs of love. Only the details were different.

Three men engineered the **Philadelphia sound**: Kenny Gamble (b. 1943), Leon Huff (b. 1942), and Thom Bell (b. 1941). All were veterans of the Philadelphia music scene; they had worked together off and on during the early sixties in a group called Kenny Gamble and the Romeos. By mid-decade, Gamble and Huff had begun producing records together. They enjoyed their first extended success with Jerry Butler, who revived his career under their guidance. Their big break came in 1971, when Clive Davis, the head of Columbia Records, helped them form Philadelphia International Records. The connection with Columbia assured them of widespread distribution, especially in white markets.

The artist roster at Philadelphia International included the O'Jays, Harold Melvin and the Blue Notes, Teddy Pendergrass (who left the group to go solo), Billy Paul, and MFSB, which was the house band. Their competition came mainly from Thom Bell, who produced the Stylistics and the Spinners, a Detroit group who went nowhere at Motown but took off when paired with Bell in 1972.

The O'Jays' "Back Stabbers" (1972) shows how Gamble, Huff, and Bell extended and updated the black pop style developed at Motown. The instrumental introduction of "Back Stabbers" runs for 40 seconds—far longer than any of the Motown intros. It begins with a quasi-classical piano tremolo, an ominous rumble that helps establish the dark mood of the song. The unaccompanied piano riff that follows simply hangs in sonic space; there is still no regular beat-keeping. Finally, the rest of the rhythm section enters, with the guitarist playing a jazz-style riff.

The rhythm sound is fuller than late sixties Motown records, not just because of the addition of Latin percussion instruments (Motown had been using them for years) but because there are more of them, and the reinforcement of the beat and the eight-beat layer is more prominent. After the conclusion of the opening phrase, the strings and, later, brass enter; all combine to create a lush backdrop for the O'Jays.

The song, co-written by Huff, advises a hypothetical person to guard against "friends" who are out to steal his woman. Like so much black pop, the song is about love, or at least a relationship. What's different about the lyric is that the narrator is an outside observer, rather than the person in the relationship. In effect, it's "I Heard It Through the Grapevine" told from the other side of the grapevine, but up-close and personal. It was the first of a series of such songs by the O'Jays.

The Philadelphia sound, as typified in this song, is the Motown formula—revised, expanded, and modernized. The instrumental introductions are grander; the texture is richer; the songs themselves are more complicated; the spotlighted instruments are more contemporary sounding (in the case of the guitar) or more exotic (in the case of the vibraphone); and there is greater rhythmic freedom, not

Philadelphia sound An early 70s style which revised, expanded upon, and modernized the Motown sound.

only in the opening but also in the syncopated riffs that are the instrumental hooks of the songs.

The formula behind the Philadelphia sound worked well for the better part of the decade. By the late seventies, however, it would be largely superseded by a more musically obvious version of itself: disco.

12-3a Barry White

Barry White (1944–2003) outdid both Motown and the Philadelphia producers in the elaborateness of his production and the explicitness of his message, which re-created the sexual experience in music over and over. White might be best described as the "minister of love." Most of his hit songs begin with a spoken erotic fantasy set over a pulsating rhythm track. Like a black preacher whipping his congregation into a frenzy, he lets the music build until he finally breaks into song. The most immediate precedent for his spoken prologues is the music of Stax veteran Isaac Hayes, but the idea of a smooth transition from speech to song goes back to the black church. All this unfolds on an epic scale. The prologue to **"I'm Gonna Love You Just a Little More Baby,"** his first big hit, lasts over a minute and a half, and the song proper doesn't get underway until almost two minutes have passed.

The songs themselves are effective, but the prologues are public pillow talk— soft porn in music. As such, they lend themselves to parody. In an early *Saturday Night Live* sketch, Chevy Chase lampooned White: dressed in a white suit, sitting at a white piano, and billing himself as "Very White," he let the spoken prologues build—as if toward climax—but never sang the song: the shtick was all foreplay.

12-4 Black Films, Black Music

Among the most visible consequences of the civil rights movement was the emergence of a film genre created by blacks for a predominantly black audience. Called blaxploitation ("black" + "exploitation"), these were a black take on the action films of the sixties. The first two big-budget blaxploitation films were *Shaft* (1971), which is still the signature film of the genre (and which was remade in 2000), and *Superfly* (1972). In *Shaft* the main character was a hero: Shaft, a private detective, portrayed by Richard Roundtree. By contrast, the main character in *Superfly* was an anti hero; Ron O'Neal portrayed a drug dealer. Both were set in the ghetto, a gritty backdrop that resonated well with black audiences, rather than a middle-class neighborhood.

To create music in tune with the plot and atmosphere of these films, producers turned to experienced black musicians. For the film score to *Shaft*, producers tapped Isaac Hayes, who helped mastermind the Stax soul sound during the mid-sixties and had just begun a solo career. For *Superfly*, they turned to Curtis Mayfield (1942–1999). In 1958 Mayfield had joined the Impressions, one of the top black vocal groups of the sixties, and he stayed with them throughout the sixties. During this same period, he became increasingly active as a songwriter and producer. He left the Impressions at the end of the decade and released his first solo album in 1970. His score for *Superfly* was his most significant commercial and artistic success. It topped the album charts for a month in 1972. His ability to marry insightful social commentary with compelling grooves would inspire numerous rhythm-and-blues and rap acts: Ice-T, Public Enemy, and Lenny Kravitz cite his music as an important influence.

The title track single from *Superfly*, which reached the Top 10, shows how Mayfield told it like it was over music that evoked the setting of the film as it found a funky groove. The lyric is a description of the main character, Youngblood Priest. Singing in his soulful falsetto, Mayfield functions as a one-man chorus in a classical Greek tragedy: a disinterested observer commenting on the drama. He portrays Priest frankly, ticking off his attributes in terse phrases even as he figuratively shakes his head at Priest's errant path.

Musically, "Superfly" finds substantial common ground with Gaye's "Inner City Blues": the prominent role of Latin percussion instruments and the active rhythms they help create; the short vocal phrases; static harmony through long stretches of the song; the bass as the focal rhythm instrument; the open-sounding middle register, occupied primarily by the vocal line. In the early seventies, these seemed to evoke the inner-city landscape. But the tempo is quicker, Mayfield's voice is lighter, the horn riffs are brighter, and Mayfield's wah-wah guitar adds a distinctive color. These and other features help convey a more upbeat mood.

Interestingly, the music for *Superfly* (and *Shaft*) had far more crossover appeal than the films themselves: gross revenue from the soundtrack album exceeded the gross from the film. Indeed, the blaxploitation genre died off in the latter part of the seventies, due in no small part to the backlash from the black community about the negative role models featured in the films. Mayfield would never match the commercial peak that he achieved with this soundtrack, which remains one of the landmark albums of the decade.

12-5 Soul in the Seventies

By the early seventies, soul had fallen on hard times. After 1970, the hits stopped coming for most of the southern soul stars. Nevertheless, positive reverberations of the soul style helped diversify the sound of black music in the early seventies. The music of Aretha Franklin and James Brown, soul music's most powerful voices, changed in the seventies. In Franklin's case it came about through an expansion of her stylistic range; in Brown's case through the continuing rhythmic evolution of his music. Soul music's new voice—and its last great one—was Al Green.

12–5a Al Green

Like virtually all other soul stars, Al Green (b. 1946) grew up singing in church. When he was nine, he and some of his brothers formed a gospel quartet that performed first in and around his Arkansas hometown, about 40 miles west of Memphis, then in Michigan, where his family moved when he was twelve. And like many other soul singers, he began his career in his teens. The crucial event early in his professional life was his encounter with Willie Mitchell, who owned Hi Records in Memphis. Mitchell became not only his boss but also his partner, coproducing his records and co-writing many of Green's hits.

Although he had an isolated hit in 1967, Green's career effectively began in 1970. Within a year, he had crossed over to the pop charts: "Let's Stay Together," his biggest hit, topped both the R&B and pop charts in late 1971. He remained a presence on the charts for most of the decade.

Green brought subtlety and sophistication to both his songwriting and singing without sacrificing its soulfulness. All qualities are evident in his first big crossover hit, "Tired of Being Alone" (1971). Its basic design is the "refrain-frame" form that dates back to "Maybellene," but the verse is in a different key from the chorus and quite long. In addition, there is an open-ended section where Green simply "goes off." In general design, then, the song is in step with rock-era songwriting, but the details make Green's song distinctive almost to the point of idiosyncrasy.

However, it is his singing—and the man behind the voice—that is the main focus here. Green's voice is a remarkably flexible instrument. He is a tenor: his basic sound is higher-pitched and lighter than most other soul singers. Even more distinctive, however, are the variations in the basic sound. Less than a minute into the recording, we have already heard several different vocal qualities:

- A plaintive sound in the chorus
- A huskier sound for the first phrase of the verse (at about 23 seconds)
- A more matter-of-fact sound on the second phrase (at about 35 seconds)
- He even changes sound on a single note: each pulsation on the syllable "me" (at 30 seconds) features a different shade of vocal color.

This variety is evident even before Green goes into high, head-voice singing, or falsetto (his effortless, floating lines anticipate the buoyant sound of the Bee Gees), or begins to use the moans, stutters, melismas, and other devices that are part of his vocal arsenal. All these dimensions make his singing more varied and subtle than the other soul singers, who tended to rely more on brute power. Al Green is Muhammad Ali to the sixties soul singers' Joe Frazier, Sonny Liston, and George Foreman: his voice can float like a butterfly and sting like a bee, as well as punch with authority.

As a result, Green's singing was intimate: women took its erotic messages personally. His appearance and stage manner certainly encouraged this perception. During his heyday, he had the svelte physique of a welterweight in fighting trim; photographs show him bare-chested, even in performance. And he teased his audience with his moves as well as his voice. Women, certain that he was singing only to them, showered him with gifts: bras and panties were thrown on stage as a token of his female fans' affection and excitement.

Green's sensuality soon led to tragedy. In 1974, one of his girlfriends poured hot grits on him, burning him over several parts of his body, and then shot herself. Green took it as a sign that he had become too worldly—his father had expelled him from the family gospel group while he was in his early teens for listening to "profane music"—so he turned back to religion. In 1976, he started his own church in Memphis but continued to tour. Another incident in 1979, when he fell off the stage but escaped serious injury, convinced him to retire from secular music, which he has largely done. Since then, Green has devoted himself mainly to gospel music, although he has appeared and recorded occasionally with other rock artists.

Green was the last and one of the greatest of the soul singers. Certain features of his style—especially the stutters, moans, and yelps—recall more directly than any other the singing of Ray Charles, the artist most responsible for the sound of soul. So in effect Green's career completes the circle. And his decision to enter the ministry closes a larger circle. With "I Got a Woman," Ray Charles helped shape soul by expropriating music from the black church; Green helped reinvigorate black gospel music with a large helping of soul.

12-6 Crossroads: The Blues in Black and White

The musicians who began their careers in the seventies represent the first generation of rock-era artists whose music was not shaped directly by the blues. Both fifties rock and roll and rhythm and blues grew out of blues styles, and the core-defining rock of the sixties grew out of a further infusion of blues. By 1970, however, both black and white musicians were far less likely to encounter the blues directly and to bring it into their music.

The diminishing influence of the blues was due principally to two factors: the evolutionary stasis of the blues and the commercial ascendancy of rock and rhythm and blues. During the first half of the twentieth century, blues was not one style but several. Moreover, blues was the cutting-edge music during this time. From the hot new dance music of the 1910s and 1920s to post–World War II rhythm and blues and rock and roll, blues drove the evolution of popular music; it helped shape the rhythms of the fox-trot, swing, rhythm and blues, and rock.

However, by the early sixties, blues was no longer a current music or an evolving music. For rock-era audiences, blues usually meant either the country bluesmen, living and dead, whose careers were resurrected by the folk revival, or electric bluesmen like Muddy Waters, B. B. King, and Elmore James. And even electric blues had settled into a groove, where it still is. The style is, in essence, frozen in time. As a result, blues would play no direct role in shaping the more active rhythms of the seventies.

By the end of the sixties, rock had become the dominant popular music. The majority of aspiring rock and rhythm-and-blues musicians listened to this current music, rather than more dated roots music, to find inspiration for their music. The next wave of "outsider" styles would find inspiration from outside the United States. Reggae and Latin music would play a more crucial role than the blues in shaping the music of the late seventies and eighties.

Because the direct influence of the blues on rock-era music was essentially complete by 1970, we can assess the extent and nature of its impact. What is most fascinating is that the influence does not divide along racial lines. In previous chapters, we have documented the influence of blues on the rhythms of rock-era music, the extensive use of blues form, the influence of blues style in singing and playing, and the emphasis on being "real" that comes most directly from the blues. The final area of blues influence came from its harmony—not so much in the use of a blues progression, but in the fundamentally different approach to harmony implicit in the most authentic blues styles, such as those of Robert Johnson and Muddy Waters.

There are two features of blues harmony in these styles that found their way into seventies music. One is the slow rate of chord change—indeed, some blues songs have no change of harmony. The other is that chords simply follow one another, instead of departing from and returning to the home chord by a conventional path. More specifically, chords that are unstable in a pop song or church hymn because they imply movement to another chord are stable harmonies in the blues. So, although the chords are familiar, they do not operate in the same way that they do in their original context.

The music most influenced by the harmonic aspect of the blues was the rock heard in **Chapters 8** and 9; up-tempo soul songs, especially those of James Brown; the music of Sly and the Family Stone; and Marvin Gaye and—to a lesser extent—Stevie Wonder and Curtis Mayfield in this chapter. For rock musicians, blues harmony was a springboard to develop a new harmonic approach, one that abandoned the tension and release present in conventional harmony. For black musicians, it was evident in slowly changing or static harmonies as well as the use of chord sequences that also avoided conventional progressions. In either case, harmony of this kind was capable of projecting a darker mood than conventional harmony, as we heard in songs as diverse as "Paranoid" and "Inner City Blues."

From the mid-sixties on, the influence of blues style on harmony has more to do with the orientation of the music than it does with race. Melodically oriented music—Beatles or Motown, singer-songwriters or Philadelphia—will show relatively little blues influence. By contrast, music more oriented to rhythm and sound tends to make use of blues-influenced harmonies and other features.

12-7 The Continuing Evolution of Black Music

Most of the most popular black music of the seventies built on the innovations of Motown. The music coming from Philadelphia and Motown expanded upon the formula that worked so successfully during the sixties. More innovative music came from the two artists who emancipated themselves from Motown's artistic control: Stevie Wonder's cutting-edge use of technology and musical variety and Marvin Gaye's social commentary. These strands of black pop would continue to evolve. It would help shape disco and eventually lead not only to the black pop of the eighties and beyond but also the dance-oriented pop of Michael Jackson, Madonna, and the wave of rising stars—black, white, and Latin—who followed along this path.

Other contemporary black pop styles also appeared in the early seventies, including the more mature pop styles of Roberta Flack and Bill Withers, both of whom were in their thirties by the time they broke through. And there were the jazz/R&B/pop blends of Grover Washington Jr. and especially George Benson—a first-rate jazz guitarist as well as a fine singer—who became the first artist to have an album top the pop, R&B, and jazz charts simultaneously when *Breezin'* hit No. 1 in 1976.

By contrast, soul largely disappeared from the scene with Al Green's decision to give up his career in popular music to return to the church. However, it helped shape several important developments in seventies black music, including the jazz/R&B fusions of groups such as the Crusaders, funk, and a new wave of black gospel music.

The use of black music in a black film genre was a major commercial breakthrough for black music. The success of film scores such as *Shaft* and *Superfly* gave black musicians a toehold in this part of the music industry.

These black music styles were comfortably inside the music industry. Despite the implicit segregation of AOR playlists, black pop artists continued to chart well and tour successfully. Indeed, Stevie Wonder was one of only five acts among the Top 20 recording artists on both the singles and album charts during the seventies. (The others were Elton John, Paul McCartney and Wings, Chicago, and Neil Diamond.)

Two other black musical styles—reggae from Jamaica and funk from the United States—were largely on the outside looking in during the early seventies. Their time would come later in the decade, as we discover in **Chapter 15**.

PART III

The Rock Era, 1975–1995: Rock's Second Generation

Part Introduction

If you'd walked by Comiskey Park in Chicago's South Side on the evening of July 12th, 1979, you might have heard a stadium full of people chanting "disco sucks." That evening, between games of a twi-night doubleheader between the White Sox and the Detroit Tigers, Steve Dahl, a disc jockey at WLUP (97.9), was leading the fans in the chant.

The "disco sucks" chant was part of a promotion scheduled to take place between games. Dahl, who had recently lost his job at a competing radio station when they converted from rock to disco, was making a name for himself at his new station by destroying disco records on the air: he'd begin playing a track (using vinyl discs), then drag the needle across the disc. The shtick quickly gained him local notoriety and an invitation from White Sox management—the team was owned by Bill Veeck, one of baseball's all-time great promoters—to schedule what came to be called "Disco Demolition Night." Fans who brought a disco LP paid only 98¢ for admission, and a beer was only 90¢. It was a rowdy crowd, with fans flinging the discs as if they were frisbees. After the first game ended, Dahl and his team put a box in the middle of center field, filled it with disco records, and blew it up. Records flew up into the air through a cloud of smoke, as high as 30 feet. Dahl and his entourage were doused in beer as they drove off the field. Then some of the fans stormed the field, tore up toilets, and started a bonfire from the seat cushions in the left field bleachers. The demolition was a disaster—utter chaos. The field was rendered unplayable, ball players and stadium staff feared for their safety, and the White Sox had to forfeit the second game to the Tigers.

Why did the people who came to the stadium hate disco so much? One reason was the lifestyle associated with the music—the glitz and glamour of the discotheques. Dahl claimed that he hated disco so much because he couldn't buy a three-piece white suit off the rack. Another seemed to be prejudice against the minorities that were among disco's earliest fans: Hispanics, blacks, and gays. Vince Lawrence, a black teenager who was a ballpark usher, remembers people in the crowd running up to him, breaking records of nondisco black artists like Curtis Mayfield in half and screaming "disco sucks" in his face. (Lawrence salvaged several of the discs and later used them to help create Chicago house, an early techno style that grew out of disco.) However, the hatred also seems to reflect a generational split among fans of rock-era music. For those who loved "old time rock and roll"—who didn't want to be out on the dance floor and avoided discos like the plague—disco seems to have been a rejection of what they liked about their music in almost every feature: different sounds and instruments, different beat, different look, different environment. Disco was brand new; rock had become, in about one decade, "old time."

Disco was the most prominent of a wave of new styles that emerged in the middle of the seventies. All grew out of earlier rock-era styles, and all began outside of mainstream rock. Reggae blended late fifties and sixties rhythm and blues with existing Jamaican popular music to produce a recognizably new rock-era style. It caught the ear of musicians, first in the United Kingdom, and then in the United States. Funk traces back to the music of James Brown and Sly and the Family Stone with its focus on dense, active rhythms and repeated riffs. Disco was a streamlined, more commercial cousin of funk. It was the most important new dance music since rock and roll, and it mainstreamed sixteen-beat rhythms. In its purest form, punk was a full-band intensification of rock and roll: the characteristic rhythmic layer of early rock hammered out fast and loud. In its emphatic return to the simpler sounds and rhythms of early rock it was an emphatic rejection of the expansion and commercialization of mainstream rock. New wave was similarly stripped down, but not as amped up, and more variable in rhythm and sound. It too was oppositional, but in a less deviant, more quirky—occasionally even humorous— manner.

As the account of "Disco Demolition Night" implies, these new styles coexisted with the established rock of the seventies. Only disco had a significant commercial presence during the latter part of the seventies, and that was short-lived. Punk and new wave bands performed in venues that held only a few hundred fans while mainstream rock acts filled stadiums.

The influence of these five styles far outstripped their commercial impact. Collectively they would help shape the most distinctive music of the next decade. Music that sounds as if it could have only come from the eighties reflects the influence of at least one of these styles, and often more than one. Rap, the most important new sound of the decade, developed mainly from disco, reggae, and funk. Disco popularized the technology that was adopted by early techno DJs; disco recordings provided some of their raw material. Eighties pop—Michael Jackson, Madonna, et al.—is distinguished from the pop of the previous decade by disco-influenced sounds and rhythms. The combined influence of disco and punk, in varying proportions, shaped much of the new rock of the eighties, most spectacularly in the music of Prince and U2. A key difference between mainstream rock and alternative was the extent to which the latter drew on punk/new wave and funk. Reggae was the source for more subtle rhythms in eighties pop and R&B, and its international success ignited the world-music movement and numerous world-based fusions. These were among the sounds that belonged to the eighties, and not before.

Earlier styles continued to flourish. New acts—from sophisticated metal acts like Metallica and hard rock bands like Guns N' Roses to roots rockers like John Mellencamp and Bonnie Raitt—expanded the range of important substyles from the late sixties and seventies. The music of top seventies acts, like Bruce Springsteen to Billy Joel, continued to evolve. They and others continued to explore the richness of established rock styles.

As we have noted, rock-era music has been remarkably diverse from the time it coalesced into the dominant new music of a generation. Even as the Stones and others defined its core, the Beatles expanded its range. Even as Motown defined a new and appealing black pop style, soul acts brought the passion of the blues and the rhythmic excitement of a culture into the present. The music of the early seventies only continued the fragmentation of rock-era music.

However, the reverberations from the new music of the late seventies added another dimension to the diversification of rock-era music: it was not only white and black, or center and boundaries, but also new and old. Rock-era music began a new generation with punk and disco, and the music that developed from it. Most fundamentally, from an evolutionary perspective, the new generation was defined by new approaches to rhythm: the intensified eight-beat rhythm of punk, and the sixteen-beat rhythms mainstreamed by disco. There was also a new sound vocabulary heard in much of this music. Cutting-edge technology, much of it based on digital audio processing, helped create synthesized analogs to conventional instruments as well as more sophisticated techniques for recycling existing recorded material.

In this part, we sample music from first- and second-generation rock-era music, from the inside and outside, and from black and white, and from both regional and international perspectives. We will outline the decisive split between disco and punk that initially divided second-generation rock-era music, and then watch the interplay between these two streams in so much music of the eighties. And we will continue to monitor the continued development of first-generation rock and R&B through the end of the eighties.

All of this music benefited from new technologies that impacted every aspect of the music business: creation, production, promotion, dissemination, and consumption.

Audio Cassettes

In the sixties, two important tape-based consumer formats emerged. One was the four- or eight-track tape. These tape players began to appear in cars (and Learjets) in 1965. (Bill Lear had the technology developed for his line of corporate jets.) They remained popular through the seventies. The other, more enduring, playback device was the audio cassette. A number of manufacturers, most notably Philips, Sony, and Grundig, worked to develop cassettes and cassette players and to come up with a common standard for them.

This new format had many advantages. The units were smaller, and so were the playback devices. Some were portable; others went into car consoles. By the mid-seventies, boom boxes had appeared; they offered a low-priced and portable alternative to the home stereo. The first Walkman came from the Sony factory in 1979; other companies quickly followed suit. All of these devices made listeners' personal recordings as accessible as the radio.

Cassette players also made it possible for consumers to assemble their own playlists, using blank tapes. With improvements in recording quality, most notably the Dolby noise-reduction technology, there was less loss in quality during duplication. People could now take their own music with them wherever they went. By the seventies, this new technology had caught on: cassette sales grew much faster than LPs (vinyl); by 1982, they would exceed them. However, cassette's reign as the dominant playback modality would be short-lived.

In 1984, the first CD pressing plant in the United States—in Terre Haute, Indiana—started producing CDs. The first CDs were expensive because the production process was seriously flawed; only a relatively small percentage of the CDs produced were good enough for release. As a result, the cost of a CD was high—higher than cassette or vinyl. (Not surprisingly, given the nature of the music business, the cost of a CD has remained higher than that of a cassette, even though production costs are now much lower.)

By 1993, unit sales of audio CDs exceeded sales of cassettes, and by 2003, cassettes had all but disappeared from the marketplace. The growth of these multiple platforms—and the high price of CDs—fueled a comparable rise in both unit sales and revenue. Unit sales reached a new high in 1988, and a new revenue high (adjusted for inflation) in 1993.

The audio CD was part of a digital revolution that would transform every aspect of the music business in the last quarter of the twentieth century—and beyond.

The Digital Revolution

What made electronic technology—the microphone, the radio, and improved recording quality—possible was the ability to convert sound waves into electrical signals and electrical signals back into sound. What made digital audio possible was the ability to encode the waveform generated by the electrical signal into a binary format. This was accomplished by sampling the wave at regular intervals, with several possible gradations. On a standard CD, the wave is sampled 44,100 times a second; there are 65,536 ($16 \times 16 \times 16 \times 16$) possible gradations of the wave. What happens is that this high sampling rate, coupled with the thousands of gradations, makes it possible to simulate the shape of the wave so closely that the original waveform and the digital sampling of it are virtually identical.

Digital audio fools our ears in much the same way that digital images fool our eyes. Open a visual image on your computer and magnify it. You'll notice that it is a grid of squares, each a single color or shade of gray. However, the size of each square is so small that our eyes are fooled into seeing color blends, curves, and other continuous images. (By contrast, dot-matrix printers typically have a resolution of only 200 dots per inch, so curves seem more jagged, especially in larger font sizes.)

This ability to encode waveform data digitally has had several benefits. First, it eliminates signal degradation. In analog tape recording, there were inevitably some unwelcome sounds: one can hear tape hiss on pre-digital recordings that have not been remastered or on cassette copies of recordings. The more a tape is copied, the more pronounced the extraneous sounds become. By contrast, digital information can be copied an infinite number of times with no loss of audio quality, as anyone who has burned a CD or used a file-sharing service knows.

Second, it became possible to maintain quality despite unlimited use. Because of the physical contact of a stylus with a record groove, or tape with the tape head, the quality of sound degraded over time. A recording played for the one-hundredth time on a turntable or cassette player will sound worse than the first time, no matter how much care is taken. This problem disappeared with digital audio.

Third, the high sampling rate has enabled those working with computer audio to isolate musical events with a precision that earlier generations could only dream about. Instead of shuttling a tape head back and forth to find the right starting point, those working in the digital domain can quickly identify and mark the beginning and end of a musical event. Once isolated, they can manipulate it at will—compressing or expanding it, changing its pitch higher or lower, changing its timbre, enhancing it with special effects. Three new applications of this technology found widespread use in the creation and production of music.

MIDI

Musical instrument digital interface, or MIDI, is an industry standard that allows electronic instruments to communicate with one another and with a computer. In theory, this seems like a natural and modest step. In practice, it was a tremendous breakthrough, for two main reasons. First, it enabled a single person to simulate an orchestra, a rock band, or a swing band, using just one instrument. Using a MIDI-enabled electronic keyboard or other similarly configured device, musicians could choose from an array of MIDI-out sounds—usually no less than 128. They could play the passage, as if playing a piano or organ, but the sound coming out would be like a trumpet, or bells, or violins, or a host of others.

Second, MIDI devices could interact with sequencers. A sequencer is a device that enables a person to assemble a sound file, track by track. Using a sequencer that can store eight tracks, a person can re-create the sound of a band: one track for the bass, another for the rhythm guitar, and so on.

Sequencers can also be used to create loops. A loop is a short sound file—such as a drum pattern or a bass line—that can be repeated and combined with other loops or freely created material to create a background for a song, whether it's rap, pop, techno, house, or something else. To make this process easier, loops are usually a standard length: eight beats (two measures), sixteen beats (four measures), and so on. With these kinds of resources, assembling the rhythm track to a song can be like building with Lego: users simply snap them into a track in their digital audio software.

Sampling

A sample is a small sound file. (Please note that this meaning of sample is different from the sample of a waveform; the two meanings are related but different, much like the multiple meanings of beat.) There are two basic kinds of samples in common use. One is the recorded sound of a voice or group of voices, an instrument (for example, a grand piano) or group of instruments (such as a violin section), or some other sound. This sound can then be activated through some other device. For instance, one can buy a disc with the sampled sound of several cellos playing every note on the usable range of the instrument, recorded in many different ways. Then the buyer can install it on a computer, activate it inside the appropriate software, and produce a passage that sounds like a recording of the cello section of a first-rate symphony orchestra.

This kind of sampling has been available since the sixties. The first commercial "sampler" to achieve any kind of currency was the Mellotron. It was a keyboard instrument in which depressing a key would activate a looped tape of a string sound. It was not very flexible, but it was a cost-efficient alternative to hiring violinists. However, sampling didn't really become practical until digital technology.

Now, sampling has reached such a level of sophistication that it is often impossible to determine whether a passage was recorded live or created using samples. In effect, this kind of sampling is a more advanced version of MIDI playback, because the sounds are rendered more accurately.

The other primary kind of sampling involves lifting short excerpts from existing recordings to use in a new recording, much like a visual artist will use found objects to create a collage or assemblage. It has been a staple of rap background tracks since the technology became available in the mid-eighties.

Computer Audio

In 1965, Gordon Moore, one of the founders of Intel, predicted that the number of transistors on a computer chip would double every couple of years. Moore's law, as it has been called, has largely held true. What this has meant is that the amount of computing power one can buy for $1,000 has doubled every eighteen months or so.

Because CD-quality digital audio requires over one million samples per second, the first personal computers could not handle audio processing in real time. However, with rapid increases in computer speed, computer audio became a reality at the end of the eighties. In 1989, Digidesign released the first digital audio workstation, which effectively enabled a computer to fulfill many of the functions of a recording studio. Other companies followed suit in the early nineties, developing software and sound cards for both Macs and PCs.

Those who have come of age with this technology in place may not find it to be unusual. However, for those of us who have seen it emerge, it is awe-inspiring. For just a few thousand dollars, anyone can create a home studio that can do just about anything that could only have been done in a million-dollar studio less than a generation ago. One of the images of this time that is sure to endure is the creative person sitting not at an instrument or a desk, but at a workstation, surrounded by displays, keyboards, CPUs, and other computer audio equipment.

The advances in computer-based digital audio have put high-end music production within almost everyone's budget. For the aspiring creative artist, the financial investment is a fraction of what it once was. The larger investment is time, not only to develop the necessary musical skills but also to master the applications necessary to create the desired result. And there are plenty of role models, from Stevie Wonder, Brian Eno, and Grandmaster Flash to Trent Reznor, Juan Atkins, and Richard James.

Digital audio was a new technology for the ears. Cable TV opened up new possibilities for ears and eyes.

Cable TV, MTV, and Music Videos

Those who have grown up with hundreds of networks may find it difficult to imagine a time when television viewing options consisted almost exclusively of three networks: NBC, CBS, and ABC. Larger metropolitan areas had public television and perhaps a few independent stations. But until the early seventies, most viewers had only NBC, CBS, and ABC to choose from. That would change with the emergence of cable television.

Cable TV is almost as old as commercial broadcasting. The first cable TV services were launched in 1948; a well-situated antenna brought television signals to homes in remote rural regions. There was some growth during the fifties and sixties; however, cable TV as we currently know it didn't get off the ground until the seventies. Two key developments—the launching of communications satellites and significant deregulation of the broadcast industry—made cable television economically viable.

Cable changed the economics of the television industry and transformed it in the process. Prior to its emergence, networks relied exclusively on advertising for their revenue. The signal was free. Cable TV services charged subscribers a fee. In turn, they passed on a percentage of the fee to the channels that they offered their subscribers. This new source of revenue made possible the fragmentation of the television market. A network that could command only 1 or 2 percent of the market would have no chance for success against the major networks. But that same 1 or 2 percent of the cable market could provide enough income to keep the network on the air and make money for its owners.

MTV

Among the first of these new cable networks was MTV. The network began broadcasting on August 1, 1981. Symbolically, the first music video that MTV broadcast was "Video Killed the Radio Star." The original format of the network was analogous to Top 40-style radio stations: videos replaced songs, and VJs (video jockeys) assumed a role similar to radio disc jockeys.

Perhaps because cable originally serviced mainly rural parts of the country, MTV took an AOR-type approach to programming. For the first couple of years, programming targeted a young, white audience: bands were almost exclusively white—Duran Duran, a British pop group with a keen visual sense, was one of the early MTV bands. Black acts cried "racism," with some justification. The most notorious incident involved jazz keyboardist Herbie Hancock, whose song "Rockit" was a hit in 1983. The video for the song received airplay on MTV. It features a Dali-esque collage of white mannequins—some whole, some only partly present—moving to the music. Hancock appears fleetingly, as if he were on a television show. Later, it was revealed that MTV insisted on his limited visibility, because of their white orientation. However, change was in the air: that video would win awards in five categories at the first MTV Video Music Awards ceremony the following year.

It was Michael Jackson who obliterated MTV's color barrier. The demand for his spectacular music videos—made in conjunction with his 1982 album Thriller—was so overwhelming that the network changed their policy. Race was suddenly a nonissue.

The Cable Act of 1984 effectively deregulated the television industry. In its wake, the cable industry wired the nation. With new revenues came new and improved programming. MTV started VH1 in 1985 and diversified their programming in several ways, adding documentaries, cartoons, and talk shows and continuing to broaden their programming. In particular, their segments on rap helped bring it out of the inner city.

MTV has affected both consumers and creators. The network has become a key tastemaker for young people around the world. It has influenced not only whom they listen to but also many other aspects of youth culture: dress, looks, body language, vocabulary, attitudes. The emergence of MTV has also reshaped the sound of pop, as we consider shortly.

Music Videos

From the start, rock had been a look as well as a sound. Elvis was a sensation on television, then in films. Other rock-and-roll stars made their way into films as well, although not as stars; the 1956 film *The Girl Can't Help It*, which starred Jayne Mansfield, featured Little Richard, Gene Vincent, and Fats Domino. The Beatles' breakthrough film feature, *A Hard Day's Night* (1964), showed the power of film to enhance music, especially when the visual element was so well in tune with the music and the spirit of the band.

During the late sixties—the twilight of the Beatles' career—the idea of using videos as promotional tools began to emerge. At the same time, live performances were captured on video, or on film: documentaries of the Monterey Pop Festival in 1967 and Woodstock in 1969 remain treasures. With its opening scene clearly differentiated from live performance, Queen's video of their 1976 hit "Bohemian Rhapsody" was an important step in moving music video beyond capturing a live performance. Further experiments, especially by new wave acts like Devo, moved closer to the integration of sound and image that characterizes contemporary music video. In their hilarious video of "Jocko Homo," they make no pretense of performing the song.

The Impact of Music Videos

Sparked by the emergence of MTV, the music video producers of the early eighties inverted the conventional relationship among sound, story, and image. In music theater and film musicals, songs were written for the story. Ideally, songs enhanced those moments when what the character felt was too much for mere words. In early music videos, the relationship was the opposite: the visual element was designed to enhance the song. However, because MTV provided an important and attractive new outlet for videos, the music video became more than a promotional tool. Songs could be conceived with their potential as videos in mind. Acts could create song and video as an integrated and balanced whole, where the song is more than a soundtrack, and the visual elements are more than enhancements of the song. With this shift in approach, the music video effectively became a genre unto itself, rather than simply a visual enhancement of an audio recording.

All of these developments altered the musical landscape. Cassettes made listening to music more portable and personal. The digital technologies—sampling, digital instruments, MIDI, and by the early nineties computer audio—effectively created techno and rap, and transformed the sound of pop. CDs preserved the sound of all of the music at a higher quality on a medium that would experience minimal degradation over time. Music videos effectively created a new multidisciplinary art form that integrated story, sound, and image, and movement. Cable TV became its outlet. We trace its impact on the music of two decades in the chapters that follow. (See MINDTAP)

CHAPTER 13

CLASSIC ROCK, 1975–1995

Learning Objectives:

1) Define the "classic rock" sound.

2) Discuss the role of album-oriented radio in classic rock.

3) Describe the groundbreaking elements found within Aerosmith's 1986 collaborative version of "Walk This Way."

4) Recall the musical characteristics of the power ballad.

5) Comment on the musical contributions of David Bowie to the 1980s new rock sound.

6) Compare the key components of **significant rock** to **grunge**.

Chapter Introduction

album-oriented radio A type of FM radio format that emphasized a restricted playlist.

The classic rock format evolved from AOR, **album-oriented radio**. AOR radically redefined the relationship between rock and radio. In the early years of rock, radio had been an important part of the music's "outsider" image: Alan Freed and other like-minded disc jockeys in the fifties; "underground" FM stations in the sixties. However, in the seventies, disc jockeys at AOR stations could no longer choose the songs they played. Instead, program directors selected a limited number of songs designed to attract a broad audience while offending as few as possible. Often, stations bought syndicated packages, further homogenizing radio content. Classic rock stations have maintained the rigidly structured playlists of AOR—at some stations deviating from the playlist will get a DJ fired—but increasingly restricted their choices to hit songs from the previous decades.

The emergence of classic rock radio was a reactionary trend. Those responsible for the initial success of the genre realized that there was still a substantial, mainly older audience who preferred the music they'd grown up with to the new music that their kids were watching on **MTV**. Although dismissed early on by some insiders as passing fad, the format remains popular: a younger audience has discovered the music of their parents and grandparents.

MTV A cable network which began broadcasting music videos in 1981.

In the spring of 2014, Walt Hickey, recently graduated from college and newly employed at **FiveThirtyEight.com**, heard Green Day's "**American Idiot**" on a classic rock station. The unexpected appearance of the song on the station's playlist prompted Hickey to "wonder, what precisely is classic rock?" He sought an answer by tabulating a week's worth of songs on 25 major-market classic rock stations and talking with a couple of people directly involved with classic rock programming. Given that the roots of the format are in AOR, it should not be surprising to find that program directors use a data-driven approach to creating playlists: sampling listeners' preferences directly and creating music analysis software to find similar

Experience an interactive version of this era in ⚡ MINDTAP

songs. Their approach has been to start at the center—for example, Led Zeppelin and Pink Floyd—then identify what other music that people who like these two bands listen to.

The results of Hickey's listening-intensive survey reveal that the heart of the playlist comes from the latter half of the seventies: a third of the songs on the list were released between 1975 and 1979, and the rest form a slightly skewed bell curve with functional end points (<h1%) at 1967 and 1991. The music ranges from songs by bands that defined and reinforced the core rock style—The Rolling Stones, AC/DC, Kiss—to those who stretched its boundaries to some extent—Pink Floyd, Queen, Fleetwood Mac—and those who did both—the Beatles, Led Zeppelin.

13-1 Rock 'N' Roll: the "Classic" Classic Rock Sound

The Rolling Stones were introduced as "the greatest rock 'n' roll band in the world" at a concert appearance in 1969. With tracks like Led Zeppelin's "**Rock and Roll**," from *IV* (1971) and the Rolling Stones' "It's Only Rock 'N' Roll (But I Like It)" from *It's Only Rock 'N' Roll* (1974), "rock 'n' roll" (in various spellings) became the label for the core rock style. By 1978, it was already "old time" and (for Bob Seger) a bulwark against disco. By that time, "rock 'n' roll" was already a timeless style. Nowhere has that been more clear than in the music of AC/DC. From "**It's a Long Way to the Top (If You Wanna Rock 'n' Roll)**" (1976), "**Let There Be Rock**" (1977), and "**Rock 'n' Roll Damnation**" (1978) to "**Rock And Roll Train**" 30 years later, the band has codified the sound of the core rock sound. We can hear their early mastery of the style—and some funky bagpipes, a unique touch—in their video of the song.

In the opening chapter, we described AC/DC's timeless approach to the core rock style in some detail. Our initial purpose in reintroducing their music here is to provide a central reference point for our survey of classic rock. In this song we hear:

- A core rock band: two guitars, bass, and drums behind the lead vocalist
- Playing loudly throughout
- With noticeable but not excessive distortion in the guitars
- Layers of syncopated riffs, which interact with the steady drums to provide a good beat and which become memorable through incessant repetition
- Expressive, blues-tinged guitar playing during Young's solo
- Syncopation also in the vocal—and bagpipe—lines
- An easy-to-follow verse/chorus form

As we sample about twenty years of classic rock (with some roots rock included for good measure), we can use these musical features to assess range and change in classic rock. We resume our survey with four examples of classic rock from the late seventies.

13-1a The Boundaries of Seventies Rock

Classic rock would eventually merge two bodies of music that were largely separate in the latter half of the seventies. One was the hard rock and heavy metal that was prominent in the first part of the decade but flew under the radar to some extent later on. The other was a group of rock-related acts whose music aligned with the middle-of-the-road goals of AOR radio. They were the main beneficiaries of the marketing muscle and media control of the music business. Their music was typically rock, but not the core rock style. Rather, it tended to be more accessible and melodic, and occasionally powerful, but not threatening, at least in sound. A majority of the chart-topping acts between 1975 and 1979—the Eagles, Fleetwood Mac, Billy Joel, Supertramp, Wings, Elton John, Peter Frampton—fit this general description. However, the best-selling albums of the same period tell a somewhat different story. Harder-rocking bands like AC/DC, Aerosmith, Bob Seger's Silver Bullet Band, Bruce Springsteen's E Street Band, and Van Halen eventually sold more recordings than these higher-charting acts. This suggests both the influence of radio airplay on the charts and the more enduring appeal of hard rock bands during this period. We consider each in turn.

13-1b Queen: The Champions of Camp?

Queen was a band fronted by songwriter-pianist-vocalist Freddie Mercury, born Farrokh Bulsara (1946–1991); the other band members were bassist John Deacon (b. 1951), guitarist Brian May (b. 1947), and drummer Roger Taylor (b. 1949).

Even by rock standards, Mercury was an outsider. His family is Parsi, those based in India who follow the teachings of Zoroaster. Parsis fled to India from Iran centuries ago to avoid persecution by Muslims; they eventually formed a close-knit community around Bombay, where they prospered after the arrival of the British colonists. Mercury's father worked for the British colonial government; Bulsara/Mercury was born in Zanzibar, off the coast of Tanzania. His family returned to India, where he received a proper British education, followed by further training at art college in London.

The band came together in 1971 and released their first album two years later. They waited four years for their first hit, "**Killer Queen**," and broke through the following year with their fourth album, *A Night at the Opera*, which contained "**Bohemian Rhapsody**," arguably the band's finest moment and still a top contender for the most outrageous rock track of all time. (There is an "operatic" section in "Bohemian Rhapsody," but the titles of the album and the next one, *A Day at the Races*, were taken from Marx Brothers films.)

Queen presented dynamic and visually exciting stage shows in large arenas: Freddie Mercury was among the most flamboyant performers of the era. The visual element was key to their success: a promotional video of "Bohemian Rhapsody" anticipated the music videos of the eighties.

In "Bohemian Rhapsody," the hit that catapulted them to stardom and got them out of debt, they packed remarkably varied material into a single track: there are jarring contrasts from section to section within this six-minute track. It begins with close harmony vocals accompanied only by Mercury's piano playing. A rock-ballad-style section follows; the other instruments join in as Mercury sings alone. Guitarist Brian May takes a brief solo, which is based on the melody of Mercury's vocal. There is an abrupt transition to a spoof of operatic style, followed by a heavy metal-sounding instrumental section, which dissolves into a return to the main vocal material.

The title of the album has a multilevel connection with "Bohemian Rhapsody," the only track on the album that blatantly parodies opera. There is the obvious link: *Opera* in the album title and the operatic interlude. However, this clear connection may mask a more subtle and pervasive connection between the madcap humor of the Marx Brothers and Queen's evocation of it in this song. If the dissonance between words and music is intentional, then "Bohemian Rhapsody" is unashamedly camp. The lush close harmony of the opening recalls the fantasy world of doo-wop love songs: even as the lyrics promise no escape from reality, the music provides it. This sets the stage for the even stronger words–music disconnect of the next section.

Because the words tell the horrific tale so melodramatically and because there is no emotional resonance between words and music (the musical style in this section is associated with love songs, not murder), it would seem that Mercury is crying crocodile tears. Indeed, the entire section would seem to be a send-up. Unlike the previous sections, the operatic section is explicitly silly, and the jarring contrasts between sections simply add to the comedic effect. Like the Marx Brothers' 1935 film *A Night at the Opera*, "Bohemian Rhapsody" is a marvelous parody, created with great skill (and at great cost; it was one of the most expensive albums to record up to that point in time) and combining well-executed slapstick moments (especially the operatic section) with more artfully disguised humor.

Band members refuse to acknowledge whether "Bohemian Rhapsody" was indeed a parody. In a 2005 interview, Brian May said:

> I have a perfectly clear idea of what was in Freddie's mind. But it was unwritten law among us in those days that the real core of a song lyric was a private matter for the composer, whoever that might be. So I still respect that.

His remark is reminiscent of John Lennon's disingenuous denial of any connection between LSD and "Lucy in the Sky with Diamonds." Like "Bohemian Rhapsody," the music of that Beatles' song conveys the mood and message far more clearly than the lyrics. It is difficult to take either statement at face value.

Freddie Mercury described Queen as "the Cecil B. DeMille of rock and roll, always wanting to do things bigger and better." Despite their subsequent success, they never created another track on the scale of "Bohemian Rhapsody." The song returned to the charts in 1992 when music and video were included in the film *Wayne's World*. It is still part of Queen's show; the band now tours with Paul Rodgers taking Freddie Mercury's place.

13–1c Fleetwood Mac: Old Troubles for New Women

Among the reverberations from the feminist movement was a series of No. 1 hits featuring female singers speaking their mind. Helen Reddy's 1972 hit **"I Am Woman"** became an anthem for women's rights. A year later, **"You're So Vain,"** Carly Simon's diatribe against clueless men, topped the charts; Linda Ronstadt's first big hit, **"You're No Good"** (1975), mined the same vein with comparable success. In the lyrics, these women vented with a frankness that was virtually absent from pre-rock pop and seldom found in rock. Only in country music had women regularly sung about troublesome issues: songs like Tammy Wynette's 1968 hit **"D-I-V-O-R-C-E"** were still in—and on—the air in the early seventies. Fleetwood Mac's 1977 album *Rumours*, an album that traversed the difficult terrain of fracturing relationships from both female and male vantage points, would enjoy even more success.

Fleetwood Mac was an unusual group for the time, or any time: a rock band with two female lead singers, both of whom had romantic liaisons with other members of the band. This distinctive lineup grew out of a chance encounter, well after the band's career was underway. In 1967, drummer Mick Fleetwood (b. 1942) and bassist John McVie (b. 1945), who had worked together in John Mayall's Bluesbreakers, joined fellow Bluesbreakers alumnus Peter Green (b. 1946) to form Fleetwood Mac. The band went through three incarnations: a blues band in the late sixties, a more progressive group in the early seventies, and a top, thoughtful pop act in the late seventies. Singer-keyboardist Christine Perfect (b. 1943) joined the band after marrying John McVie. After a turbulent period in the early seventies, the band's membership stabilized when Fleetwood was scouting out a recording studio in southern California, heard a demo tape of guitarist Lindsey Buckingham (b. 1949) and vocalist Stevie Nicks (b. 1948), and invited Buckingham to join the band after the departure of guitarist Bob Welch (1946–2012). Buckingham accepted, on the condition that his partner also be part of the group.

This new incarnation of the band, now based in southern California, debuted in 1975 and would, barely, remain intact during the group's most successful period. *Fleetwood Mac*, their first album together, would top the charts in 1975. *Rumours*, their next album, released in 1977, would become one of the most successful albums of all time, ultimately selling over 19 million units.

Part of the appeal of *Rumours* was the autobiographical nature of the lyrics, which reflected the turbulent relationships involving all of the band members. The marriage between John and Christine McVie was headed for divorce, Nicks and Buckingham's personal partnership was on the rocks, and Fleetwood was in the process of divorcing his wife. All relationships were strained during the time the group recorded *Rumours*, and the songs on the album speak directly to the problems the couples were having. It was, in effect, the seventies musical counterpart to reality TV.

More than any other major album of the seventies, *Rumours* evidenced the frankness with which rock-era artists could speak about difficult personal issues. In the early years of the rock era, divorce was a dirty word, and problems in relationships were often hidden from public view: one simply didn't discuss such things openly. That would change in the aftermath of the free love of the sixties. What was remarkable about *Rumours* was the willingness of the members of Fleetwood Mac to allude to their troubled relationships in their music.

Their collective experiences, which they explored from both female and male points of view, resonated with the mood of the times. Divorce rates in the United States peaked in the late seventies to 40 per 1,000 married women. The number was almost three times higher than the rate of 15 per 1,000 women during the fifties. Divorce rates have steadily declined since that time.

Another reason for the success of *Rumours* was the way in which the music enhanced the impact of the lyric without overwhelming it. For example, in **"Dreams,"** written by Stevie Nicks and the most successful single from the album, the music creates a dark, unsettled atmosphere underneath Nicks's despairing lyric. In the song, Nicks fatalistically accepts Buckingham's urge to roam but warns him of the likely consequences. She laces her lyric with words like "loneliness" and "lost" and phrases like "drives you mad/In the stillness of remembering what you had/And what you lost." Her vision of his life without her is bleak indeed.

The music helps convey this mood. The harmony oscillates between two chords; it is rootless, like a relationship that is going nowhere. In the verse, the background is empty: modest bass and drum parts are the most consistent features. The transition and chorus, where the background vocals and other instruments join in or become more active, do not completely dispel the emptiness of the verse; it is as if there is always something missing—in the music, as well as in Nicks's relationship with Buckingham.

Despite their collective personal issues, the musical result worked. The group assembled words, melody, and setting skillfully and imaginatively, so that everything worked synergistically and presented the idea in a fresh way. This was thoughtful pop for adults, many of whom were wrestling with the same problems as the band members or could empathize with them.

Rumours was the high point of Fleetwood Mac's career. They have continued to enjoy some success despite domestic difficulties and substance abuse problems. Still, musically and personally, they remain strongly connected to the seventies. Their formula for mainstream success during their decade-long run: lyrics that engaged their audience, delivered in an easily understood manner; settings that placed the melody and the lead vocalist very much in the spotlight; and imaginative backgrounds that responded to the mood of the lyrics.

13-2 The Future of Rock and Roll

On Thursday, May 9, 1974, Jon Landau went to a concert at the Harvard Square Theater in Cambridge, Massachusetts. The headliner was Bonnie Raitt; opening for her was Bruce Springsteen and the E Street Band. Springsteen had built a small but fervent following among the college crowd throughout the Northeast, but his albums had sold poorly. At the time, Landau was an influential and opinionated critic: he had written record reviews for *Rolling Stone* since their first issue and at the time was also writing for *The Real Paper*, an alternative Boston newsweekly. His review of the concert in the May 22 issue of *The Real Paper*, which begins with a long, rambling account of his relationship with rock music, finally gets to the main point: an ecstatic review of Springsteen's performance. The Springsteen part of the review begins:

> Last Thursday, at the Harvard Square theater, I saw my rock 'n' roll past flash before my eyes. And I saw something else: I saw rock and roll future and its name is Bruce Springsteen. And on a night when I needed to feel young, he made me feel like I was hearing music for the very first time.

The experience changed Springsteen's and Landau's lives. Landau's oft-quoted review gave Springsteen's career a huge boost. Later that year, Landau developed a friendship with Springsteen that quickly became much more than that. He took over as Springsteen's manager and producer while disentangling him from a messy business relationship with Mike Appel, Springsteen's manager at the time; he still holds that position.

In his review, Landau listed music that he felt passionate about—music that, in his mind, spoke to the head and the gut and that was not pretentious. His personal playlist ranged from James Taylor, Randy Newman, and Stevie Wonder to (good) Rolling Stones and Neil Young. In Springsteen he found music that covered just about that entire range.

The "future" in Landau's review seems to refer to Springsteen's new way of reaffirming what he felt were rock's core values. In this sense, he was prophetic. Springsteen's music has never strayed far from these values, although it has been realized in diverse ways, from all-acoustic music to what Landau called "street trash rockers," and he has been among the most admired rock artists for decades.

Another Northeast-based band would offer another vision of rock-and-roll's future. Aerosmith, formed in 1970, would create music that would connect the good rock of the early seventies with the funk-influenced rock of the eighties and beyond. We consider two memorable songs released in 1975—Springsteen's "**Born to Run**" and Aerosmith's "Walk This Way"—as part of a discussion of the future of rock and roll.

13-2a Bruce Springsteen and the Rebirth of Important Rock

Asbury Park is a New Jersey beach town about an hour's drive from New York City. Bruce Springsteen (b. 1949) grew up in and around the town. Early on, he forged the musical split personality that has been his trademark: he worked with bar bands close to home and also played solo gigs in Greenwich Village clubs, where he mingled with Patti Smith and other early punk rockers. This helps account for the huge swings in his music, from the all-acoustic *Nebraska* album to the hard-rocking *Born in the U.S.A.*

Springsteen's enormous success comes in part from his ability to integrate seemingly contradictory aspects of his life and work. He is a superstar and a man of the people, a musician who plays to sold-out arenas and shows up unannounced to sit in with local bands. Throughout his career, he has stayed close to his working-class roots and has written songs that reflect their concerns. At the same time, he is larger than life: he is "the Boss" to his fiercely loyal fans.

This sense of being larger than life emanates directly from his music. In the course of his forty-plus year recording career, Springsteen has created music that has covered an enormous range of moods, styles, and resources: anthems like his **"Born"** songs and **"Counting on a Miracle"** from *The Rising*, his response to 9/11; the acoustic *Nebraska*; and more subdued songs like **"Streets of Philadelphia,"** his Grammy-winning song written for the 1993 film *Philadelphia*. If there is a consistent element running through his music, acoustic or electric, early or late, with or without the E Street Band, it is that it sounds big.

This sense of bigness is comprehensive and coherent. It touches every important aspect of his music: its message, its sound, its scale. It begins with Springsteen's lyrics, which always have something meaningful to say, whether it's a first-person issue or a social or political statement.

The bigness of the sound begins with his voice. Springsteen's singing—over his band blasting away or in a more intimate setting—is true: in pitch and in the emotions that it conveys. There are no obvious tricks—high falsetto singing, virtuosic melismas, stutters, or other vocal effects—nothing that says "listen to what I can do." Rather, Springsteen sings honestly and expressively, with a rough but resonant voice that delivers words and melody plainly, whether at full volume in front of a band, or more intimately, when he simply accompanies himself on the guitar.

Springsteen often augments this core sound with a large band, strong musical gestures (like the opening guitar riff in "Born to Run"), effective use of registral spacing to give depth and richness to the setting, expansive melodic ideas, and a lot of reverb in the mix. He casts his songs on a large scale: three minutes is typically way too short, and in "Born to Run," it takes a full 4 minutes 30 seconds to traverse the form once. This distinctive sense of bigness has been present virtually from the start of his career. We hear how he did it in his first big hit, the 1975 song "Born to Run."

"Born to Run" is a big song, in every respect. It shows how Springsteen expanded rock style in virtually every important dimension. The song has a strong beat, with the rhythm section hammering out the eight-beat rhythmic layer. There is none of the rhythmic play that we have heard in other rock songs. We might consider this a no-nonsense rock beat: Springsteen seems to use this straightforward version of rock rhythm to convey seriousness of purpose.

On this recording, Springsteen's E Street Band is big: several guitars, saxophone, keyboards, bass, and drums, and so is their range. In this song, moments of great power, such as the reprise of the opening guitar riff right after the instrumental break (and Springsteen's "1-2-3-4") contrast with the more delicate sections in the bridge.

"Born to Run" is cast on a large scale. The opening guitar riff is long; the narrative sections take a while to unfold; the extended interlude before the final statement of the original melody is also more elaborate harmonically, rhythmically, and texturally than good but more conventional rock.

In this song Springsteen connects directly to recent American culture. It builds on Dylan's electric phase: the same concern for the primacy of the words in the midst of a dense, loud accompaniment pervades his music. Springsteen's singing also connects his music with Dylan: his quasi-spoken, rough-edged vocal style borrows directly from Dylan's delivery. The lyric, and the attitude it conveys, goes back another decade, to Hollywood images of rebellion: Marlon Brando astride his motorcycle in *The Wild One* (1954) and James Dean in *Rebel Without a Cause* (1955).

"Born to Run" is at once down home and downtown. It is easy to imagine Springsteen dressed in torn jeans and a T-shirt, wearing his trademark bandanna, seated on a Harley and ready to ride off into the sunset with his girl. Certain aspects of the music—Springsteen's singing, the beat, the big guitar riff—communicate this look in sound. However, such features as the bell-like effects just before the title phrase and the complex harmonies and slithering scale of the instrumental break suggest a level of sophistication far greater than one would expect from the average bar band. Springsteen brings it off: he integrates these contrasting signals into a song with real impact.

Springsteen's stature has grown since this early success. He has been one of rock's superstars since the early eighties, and one of the few whose integrity and passion seem unflagging. From *Nebraska* and *Born in the U.S.A.* through the 1995 *Ghost of Tom Joad* (with its allusion to Steinbeck's *Grapes of Wrath* and connection with Dylan's idol Woody Guthrie) and his response to 9/11, *The Rising* (2002), he has continued to express his ideas honestly and powerfully.

13–2b Aerosmith: Bridging Rock's Generation Gap

The video that featured Aerosmith's 1986 collaboration with Run-D.M.C. on the rap group's remake of "**Walk This Way**" begins with the two parties in adjoining rooms separated by a flimsy and far-from-soundproof wall. As lead guitarist Joe Perry jams away, the rappers yell at the band to turn the volume down, to no avail. So when Aerosmith (bassist Tom Hamilton [b. 1951], drummer Joey Kramer [b. 1950], guitarist Joe Perry [b. 1950], vocalist Steven Tyler [born Steven Tallarico, 1948], and guitarist Brad Whitford [b. 1952]) begin to replay the song, Run-D.M.C. decides to fight fire with fire: we hear the rappers' version of the verse. This in turn sets lead vocalist Steven Tyler off. He begins to throw things at the wall, then hammers away at it with the base of the microphone stand. He breaks through just in time to sing the chorus. The video ends with Run-D.M.C. sandwiching Tyler; the three are moving together to the collective groove of the band and the DJ.

The song and video of "Walk This Way" were a breakthrough for Run-D.M.C. and rap. The collaborative version of the song reached No. 4, which was higher than the chart position (No. 10) of Aerosmith's 1975 original version. More significantly, it was the first rap video to get extensive airplay on MTV (hard to believe in our time!). It was an important step in bringing rap into the mainstream. The use of a familiar song seemed to give listeners who were new to rap a comfortable point of entry.

The new version of "Walk This Way" also sparked a breakthrough for Aerosmith. The band had seen their career go down the toilet through substance abuse that was excessive even by rock star standards. Perry left the band in 1979, swearing that he would never play with Aerosmith again. Five years later, with all of the band members strung out and broke, the group decided to reunite. Their well-known drug problems made music industry people reluctant to book them, although they toured in 1984 and secured a recording contract from Geffen Records. However, their first reunion record did not sell well. Their collaboration with Run-D.M.C., orchestrated by Def Jam producer Rick Rubin, opened the door to a return to the top. In the wake of the song's success, the band decided to get sober; by early 1987, they were clean.

"Walk This Way" has served as a musical bridge—for Aerosmith, for rock, and for the music industry. For Aerosmith it was the key to their phoenix-like rebirth; they have been even more successful in their second incarnation than they were initially. For rock, Aerosmith's music, most notably in songs like "Walk This Way," was a bridge between the classic hard rock of the late sixties and early seventies and important alternative styles that emerged in the latter part of the eighties. And the cover of "Walk This Way" was a bridge between rock and rap, which inhabited almost completely separate musical worlds at that time. We focus on the bridge between classic and more contemporary rock in the discussion of "Walk This Way" following.

In its first version, "Walk This Way" was a track on the group's third album, *Toys in Our Attic*, which the group recorded in 1975. The album went platinum and helped establish the band as a top stadium attraction. It was the high point of their career in the seventies.

The original song begins with drummer Joey Kramer laying down a good rock beat with a lot of bass drum and a strong backbeat. Perry enters two measures later with the signature instrumental riff of the song. This leads into Tyler's proto-rap verse—recall that the song dates from 1975. Behind his singing are active guitar parts, Whitford strumming on a chord, and Perry repeating a busy riff. In the first 30 seconds of the song we hear the past, present, and future of hard rock circa 1975. The sound of Aerosmith clearly grew out of the British blues bands that shaped rock and roll and heavy metal. The basic instrumentation of the band, the volume level, the power chords, the complex riffs based on the black pentatonic scale, the heavy distortion—these and other features connect directly to this earlier generation of hard rock. To cite an obvious example: in that both songs begin with a complex line built from a pentatonic scale and are accompanied only by drums, there is an underlying similarity between the guitar/bass riff in Led Zeppelin's "Black Dog" and the opening guitar riff in "Walk This Way." Moreover, the connection was obvious to their audience: early in their career, Aerosmith was derided in the rock press as an American clone of the Rolling Stones.

By contrast, it is the rhythm of the opening riff, the vocals in the verse, and the guitar chords and riffs underneath the vocals that move the sound of hard rock into the seventies and toward the eighties. All three map onto a steady rhythm that moves twice as fast as Kramer's rock beat. As with much of the other music using 16-beat rhythms heard thus far, these faster rhythms make possible a richer, more complex, and more syncopated rhythmic texture. It is this aspect of the music that made it an ideal choice for the rap collaboration and that anticipates the funk-tinged stream of alternative rock that appeared in the latter part of the eighties in the music of groups such as the Red Hot Chili Peppers, Fishbone, and Primus.

All of this supports a lyric that tells the story of a naive young man's introduction to sex via an experienced and promiscuous cheerleader. This reaffirms the erotic element that has underlain good-time rhythm and blues ("Shake, Rattle and Roll" was one of many such songs) and rock from the beginning. And it is in sharp contrast to the other music included in this chapter.

In these recordings by Springsteen and Aerosmith, we hear continuations of two important dimensions of sixties rock: Aerosmith's Rolling Stones–type rock and roll exemplifies what makes rock "rock"; Springsteen's rock exemplifies what makes rock important. Both are exemplars of their particular branch of rock, and each represents an important new synthesis within their particular domain. In their strong connection to the spirit of the sixties, they represent a countercurrent to the other music discussed in this chapter.

At the same time, this pair of examples highlights the seemingly dialectical relationship between rock as a thinking music and rock as an action music—that is, rock that makes a significant statement versus rock as music to rock to—that emerged around the middle of the seventies. For major acts, the challenge was creating music that fed the brain and shook the booty at the same time. This is apparent in the lyrics of the songs. Springsteen's James Dean–like lyrics invite us to engage in their content; the music amplifies their message. In "Walk This Way," only the chorus is easily comprehended on the first listening. The lyrics, learned after the fact, simply explain the erotic thrust of the music.

Musically, perhaps the most significant difference is the ratio of timekeeping to syncopation. In Springsteen's "Born to Run," rhythm guitar, bass, and drums consistently mark the rock-beat layer; what syncopation there is occurs mainly in the lead guitar riff and the vocal line. By contrast, "Walk This Way" is rich in rhythmic play; there is much more rhythmic activity against the beat than there is beat marking. The underlying message seems to be that when the beat is as seductive as it is in Aerosmith's song, it is difficult to detach oneself sufficiently from the groove to think about important things.

The two tracks anticipate the two important rhythmic approaches that would characterize the majority of rock-era music in the last quarter of the twentieth century. One was the intensified rock rhythm heard in "Born to Run." This would surface in even more concentrated form in punk and reverberate through a broad spectrum of music: from post-punk to pop. The other is the **sixteen-beat rhythm** heard in "Walk This Way." It became a more mainstream option through disco, and as the remake with Run-D.M.C. verified, worked well with rap. It would become the most widely used rhythmic template of the eighties and nineties: in pop, techno, rap, world music, R&B, and a broad range of rock.

In retrospect, the accuracy of Landau's remark about Springsteen and the future of rock 'n' roll depends on how we interpret "rock 'n' roll." If we understand it as identifying music closely related to the core rock style—for example, AC/DC or Bob Seger—then the remark makes sense. Springsteen engaged not only the hips, but also the heads and hearts of his listeners. And certainly his later music covers a broad stylistic range while remaining rooted in rock's center. However, if we interpret Landau's "rock 'n' roll" more generally to encompass all rock, then its accuracy diminishes. Much of post-1980 rock follows different paths, as we will hear in later chapters. By contrast, Springsteen has remained largely true to his rock 'n' roll roots, although he has blended more contemporary elements into his music.

> **sixteen-beat rhythm**
> A rhythmic template in which the fastest rhythmic layer moves four times the speed of the beat: 4 times per beat 3 4 beats 5 16-beat rhythm. First popularized in disco and funk, it has been the most widely used style beat since the early eighties.

13-3 Revitalizing Classic Rock in the Eighties

What would become classic rock pulled in its boundaries as it entered the eighties. The AOR-friendly branch of classic rock began to fade away around 1980. The top-selling acts of the late seventies, especially Fleetwood Mac and the Eagles, dropped off the charts in the first part of the eighties, and the periphery of rock, always more responsive to innovation, went in directions influenced by the outsider music of the late seventies. (We will hear an early example of that influence in the Eagles' "Hotel California" in **Chapter 16**.)

What remained were rock subgenres more aligned with the core style. Among the most commercially successful were those acts whose music included power ballads and pop-leaning heavy metal acts. For both, innovation involved rhythm and/or sound—a different approach to rock rhythm and the incorporation of synthesized sounds in addition to—or even in place of—the standard rock band instrumentation.

13-3a The Power Ballad

A ballad is a poetic form. In Medieval France, a ballad (ballade) emerged as a lyric for dance music—ballade and ballet come from the same Latin root word: *ballare* (to dance). Since at least the sixteenth century, in Europe and the Americas, a ballad has been a poem that tells a story and is ideal for setting to music. Several of the folk songs popular during the folk revival, like "Barbara Allen," were ballads. For pre-rock popular musicians, a ballad is both a dance song and a story. Typically, the song tells a story about love, and is performed for dancing at a slow tempo. The Flamingos' **"I Only Have Eyes For You"** is an especially slow example of a pre-rock ballad (but sung by a rock-era doo-wop group); Sam Cooke's **"You Send Me"** is an original song written in pre-rock ballad style.

As its name implies, a power ballad is a rock subgenre that combines the slow tempo and (often) focus on love or other ennobling experience with the power of massive amplification. In its length and gradual progress from soft and slow to faster and louder, Led Zeppelin's 1971 anthem **"Stairway To Heaven"** was a prototype for the power ballads. Its influence had more to do with the overall sweep of the song—and its resounding success despite its eight-minute length—than on the content of the lyric or the form of the song.

The eighties was the heyday of the power ballad. From Journey's 1981 hit **"Don't Stop Believin',"** which has continued to enjoy success as an inspiration for numerous sports teams, to Poison's **"Every Rose Has Its Thorn,"** the band's biggest hit, power ballads became a standard feature of a rock bands' set. The songs often served as a Sinatra-esque contrast in sound and mood to medium and up-tempo rockers.

Among the bands that rose to prominence in the late seventies was Foreigner, a six-man group whose original personnel included three musicians from the United Kingdom, including leader Mick Jones (b. 1944), and three from the United States, including lead vocalist Lou Gramm (b. Louis Grammatico, 1950). (The name apparently derives from the fact that no matter where the original Foreigner performed, at least half of the band members would be foreigners.)

More than most rock-oriented bands of the era, Foreigner recorded numerous power ballads: enough to warrant a compilation CD in 2014 entitled **I Want To Know What Love Is—The Ballads**. The most popular has been the lead track on their ballad compilation, and on their 1984 album, *Agent Provocateur*, **"I Want To Know What Love Is."**

Like so many power ballads, this song is about love (flick your lighters, please). In this case, it's about the search for love, as the title of the song makes clear. It is the music—both the melody and the setting of it—that bring the lyrics to life. The song is a showcase for Gramm's warm and passionate singing, which has echoes of the great soul singers. Like them, he moves easily from the lower register of the verse to the soaring title-phrase hook at the top of his range.

Power ballads tend to be more melodic than other classic rock tracks, and "I Want To Know What Love Is" is no exception. The melodic line is the primary focus, and it builds gradually and inexorably to the chorus. The flow is continuous. The setting of the song—layers of synth chords and riffs, instead of the usual guitars, supported by steady but not overpowering bass and drums, and at the end, Jennifer Holiday and the New Jersey Mass Choir—is like a halo of sound around Gramm's voice, and the overall effect is like listening to the sun come up: from just before dawn to sunrise.

This approach is a clear departure from the norms of classic rock: slow tempo, dominant melody, no guitars, black gospel choir in support. This is music that helps define the periphery of classic rock, and its deep emotion—in words, singing, and setting—helps explain why classic rock remains popular.

13–4 Heavy Metal in the Eighties

Heavy metal, such a powerful force in rock during the early seventies, seemed to be merely a cartoon parody of itself by mid decade. The most visible metal band was Kiss, who made their reputation on their clownish makeup and over-the-top stage show. However, metal didn't go away; it simply went on the road.

Although dismissed or ignored by rock critics—Lester Bangs pronounced it all but dead in the late seventies—heavy metal developed a loyal and steadily increasing fan base through the late seventies and eighties through frequent touring. Fans packed arenas to hear their favorite bands, bought their recordings, and kept up to date through fanzines. Exposure on radio and MTV was minimal, especially early in the decade.

13–4a The Revival of Heavy Metal

However, by the end of the decade, it was clear that heavy metal was the most popular genre in a heavily segmented rock marketplace. To cite just one piece of evidence, Guns N' Roses' debut album, **Appetite for Destruction** (1987), has sold over 20 million units. Numerous other metal bands, among them Van Halen, Def Leppard, Metallica, and Living Color, also racked up platinum/multiplatinum record sales.

Male teens and males slightly older made up most of the heavy metal fan base in the eighties. In the wake of the economic hard times in both Great Britain and the United States, many faced a bleak future. They felt out of the loop, especially during the eighties, when the gap between rich and poor widened so dramatically. They responded to the recurrent themes in heavy metal: the occult, sexual dominance (often to the point of misogyny), rage, frustration, protest, and—above all—power. Band names tell the story—Megadeth, AC/DC, Motörhead, Judas Priest, Iron Maiden, Twisted Sister, Scorpions—all were worthy sequels to the original: Black Sabbath.

And it was the music above all that conveyed the power. Most characteristically, it was loud to the point where a listener *felt* it as much as heard it. And the sound was heavily distorted, a sign both of power (distortion originally came from overdriving amplifiers) and defiance (distortion was originally an undesirable byproduct of amplification, to be avoided if possible).

Performances were a communion between musicians and their audience. Bands preached to the converted. Fans knew the words to songs, even though they were often unintelligible (fans learned the lyrics from record jackets). Stage shows were typically spectacles on a grand scale, comparable to an elaborate pagan ritual. In response, metalheads engaged in **headbanging**, heavy metal's version of dancing. In the familiarity of the audience/congregation with the songs, in their involvement in the performance, and in the sense of power that they experienced during the event, a heavy metal concert was more like a religious rite than anything else.

All of this occurred outside the purview of the mainstream media. Few "unconverted" listeners were willing to go past the distortion, the lyrics, and the visual images. The music, and what it stood for, was almost universally misunderstood and underappreciated. Those who attended the symphony would probably have been horrified to learn of the wholescale expropriation of classical music by metal guitarists such as Eddie Van Halen, Randy Rhoads, Yngwie Malmsteen, James Hetfield, and Dave Mustaine. They might well be scandalized at the suggestion that the degree to which Van Halen expanded the sound possibilities

> **headbanging** An high-energy, violent dance which evolved around heavy metal.

and raised the level of virtuosity on his instrument recalls the work of the diabolical nineteenth-century violinist Niccolo Paganini. For many, these developments were a well-kept secret. Heavy metal remained insulated in its own world: the bands and their fans.

Heavy metal was never a monolithic style, as we have seen, but in the eighties it became even more diverse. Substyles, often based on a single feature, proliferated. By the end of the decade there was speed metal, thrash metal, death metal, industrial metal, and more. Its diversity was also due to its blending with other styles; during the eighties, heavy metal came in several grades of purity. Distortion remained metal's sound signature, but "pure" heavy metal was far more than a rock song played with distortion.

As evidenced in the music of top acts like Metallica, heavy metal features these musical elements, many of which distinguish it from other rock styles, and even more from pop, R&B, and the like.

1. *Distortion is typically more extreme*. Because it is the most easily borrowed feature of heavy metal style, serious metal bands compensated by increasing the distortion to the point that the notes being played may be almost impossible to discern because of the halo of white noise around them.

2. *Instrumentation is basic*. It consists of one or two guitars, bass, and drums. Use of additional instruments—synths, saxes, extra percussion—is a stylistic impurity.

3. *It is not tuneful music*. This is especially evident in the vocal line, which is typically more incantation than melody. The vocalists chant, wail, even spit out the words. They seldom sing a catchy melodic phrase.

4. *The ratio of instrumental sections to vocal sections is much higher than in most other rock-based styles*. In addition to extended solos, where lead guitarists show off their prowess, there are also long passages with no vocal lines. These typically consist of a series of intricate riffs.

5. *It typically avoids conventional harmony*. Bands may play power chords, but complete harmonies and chord progressions are the exception rather than the rule. Instead, the music tends to be linear, with both solos and group riffs built on modes. Variety in pitch choice comes about through shifts from one mode to another, or shifting the central tone of a mode. (It should be noted that the avoidance of conventional harmony in heavy metal is a choice, not a limitation. Numerous metal songs begin with delicate slow introductions; these often contain sophisticated harmony. Apparently, eighties metal bands, like their predecessors from the early seventies, felt that the use of standard or even alternative chord progressions would undermine the power of their music.)

6. *The best metal bands are virtuosic*. This applies not only to the guitarist(s) who play solos, but to the entire band, who create and perform intricate riffs, often at breathtakingly fast tempos, with a level of precision comparable to a fine string quartet or jazz combo.

7. *Metal "songs" tend to be long, sprawling, multisectional works*. They avoid the standard verse/bridge/chorus formula of rock-era music. Instead, the work typically consists of blocks of sound, often in different tempos and with different key centers, all arranged in complex, unpredictable sequences.

These features occur in heavy metal tracks undiluted with other stylistic elements. What was labeled heavy metal in the eighties ranged from mainstream rock covered with a metal sheen to the music of high-minded bands such as Metallica. We consider these two extremes in two songs with one-word titles: Van Halen's "Jump," and Metallica's "One," a track from their 1988 album *And Justice for All*.

13-4b Light Metal and a New Eighties Rock Sound

Rock got a "beatlift" around 1980. The new sound was lean, clean, vibrant, and colored with an array of synthesizer timbres and effects. It harnessed the energy of punk, but its most direct antecedent was the music of David Bowie, himself one of punk's seminal influences. From these sources, it distilled a purer form of rock rhythm, typically spread throughout the texture, from bass and kick drum to high-pitched percussion and synth parts. Its leanness and cleanness came in large part from an open-sounding midrange: crisp single-note lines and sustained chords replaced thick guitar chords and riffs.

Bowie himself was a major contributor to this new sound. So were new wave artists such as Elvis Costello, Blondie, the Pretenders, the Talking Heads, Devo, and the B-52s. However, there were also groups that had neither punk's rage nor new wave's weirdness.

The Go-Go's' "**We Got the Beat**" (1981) could easily be the signature song of this new rock sound. Like a typical Ramones' song, it has a simple lyric, mostly the repeated title phrase. And it has punk's saturated rock rhythm—not only in the drum part but also in repeated notes and chords from top (high piano chords) to bottom (bass and low guitar). But the spirit of the song is completely different: it is almost mindlessly happy—much closer to fifties rock and roll than it is to punk or new wave. However, the rhythmic approach clearly places it in the eighties.

So does the makeup of the band. The Go-Go's were among the first of the all-girl rock groups. "We Got the Beat" also shows how the point of punk's rhythmic innovation had been turned completely on its head within five years. In the Sex Pistols' music, the rhythm was aggressive and confrontational. Here it's simply bouncy: lead singer Belinda Carlisle (b. 1958) had been a cheerleader in high school. It's as if someone put one of those yellow smiley faces on Johnny Rotten.

Van Halen

Among the bands to utilize this new approach was Van Halen, an excellent second-generation heavy metal band. Two brothers, drummer Alex (b. 1953) and guitarist Eddie (b. 1955) formed the band with bassist Michael Anthony (b. 1954) and lead vocalist David Lee Roth (b. 1954). Their 1978 debut album, simply titled *Van Halen*, showcased Eddie Van Halen's breathtaking virtuosity. The appropriately titled "**Eruption**," a free-form solo by Van Halen, immediately raised the bar for guitarists. The album was an immediate success and one of the most spectacular debut albums in rock history. It would be the first of an almost unbroken string of platinum albums by the band.

Although associated with heavy metal because of the guitar-centric songs and Eddie Van Halen's playing, Van Halen was, from the start, more than a heavy metal band. During the early eighties, in the latter part of Roth's tenure with the band, Eddie Van Halen sought to move more toward the mainstream, in part by incorporating synthesizers into their sound—he is also a skilled pianist. Among the fruits of this particular direction was "**Jump**," from their sixth album, *1984*; it was the band's first No. 1 single.

"Jump" (1983) exemplifies the new sound of punk-inspired and pop-oriented rock that emerged in the early eighties. The features that most clearly identify this sound are the prominent place of synthesizers, the open texture, and the rhythmic conception. For most of the song, including the opening signature riff, synths rule: in addition to replacing the lead guitar as the source of the opening instrumental hook, they provide most of the accompaniment for Roth's vocal. Van Halen plays guitar only in the contrasting section and in a brief tantalizing solo, which only hints at his technical mastery and sonic imagination. This soon gives way to a synthesizer solo that is more extended but less virtuosic. The synth riff lies mainly in a medium-high register; it is in a higher range than Roth's vocal line much of the time. By contrast, the bass line, played by Anthony (on bass) and Van Halen (on a synthesizer—synthesizers are now polyphonic and can play several parts simultaneously), is in a low register. What's missing—or very much in the background—most of the time are chords played by a rhythm guitarist. By omitting this typically prominent part of the texture, Van Halen gives the song a more spacious sound. This sound is a defining characteristic of the new rock sound of the eighties.

Underpinning Roth's vocal and the synthesizer and guitar parts is a bass line that is mostly a single note repeated at rock-beat speed. It changes infrequently in the heart of the song: mainly at the end of phrases, in the contrasting section, and during Van Halen's guitar solo. By presenting the rock-rhythm layer most prominently in a repeated-note bass line, Van Halen (and the other eighties bands that also used this strategy) further concentrates this already distilled form of rock rhythm. Here, the bass part turns rock rhythm into a musical trampoline, on which the rest of the texture bounces. In this form, the rhythm is vibrant, not aggressive and confrontational. Indeed, "Jump" is a good-humored song; we can almost see Roth smirking as he sings the song.

The most tuneful aspect of the song is the high midrange part, which runs continuously through the opening section and its several repetitions. Roth's vocal line is almost hidden behind it. This accessible line has more to do with pop than heavy metal, like most of the song.

Shortly after recording *1984*, Roth left the band. Sammy Hagar (b. 1947) replaced him for the better part of a decade. He too left, in 1996. Gary Cherone (b. 1961) then began his brief tenure as lead vocalist. The band has been inactive since 2004. Although Roth claims that a reunion is "inevitable," it remains (as of this writing) a dream for Van Halen fans pining for a return to the glory days of the early eighties.

The sounds and rhythms popularized in songs like "Jump" were one of the freshest trends in rock during the eighties. Other acts—including the Eurythmics, Cyndi Lauper, and the Smiths—also featured it in their music. It is these qualities—the livelier, cleaner rhythmic textures and the expanded sound palette created by the new synth timbres—that make the music sound distinctly different from almost all of the music of the seventies and before.

The connection with heavy metal is limited exclusively to the guitar solo, and to Van Halen's reputation as a superb and innovative guitarist fluent in heavy metal styles. And even the connection of the guitar solo to heavy metal is undermined somewhat by the syncopated rhythms in bass and drums. By contrast, Eddie Van Halen's keyboard playing, not only in the tuneful synth part but throughout the texture, and especially in the free-form keyboard solo that follows Van Halen's guitar burst (Eddie had recently built a recording studio in his backyard and was making extensive use of it for the band's recording projects), is central to the song and its dominant feature.

"Jump" is a mixture of eighties pop rock and metal: commercially successful, but not true to the genre. That's not the case with Metallica's music.

13-4c Extreme Virtuosity: the Music of Metallica

Metallica began the eighties toiling in relative obscurity. The group, formed in 1981 by guitarist-vocalist James Hetfield (b. 1963) and drummer Lars Ulrich (b. 1963), built an ardent cult following during the first part of eighties even as they went through a string of guitarists, including Dave Mustaine (b. 1961), who would later form

Megadeth. In 1983, Hetfield and Ulrich recruited Kirk Hammett (b. 1962); Hammett remains the lead guitarist with the group. Cliff Burton (1962–1986), the bassist for Metallica's first three albums, died in a freak accident during a 1986 Swedish tour. Jason Newsted (b. 1963) replaced him; he would remain with the group through 2001.

Like those of other top metal bands, Metallica's record sales were brisk, although the band got almost no exposure on radio or television. The group eventually broke through on radio in 1988 with "**One**," a single from their fourth album (and first with Newsted), *And Justice for All*, which peaked at No. 6 on the charts.

Even a cursory listening to "One" makes clear that the market came to Metallica, not the other way around. "One" is a grim antiwar statement that unfolds on a large scale: the work is well over seven minutes long. It makes few concessions to mainstream rock—in lyrics, music, or length. The form of the song takes its shape from the images in the lyrics; it is an especially graphic depiction of the horrors of war, as experienced by one of its many casualties.

The song unfolds slowly, and gently at first, after the faint chatter of machine guns and other war noises: the extended instrumental introduction features a guitar duet. The first flash of typical metal comes about two minutes later, in the chorus; the burst of distortion seems to depict a flashback by the protagonist. For the next two minutes, the track alternates between the gentler Flamenco-tinged music and the more aggressive and distorted music of the chorus, as the protagonist moves back and forth from faint memories to the painful present. About halfway through, the music abandons the gentler music of the opening section. With the entry of the "machine gun" rhythm—first on drums, then with the entire band—it is as if the scene shifts from the hospital ward to the battlefield. The action escalates, first in an ensemble section dominated by the "machine gun" rhythm, then in a guitar solo. The song ends abruptly.

In its sprawling form, relatively little emphasis on vocal lines, musical sophistication (for instance, there are several shifts from four-beat to three-beat measures), deep contrast from dark and moody beginning to powerful conclusion, "One" demands a lot from its listeners. The music is as uncompromising and grim as its message.

"One" has more in common with a film soundtrack than a conventional rock song. Indeed, after recording the song, Metallica discovered the similarities between their song and *Johnny Get Your Gun*, a 1939 antiwar novel that author Dalton Trumbo later turned into a film. The music video of "One" juxtaposes scenes from Trumbo's film with footage of the band and adds dialog from the film to the music. Curiously, many of Metallica's fans objected to the video, the band's first. Perhaps it was the fact of the video that troubled them, because the video, with its skillful mixing of band scenes with film footage, makes the antiwar message of the track even more compelling.

Metallica's "One" is significant rock. With its long narrative-based form, dramatic shifts in mood, masterful playing, and vivid sound images, "One" exemplifies Metallica's uncompromising approach to music making; there is nothing in the track that suggests any effort to accommodate more mainstream tastes. Despite this, the band has enjoyed commercial success as well as critical acclaim.

Despite its growing popularity, no rock music of the eighties was less understood or less appreciated than heavy metal. However, even though critics and audiences may have scorned it early on, musicians didn't. Not only did it develop into one of the important directions of the late eighties and nineties, but it bled into the exciting new fusions of the alternative bands that began to surface at the end of the decade. It remained a significant part of the rock music scene through the end of the century.

13-5 Significant Rock

In 1984, Bob Geldof (b. 1954), the lead singer with the Irish new wave band the Boomtown Rats, saw a film broadcast on the BBC that showed thousands of people in Ethiopia dying from starvation, because of drought-induced famine. Geldof was so moved that he resolved to organize a musical event to raise money for famine relief and to raise people's awareness of the crisis; he would call his project Band Aid. He recruited top performers like Paul McCartney, Bono, Sting, Boy George, and Phil Collins to record a song co-written with Midge Ure entitled "Do They Know It's Christmas?" The single topped the charts in the United Kingdom late that year, and Geldof created the Band Aid Trust to funnel all of the revenues for famine relief. A similar project in the United States early the following year: "**We Are the World**," written by Michael Jackson and Lionel Richie and featuring an all-star cast—including Paul Simon, Tina Turner, Diana Ross, Willie Nelson, Bruce Springsteen, Bob Dylan, and Ray Charles—came out in March, 1985. On Good Friday (April 5 that year), 5,000 radio stations played the song simultaneously. The single and an album spun off from the single both went multiplatinum. The project, called USA (United Support of Artists) for Africa, raised over $50 million for famine relief.

Capitalizing on the goodwill generated by the Band Aid project, Geldof organized Live Aid, the most massive fund-raising event in the history of the music business. His idea was to create a "global jukebox" with broadcasts of concerts from stadiums in London and Philadelphia. The concerts—over 22 hours between the two venues—and live performances from other venues throughout the world—for example, Moscow, Sydney, the Hague—would be broadcast throughout the world via satellite. The roster of acts performing at the multiple venues reads like a Who's Who of rock. Live Aid, performed July 13, 1985, drew a worldwide audience estimated at over 1 billion viewers; at one point during the broadcast, Billy Connolly, a Scottish comedian and actor who was opening for Elton John, announced that he had been informed that 95 percent of the world's television sets were watching the event. Live Aid eventually raised over $260 million for famine relief in Africa. Even more important, the events and the recordings called attention to the plight in Africa; shipments of grain surpluses from the United States and elsewhere soon alleviated the suffering in Ethiopia.

These events and others like them (such as Farm Aid) put the "we" back in rock. In the sixties, rock had defined itself as a "we" music: first in the bands themselves (names like the Beatles, the Beach Boys, the Who, the Rolling Stones gave bands a collective identity), then in the bond between music and audience. The "we" in rock was a generation that didn't trust anyone over 30. The seventies, by contrast, have been dubbed as the "me" decade: in music, self-involvement (what about me?) and the pursuit of success seemed to negate the sense of community created in the sixties. There was no Woodstock in the seventies.

The massive fund-raising events of the eighties signaled the return of rock's conscience, but with a huge difference. In the sixties, rock gave voice to a generational revolution. It provided the soundtrack for an assault on the establishment, and by overthrowing the pop music establishment, it led by example. In the eighties, rock *was* the establishment, the dominant segment of the music industry. As a result, it could leverage the celebrity of its artists in projects that served a greater good. In the eighties, "we" in rock not only included the musicians, the music industry, and the audience, but also those whom they sought to help. The success of their efforts was a strong signal of the enormous cultural presence of rock-era music in the latter part of the twentieth century.

Idealism and altruism came into rock via the folk tradition, most notably in the early music of Bob Dylan. In this music, the words delivered the message—whether it was a trenchant critique of contemporary life or a call to action. The music amplified its impact because the words were sung, not spoken, but melody and accompaniment were, for the most part, expressively neutral. As in the songs of Woody Guthrie, there was little or nothing in a guitar accompaniment that resonated directly with the message of the lyrics. By contrast, electric Dylan and those he influenced moved away from the idealistic, socially involved themes of early sixties folk. It often took an extraordinary event to prompt a musical response: "Ohio," which Neil Young wrote for his supergroup Crosby, Stills, Nash, and Young in response to the shootings at Kent State, is a well-known example.

Significance returned to rock at a time when rock had matured to the point that it could convey importance in music as well as words. This is the musical corollary to the fund-raising events created to help those in need. Celebrity was a resource for these artists that they could leverage to gain support for a good cause. The folkies of the early sixties could have only dreamed about the huge amounts of money that Geldof and others raised. And for a few eighties acts, a generation of musical development provided resources to create a music that sounded significant before the first phrase of the lyric. The opening seconds of a song by Bruce Springsteen can send a message far more powerful than even the most artfully constructed acoustic accompaniment, a point that we explore in the following discussion.

13-5a Springsteen in the Eighties

After "Born to Run," Springsteen's career was primed for takeoff. However, a drawn-out legal battle involving Jon Landau, his new manager, and Springsteen's first producer, Mike Appel, kept Springsteen out of the studios for about three years. He returned with a string of critically acclaimed and mildly (for 1980) popular albums: *Darkness on the Edge of Town* (1978), *The River* (1980), and the acoustic *Nebraska* (1982). He finally broke through to a mass audience in 1984 with *Born in the U.S.A.* It was in this album that Springsteen fully realized the big conception first expressed in songs like "Born to Run."

In the title track, as in "Born to Run," Springsteen mixes a strong story line, simple riffs and rhythms, and subtle details. However, in this song, Springsteen adopts a less-is-more approach, with telling effect. The lyric paints a brutal portrait of a Vietnam War veteran through powerful, almost posterized images: "sent me off to a foreign land/to go and kill the yellow man." The verses telegraph defining moments in the protagonist's life, from early childhood to his inability to get a job and the insensitivity of the government in supporting veterans. Springsteen's words put an ironic spin on the title phrase. In this context, what could be a prideful affirmation of patriotism becomes a jingoistic mantra—a badge of shame for a country that sends its less fortunate off to fight in a senseless war, then does little to help those who return.

Springsteen sets his trenchant lyric in an almost minimalist musical environment. The song begins with only a single octave on the piano, a heavy backbeat, and a synthesizer riff. The spacing of these three elements—low, middle, high—and a judicious amount of reverb (which makes the backbeat sound uncomfortably close to a rifle shot) give the introduction a big sound by defining a wide open space waiting to be filled in. As the song unfolds, Springsteen fills in the middle; the most prominent of the additional parts either strengthen the bass or fill in the upper range—most notably, the piano part presents a more active version of the synthesizer riff. These and other instruments weave in and out of the texture, but the riff and backbeat are constants—even through Max Weinberg's "war zone" drum solo.

In "Born in the U.S.A.," Springsteen is at once simpler and subtler than he was in "Born to Run." The prominent elements in "Born in the U.S.A." are even more basic than the driving rhythm and opening guitar riff of the earlier song, whereas the spacing of the texture and the balance between the prominent features and background support is more sophisticated, because it is less obvious.

Springsteen's "significant" sound, as evidenced in "Born in the U.S.A.," was one of several musical options that he would employ in his music from the early eighties on. Other tracks on the album range from the punk-drenched "**No Surrender**" and the country-flavored "**Darlington County**" to the synth rock of "**Dancing in the Dark**" and the moody ballad "**My Hometown**."

13-6 Renewing Rock and Roll

Among the most important acts to debut in 1988 was a group known as the Traveling Wilburys. The group presented themselves as half-brothers who were all sons of the late Charles T. Wilbury Sr.: Lucky, Otis, Charles T. Jr., Nelson, and Lefty. In fact, the Traveling Wilburys were one of the great supergroups of any era. On their first album, released in the fall of that year, the Wilburys included Bob Dylan, Jeff Lynne, Tom Petty, George Harrison, and Roy Orbison. This recording was the only one to include all of the original members; Orbison passed away later that year.

Lynne (b. 1947) was the catalyst for the formation of the group. After leading the Electric Light Orchestra throughout the seventies and into the eighties, Lynne dissolved the band in 1986 to move into solo work and production. While at lunch, Harrison and Lynne called Bob Dylan to ask whether they could use his home studio to record a song. Orbison was in town and agreed to sing on the track. Petty (b. 1950) and Dylan joined in. The good times led to an album assembled over a ten-day period.

There is symbolic significance to the coming together of Dylan, Orbison, and Harrison just before Orbison's death. The path from Anglo-American folk music to rock forked with the birth of country music in the twenties and split even farther apart with the reclamation of the folk heritage and the emergence of contemporary folk music in the thirties. Until the sixties, they evolved along largely separate paths. Rock-and-roll acts found little common ground with folk counterparts other than their shared heritage and a mostly young audience; Buddy Holly and The Kingston Trio were in different worlds musically. Their intersection with— and through—rock began in the early sixties, in large part because of the work of Orbison and Dylan. By the late eighties, the schism was ancient history; the formation of the Wilburys celebrated that fact.

The Wilburys' collaboration was one branch of a neo-traditional trend within rock during the eighties and nineties. Another was the music of John Mellencamp.

13-6a John Mellencamp

Perhaps the most down-to-earth of the newer rock acts was John Mellencamp— literally: "**Rain On The Scarecrow**" (1986), one of his most powerful songs, presents the plight of the small-time farmer through a tale about a family that's losing their farm. So it's not surprising that Mellencamp was one of the main forces behind the Farm Aid benefits.

Mellencamp, known as John Cougar at the beginning of his career ("Cougar" was his first manager's invention; Mellencamp learned about it only after seeing the name on the cover of his debut album), began his career in the mid-seventies, but it didn't take off until the early eighties. His breakthrough album was *American Fool* (1982), which included the No. 1 single "**Jack & Diane**." It was the first of five Mellencamp albums released in the eighties to reach the Top 10 on the album charts and go platinum. Mellencamp's "**Paper in Fire**," a hit single from the 1987 album *The Lonesome Jubilee*, shows his connection with, and expansion of, the American rock-and-roll tradition exemplified by Creedence Clearwater Revival, the Grateful Dead, and the Band. Mellencamp encases an excellent story, which unfolds slowly and suspensefully, in a well-grooved rock-and-roll setting. The lyric tells a cautionary tale about the fate of those who get but don't give. Mellencamp sets up the chorus beautifully by presenting the verse with a subdued, static accompaniment, then exploding with siren-like syncopated chords at the chorus.

Through the instrumentation of the song, Mellencamp deepens the country/blues fusion that typified the "American" sound, ca. 1970 by drawing on both sound worlds. Among the backup instruments are a banjo (bluegrass), slide guitar (deep blues), fiddle (country), and accordion (zydeco); the tambourine shaking out a double-time rhythm throughout the song was a staple in the minstrel show and in numerous rock bands of the sixties.

"Paper in Fire" is an especially successful continuation of the storytelling tradition within rock that dates back to Bob Dylan. Like Dylan, Mellencamp uses the musical setting to amplify the sense of the text; the music behind the words and melody are integral to the impact of the song. It demonstrates that fresh approaches to the by-now-timeless rock style produce memorable music. In the early nineties, one of the most creative reconceptions of American-sounding rock came from the plainly named Dave Matthews Band.

13-6b The Dave Matthews Band

The Dave Matthews Band is a "what you see is what you get"–type name: Dave Matthews and four others. Its simplicity harks back to the fifties when rock-and-roll acts were identified by their names: Elvis, Jerry Lee Lewis, Little Richard, Chuck Berry.

Dave Matthews (b. 1967) was born in South Africa, but his parents moved to New York in 1969. In 1986 he moved to Charlottesville, Virginia; by the end of the eighties, he was tending bar in a jazz club, admiring musicians like saxophonist LeRoi Moore, and keeping his music to himself. After a trip home to South Africa, he returned to Charlottesville and decided to record some songs that he'd written. To help make a demo, he recruited jazz musicians, among them several he'd heard in the club where he tended bar. Four of the musicians on his demo—violinist Boyd Tinsley (b. 1964), saxophonist LeRoi Moore (1961–2008), drummer Carter Beauford (b. 1957), and bassist Stefan Lessard (b. 1974)—were the nucleus of his band until Moore's untimely death. Guitarist Tim Reynolds (b. 1957) has remained a long-time collaborator.

The Dave Matthews Band played their first gig in 1991 and quickly built a large and enthusiastic fan base. Their first album, drawn from a live performance and issued on the group's own label, Bama Rags, was released in 1993. From start to finish, it showed the kind of energy and enterprise for which the band is famous. It sold well enough that the band could choose which of the majors they would sign with: they opted for RCA—now BMG as of this writing (there are rumors of yet another big merger). By the end of the decade, their albums started at the top of the charts. In the fall of 2003, they played to over 85,000 people in New York's Central Park to raise money for the New York City school system.

The musicians that Matthews chose for his band set it apart from more conventional rock acts. It has the guitar/bass/drums nucleus. But both Beauford and Lessard are skilled jazz musicians, who brought a jazz-like freedom to their playing. The two lead instruments, saxophone and violin, are the trademark solo instruments of rhythm and blues and country music, respectively. Both get plenty of space to solo. The influence of jazz, not only in the instrumental interludes but also in the interplay of the rhythm section, and the R&B and country connections, give the Dave Matthews Band an all-American sound, as we hear in one of the fan favorites from their early years, "**Ants Marching**."

The song begins with three sharp raps by the drummer. Only when violin and saxophone enter with the song's signature riff do we discover that Beauford has been playing the backbeat, not the beat. Bass and guitar join in with a complementary riff; the four oscillate between two chords for the verse of the song.

"Ants Marching" follows a familiar rock path: alternating verse and chorus, with a climactic section toward the end where the marching ants make their debut. The solos and the wonderfully expansive final section help separate the song from the run of the mill; so does the great groove. It doesn't seem to matter that the lyric is a somber commentary on those who go through life without reflection or growth—the kind that words-first singer-songwriters seem to write. It's a safe bet that many more left Matthews's concerts humming the signature riff than pondering the connection between ants marching and inflexible personalities. One can understand why it has been a favorite on tour.

The music of the Dave Matthews Band offers compelling evidence of the continued vitality of rock and roll. It demonstrates not only that rock and roll is still full of life, but also that it is possible to bring new sounds and ideas into the basic conception without losing its essence. On the other side of the continent, in the foggy coastal town of Aberdeen, Washington, another creative band would enjoy even more spectacular, albeit short-lived success, speaking to a different generation.

13-7 Generation X

Generation X is a term popularized by the Canadian novelist Douglas Coupland: it identifies the children of the baby boomers—those born mainly in the latter part of the sixties and the seventies. Most were born during the hangover from the sixties, with race riots, the squalid end to the Vietnam War, the rise of the "silent majority," the impeachment of Nixon, and rampant inflation all but obliterating the optimism with which the decade began. The members of Generation X, some of whom came from counterculture families, came of age during the "greed is good" eighties. Many, and especially those stuck in service-industry "McJobs" (another term coined by Coupland), felt completely estranged from their baby-boomer parents and the world portrayed in the media. They saw little hope for advancement in their work; many felt that their odds of enjoying the lifestyle of the rich, if not the famous, were about as good as winning the lottery. They were more in tune with the "no future" mindset broadcast by the disaffected youth in Great Britain and North America and the punk bands that set it to music. The "X" used to identify them underscored their lack of identity and power. As a result, they turned away from mainstream society and turned toward the music that expressed their anger, frustration, and alienation. Their anthem was Nirvana's 1991 hit "**Smells Like Teen Spirit**."

13–7a Grunge

The pivotal song in the history of alternative rock as a commercial music was Nirvana's "Smells Like Teen Spirit," from their 1991 album, *Nevermind*. For this recording, Nirvana consisted of singer-guitarist Kurt Cobain (1967–1994), bassist Krist Novoselic (b. 1965), and drummer Dave Grohl (b. 1969). Grohl replaced the drummers on Nirvana's first album, *Bleach* (1989), which the group recorded for just over $600. In the wake of its surprising success, Nirvana signed with Geffen Records. As a result, *Nevermind* was a far more elaborately produced album.

"Smells Like Teen Spirit" got incessant airplay from MTV and the album soared to No. 1, dethroning Michael Jackson's *Dangerous*. All of a sudden the nineties had an anthem: it is still among the best-known songs of the decade. Alternative had crossed over.

Nirvana's particular brand of alternative was called grunge. Grunge fused punk disaffection with the power of hard rock and distortion of heavy metal. Like so many other alternative styles, it started on the fringes—literally. Cobain and Novoselic formed Nirvana in Aberdeen, Washington, which is on the fringe of North America. The group's first single appeared on one of the many indie labels: the appropriately named Sub-Pop, which was based in Seattle. Nirvana's sudden success made Seattle the mecca for grunge, but the sound had already surfaced in several locations around the United States.

In retrospect, it is easy to understand the enormous appeal of "Smells Like Teen Spirit," especially to its target audience: angry young people who were not ready to buy into the system. The lyrics jerk from image to idea, like a trigger-happy video editor. Their power comes not from their coherence but from the jarring juxtapositions—mulatto, albino, mosquito, libido; hello, how low.

The music amplifies this sense of dislocation. The song begins with a distinctive four-chord pattern. It is barely amplified; it sounds almost as if Cobain is trying it out for a song he's writing. Suddenly, we hear the same riff, this time with the whole band in heavy metal mode. Just as suddenly, the middle falls out—we are left with just bass, simple drum timekeeping, and a haunting two-note riff, which serves as an introduction to the verse; it continues underneath Cobain's singing. The two-note riff speeds up under the "hello/how low." The two-note vocal riff that sets "hello" then becomes the raw melodic material for the climactic section of the refrain. Here Cobain sings as if his throat is being ripped out. A short instrumental interlude, which interrupts the four-chord progression, bridges the refrain and the verse that follows.

We hear this same sequence of events, then a loud instrumental version of the verse and "hello" section. Instead of the refrain, however, the song shifts to a third verse; we hear the entire verse/bridge/refrain sequence again, followed by primal screams on the word "denial."

"Smells Like Teen Spirit" is a dark song. Everything about it conveys that message; its enormous impact comes in part from the reinforcement of this mood on so many levels. The chord progression does not follow a well-established path; because of this we respond more to its rise and fall. It is like a hole that one cannot climb out of: every time the band arrives at the fourth and highest chord, they drop back down. Because the bass line/outline runs through almost all of the song, despite all of the contrasts, it seems to suggest a depressed state of mind that's impossible to shake. In this context, the instrumental break following the refrain sounds absolutely demonic; it is purposefully ugly, even mocking.

"Smells Like Teen Spirit" is a remarkable synthesis of several different, almost contradictory, elements. The melodic material—especially the several instrumental hooks, the "hello" section, and the vocal refrain—embed themselves in the listener's ear; they offer immediate points of entry. At the same time, they don't sound like music calculated to be appealing. Rather, they seem to be a direct expression of the mood of the song; that they are catchy at the same time is a bonus.

The sharp contrasts and abrupt shifts from section to section help "Smells Like Teen Spirit" portray the darkest depression: an oppressive weight that cannot be thrown off. It is easy to understand why "Smells Like Teen Spirit" was the song of the nineties. And it makes Cobain's subsequent suicide even harder to take; it is as if he let us into his mind so that we can feel his despair.

"Smells Like Teen Spirit" is a punk song in spirit: it expresses rage, alienation, and frustration in both words and music. However, the musical setting connects more closely to the established conventions of hard rock—in sound and rhythm— than it does to punk. It is as if the one gear available in pure punk, no matter how intense, is insufficient to convey the range of emotions communicated in the track. The eclectic mix of styles—power trio intro, understated verse, metal breaks— serves an expressive purpose here, because the quiet of the verse makes the louder sections, especially the chorus with its short vocal riffs, more powerful by contrast.

The more traditional approach to rock style in "Smells Like Teen Spirit" is also characteristic of *Nevermind*, and more generally the grunge of Nirvana and Pearl Jam. For them, a punk-influenced approach to rhythm and tempo was a less frequent option.

The most striking innovation in "Smells Like Teen Spirit" is the schizophrenic shift from section to section. Nirvana creates sharply defined sound worlds within each section of the song. They are haunting, mocking, and angry in turn. They create sharp contrasts from section to section: the kind one would more likely encounter between one song and the next, rather than within a song. When combined with the relentless chord progression and the repetition of the 2 two-note melodic fragments, they project a mood of utter despair: one can rage against the wind—or the machine—or fall into an almost apathetic state, but it is impossible to shake off the dark mood.

Sudden contrasts within a song was a widely used device in much nineties alternative rock. Another less prominent feature is the constant chord cycling: the same sequence of chords heard in the introduction runs throughout the song, except for the break after the chorus. The bass line outlines the harmony in the verse; Cobain joins in at the bridge and continues through the chorus. The practice of cycling chords in a regular rhythm throughout a song is not without precedent— the "Heart and Soul" progression is a familiar example that is still in use (e.g., Justin Bieber's 2010 hit "Baby"). However, creating the cycle from a distinctive, rather than generic, series of chords was novel. It has become a common feature in popular music since the early nineties.

The sound of traditional rock would continue through to the new century, not only with bands from the sixties through the eighties, but also with new stars, from both rock and country music. We revisit first generation rock-era music in **Chapter 19**.

13-8 What Is Classic Rock

To return to Walt Hickey's "what (precisely) is classic rock?", we can approach the question from both a commercial and a musical perspective. As a business enterprise, classic rock plays it safe, by relying mainly on chart-topping songs before 1990, and by being responsive to its audience. In a 2013 web post, Fred Jacobs, a pioneer in classic rock radio during the mid-eighties and now a consultant, bemoaned the fact that the artists featured on classic rock radio stations cannot get airplay of their post-1990 work. As a case in point, he cited Paul McCartney's 2013 album *New*, which has apparently not gained any traction on classic rock stations. And Hickey pointed out that playlists for classic rock stations are regionally responsive: Billy Joel is bigger in New York than any other city; the Allman Brothers are big in Boston; and grunge bands top California markets. Despite these regional variations, it should not be surprising that there are no surprises among the most frequently played acts: all of the ten top classical rock acts on Hickey's list came to prominence in the sixties (Beatles, Stones) or seventies (AC/DC and Aerosmith to Led Zeppelin and ZZ Top). The center of the classic rock repertoire seems to be holding; change seems to be mainly on the fringes.

Considering the "what is classic rock?" question from a musical perspective offers a unique—and fascinating—opportunity to study rock-era music generationally. The "rock and roll" at the musical core of classic rock is a timeless style. AC/DC, whose music epitomizes this core rock style, sounds much the same in the 2010s as they did in the late seventies and early eighties. If the Rolling Stones set-lists are any indication, people flock to hear the band perform their classic hits, from **"Satisfaction"** and **"Jumping Jack Flash"** to **"Brown Sugar"** and **"It's Only Rock 'n' Roll (But I Like It)."**

Using this timeless style as a reference, we can compare other music on classic rock playlists over time, to observe how the music surrounding this classic sound changes over time: from the more restrained late seventies music of Fleetwood Mac and the synth-supported eighties music of Foreigner and Van Halen to the more intense heavy metal of late eighties Metallica and the abrupt contrasts in Nirvana's early nineties music.

At the heart of just about all of this music is the traditional approach to rock rhythm—the approach most clearly realized in the core rock style. The use of this more traditional kind of rock rhythm clearly distinguishes it generationally from the sixteen-beat rhythms of much seventies black music, disco, and a host of eighties and nineties music: rap, techno, R&B, pop, and multiple rock/R&B fusions. The difference from punk is more subtle, because the rhythmic template is the same. But the punk-influenced approach intensifies the rock rhythmic layer and typically offers less rhythmic interplay than the characteristic rhythms of classic rock. There's a continuum between AC/DC and the Ramones (as we'll explore shortly), but also a clear difference in approach and end result.

Classic rock has become a classical music in the more familiar connotation of the term: it is a finite body of music from a previous generation that remains more popular than current music. Just as we are more likely to hear "classical" music from 200 to 300 years ago—Bach, Mozart, Beethoven—than we are to encounter music by more recent "classical" composers, we are more likely to hear "classic" rock than other kinds of rock music. So far, it is the first classic style in popular music to maintain a strong commercial presence decades after its initial appearance.

CHAPTER 14

REGGAE, FUNK, AND DISCO: VIEWS FROM THE OUTSIDE

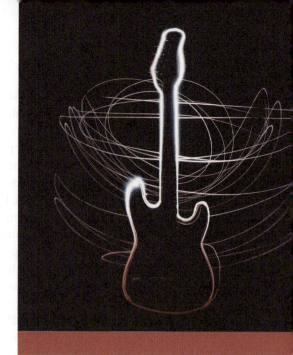

Learning Objectives:

1) Comment on the key innovations of rock-era music in the 1980s that were rooted in reggae, funk, and disco.

2) Compare the rhythmic characteristics of **ska**, **rock steady**, and **reggae**.

3) Discuss Bob Marley's contributions to reggae.

4) Recall the evolutionary journey of **funk**.

5) Describe the two distinct trends in early seventies black pop.

6) Ascertain the symbiotic relationship between **disco** and dance.

Chapter Introduction

toasting The practice developed by Jamaican disc jockeys of delivering a steady stream of patter. Much of it was topical, even personal: they would pick out, and sometimes pick on, people in the crowd that had gathered around. Toasting is a direct forerunner of rap: both initially featured topical, humorous commentary over pre-existing music.

"Rapper's Delight" was arguably the surprise hit of 1979. Released in the fall of 1979 as a twelve-minute single, it reached No. 4 on the R&B charts and crossed over to the pop charts early in 1980. It would become the first rap record to go gold. The recording was the brainchild of record executive Sylvia Robinson. She had become aware of block parties in the South Bronx where enterprising blacks hotwired into the streetlamps to get power for their sound systems, then rapped over pre-recorded music. So she had her son Joey recruit the three rappers who would become the Sugarhill Gang—Wonder Mike, Big Bank Hank, and Master Gee—then brought them into the studio. While a studio band re-created the instrumental accompaniment to Chic's 1979 hit **"Good Times,"** the trio rapped for almost fourteen minutes.

It is worth noting that the first hit song of the most significant new style during the last part of the century is a synthesis of three Afro-centric styles that came to prominence in the seventies. The most easily detected connection in "Rapper's Delight" is with disco. The borrowing from "Good Times" anticipates the sampling that would become common practice by the mid-eighties. Rapping is a black adaptation of **"toasting**, a Jamaican practice of talking over a recording, often a rhythm track without vocals. And most generally and most directly, rap connects to funk; it is the seemingly inevitable continuation of the increasing emphasis on rhythm and sound over melody that has characterized one stream of black music throughout the twentieth century.

Experience an interactive version of this era in ⟡ MINDTAP

Reggae, funk, and disco share much common ground. All three are musical styles created mainly by members of the African diaspora. All have their beginnings in the sixties and emerged as mature styles in the seventies. All three began very much outside the mainstream: reggae is Jamaican music; funk found most of its audience among blacks; disco was part of the largely underground dance club scene in the United States and Europe before the release of *Saturday Night Fever*. These styles would enjoy varying degrees of crossover success; disco was briefly a mainstream style.

Collectively, the three styles have had enormous influence on rock-era music since 1980. Many of the important innovations of late twentieth-century and early twenty-first-century music—most notably, more active and free rhythms, the extensive use of electronics, the use of musical quotation, the practice of mixing songs into a larger musical entity—have their roots in these styles. In this respect, they played a role comparable to the blues in the early years of rock. Indeed, they replaced the blues as the primary influences on a new musical generation. The music of the last quarter century was the first generation of twentieth-century popular music *not* to be shaped by an infusion of the blues.

Despite their obvious affinities and mutual influence, they were distinct musical styles, with different audiences, different esthetics, and different expressive objectives. We consider each in turn, then discuss their impact on the music of the eighties and beyond.

14-1 Reggae

Most Jamaicans are of African descent—about 90 percent at the turn of the twenty-first century. Most trace their roots back to slavery: like the United States, Cuba, and Brazil, Jamaica was a destination for the slave traders. More than 600,000 slaves arrived in Jamaica between 1665 and 1838, the year in which the slave trade ended. British colonial rule continued for more than a century. Great Britain gradually transferred authority to Jamaicans, with the final step—independence—taken in 1962. However, the economic and social inequities of colonialism did not keep pace with the political changes. One result was a great deal of social unrest in the sixties. Two mid-century movements that emerged in response to Jamaican social conditions stand out: Rastafarianism and "rude boys."

14-1a Rastafarianism

An important consequence of Marcus Garvey's crusade to elevate the status of people of African descent is Rastafarianism. Garvey, born in Jamaica, agitated for black power in the United States during the twenties, in response to the dire poverty and discrimination that the vast majority of blacks living in the New World faced. His efforts blended church and state: even as he pressed for an African homeland to which former slaves could return (it never materialized), he prophesied that Christ would come again as a black man. After serving half of a five-year sentence for mail fraud in an Atlanta prison (the charge was almost certainly politically motivated), he was exiled from the United States and returned to Jamaica.

For centuries, African slaves and their descendants had been confronting the historically inaccurate image of Jesus as a pale-skinned Caucasian. Moreover, it was inevitable that they would connect this image with the colonial empires that brought it to them. At the same time, those slaves who had become Christians saw parallels between the Jews' enslavement by the Egyptians and the slavery of

Africans in the New World. Black spirituals are rich with such connections. In this context, Garvey's prophecy about Christ's second coming and his emphasis on the Jewish/African slavery connection was a logical, if controversial, extension of these circumstances. In effect, they were the religious analogue to his black nationalism.

Rastafarians took Garvey's ideas several steps further. They claimed that Jesus had indeed come again, in the person of Haile Selassie (Prince Ras Tafari), the former emperor of Ethiopia. Selassie claimed lineage back to King Solomon, which Rastafarians have taken as further proof of Selassie's divine status. In line with Selassie's personal genealogy, Rastafarians also claim to be descendants of the twelve tribes of Israel.

These beliefs, which have never come together as "official" doctrine (as has happened in organized religions), are the religious dimension of Rastafarians' efforts to promote a more positive image of Africa and Africans. This has largely come from within the movement. For those on the outside, the most vivid impressions of Rastafarianism are images and sounds: dreadlocks, ganja (marijuana that they ingest as part of their religious practice), and the music. To Jamaican music, they gave a sound, Rastafarian drums, and reggae's one superstar, Bob Marley.

14-1b Rude Boys

The other response to the social unrest during the transition to independence was more violent: it came in the form of rude boys, young black Jamaicans who grew up in the most disadvantaged sections of Kingston. They were stylish dressers and often carried sharp knives. For many Jamaicans, including the police, they were outlaws. However, others saw them as heroes, much as the James Brothers and Billy the Kid were heroes to earlier generations of Americans, or as today's gangsta rappers are heroes to some of today's youth.

14-1c From Ska to Reggae: The Evolution of Rock-Era Jamaican Music

It is no coincidence that a distinctive Jamaican popular music during the drive for independence often had a political orientation. Nor is it a coincidence that this music drew heavily on the American rhythm and blues popular in the years around 1960: the proximity of the two countries made it available in multiple ways.

American Radio in Jamaica

Rhythm and blues reached Jamaica in two ways: through radio broadcasts and via sound systems used to create impromptu block parties. Since the development of networks in the twenties and clear-channel stations in the thirties, radio has been able to ignore borders; it is limited only by distance and wattage. So it should not surprise us that Jamaicans tuned in their radios to American stations in the years after World War II. Kingston, the capital city, is just over 500 miles from Miami as the crow flies, and about 1,000 miles from New Orleans. Stations from all over the southern United States were within reach, at least after dark. Like Buddy Holly, many young Jamaicans listened to rhythm and blues. For them, it replaced **mento**, the Jamaican popular music of the early fifties. Some would transform it into ska.

Sound Systems and Street Parties

Sound systems, the mobile discos so much a part of daily life in Jamaica, offered another way to hear new music from America. Sound systems were trucks outfitted with the musical necessities for a street party: records, turntables, speakers, and a microphone for the DJ. Operators would drive around, pick a place to set up, and begin to play the R&B hits that enterprising operators had gone to the United States

> **mento** The Jamaican popular music of the early 1950s.

to fetch. Between songs, DJs delivered a steady stream of patter. Much of it was topical, even personal: they would pick out, and sometimes pick on, people in the crowd that had gathered around.

This practice was called toasting. It became so popular, and so much a feature of the sound system party, that Jamaican record producers like Lee "Scratch" Perry began releasing discs in which the "B" side was the "A" side without the vocal track. The instrumental track would then serve as the musical backdrop for the DJ's toasting. As we noted earlier, toasting is a direct forerunner of rap: both initially featured topical, humorous commentary over pre-existing music.

From Ska to Reggae

By the end of the fifties, Jamaican music had begun to absorb, then transform, the R&B brought to the country. The first wave of new Jamaican music was ska. Ska emerged around 1960 and was the dominant Jamaican sound through the first part of the sixties. The most distinctive rhythmic feature of ska is a strong afterbeat, a strong, crisp "chunk" on the latter part of each beat. This was a Jamaican take on the shuffle rhythm heard in so much fifties R&B. It kept the basic rhythm but reversed the pattern of emphasis within each beat. In the standard shuffle rhythm, the note that falls *on* the beat gets the weight; the afterbeat is lighter. In ska, it is just the opposite, at times to the extent that the note on the beat is absent—there is just the afterbeat. Whether this was an intentional decision by ska musicians such as Derrick Morgan and Prince Buster, a product of the relatively primitive recording studios in Jamaica during this time (recall that early electrical recording did not pick up bass sounds very well), or the lack of bass instruments and people to play them, we don't know; perhaps it was a combination of all of these factors. Whatever the reason, the strong afterbeat remains the aural trademark of ska and part of the rhythmic foundation of reggae.

Rock steady, a new Jamaican style that emerged in the latter part of the sixties, combined the persistent afterbeat of ska with a backbeat. The backbeat is typically played on a different instrument, so that the two layers—the afterbeat and the backbeat—are distinguished by timbre.

Both off-beat layers stand out because the beat is either marked lightly or not at all. In particular, the bass, which was the main beat-keeping instrument in rhythm and blues, now roams freely, typically playing a line not tied to a timekeeping role.

With the creation of the composite afterbeat rhythm and the addition of the bass, the rhythmic foundation of reggae was in place. In reggae, the basic rhythmic texture of rock steady is treated more flexibly, and with greater complexity, much as late-sixties rock treated rock rhythm more flexibly than early-sixties rock. In the music of its biggest stars, reggae's rhythmic texture is typically denser and more subtle, often with several additional rhythmic layers. In addition, the backbeat is generally stronger, which then establishes the trademark "ka-CHUN-ka" pattern.

The distinctive rhythm of reggae is typically a pattern of emphasis: light or no sound on the beat, strong afterbeats, even stronger backbeats. It works equally well with any rhythm that divides the beat into two parts: we will hear it superimposed on the rock-rhythm–like even division of the beat in Jimmy Cliff's "**The Harder They Come**" and on a shuffle-rhythm–like uneven division of the beat in Bob Marley's "**Is This Love**." In this respect, reggae rhythm is different in kind from a style beat like rock rhythm, which describes a more fundamental relationship.

In about a decade, the rhythms of Jamaican music had mutated from an adaptation of the shuffle rhythm of post–World War II rhythm and blues into a rhythm that was unique in the early seventies. Early on, its development went largely unnoticed outside of Jamaica. Jimmy Cliff's film *The Harder They Come*,

Rock steady Ska's evolution in the latter half of the sixties, in which musicians added a backbeat layer over the afterbeats.

released in 1972, attracted attention in England, then in the United States when it was released there the following year. But it wasn't until Eric Clapton scored a No. 1 in 1974 with a cover of Bob Marley's "**I Shot the Sheriff**" that reggae got real mainstream exposure.

Jimmy Cliff and Reggae as Protest Music

Jimmy Cliff (born James Chambers, 1948) was one of reggae's first stars. Born in Jamaica, he emigrated to England in 1964. By the time he landed the lead role in the film *The Harder They Come*, he had gained a modest international reputation as a singer and songwriter. His appearance in the film, and the songs that he recorded for the sound, cemented his place in popular music history.

In *The Harder They Come*, Cliff played Ivanhoe Martin, a naive musician who becomes a dope dealer after being ripped off by his record producer and hassled by a corrupt police force. Cliff wrote several songs for the film, including the title track. Although his character is loosely based on a real-life person from the forties, the film is set in the present: Martin is a reggae singer. The film, widely acclaimed at home and abroad, helped introduce reggae, still a new sound at that time, to an international audience. It also exposed the difficult conditions under which so many Jamaicans lived.

The lyric of the title song sets the tone of the film. It resonates with overtones of social injustice and police oppression and brutality, even as it outlines how the character will respond: "I'm gonna get my share now of what's mine." Cliff does not sugarcoat his message at all. Lines like "But I'd rather be a free man in my grave/ Than living as a puppet or a slave" brutally clarify the options he saw.

In "The Harder They Come," the characteristic reggae rhythm is embedded in a dense rhythmic texture. Two keyboards outline the rhythm: an abrasive-sounding organ chord occurs on the backbeat, while another keyboard plays the afterbeats more faintly. All of this happens over a muted rock rhythm in the drums; an active bass line and other percussion sounds enrich the rhythmic texture. The rhythm serves as a cushion for Cliff's lyric, set to a gently flowing melody that is harmonized with basic chords and that follows the familiar verse/bridge/refrain form heard in many Motown songs and much other rock-era music.

Topical Tropical Music: Reggae and Music with a Message

In "The Harder They Come," we are faced with the seeming contradiction between words and music. The lyrics are dark, even menacing. But the music can't help bringing a smile to one's face and a body movement somewhere. This is happy music: in its rhythm, in the lilt in Cliff's voice, in the Motown-inspired form, and in the gently undulating melody. Is the music the candy that entices us to listen to the message of the lyrics, or is it a way to forget for the moment the situation that the lyrics depict, or something else altogether? What we do know is that many of the songs that put reggae on the international musical map—like this one and Bob Marley's "I Shot the Sheriff" and "**Get Up, Stand Up**"—embedded hard messages within reggae's infectious rhythms and sounds.

The use of popular song as a vehicle for social commentary was largely a rock-era phenomenon. There were isolated examples in modern-era popular songs—Andy Razaf and Fats Waller's 1929 song "**Black and Blue**," a lament on the disadvantages of dark skin color, is a memorable example; so was Billie Holiday's 1939 recording of "**Strange Fruit**," a powerful song about lynching. But songs like these were the exceptions. What topical music there was in the thirties and forties came mostly from singer-commentators like Woody Guthrie and, to a lesser extent, the blues (for example, some maintain that Nat Cole's **"Straighten Up and Fly Right"** is an allegory on race relations).

The music of Dylan and the other folksingers of the early sixties brought topical song into popular music, and reshaped it in the process, as we have seen. During the sixties and early seventies, a few black performers—most notably James Brown and Sly Stone among popular musicians and jazz saxophonists John Coltrane and Archie Shepp—dealt powerfully with racial issues and their emotional consequences in their music. But the efforts of all these musicians represented only a fraction of their total output, and an even smaller fraction of the musical activity in rock and soul.

Reggae was different, in that it first became known outside of Jamaica as a music with a message. The music of Marley, Cliff, and other early reggae stars called attention to the social inequities in Jamaica. Moreover, it came at a time when rock had largely forsaken its role as a vehicle for social commentary. Marley would help fill that void, becoming a powerful voice on social issues. In this respect, reggae anticipated both punk and rap. And like these later styles, its musical features soon found their way into songs that had no literal or emotional connection to the social issues that the first hits introduced. Marley would lead the way in this respect as well.

Bob Marley

Bob Marley (1945–1981) was born in Nine Miles, a small Jamaican village. His recording career began in the early sixties and took off in 1964, after he formed the first edition of his backup group, the Wailers, which included longtime associates Bunny Livingston (b. 1947) and Peter Tosh (1944–1987). By the early seventies, he was extremely popular in Jamaica. However, it wasn't until he signed with Island Records that his reputation spread throughout the world.

His success on record and in concert gave him and his country's music unprecedented exposure. For many people, Bob Marley *was* reggae. Worldwide, he was its most popular artist. He was also the decade's most visible spokesperson for peace and brotherhood, carrying the torch of sixties social activism and idealism into the seventies. He also made clear his affiliation with Rastafarian practice, which he had begun in the mid-sixties. While Marley's stance didn't completely legitimize Rastafarianism, it certainly raised its status in Jamaica and elsewhere.

However, Marley's music left the deepest impression. It made possible his popularity, which in turn gave him the leverage to work for meaningful change in Jamaican society. His first hits, most notably "I Shot the Sheriff" and "Get Up, Stand Up," both recorded in 1973, show his political side. Both were recorded with the original version of the Wailers, which dissolved in 1974. Marley re-formed the Wailers with the Barrett brothers (Aston "Family Man" Barrett [b. 1946] on bass and Carlton Barrett [1950–1987] on drums), plus several other musicians and the I Threes, a backup vocal group that included Marley's wife Rita (b. 1946). In addition to politically charged songs, Marley also scored with gently themed songs, including the lilting 1978 hit, "Is This Love." In keeping with the content and tone of the lyric, the form of this song sprawls lazily through time, moving at a relaxed tempo.

A comparison of the rhythm in the two songs suggests the flexibility of reggae rhythm: in "Is This Love," Marley adapts the characteristic reggae afterbeat/backbeat pattern to a shuffle rhythm, rather than a rock rhythm. Combined with a slower tempo, it projects a quite different rhythmic feel from Cliff 's "The Harder They Come." Note that in both songs the slower offbeat rhythm is the same: a backbeat. It is only the faster-moving layer that is different.

The gentle pulsations of the drum and tambourine, prompted by the fast shuffle-based reggae rhythm in the keyboards, keep the rhythm afloat, while the vocal parts—Marley's slow-moving melody and the sustained harmonies of the I Threes—and in-and-out bass slow the beat down to a speed below typical body rhythms, even the heartbeat at rest or the pace of a relaxed stroll. As a result, the rhythm of the song is buoyant and lazy at the same time. All of this evokes a feeling of languid lovemaking in the tropics, a perfect musical counterpoint to the lyric of the song.

Bob Marley was reggae's greatest ambassador. With his death in 1981, reggae lost an important world presence. Reggae is still a dominant music in Jamaica, and its sounds and rhythms have shaped diverse styles in the last quarter century— and so has its look: Rastafarian dreadlocks are still fashionable. However, it is ska, its antecedent, that has enjoyed a resurgence in popularity in both the United Kingdom and the United States.

14-1d Reggae as an International Music

Within popular music, and particularly within rock-era music, patterns of influence have often had a geographic component: the long journey of deep blues from the Delta to England via Chicago and Memphis, then back to the United States, is the most spectacular of numerous examples. In the process, the music undergoes a thorough transformation, coming back to its original home significantly changed and profoundly influential. In the seventies, the most dramatic instance of a long and winding pattern of influence was reggae. Like the blues-based rock of the late sixties, reggae also drew heavily on the music of black Americans, flourished in Great Britain, then returned to the United States via England.

Reggae's popularity outside of Jamaica owed much to the heavy concentrations of Jamaicans in England. As part of the transition from colonialism, Great Britain opened its doors—or at least its ports—to people from its colonies. During the fifties and early sixties, around 250,000 people arrived from the Caribbean, more than from any other former colonial region. By the end of the sixties, the British government had enacted legislation that severely restricted immigration. By that time, however, several generations of Jamaicans were already in England, where they re-created much of their culture. All the types of Jamaican music of the sixties and seventies found a supportive audience in England, among Jamaicans eager for this link to their homeland and among British whites intrigued by this quite different music.

For a new generation of British musicians in search of "real" music, reggae (and ska) provided an at-home alternative to the blues. Eric Clapton, who had immersed himself so deeply in the blues during the sixties, led the way with his cover of Marley's "I Shot the Sheriff." The recording topped the charts in 1974. A wave of new British acts—among them the Clash, Elvis Costello, and the Police—wove the fresh sounds of reggae into their music.

Reggae's path to America seems unnecessarily roundabout: the music didn't find a substantial audience in the United States until after it had become popular in England. Once known, however, its influence was in some respects even more widespread and more divorced from the social context of the music. For example, we hear echoes of the distinctive rhythm of reggae in the Eagles' huge 1977 hit **"Hotel California."** It had a deeper and more sustained impact on black popular music in two quite different ways. One was its influence on rap: the toasting of Jamaican DJs soon evolved into rapping, as we have noted. The other was the continuing liberation of the rhythm section in black pop. Because reggae embedded the pulse of a song in the distinctive rhythms played by midrange instruments, bass players were free to roam at will, largely independent of a specific rhythmic or harmonic role. Because of this, reggae offered eighties black romantic music the next step beyond the advances of Motown and the Philadelphia sound. We hear its influence in such diverse hits as **"Sexual Healing,"** Marvin Gaye's 1982 ode to carnal love, and **"What's Love Got to Do with It,"** Tina Turner's 1984 cynical rejection of it.

14-2 Funk

Like *blues*, *jazz*, *rock*, *soul*, and *rap*, *funk* is a one-syllable word from African American culture that began as nonmusical slang, then found its way into music, and eventually became a style label.

"Funk" originally targeted not the ears but the nose. As far back as the early years of the twentieth century, "funky" meant foul or unpleasant: a person who neglected to bathe for several days usually gave off a funky odor. Over time, it acquired another meaning: hip. Stylish clothes were funky threads. When James Brown sings "Ain't It Funky Now," he is referring to the ambience, not the smell.

Funk and funky came into popular music through jazz. Beginning in the mid-fifties, funk referred to a simpler, more blues-oriented style—a return to roots and away from the complexities of hard bop. By the sixties, it had also come to mean soulful. (It also retained the other meanings; context and delivery determined which meaning was appropriate.) By the early seventies, it had come to identify a particularly rhythmic strain of black music.

James Brown was the father of funk as well as the godfather of soul—and the grandfather of rap. Funk musicians built their music on both the basic concept of Brown's music and many of its key musical features. Whether he was talking about feeling good or exhorting his listeners to get up and get involved, Brown embedded his message in a powerful groove. Those who followed his path—first Sly and the Family Stone, then the funk bands of the seventies—expanded both the range of messages and the musical resources. Brown's music was relentlessly upbeat; Sly and the Family Stone and funk bands occasionally expressed the gloomier side of the black experience. Funk bands used the same basic lineup—vocal, horns, rhythm instruments—but they were bigger. Not surprisingly, textures thickened and rhythms became even denser and more complex.

14-2a George Clinton and Funk

Nowhere are these developments more evident than in the music of George Clinton (b. 1940). Clinton was the mastermind behind two important funk bands: Parliament and Funkadelic. While still a teen, he formed Parliament, but as a doo-wop group. They signed on with Motown in 1964 but did not break through. When Clinton left Motown, he had to relinquish the Parliament name to them. So he formed Funkadelic while battling to regain ownership of his group's name. Funkadelic represented a major change of direction. As the group's name implies, it brought together funk and psychedelic rock: James Brown and Sly Stone meeting Jimi Hendrix. When Clinton regained control of the Parliament name in 1974, he used two names for the same band. He recorded the more outrageous material under the Funkadelic name and the tighter, more polished material as Parliament.

The formation of Funkadelic signaled Clinton's transformation into Dr. Funkenstein (he also referred to himself as Maggot Overlord); the title of his 1970 album *Free Your Ass and Your Mind Will Follow* shows another side of his funky sense of humor. While Clinton certainly enjoyed being provocative and playing with words, there is in many of his songs a sense that he is laughing to keep from crying. He tucks his darker messages inside humorous packages, set to a good-time groove. When he asks people to "Tear the Roof Off the Sucker," he could be urging them to party hard—or riot.

Without question, there is an escapist aspect to his work: his many aliases, the flamboyant costumes he and his bands wore in performance, the sci-fi world he created (the Mothership Connection), the spectacular stage shows that were a major attraction during the seventies.

In a very real way, this is the opposite of punk, in attitude and music; there is no doubt about the message of a punk song like "**God Save the Queen**," either in words or music, which hammers the listener. By contrast, Clinton seems to invite listeners to become "one nation under a groove"; surrendering to the rhythm offers momentary relief from the pain of daily life as a black person in the United States. Whatever the motivation, there is no question that Clinton's groups could create a groove. We experience this in his 1976 hit **"Tear the Roof Off the Sucker (Give Up the Funk)**," which his band recorded as Parliament.

"Tear the Roof Off the Sucker (Give Up the Funk)"

The song shows both Clinton's debt to James Brown and Sly and the Family Stone and the ways in which his music went beyond theirs. The instrumentation is similar: vocal, horns, and rhythm, but the sound is fuller than either James Brown's or Sly Stone's because there are more instruments and all of them are busy. Clinton's debt to Brown goes beyond these general features; after 1975, his roster included two important James Brown alumni: bassist Bootsy Collins (b. 1951) and saxophonist Maceo Parker (b. 1943). They were key members of his large band, which included as many as twelve musicians.

Like Brown and Stone, Clinton creates the groove over static harmony: this is a one-chord song. The texture is dense. There are riffs and sustained chords from both horns and keyboards, high obbligato lines from a synthesizer, an active but open bass line, lots of percussion, and voices—both the choral effect of the backup singers and Clinton's proto-rap. Clinton gives Collins a chance to stretch out. Collins's lines are active, syncopated, and melodic; they call attention to the increasingly prominent role of the bass in this branch of black music. (Within another generation, **hip-hop** artists would take this direction to its logical end, by creating backgrounds that emphasized bass and percussion sounds to the exclusion of almost everything else.) The rhythm has a sixteen-beat feel over the eight-beat rhythm laid down in the drum part. Clinton's rap-like introduction moves at this faster rhythm; so do the horn riffs, the bass line, and guitar parts. This is the same approach heard in the music of Brown and Stone; it is a thicker sound because there is more going on. It is a darker sound, mainly because of Clinton's voice and the prominence of the bass.

Clinton's various bands—Parliament and Funkadelic were recording for two different labels, and there were other offshoots in addition to these two—ran into trouble in the late seventies, mainly because of bad money management, sloppy business practices, and drug abuse. By 1981, Clinton consolidated the two versions of the band under one name: the P-Funk All Stars. Around the same time, Clinton began to concentrate on producing, not only his own music but also groups like the Red Hot Chili Peppers.

Funk, by Clinton's band and other groups, never crossed over to the pop mainstream in its pure form. "Tear the Roof Off the Sucker" was Parliament's highest-charting song; it made it only to No. 15. However, the music would prove to

hip-hop A term used to describe the African American culture from which rap emerged. Its artistic expressions include not only rap but also break dancing and graffiti.

be enormously influential; most immediately, it helped shape disco and other black styles. And with the advent of digital technology, rappers sampled Clinton's music mercilessly. Among the bands that borrowed heavily from funk was the leading black act of the late seventies: Earth, Wind & Fire.

14–2b Earth, Wind & Fire: A Black Music Synthesis

Like *rock, rhythm and blues* has been an inclusive term. Precisely because it has identified such a wide range of music, it has not been—indeed, cannot be—completely precise. From the time Jerry Wexler coined the term, *rhythm and blues* has also embraced not only rhythmic and bluesy music, but also black pop, which emphasizes melody and harmony over strong rhythm and deep blues feeling.

Two Streams in Rock-Era Black Music

From doo-wop through Motown to the several streams of black romantic music in the early seventies, black pop had grown dramatically—in presence, in variety, and in market share. During the same time-frame, more rhythm-and-blues–oriented black music had also grown, musically and commercially: from the big-beat music of the fifties through soul in the sixties and funk in the seventies.

These two paths were the most significant trends in black music during the third quarter of the twentieth century. And throughout these 25 years, there has been a clear distinction between the two—at least in retrospect. James Brown didn't sing black pop; Diana Ross didn't sing soul. Similarly, Roberta Flack and George Clinton inhabit different musical worlds.

Few artists have successfully fused these two streams. Among the few are two truly great performers: Ray Charles and Aretha Franklin. Both brought soul into pop, and vice versa. In the early seventies, Marvin Gaye and Stevie Wonder, the two newly independent Motown artists, found a fruitful middle ground between funk and romantic pop. Gaye's music in the seventies ranged from the bleakness of **"Inner City Blues"** and **"Trouble Man"** to the rapture of **"Let's Get It On"** and **"Got to Give It Up."** Wonder's music ranged from funky songs like **"Superstition"** to romantic ballads like **"Send One Your Love."** In the latter part of the decade, Earth, Wind & Fire joined them: all three acts moved easily between the two styles and at times blended them within a single song.

Earth, Wind & Fire

Maurice White (1941–2016), the founder and leader of Earth, Wind & Fire, named the group after his astrological sign. He was a Sagittarian: the sign contains three of the four elements—earth, wind, and fire—but not water.

After a successful career as a session drummer at Chess Records and with jazz pianist Ramsey Lewis, White set out in 1969 to create a new kind of group. By 1971, they were Earth, Wind & Fire. The next year, they moved to Columbia (now Sony) Records and continued to climb up the charts. By 1975, they had become one of the elite groups of the decade, both on record and in live performance, and remained a top act through the end of the decade.

Earth, Wind & Fire was a big group. In this respect, they were in step not only with black acts like George Clinton's funk bands, Barry White's Love Unlimited Orchestra, and the various Philadelphia groups. As many as fourteen musicians could be on stage; the nucleus of the band was White, who sang and played a kalimba, an African thumb piano: his brothers Verdine (b. 1951) on bass and Freddie (b. 1955) on drums, plus singer Philip Bailey (b. 1951).

The group was comparable in many respects to George Clinton's groups. Both were big bands; they created great grooves by layering piles of riffs on top of sixteen-beat rhythms. But there was a marked difference in attitude, as we hear in their first No. 1 single, the 1975 hit **"Shining Star."**

The title and refrain line of this song projects the optimistic, hopeful mood that runs through so many of the group's songs: "Shining star for you to see, what your life can truly be." The song itself has a clear division between verse and refrain. The verse sets up a complex funk-style groove over a single chord, much like that heard in "Tear the Roof Off the Sucker (Give Up the Funk)." However, the refrain underpins a more coherent, riff-based melodic line with rapidly changing harmonies. As in gospel and love songs, rich harmony is used to send a message of hope; that also seems to be the case here.

Earth, Wind & Fire's ability to meld funk-like grooves with more melodious material is one key to their crossover success. This versatility is evident in the range of their hit songs, from soulful ballads like **"That's the Way of the World"** to up-tempo songs like **"Serpentine Fire."** Few seventies acts were at home in both funk and black pop styles; fewer still succeeded in blending the two. Earth, Wind & Fire was one of them.

14-3 Disco

Disco is short for *discothèque*. *Discothèque* is a French word meaning record library (by analogy with *bibliothèque*, meaning book library). It came into use during World War II, first as the name of a nightclub—Le Discothèque—then as a code word for underground nightclubs where jazz records were played. Because of the German occupation, these clubs were run like American speakeasies during the Prohibition era.

14-3a The Roots of the Club Scene

Discothèques survived the war, becoming increasingly popular in France. The first of the famous discos was the Whiskey-a-Go-Go, which featured American liquors and American dance music, both live and on record. Others sprang up in the postwar years, eventually becoming a favored destination of jet setters. By 1960, the idea of a discothèque had moved to New York. The Peppermint Lounge, where Chubby Checker and the rich and famous did the twist, opened in 1961.

This rags-to-riches-and-back-to-new-rags story would become the recurrent theme of dance music in the latter part of the century. As dance fads like the twist moved out of the clubs into mainstream society, the original audience sought out new music in different, less exclusive, and less pricey venues.

By the end of the sixties, a new club culture was thriving. It was an egalitarian, non-restrictive environment. The new, danceable black music of the late sixties and early seventies provided the soundtrack: Sly and the Family Stone, Funkadelic, Stevie Wonder, Marvin Gaye, Curtis Mayfield, Barry White, and above all the Philadelphia acts. Clubbers included not only blacks but also Latinos, working-class women, and gays, for whom clubbing had become a welcome chance to come out of the closet and express themselves. Despite the gains of the various "rights" movements in the sixties and seventies, these were still marginalized constituencies.

14-3b The Mainstreaming of Disco

By mid decade, however, disco had become not only a venue but also a music for the venue. Integrated bands like KC and the Sunshine Band, which exploded onto the singles charts in 1975, began making music expressly for discos. **Saturday Night**

Fever was the commercial breakthrough for the music. Almost overnight, what had been a largely underground scene briefly became the thing to do.

In New York, the favored venue was Studio 54, a converted theater on 54th Street in Manhattan. It became so popular that crowds clamoring to get in stretched around the corner. It was the place to see and be seen. Writing about Studio 54 at the end of the seventies, Truman Capote noted, "Disco is the best floor show in town. It's very democratic, boys with boys, girls with girls, girls with boys, blacks and whites, capitalists and Marxists, Chinese and everything else, all in one big mix."

14–3c Disco and Electronics

Meanwhile, the discothèque scene continued to flourish in Europe. The new element in the music there was the innovative use of synthesizers to create dance tracks. Among the most important figures in this new music were Kraftwerk, a two-person German group, and Giorgio Moroder, an Italian-born, Germany-based producer and electronics wizard who provided the musical setting for many of Donna Summer's disco-era hits.

Kraftwerk and Moroder exemplified the increasingly central role of the producer and the technology. Disco became a producer's music, even more than the music of the sixties girl groups. Just as Phil Spector's "wall of sound" was more famous than the singers in front of it, so did the sound of disco belong more to the men in the studio than the vocalists. Here, the wall of sound was laced with electronic as well as acoustic instruments. Singers were relatively unimportant and interchangeable; there were numerous one-hit wonders. We hear a seminal example of electronically driven disco in Donna Summer's **"I Feel Love."**

14–3d Donna Summer: The Queen of Disco

If there is one performer whose career embodies disco—its brief history, its geography, and its message—it is Donna Summer (b. Donna Adrian Gaines, 1948–2012). Summer grew up in the Boston area and moved to Europe while in her teens to pursue a career in musical theater and light opera. While working as a backup vocalist, she met Giorgio Moroder (b. 1940), who would collaborate with her on her major seventies hits. Her first international hit, **"Love to Love You Baby,"** was released in 1975; it was a hit in both the United States and Europe. The most striking feature of the song was Summer's erotic moans. In its graphic evocation of the bedroom experience, it is in spirit an answer song to Barry White's orgasmic episodes.

As the song title suggests, "I Feel Love" (1977), her next big American hit, explores the erotic dimension of love, although not as blatantly as in the earlier song. Here, Summer's deliberately wispy voice floats above Moroder's sea of synthesized sound. Summer's vocal may be the most prominent element of the music, but the background is certainly the more innovative. The innovation begins with Moroder's use of electronic counterparts to a traditional drum set; there is not one conventional instrument on the track. Even more noteworthy is the idiomatic writing for synthesizers. Moroder creates a rich tapestry of sound by layering in a large quantity of repetitive patterns, some constantly in the foreground, others in the background and often intermittent. None of them really corresponds to traditional rock guitar or bass lines: it is not only the sounds that are novel, but also the lines that create the dense texture behind Summer's vocal.

Rhythmically, the song converts the sixteen-beat rhythms of funk and black pop into an accessible dance music by making the beat and the sixteen-beat layer more explicit. From the start we hear the steady thud of a bass drum–like sound on every beat and an equally steady synthesized percussion sound moving four times the speed of the beat in a midrange register. Other parts, most obviously the synthesized ascending pattern that runs through the song, also confirm regular rhythms. Compared to previous examples that used this more active rhythm, "I Feel Love" is far less syncopated and much more obvious in its timekeeping. This is certainly due in large part to its use as dance music.

The busy rhythms of the accompaniment contrast sharply with Summer's leisurely unfolding vocal line and the slow rate of harmonic change. These two seemingly conflicting messages about time in fact invoke two aspects of the disco scene: the activity of the dancers to the throbbing beat and the endlessness of the experience, as one song mixes into the next. (The abrupt ending of the song suggests its use in a disco: the DJ would fade it away before the end as he brought up the next song.)

Summer's career started before disco went mainstream, then crested during the late seventies. Perhaps anticipating the imminent commercial decline of disco, she took her music in new directions in songs like "**Bad Girls**." This helped sustain her popularity through the end of the seventies; her last three albums of the decade each went to No 1.

Among the most loyal members of Summer's fan base were gays. Their connection to disco took on a public face in the music of the Village People.

14–3e The Village People: Disco Out of the Closet

The Village People was the brainchild of Jacques Morali (1946–1991), a French producer living in New York. Morali's various accounts of the formation of the Village People are conflicting, but what is certain is that he recruited men to front his act literally from off the street and from gay clubs.

The public image of the Village People is six guys dressed up as macho stereotypes: the Native American (in full costume, including headdress), the leather man (missing only the Harley), the construction worker, the policeman, the cowboy, and the soldier. These expressions of hyper-maleness were, in effect, gay pinups. Their look was more important than their sound, although after a disastrous appearance on *Soul Train*, Morali fired five of the six men and replaced them with new recruits.

The whole act was an inside joke. Morali and gay audiences laughed while straight America bought their records by the millions and copied the look—mustaches, lumber jackets, and the like. Many listeners were not aware of the gay undertone to the lyrics—or if they were, they didn't care.

The group's song "**Y.M.C.A.**," their biggest hit on the singles charts (No. 2 in 1978), shows the macho men at work. In most cities and towns around the United States, a Y.M.C.A. is a place for families to participate in an array of activities. Some are athletic: basketball, swimming, gymnastics. Others are social and humanitarian, such as meals for senior citizens. In larger cities, a Y.M.C.A. can also accommodate residents. In cities like New York, these became meeting places for gays.

The lyrics of the song have fun with this situation. Seemingly innocuous lines like "They have everything for men to enjoy/You can hang out with all the boys" take on a quite different meaning when understood in the context of the Y as a gay gathering spot.

The music is quintessential disco. Here are some of its characteristic features:

- The tempo: most disco songs had a tempo right around 120 beats a minute—the same speed as a Sousa **march**—so that the DJ could seamlessly **mix** one song into the next.

march Music composed in regularly accented, usually duple meter that is appropriate to accompany marching; a composition in the style of march music.

mix A series of songs or dance tracks seamlessly connected by a disc jockey.

- The four-on-the-floor bass drum: many disco songs featured a rock-solid beat, marked on the bass drum (or its drum-machine counterpart). This song is no exception.
- Active, sixteen-beat-based rhythms: the conga drum most clearly marks the sixteen-beat rhythmic layer. Often the bass line and drums add a "dum-diddy" rhythm. And the drummer plays on the off-beat of every beat. The rhythm in disco songs like "Y.M.C.A." derives its density and activity from both funk and dance-oriented black pop. The biggest difference is that the beat is much more obvious, not only from the beat-keeping bass drum, but also the bass line and other rhythm parts. Compared to funk, there is not much syncopation.
- A rich, almost orchestral, accompaniment, featuring an augmented rhythm section, electronic instruments, and strings: here, there is all of that, with brilliant string lines, horn parts, plus "solos" for the synthesizer in the disco mix version.
- A catchy tune, delivered in chunks and sung without much finesse: this is a simple verse/refrain song, put together in short phrases. The vocalists are enthusiastic but not terribly skilled.
- Repetitive harmony: disco songs often cycle familiar progressions endlessly, the better to suggest the endless disco experience—with continuous music, no clocks on the wall, or any other method of marking time. Here, the harmony is a stretched-out version of that perennial favorite, the "Heart and Soul" progression, in both verse and chorus. When simply recycled, as it is here, it loses its sense of direction to a home chord; it recontextualizes the progression into something quite different in meaning: from clear boundaries to no boundaries.

14-3f Dance Fads and the Influence of Disco

Disco was widely popular during the last part of the seventies. During that three-year window, it spread from urban dance clubs to the suburbs, and its audience grew considerably. While it had clear and strong gay associations, as "Y.M.C.A." makes clear, it was more than music for gays and blacks. In this respect, *Saturday Night Fever* was a slice of life: there were many working-class urban youth who used disco dancing as an outlet.

Disco was more than the music, or even the culture that had produced it. For many, it became a lifestyle. It was hedonistic: dancing was simply a prelude to more intimate forms of contact. It was exhibitionistic: fake Afro wigs; skin-tight, revealing clothes; flamboyant accessories; platform shoes; everything glittering. It was drug-ridden: with disco, cocaine became a mainstream drug; the logo for Studio 54 showed the man on the moon seemingly ingesting cocaine from a silver spoon.

14-3g Reactions Against Disco

All this, plus the inevitable stream of mindless disco songs (the ratio of wheat to chaff in any genre is low; disco was no exception) gave disco's detractors plenty of ammunition. They trashed the music and the culture. Ostensibly, it was simply a reaction against disco's many excesses, but there was also a strong homophobic undercurrent. When disco disappeared from the charts and the radio, there was an "I told you so" response from those who hated it. But in retrospect, it would have been surprising if it had lasted much longer, given the history of earlier dance fads.

14-3h Disco and Twentieth-Century Dance Fads

The major dance fads in the twentieth century have had short lifespans: the Charleston and black bottom in the early twenties; jitterbugging and lindy hopping around 1940; the twist and other rock-and-roll dances around 1960. The Charleston and the twist were dance fads that caught on somewhat after the introduction of new rhythms: the two-beat fox-trot in the 1910s and early 1920s, and the eight-beat rhythm of rock and roll in the fifties. Disco, like the jitterbug, was a dance fad that came with the division of popular music into two related rhythmic streams. In the thirties, it was sweet (two-beat) and swing (four-beat). In the seventies, it was rock (eight-beat) and disco (sixteen-beat).

Both swing and disco were brief windows when the more active rhythms of black and black-inspired music became a truly popular music. In both cases, much of the music was rhythmically more obvious than the music that had spawned it. Many of the hits of the swing era, especially by the white bands, laid down the beat but lacked the rhythmic play of music by Basie, Ellington, or Goodman. Similarly, disco was more straightforward rhythmically than funk or black pop, as we have discussed. This made it accessible to a greater number of dancers, but sacrificed musical interest in the process.

So it shouldn't be surprising that disco faded away so quickly. It was following much the same path as the other dance fads that signaled the arrival of a new beat. And it should not be surprising that the new beat took root following disco's demise.

Disco was an influential music, far more so than its brief lifespan would suggest. It brought a new, more active rhythm and electronic sounds into the mainstream, and reconfigured the relationship between creator, performer, and musical result. It would help shape the sound of a broad range of music, including techno, rap, pop, R&B, and some new directions in rock. It's a substantial legacy for a music scorned by those who preserved the music that had been considered revolutionary only a decade before.

14-4 Moving Beyond Rock

It's a long way geographically and culturally from the ghettos of Kingston, Jamaica, to the glitz of Studio 54 in New York. Jimmy Cliff's pointed commentary in "The Harder They Come" sends a strikingly different message from the Village People's puckish humor in "Y.M.C.A." Reggae, funk, and disco inhabited largely independent worlds during the seventies, although some funk bands tried to hop on the disco bandwagon in an attempt to cross over to the pop charts. And only disco had a significant commercial presence, however brief.

Nevertheless, they are linked not only temporally, but also musically and socially, despite their differences in message, milieu, and musical substance. Each was a minority music: reggae took shape outside the US–UK axis; funk was less popular than other forms of black music, even within the black community; disco's original fan base included multiple minorities: race, ethnicity, and sexual preference. And each represented a significant departure from mainstream rock—in subject, style, and sound.

Their musical common ground is extensive. Most fundamentally, it includes an emphasis on large bands (or their electronic counterparts); more active and often more syncopated rhythms, typically based on a sixteen-beat rhythmic foundation; dense, multilayered textures; and a predilection for electronic sounds. Collectively, these style features laid the foundation for the most far-reaching developments in post-1980 rock-era music. We have already noted rap's debt to these styles. However, other distinctive trends—including the new pop of the eighties and beyond, the numerous forms of dance music, and world music fusions—also connect directly to this music. In particular, disco was the gateway for the wholesale infusion of electronica. And it created a new kind of underground dance club culture, which would continue through the eighties and flower in the nineties. Funk, especially that of George Clinton, became a sampling ground for rap and a primary source for an important direction in alternative rock. Reggae was arguably the first world music with a significant commercial presence: similar rock/R&B/ regional fusions emerged elsewhere in the Caribbean (for example, soca, zouk) and in Africa (such as new forms of juju, **Afropop**, mbalax).

In the remaining chapters, we will hear rock-era music evolve far away from the core rock discussed in earlier chapters. These three styles—reggae, funk, and disco—and the cultures that they represented, contributed more to this evolutionary momentum than any other music of the seventies.

Afropop A fusion of West African and pop music.

CHAPTER 15

PUNK AND ITS AFTERMATH

Learning Objectives:

1) Exemplify the origin of the **punk** genre.

2) List the key components of "pure" punk.

3) Describe the Ramones' contributions to the punk genre.

4) Compare and contrast **new wave** to punk.

5) Comment on the unique characteristics of Devo.

6) Discuss the lasting effect of punk on future musical styles.

Chapter Introduction

CBGB is a small club located in the Bowery section of New York City. Originally, it was the bar in the Palace Hotel. By 1973, the year that CBGB opened, the hotel had gone from palatial to poverty-stricken: it was a cheap rooming house for the alcoholics and druggies that inhabited the neighborhood.

The full name of the club is CBGB & OMFUG: Country, Blue Grass, and Blues, and Other Music for Uplifting Gormandizers. Owner Hilly Kristal's original plan was to book these kinds of acts into his new club. However, an encounter with Richard Hell, Richard Lloyd, and Tom Verlaine of Television—Kristal was repairing the awning over the club entrance when the three band members walked by and struck up a conversation with him—led Kristal to hire the band for a gig at Kristal's club, followed by another with another newly formed band: the Ramones. Neither date attracted much of a crowd.

Nevertheless, Kristal persevered and promoted. After some success with Patti Smith early in 1975, he decided to present "A Festival of the Top 40 New York Rock Bands." He scheduled it in the summer to coincide with the Newport Jazz Festival, a big-time event. It was a gamble—he spent a lot of money on advertising—that paid off. Critics came to hear the bands, and the audience for punk exploded almost overnight.

Among Kristal's customers was Malcolm McLaren, who came to New York in 1974 to attend a boutique fair. Three years earlier, McLaren had opened a clothing boutique in London with Vivienne Westwood called Let It Rock, which featured vintage and retro styles; he and Westwood also created theater costumes. However, McLaren saw himself as a political provocateur. He wanted to be able to thumb his nose at the establishment and make money on it at the same time. McLaren viewed rock music as a vehicle for his politics; bands would make a statement with images as well as sound.

While in New York, McLaren persuaded the New York Dolls, who had just been dropped by Mercury Records, to let him manage them and design their outfits.

He costumed them in red leather and had them perform in front of a hammer and sickle. For the Dolls, the shock strategy backfired: the blatant nod to the Soviet Union apparently turned off other labels, and the band broke up the following year. For McLaren, it was simply the prelude to an even bolder statement. After hearing early punk bands like the Ramones and Neon Boys (who would become Television) and seeing Richard Hell's torn clothing and studded collars, McLaren returned to England, changed the name of his boutique to SEX, and started carrying fetish clothing and original punk-inspired items. This in turn attracted a clientele from which McLaren would eventually assemble the Sex Pistols.

That a boutique storeowner and fashion designer would form and manage the United kingdom's seminal punk band says a lot about the movement. At least in McLaren's realization of it with the Sex Pistols, punk was part of a larger package. It was only one component of a presence designed to stand out, outrage, and affront those on the outside. Hand in hand with the noise of punk went the hostile attitude and—even more obvious from a distance—the look: spiked hair in a rainbow of colors, tattoos and body piercings, torn clothes ornamented or even held together with safety pins.

Punk was an extreme form of a wave of new music that emerged in the mid-seventies, first in New York, then in other parts of the United States and in England. Rather than stadiums with thousands listening and watching, it flourished in small clubs like CBGB, with audiences in the hundreds. In the sense that it sought to recapture the revolutionary fervor and the relative simplicity of early rock, it was a reactionary movement—a counterrevolution against what its adherents saw as the growing commercialism of mainstream rock. However, in its reconception of these values, it established an important and influential new direction in rock, which continues to the present.

15-1 The Punk Movement

The most powerful and enduring image in rock has been the rebellious outsider as hero. From Elvis, Little Richard, and Jerry Lee Lewis to the latest flavor of indie band, rock has glorified those who outraged a complacent, corporate-minded establishment while delivering their message loudly, if not always clearly. In rock's early years, it was rock on the outside versus the pop establishment. However, when rock became the dominant commercial music, the rebellion happened on the inside. As before, it was David and Goliath. With punk, however, Goliath was the rock establishment. The power of this image can be gauged by the ratio of commercial success to critical attention. Few punk or new wave bands enjoyed much commercial success; nevertheless, far more has been written about the early years of punk than about more mainstream rock in the seventies.

15-1a The Roots of Punk

Punk took shape in New York. Much like the folksingers of the sixties, bands performed in small clubs located in Greenwich Village and Soho. CBGB, the most famous of these clubs, launched the careers of a host of punk and new wave bands. Among the CBGB graduates were Patti Smith, Richard Hell (in the Neon Boys, then Television, and finally as Richard Hell and the Voidoids), the Ramones, and the Talking Heads. Ohio was another spawning ground: Pere Ubu, from Cleveland, and Devo, from Dayton, both had careers underway by 1975.

Among the major influences on punk in New York were the Velvet Underground and the New York Dolls. The Velvet Underground embraced the

New York City subculture sensibility and nurtured it in their music. Their songs (for example, "Heroin") were dark, which foreshadowed punk's "no future" mentality, and the sound of their music was often abrasive and minimalist. They presented an anti-artistic approach to art, which was a rejection of the artistic aspirations of the Beatles and other like-minded bands. In addition, their impresario was an artist, Andy Warhol, who packaged them as part of a multimedia experience (the famous Exploding Plastic Inevitable); this presaged McLaren's vision of punk as a fusion of image and sound in the service of outrage.

The New York Dolls, led by David Johansen, were America's answer to David Bowie, Marc Bolan, and the rest of the British glam bands. They lacked Bowie's musical craft and vision; their musical heroes were not only the Velvet Underground but also MC5 and Iggy Pop and the Stooges. In effect, they dressed up the latter groups' proto-punk and made it even more outrageous, wearing makeup and cross-dressing outlandishly—they out-Bowied Bowie in this respect—and taking bold risks in performance. Brinksmanship came easily to them, as they were, in the words of one critic, "semi-professional" at best.

Patti Smith, a rock critic turned poet-performer, was the first major figure in the punk movement to emerge from the New York club subculture. Smith was its poet laureate, a performer for whom words were primary. There is nothing groundbreaking in the sound of her music. Indeed, she wanted to recapture rock's brief glory period in the mid-sixties, to have her music make a statement, not a spectacle. Her work had much of the purity and power of punk: purity in the sense that it returned rock to its garage-band spirit, and power in the outrage. But it was not outrageous, at least not by the Sex Pistols' standards. Smith was also important because she was a woman in charge: she played a seminal role in the creation of this new/old style. Partly because of her presence, punk and new wave music were much more receptive to strong women than conventional rock.

In the United Kingdom, punk was a music waiting to happen. All the components were in place, except the sound. Disaffected working-class youth wanted an outlet for their frustration: pierced body parts, Technicolor hair, and torn clothes made a statement, but they weren't loud enough, and they didn't articulate the message. Following McLaren's return to London and the Ramones' 1976 tour, punk took off in England as well as in the United States, most notably in the music of the Sex Pistols. Elvis Costello quickly became the bard of the new wave. The Clash, the Pretenders (fronted by Akron, Ohio native Chrissie Hynde), and the Buzzcocks were among other leading UK bands in the late seventies.

The attitudes expressed in the punk movement reflected deeply rooted contradictions in everyday life during the seventies. The "we" mindset of the sixties—the sense of collective energy directed toward a common goal— gave way to a "me" mindset, where everyone looked out for themselves. The various rights movements and the move toward a more democratic society eroded class distinctions at a rapid rate. Still, there was a strong conservative backlash in both Britain and the United States. At the same time, a prolonged recession, driven in part by the absence of fuel due to the Arab oil embargo, gave working- and middle-class people little opportunity to take advantage of their new social mobility. And sky-high interest rates and inflation created the fear that today's savings would be worth far less in the future. "No Future," the nihilistic battle cry of the Sex Pistols, was in part a product of this bleak economic outlook.

15–1b The Power of Punk

Although the look screams outrage and the words scream rebellion, the power of punk is in the music; it is the sounds and rhythms of punk that most strongly convey its energy and attitude. Especially when experienced in its native environment, a small club overflowing with people, the music overwhelms, injecting the crowd with massive shots of energy.

Punk is to rock and roll what heroin is to opium: it gains its potency by distilling its most potent elements and presenting them in concentrated form. "Pure" punk songs are short: they say what they have to say quickly and move on. In their mid-seventies heyday, the Ramones would play thirty-minute sets, in which all of the songs lasted about two minutes. Within such brief timespans, punk offers songs that intensify the dangerous aspects of rock and roll: the loudness, the sounds, the rhythms.

Punk is loud. Typically, subtlety is not part of the equation; neither is contrast in volume. It's full-bore volume from beginning to end. Punk is noise: guitarists and bassists routinely use heavy distortion. Punk singing is the triumph of chutzpah over expertise. Indeed, the lack of vocal skill or sophistication was a virtual requirement; one couldn't credibly croon a punk song. Part of the message was that anyone could sing a punk song, if they had the nerve. Punk is fast: tempos typically exceed the pace of normally energetic movement—walking, marching, disco dancing. However, the most compelling feature of punk is its approach to rock rhythm.

15–1c Saturated Rock Rhythm

A brief recap of twenty years of rock rhythm: Recall that what distinguished rock and roll from rhythm and blues was the eight-beat rhythm. We heard it in the guitar lines of Chuck Berry and the piano playing of Little Richard and gradually in other rhythm instruments, as musicians caught on to this new rhythmic conception. Move ahead to the late sixties and early seventies: as rock musicians became comfortable with rock rhythm, the basic rock beat became a springboard for rhythmic play, as we heard in the music of the Who, Led Zeppelin, and others.

Punk restored the essence of rock rhythm. Punk bands extracted the eight-beat rock rhythmic layer, sped it up, then intensified it by isolating its defining feature, making it the most prominent feature of the rhythm and saturating the rhythmic texture with it. In punk, the "default" way of playing the rock rhythmic layer was simply to repeat a note, a chord, or a drum stroke over and over at rock-beat speed. Musicians could graft riffs onto this rhythm to create variety and interest, but this was an overlay; typically, the eight-beat rhythm continues through the notes of the riffs. By contrast, Chuck Berry's rhythm guitar patterns typically oscillate every beat between two chords. This oscillation creates slower rhythms that attenuate the impact of the faster rhythm. Punk strips away these slower rhythms, presenting rock rhythm in a purer form.

Punk made this "purer" form of rock rhythm stand out through a two-part strategy. First, the entire rhythm section typically reinforced it: guitar(s), bass, and drums all hammer it out. Indeed, depending on the speed of the song and the skill of the drummer, the reinforcement could be heard on the bass drum as well as the drums or cymbals. Second, it favored explicit timekeeping over syncopation and other forms of rhythmic play. This reverses the prevailing direction of the evolution of rock rhythm, which was toward greater rhythmic complexity—more syncopation, more activity, more implicit timekeeping—as we heard in **Chapter 9**. We sample the power of punk in songs by the Ramones and the Sex Pistols.

15–1d The Ramones

The Ramones—vocalist Joey Ramone (Jeffrey Hyman, 1951–2001); guitarist Johnny Ramone (John Cummings, 1948–2004); bassist Dee Dee Ramone (Doug Colvin, 1951–2002); and original drummer Tommy Ramone (Tommy Erdelyi, 1949–2014)—were the poster boys of punk. With their trademark look—torn jeans, T-shirts, leather jackets, and long dark hair—and electrifying half-hour sets that consisted of a nonstop string of high-voltage songs, they put punk on the map, first in New York, then in the rest of the United States and in England, where they inspired groups such as the Sex Pistols and the Clash.

The Ramones were brothers only on the bandstand. All had been students at Forest Hills High School in Queens, New York, but were not related. They formed the Ramones in 1974 and quickly reclaimed the spirit of early rock and reworked it into punk. They began with the essence of the garage band: a singer backed by guitar, bass, and drums playing three-chord songs built from simple riffs. However, they jacked up the tempo to breakneck speed: a typical Ramones song has a tempo of over 170 beats per minute, well above the 120 to 126 beats per minute of a disco song. Such fast tempos tax any drummer's physical ability, and certainly approached the limit of Tommy Ramone's skill and endurance. A set of ten or twelve songs at maximum tempo and volume was exhilarating for band and audience.

Partly because of the extremely fast tempo, Ramones' songs are not rhythmically subtle. The three essential layers of rock rhythm—the beat, the backbeat, and the rock-rhythm layer—are in the forefront during the instrumental sections and clearly audible underneath the vocals. There is little syncopation, and they are basic. Compared to pre-punk rock, a set of Ramones' music amounts to mainlining rock rhythm.

"**Blitzkrieg Bop**" was the Ramones' first single: it was released in November 1975 in the United States and in July 1976 in England. The song, which also appeared on the band's first album, introduced the sound for which the Ramones would become famous and which would outline the key elements of pure punk.

> The title of the song is worth a comment: "Blitzkrieg" ("lightning war") was a term that the German military used during World War II to identify a quick strike; it has a clear association with Nazis. Although there are no obvious neo-Nazi overtones in "Blitzkrieg Bop," Nazi images were a big part of the punk scene in the United Kingdom. Among the provocative fashions sold at McLaren's shop was a short leather skirt with a swastika in studs on the back panel, and Siouxsie (of the Banshees) regularly sported an armband with a swastika.

The song begins by repeating a three-chord pattern: I, IV, and V, with a syncopation on the V chord. We hear distorted guitar, bass, and drums, all at full volume, and all hammering out the rock beat. The first vocal chorus is a primer on the punk take on rock rhythm. Underneath the famous "Hey ho/let's go" we hear Tommy Ramone beating out a straight rock rhythm and the backbeat. Soon, Dee Dee joins in, playing the same note over and over at rock-beat speed. Johnny joins in next, playing a repeated chord, also at rock-beat speed. In these ten seconds, we can hear the role of each rhythm-section instrument in creating the distilled essence of rock rhythm: everyone pumps out the rock rhythmic layer—on a drum, on a single note, on a single chord. The only other rhythmic feature is the backbeat, the other main component of rock rhythm. No other rhythms are implied. This is as pure, and as energetic, as rock rhythm gets.

In several other respects, the song recalls early rock. The melody consists of simple riffs that lead to the short hook that is the title riff. It uses the AABA form typical not only of pre-rock pop but also those many rock-and-roll songs that emulated the older style. The lyric seems teen-themed ("climbing in the back seat/... steam heat"), but with an edge ("shoot 'em in the back now"); but the overall effect is disconnection—between the title phrase, the events described in the lyric, and the exhortation ("Hey ho/let's go"). This has the effect of focusing attention on the music: the real message of the song is its unbridled energy.

The Ramones were one of the most prolific punk bands, playing over 2,000 performances during their twenty-plus years and recording fourteen studio albums. They were also punk's premier ambassadors, fueling the punk revolution in Britain with their appearance there in 1976. Among the bands that heard them perform were the Sex Pistols.

15-1e The Sex Pistols

We think of rebels as independent figures standing apart from the crowd. So there is an uncomfortable irony to the fact that the most rebellious act in the history of rock music was part of perhaps the most complex and manipulative relationship between a major rock act and its management. Malcolm McLaren, a radical and an entrepreneur, made the Sex Pistols: vocalist Johnny Rotten (John Lydon, b. 1956), guitarist Steve Jones (b. 1955), bassists Glen Matlock (b. 1956) and Sid Vicious (John Ritchie, 1957–1979), and drummer Paul Cook (b. 1956); he also made them an instrument that enabled him to realize his own provocative ends.

McLaren found the Sex Pistols in his shop. Glen Matlock, the original bassist with the group, worked for McLaren. When he let McLaren know that he and two of his friends, guitarist Steve Jones and drummer Paul Cook, were putting together a band, McLaren found them rehearsal space, took over their management, and recruited a lead singer for them. John Lydon, who became Johnny Rotten (allegedly because of his less-than-meticulous personal hygiene), had been hanging around SEX for a while. McLaren had gotten to know him and felt that he had the capacity for outrage that he'd been looking for. (Another SEX shop hanger-on, Sid Vicious [John Ritchie], would eventually replace Matlock.)

In fact, none of the four had much musical skill at the time they formed the band. Jones was more adept at thievery than guitar playing: he stole the group's first sound system. McLaren booked the group into small clubs, where they acquired more of a reputation for outrageous conduct than for musicianship. Word spread about the group through word of mouth, newspaper reviews, and subculture fanzines. (*Punk*, a fanzine started by two high school friends from suburban Connecticut, gave the new movement its name.)

The Sex Pistols found their musical direction after hearing the Ramones and learning the basics of their instruments. What they had from the beginning, however, was the ability to shock, provoke, confront, and incite to riot. When they added the musical energy of the Ramones to this stew, they were ready to overthrow the ruling class, a stance that is evident in two of their best-known songs, "**Anarchy in the UK**" and "**God Save the Queen**." Johnny Rotten opens "Anarchy in the UK" with "I am an Anti-Christ; I am an anarchist" and ends with a drawn out "Destroy." The opening line lances both church and state; the final word makes clear their agenda. Rotten, a skinny kid who knew no bounds, sings/screams/snarls the lyrics. In "God Save the Queen," we can imagine the sneer on Rotten's face as he delivers the opening line, "God Save the Queen, the fascist regime."

All of this was music to McLaren's ears. He hated the liberal attitudes of the sixties and was canny enough to exploit their openness, so that he could take aim at both the ruling class and the "peace and love" generation. In his mind, punk was nihilistic: "no future" was the motto. For McLaren, the Sex Pistols were another expression of his business philosophy. The bondage gear sold in McLaren's boutique promoted sex as pain, not pleasure. Although Rotten railed against the "fascist regime," punk's use of the swastika image evoked the ultimate fascist regime. And the Sex Pistols' sets often ended in some kind of fracas: their attitude was more than words and symbols.

The music behind the words was, if anything, even more provocative. It was not just that it was loud, particularly when heard in the small venues where the punk bands played, or simple—power chords up and down the fretboard. It was the beat. Punk fulfilled the confrontational promise of the very first rock-and-roll records. Rock-and-roll's signature was a repetitive eight-beat rhythm, whether pumped out by Chuck Berry or hammered out by Little Richard and Jerry Lee Lewis. It was the subversive element that got the revolutionary message across loud and clear, even when the lyrics didn't (after all, what is "Tutti Frutti" about?).

In "God Save the Queen," guitar and bass move in tandem to hammer out a relentless rock rhythm almost all the way through; only the periodic guitar riffs that answer Rotten's vocals give it a distinctive shape. The drummer reinforces this rock rhythm by pounding it out on the bass drum and either a tom-tom or hi-hat. Like the Ramones, the band distilled and intensified rock and roll's revolutionary rhythmic essence. There is no way that a rock beat could be more pervasive or powerful.

As expressed in the Sex Pistols' music, the beat is the primary source of punk's power, but its impact ultimately grows out of its remarkable stylistic coherence. Every aspect of the song—the lyrics, Rotten's vocal style, the absence of melody, simple power chords, the heavily distorted sounds, and the relentless, fast-paced beat—conveys the same basic message: they are mutually reinforcing.

The message of the Sex Pistols resonated throughout the United Kingdom. Many working- and middle-class youths were tired of the rigid class system that they inherited and foresaw a bleak future. The Sex Pistols' songs encapsulated the frustration and rage they felt.

The group achieved their main ambition—to be rock-and-roll stars. So did McLaren. Through the band, he made a statement, although the fact that he made a statement seemed to be far more important than its message. McLaren had his cake and ate it, too: he made a lot of money off the Sex Pistols, some of which he had to turn over to the band after they sued him. His dishonest management certainly suggests that punk, for him, was more a business proposition than a matter of political principle.

Despite their meteoric rise and fall (Lydon announced the breakup of the group in January 1978), the Sex Pistols were enormously influential: no group in the history of rock had more impact with such a brief career. They embodied the essence of punk in every respect. No one projected its sense of outrage and its outrageousness more baldly. The Ramones were comparably influential, not only because their fast and loud sound inspired the Sex Pistols and countless other groups, but also because their facelessness—assumed names and punk "uniform" (torn jeans, T-shirts)—and cryptic lyrics projected a different form of nihilism: loss of identity and meaning.

15-2 New Wave

The punk of the Ramones and the Sex Pistols was an extreme form of a new wave of music that began to emerge around the middle of the seventies, mainly in New York and London. Other bands, most notably, the Talking Heads and Devo in the

United States and Elvis Costello and the Attractions and the Clash in England found a similar audience.

These diverse acts shared considerable common ground. Most obvious, perhaps, were the venues and the audiences who filled them. Both bands and audience assumed an anti-mainstream position: with few exceptions, their music, whatever form it took, was a reaction against prevailing tastes. The reaction could be rage, weirdness, cleverness, humor, and more; but it was typically a reaction. Musically, their shared values included such features as the directness of the rhythm and instrumentation that was typically limited to the nuclear rock band: vocalist, guitar, bass, and drums. The varied musical products reflected their equally varied responses to mainstream rock. Most of it was called either punk or new wave, often interchangeably.

In retrospect, one of the significant distinctions between punk, or at least the "pure" punk of the Ramones and Sex Pistols, and the new wave styles that emerged at the same time is the aim of the music: punk aims for the gut; new wave aims for the brain or perhaps the funny bone. The Sex Pistols' biggest songs express rage. The lyrics of Ramones' songs seem calculated to deflect attention away from the words to the high-energy sounds; we hear them, but we don't always process them as a coherent statement. By contrast, the songs of new wave acts such as the Talking Heads and Elvis Costello demand attention to the words, and the musical setting puts the lyrics in the forefront.

To support clear delivery of the lyrics, bands favored a stripped-down, streamlined sound. Many groups were garage-band graduates. They kept their basic three- or four-piece instrumentation: guitar(s), bass, and drums, with the occasional keyboard. (Elvis Costello seemed fond of cheesy-sounding synthesizers.) The rhythmic texture was relatively clean, with little syncopation or rhythmic interplay. This energized the songs without overpowering or deflecting attention from the vocals. Instrumental solos were at a minimum; the primary role of the music was to enhance the words.

Within these relatively general boundaries, there was considerable variation in content and result, which we sample following in the music of the Talking Heads and Elvis Costello and the Attractions.

15-2a The Talking Heads

Like so many British rock musicians, the Talking Heads started out in art school: lead singer David Byrne (b. 1952) and drummer Chris Frantz (b. 1951) attended the Rhode Island School of Design together before moving to New York. They formed the group in 1975, with Tina Weymouth (b. 1950), Frantz's then-girlfriend (and later wife), playing bass, and added guitarist/keyboardist Jerry Harrison (b. 1949) two years later.

Although they operated in the same CBGB milieu as the Ramones and other similar punk bands, the Talking Heads came from an opposite place conceptually. Where the Ramones' sound remained remarkably consistent from song to song, the Talking Heads' music, beginning with their debut album *Talking Heads '77* and continuing throughout their sixteen-year career together, offers considerable variety. In their earlier albums, this is especially remarkable, given their limited instrumental resources and Byrne's vocal limitations.

Their music reflects both their seemingly insatiable curiosity regarding the world of music and their art-school training. Byrne would become one of the leaders of the world music movement in the eighties; *Naked*, their last studio album, released in 1988, featured African musicians. Many of their early songs draw on the rock and rhythm and blues with which they were surrounded in their formative years. However, they process it in their songs much as cubist painters like Picasso and Braque processed the scenes and objects that they portrayed in their paintings. These once-familiar sounds often occur as distorted or fragmented in the Talking Heads' music, to the extent that the connection with an earlier style is all but broken. This manipulation of familiar sounds provided an instrumental setting that enhanced the impact of Byrne's quirky lyrics and quavery voice, which was ideally suited to convey a person who has drunk way too much coffee or is simply over the edge.

"Psycho Killer" (1977), a surprise hit from their first album, evidences salient features of their sound: lyrics and Byrne's singing in the forefront, varied accompaniment, with several subtle features in support. Rhythm and texture are simple and clean: the bass line marks the beat with a repeated note, while guitar and keyboard move at rock-beat speed. The jangly guitar—first in the arpeggiated accompaniment of the verse, then in the chords under the chorus—echoes Byrne's words and sound. This spare backdrop—perhaps a musical counterpart to the white cell of the psycho ward—is an ideal foil for Byrne's vocal. The lyric is inflammatory. Byrne announces quite clearly that he's crazy ("a real live wire"), and his neutral delivery makes his portrayal especially effective: as if he's a time bomb waiting to explode. In contrast to the punk songs heard previously, which go full bore from beginning to end, there are numerous changes in accompaniment, from the edgy beginning to the brutal beat-by-beat chords in the interlude where Byrne shifts to French.

As "Psycho Killer" demonstrates, the sound of the Talking Heads was fueled more by imagination than craft. There is nothing particularly challenging in any of the instrumental parts, nor is Byrne a vocalist with a wide expressive range. There is none of the virtuosity heard in such diverse acts as Steely Dan, Yes, or Led Zeppelin, nor is there the rhythmic complexity heard in hard rock or funk, or the lavish instrumentation of much black pop or disco. Yet, the Talking Heads created one of the most innovative sound worlds of the seventies.

15–2b Elvis Costello

In the United Kingdom, the most distinctive new voice of the new wave belonged to Elvis Costello (born Declan McManus, 1954). Costello began with the great singer-songwriter's storytelling gift and a fertile musical imagination. He nurtured it in an early-seventies apprenticeship with pub rock bands, which fueled his ambition to obtain a recording contract. Punk and reggae gave his music an edge, evident in some of the tracks from his first album, *My Aim Is True*. Flush from the success of this album, he recruited the Attractions, who would be his collaborators for the better part of a decade. The group included keyboardist Steve Nieve (born Steve Nason, 1960), bassist Bruce Thomas (b. 1948), and drummer Pete Thomas (b. 1954) (the two are not related). The group helped him realize songs that grew out of what Costello acknowledged in an interview as his main motivations: revenge and guilt.

The anger in his music was more complex than that of the Sex Pistols, whose music inspired him. Instead of a frontal assault, Costello would often seduce his listeners, in words and music, then gradually reveal the underlying message of the song. We hear this in one of his first hits.

"Radio, Radio" was originally released as a single in 1977 and later included on Costello's second album, *This Year's Model*, which was released in 1979. The storyline is easy to follow, and the music, from the opening organ hook on, is as accessible as a mainstream rock song. Costello's genius becomes apparent as the song unfolds. What seems like a simple paean to radio in the verse develops Orwellian overtones (1984 was less than a decade away!) by the chorus. And the complexity of his ideas is matched by the complexity of the form of the song. Although it is a verse/chorus song, with sections clearly marked off by restatements of the opening organ hook, the chorus goes through a tunnel full of twists and turns before returning to the verse.

The setting is likewise a complex realization of the basic punk/pop sound. Costello's texture is almost orchestral. The opening organ hook is thickly textured, the punk band equivalent of a full orchestra. As Costello enters with the verse, the texture thins drastically with only the three rhythm instruments playing a bottom-heavy version of rock rhythm. The organ returns in the chorus, along with some special effects, and there is a nice stop-time section at the end. The basic texture has a clear affinity with punk, but the orchestral-like variation in rhythm and texture has much more in common with the Talking Heads than it does with the Ramones or the Sex Pistols.

Both Costello and the Attractions and the Talking Heads explored dark and difficult themes (a demented killer; oppressive control through the media). They did so through songs that put the words in the forefront and that backed them up with musical settings that helped evoke the ominous lyrics, despite relatively modest instrumental resources. Like punk, new wave often projected rage or frustration, but it did so with more finesse: a sharp stick instead of a bludgeon.

15-3 Punk: Devolution and Evolution

The next two examples offer additional perspectives on the punk/new wave movement of the late seventies. In the music of Devo, we hear the humorous side of the new wave movement; in the music of the Clash, we hear the rapid evolution of punk beyond the raw, manic energy of the Ramones and the Sex Pistols.

15-3a New Wave Humor

If there are emotions that seem to dominate punk and new wave music, they are rage and frustration. They spill out from the words and even more from the music. It is explicit in the music of the Sex Pistols and present, albeit more obliquely, in the music of the Ramones, the Talking Heads, and Elvis Costello and the Attractions. However, a small minority of new wave bands, some emerging from such unlikely locales as Athens, Georgia, and Akron, Ohio, rechanneled the energy and streamlined simplicity of punk and new wave into music that revisited humor in rock. The B-52s, the first of several noteworthy bands to get started in Athens, brought kitsch into rock—in image (their name came from the beehive hairdos popular in the years around 1960), words, and sound. Devo, like Pere Ubu, was formed in Ohio; the three founding band members were students at Kent State University.

Devo

The founding members of Devo were bassist Gerald Casale (b. 1948), lead singer and keyboardist Mark Mothersbaugh (b. 1950), and guitarist Bob Lewis (b. 1947). The band quickly evolved into a two-family affair: Casale's brother Bob joined the band shortly after its formation as a rhythm guitarist, as did Mothersbaugh's brothers Bob and Jim: Bob (Bob II) replaced Lewis on lead guitar, while Jim replaced original drummer Rod Reisman. Alan Myers would soon replace Jim Mothersbaugh.

Devo the band was the vehicle created mainly by Mark Mothersbaugh and Jerry Casale to convey their response to the senseless shootings at Kent State in 1970. After the incident, the two friends began formulating a Dada-esque theory of devolution, which they promulgated in an obscure journal. They maintained that at the end of the twentieth century, man was devolving, not evolving. They expressed this viewpoint not only in their music but also in a short film entitled *The Truth About De-Evolution*, which caught the attention of David Bowie and Iggy Pop when presented at the 1976 Ann Arbor Film Festival. This led to a recording contract with Warner Bros. and an association with Brian Eno, who produced their debut album: *Q: Are We Not Men? A: We Are Devo!* (1977). By this time, their anger at the absurdity of modern life had devolved into weirdness, as is evident in their first hit, "**Jocko Homo**," a single taken from the album.

The weirdness is apparent from the start: The sound of the opening instrumental riff is a blend of distorted guitar and other rock band instruments and synthesizer. The mix gives the distortion an eerie quality that evokes the soundtracks to underfunded science fiction films. (Synthesizers, or synths, always a key element in Devo's sound, would become the dominant instrumental resource in the eighties.) The rhythm is even more unusual than the sound: the riff lasts seven equally spaced notes per measure, rather than the eight used in conventional rock rhythm. This necessarily creates an asymmetrical pattern (4 + 3 notes), which puts the song off-balance from the start. The asymmetry is maintained through much of the song; a familiar rock rhythm occurs only in the interlude. This almost minimalist setting supports the almost mechanical delivery of the lyric, which the vocal distortion simply underscores in the answering phrase of the refrain: ("Are we not men?) We are DEVO." The absurdist element continues in the interlude, which interrupts their succinct account of human evolution and social commentary with the riddle "What's round at the ends and high in the middle? (O-hi-o)."

Devo would carve out a niche for themselves, both on disc and on video, that sustained their career into the eighties. Their videos, which typically featured them in "uniforms" of various kinds (the geek analogs to the Ramones' look) and wearing unusual headgear, like flowerpots, enjoyed a brief vogue in the early years of MTV. Their commitment to weirdness may have cost them popular success but preserved their special place in the history of punk.

The Clash

Like the Rolling Stones, the Clash grew out of a chance encounter. However, the meeting between guitarists Mick Jones and Joe Strummer took place not in a train station over an armful of blues records, but while waiting in line for an unemployment check. As in the United States, rampant inflation in the United Kingdom had had a devastating effect on the economy. An influx of people from the former British colonies (Jamaicans, East Indians, Nigerians, and others) strained social services and heightened racial tension. At the same time, the class distinctions that had been part of British life for centuries were under assault—as was made manifest in "God Save the Queen." All of this fueled the punk movement in the United Kingdom.

The Clash came together in 1976, when Strummer (1952–2002) and Jones (b. 1955) teamed up with bassist Paul Simonon (b. 1955) and drummer Terry Chimes (b. 1955). Topper Headon (b. 1955) soon replaced Chimes. Simonon gave the group its name, which suited the confrontational personality of the group and their on-stage persona. In the summer of 1976, Strummer and Simonon found themselves in the middle of a riot between Jamaican immigrants and police. "**White Riot**," the song that they wrote in response to the incident, was the group's first major hit. It not only got the group noticed but also set the tone for their career: many of their songs railed against political and social injustices.

"White Riot" and many other early songs follow the lead of the Ramones: they are fast, loud, and crude. However, the group quickly evolved into a much more skilled and versatile band. By 1979, the year in which they released *London Calling*, the highpoint of their recording career, the Clash were at home in a variety of styles. However, they never lost the passion that informed their first work. It is evident in virtually all of their music, regardless of subject.

"**Death or Glory**," a track from the album, comments on a central issue for the group: whether money will motivate a group to sell out. The lyric reeks attitude: the cast of characters includes a "cheap hood" and a "gimmick hungry yob" ("yob" is British slang for a young working-class male). The images are brutal: the hood beats his kids; bands who haven't got it should give it up. The refrain sums up the disillusionment that pervades the song.

The music that supports it is simply good rock, rather than high-energy pure punk. The song uses the conventional verse/chorus form; the refrain features catchy melodic hooks that embed themselves in listeners' ears. Once underway, the song maintains a driving beat enriched with rhythmic interplay among the rhythm section players, except for an adventurous interlude that spotlights Headon. The texture is dense in a way that is typical of rock, with melodic lines in both guitars and bass, and there is an array of timbres, from the distorted chords that announce the refrain to the more mellow bass and guitar sounds in the introduction.

"Death or Glory" is not representative of *London Calling*, a double album with nineteen tracks. Neither is any other track on the album; each song has a distinct character and musical setting; they range from swing-evoking "**Jimmy Jazz**" and reggae-inspired "**Revolution Rock**" to the clever punk-style "**Koka Kola**" and the more conventional rock of "Death or Glory." However, throughout the album, the Clash infuse their music with the power and passion of punk. Regardless of the style or influences of the music, the songs matter—because of the lyrics and because the music backs up the lyrics.

More than any other group of the late seventies, the Clash demonstrated by example how to revitalize rock with words and music that mattered, because, unlike the "gimmick hungry yob," they refused to compromise. (Interestingly, their record company undermined their integrity by marketing them as the "The Only Band That Matters," a phrase created by their fans.)

15–3b The Reverberations of Punk

Many commentators regard *London Calling* as the most significant album of the decade: for example, it is the only album by a band formed after 1970 to make the Top 10 of *Rolling Stone*'s list of the 500 greatest albums of all time. That the most significant music would be released in the United Kingdom in December 1979, the last month of the last year, is the ultimate comment on rock in the seventies. It was as if rock in the seventies had to wait until the last possible moment to be reminded of its ability to send a strong message.

Punk and new wave restored the soul of rock and roll. The important bands resurrected rock's sense of daring and amped it up well beyond what had gone before. As with Dylan's pre-electric and early electric work, the anthemic sixties songs of the Who and the Rolling Stones, and reggae, there is a powerful message: political, social, personal. However, in punk it is embedded not in a simple acoustic setting, the coming-together rock of the mid-sixties, or the transparent rhythms of reggae. In punk, the rock can be as brutally blunt in its musical message as in the lyrics. There is a synergy among attitude, words, and music that gives both punk and new wave unprecedented impact. Once again, this is rock music that sought to change the world.

In its intent, punk stands apart from almost all other music of the seventies that we have heard, in that the music is not an end in itself but a means to convey a meaningful message. It is not music for dancing, like disco; for entertainment, like mainstream rock; for expressing personal feelings and experiences in an almost private way, like the singer-songwriters' melodies; or for appreciation as an art artifact, like the music of Yes. Instead, the message is primary, whether it is expressed directly, as in "God Save the Queen" or "Death or Glory," or more obliquely, as in "Blitzkrieg Bop" or "Radio, Radio." This helps account for the relative simplicity of the musical materials—whether presented as a sound-blitz (as in the Ramones' music) or with imagination (as in the music of the Clash and the Talking Heads): if the musical setting were too elaborate, it would deflect attention away from the underlying intent of the song.

As with any significant new music, punk and new wave would reverberate through the music of the next generation. Punk, and especially the music of the Clash, served as a bridge between the significant rock of the sixties and the significant rock of the eighties, most notably the work of U2. It introduced a new conception of rock rhythm that would filter into numerous mainstream and alternative styles: this was one reason that much of the rock from the eighties sounds as though it is from that decade and not from an earlier time. It sharpened the edge of much rock-era music, even the pop of Michael Jackson and Madonna. It opened the door for those outside corporate rock: the alternative movement that began in the early eighties continues the independent spirit that typified the punk and new wave music of the late seventies. That spirit lives on most fully in the post-punk bands that have emerged since 1980.

CHAPTER 16

ALTERNATIVES: THE NEW SYNTHESES OF ROCK'S SECOND GENERATION

Learning Objectives:

1) Starting from the 1970s, articulate the evolution of world music in popular culture.

2) Identify the unique musical characteristics of Paul Simon's solo works.

3) Define the term **dance-oriented rock**.

4) Describe the common instrumental and rhythmic textures employed in the music of U2.

5) Contrast "pure" punk to post-punk styles.

6) Recall key female musicians involved in the alternative movement.

Chapter Introduction

In a 2012 interview for *musicradar* prior to the release of *Road to Forever*, his first solo album in 30 years, ex-Eagles guitarist Don Felder discussed at length the genesis of "Hotel California." Felder joined the Eagles in 1974, a day after being asked to play slide guitar during a recording session. A year later, Joe Walsh, a hard rock guitarist who had a long-term acquaintance with the Eagles, also joined the band, replacing founding member Bernie Leadon. Frey and Henley recruited Walsh for the band because they wanted to give their music more of a rock edge.

In 1976, the Eagles released *Hotel California*, their first album with the new line up. With the addition of Felder and Walsh, the band could rock harder than before. That's evident in "**Life In The Fast Lane**," one of three singles from the album. However, the majority of the tracks explore musical territory that's removed some distance from the core rock style. Nowhere is that more evident than in the title track from the album, which would become the band's signature song.

Felder wrote the song along with several others and recorded demos of them at his home using a simple recorder on which he overdubbed guitar and bass lines and used an early drum machine for percussion. In the interview, he explained how he presented the songs to Henley and Frey.

I would write track ideas—introductions, verses, choruses, solos—and I'd put them on a cassette and give them to Don and Glenn. I did this with the songs for

Hotel California, and I said, "If there's anything you like on these cassettes and you want to finish writing, let's do that." Henley said, "I like that song that sounds like a Mexican reggae or Bolero."

With a fair amount of massaging and a couple of name changes, the "Mexican reggae" became "**Hotel California**." The prominent role of reggae elements gave listeners a foretaste of a new relationship between inside and outside in rock-era music, one that would shape much of the music of the eighties.

From the start, rock has been a musical melting pot. It has seamlessly absorbed markedly different musical styles and produced vital new music. During the sixties alone rock absorbed folk, pop, classical music, jazz, Latin music, musical theater, and traditional country. It made no difference whether a style began on the opposite side of the cultural fence: rock assimilated it. Rock's openness to outside influences and sources, regardless of provenance, has been one of its hallmarks.

As rock became the dominant popular music, the dynamic between inside and outside changed. It was no longer rock and nonrock styles coming together, but mainstream and nonmainstream styles. In the seventies, reggae, punk, funk, and disco began outside the mainstream. The initial audience for each was small and a minority of some kind: Jamaicans, disaffected "no future" youths, a subset of (mostly) black listeners, minorities and gays. In their most authentic form, the styles were different from mainstream rock, and also recognizably different from each other, musically and culturally.

Despite their obvious musical differences, rock-era musicians of the eighties drew on these distinct, seemingly conflicting styles to produce a dazzling array of new syntheses. The best were master painters in sound using an expanded palette. We sample several of these fusions, from reggae and world music to intersections of punk and funk.

16-1 Reggae and World Music Fusions

The influence of reggae on other rock-era styles is most evident in rhythm: reggae liberates rhythm from the tyranny of the rhythmic template. This freedom is evident mainly in two ways: the various off-beat rhythmic patterns that make beat-keeping implicit, rather than explicit, and the freely roaming bass lines, which typically avoid marking the beat or locking into a repetitive rhythmic pattern. The characteristic off-beat patterns usually take one of two forms. One is the "ka-CHUN-ka" after beat/backbeat combination heard in "**The Harder They Come**" and "**Is This Love**." These overlay and attenuate a rock beat (as in Cliff's song) or a shuffle rhythm (as in Marley's song). The other is related: rebound afterbeats on either side of the backbeat ("ka-ka-CHUN-ka-ka"); this version maps onto a sixteen-beat rhythm.

Both of these contrast sharply with the saturated eight-beat rhythm of punk and the relentless fast-moving streams of notes heard in disco songs like Donna Summer's "I Feel Love." The difference is not just between insistent and intermittent rhythms. It's also a difference in texture: tracks that feature the saturated eight-beat rhythm (e.g., "**Blitzkrieg Bop**," "**Highway Star**," "**Born To Run**") tend to concentrate these insistent rhythms in a lower register, which thickens the sound. By contrast, the intermittent rhythms of reggae and the relative unpredictability of the bass line create a sound that seems to float over time, even as it supports the melody.

We explore two songs supported by buoyant reggae-influenced rhythms, "Hotel California" and "**Don't Stand So Close To Me**," by the Police.

16-1a "Hotel California"

When he created the demo of what would become "Hotel California," Felder added an extended solo to the end of the track in which he simulated the sound of dueling guitarists by using two different guitars, his own Les Paul and a Fender Stratocaster for his Walsh-like answers.

During the time that they recorded *Hotel California*, the Eagles included three guitarists—Glenn Frey was the one remaining guitarist from the band's original lineup. To simply note that the band has three guitarist gives almost no indication as to the extraordinary range of sounds that the guitarists produce. The song opens with Felder's delicate 12-string solo. Walsh joins in with a resonant, slow-moving, almost horn-like line. Frey adds the crisp reggae-inspired rebound afterbeats under Henley's singing of the verse. In the chorus, guitar lines are constantly interweaving, answering Henley's vocals, and generally creating a rich midrange texture, which is supported by Henley's drumming and Meisner's bass, and which in turn supports the close harmony vocals. The guitar highpoint is, of course, the extended exchange/duet at the end. Felder had assembled this part of this song simply as a demonstration, but Henley insisted that he and Walsh recreate it note-for-note in the recording. It took Felder and Walsh three days to work out the intricate interplay. So have many others: the solo remains one of the most admired and frequently covered solos in all of rock.

All of this is the backdrop to a cryptic lyric, for which Henley has offered several different interpretations. Its subtlety and ambiguity (for example, "colitas" a possible reference to marijuana, "Mercedes Bends" a play on the name of the automobile, etc.) resist literal interpretation. The connection between words and music is more a matter of atmosphere—the languid tempo and active but not overpowering rhythms suit phrases like "a warm smell of colitas, rising up through the air." But the music can almost stand apart from the words: the extended introduction and even more extended guitar exchange at the end comprise half of the length of the song.

The use of reggae rhythm in "Hotel California" reflects a growing awareness of this heretofore regional music. Reggae began to attract an international audience in the early seventies and its distinctive rhythms and textures had time to gain traction. This enormously successful song—successful both critically and commercially—provided an early demonstration of how musicians could seamlessly integrate the new sounds and rhythms of the seventies into a more commercially-oriented setting (Henley: "That's gonna be our single."). Many other important songs that blended multiple styles would follow, including more reggae-inspired hits. Among them was "Don't Stand So Close To Me."

16-1b Reggatta de Blanc: The Police

"Reggatta de blanc" translates as "white reggae." *Reggatta de Blanc* (1979) was the title of the second album by the Police. With this title, the group positioned themselves in the musical world of the late seventies.

For almost all of their decade-long career together, the Police was a trio: drummer Stewart Copeland (b. 1952), bassist and lead singer Sting (born Gordon Sumner, 1951), and guitarist Andy Summers (b. 1942). Although linked with the new wave movement in Great Britain, the group traced a different trajectory from the start. At the time the group formed in early 1977, its members were 24, 25, and 34—long in the tooth by punk standards. In particular, Andy Summers was an experienced musician whose credits included a stint with Eric Burdon and the New Animals as well as extensive session work in the early seventies. In part because of their wide-ranging backgrounds, their career as the Police lasted well into the eighties, peaking during the early eighties, well after the first wave of punk and new wave bands gained notoriety and commercial success. Each member has enjoyed success since they dissolved the band in 1986: Sting as a solo artist, and Copeland and Summers mainly in film scoring.

The pared-down, reggae-influenced style that served them so well throughout their time together was a choice, one that enabled them to project the words effortlessly and explore subtle nuances in rhythm and sound. Although linked to the punk and new wave movement, their music is different temperamentally from both. For them, reggae was not a way to project a political message, as it was with the Clash, but a point of departure for a new pop style.

In their first recordings, the reggae elements are distinct: in "**Roxanne,**" a hit single from their first album, the off-beat bass and repeated guitar chords connect directly to the Jamaican music. However, they quickly transformed the reggae elements into a new approach—one that captured the airy texture and floating rhythms of reggae without precisely replicating its rhythmic features. We hear this sound in a 1980 recording, "Don't Stand So Close to Me."

Before forming the Police, Sting was the British counterpart of a high school English teacher. His background in literature helps explain the prominence of the lyrics in the songs of the Police; his prior teaching experience certainly sheds some light on the subject of the song. Much later, Sting claimed the experience described in the lyric was not autobiographical, although he was a young man when he taught secondary school. If in fact he were not dissembling, he almost certainly would have witnessed it happen to a colleague. Certainly, he found it all too easy to imagine the tensions felt by the teacher who is the protagonist in the lyric.

Rather than relating a story, Sting's lyric simply describes a dilemma. It is deliberately inconclusive; he leaves it to our imagination to determine whether lust or honor wins out. The musical setting connects to this tension in numerous ways—some obvious and some more subtle. The obvious ones include the suspenseful opening and the voiceless final statement of the verse: instead of another installment of the lyric, where we would certainly learn which path the teacher and student took, we hear synthesized washes of sound.

The more subtle touches include the harmony and the rhythm. The harmony oscillates between two keys: one in the verse and the other in the chorus. Neither resolves conclusively; the end of the song leaves listeners hanging—in this respect, it's a musical analog to the teacher's emotions. The rhythmic texture uses reggae-inspired rhythms to convey a sense of uncertainty. It begins with the sustained synthesized bass sound and the guitar noodle, continues with the off-beat guitar chords, then settles in to a pattern that features little or no sound on the first beat of every measure, in both verse and chorus. The timekeeping is subtle; the most prominent rhythm is the guitar riff, which always starts on the second beat. This is an adaptation of the reggae off-beat rhythm; it has the similar effect of making the rhythmic texture buoyant. Here, it underscores the unsettled state of mind of the young teacher who may ask the student to keep her distance but wish her next to him as he says it.

The combination of buoyant rhythms, prominent words and melody, and an open texture dominated by single-line parts rather than chords exemplifies one of the freshest rock sounds of the eighties. It was a sound that listeners found especially appealing; a 1983 *Rolling Stone* feature article declared them "today's best-loved band."

The impact of reggae, both directly in the music of Bob Marley and other Jamaican musicians, and indirectly in the music of pop and rock acts like the

Eagles, the Clash, and the Police, gave impetus to other regional-rock fusions, especially those from African countries. In the eighties, these new syntheses were part of the world music movement.

16-2 World Music

In discussing his involvement with World of Music, Arts, and Dance (WOMAD), Peter Gabriel, the lead vocalist in Genesis and an important solo artist since the late seventies, noted:

> Pure enthusiasm for music from around the world led us to the idea of WOMAD in 1980 and thus to the first WOMAD festival in 1982. The festivals have always been wonderful and unique occasions and have succeeded in introducing many talented artists to an international audience. Equally important, the festivals have also allowed many different audiences to gain an insight into cultures other than their own through the enjoyment of music. Music is a universal language, it draws people together and proves, as well as anything, the stupidity of racism.

Gabriel was one of the founders of the World of Music, Art, and Dance. Since the first festival in the United Kingdom in 1982, WOMAD has grown into a multifaceted organization. Its festivals are huge events that take place around the world: In the 2001 Guinness Book of Records, it was cited as the biggest International Music Festival. It has provided a platform for numerous world music performers. Since its inception, its mission has been to use the arts to open minds and hearts to the world around us. As they state on their website (**http://womad.org**), "at festivals, performance events, through recorded releases and through educational projects, we aim to excite, to inform, and to create awareness of the worth and potential of a multicultural society."

16-2a The Roots of the World Music Movement

The roots of the world music movement that took shape in the early eighties go back to the late forties, in the music of the Weavers. Among their biggest hits were songs from Israel ("Tzena, Tzena, Tzena") and South Africa ("Wimoweh"). In the latter part of the fifties, Harry Belafonte would enjoy comparable success with his versions of calypso songs like "Banana Boat (Day O)." Although their music doesn't sound much like authentic versions of the songs, their advocacy of folk music from then-exotic locales and their effort to capture something of its spirit played a large role in creating the open-minded attitude that has characterized rock-era music. Belafonte also played a key role in introducing South African singer Miriam Makeba to US audiences. She would enjoy a long run in the sixties, but her success did not lead to widespread interest in South African music.

During the sixties, both the bossa nova craze and the Beatles played a big part in expanding the popular-music worldview. Bossa nova was an international/regional fusion—jazz met samba in Brazil and returned as the bossa nova—that gained significant traction in the United States and elsewhere. The appeal of the music surmounted the language barrier. The Beatles spearheaded a more inclusive musical attitude on multiple levels. One was the simple fact of their success. The British Invasion of the mid-sixties made rock—and, by extension, popular music—an international music. The second level of influence was their musical daring: they were not afraid to try anything or use music from any source. By their example, they nurtured the open-mindedness of rock and folk artists. Most specifically, they helped bring Indian music to a much wider western audience. George Harrison's flirtation with the sitar and his use of it in songs like "Norwegian Wood" helped build a western audience for Indian musicians like Ravi Shankar.

The seventies were the prelude to the world music explosion of the eighties. The most significant development was the emergence of reggae. Its popularity and influence outside of Jamaica inspired artists and industry members in other Afrocentric styles, such as juju and calypso, to promote their music to a wider audience. Moreover, reggae's role as the conscience of popular music in the seventies demonstrated once again that music could go beyond mere entertainment to be a force for social change. Artists in other Afrocentric styles also embraced this concept.

16-2b The Emergence of World Music

All of this laid the groundwork for the world music movement that flowered during the eighties. Five key ingredients were in place: the use of music as an expression of national or cultural identity, the growing international recognition of regional popular styles, deep interest from a few mainstream popular musicians, the drive to reclaim folk heritages around the world, and audience interest.

In many cases, the revival and promotion of traditional music had a political dimension. This was particularly the case in Africa and the Caribbean. Almost all of the countries had formerly been colonies of England or France, and most had gained their independence only in the sixties and seventies. As the countries shook off colonial rule, traditional music became an expression of cultural identity and national pride, especially in Africa. For example, Kwame Nkrumah, Ghana's first president, made the restoration of traditional music a matter of government policy.

After independence, both England and France had liberal policies with regard to immigration from former colonies. Indeed, the Caribbean islands Guadeloupe and Martinique are *départements* of France. As a result, London and Paris became the centers of world beat because of the large expatriate colonies in both cities. These European capitals were homes away from home for both musicians and audience.

Reggae's popularity during the seventies helped spark interest in other Afrocentric music. Among the regional styles to gain a toehold in the international market were calypso and soca (soul calypso, a regional/international hybrid that had emerged during the seventies) from Trinidad, *zouk* and cadence from the French Caribbean, samba from Brazil, and Afropop styles like *juju* from Nigeria (King Sunny Ade was the best-known Nigerian musician).

None of these styles has succeeded on the same scale as reggae—many, especially the West African styles, must overcome the language barrier—but all have an international presence. Most were already in existence well before the eighties (e.g., calypso dates back to the 1910s). Their emergence in the eighties reflects both changes in the music—a more updated sound, through the addition of electronic instruments and the incorporation of elements from the international style—and the growing interest of musicians and audience from other parts of the world in new sounds.

The complement to regional musicians blending elements of the international style with their local music was the mainstream musicians bringing these regional styles into their music. Three musicians stand out: Paul Simon, David Byrne of Talking Heads, and Peter Gabriel. All played an active role in promoting world music by using African musicians on their recording dates (e.g., Youssou N'Dour with Peter Gabriel), and by seeking out and promoting regional music. Among the most acclaimed and successful of these collaborations was Paul Simon's 1986 album, *Graceland*.

16-2c Global/Pop Fusions

Ethan Zuckerman, a fellow at The Berkman Center for Internet and Society at Harvard Law and a cofounder of Global Voices, maintains the blog *My Heart's in Accra* (**http://ethanzuckerman.com**) to share his thoughts on "Africa, international development, and hacking the media." In an April 2009 entry entitled "From Protest to Collaboration: Paul Simon's *Graceland* and Lessons for Xenophiles," he discusses the creative process that eventually produced Simon's album in the context of the anti-apartheid movement. *Graceland* was ultimately a huge success for Simon and many of his fellow musicians, but its production and release generated considerable controversy.

16-2d Music, Race, and Cultural Change

Among the sources of increasing pressure on the South African government to eliminate apartheid was a widespread cultural boycott begun in 1961 by the British Musicians' Union and later overseen by the UN Centre against Apartheid. This boycott got a boost in 1985 when Steven Van Zandt, Bruce Springsteen's longtime on-and-off guitarist, created Artists United Against Apartheid and recorded "Sun City," a seven and a half minute video with a simple message: Artists with a conscience don't perform in Sun City.

Sun City was a luxurious resort and casino built in 1979 in a *bantustan*—a black African homeland created by the South African government. Gambling, pornography, and other Las Vegas–type vices were illegal in white South Africa, so the government permitted the casino to be built in a black area. In response, Van Zandt mobilized an all-star aggregation of artists to promote a boycott of the resort. The video juxtaposes images of the casino, clips of police brutality in South Africa, and scenes from the American civil rights movement of the sixties with cameos of the artists.

It was in this context that Simon recorded *Graceland*. Not surprisingly, he took an enormous amount of flak from several quarters, much of it misinformed. Among the most common criticisms involved "exploitation" and "musical colonialism." The facts tell a different story: Simon paid the musicians triple scale, shared songwriting credits, brought several musicians to New York to finish the album, and toured for a year with Miriam Makeba and Hugh Masakela, both South African exiles. That Simon would choose to go to South Africa to record was a logical step in his musical evolution.

Paul Simon

Paul Simon (b. 1941) has had a long history of collaboration that goes back to the beginning of his career, and as a solo artist he has been willing to integrate his musical identity with outside influences. His first professional success came from songs written with Carole King, and he first gained fame as a performer with Art Garfunkel (b. 1941). Their successes included the soundtrack for the (1967) film **The Graduate** (a rock first) and three chart-topping albums.

When Simon and Garfunkel dissolved their partnership in 1970, Simon immediately embarked on a solo career. The split seemed to liberate Simon musically: It was a case of addition by subtraction. Both Simon and Garfunkel have pleasant voices that do not project a strong and distinctive personality. Yet because there are two voices, usually in harmony, the vocal sound is typically the dominant element, even in a song like "**The Boxer**," which features a rich instrumental backdrop laced with unusual timbres.

However, in Simon's solo work, the musical settings became as important expressively as the words, melody, and Simon's singing, The settings often drew on a broad range of distinctive styles, for example, Latin music, both black and white gospel, and reggae. In this respect, Simon, more than any other post-1970 artist, has furthered the Beatles' revolutionary reconception of song, one in which setting, like words and melody, plays a key role in projecting meaning. In **Graceland**, he went beyond his work in the seventies, geographically and musically.

In 1984, Simon was at a low point in his career. *Hearts and Bones*, released the previous year and his first album since 1975, had not done well. A friend shared a cassette of township jive (a popular style created by black South Africans) by the Boyoyo Boys. Inspired by this unfamiliar music, Simon sought out Hilton Rosenthal, the record's producer, about recording with South African musicians. Rosenthal assured Simon that collaboration was possible and sent him numerous recordings. However, because of the intense international opposition to apartheid, Simon consulted Quincy Jones and Harry Belafonte, who had been involved in the USA for Africa project, and received their assurance that his project was ethical. Encouraged, Simon went to South Africa, enlisted South Africans as cowriters, then had the black South African musicians record rhythm tracks. Only then did he begin to write the songs on top of tracks that he pieced together.

By reversing the conventional sequence of events in recording, Simon virtually guaranteed that the African element in the recording would be organic, not cosmetic. "**Diamonds on the Soles of Her Shoes**" exemplifies the extent of the African influence. It begins with the choral group Ladysmith Black Mambazo singing in Zulu; one translation of their lyrics is "Even though you saved that man today,/He will be ruined no matter what./Come on, girl." In the main section of the song, Simon describes the rich girl/poor boy relationship in a series of images as he rides the distinctively African sounds, rhythms, and harmonies—in this case, a revolving three-chord progression. In effect, Simon merges his distinctive songwriting esthetic into the infectious music of his African collaborators.

The track and the album are a true global fusion, an outstanding example of the blending of regional and international music. *Graceland* was Simon's most successful album, commercially and critically, and the album and tour helped promote the careers of many of the artists involved, most notably Ladysmith Black Mambazo.

16-2e Music as a Force for Global Understanding

Apartheid was dismantled during the early nineties, and in 1994 Nelson Mandela became the first South African president elected by a fully democratic vote. At Mandela's invitation, Simon became the first American to perform in post-apartheid South Africa. For Simon, it was not only a triumphant experience but also a moment of vindication in the wake of the controversy surrounding *Graceland*. As such, it is an object lesson on how complicated mixing art and politics can become. Ethan Zuckerman's perspective on this matter is enlightening:

> Steven Van Zandt's position, a principled stance against engaging with South Africa under apartheid, is a cleaner, neater position than the complex compromise Simon chose, but I doubt it was as effective. Van Zandt helped call attention to a nasty situation in the waning days of the Botha regime—Simon introduced the wider world to a soundtrack for both a revolution and for a new South Africa.

As we listen to "Diamonds on the Soles of Her Shoes," it's easy to be caught up in the flow of the music and intrigued by Simon's quirky lyric. But the circumstances of its creation remind us how music is so much a part of our world even as it can carry us apart from it.

16-3 Post-Punk/Post-Disco Fusions

Punk and disco seem as easy to blend as oil and water. As they emerged in the late seventies, they seemed to demarcate contrasting ideologies and musical approaches. Punk was real while disco, as experienced in a club, was an escape into a timeless world. Punk was about grit; disco was about glitter. Punk was performed by live bands on conventional rock instruments, hammering out a concentrated rock rhythm; disco was performed by DJs mixing a string of recordings, most of which combined a strong beat with active sixteen-beat rhythms. The lyrics of punk songs usually said something; disco lyrics often descended into banality.

However, in *Christgau's Record Guide*, his 1990 survey of 3,000 recordings from the eighties, Robert Christgau, the dean of American rock critics, described "post-punk/post-disco fusion" as a key development of the decade. He described a synthesis of the two in what he called DOR, or dance-oriented rock, an umbrella term he coined to identify an array of eighties styles. What Christgau called DOR was just one of several new sounds that emerged in the eighties that showed the joint influence of punk and disco. The most significant pop musician to draw on both styles in his music was Prince, a multifaceted musician who, more than any other figure of the decade, forged a new middle-ground consensus from a broad spectrum of sixties and seventies musical styles.

16-3a Prince

It would be difficult to find any rock artist who embodies more confluences and contradictions than Prince (born Prince Rogers Nelson, 1958–2016). His music is a rock and rhythm-and-blues melting pot: one hears elements of funk, punk, hard rock, disco, black and white pop, and more, in varying proportions. His touring bands, like Sly and the Family Stone, have included blacks and whites, women and men. His particular syntheses came to be known as "the Minneapolis sound," after the city where he was born and where he continued to make his home base (he opened Paisley Park Studios there in 1987). The confluences extend to his personal life: the unpronounceable symbol that he used in lieu of his name from 1993 to 2000 (when he became "the artist formerly known as Prince") reputedly represents a merging of the symbols for male and female.

The contradictions are present in his life and his music. He created a public persona so blatantly erotic at times that his music sparked the campaign to put parental advisory labels on recordings, but he led an extremely reclusive private life, which had a strong spiritual dimension. (He claimed that God directed him to change his name to a symbol.) He was an artist sufficiently drawn to the spotlight that he coauthored and starred in a quasi-autobiographical film (*Purple Rain*) and a musician who willingly and anonymously wrote for, produced, and accompanied other artists. (Prince often used aliases when he appeared on others' recordings.) His music was deeply rooted in the valued music of earlier generations: in a 1985 *Rolling Stone* interview he acknowledged artists as diverse as Stevie Wonder, Joni Mitchell, Miles Davis, Santana, and George Clinton. Yet his music grew by absorbing numerous contemporary influences some distance from his musical roots—such as new wave—and by blending sounds produced by cutting-edge technology— for example, drum machines in the early eighties—with more conventional instruments, all of which he played masterfully.

One measure of Prince's greatness as an artist was his ability to reconcile the contrasting, even contradictory, elements of his musical life into a personal style that retained its identity despite its great stylistic and emotional range. Most songs exhibited qualities, particularly in the approach to texture and rhythm, that gave evidence of a consistent musical conception, despite considerable differences from song to song. Listening to a Prince album can be like taking a course in rock history. Prince mastered virtually all rock-era styles. For Prince, style mastery was not simply the ability to cover a style; he seldom did just that. Instead, he drew on disparate style elements and mixed them together to evoke a particular mood. For him, beat patterns, sounds, and rhythmic textures were like ingredients in a gourmet dish; they are used to flavor the song. More importantly, he also added original ideas to create the nouvelle cuisine of eighties pop.

Prince was the son of musicians: jazz pianist John Nelson and singer Mattie Shaw. To escape his parents' troubled relationship (they divorced when Prince was ten), Prince sought refuge in music. By his teens, he had mastered not only the full array of rhythm instruments, but he had begun writing his own material and had learned production skills. Although not a child star, he was more precocious in some respects than Michael Jackson as both musician and producer. He played all the instruments on his first five albums and produced them as well. Stevie Wonder had pioneered this electronic version of the one-man band in the early seventies; Prince grew up with it.

He secured his first recording contract, which gave him total freedom in the studio, in 1977. The hits began coming two years later, beginning with "**I Wanna Be Your Lover**." The success of **Purple Rain** (1984) brought him commercial success (sales of thirteen million units; three hit singles) and critical recognition (the soundtrack won three Grammy awards); in its wake, he became one of the few superstars of the eighties. His subsequent work continued to explore new territory. As he remarked in the *Rolling Stone* interview, "I always try to do something different and conquer new ground." He reached what many commentators feel was an artistic high point in 1987 with the release of the double album *Sign 'O' the Times*. We consider the title track following.

"**Sign 'O' the Times**," one of three singles from the album to chart, presents a bleak vision of contemporary life: gangs, AIDS, drugs, natural disasters, interlaced with anecdotal accounts of the fallout from drug use. The music is correspondingly bleak. The track begins with an intricate rhythm formed from a syncopated synthesizer riff and two electronically generated percussion sounds. This texture continues throughout the song. In the larger context of Prince's music, the repetition seems purposeful: it seems to suggest a despair that knows no end. In effect, it serves as a substitute for a standard rhythm section, and it is the accompaniment for Prince's vocal in the verse section. Other consistent elements include a strong backbeat and a synthesized bass riff, which often provides a response to the vocal line. Funky, jazz-influenced guitar figures, then sustained synthesizer chords, which provide the first harmonic change, highlight the buildup to the crux of the song: one finds happiness only in death. To underscore this difficult idea, the music returns to the empty sound of the opening—an abrupt and disconcerting return to reality. Only a blues-tinged guitar solo, again over the relentless synthesizer riffs and intricate percussion rhythms, provide relief from the misery portrayed in the lyric; this is interrupted by percussion sounds that evoke the fire of a machine gun. (Shades of U2?)

"Sign 'O' the Times" gains its impact as much from what's missing as from what's present. There is no rhythm guitar, no bass line, and no routine timekeeping on a drum set. There is no hook at the highpoint of the chorus to latch onto. There are no familiar chord progressions and few other clues that help us navigate through the song. The rhythms are complex, as in funk, but disciplined; the texture is spare, not dense. These features help create a sound world that is as vivid and powerful as a black and white photograph of a gray day in the ghetto.

"Sign 'O' the Times" shows how Prince mixed disparate elements into a coherent and effective whole. From punk, via rap, he took realness: there is no fantasy, or escape, in this song. From funk, he took complex layered rhythms, which he pared down to convey the mood of the song. He adapted blues-influenced rock guitar to the context, supporting it unconventionally with the minimalist synthesizer riffs and rhythms.

Almost any other Prince song will sound quite different in many respects; that is one reason for his commercial and critical success. The most consistent elements are likely to be the mix of synthesized and conventional instruments; an open-sounding, intricately worked-out texture that puts a different spin on the conventional interplay between regular timekeeping and syncopated patterns; and a few distinctive features that help set the song apart from the sources that inspired it. In this song, it is the absence of bass and drum set and the rich sustained harmonies in the first part of the chorus. But the distinctive element can be anything: "**U Got the Look**," another top hit from *Sign 'O' the Times*, offers a radically transformed version of the **twelve-bar blues** progression.

Even by rock standards, Prince was an eccentric. Still, the odd, often contradictory aspects of his personal life cannot obscure or diminish Prince's remarkable musical achievement: there has been no more multitalented, multidimensional musician in the history of rock.

Prince was a musical chameleon. By contrast, U2 was a band that drew on both punk and disco to forge a distinctive sound that made them one of the most significant acts of the eighties and beyond.

16–3b U2

From the start, U2—lead vocalist Bono (born Paul Hewson, 1960), guitarist-keyboardist The Edge (born David Evans, 1961), bassist Adam Clayton (b. 1960), and drummer Larry Mullen (b. 1961)—have had a sense of their destiny. In 1981, three years after the group came together, Bono told *Rolling Stone*, "Even at this stage, I do feel we are meant to be one of the great bands. There's a certain spark, a certain chemistry, that was special about the Stones, the Who, and the Beatles, and I think it's also special about U2." They have fulfilled their destiny because they have stayed together and because they have never lost their passion for rock and what it can be. As recently as 2000, after more than two decades of touring, recording, and sending their message out into the world, Bono told *USA Today* that "There is a transcendence that I want from rock.... I'm still drunk on the idea that rock and roll can be a force for change. We haven't lost that idea."

U2 soon made Bono a prophet. In their first two albums, *Boy* (1980) and *October* (1981), the group addressed personal issues, among them relationships and their faith. By 1983, the year that they released *War*, their third album, the band had defined its purpose, found its audience, and had begun to define its sound. With this album, their music took on the politically and socially aware edge that would characterize it through the rest of the eighties. "**Sunday Bloody Sunday**," a track from the album and their first No. 1 hit in the United Kingdom, for example, recounts an especially bloody incident in the ongoing strife between Catholics and Protestants in Northern Ireland, and the musical setting reinforces the message of the lyrics: the five-note bursts played by the entire band underneath Bono's vocal line evokes the sound of gunfire.

The following year, they began their long and fruitful collaboration with Brian Eno (b. 1948)—a founding member of Roxy Music, an **electronica** pioneer, the father of **ambient music**, and by 1984, a much-in-demand producer. (More recently,

twelve-bar blues
The most widely used form for one chorus of a blues song. It is defined principally by its chord progression, which features I, IV, and V in a consistent pattern over twelve bars: I(1), I(3) / IV(5), I(7) / V(9), I(11). The 12- bar blues form is used in both vocal and instrumental songs. In sung 12- bar blues songs, the typical lyric is a rhymed couplet, with the first line repeated.

electronica The umbrella term for a large and varied family of musical styles: house, techno, trance, ambient, jungle, drum & bass, industrial dance, and many more.

Eno has identified himself as a "sonic landscaper," a label that also applies readily to his work with U2.) Eno brought a polish to U2's music, while preserving the distinctive sound world that they had begun to create. Their first album together was the 1984 release *The Unforgettable Fire*; he would collaborate on four of their albums. By 1985, *Rolling Stone* had dubbed them the band of the eighties, but it wasn't until *Joshua Tree* (1987) that they achieved the overwhelming commercial success to match their critical acclaim.

Virtually from the start of their career, U2 cultivated a sound world that made their music sound significant. They put the essential components in place in their first albums, enhanced them with the help of Brian Eno, and maintained them through the eighties. The sound grows out of punk but already has a distinct identity in songs like **"Gloria"** (1981) from their second album. Surrounding Bono's vocals is a four-strand texture, separated into low, middle, and high:

- Two low range sounds: repeated notes at rock-beat speed in the bass and beat-keeping on the bass drum
- A midrange percussion sound: a rock-rhythm layer on the hi-hat
- A medium high range sound: the angular guitar line, also moving at rock-beat speed

The insistent rock rhythmic layer, played by the entire band, derives from punk, but U2 has already put their personal stamp on it, in the spacing of the instruments and in The Edge's asymmetrically patterned single-line guitar figures. Because of the registral openness and the angular guitar lines, the effect is quite different from punk. Whereas the sound of Ramones-style punk rams the listener head-on, the sound of U2, even at this early stage, envelops the listener.

This distinctive sound world is built on contrast: between high and low and between slow and fast. As the band's music evolved during the eighties, the contrast deepened. One significant change came from within the band: the active rhythms doubled in speed, from rock rhythm to the sixteen-beat rhythms of disco, while such features as chord rhythm often moved at even slower speeds. In his work with U2, Eno enriched the "sonic landscape" by deepening the contrast between slow and fast with sustained synthesizer sounds and introducing stronger textural contrasts. These changes gave U2's music an even more sharply defined profile, as we hear in **"Where the Streets Have No Name,"** a hit track from their 1987 album *Joshua Tree*.

"Where the Streets Have No Name" continues U2's predilection for meaningful words encased in meaningful-sounding music. The lyrics describe a universal longing for the harmony that can be created when divisions by class, race, and wealth disappear. They are general enough to have spawned multiple interpretations. Some connect the song's message to Ethiopia, where Bono and his wife had done relief work. Others link it to Los Angeles, where the video of the song was filmed. Still others associate it with Dublin, where the street one lives on could identify one's social and economic status. And most connect it to the world beyond.

Bono presents the lyric through a melody whose simplicity is obscured by the rich instrumental backdrop. If we tune out the instruments and simply listen to Bono's voice, we hear a folksong-like melody: short phrases that gently rise and fall within a narrow range. This melody is coherent even without accompaniment, and it would work with a simple folk guitar accompaniment.

It is U2 and Eno's grand setting that relocates this simple melody from the front porch to the stage. The extended instrumental introduction—almost two minutes in length—begins with sustained organ and synthesizer sounds. The Edge's busy guitar pattern slowly emerges out of this sound cushion. At first it is in a rhythm that oscillates once for every six notes, like a jig in slow motion. Imperceptibly, he converts the pattern to the sixteen-beat rhythm that is sustained through the rest of the song. The rhythmic patterns range from the sustained synthesizer chords, which may last four measures before changing, through the beat-speed thump of Mullen's bass drum, Clayton's rock-beat-speed repeated note, and the sixteen-beat rhythms of the guitar(s)—there are two guitar sounds much of the time—and drums. All of this encases Bono's singing in a musical halo.

The sound world that U2 created in "Where the Streets Have No Name" was the band's musical signature during the eighties. It is heard in many of their hits during that decade, and it becomes progressively more sophisticated from album to album. It has the effect of elevating the simple melody that lies at its center, investing it with a power and impact that it could not have had in a simpler setting. In this sense, the music of U2 is the ultimate folk rock: one in which the power of the words is matched by the power of the music.

16-4 Significant-Sounding Rock

U2 was one of the few major acts of the eighties that attempted to rekindle the spirit of the sixties, when rock meant something. As Springsteen did with the aftermath of the Vietnam War, U2 confronted difficult problems in which they had a deep personal involvement: the conflict in Northern Ireland, and the suffering in Africa. And like Springsteen, they wore their hearts on their sleeves: they would rather be too passionate than too reserved.

The power of their music comes in large part from applying two principles: simplifying and highlighting basic rhythms and creating a full, yet open sound. By emphasizing regular timekeeping over syncopation, and maintaining the same basic texture with only subtle variation through long stretches of time, the instrumental settings convey both simplicity and seriousness. Their function is to enhance the power and presence of the lyric.

The simplicity and directness of the rhythms connect to the rhythmic approach, if not the sound, of punk, while the sixteen-beat rhythms in the guitar and drum parts connect to the more active rhythms' mainstream via disco. It is a distinctive synthesis of the two streams, one that leaves other aspects of the styles out of the equation. And it is a compelling example of how 1980s musicians adapted novel elements of these "outsider" rock-era styles and reshaped them into a new esthetic.

This rhythmic approach cuts the cord with good-time rock. As we have noted in earlier chapters, the rock groove that makes people want to get up and dance grows out of the interplay between regular rhythms and rhythms that conflict with it or transcend it. In "Where the Streets Have No Name" rhythmic play occurs only in the irregular *patterns* of The Edge's active accompaniment, not in the rhythm itself, which is regular. It is as if U2 are saying that they want listeners to hear the message in the lyrics. Listeners can draw power from the music, but they should not be distracted by rhythms that are too playful for the lyric. In post-punk rock-era music, a serious message virtually demands music with minimal syncopation.

16-5 Post-punk Alternatives

The boundary between punk and new wave on the one hand and alternative on the other seems more geographic than temporal or musical. The formation of the first alternative bands occurred around 1980, when the careers of bands like the Clash, Elvis Costello and the Attractions, and the Talking Heads were at a high point. The music of the first alternative bands music represents a stylistic continuation of punk and new wave; there is no radical difference between the two at the beginning, although alternative would soon diversify into a much more varied music.

However, alternative took root in college towns throughout the United States, rather than in major metropolitan areas. Small clubs were its first venues, and college radio stations were among the first to broadcast the music of alternative bands. The size of the town was not as important as the size of the university: it was the student body that provided the most enthusiastic support for these bands. Active regional scenes, in the United States and ultimately throughout the world, would become a hallmark of alternative music.

16-5a Early Alternative

The two bands most responsible for starting the alternative music movement were Hüsker Dü, based in Minneapolis (the home of the University of Minnesota), and R.E.M., formed in Athens, Georgia (the home of the University of Georgia). Both locales were well outside the New York–London axis where punk and new wave flourished. Hüsker Dü (the group took their name from a Danish board game) began as a hardcore punk band trying to out-Ramone the Ramones. Their music occasionally ventured beyond this frenetic-paced music toward a more moderate and melodic style. Although admired as an important influence on the new alternative movement, Hüsker Dü never crossed over to a more mainstream audience. That was not the case with R.E.M.

R.E.M.

R.E.M. as formed in 1980 by guitarist Peter Buck (b. 1956) and vocalist Michael Stipe (b. 1960); they began as one of the numerous do-it-yourself groups that sprang up in punk's wake. Buck and Stipe recruited bassist Mike Mills (b. 1958) and drummer Bill Berry (b. 1958), agreed on a name (R.E.M. is the acronym for rapid eye movement, a defining characteristic of the lightest stage of sleep), then performed relentlessly. They quickly became favorites of the local underground rock scene, playing college bars and small clubs.

"**Radio Free Europe**" (1981), their first hit, helped put the band on the rock music map and establish the essentially retrospective orientation of alternative music. It has the bright tempo, clean rhythm, and lean sound associated with David Bowie and new wave bands. The texture is spare in the verse; by contrast, the chorus features a much richer texture because of the jangly, reverberant guitar figuration and the active bass line underneath Stipe's vocals.

Characteristically for R.E.M., the lyric is as elliptical as the music is clear. The words are intelligible but what do they mean? By their own admission, the band has deliberately written nonspecific lyrics. As Michael Stipe said in a late-eighties interview, "I've always left myself pretty open to interpretation."

The sharp and sudden contrasts between verse and chorus provide a foretaste of what would become a defining feature of alternative music: dramatic, often jarring contrasts within songs. And Buck's flashback to a guitar sound directly descended from the Byrds' Roger McGuinn provides an early instance of the infusion of alternative's punk base with elements from other retro styles.

By the late eighties, R.E.M. had begun to bring alternative into the mainstream: **"The One I Love"** (1987) was their first Top 10 single. They would remain a popular band through the nineties, although Berry retired from performing in 1997.

In their determination to follow their own creative path, even if it circled back to the past instead of toward the future, the group set the tone for the alternative movement. And the simplicity of their sound—basic instrumentation, clear textures, little if any electronic wizardry—was a model for the alternative bands that followed.

16-6 The Persistence of Punk

Even as reverberations from the punk movement touched much of the new music of the eighties, "pure" punk—that is, the music that was most in tune with the attitude and sound of late seventies punk—went underground. With its breakneck tempos, screamed-out vocals, loud and crude riffs, and confrontational, politically charged lyrics, hardcore punk (or simply hardcore) was the most direct continuation of the punk esthetic established by the Sex Pistols. Bands such as Hüsker Dü, the Dead Kennedys, and Bad Religion were among the leading hardcore bands of the eighties.

The movement known as post-punk identifies a family of styles that merged the aggressive elements of punk with more experimental elements and outside influences, such as synthesizers. Joy Division, which dissolved in 1980 after the suicide of lead singer Ian Curtis, is generally regarded as a seminal post-punk band. The early industrial group Throbbing Gristle is often associated with post-punk. Other noteworthy bands include Public Image, Ltd. (fronted by John Lydon), Sisters of Mercy, and Sonic Youth.

> The proliferation of punk-related substyles and sub-substyles in the eighties and nineties—for example, hardcore (leading to thrashcore, emo, and skate punk); post-punk (leading to gothic rock); and **no wave**—highlights the seemingly causal relationship between the number of styles and the enthusiasm and isolation of the fan base. Since 1980, the three most subdivided genres have been the second waves of punk, heavy metal, and dance music. Each has relatively small but extremely supportive followings, and each exists in a cocoonlike world well outside the mainstream. The profusion of substyle labels is certainly due in part to the desire of fans and commentators (who are often one and the same) to provide the bands that they support with something that quickly and easily distinguishes them from other similar bands. In practice, the labels often overlap, and bands often find the distinguishing feature of a substyle (for example, breakneck tempos or extremely loud power chords) too confining.

no wave Post-punk substyle, characterized by the music of Sonic Youth.

16-6a Enhancing Punk

From the start, the fundamental creative tension in punk has been between power and expressive range. The challenge for bands was to broaden the range without dampening the impact. In the seventies, this tension was manifested in the different paths of punk and new wave music. In the eighties, it was evident in the numerous punk offshoots, most notably in the numerous post-punk substyles, such as no wave. The most successful no wave band, critically and commercially, is Sonic Youth.

Sonic Youth

Sonic Youth is a four-person band formed in 1981. During the peak of its career in the latter part of the eighties and early nineties, the band members were guitarists Thurston Moore (b. 1958) and Lee Ranaldo (b. 1956), bassist-guitarist Kim Gordon (b. 1953), and drummer Steve Shelley (b. 1963).

Like other no wave bands, Sonic Youth brought a rock-as-art sensibility to their work. Using the basic instrumentation, fast tempos, and clear timekeeping as a point of departure for their style, they overlaid it with unusual guitar sounds, noise, exotic harmonies, and sharp contrasts in texture. This sound world supported lyrics that put a fresh spin on familiar themes, sung/shouted accessibly to a simple melody. We hear these qualities in "**Hey Joni**," a track from their critically acclaimed double album *Daydream Nation* (1988).

"Hey Joni" begins with a low synthesizer drone that is gradually surrounded by extraneous noises. This abruptly gives way to the refrain of the song, in which both the connection and the distance from punk are evident. Drummer Shelley raps out a fast, straightforward rock rhythm—the kind that one expects to hear in a typical punk song. However, both guitarists alternate between conventional power chords and more dissonant and intricate figuration. An alternative effect comes to the forefront during the interlude between refrain and verse: syncopated riffs in one guitar part compete with high-register figuration that uses the more delicate sound of **harmonics** (musicians create the sound of harmonics on a stringed instrument by depressing the string only partway at certain points; this creates higher-pitched sounds with a distinctive ring). Other similar effects, such as the "Wipeout"-inspired glissando, follow in the verse and subsequent instrumental interludes. The changes in texture, which are concentrated in the middle registers, create a kaleidoscopic effect.

For Sonic Youth, sonic variety is key. Although they start from a basic rock-band instrumentation, they create magical sounds with the interplay of often discordant riffs and figuration and by employing special effects, such as the harmonics used here. The song melds the energy of punk with the glorious guitar sounds and noises for which the group is known.

Although *Daydream Nation* remains their most respected and best-known album, Sonic Youth has continued to evolve and explore new directions. Their tour with then barely known Nirvana was captured on the DVD *1991: The Year Punk Broke*. Their work, and especially the innovative guitar sounds and noises, have influenced more recent alternative bands.

> **harmonics** Sound created on a stringed instrument by depressing the string only partway at certain points, creating higher-pitched sounds with a distinctive ring.

16-7 Beyond Punk: Infusions of Funk and Metal

Among the most eclectic and electric new sounds of the late eighties and early nineties alternative scene was the music created by bands such as the Red Hot Chili Peppers, Primus, Jane's Addiction, Living Colour, Rage Against the Machine, and the Spin Doctors. Like the pop middle ground surveyed in the next chapter, this alternative music thoroughly integrated black and white music. But all of it was almost militantly antipop.

The songs expressed wildly different attitudes, from rage to razor-sharp humor. However, they shared stylistic common ground, which comes mainly from two features. One was deep roots in soul and sixties hard rock. This connection is evident in the complex, active, syncopated rhythms and the reaffirmation of the basic rock-band instrumentation. The other was the infusion of elements from important nonpop styles of the late seventies and eighties, most commonly funk, heavy metal, and rap. From funk, they took complex, active sixteen-beat rhythms. From heavy metal, they took bold guitar playing, extreme distortion, and virtuosity: Les Claypool of Primus is a strong candidate for the Van Halen of the electric bass. They occasionally overlaid these mixes with rap-inspired voice parts, more spoken than sung.

In 1985, none of these sources was new. Neither was the idea of forging new styles by mixing black and white sources: that is rock's most time-honored tradition. What gave the music a late-eighties sound was its thorough integration of rock and soul, and punk and funk, and the currency of its sources. We hear this interplay in **"Good Time Boys,"** a track from the Red Hot Chili Peppers' 1989 album *Mother's Milk*.

16–7a The Red Hot Chili Peppers

The Red Hot Chili Peppers was formed in 1983 by four alumni of Fairfax High School of West Hollywood, California. Two of the original four, bassist Michael "Flea" Balzary (b. 1962) and vocalist Anthony Kiedis (b. 1962), are still band members. Hillel Slovak (1962–1988), the original guitarist, died of a heroin overdose in 1988; his death prompted drummer Jack Irons (b. 1962) to leave the band. Drummer Chad Smith (b. 1961) and guitarist John Frusciante (b. 1970) replaced Irons and Slovak.

The Red Hot Chili Peppers received their training in funk from the highest authority. George Clinton produced their 1985 album *Freaky Styley*, which also featured Maceo Parker and Fred Wesley, both veterans of James Brown's band. Neither their self-titled debut album nor *Freaky Styley*, their second album, went anywhere commercially, but their next album, *The Uplift Mofo Party Plan* (1987), did. *Mother's Milk* (1989), with new band members Smith and Frusciante, did even better: it would become the group's first platinum album, eventually selling over two million units.

In "Good Time Boys," the Red Hot Chili Peppers merge the edge of punk with the strong bass lines of funk, the distorted guitar sounds and prominent and complex riffs of hard rock and heavy metal, and raplike vocals. Among the most innovative features of the song is the presence of both a strong bass line and a prominent guitar part. In the music that we have heard, typically either guitar or bass is dominant—guitar in rock, bass in R&B. Here they are virtually equal partners. Flea's bass lines stand out beneath the rap-style verse; Frusciante's complex guitar riffs take over in the instrumental interludes. And with its chanted, pentatonic vocal line, sung in unison by the band and doubled on the bass, the chorus recalls Parliament-style funk. All this supports an upbeat, self-promoting lyric, much closer to rock and roll and early rap in style and spirit than it is to the anger of punk or the weirdness of new wave. A simulated spinning of the radio dial interrupts the song just after the midway point. The final radio clip ends with the phrase "She's a white girl..." sung to a vanilla accompaniment; the abrupt return to the funky groove underscores the strong black influence in this song.

The influence is especially evident in the rhythm. From the very opening riff to the end of the song, the rhythms are complex, active, and highly syncopated. Smith lays down a rock beat, but Frusciante's riffs, Flea's bass lines, and Kiedis's rap-style vocals in the verse all move at sixteen-beat speed.

"Good Time Boys" illustrates the punk/funk fusion of the latter part of the eighties and early nineties. The infusion of funk and rap elements helped introduce a different tone in alternative music and broaden its horizons. The success of the Red Hot Chili Peppers helped put alternative on the music industry's radar and blur the musical, commercial, ecological, and ideological boundaries that distinguished alternative from other genres.

The band's well-documented problems with drugs—Kiedis, Frusciante, and Flea were addicts—crippled the band during the nineties; Frusciante left the band in 1992 and was invited to return in 1998 after quitting drugs. They have remained one of the leading "modern rock" acts in the music industry. Like other acts that have moved from the fringes of the industry to stardom, they have left the alternative world behind. And they were never at the center of it, as was R.E.M. during its early years. For the Red Hot Chili Peppers, "alternative" is increasingly just a label.

16-8 Women's Voices

Women quickly found a home in the alternative movement. Their growing presence can be understood as still another dimension of the more prominent place of women in popular music: the eighties were the decade not only of Madonna but also Joan Jett, the Go-Go's, and the Bangles. What made the work of women in alternative music distinctive was that their voices were not constrained in any way by the expectations of more mainstream music. Alternative gave feminists a forum and enabled women of every persuasion to speak their mind.

The women's movement within alternative music took root in the latter part of the eighties and flourished in the nineties. Among the important trends was the **riot grrrl** movement, which supported a militant feminist agenda with post-punk music that favored confrontation over chops (that is, musical skill). The music was part of a self-contained subculture: Bands such as Bratmobile and Bikini Kill played in clubs and at music festivals that promoted feminist solidarity. Feminist fanzines nurtured and promoted them and other acts, and independent labels released their recordings The **queercore** movement, which reacted against the more mainstream gay and lesbian views, found a musical voice in the work of bands such as Sister George, Tribe 8, and Team Dresch, whose founder Donna Dresch also created the fanzine *Chainsaw*, which she spun off into a still-active record label.

Alternative music also supported a revival of singer-songwriters, many of them women. Even as artists such as Tracy Chapman, Suzanne Vega, k.d. lang, and Alanis Morrissette garnered major label contracts and the occasional Grammy award (Tracy Chapman's **"Give Me One Reason"** won a Grammy in 1996 for Best Rock Song), other singer-songwriters such as Patty Larkin, Dar Williams, and Ani DiFranco also toured and recorded extensively.

That the music of women within the alternative movement would take these two directions should not be surprising, because they have their roots in the two seventies styles most open to women. Patti Smith was a punk pioneer, and musicians like Talking Heads bassist Tina Weymouth made women instrumentalists less exceptional—Kim Gordon, the bassist with Sonic Youth, followed in her footsteps. Similarly, singer-songwriters like Joni Mitchell and Carly Simon brought a feminine perspective to the forefront of popular music; the music of contemporary artists such as Ani DiFranco continues that tradition.

16-8a Ani DiFranco

Although her music has evolved away from what she calls the "folk punk" of her early recordings, Ani DiFranco (b. 1970) embodies the entrepreneurial spirit of alternative music as fully as any artist. She started her own record company, Righteous Babe Records, in 1989 and put out her first album the following year.

riot grrrl A 90s militant feminist movement which supported post-punk bands.

queercore A movement which reacted against mainstream gay and lesbian views and musically centered around punk and industrial rock.

While in college at New York City's New School, she began touring actively, performing in small clubs and other venues where she built up a loyal following. As she and her label grew more successful (it now offers all of her recordings, plus recordings by twelve other acts), she established the Righteous Babe Foundation, to give support to causes in which she believes, including queer visibility, opposition to the death penalty, and historic preservation. (The new headquarters of Righteous Babe is a formerly abandoned church in Buffalo.)

Like Joni Mitchell, whose music has reflected a similarly wide-ranging curiosity and a from-the-heart perspective, DiFranco's music has ranged from contemporary takes on the urban folk style to collaborations with major artists such as Prince, Janis Ian, Maceo Parker, and the Buffalo Philharmonic Orchestra. The three constants have been incisive lyrics, which usually speak either to social and political issues dear to her heart or the current take on her personal life; her affecting voice; and her fluent and imaginative acoustic guitar playing. We hear her mordant view on a failed relationship in **"32 Flavors,"** a track from her 1995 album *Not a Pretty Girl*.

"32 Flavors" is the product of just two musicians: DiFranco and percussionist Andy Stochansky, a longtime collaborator. Together, they update the work of the great singer-songwriters of the early seventies. DiFranco's guitar accompaniment, which remains consistent throughout the song, is more elaborate and melodic than the accompaniments typically heard in the folk and folk-inspired music of the sixties and seventies. Guitar(s)—DiFranco added a discreet bass guitar part— and percussion provide a buoyant cushion for DiFranco's scathing indictment of a former partner. Lines like "cuz some day you are going to get hungry/and eat most of the words you just said" cut like a scalpel because they are funny and true. DiFranco's warm, low-key vocal style in this song resonates with the gentle accompaniment; its understated quality gives the lyrics even more bite, because of the contrast between the message and its delivery. The extended percussion outro is a nice bonus, although not connected thematically to the lyric.

The gently flowing music of Ani DiFranco heard here is some distance stylistically from the punk-inspired sounds that typify alternative music. However, her do-it-yourself approach to all aspects of her career—performing, recording, managing, promoting, and support for other grassroots efforts in causes that are important to her—embodies the spirit of alternative music; so does her high-mindedness. Her enterprise and determination in charting her own career path, unbeholden to authority figures in any branch of the music industry, has been an inspiration to numerous young musicians.

By the time DiFranco released *Not a Pretty Girl*, the charts were filled with a wave of female pop and R&B stars, among them Janet Jackson, Mariah Carey, Toni Braxton, and Celine Dion. Their music was part of a new post-1980 pop. We examine this new pop in the next chapter.

CHAPTER 17

NEW SOUND OF POP IN THE EIGHTIES

Learning Objectives:

1) List the three developments in the eighties music industry that directly influenced the pop music genre.

2) Describe Michael Jackson's unique music style.

3) Articulate how the pairing of video and music contributed to the success of Madonna.

4) Contrast sixties black pop to the "mature" eighties style.

5) Extrapolate how the theme of "love" permeated pop music through the latter half of the twentieth century.

6) Summarize the six qualities that distinguish eighties pop music from the earlier decade.

Chapter Introduction

Perhaps it's karma. Coincidence or not, it is certainly intriguing that two of the biggest pop acts of Ronald Reagan's presidency were Michael Jackson and Madonna. In an era of political and social conservatism, both Michael Jackson and Madonna presented complex, provocative, and at times confusing images of race and gender. Michael Jackson's gradual metamorphosis to paleness, questions about his sexual and generational preferences, and his erratic behavior were tabloid fodder for over two decades. Madonna broke down barriers on stage, in the media, and behind the scenes. People noticed what she did and what she thought; both were often controversial. More tellingly, she was the first female pop star to chart her own career path. Madonna quickly ascended to one-name celebrity status. Michael Jackson might well have if it weren't for basketball's Michael J.

Both were extraordinarily visible; what people can see has been very much part of their success. Michael Jackson broke through first. He appeared as the scarecrow in the 1978 film *The Wiz*, a black take on *The Wizard of Oz*. There he met Quincy Jones, who was instrumental in shaping his career. He made his mark in a series of landmark music videos, which displayed the full range of his talents. By the time he broke through MTV's color barrier, Madonna's career was well underway; she would star in music videos, films (such as the 1985 *Desperately Seeking Susan*), and stage musicals. Both Michael Jackson and Madonna capitalized on a newly emerging genre (the music video) that became a staple on a new network (MTV) in a still-emerging new medium (cable television).

Experience an interactive version of this era in MINDTAP

17-1 The Transformation of Pop

The most obvious, and most widely discussed, consequence of MTV's new-found importance as an outlet for music videos was the suddenly increased emphasis on the look of an act, and the look of the video, as a determinant of success. However, its impact went beyond that, especially in the work of Michael Jackson and Madonna, the two stars who defined music video in the eighties. Jackson is a sensational, innovative dancer, and Madonna began her career as a dancer. Both were in touch with the new dance music; Madonna started her career in the New York club scene. **Off the Wall** (1979), Michael Jackson's first big post-*Wiz* success, drew on disco, and much of his eighties music had a punk/funk/disco-derived edge. With both of them, movement became an expressive third element in the music video, joining words and music.

The new sound of pop that emerged in the eighties was the confluence of three developments: the emergence of MTV and music videos; the more active rhythms and richer, synth-driven textures of dance music; and the return of the all-around performer, whose skill as a dancer more than matched his or her vocal ability. (Michael Jackson's most illustrious predecessor would be Fred Astaire.) The result was a new kind of pop, where much of the momentum in the song shifted from the melody to the dance-track rhythms. At the same time, dancer–singers like Michael Jackson and Madonna put on exhilarating displays. The songs were still tuneful, but they left room for plenty of movement.

In the last years of the twentieth century, the pop singer who simply stood in front of a microphone and sang a tuneful melody was the exception, not the rule, especially at the top of the pop charts. Vigorous movement was in, from groups like the Backstreet Boys and 'N Sync or solo acts like Mariah Carey, Britney Spears, Christine Aguilera, and Mary J. Blige. The music matches the movement. Much of it draws on the sixteen-beat rhythms also heard in dance music and rap. An overlay of tuneful melody and pleasant voices cannot obscure the fact that the major new pop acts of the eighties took rock-era pop music in a new, visually exciting direction.

17-2 Michael Jackson and Madonna: Redefining Pop in the Eighties

Both Michael Jackson and Madonna integrated image and movement into their performing persona to an unprecedented degree. For Jackson, song and dance were complementary components of the same conception. In his videos, we experience them as a unified expressive gesture, even though we are well aware that he lip-syncs the vocal. For Madonna, song and dance were components of the mini-dramas that she compressed onto video and disc.

17-2a Michael Jackson

Although only 24 when *Thriller* (1982) was released, Michael Jackson (1958–2009) had been a professional entertainer for three-fourths of his life and a star for half of it. He had released solo singles in the early seventies, but Jackson's solo career didn't take off until 1978, when he starred in the film *The Wiz*. During the filming, he met composer/ arranger/producer Quincy Jones, who collaborated with him on *Off the Wall* (1979), his first major album, and *Thriller*. Jones's skill and creativity proved to be the ideal complement to Jackson's abilities.

There are precedents for Michael Jackson's exuberant dancing in rock-era music: for example, Elvis's stage and film performances; the stylized choreography of the Motown groups, including the Jackson 5; James Brown's stage shows, which featured "the hardest working man in show business" moving and grooving all over the stage; and the dance scenes in such films as *Saturday Night Fever*. However, it was the musical that offered a more direct precedent for the integration of song, dance, and story. This connection is evident in the video of "**Thriller**." The group dance scene recalls the marvelous dance scene to the song "Cool" in the film version of Leonard Bernstein's landmark musical *West Side Story*.

As with so many other rock artists, Michael Jackson was fortunate to be in the right place at the right time. MTV had gone on the air in 1981; *Thriller* was released a year later. Jackson helped transform the music video from a song-with-video into a mini-film that used a song as the focal point: for example, the video of *"Thriller"* is over twice the length of the track on the album. Jackson made it work through his dancing: no earlier rock-era performer had danced with his virtuosity and expressiveness.

The title track to *Thriller* shows the musical side of these changes. It is a long song by pop standards, in part because of the long build-up at the beginning and the voice-over at the end by Vincent Price, one of Hollywood's masters of the macabre. But the heart of the song is a Disney-esque version of scary: Michael's voice, the skillful orchestration, the security of the four-on-the-floor bass drum and heavy backbeat, and the busy rhythms all ensure a cartoonish kind of spooky music more reminiscent of *Scooby Doo* than *Friday the 13th*. The video reinforces this as each of the nightmarish scenes dissolves into fiction. This is not to say that it wasn't well done, or deserving of its enormous popularity. But compared to the Black Sabbath version of a scary night, this one is safe—at least until the music drops out and Price has his last laugh—or Jackson's cat eyes return.

Thriller also reveals several distinctive characteristics of post-1980 pop. One is the extensive use of electronic instruments in combination with conventional instruments. Among the most prominent electronic sounds are the repeated bass riff, the sustained harmonies behind Michael's vocals, and the brash chords of the opening: all are played on synthesizers. The basic rhythm grows out of disco: we hear a strong backbeat, a relentless bass-drum thump on each beat, and several layers of percussion marking off a sixteen-beat rhythm. However, the other instrumental parts, especially those played on rhythm section instruments or their electronic counterparts, create a texture that is denser and more complex than that usually heard in a conventional disco song. (This is certainly appropriate, since the dancing of Jackson and his cohorts is more expressive and complex than social dancing to disco.) Jackson's vocal line is simply one strand in the texture. In the verse, it is in the forefront, but in the chorus sections the backup vocals and instruments playing the title-phrase riff all but drown him out. It floats on the busy rhythms and riffs that provide much of the song's momentum—indeed, in the video, the basic rhythm track sustains the flow through the graveyard scene, and, after a short break, through the first part of the extended dance number that is the heart of the video.

Although only three of the tracks were shot as music videos, all of the songs on *Thriller* have a distinct identity. There is considerable contrast from song to song, as the musical settings capture the tone and content of the lyric. For example, the hard-edged riffs that open "**Wanna Be Startin'** Somethin'" anticipate the lyric's school-yard-style provocation. The punk-inspired beat and Eddie Van Halen's guitar underscore the message of "**Beat It.**" The loping rhythm (a shuffle beat on top of a rock beat), the use of pre-rock pop harmony, and the soft synth sounds reinforce the friendly rivalry between Michael and Paul McCartney in **"The Girl Is Mine."** And a setting that mixes an open middle range—just a simple synthesizer riff—with the irritation of a persistent bass riff and percussion sound characterizes the emptiness of the groupie-style relationships in **"Billie Jean."** Both the songs and Quincy Jones's masterful settings give the album an expressive range that compensates for the one-dimensional quality of Jackson's singing.

There is no doubt that *Thriller* would have been a successful album without the videos. But it also seems certain that the videos, and the fact that the songs were so "video-ready," played a crucial role in its overwhelming success. *Thriller* was the crowning achievement of Jackson's career; nothing before or afterward matched its success.

17–2b Madonna

In Renaissance-era Italian, *madonna* was originally a variant of *mia donna*, or "my lady." The term eventually came to refer more specifically to Mary, the mother of Jesus: for example, the phrase "Madonna and Child" identifies those works of art that depict Mary with the infant Jesus. In the eighties, "Madonna" acquired an even more concrete image: the pop star whose given name soon was enough to identify her to the world at large.

Madonna (born Madonna Ciccone, 1958) was born the same year as Michael Jackson. In 1978, while Jackson was starring in *The Wiz*, Madonna moved to New York to further her career as a dancer. She soon became active in the club scene, while she struggled to pay the rent. Her star rose quickly. Her first records, released in the early eighties, gained her a following mainly among clubbers. Although these songs didn't cross over, they created enough of a buzz that she received a contract to record her first album, *Madonna*, which was released in 1983.

In 1984, she took one of the many bold steps that have characterized her career, releasing the video of **"Like a Virgin."** Shot in Venice, Italy, the video rapidly juxtaposes images of Madonna in a white wedding dress with her in street clothes and a provocative evening dress—attire that suggests she is anything but a virgin. The video established a formula that would set the tone for her subsequent work: combine provocative, shocking, and controversial themes and images with bright, accessible music.

Among her most controversial projects of the eighties was the video **"Like a Prayer"**; the song was the title track from her 1989 album of the same name. The video conflates religious images (e.g., a scene in which she grasps a knife, and it cuts her in a way that evokes the stigmata of the crucified Christ); symbols of racism (burning crosses); numerous incongruities and impossibilities (a black gospel choir in a Catholic chapel; the statue of a black saint who comes to life, then doubles as the black man wrongly accused of murdering a woman); and the one constant: Madonna in a revealing dress. All of this outraged numerous religious groups, who threatened to boycott Pepsi, which had recruited Madonna as a spokesperson. The controversy served as free publicity: the album topped the charts.

The video of "Like a Prayer" dramatically evidences the emergence of the music video as an entity distinct from the song that spawned it, and from other expressive forms that merge song, image, and movement. The messages of the song—among them, racism is wrong, we are all brothers and sisters in Christ, and Madonna is sexy—come through mainly in the rapid-fire series of images/scenes/song fragments. There is little sense of continuity in the narrative, visually or in the lyric, and there are long stretches where Madonna makes no attempt to sing in the video, even as we hear her voice in the song. This shows the rapid evolution of the music video, not only in Madonna's own work but also in the medium overall. It has moved well beyond simply capturing a live performance, as was the case in "**Everybody**," her first video; at this point of her career and in the brief history of the medium, such videos seem a distant memory.

Musically, Madonna's winning formula has been to combine a simple, catchy melody with trendy sounds and rhythms and skillful production. The melody of "Like a Prayer" flows in gently undulating phrases, with little or no syncopation. When isolated from its setting, the melody bears a closer resemblance to a children's song or a folk melody than to a dance-inspired song from the eighties. And like a folk melody, it is easily absorbed and remembered. The support for this melody oscillates between sustained chords sung by a choir and played on an organ and a Caribbean-flavored background that bears a striking resemblance to Steve Winwood's 1986 No. 1 hit "**Higher Love**." As with much post-1980 pop, the active accompaniment is dense, rhythmically active, and rich in both electronic and conventional instrumental sounds. The steady flow of Madonna's melody allows her to alternate between the dance-like sections and those sections with only sustained harmonies and extremely light percussion sounds.

"Like A Prayer" breaks no new ground musically, but it does merge disparate and seemingly contradictory musical features into an effective song, just as the video does.

Artistically, Madonna has not been an innovator. The most ground-breaking aspect of Madonna's career has been her ascension to a position of complete control of her career: writing her songs, producing her recordings, choreographing her performances, and making the key decisions about every aspect of its production and promotion. This owes more to her ambition, business acumen, and chutzpah than it does to her talent. In achieving elite celebrity status (single-name recognition, constant tabloid fodder) as she directed her career, she has become a role model for a new generation of women performers.

Many have found her public persona liberating. Without question, her success added a new dimension to sexual equality within the pop music business: women, or at least women like her, no longer had to be front persons for men. Cynical observers have dismissed the provocative images that she presents, such as those encountered in the "Like a Prayer" video, as attention-getting stunts whose shock value obscures a lack of talent and imagination. It is true that Madonna is not spectacularly creative in any artistic dimension of the music business: she is neither equal to Michael Jackson as a dancer nor equal to Tina Turner as a vocalist. However, to dismiss her talents out of hand would be to ignore the sense of conviction with which Madonna presents these controversial juxtapositions, and to dismiss their role in challenging value systems that have grown rigid over time.

17-3 The Maturation of Black Pop

The more traditional black pop, the one that charted the ups and downs of romantic love, got a makeover in the eighties. A new generation of singers— among them Lionel Richie, Natalie Cole (daughter of the great Nat Cole), Whitney Houston, and Luther Vandross—were among the brightest stars of the eighties and nineties. Top acts from the past continued to make great music: Tina Turner, Marvin Gaye (until his untimely death in 1984), Aretha Franklin, Stevie Wonder, and Diana Ross stand out.

Tina Turner was 44 in 1984, when she scored her first No. 1 hit as a solo act with **"What's Love Got to Do with It."** At 44, she was the most senior of the prominent black pop singers, but most of the others were not far behind. Among the singers mentioned earlier, only Whitney Houston was not yet 30 in 1984. By contrast, the Shirelles were still in their teens when they first hit the charts, and Diana Ross had just turned twenty when the Supremes' **"Where Did Our Love Go"** reached No. 1 on the pop charts.

Not surprisingly, these artists sang about love in a more mature and real way than the black pop artists from the sixties usually did. They and their audience had grown up in the intervening years; in most cases, the tone of the lyrics connected more directly to the mature black romantic music of the early seventies, most notably the music of Roberta Flack and Bill Withers, than it did to the bright-eyed, more innocent lyrics of sixties black pop.

The music is comparably more mature. In the songs of the early sixties girl groups and early Motown recordings, there is a sense of discovery; the occasional rough edges in conception and production evidence that it is hard to get everything right when you're inventing a dramatically new style and sound. By contrast, the black pop of the eighties is exquisitely produced, not only because of the improved technology but also because of the improved skill of the recording engineers and producers. And like the pop of Michael Jackson and others, the songs make use of the new rhythms and synthesized sounds of the late seventies and eighties.

However, these are songs about love—or more accurately, about the problems of relationships—and the singers deliver them in a manner that makes the lyrics credible. For example, in the video of "What's Love Got to Do with It," Tina Turner alternates between simply standing and singing and walking. Her walk is stylish and in the rhythm of the song, but it is light-years away from the elaborate dance numbers seen in "Thriller." And the song is not in the service of a larger message that is evident only when the video is viewed. Here, the video simply presents an enhanced version of the song; the song is the defining element.

17-4 Musical Features of the New Black Pop

The sound of the eighties black pop resulted mainly from two significant changes: the use of synthesized sounds to replace most, if not all, of the traditional instruments, and more adventurous rhythms. The sumptuous backgrounds that were so much a part of the sound of later doo-wop, Motown, Philadelphia, and Barry White are parts of this updated black pop sound. The difference is that producers use electronic analogs to the strings, horns, and even rhythm instruments. Their function is much the same, but the sounds are new. This fresh sound palette gives the music a more contemporary flavor.

The other major change had to do with rhythm. By the beginning of the eighties, sixteen-beat rhythms were the norm throughout rock-era music, and especially black music: we hear these more active rhythms in all of the songs discussed in this and the previous chapters and in much of the music in the subsequent chapters. At comparable tempos, sixteen-beat rhythms offer many more opportunities for rhythmic play than rock rhythm, simply because there are so many more combinations of sound and silence. When applied to a Motown-style conception of rhythmic texture, the results are liberating.

Recall that one of the distinctive features of Motown songs was subtle timekeeping, except for a strong backbeat. Generally, only the drummer (and conga player, if present) kept the rock rhythm; no instrument marked the beat. In the black pop of the eighties, timekeeping became not only more active, but also often more implicit. Any regular timekeeping was generally in the background, and at times it was dispensed with altogether. The dominant rhythms moved either much slower (for instance, sustained chords) or faster than the beat; the faster rhythms typically played against the beat, with irregular patterns or syncopations.

In this connection, it is worth noting the impact of reggae on this new kind of rhythmic freedom. Recall that the black pop and R&B of the late fifties and early sixties was a major influence on Jamaican music in the sixties, which developed into reggae by the end of the decade. The characteristic sound of reggae comes largely from the off-beat rhythms in the middle of the texture and the free bass line underneath. In the late seventies and eighties, both black and white acts wove reggae rhythms into other styles. Its impact on black music can be heard in such songs as Marvin Gaye's **"Sexual Healing"** (1982) and Tina Turner's "What's Love Got to Do with It" (1984). With this development, the exchange between black pop and Jamaican music has come full circle, much as Ray Charles's fusion of gospel and blues closed the connection begun by Thomas A. Dorsey/Georgia Tom. We hear the influence of reggae in "What's Love Got to Do with It."

17–4a Tina Turner

If anyone was entitled to be cynical about love, it would be Tina Turner (born Annie Mae Bullock, 1939). In 1956, as a young woman still in her teens, she connected with Ike Turner, eight years her senior and already a music business veteran. (Recall that he was the musician behind the seminal **"Rocket 88,"** which came out under Jackie Brenston's name in 1951.) The connection soon became personal as well as professional: they married in 1962, and for more than a decade, they prospered professionally as the Ike and Tina Turner **Revue**; they had a huge hit in 1971 with a cover of CCR's **"Proud Mary."**

However, for much of their relationship, Ike abused Tina emotionally and physically. The abuse grew worse as their career declined; Ike's alleged drug use and almost paranoid distrust of outside management was a main factor in their career decline. Their professional relationship complicated any personal breakup. When she finally broke free of Turner—in the middle of a tour—she also broke contractual obligations. Because of this, the divorce settlement devastated her financially; she retained only her name.

It took Tina the better part of a decade to get her solo career on track. Her break came in 1983, when she covered Al Green's **"Let's Stay Together"** for B.E.F. (British Electric Foundation), the production side of a synth-pop group doing some serious soul searching. (B.E.F. would eventually record with not only Turner but also with Chaka Khan, Mavis Staples, and other major black artists.) The next year saw the release of *Private Dancer*, an album that included "What's Love Got to Do with It" among its three charting singles. The song would win three Grammys the following year.

Turner's song and her singing are in tune with each other. Both project an embittered view of love: any excitement found in the physical aspects of a relationship is tempered by the foreknowledge that the relationship will never mature into love. She sings from the heart: close to two decades of pain spill out in her soulful singing.

The song uses the verse/chorus template as a point of departure: the verse builds inexorably to a magnetic hook, which Turner's gritty voice invests with deep feeling. By contrast, the musical setting is muted—almost arid. Synthesizer sounds

Revue A type of stage entertainment popular in the first third of the century. Revues were topical; they often lampooned prominent public figures. They had a flimsy plot, designed to link—however loosely—a series of songs, dance numbers, and comedy routines.

are prominent: sustained synthesizer chords and obbligatos. The rhythm shows the influence of reggae in the persistent rebound pattern on the off-beat, the open texture, and a free-roaming bass in the chorus. The accompaniment never matches the intensity of Turner's singing; it is almost as if the accompaniment is indifferent to her pain. This has the effect of casting Turner's pain into relief: in the song, she grieves alone.

Turner's song blends the urgency of soul singing with an accompaniment that connects directly back to Motown. The next example surrounds one of the great black pop voices of the late twentieth century in a rich, and synth-rich, setting.

17–4b Luther Vandross

Like so many black pop singers, Luther Vandross (1951–2005) grew up singing gospel. He began his career largely out of the limelight, composing jingles and doing session work as a backup singer for numerous top acts. A guest appearance on an album by Change, *The Glow of Love* (1980), led to a recording contract and a jumpstart to a solo career. By the middle of the decade, he had become one of the most prominent of the new generation of black pop singers.

"**Don't Want to Be a Fool**," a track from his successful 1991 album, *Power of Love*, continues the evolution of the black pop style that began with Motown and continued through the seventies. The song updates form, rhythm, and sound, while retaining its most timeless elements: lyrics about love, set to an appealing melody and sung by a singer with a rich, pleasing voice.

"Don't Want to Be a Fool" is a more expansive version of a classic Motown song form: a verse/chorus format where the first part of the chorus builds to the hook, plus an intense bridge that replaces the final verse. There are no real surprises in the form, except perhaps that the form itself continues to be viable after over twenty-five years. However, it unfolds more slowly than typical Motown songs: once through the form takes over four minutes.

The rhythmic texture of "Don't Want to Be a Fool" has its roots in the black pop of the sixties but also evidences the greater rhythmic complexity of post-1980 music. There is a strong backbeat and a discreet rock beat most of the time. Other rhythms, mostly at sixteen-beat speed, dance over this basic backdrop; in particular, the bass line is free and highly syncopated.

The introduction and the first phrase of the verse have almost no timekeeping from percussion instruments; we hear mainly electronic keyboards and Luther's voice. Things get busier as the song builds to the refrain. By the refrain, the fast rhythm is present but spread out among several different percussion sounds. The bass line moves occasionally in these quicker rhythms, but there is never a time when the sixteen-beat rhythm is hammered out, as it so often is in rap and dance music. Indeed, the heart of the song—Luther's vocal, the background vocals, the background instrumental harmony and melodic riffs—are in the eight-beat rhythm of a rock song for most of the song.

This combination of the two rhythmic levels—eight- and sixteen-beat rhythms—plus the more implicit approach to timekeeping seem to match the mood of the song better than the more explicit, active rhythms of dance music. It would be harder to focus on the words and the story they're telling if they had to compete with insistent dance rhythms.

We can hear this rhythmic texture as a more sophisticated continuation of the rhythms heard in the black pop of the sixties and seventies. Recall that one of Motown's innovations was a more implicit approach to rock and shuffle rhythms: the bass was strong, but free, while the midrange timekeeping was very much in the background: the song still had a great beat, but rhythm did not overpower the melody and rich accompaniment. The rhythms heard in "Don't Want to Be a Fool" take this innovation several steps beyond. Such a sound was possible only in the eighties, after the textural possibilities of the new sixteen-beat rhythms had been thoroughly assimilated.

"Don't Want to Be a Fool" also updates the sound world of rock-era black pop. A classic Motown song had a full orchestra behind the singer(s): rhythm section, horns, and strings. Vandross and bassist Marcus Miller (b. 1959), who collaborated with Vandross on this song, not only create electronic counterparts to most of the conventional instrumental sounds (such as the sustained chords that sound like strings, the shaker-like percussion sounds in the background), but also add an array of new timbres (e.g., bell-like timbres). They provide evidence of the way in which electronic sound generation and sampling have enriched the sound world of contemporary popular music.

17–4c The Persistence of Love

Songs such as "What's Love Got to Do with It" and "Don't Want to Be a Fool" continue black pop's romance with romance. It dates back to the very beginnings of the rock era, with the first doo-wop songs from the late forties. The constants that have informed this music throughout its history have been not only the focus on love, but also on gospel-tinged vocalists singing tuneful melodies with rich accompaniments that featured harmonies typically found in pre-rock pop.

Among the reasons for this continuity is the strong connection with gospel music: so many of the black pop stars came out of the gospel tradition. The correspondences in the message of the words and the musical means to support it continued through the seventies. In fact, gospel acts occasionally crossed over to the pop charts in the years around 1970: **"Oh Happy Day"** was a surprise No. 4 hit for the Edwin Hawkins Singers in 1969, and the Staples Singers' **"I'll Take You There"** topped the charts in 1972.

Another reason might have been the relative novelty in black music of connecting not only the song but also the singer to romance. Ever since Bing Crosby began to croon into a microphone, audiences, or at least those of the opposite sex, personified their relationship with the singer: they could imagine Crosby and other crooners singing to them alone, and meaning it. Frank Sinatra would soon become the first pop-singing heartthrob; thousands of adoring fans swooned during his performances, much as they would for Elvis fifteen years later. Sinatra, Crosby, and several other singers parlayed their pop success into film careers; even Fred Astaire, in appearance an extremely unlikely leading man, succeeded in winning the affection of Ginger Rogers, at least on the screen.

By contrast, Ethel Waters, the top black pop singer, could sing "my man and I ain't together" (from Harold Arlen's bluesy standard **"Stormy Weather"**) to Cotton Club audiences and on disc, but her most significant film role before 1950 came as Petunia (!) in the 1943 all-black film *Cabin in the Sky*. In it, she sings another great pop standard, **"Taking a Chance on Love,"** to Eddie Anderson, who would later become famous as Jack Benny's servant Rochester. She is dressed dowdily, and simply rolls her eyes back and forth as she sings. The song and the singing are great, the message is romantic, but their interaction is anything but romantic. Indeed, the scene reminds contemporary viewers that minstrelsy was not ancient history in 1943; Hollywood would not portray blacks romantically. In the late forties and fifties, Nat Cole thrilled black and white audiences with beautiful love songs like **"Unforgettable."** but his appeal was limited to his voice, at least among white audiences.

The personification of romantic song in popular music began to transcend race in the sixties, as we noted in Chapter 5. This wholesale shift in attitude was evident by the time Tina Turner recorded "What's Love Got to Do with It." Turner's sex appeal was certainly not delimited by her ethnicity in North America, and even more in Europe, where she has had an ardent fan base (and where she currently resides): her video won MTV's Best Female Video Award in 1985.

As the century came to its end, race and ethnic heritage became virtually a nonissue in romantic music. A big reason was the overwhelming success of Whitney Houston.

17–4d From Black Pop to Pop: The Rise of Whitney Houston

If there was ever anyone destined for pop stardom, it was Whitney Houston (1963–2012). She had the complete package: she was beautiful and had a beautiful voice, and she projected a sunny personality. Her mother is a fine gospel singer who sang backup for Aretha Franklin and others; her cousin is Dionne Warwick, Burt Bacharach's voice for several hits during the sixties. Like many black stars, she grew up singing in church, and also occasionally joined her mother on stage. A performance with her mother at Carnegie Hall led to work as a model. Her first record contract, which she signed in 1983, was with a top label: Arista. She released her first album, entitled *Whitney Houston*, two years later. It went platinum within six months and has sold over 13,000,000 copies in the United States alone; three singles from the album reached the top of the charts. For her next album, released in 1987, she dropped her last name from the title; it's entitled simply *Whitney*. Among the tracks on the album was the enormously successful **"I Wanna Dance With Somebody (Who Loves Me)**," which reached No. 1 in 1987 and was certified platinum two years later.

The track highlights both the connection of eighties pop to Motown and how and in what ways this new pop gave the Motown sound a makeover. The connection is clear in the upbeat, romantic tone of the lyrics, the general outlines of the form, the use of familiar chord progressions, and the overall balance among sound, melody, and rhythm. However, all elements, and especially sound and rhythm, have been reworked to reflect the new, more active rhythms of the late seventies and eighties and the novel sound possibilities of synthesizers and drum machines.

The lyric seems to have been written with the video in mind. There's nothing particularly deep about it, and we are reminded for the last minute and a half that Whitney does just want to dance. In that respect, she's in step with Michael, Madonna, and others.

The harmony revisits the familiar chords that continued from pre-rock pop through Motown and other black pop. This is clear in the chorus of the song, which features the "Heart And Soul" chords so familiar in doo-wop in a distinctive rhythm. The vocal melody builds nicely from the darker, low range verse to the climactic title phrase, and—true to Motown practice—memorable riffs are heard in the accompanying instrumental parts. The form follows the familiar verse/bridge/chorus widely used in Motown (and elsewhere!), but a long introduction, interlude, and outro almost double the length of the track from what the heart of the song would otherwise dictate.

The instrumental sounds in the recording are almost entirely generated by synthesizers: counterparts to conventional drums, percussion instruments, bass, guitar, and horns. The functions of these groups of sounds is similar to earlier black pop, but the results are strikingly different. Much of the difference has to do with the timbres generated by the synthesizers. Two groups of sounds stand out in this regard. One is the array of percussion timbres, from the deep reverberant sound on the backbeat (the signature percussion sound of so much rock and pop from the eighties) to the simulated clapping sounds, shakers, and more. The interplay among these various timbres helps highlight the intricate rhythmic interplay (discussed directly below).

The track begins with just percussion sounds. The first pitched instrument to enter is the synth bass, offering a riff that's repeated again and again. The next instrumental sound is a high-register harmonized riff that evokes the sound of a trumpet section. The low-high halo around Houston's voice continues the Motown practice of surrounding midrange voices with a strong bass and mid- and high-range riffs and sustained chords to keep the focus squarely on the singers. Nineteen-eightees pop extends this practice by placing this prominent background riff in a register well above the range in which Houston sings most of the song. For conventional trumpets, the riff is at the top of the range of the instrument, and hard to play brilliantly without overpowering the voice. However, the timbre of the synth analog is brilliant enough to stand out and project a bright mood, but still subordinate to the voice. In this track, we can hear how new technology enables an updated sound.

The rhythm is similarly updated through an inventive, technology-driven approach to sixteen-beat rhythm heard in so much eighties and nineties pop. If we compare eight- and sixteen-beat rhythmic templates, we immediately see and hear that a sixteen-beat rhythm is twice as active as an eight-beat, heard in relation to the beat and backbeat. However, the number of possible sounds (percussion or pitched instruments) per beat quadruples. An eight-beat rhythm offers four possible sounds per beat: none, one on either half of the beat, and sounds on both halves. By contrast, a sixteen-beat rhythm offers sixteen different combinations, from none to four.

In the extended introduction to "I Wanna Dance With Somebody (Who Loves Me), the only regular rhythms are the backbeat and a faint shaker-like sound at sixteen-beat speed. The rhythms of the other parts are irregular; no one strand of percussion or marks the beat. The almost random patterns from several parts align with the template, but we feel the beat only by implication. This kind of intricate interaction would be challenging even for good musicians in real time; programming these interactions makes the end result foolproof. This kind of interaction, which is heard in all of tracks discussed in this chapter to some degree, in other chapters as well (e.g., Prince's **"Sign 'O' The Times"**), and in its most extreme form in this song, is the rhythmic opposite of U2's **"Where The Streets Have No Name**." There, the band relentlessly reinforces three layers of the template. In eighties pop of this kind, the shift to a more active rhythm and the incorporation of technology to realize more complex patterns opens up new and engaging rhythms. From this point, it was only a short step to abandoning rhythms that outlined the template, as we will hear in much more recent music.

The new sounds and rhythms of eighties pop give this music an undeniably contemporary sound. We can best understand this more contemporary approach to pop in the music of top stars like Michael Jackson, Madonna, and Whitney Houston as an extension of the Motown conception of a black popular style that effectively transcends race to a great extent.

17–5 The Legacy of Motown

The early eighties ushered in a new generation of pop stars. In many respects, their music was dramatically different from the music of the previous decade. Six qualities distinguish it:

- *It made gender, race, and sexual preference a nonfactor in commercial success.* During the eighties, its leading acts were Michael Jackson, Madonna, and

Whitney Houston. None of them are heterosexual, white males. Other successful performers during that decade included Boy George, Cyndi Lauper, and Tina Turner.

- *It exploited new media resources.* Michael Jackson was not the first to make music videos, but he raised the music video to an art form. Video and film were essential in boosting both Madonna and Whitney Houston to superstardom; the three set the tone for the pop music videos of the next decades.

- *It brought back the multifaceted entertainer.* It was no longer enough to be just a good singer or musician; one had to be able to move well, although no one topped Michael Jackson in skill or imagination. Conversely, those who could present themselves well, dance expressively, and use the music video as a new meaningful medium (think Madonna) could achieve stardom with more limited vocal ability.

- *It was a musical melting pot.* Although the new pop of the eighties and beyond connects most directly to the black pop tradition of the sixties and seventies, the music was certainly open to other influences: disco, punk, reggae, funk, Latin music, and, more recently, dance music and rap.

- *Synthesizers played an increasingly important role in the sound of the music.* Some replaced guitars, basses, and conventional keyboards as the main sources of harmony; synthesized percussion sounds enriched, or even replaced, drum kits and other acoustic instruments; and sustained synth sounds put a lot of string players out of work.

- *It has been extraordinarily popular.* Michael Jackson's *Thriller* album easily surpassed the sales of the previous best-selling album. He, Madonna, and Whitney rank among the Top 20 in all time US album sales. As rock critic Robert Christgau pointed out, the sheer volume of sales was part of its significance.

Precisely because its artists drew from so many sources, there has been no single "middle-ground" style of pop in the eighties. It has not been defined by a distinctive kind of beat-keeping, like punk; or a rhythmic feel, like funk; or a special sound quality, like the distortion of heavy metal.

Instead, it was a set of principles that defined the music that topped the charts during the eighties. The songs typically have intelligible lyrics that tell a story—usually about love or its absence or about a slice of life. They are set to a "singable" melody. The melody in turn is imbedded in a rich, riff-laden texture; most layers—if not all—are played on synthesizers. The songs typically have a good beat—easy to find and danceable, neither too monotonous nor too ambiguous.

This set of principles is, more than anything else, an updated version of the Motown sound. The lyrics are more worldly, the rhythms are more complex and usually based on the more active sixteen-beat rhythms, and synthesizers replace many of the conventional instruments. Novel elements, most notably rap, give this more recent music a different sound. Still, the basic approach is clearly the same.

The Motown middle ground connection extends beyond the music. The elaborate movement and dance made possible by the music video production process upgrade the choreography of the Motown acts, and Motown's pyramid-like creative structure evolved into the elaborate production of post-eighties pop.

Michael Jackson is the direct link between the two traditions: as a member of the Jackson 5, he was part of the last great act in Motown's heyday. As a solo performer in the late seventies and early eighties, he helped define the new pop middle ground musically, revive the all-round performer, and establish the music video as a new, integrated mode of expression. Moreover, his dancing raised the bar to a virtually unattainable height. His growth as an artist parallels the evolution and transformation of the Motown paradigm into the new pop of the eighties.

Berry Gordy's vision was a black pop style whose appeal transcended the black community. One branch of its legacy was the post-eighties pop middle ground marked out by Michael Jackson, which continues to flourish in the music of women and men of many races and ethnic heritages. Motown was not a force for social change during the sixties drive for civil rights; however, the fact of Motown—the enduring appeal and popularity of the music—has helped bring us to a musical world where the boundaries between black and white—and Hispanic—are all but invisible, and inaudible. This is in turn both cause and consequence of more open attitudes with regard to race and gender, not only in music but in society.

This openness, which we take for granted in the twenty-first century, was unthinkable in the middle of the previous century. Nat Cole was the first black performer to host a network television show. It would air for only thirteen months, from November 1956 to December 1957, because NBC could not convince potential sponsors to advertise their products on a show headlined by a black man. Today, blacks and Hispanics not only attract sponsors but also help sell their products. This stream of rock-era music, from Motown through the eighties and then the divas of the nineties and beyond, has helped bring us to this far more open society.

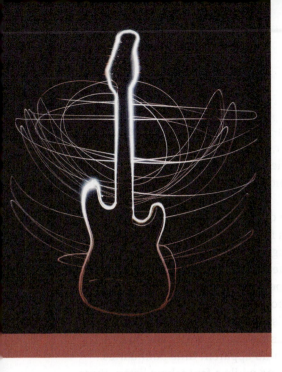

CHAPTER 18

ELECTRONICA AND RAP

Learning Objectives:

1) List the musical styles associated with **electronica**.

2) Articulate the reasoning behind *musique concrète* (concrete music).

3) Define the musical terms: **house** music, **techno**, and **rave**.

4) Describe the relationship between a recording, a **mix,** and a **set**.

5) Discuss Richard James's contributions to **ambient electronica**.

6) Determine key themes addressed in **rap** music.

Chapter Introduction

The welcome page of Joseph Saddler's website (**www.grandmasterflash.com**) features a video in which Saddler, better known as Grandmaster Flash, explains how DJs from the seventies never put their hands on the grooves of the vinyl discs they played. He goes on to say that he was the first to put his hands on the grooves, which enabled him to develop an array of innovative techniques, including cutting, scratching, back-spinning, and flaring. Soon, he would mark particular spots on a disc with tape or crayon so that he could access a particular spot on the fly. Armed with two turntables, a mixer, and a stack of discs, including doubles of the tracks he planned to use, Flash could transform the playback of a song—to this point as predictable an event as the sun rising in the east—into a unique, spontaneously crafted experience.

In the sense that it became a device with which one could shape musical sound in-the-moment, Flash turned the turntable into a musical instrument. But because the musical sounds involved an extra layer of creativity—the sounds had already been recorded—the turntable was different in kind from more conventional instruments, such as those used in a rock band. Although the use of prerecorded sounds in live performance was not new, Flash's techniques brought a new, richer, and more improvisatory dimension to the experience. They were one sign of a movement that would radically transform cutting-edge rock-era music in the eighties and beyond.

It should be noted that there was a good reason that other DJs handled recordings by the edge: bringing the grooves into contact with anything—fingers, crayons, errant tonearm needles—would damage the disc and eventually render it unplayable. While Grandmaster Flash was perfecting his novel techniques, the digital revolution that would render them all but obsolete was underway.

Digital technology facilitated the creation and development of a radically new esthetic, one that focused on sound and rhythm more than melody. This new esthetic shaped the two most innovative musical styles of the eighties, electronica and rap.

18-1 Electronica

Among the most enduring images in twentieth-century music is the singer with guitar. The image transcends style, race, gender, locale, theme: Blind Lemon Jefferson, Jimmie Rodgers, Gene Autry, Maybelle Carter, Robert Johnson, Woody Guthrie, Bob Dylan, Joan Baez, Joni Mitchell, and countless others—country and city, traditional and topical.

Now imagine a sound that is its complete opposite. There is little or no singing—and what vocals there are have been filtered through an electronic device. There is no melody with accompanying chords; instead there might be wisps of riffs or some sustained notes. Instead of the simple rhythm of the accompaniment, there is the thump of a low percussion sound marking the beat, several fast-moving patterns, plus other electronically generated **loops** Instead of the strumming of an acoustic guitar, there is an array of electronic sounds, complete with special effects (fx). Instead of a story with a beginning and end, there is total immersion in a sound world with no apparent time boundaries. Instead of a single performer singing and playing while a few others listen, there is a DJ in a booth, surveying a dance floor filled with bobbing and weaving bodies as the DJ mixes the music.

> **loops** A short sound file that can be repeated or combined with other loops to create a background for a song.

You will find examples of this totally opposite sound in the dance/electronica section of your favorite record store—on the street, in the mall, or online. Electronica has become the umbrella term for a large and varied family of styles: house, techno, trance, ambient, jungle, drum 'n' bass, industrial dance, and many more.

The almost total contrast between electronica and the folk/blues/country singer underscores how radically different the electronic-based music of the eighties, nineties, and the twenty-first century is from so much earlier music, including much of the music of the early rock era. The differences begin with its origins, continue with its venues, its performance, and ultimately its intent.

18-1a The Antecedents of Electronica

Most popular music genres have evolved through the influence of music from "below": that is, music from "plain folk" who live outside and beneath the realm of high culture. We use the word *roots* to convey this. Electronica is different. Its origins are in the most cerebral and esoteric music of the midtwentieth century, the classical music avant-garde.

During the middle of the twentieth century, composers in Europe and the United States, using equipment as cutting-edge as the first tape recorders and synthesizers and as everyday as nuts and bolts, explored virgin musical territory. Shortly after World War II, the French composer Pierre Schaeffer began creating music using recorded sounds, rather than musical ideas inside his head, as raw material. The recordings could be of any sounds at all, and they could be modified or transformed before being assembled into a music event. Schaeffer called this process *musique concrète* (concrete music).

Others—among them the German composer Karlheinz Stockhausen, the French American composer Edgard Varèse, and the American John Cage—assembled compositions completely from synthesized sounds, recorded, then spliced together to form a complete composition. In 1958, Lejaren Hiller set up the first computer-music studio at the University of Illinois. Among these new electronic works were the first examples of the recording as the creative document—with no performer involved in the creative process.

Much of this music was conceptual: it grew out of a particular idea that the composer wanted to investigate. The results explored every possible extreme. American composer Milton Babbitt created works in which every musical parameter was regulated by a predetermined series: total serialism. In effect, his compositions using this procedure were precomposed. At the other end of the spectrum were works by John Cage. One famous work required the performer to sit perfectly still for 4 minutes 33 seconds; the composition was the ambient sounds in the performing space. Stockhausen composed a work for piano in which fragments of music were printed on an oversized score; the performer determined the sequence of the fragments during the performance. Cage created works in which events were determined by chance. Varèse created *Poème électronique*, an electronic piece that mixes synthesized and *concrète* sounds, for the 1958 World's Fair in Brussels. It was played over 425 loudspeakers.

All of these concepts have found their way into the various electronica styles. For example, the loudspeaker setup for *Poème électronique* anticipates the "total immersion" sound systems of dance clubs. Stockhausen's piano piece, where the performer switches arbitrarily from fragment to fragment, anticipates the DJ mixing on the fly. *Musique concrète* anticipates the found sounds that appear in so much electronica and related styles, like rap. And totally electronic pieces anticipate the millions of synthesizer-generated dance tracks.

Needless to say that there is a straightforward causal connection between midcentury avant-garde music and the electronica of the last twenty-five years. Rather, it is to suggest three things. First, even the most esoteric ideas and concepts have a way of filtering down; in this case, they made it all the way to the underground—the club scene that has nurtured this music. Second, electronica could blossom only when the necessary equipment became accessible and affordable. Third, electronica involves more than simply making dance music on computers. Its most imaginative creators have radically altered or overturned conventional assumptions about music making.

18–1b Music for Dancing, Places to Dance

The dance club is the home of electronica. The dance scene that has nurtured the music since the early eighties has been an underground continuation of disco: the music of Donna Summer and Giorgio Moroder were among the best and most successful examples of early electronica. In essence, there were people who still wanted to dance after disco declined in popularity; the club scene, and the music created for it, gave them the outlet.

During the eighties, two major club scenes emerged in the Midwest: **house music** in Chicago and **techno** in Detroit. Both would have a profound influence on dance music throughout the world. House music was a low-budget continuation of disco; DJs like Frankie Knuckles would use bare-bones rhythm tracks as part of mixes that included disco hits and current disco-inspired songs. The Detroit scene was almost exclusively the work of three friends and colleagues—Juan Atkins, Derrick May, and Kevin Saunderson—who had known one another since junior high. Despite their Detroit base, they were more interested in techno pioneers like Kraftwerk than Motown. Atkins said in an interview that "I'm probably more interested in Ford's robots than in Berry Gordy's music." As DJs and producers, they delivered a stark, dark kind of dance music under numerous guises, including Atkins's Model 500 and May's Rhythim Is Rhythim.

By the mideighties, the music had migrated to Great Britain. The event that brought the music, the culture, and the drugs up from the underground and into

house music An early techno style based originally in Chicago; it was a low-budget continuation of disco.

techno Post-disco dance music in which most or all of the sounds are electronically generated.

rave A huge dance party conducted in a large space: outdoors, an abandoned warehouse, or even a large club. Ecstasy and other "designer" drugs were very much part of the scene; they suppressed the need to eat or sleep.

the public eye was the 1988 "Summer of Love," a **rave** that went on for weeks. A rave is a huge dance party conducted in a large space: outdoors, an abandoned warehouse, or even a large club. Ecstasy and other designer drugs were very much part of the scene; they suppressed the need to eat or sleep. (Never mind that the drugs are dangerous—even deadly—especially when consumed with alcohol.)

18-1c Hearing Electronica

Dance music has defined a new performance paradigm for popular music. The nature of the venue—the dance club, rather than the arena, auditorium, night club, or coffeehouse—has fundamentally altered what is performed, how it's performed, how it's created, and how it's experienced.

The obvious difference, of course, is the use of recordings, rather than live musicians, to create the music being heard. That doesn't mean that there isn't the spontaneity and performer-crowd interaction that can be part of a live performance; it's just that it comes from a different source: the DJ.

The idea of stringing together a series of songs has a long history in popular music. From the thirties on, dance orchestras and small dance combos would occasionally play a **medley**, a group of songs connected by musical interludes. Often medleys were slow dance numbers; bands would play one chorus of each song, rather than several choruses of one song. But they could be any tempo.

medley A group of songs connected by musical interludes.

Medleys were harder to create in real time during the early years of the rock era because the identity of a song was more comprehensive. It was more than just the melody and harmony; it included every aspect of the song, as preserved on the recording. It was more difficult to alter songs so that one would flow easily into the next. Still, the idea of connecting songs did not disappear, as landmark albums such as *Sgt. Pepper* and *The Dark Side of the Moon* evidence.

Still, it wasn't until disco that the idea of creating medleys resurfaced, in a much updated form. It was the DJ who transformed the practice of connecting songs into an art. A DJ with a two-turntable setup was able to mix a series of songs into a set, an unbroken string of songs that could last longer than even the most extended Grateful Dead jam.

The art of the DJ begins with music that he or she selects. For this reason, many DJs create their own music: it helps them develop a signature style. In performance—in the dance club—skilled DJs string together a series of dance tracks with seamless transitions. It is not just that they blend one record into the next without dropping a beat—unless they plan to. They orchestrate the sequence of songs, how much they'll use of each song, and the kind of transition they'll use to give a sense of architecture to the set. It is in this context that they can respond to the dancers' energy, building to a climactic moment or moments as the set unfolds.

In the discussion of rock and rhythm and blues in the sixties, we noted that the record had become the document, the fullest and most direct expression of the musicians' creative intent. This changes in dance music. The musical unit is no longer the *recording*—which is seldom if ever played in its entirety—but the *set*. The recording is the raw material for the set; recordings are the building blocks—much as riffs are the building blocks of so many songs.

This in turn changes the nature of a dance track. It is not just that it is music for dancing. It is that the dance track is often created with the idea that it is a component of a larger structure—the set—rather than an entity complete unto itself—the song. This is a radical departure from mainstream rock; rock gave the song an integrity that it could not have had in earlier generations.

Moreover, music for club use employs a different sonic spectrum. Since the early sixties, popular music designed for airplay concentrates on midrange frequencies because these come across better on radio than high or low frequencies do. By contrast, dance clubs typically have good sound systems, so producers can take advantage of the range of audible frequencies. Electronica styles typically make full use of this, especially low-end frequencies.

This combination of a full sonic spectrum and relentless dance beat, all in an enclosed space, produces a kind of sensory inundation. It is virtually the opposite extreme of sensory deprivation, and it seems to have many of the same mind-altering consequences.

18-1d Electronica and Dance Music

We hear an influential example of electronica: "**Nude Photo**" by Rhythim Is Rhythim (Derrick May, b. 1963), is a good early sample of Detroit techno. "Nude Photo" establishes a characteristic techno groove almost immediately. The heart of it is the beat: a bass drum-like sound on every beat, a strong backbeat, and a fast-moving percussion part. Layered over that is some more melodic material: complicated, syncopated synthesizer figures, one in midrange and two in a lower register. After the track gets underway, a slow-moving melodic fragment comes in and out. There is some variety: a short rap-like vocal, some other vocal sounds, addition and subtraction of the various layers, some new versions of the melodic figures toward the end. These are the musical counterparts to the disco ball: rotating, and slightly different because of that, but essentially the same throughout. The track begins and ends abruptly; one can imagine it as part of a mix where we would never hear beginning or end.

This example can only hint at the range of sounds, rhythms, and textures possible within the world of electronica. Still, it highlights key features of dance-oriented expressions of the genre: a steadily marked beat at about 120 beats per minute; rich, complex textures featuring electronically generated percussive and pitched sounds; very little singing; subtle changes within a generally repetitive, modularly constructed form; and little sense of beginning or end. These tracks are not telling a story; rather, they're sustaining a mood. At the opposite end of the electronica spectrum is the early ambient music of Richard James, best known professionally by his pseudonym Aphex Twin.

18-1e Ambient Electronica

The cover of Aphex Twin's 1999 EP **Windowlicker** shows James's smiling face photoshopped onto the body of a generously endowed woman clad in a skimpy bikini. It is one of several jarring album covers that show his face distorted in various ways. The provocative covers allow James to have his cake and eat it too. As he acknowledged in an interview, by putting his face on album covers, he was violating what he called an "unwritten rule" about not putting one's image on an album cover. However, the images are so grotesque that he is likely to be unrecognizable to anyone who does not know already what he looks like.

They contrast sharply with more candid photos, where he looks more like a grown-up version of a self-described "irritating, lying, ginger kid from Cornwall who should have been locked up in some youth detention centre." However, instead of being locked up, James (b. 1971) won a competition at age eleven by figuring out how to get sound from a primitive home computer with no sound hardware, and graduated from Cornwall College at nineteen with a degree in engineering. By that time, he had been producing music and working as a DJ for over five years. His first album as Aphex Twin, *Selected Ambient Works, 85–92*—where he uses an amorphous A instead of his distorted face as the cover—includes music created when he was fourteen. The album was a milestone in the development of ambient electronic music.

Ambient music, a quite different branch of electronica, dates back to the seventies. Its early history includes Pink Floyd, Kraftwerk, and Tangerine Dream. The father of ambient music is Brian Eno; his recording **Ambient I: Music for Airports** (1979) is seminal.

As its name suggests, ambient music is more atmospheric and less dance driven, with more attention to sound and texture and less emphasis on rhythm. As a genre within electronica, it has often merged with both house and techno, introducing a more varied sound world into both. In these hybrid genres, it began to catch on in the late eighties and early nineties.

However, its influence, and especially the influence of James's music, extended well beyond electronica. In his first album as Aphex Twin and its 1994 sequel, **Selected Ambient Works, Volume II**, James contributed significantly to a rebalancing of rock-era music away from other elements, especially melody and rhythm. It's evident in its most extreme form in "#3", the third of 24 tracks on his second album identified only by number. The track begins with a series of five chords moving in a slow steady rhythm that remains largely unchanged through almost eight minutes. There is melody, but only in the broadest understanding of the term: a simple oscillation between two notes a step apart. There is a timekeeping beat, but it is soothingly simple and slow. There are no prominent percussive sounds; the dominant synth sounds resemble the sonority of bass flutes through much of the track. The texture changes over time, but the changes are infrequent and subtle: the effect is like a slowly twisting kaleidoscope. By suppressing both melody and rhythm as points of entry into the music, James spotlights the gentle synth sounds that pervade the track.

Tracks like "#3", and James's music in general, helped define the most important new path in the music of the nineties and twenty-first century: the prioritizing of sound over melody and rhythm. Thom Yorke, the lead singer for Radiohead, credits James as a decisive influence in changing the group's focus. In a 2013 interview where he was asked to identify his biggest influence, Yorke said:

> Aphex opened up another world that didn't involve my f*cking electric guitar, and I was just so jealous of that whole crew. They were off on their own planet. I hated all the music that was around Radiohead at the time, it was completely f*cking meaningless. I hated the Britpop thing and what was happening in America, but Aphex was totally beautiful, and he's kind of my age too. He's a massive influence.

In its countless permutations, electronica gained a more substantial commercial presence in the nineties. Fueled in part by the growth of the club scene, a proliferation of styles came about not only through the combination and recombination of existing styles (such as ambient house) but also through the absorption of outside influences, which led to an array of hardcore techno substyles. Electronica began to appear on the pop charts, in the music of acts such as Daft Punk, Chemical Brothers, and Moby.

Still, electronica has remained the most faceless music of the recent past. Its creators work almost anonymously in studios—often alone. They assume aliases: Aphex Twin is Richard James; Rhythim Is Rhythim is Derrick May. The music they produce—largely instrumental and without the melodic points of entry common to other kinds of popular music—does little to encourage the listener to identify with them in the same way that they would identify with the lead singer or lead guitarist of a rock band. In many ways, this recalls the structure of the music business at the turn of the previous century, when largely anonymous songwriters turned out reams of songs for Tin Pan Alley publishers. For the most part, DJs are the stars of electronica, but it is a very localized form of stardom. That's not the case in rap.

18-2 Rap

Several years ago, students at the university where I was teaching asked me to participate in a discussion titled, "Is rap music?" To get the discussion started, one of the students read a definition of *music*. As it turned out, rap would not have been music according to the dictionary definition. However, at no time in the discussion did anyone challenge the question itself. For me, the correct answer to the question, "Is rap music?" is simply, "It doesn't matter." Rap is rap. **Rap** is a form of creative expression that uses musical sounds to get its message across. (Indeed, one could argue convincingly that the rap video is the first total-arts genre, since it combines poetry, drama, visual arts, dancing, and music.) Whether it's music should be a nonissue, and it is a nonissue to the millions who enjoy it.

18-2a Forerunners of Rap

The practice of talking over a musical accompaniment has a long history in popular music. Al Jolson used to talk over instrumental statements of the melody in the twenties; bluesmen and contemporary folk artists like Woody Guthrie would routinely strum and talk. Within the popular tradition, the practice of reciting poetry over a musical accompaniment goes back to the fifties, when Beat poets such as Kenneth Rexroth presented their work backed by a jazz combo. Somewhat later, black poets such as Amiri Bakara (LeRoi Jones) often delivered their work with jazz in the background. In the sixties, acts as different as Bob Dylan and James Brown delivered words that were both rhymed and rhythmic, using a vocal style that fell somewhere between everyday speech and singing.

However, the most direct antecedent of rap was the toasting of the Jamaican DJs who ran the mobile sound systems and who kept up a steady stream of patter as they changed discs. Recall that some Jamaican record companies began issuing the instrumental background of a recording as the "B" side of a song, so that the DJs could prolong their toasts. The Sugarhill Gang's "**Rapper's Delight**," the single widely acknowledged as the first commercial rap, uses a similar approach: much of the rap takes place over a sample of Chic's "**Good Times**." Another source of rap, this one closer to home, was George Clinton's funk; we heard a proto-rap at the beginning of "**Tear the Roof Off the Sucker (Give Up the Funk)**."

18-2b Rap and African American Culture

There are numerous parallels between the Mississippi Delta in the first half of the twentieth century and the South Bronx in the latter half. Both regions are heavily black. Both are heartbreakingly poor: there is either no work or work at such low pay that one cannot make ends meet. They are violent, even lawless places. Health and living conditions are closer to life in a Third World country than the suburbs of New York or Memphis: out-of-wedlock children born to young teens; rats and roaches everywhere; segregated, underfunded schools, where the playground may become a battleground.

There are differences, of course. The Delta was—and is—rural. Geography, prejudice, and poverty kept the people who lived there thoroughly isolated from mainstream culture. The South Bronx is urban. Fifth Avenue in Manhattan is a short subway ride away. But it might as well have been another world for those who lived in the ghetto. In effect, there has been, in both cases, an invisible barrier that has prohibited meaningful contact between blacks and whites. However, television brought the rich and famous into the living rooms of South Bronx residents; they had a much sharper sense of what they didn't have than their early-twentieth-century Delta counterparts.

Both are depressing, demoralizing environments, environments that can suck hope out of one's mind, body, and spirit. So it is a testament to the resiliency of African Americans and the vitality of their culture that the Delta and the South Bronx have been home to two of the most vital, important, and influential forms of artistic expression to emerge in the twentieth century. Just as the Delta is the spiritual home of the blues, so is the South Bronx the home of rap.

Ask those who listen to rap what draws them to it. Chances are they'll say, "It's real." Like the blues, the realness of rap is not just in what it says, but how it says it. Rap gives us a window into life in the ghetto: the good, the bad, the ugly . . . and the beautiful. There is humor; bleak visions of the past, present, and future; posturing; misogyny, and responses to it; slices of gang life and pleas to bring an end to it; brutal depictions of current conditions and forceful demands for action. Like other roots music—blues, folk, country—this is music by and for its constituency. That rap has found a much wider audience is great but incidental to its original mission. The power comes from its emotional urgency: as with the blues, we can feel it's real. It has much more of an edge, in words and sound. It's as if blacks are saying, "We're tired of this s@#t."

Rap is a contemporary instance of a popular style speaking to and for its audience. In a 1992 *Newsweek* article, Public Enemy's Chuck D called rap "Black America's CNN." In his view, it provides information and opinions for the inner city, viewpoints not available through conventional media. Chuck D feels that rap and rap videos give whites exposure to a side of black life that they could not get short of living in a ghetto.

18–2c Rap and Hip-Hop

break dancing A vigorous dance form associated with hip-hop music and culture.

Rap emerged as one artistic dimension of hip-hop culture, along with **break dancing** and graffiti. All three were unconventional forms of expression that required considerable skill and preparation. Break dancing is extremely athletic; its vigorous moves parallel the energy of the music to which it's performed. Graffiti artists prepared their work much like a military campaign. They would plan the graffito through a series of sketches, scout out the train yards, sneak in and paint the cars, then sneak out. Their use of trains and buses as "canvases" suggests that graffiti was another way to get their message out of the ghetto.

There is a kind of defiance built into all three: rap, graffiti art, and break dancing. The implicit message is "You can put us down, but you can't keep us down." You—the man, the establishment—can subject us to subhuman living conditions. You can ignore us. But you can't break our spirit. We can create something that comes from us, not you, and you can't do what we do, even though you want to. (Keep in mind that before Eminem there was Vanilla Ice.)

18-2d Rap and Technology

Rap is a fascinating blend of low- and high-tech; and of the creative use and reuse of whatever is at hand. One can rap without any accompaniment at all. In this sense, it is about as low-tech as one can get. The first raps happened over existing music, but it wasn't long before DJs such as Grandmaster Flash found ways to put a new (back)spin on playing discs. With Grandmaster Flash, the turntable went from simple playback device to musical instrument. Equipped with two turntables, each with a copy of the record being played, DJs would scratch (move the turntable in a steady rhythm while the needle was still in the record groove to produce a percussive sound) and create breaks by repeating a segment of a song over and over on alternate turntables. In order to do this, DJs had to know exactly how far back to spin the turntable. Affordable samplers have rendered this technique obsolete.

These techniques were two more in a long string of found sounds within black music: the bottleneck for the guitar, the toilet plunger for the trumpet and trombone, the diddley bow and washtub bass. The resources may have been more sophisticated, but the principle remains the same: an imaginative search for new sound resources.

18-2e Grandmaster Flash: Messages and Techniques

Rap evolved quickly from this point—in content, style, and appeal. Among the pioneers was Grandmaster Flash. Flash (born Joseph Saddler, 1958) was born in Barbados but moved with his family to the Bronx at a young age. He grew up with passionate interests in his father's jazz records and electronics, which he merged as a budding DJ at block parties and in public parks.

> **Performing Aliases**
>
> In the twentieth century, there have three groups of musicians who have routinely assumed performing aliases: rappers, rural bluesmen, and calypsonians. For every Grandmaster Flash, Ice-T, or Notorious B.I.G., there were bluesmen like Leadbelly, Lightnin' Hopkins, and Howlin' Wolf, and calypsonians from Attila the Hun and Lord Kitchener to Mighty Sparrow and Lord Stalin. Calypso is an Afro-centric genre associated with the Carnaval celebration in Trinidad. Soca is a more modern offshoot.

Inspired by Kool Herc, the first great hip-hop DJ, Flash developed the array of turntable techniques that would revolutionize rap. Even more significantly, he translated these techniques into a radically new musical conception: the sound collage. In the visual arts, an artist creating a collage assembles found materials (artifacts such as print materials, photographs, or machine parts) or natural objects (such as seashells, flowers, or leaves) into a work of art. The collage can consist exclusively of the preexisting materials, or it can be integrated into the work of the artist. What the visual artist does with found materials, Flash did with sound. In effect, he cut and pasted sound clips from recordings into his music. The clips could range in length from a fraction of a second to several seconds; in either case, Flash completely recontextualized them.

The first song in which he showcased these skills was "**The Adventures of Grandmaster Flash and the Wheels of Steel**," which he recorded with the Furious Five, featuring Melle Mel (Melvin Glover) and ex–Sugarhill Gang percussionist

Duke Bootee (Ed Fletcher). The song, a minor R&B hit in 1981, included excerpts from Chic's "Good Times," Blondie's "**Rapture**," and Queen's "**Another One Bites the Dust**," as well as samples from other songs and sources; it would become a textbook for the creative possibilities of sampling.

This was a radical transformation of the age-old practice of musical quotation. Instead of interpolating snippets of just the melody, Flash mixed in the entire musical event, as preserved on record. The result was a redefinition of "song."

Flash's other major contributions came with "**The Message**," which reached No. 4 on the R&B charts in 1982 and also crossed over to the pop charts. It was innovative in both subject and setting. "The Message" presents a brutal picture of life in the ghetto. Its impact begins with the rap itself, which describes the oppressive and parlous circumstances of everyday life for those who live there. Another noteworthy feature was "arrest" at the end of the track, a "slice of life" interpolation that interrupts the musical accompaniment for several seconds. When the accompaniment resumes, it is as if the arrest was barely a blip on the radar screen—a virtual nonevent in the ongoing misery of life in the ghetto. Such real-life nonmusical sounds were not an innovation with rap; in rock-era music they date back to the Beatles. However, rap captured more powerful clips and used them more extensively. Both the rap and the arrest scene convey a much more serious message. With "The Message," rap graduated from party music to serious social commentary.

The other major innovation in "The Message" is the coordination of the musical setting with the message of the rap. There are many layers of activity, most of it generated on synthesizers and drum machines. The most prominent are the strong backbeat and the high synthesizer riff, the closest thing to melodic material on the entire track. However, none of the many layers establishes a consistent, active rhythm: the bass part, percussive guitarlike midrange part, and the multiple percussion parts dart in and out of the texture; the overall effect evokes James Brown's music, but it is much emptier-sounding than the textures typically heard in his music. The sixteen-beat rhythm that is implicit in the instrumental sections becomes explicit only when the rap begins. An abrupt change in the rhythm of the rap, from the sixteen-beat stream to a variant of the clave pattern, signals the arrival at the "chorus": "Don't push me cuz I'm close to the edge."

The spare, widely spaced sounds, and the way in which the synthesizer riff trails off seem to communicate the desolation of the ghetto environment; the lack of change in the setting seems to imply the difficulties faced in ameliorating this depressing environment.

Rap crossed over to the mainstream with Run-D.M.C.'s version of "**Walk This Way**." As with earlier rap songs, "Walk This Way" built the rap on a preexisting musical foundation, in this case, Aerosmith's 1976 hit, "Walk This Way." The new twist was that Aerosmith members Steven Tyler and Joe Perry participated in the recording session. This new version made the charts exactly a decade after the original in 1986. A year later, LL Cool J and the Beastie Boys (who were signed to Def Jam Records, the most prominent rap label) found the charts; with their emergence, rap burst out of the ghetto and into the burbs.

18-2f Public Enemy: Rap as a Political Music

Among the major rap acts of the late eighties and nineties was Public Enemy. The group's key figures were Chuck D (born Carlton Ridenhour, 1960), Flavor Flav (born William Drayton, 1959), and DJ Terminator X (born Norman Rogers, 1966). They surrounded themselves with a substantial posse, some of whom contributed to their work.

Public Enemy was the most political of the rap acts to emerge during the late eighties. Their look kindled memories of the black radicals from the sixties: paramilitary uniforms, Black Panther evocations, fake Uzis carried by their entourage as they appeared on stage. The look was the smaller part of the equation. Far more telling were the raps themselves.

In "**1 Million Bottlebags**," a track from their 1991 album *Apocalypse 91 . . . The Enemy Strikes Black*, Public Enemy takes on everyone. The rap is an indictment of alcohol abuse. It takes on all of those responsible for the problem: not only those who consume it and can't stop, but also the companies that prey on blacks by advertising their liquor products heavily in the ghetto. The language is powerful and direct; it is from the street. The frustration and anger behind it are palpable.

The rap begins with a collage of sounds: a bottle breaking, a "news bulletin" about target advertising by liquor companies in the black communities, the rhythm track, the sound of beer (or malt liquor) being poured, a beer belch, then hornlike synthesizer chords. The rap begins. Sirens and more prominent rhythm sounds signal the arrival of a refrain-like section. The end of the track simulates changing stations on a radio. Juxtaposed are a long statement about the immorality of making money off the impoverished and a scathing critique of the way in which racist corporate types dismiss the problem.

There are five kinds of sounds here: the rap, the spoken elements, the real-world sounds (e.g., the bottle breaking), the rhythm tracks, and the pitched sounds, such as the siren screeches that mark the refrain. Collectively, they amplify the message of the rap through the sharp juxtaposition of sounds and images. The siren screeches are both a musical sound, a two-note riff, and an evocation of a too-familiar real-life sound. There is complexity in the density of information, which matches the multiple levels of commentary.

The rhythm track, which combines a strong backbeat with interlocked patterns that collectively mark the sixteen-beat rhythm, serves several purposes. It is the glue that holds the track together, through the changes of voice, the spoken clips, and other sounds. It reinforces the delivery of the rap. Because both move at sixteen-beat speed, the percussion sounds give the rap support and strength. And it creates a groove: even more than in funk, you can move to the groove even as you take in the message.

"1 Million Bottlebags" is even less melodic than "The Message." The only easily identifiable melodic elements are the siren-like sound and the repeated chord: in both cases, the same pitch is repeated again and again. The absence of melody is a strength, not a shortcoming. Its presence would dilute the impact of the rap. It would soften the edge that is present everywhere else: in the delivery of the rap, in the rhythm track and other musical sounds, in the sound clips.

The moral high ground staked out by Public Enemy in tracks like "1 Million Bottlebags" was undermined by incidents such as the 1989 *Washington Post* interview with Professor Griff (born Richard Griffin, 1960), Public Enemy's "minister of information," in which he made numerous provocatively anti-Semitic remarks, including claiming that Jews were responsible for the majority of wickedness that goes on throughout the world. It was the most flagrant of several anti-Semitic public incidents in Public Enemy's career; others included an endorsement of Nation of Islam leader Louis Farrakhan. The controversy surrounding such incidents created dissent within the group and a sudden decline in their fortunes. By 1993, Chuck D put the group's career on hold; he would revive Public Enemy later in the decade, where they recaptured some of the success that they had previously enjoyed. Still, their most substantial contribution came in the late eighties and early nineties; more than any other group of the era, they made rap relevant—the black CNN—to both blacks and nonblacks and created sound worlds that amplified the impact of the lyrics.

18-2g Rap as Thoughtful Commentary: Nas

Among the new rap stars of the midnineties was Nas (Nasir Jones, b. 1973). The son of jazz trumpeter Olu Dara, Nas grew up in Queensbridge, a massive, dangerous, and desolate housing project in New York. Despite dropping out of school in the eighth grade, he developed into one of the more thoughtful and literate rappers of the nineties. *Illmatic,* his 1994 debut album recorded when he was only twenty, drew widespread praise as a quintessential example of "street flow," a seemingly endless stream of inventive and provocative observations about life in the projects.

"**Life's a B******," one of the most admired tracks on the CD, contains two raps, one by AZ (Anthony Cruz) and the other by Nas, with a refrain by AZ tying them together. The raps express powerfully a fundamental contradiction in rap. Both title and content portray the despair of life in the projects, and the rappers' complex response to it. They stress that life is short and get what you can while you can; as one reviewer noted, the message is not "life's a b**** and then you die" but "life's a b**** because you die." The raps are full of conflicting messages: Nas celebrating the first quarter of his life even as both acknowledge that living to an old age is unlikely; AZ proclaiming an amoral value system while acknowledging sinners; Nas matter-of-factly describing his early encounters with sex and drugs yet seeming to put these encounters behind him.

However, the biggest conflict is between the content of the raps and the fact of them. That AZ and Nas would devote the time, energy, and passion to create meaningful statements about their lives is an affirmation of their lives and their culture. It is, in the most fundamental way, vital. It says that they have chosen to spend at least part of their lives creatively rather than giving in completely to the "sin" ("cause all of us turned to sinners") that has brought so many of their peers down. It suggests the same spirit as those community gardens one occasionally finds growing in an empty lot in a rundown neighborhood. In this respect, rap is the postmodern urban counterpart to the blues: just as a bluesman sings the blues to chase away the blues, so does a creative rapper rap to convey hope in an environment of despair.

The musical setting serves as a foil for the raps; it is integral to its presentation and impact. Here, the understated, unchanging backdrop—dark bass and percussion, a pair of chords that never resolves, and a high string synthesizer sound, all at a slow tempo— immediately sets a gray mood. Moreover, it does not change, as if to suggest that the environment is permanent. The accompaniment sets up a powerful contrast between the brevity of life and the endlessly hopeless environment that makes lives short. The mournful muted trumpet at the end, by Nas's father Olu Dara, sustains the bleak mood through the end of the track. The result is an innovative mix of poetry and music, where the interaction between two works synergistically.

18-2h Mainstreaming Rap: The Case of Gangsta Rap

gangsta rap A form of rap which emerged in the late 80s and expressed the violence of inner-city life.

In rap, the boundary between life and art is all but invisible. The work of rappers often comes directly from their life experiences; the raps may simply document them. Nowhere has this been more evident than in **gangsta rap**. Gangsta rap, which emerged in the latter part of the eighties, brought the violence of inner-city life into the music and out into the world.

Gangsta rap might well be written gang-sta rap because its strongest undercurrent was the association with gang life. A visual image of this life was the 1988 film *Colors,* starring Robert Duvall and Sean Penn as police officers trying to control violence between the Bloods and the Crips, two rival Los Angeles gangs. Ice-T, among the first of the gangsta rappers, recorded the title track of the film.

Although Schoolly D, a Philadelphia-based rapper, is credited with the rap that sparked the genre (the 1986 single "**P.S.K.**"), gangsta rap has been perceived as a west coast phenomenon because of the success of rap artists and groups such as N.W.A. and Ice-T, then Dr. Dre (a former N.W.A. member), Snoop Doggy Dogg, and 2Pac (Tupac Shakur). The success of these groups escalated the territorial animosity from rival gangs within a community to the communities themselves. Bad blood developed between west coast gangsta rappers and New York hip-hop artists; both groups used lyrics to diss the opposing camp. The violence portrayed in the lyrics often spilled over into real life: Snoop Doggy Dog and Tupac Shakur were among the notable gangsta rap artists who served jail time ("**California Love**" was Shakur's first recording after his release from jail); the shooting deaths of Shakur and Notorious B.I.G. are commonly regarded as gang retribution for earlier offenses.

The violence was not the only controversial aspect of the music. Raps were often pornographic and misogynistic, and richly scatological. Most recordings routinely earned the "parental advisory" label from the RIAA (Recording Industry Association of America). For suburban whites, gangsta rap must have seemed like forbidden fruit; the genre would enjoy a large following among whites, most of whom experienced the rappers' world only vicariously.

Although its audience had grown steadily throughout the late eighties and early nineties, gangsta rap crossed over to the mainstream in large part because of a musical decision: to work pop elements into hardcore rap in an effort to give the music more widespread appeal. It first appeared in the music of New York hip-hop artists such as Notorious B.I.G. and Nas, and quickly spread to the west coast: Tupac Shakur's "California Love," which topped the pop, R&B, and rap charts in 1996, epitomizes this new approach.

Tupac Shakur

If ever an artist seemed destined to live and die by the sword, it would be Tupac Shakur (1971–1996). His parents were active in the Black Panthers; his mother was acquitted on a conspiracy charge only a month before Shakur's birth; his father is currently incarcerated in Florida; and others close to his mother during his childhood were either in and out of prison or fugitives.

What made his too-short life doubly tragic was the terrible conflict between the sensitive and violent sides of his personality. He was intelligent and curious—reading Machiavelli during his prison term—and creative and multitalented, with obvious gifts as an actor, poet, dancer, and musician. Yet in his personal and professional lives, he gave vent to the violent side: run-ins with the law; a sexual abuse lawsuit and scandal; the track "**Hit 'Em Up**," a personal attack on Notorious B.I.G., in which he claimed to have slept with B.I.G.'s wife. That his life would end prematurely as a result of the ultimate violent act seems in retrospect almost a foregone conclusion.

Shortly before his death, Shakur recorded "California Love" with Dr. Dre for Death Row Records, the label headed by Suge Knight, who was also repeatedly in trouble with the law. Both the video and the song evidence the mutation of rap from an outsiders' music flourishing in inner-city parks to a big business. Both the opening scene and the action during the song itself seem inspired by the Mad Max films: it purports to present a desolate, lawless world a hundred years in the future. Although it is skillfully produced, the video has no obvious thematic connection with the song, which is very much in the present—the "'95" that Dr. Dre mentions is clearly 1995, and Tupac's first words are "out on bail fresh outta jail." What is obvious is that the video took a lot of money to produce; it is a clear sign that rap has become big business.

The song shows how rap found a mainstream audience by bringing in non-rap elements. It begins with a striking processed vocal riff; the instrumental introduction that follows spotlights the bass. The next section features a tuneful melody with a rich accompaniment; this becomes the main refrain of the song. The refrain returns after Dr. Dre's rap. It is followed by another sung section "Shake it," which gives way to Tupac's rap.

The rap lyrics offer a sizable dose of gangsta rap posturing: there are references to violence, gangs, prostitution, money, clothes, and jewelry. But the prevailing mood, in both words and music, is party hard, because "we keep it rockin'!" Especially in the refrain, it sounds more like a promo for the chamber of commerce than an incitement to riot.

Its most surprising feature, and undoubtedly one of its most appealing features, is its melodic and textural richness. The vocal melodies are the most apparent evidence of this, but woven into the texture behind both the sung sections and the raps are lush synthesizer harmonies and multiple fragments of melody. The return of the refrain features even more supplementary melodic activity, both vocal and instrumental. Almost all of this activity, and especially the synthesizer chords and lines, occurs in middle and high register, above the vocal range of the rap. This counterbalances the characteristic dark bass sound that runs throughout the song.

Additionally, several layers of percussion sounds mark the backbeat and sixteen-beat rhythms or play against these regular rhythms: the whistle stands out as a source of rhythmic play. The rhythmic texture of the song is even denser than that heard on "1 Million Bottlebags," although the tempo is considerably slower.

The sound world of the song, and the genre, is defined most fundamentally in the brief instrumental interlude just after the title-phrase riff. For a brief moment, there is only the active bass line and several percussion sounds, most prominently the high-pitched percussion sound marking the sixteen-beat rhythm. It is a sound that we associate with rap: we hear it above everything else emanating from car stereos. In Motown, soul, seventies black pop, and funk, the bass is the dominant rhythm instrument. In rap, it has become the dominant instrument, period. This sound—strong, freely moving bass and active percussion—distills the most characteristic elements of black music to their essence and pushes them into the forefront, much as the saturated rock rhythm played by a punk rock band reduces, intensifies, and projects the most basic elements of rock rhythm and sound.

In particular, the bass sound, made dark and fat by stripping away the overtones so that only low-frequency sounds remain, is a logical extension of the dark sound of electric blues. Electric blues made rural blues darker by adding a bass instrument and guitar riffs in a low register; the characteristic bass-driven sound of rap simply continues this progression.

In "California Love," we hear this essential sound by itself for about seven seconds. During the course of the song, the other elements of the song—vocal refrains, raps, other instrumental sound—covers over this foundation, which continues through the song. Especially in light of the fact that the more tuneful elements were added as a conscious effort to enhance the appeal of the style, the effect is striking; it is as if we get a glimpse of a public figure in an unguarded moment and see him as he really is, not as he portrays himself.

The rich texture created by the numerous melodic fragments and sustained chords are an important source of the enormous crossover appeal of the song. It makes the song more accessible and more familiar, and there is more to connect to—not only the two raps and the beat, but the melodies and the sound variety. The strategy to mainstream rap through melody succeeded on both coasts, and it has remained a common practice up until the present.

Fortunately for Death Row Records, Shakur had recorded a substantial amount of unreleased material. Six albums were released posthumously, the last in 2004. All went platinum. His legacy extends beyond his recordings. Following his death, his mother Afeni Shakur established the Tupac Amaru Shakur Foundation to "provide training and support for students who aspire to enhance their creative talents."

18-2i Reactions to Rap

Gangsta rap has been the most visible rap style since the late eighties because of its appeal and notoriety, but it is one of many rap styles to emerge during this period. Because it is so integral to hip-hop culture, it may be hard to divorce rap from its trappings and particularly the baggage that it carries: the controversial pronouncements, the violent world it portrays and realizes, the hedonistic lifestyle it projects. So it is not surprising that rap, like so many other genres with aggressive postures and outsider status (heavy metal, punk, techno), has gotten its share of bad press. Its critics focus on the language, the lifestyle, the lyrics, and the emergence of substyles like gangsta rap to condemn the entire genre. There is no denying rap's edge; the speed and tone of the rap and the busy rhythms underneath virtually guarantee it.

However, the act of rapping is inherently value neutral. It can be, and has been, used to deliver a variety of messages—not only dark gray portraits of life in the hood and expletive-filled rants but also humor and hope. Whether the message is negative or positive depends on the content, not the genre. A case in point: Christian rap (or, more alliteratively, holy hip-hop) also emerged in the nineties. The music of groups such as the Gospel Gangstaz sends a message far different from that heard in "California Love," "Hit 'Em Up," and other gangsta rap tracks.

At the beginning of the twenty-first century, rap—in all of its manifestations— is an enduring and significant part of the rock-era musical world. The numerous rap/rock syntheses—such as rapcore, rap-rock, and rap-metal—offer one more indication of its strong presence in popular music. At the same time, some have looked back almost nostalgically to "old school," the rap from the late seventies and eighties, when the message, whether it talked about good times or bad, seemed purer.

18-3 Moving Beyond Rock

In the summary of rock's core values that appeared at the end of **Chapter 1**, we listed features that one expects to hear in a classic rock song. A comparison of that style profile with the features typically found in techno and rap offers compelling evidence of the way in which electronica and rap, arguably the two most progressive musical styles since 1980, have moved beyond rock. Here are key differences:

- Sixteen-beat rhythms, instead of a rock beat
- A good beat of far greater complexity because of the more active rhythms and a richer texture

- Electronic instruments and samples, instead of a core rhythm section of guitar, bass, and drums
- Few if any sung riffs, and no melody to speak of; no hooks in a sung refrain or in a lead guitar part

While there is a sense of verse/chorus form in the two rap songs and recurring musical ideas in the techno track, there is little sense of arriving at the chorus and highlighting it with a memorable melodic hook.

Moreover, the very *idea* of a song as a fixed, discrete document contained on a recording comes under attack in both styles. Tracks like "Nude Photo" are pieces in a larger puzzle, a single element in a DJ's mix. And in both techno and rap, remixing songs into new versions is standard practice.

Despite these commonalities, rap and techno face in opposite directions historically. Rap is the end of a long pendulum swing from melody to rhythm that began at the beginning of the twentieth century and reached its endpoint in a genre with no melody required. Techno, more than any other late twentieth-century music, explored the expressive capabilities of sound. Its influence on the innovative music in all genres from the nineties on has been profound. We explore this in the next part.

Part Introduction

About the time that Radiohead began work on their first post-EMI/Capitol album, lead singer Thom Yorke told Time magazine, "I like the people at our record company, but the time is at hand when you have to ask why anyone needs one. And, yes, it probably would give us some perverse pleasure to say 'F__you' to this decaying business model."

Shortly before they completed work on their new album, Radiohead decided to answer—at least for themselves—Yorke's question about the need for a record company. They reserved the domain name "**inrainbows.com**"—*In Rainbows* was the album title—and offered the album, which they had produced at their own expense, exclusively as a digital download for two months: from October 10 to December 10, 2007. Those who downloaded the album chose how much they wanted to pay for it: nothing was an option. Reports vary on what percentage actually paid for it and how much they earned, but Warner Chappell, Radiohead's music publisher, reported a year later that the group had made more from their self-released digital version of the album than they had from the sales of *Hail to the Thief*, their previous album.

Radiohead's bold move shocked music industry executives. One producer told Time, "Radiohead is the best band in the world. If you can pay whatever you want for music by the best band in the world, why would you pay $13 dollars or $.99 cents for music by somebody less talented? Once you open that door and start giving music away legally, I'm not sure there's any going back."

Radiohead's pay-what-you-want marketing is not for everyone; the group is one of the few acts that have earned sufficient stature to make this kind of offer and expect something in return. And the group also offered an $80 discbox through their website and began selling physical CDs shortly after discontinuing the online downloads, making arrangements with an array of distributors and record companies throughout the world. But the mere fact that an act as important as Radiohead would—and could—undertake a marketing strategy that challenges the existing business model, underscores the upheaval in the music industry that was created by the digital revolution.

The "Death" and Transfiguration of the Music Industry

Early in 2011, blogger Michael DeGusta, in an article entitled "The REAL Death of the Music Industry," published a revised version of a chart that showed the revenue derived from recorded music sold in the United States between 1973 and 2009 and accounted for by the RIAA (Record Industry Association of America). Among the conclusions drawn from his analysis: a 64 percent drop in revenue from its 1999 peak, and a 45 percent drop from 1973, when adjusted for inflation.

It can be argued that the steep decline in revenues during the 2000s does not signal the death of the music industry so much as a long-awaited market correction. The album as the all-but-universal unit of sales for all types of recorded music is a rock-era development; before the sixties, singles were far more popular than albums in popular music. From this broader perspective, digital downloads can be understood as a legal means of restoring consumer choice: buy the entire album or just the tracks you want. Indeed, some who grew up during the era of album dominance regard peer-to-peer sites and online delivery as payback for an industry that they feel had gouged consumers for decades.

Correction or not, there is no question that the rapid and far-reaching changes brought about by digital technology have disrupted the business model of the music industry. Sales of CDs declined from over $15 billion in 1999 to under $1.2 billion in 2015. During that same year, digital revenues exceeded revenues from physical products for the first time, and have continued to grow. Paid subscriptions to streaming services doubled between 2015 and 2016, and digital revenues globally increased over 10 percent, the first significant revenue increase in almost two decades. In the United States, streaming now accounts for over half of the revenue from recording, although the modest improvement in revenues overall only amounts to about half of the revenue produced in 1999. This dramatic shift toward streaming is the inevitable consequence of the growth of the internet.

The Internet and Its Impact

The first attempts to create an "Internet", or network of networks, date back to the seventies. By 1980, a protocol that enabled different networks to communicate with one another was in place. During its early years, the internet was mainly under government supervision and control; the National Science Foundation managed it in the United States. However, in 1993, the internet backbone was opened to the private sector in the United States, and Mosaic, the first browser, became available. (Mosaic became Netscape the following year.) Browsers simplified access to the internet by providing a graphical user interface, similar to those found on Windows and Mac operating systems.

By 2000, the mechanics of the now-familiar internet experience were in place. Since then, the pace of innovation and evolution has been breathtakingly fast and remarkably comprehensive. Driving this growth were astounding technological advances, in computing power, storage, portability, access, and more. By way of example, a current iPhone is a more powerful computer by far than an iMac a decade earlier.

Internet access and speed have grown at a comparable pace. Between 2000 and 2017, global internet access grew 934 percent, an almost tenfold increase. In 2000, less than 6 percent of the world's population could go online; by March 2017, almost half have access, and in North America the ratio is eight out of nine.

Numerous new businesses and services have leveraged these technological advances to open up all aspects of commerce: as author Craig Anderson has discussed in depth, "free" is now an option. Consider the cumulative impact on the music industry of these developments:

- Napster: Napster went public in 1999 as a peer-to-peer file sharing application. By 2001, Shawn Fanning, its creator, had closed down the service after several artists sued the company. However, BitTorrent sites continue to make music available (illegally) for free. Legal and ethical issues aside, such peer-to-peer networks can function much like a greatly enhanced version of the preview clips on digital download sites such as iTunes and Amazon. They give enthusiastic listeners with more time than money the opportunity to sample a large body of music by a particular act before deciding whether to buy one or more albums.

- iTunes/iPod: iTunes appeared in 2001 as an application for organizing and playing back audio files on a Mac computer; the first iPod was introduced a few months later. The iTunes Music Store opened in April 2003, offering tracks from the top record companies and, somewhat later, numerous independent labels. In less than five years, the iTunes Store had become the No. 1 music retailer in the United States. By late 2010, Apple had sold 10 billion tracks, and by 2014, cumulative sales reached 35 billion. However, sales of digital downloads have been dropping precipitously with the rise of streaming services.

- Facebook/MySpace: Social networks such as Facebook and MySpace took off in the latter half of the 2000s. Users shared their tastes in music on both. MySpace started strong but quickly lost traction, shortly after Rupert Murdoch's News Corporation acquired the website in 2005. Facebook took off around the same time; a Facebook page is now an almost obligatory promotional tool for any music act.

- YouTube: YouTube, founded in 2005 and bought by Google a year later, has made everyone a potential video producer or distributor. Users of the site have uploaded not only their own music but also music videos, footage from live events, and audio recordings from their favorite acts. Google monetized viewing of videos; revenue in the United States from on-demand ad-supported streaming approached half a billion dollars in 2016.

- Streaming services. Digital streaming includes both free ad-supported and ad-free subscription options for radio (Pandora) and internet audio (Spotify), or simply by subscription (Apple Music, Amazon Music). Streaming services, both free and subscription, took a while to gain traction because record companies were reluctant to license their music, especially by top acts, for such services. However, streaming services, and in particular paid subscription, have proven to be a dependable revenue source, and are now the revenue stream showing the greatest growth.

A Digital Democracy

The internet was the last piece of the digital ecosystem to emerge. Its rapid growth, along with the continuing improvement in all aspects of digital audio (and video), has created a digital democracy for musicians and their audience. The advances in computer-based audio have put high-end music production within almost everyone's budget. For just a few thousand dollars, anyone can create a home studio that can do just about anything that could have been done only in a million-dollar studio less than a generation ago. Online promotion is also less expensive: the cost and ease of creating and maintaining an attractive website continues to drop, and marketing tools are comparatively inexpensive.

For the aspiring creative artist, the financial investment is a small fraction of what it once was. For the consumer, it means anywhere (there's internet), anytime access to millions of tracks for about 35¢ a day. And for the beleaguered music industry, it means a stable and growing income stream that has reversed (for now) the precipitous decline in revenue from the end of the last century to the mid-2010s.

For musicians, the music industry, and the consumers they served, the digital revolution was as comprehensive and consequential as the technological revolutions of the twenties and sixties. However, there was no musical revolution occurring in tandem with it: instead of coming together around a dominant new style there was further fragmentation of the existing marketplace, not only by genre but also by generations.

The "Comprehensive" Era

At the beginning of the twenty-first century, Billboard's Top 200 chart listed the best-selling albums, regardless of genre, that had been released within the previous eighteen months. Older albums appeared on the Top Pop Catalog Albums. However, in 2003, Billboard introduced the Top Comprehensive Albums chart, which identified the bestselling albums, regardless of release date. In 2009 when, after Michael Jackson's passing, three of his albums topped the charts, Billboard turned the relationship between current and catalog albums on its head by converting the Top Comprehensive Albums chart into the Billboard 200 and introducing a new Top Current Albums chart.

The inversion of the relationship between "catalog" (older) and "current" during the first decade of the new century acknowledged the reality of musical life in twenty-first-century America. The marketplace is more fragmented than ever before, not only by genre—rock, country, hip-hop, etc.—but also by generation. In this context, "generation" refers not just to the age(s) of the acts or the release date of their work, but also their musical approach.

Billboard's decade-end chart lists the best-selling acts of the decade. For the 2000's, the top ten included three rap/R&B acts, three rock acts, three country acts, and a pop diva.

Rap/hip-hop	Rock	Country	Pop
Eminem	Linkin Park	Toby Keith	Britney Spears
Nelly	Nickelback	Tim McGraw	
Jay-Z	Creed	Kenny Chesney	

All four categories represent well-established genres. Country is inherently traditional, or at least neo-traditional. Of the three top rock acts, only Linkin Park is at all contemporary in approach. The turn-of-the-century pop divas closely followed Madonna's lead. Rap, the newest genre—if the eighties can be considered new in the twenty-first century—has been leavened with melody. The rest of the list includes acts that reach into the more distant past: traditional pop and classical crossover singers like Josh Groban (14), Andrea Bocelli (53), and Michael Bublé (90), stars from rock's first generation like The Beatles (27), Santana (29), Elvis (102!), the Eagles (105) and Ray Charles (109), and Celtic/new-age star Enya (56).

This embrace of the past has continued into the 2010s. A 2015 Music Watch survey, sponsored by the Record Industry Association of America (RIAA), aggregates listeners' preferences by age and music delivery method (CD, streaming, etc.). The overall top choices were classic rock (sixties to eighties), Top 40, and country. Similarly, the twenty top-grossing tours of 2015 included AC/DC, U2, Fleetwood Mac, The Rolling Stones, Madonna, Paul McCartney, Elton John, Billy Joel, and Neil Diamond, along with contemporary singer/songwriters Taylor Swift and Ed Sheeran, and top country acts like Kenny Chesney, Garth Brooks, Luke Bryan, and Shania Twain. All of these data suggest that the music marketplace is stratified not only by genre but also generation.

Genres and Generations: Popular Music in the Twenty-first Century

In January, 2015, as the second half of the 2010s began, the staff at billboard.com celebrated in characteristic fashion, by making lists. Among them was the "10 defining artists of the 10s (so far)." Their list included five rappers, four pop/R&B singers—all female—and one rock group. The staff's "defining artists" and their lists of best albums and singles reflect contemporary trends, but not the marketplace as a whole. Data from MusicWatch and Billboard imply that accounting for musical preferences should factor in generations as well as genres: more people were listening to classic rock than current hits. Doing so provides a different perspective on musical life in the first part of the twenty-first century.

Twenty-first-century record sales, streaming preferences, and concert attendance suggest that there are four generations of popular music that still have significant market share and mind share, and remain a vital source of new music. In chronological order, they are:

- Classic pre-rock pop (the "Great American Songbook"), based on the postwar popular singing of Sinatra, Nat Cole, et al. The ageless Tony Bennett remains a favorite; younger stars such as Michael Bublé and Diana Krall enjoy large followings; and rock-era stars from several decades (e.g., Rod Stewart, Lady Gaga) have also delved into this music.

- First generation rock-era music (1960s+). Sixties icons such as Bob Dylan and Paul McCartney continued to record into the twenty-first century, while more recent acts such as Mumford and Sons and the Tedeschi Trucks Band bring a fresh approach to classic rock and R&B. Moreover, most contemporary country music is stylistically aligned with first generation rock: particularly its characteristic rhythms and core instruments.

- Second generation rock-era music (late 1970s+). This begins with punk, funk, and disco, and includes music from the eighties and beyond that built on the rhythms and sounds of these styles, for example, R.E.M., Michael Jackson, Madonna, and U2, as well as rappers and electronic artists. Numerous alternative bands and pop stars continue to work within these styles.

- Musicians looking to forge a distinct twenty-first-century sonic identity. Such a list would include commercially successful acts like Radiohead, Arcade Fire, Linkin Park, Drake, Beyoncé, Kanye West, recent Taylor Swift, Adele, and Lady Gaga. It's a diverse group, united more by what they're not than any common musical ground.

The generational stratification of contemporary musical life makes clear that there has not been a transformative new style, a style with sufficient gravitational pull to not only take over the market but also mirror and even change the culture. There has been new music that is identifiably from this century, but it is not the dominant music of our time. Half a century later, it seems clear that there will be no revolution comparable to the rock revolution of the sixties.

In this part, we sample music from three rock-era generations as we explore musical reasons why there has not been a significant new genre in rock since the eighties.

CHAPTER 19

FIRST-GENERATION ROCK IN THE TWENTY-FIRST CENTURY

Learning Objectives:

1) Recall three reasons behind the country genre's rise in popularity in the 1990s music industry.

2) Describe how multiple genres contributed to the style of Taylor Swift.

3) Explain Tim McGraw's use of both country and rock elements in his music.

4) Ascertain the key differences between Bob Dylan's 1960s style and his 2006 album, *Modern Times*.

5) Exemplify Alicia Key's use of the classical genre in her music.

6) Comment on the fundamental qualities shared among musicians that successfully combine genres.

Chapter Introduction

Fred Jacobs, the key figure in the development of the classic rock radio format, has been running Jacobs Media Strategies, his own consulting business for media companies since 1983. In a blog post written in 2013 entitled, "The State of Classic Rock Is . . ." he celebrates the staying power of classic rock, but laments the difficulty established acts face when they try to introduce more recent material.

While much of this has been blurred over the decades—clouded by video music discovery starting with MTV and exploding with YouTube—the fact that classic rock concerts continue to be commercially successful speaks to both the lasting power of the music and the ways in which the artists resonated with the times in which they rose to power.

Yet, most Classic Rockers have failed to score "new" hits of any kind in the 'nineties and beyond. That shouldn't surprise us. Sadly and predictably, those are the moments when concertgoers stream to the concession stands and the restrooms.

As a case in point, Jacobs cites the title track from Paul McCartney's 2013 album *New*. He laments the fact that the song got little traction on classic rock stations. Although the song charted well and the album topped the *Billboard 200*, "**New**" is unlikely to replace "**Yesterday**" as a favorite McCartney song.

For established acts like McCartney, creativity is a delicate balancing act between familiarity and novelty. That they continue to work productively is obvious evidence of the continuing vitality of first-generation rock. They are joined by two other significant sources of new music with deep roots in the rock and black music of the sixties and early seventies. Country musicians and a new generation of younger musicians bring skill and imagination to these established conventions. We sample all three, beginning with country.

19–1 Musical Cousins: Classic Rock and Contemporary Country

Rock-era music has had a Southern accent almost from the start, in the music of Sun Records stars like Elvis, Carl Perkins, and Jerry Lee Lewis. It largely disappeared in the early sixties in the wake of the British invasion, but returned toward the end of the decade and flourished in the early seventies. The embrace between country and rock came from several directions. Among the most important were the country/rock fusions of the Byrds, Flying Burrito Brothers, and Eagles; the Southern rock of the Allman Brothers, Lynyrd Skynyrd, and others; the "American" sound of Creedence Clearwater Revival, the Band, and others, which also mixed country, blues, and rock; and the incorporation of rock (and contemporary pop) elements by country musicians as diverse as Glen Campbell and Merle Haggard.

The new direction of the Eagles after 1975 seemed to symbolize the separation of rock and country. However, the separation was more cultural than musical: the rock elements assimilated into country earlier in the seventies—in particular the use of a classic rock beat and the core rock instruments—remained, especially in much of the music of a new generation of country acts. Among the most prominent were Alabama, Vince Gill, Travis Tritt, Lyle Lovett, and Clint Black. Don Was's 1994 album *Rhythm, Country, and Blues*, which featured tracks that paired country and rhythm and blues acts performing classic rock, R&B, and country hits, made clear the common ground among these rock-era musicians. Nevertheless, despite occasional crossover successes—for example, Dolly Parton's starring role in, and theme song for, the film *9 to 5*—country music operated apart from the rock and pop of the eighties.

In the nineties, country assumed a more prominent place in the music industry mainly for three reasons. One was the use of a more accurate and efficient method of calculating sales. Toward the end of 1991, *Billboard* began using Nielsen SoundScan, an information system that tracks sales through the use of barcodes scanned at registers in retail centers and record stores throughout the United States. Around the same time, the music industry started using computers to track radio airplay. In combination, the two information sources provided much more precise—and eventually more reliable—data about popularity.

Not coincidentally, the market share of country music just about doubled between 1990 and 1993, from 9.6 percent to 18.7 percent. This alerted industry executives on both coasts to something that country fans had known for decades: country music was much more popular than the music industry thought it was.

The dramatic jump in market share (which has since declined somewhat) was just one indication that country music had become a major player in the popular music industry. Country music television networks, country stars in advertisements, the emergence of Nashville as an important music center, crossover chart success—these also show the growing presence of country music.

Second was a wave of talent whose careers took off in the 1990s: among the most prominent were Garth Brooks, Alan Jackson, Shania Twain, Trisha Yearwood, and Clint Black. Brooks has been commercially dominant. As of June 2017, he has sold 148,000,000 albums, as certified by the RIAA. Only the Beatles, with sales of 178,000,000 albums, have surpassed Brooks in sales. For country music, Brooks's spectacular sales figures are neither an aberration nor an isolated instance. Of the 100 best-selling acts of all time, 24 began their recording careers in the nineties or later. Of these 24, eight are country acts: Brooks and Dunn, Kenny Chesney, Dixie Chicks, Faith Hill, Alan Jackson, Toby Keith, Tim McGraw (Faith's husband), and Shania Twain.

A third reason for the unprecedented popularity of country music at the turn of the twenty-first century would seem to have more to do with the continuing evolution of rock, pop, and rap than it does with significant evolutionary changes in country music. More than any other kind of rock-era music, contemporary country music has retained familiar points of entry: a good story told in an easy-to-understand lyric; a singable melody, sung with feeling but without histrionics; a good beat; a predilection for conventional instruments, although electronic sounds occasionally appear on tracks; and forms that are easy to follow. Stylistically, there's a smooth continuum between middle-ground country and much of the AOR rock of the seventies; the slight twang of the singers is typically the most obvious—and sometimes the only—country element.

It was precisely this continuing embrace of noncountry elements that prompted Larry Cordle and Lonesome Standard Time to release an album entitled **Murder on Music Row** (1999). The title track spelled out the divide between traditionalists and those in the country music industry who would sell out in pursuit of fame and fortune. The lyrics don't mince words:

> "But someone killed country music/
> Cut out its heart and soul/
> They got away with murder/
> Down on Music Row."

(Music Row is the Tin Pan Alley of country music, a section southwest of downtown Nashville where numerous music-related businesses are located.)

George Strait and Alan Jackson covered Cordle's song, first in a performance at the 1999 Country Music Association awards ceremony, then on Strait's **Latest Greatest Straitest Hits** (2000). The track won the 2000 CMA Vocal Event of the Year Award.

This salvo was a recent installment in the ongoing battle between trendiness and tradition that's been the central tension in country music since the music began to be heard over the radio and on recordings. Country music was the caboose of the evolutionary train of twentieth-century popular music: the connection to the past was crucial, and the give-and-take between past, present, and future continues to shape country music in the twenty-first century. We explore past, future, and present in tracks by the Dixie Chicks, Taylor Swift, and Tim McGraw.

19-1a The Dixie Chicks

While performing in London in April 2003, Natalie Maines, the lead singer of the Dixie Chicks, remarked, "Just so you know, we're ashamed the president of the United States is from Texas." She would later apologize for disrespecting the president but not for her antiwar position. It was not her first antiwar statement; previously, she had taken fellow country star Toby Keith to task for his ardent support of the war and the president. The remark provoked death threats and boycotts, and another thinly veiled barb at Keith continued to erode their support among country fans, to the point that Martie Maguire told a German reporter later that year, "We don't feel a part of the country scene any longer; it can't be our home any more." Despite a disappointing tour, the group refused to back down from their earlier position. In the lyrics to "**Not Ready to Make Nice**," a single from their acclaimed 2006 album *Taking The Long Way*, they recounted their ordeal—the death threats, a mother telling her child to hate a stranger—and made clear that they would continue to stand by their principles. Fortunately, what might have been professional suicide in an earlier time redefined their career and broadened their audience. The album entered the Top 200 album charts at No. 1 and won several Grammys.

The attention surrounding the Bush incident and their subsequent distancing of themselves from their core audience has deflected attention from the group's deep connection with traditional country music. The Dixie Chicks—currently Natalie Maines (b. 1974), Martie Maguire (born Martha Erwin, 1969), and Emily Robison (born Emily Erwin, 1972)—began as a four-person, all-girl bluegrass group busking on Dallas street corners, (bassist Laura Lynch would leave the group in 1995). The sisters are excellent instrumentalists: Maguire on violin, mandolin, and other string instruments; Robison on banjo, dobro, and numerous other instruments. As their career took off they moved away from bluegrass toward contemporary country. The pivotal point in their career came in 1995, when Maines, the daughter of top session steel guitarist Lloyd Maines, joined the group, now down to just three, as lead vocalist. Maines's singing gave the group a more mainstream sound, which in turn made them a top country act, with multiple multiplatinum albums.

Home (2002), their third album with Maines, simultaneously looked back to the past and ahead to the future. Unlike the previous two albums, it was an all-**acoustic recording**. In addition to the traditional bluegrass instruments—fiddle, banjo, dobro, mandolin, bass—there were steel guitar and Celtic instruments on several tracks. Despite this traditional orientation, the group scored a huge crossover hit with their cover of Fleetwood Mac's "**Landslide**."

"Landslide," Stevie Nicks (2002). The Dixie Chicks

For the Dixie Chicks, adapting "**Landslide**" was a relatively straightforward affair. Maines's vocal style isn't that far removed from that of Fleetwood Mac lead singer Stevie Nicks, and the original version of the song features an intricate acoustic guitar accompaniment. The group simply adapted the guitar accompaniment to banjo and mandolin, added acoustic bass, guitar, and dobro, and sang the chorus in their trademark three-part close harmony.

In covering "Landslide," the Dixie Chicks bring together the two paths by which Anglo-American folk music fed into popular music. Both the singing and guitar playing in Fleetwood Mac's original version of the song reach back through the singer/songwriters of the early seventies, to the folk revival of the early sixties, who took their inspiration from Woody Guthrie, who in turn learned the **thumb-brush** guitar style from Maybelle Carter. The setting of the song derives directly from bluegrass, a traditional style that is an outgrowth of old-time music, the folk music of the southern Appalachians that was the original country music. That music is timeless, but the Dixie Chicks' version is very much of the new century.

Their music video of "Landslide" alternates between Maines standing in surreal settings; Robison, who is proudly pregnant, lying in a stylized grassy field with a house that grows roots; and Maguire walking through an urban neighborhood.

acoustic recording An early recording process in which sound vibrations were transferred directly to the recording medium (cylinder or disc) by means of a large horn or cone. In 1925 it was replaced by electric recording.

thumb-brush An early country guitar style in which the performer plays the melody on the lower strings and, between melody notes, brushes the chords on the upper strings. It was first popularized by Maybelle Carter.

All three women are dressed fashionably: Maines and Robison wear long gowns but are barefoot; Maguire is wearing a sexy pantsuit. They are clearly worldly women, and the backgrounds have more to do with the art of Salvador Dali than with actual farms and forests. At the same time, we hear and see Robison play the dobro and Maguire play mandolin—after she plucks it out of midair. In its mix of traditional and modern, rural and urban, and real and surreal, the video seems to encapsulate the creative balance between tradition and innovation, and between down-home and sophisticated, which characterizes much contemporary country music.

It was during the tour supporting *Home* that Maines made her controversial comment. Despite the fallout from her remark, the Dixie Chicks continued to tour, but they did not record another studio album until 2006. In *Taking the Long Way* (2006), the group once again moved away from their traditional roots and away from their traditional audience. Super-producer Rick Rubin was called in to produce the album; Martie Maguire recalls him telling her, "I think this should sound like a great rock act making a country album, not a country act making a rock album." The Dixie Chicks' gravitation toward rock puts them at the cutting edge of country music, just as their political views separate them from the "my country right or wrong" mind-set associated with country music's core audience.

The career of the Dixie Chicks encapsulates the evolution of country music and the expansion of its audience. Country began as a folk tradition suddenly recorded and played over the air by amateur or semiprofessional performers. The Dixie Chicks began as bluegrass-playing buskers earning spare change. Today, they are a major act with broad commercial appeal, just as country is a major force in the music industry. They, and country generally, produce music with a distinct regional identity, but it is no longer a regional music. Their seamless transition from country traditionalists to a "great rock act making a country album" mirrors the open-ended two-way exchange between rock and country since the sixties.

19-1b Taylor Swift and "Cosmetic" Country

If Larry Cordle, George Strait, and Alan Jackson wanted to locate the murderers of country music, they could find culprits in the offices of Scott Borchetta's Big Machine Records, located along Nashville's Music Row. Borchetta founded Big Machine Records in 2005; Taylor Swift was the first act that he signed to his new label.

The prosecutors of the Music Row murderers might well try to convict Swift and Borchetta on the *lack* of evidence: songs that aren't about common country themes, a vocal style that does not have that immediately identifiable country sound, rhythms that are not countrified. There are traditional country instruments, but they are part of the mix rather than in the forefront. Swift's strongest defense would be her passionate love of country music.

Taylor Swift (b. 1989) grew up in Wyomissing, Pennsylvania, a comfortable small town about 60 miles northwest of Philadelphia and just under 800 miles from Nashville. Her interest in country music began early. Among the country artists she has cited as influences are Patsy Cline, Dolly Parton, Shania Twain and the Dixie Chicks, whom she credits for "stretching boundaries." The granddaughter of an opera singer, she began performing in grade school, made her first trip to Nashville at age eleven, where she tried without success to secure a recording contract, and started writing songs at twelve, shortly after learning three chords on the guitar. To support her intense desire for a career as a country musician, her family relocated to Hendersonville, Tennessee, a suburb of Nashville, when she was fourteen, and she signed a contract as a songwriter with Sony/ATV shortly after the move. By sixteen, she had recorded her first album, which went multiplatinum; she was a star before she graduated from high school.

Country music may have been Swift's first and deepest love, but her music also has much in common with the singer-songwriters of the early seventies and the tuneful rock and roll and rhythm and blues of the late fifties. Like the singer-songwriters, Swift's music is drawn so directly from her own experience that some of her ardent fans have attempted to match the stories in her songs to real-life incidents. And both words and music can evoke fifties teen-themed music: "**Tim McGraw**," her first hit song, describes the painful end to a summer relationship; the melody is set over a four-**chord progression** that is reminiscent of the "Heart and Soul" chords so common in doo-wop and rock-and-roll ballads. We discover another chapter in her high school life in "**You Belong with Me**," a track from her 2008 album *Fearless*.

In "You Belong With Me," Swift seems to be channeling Buddy Holly. Her lyric tells a story of teen angst, and in the music video, until her glamorous appearance at the dance, she wears big-rimmed glasses that are only slightly more stylish than Holly's thick frames. (In a nice touch, she also portrays the drama queen with whom she competes for the star wide receiver.) The song is by a high school student about the kind of crisis that seems so much a part of high school life. The locale could be anywhere in the United States where football is played; there's nothing that suggests country life. The musical setting is only cosmetically country. We hear banjo and steel guitar in the verse of the song, but they disappear in the chorus.

Stylistically, "You Belong with Me" shows the intersection of country, pop, and rock. The subsequent arc of her career to this point—gravitating away from country and toward a twenty-first-century pop—has proven to be a career-enhancing direction both creatively and commercially, and confirmation of Cordle's worst fears about the death of country music. That's not been the case with the music of Tim McGraw.

chord progression A sequence of chords. Many of the chord progressions in popular music follow well-used patterns, such as the chord progressions for "Heart and Soul" and "La Bamba."

19–1c Tim McGraw

Through age eighteen, Tim McGraw was Tim Smith. His mother Betty had become pregnant with him while she was still a student in a Jacksonville, Florida, high school, and her parents sent her to relatives in Louisiana. Soon after McGraw's birth, Betty married Horace Smith, whom she divorced in 1988. He discovered at age eleven that he had been conceived out of wedlock and that his father was the famous baseball pitcher Tug McGraw. It was seven more years before he connected with his biological father. Over time, they became closer. During that time, Tim McGraw legally changed his surname from Smith to McGraw and began his ascent to country music stardom.

His father had a hand in securing McGraw his break. In 1990, Tim gave his father a demo, who in turn passed it on to Mike Borchetta (the father of Scott Borchetta), who was the person responsible for McGraw signing with Mike Curb of Curb Records. (Twenty years later, Curb and McGraw parted ways with some animosity; McGraw now records for Scott Borchetta's Big Machine Records.)

By 1994, he was a star: *Not A Moment Too Soon*, his second album, was the top-selling country album of the year, and the winner of the Academy of Country Music Album of the Year Award. In the process, he also won the Top New Male Vocalist Award. In his earlier recordings, McGraw oscillated between hard country songs like "**Give It To Me Strait**" (pun intended, for sure) and more tender songs like the No. 1 single from the album "**Don't Take The Girl**."

Toward the end of the decade, he gravitated toward a more mainstream sound. That he would do so should not be surprising: in an interview with Larry King,

McGraw acknowledged that "I'm a huge '70s classic rock fan" and listed the Eagles, Tom Petty and the Heartbreakers, and Rush as among his favorite bands. We can hear his affinity for classic rock in his poignant song "**Live Like You Were Dying**," the title track from his eighth album.

The lyric of "Live Like You Were Dying" depicts a one-sided conversation with a middle-aged man diagnosed with a terminal disease. Craig Wiseman and Tim Nichols, the songwriting team that wrote it, got the seed for the storyline from an experience of a mutual friend who'd been misdiagnosed with a serious illness. It provoked them to think about how people might respond to that kind of news. There's a wonderful contrast in the lyric between macho activities like bullfighting and things from the heart, like forgiveness and friendship. The song must have been particularly poignant for McGraw, whose biological father had passed away early in 2004 from a brain tumor.

Like so many good country songs, "Live Like You Were Dying" tells a heartfelt story, and McGraw sings it with a recognizably country voice. However, almost every other aspect of the musical setting could easily support a tuneful rock song from the seventies, McGraw's favorite decade. Only the singing and the sound of the steel guitar are certifiably country-sounding elements. These two sounds, which are so strongly associated with country, may obscure the underlying affinity between classic rock and much country music from the last several decades. Music of country acts from Alabama to Zac Brown Band lies on a continuum that also includes Southern rock, roots rock, and other American-sounding rock styles.

In the decades around the turn of the twenty-first century, country music continues to evolve as it has almost since its emergence in the 1920s as a commercial music: by assimilating and "countrifying" existing mainstream and black music. Artists from Jimmie Rodgers, whose blue yodels brought the blues he heard growing up to a country audience, to hick-hop acts like The Lacs and Jawga Boyz, who are among the most prominent country rap artists, have integrated outside sounds into this tradition-oriented music and changed it in the process. For the past few decades, the sweet spot in country lies in a body of music situated stylistically between traditional honky-tonk and country pop. This music shares numerous common features with McGraw's cofavorite music, the classic rock of the seventies. In important features of musical style, much contemporary country is one branch of first-generation rock-era music; musically, it's the voices and the signature instruments (fiddle, steel guitar) that most obviously set it apart from more conventional classic rock.

As country music as a commercial enterprise approaches its centenary, its evolution seems to have ground to a halt. Top country artists of the 2010s, such as Luke Bryan and Blake Shelton, record and perform music in much the same style as country musicians at the end of the previous century. As we noted earlier, country music evolved from the dance tunes recorded by Fiddlin' John Carson in 1923 to the present by assimilating and "countrifying" contemporaneous styles—pop, blues, swing, and early rock. Continuing the evolution of country music beyond classic rock is problematic because its core values center around the story in the lyric, the melody to which the lyric is set, and the singing style of the vocalist. Prominently incorporating second-generation rock-era features risks diluting or dropping these core features in the search for novelty.

The greater threat by far to the integrity of country music is the gravitation toward pop. That's the Music Row development that traditionalists feel would murder country. That's a battle that's been fought throughout the history of country music: and it's likely to continue much as before.

19-2 Classic Rock and R&B in the Twenty-First Century: Three Profiles

In August 2006, Bob Dylan released (the perhaps ironically titled) *Modern Times*. The album title is ironic because so many of the tracks have musical settings that evoke pre-rock or early rock styles: pop songs, country blues, honky-tonk and other country styles. There is nothing "modern" about the songs in any conventional sense of the term. Instead, Dylan writes new material with deep roots in the past. In a 2004 interview with Robert Hilburn of the *Los Angeles Times*, Dylan described his unusual creative process:

> Well, you have to understand that I'm not a melodist . . . My songs are either based on old Protestant hymns or Carter Family songs or variations of the blues form. What happens is, I'll take a song I know and simply start playing it in my head. That's the way I meditate. A lot of people will look at a crack on the wall and meditate, or count sheep or angels or money or something, and it's a proven fact that it'll help them relax. I don't meditate on any of that stuff. I meditate on a song. I'll be playing Bob Nolan's "Tumbling Tumbleweeds" for instance, in my head constantly—while I'm driving a car or talking to a person or sitting around or whatever. People will think they are talking to me and I'm talking back, but I'm not. I'm listening to a song in my head. At a certain point, some words will change and I'll start writing a song.

The practice that Dylan describes—of fitting new words to an existing melody—dates back centuries. Our national anthem originated as an English drinking song, caught on at home and in the colonies, and served as the melody for Francis Scott Key's new text. The Civil War anthem, "The Battle Hymn of the Republic," featured new lyrics by Julia Ward Howe to the tune "John Brown's Body," which in turn developed organically from a folk hymn.

In both his approach to songwriting and the material that he uses as raw material, Dylan is deeply rooted in the past. Still, the songs on *Modern Times* sound fresh, and the album went platinum and critics reviewed it favorably. The same fresh approach to classic styles is also true of the other two tracks discussed below: Alicia Keys's, "**If I Ain't Got You**" and the Tedeschi Trucks Band's, "**Come See About Me**." We sample three varied approaches toward revitalizing the past in the work of three generations of musicians next.

19-2a Dylan Redux

Modern Times was released four decades after his time of greatest influence and three decades after his mid-seventies string of three No. 1 albums. Dylan's voice has dropped an octave or so since the sixties, and his musical support is at once loose (in the almost-improvisatory interplay of multiple layers of riffs) and tight (none of the sloppiness heard in earlier songs like "**Subterranean Homesick Blues**" and "**Like A Rolling Stone**").

In "**Someday Baby**," for which he won the 2007 Grammy Award for Best Solo Rock Vocal Performance, Dylan delves deep into the blues. He draws not on one blues style but several. One is the song itself, which first appeared in 1935 as "**Someday Baby Blues**" in a recording by Tennessee bluesman Sleepy John Estes, whom Dylan acknowledged on the liner notes of his 1965 album *Bringing It All Back Home*. Other bluesmen reframed and retitled the song: the best known is Muddy Waters's 1955 recording, it was **"Trouble No More,"** which was covered by the Allman Brothers early in their career. Like many country blues songs, Estes's original version does not use the conventional twelve-bar blues form: the phrases are of varying length and only two of the three basic blues chords are used. Dylan seems to tacitly acknowledge this by creating what is, in effect, a fifteen-bar blues form.

The supporting musicians evoke both electric blues and rockabilly. The influence of electric blues is most evident in the dense interplay among the guitarists—offbeat repeated notes, short answering riffs. All of this—even the slide guitar solo—is understated so that no one overpowers the others, or Dylan. The fast shuffle rhythm, marked most clearly by drummer George Receli, who's using brushes, recalls Carl Perkins's description of his approach to rockabilly: "I just put a little speed into some of the slow blues licks."

"Someday Baby" is yet another reinterpretation of Estes's original blues song, one that acknowledges the connection in the title. In its irregular form, dense instrumental interplay, and pulsing shuffle rhythm, it amalgamates multiple pre-rock blues traditions—country blues, electric blues, rockabilly. The flawless instrumental setting is the ideal backdrop for Dylan's low-register and low-key singing: both words and melody are in the forefront.

The core rock style became a modern music of the sixties when rock musicians brought Chuck Berry's blues-based rock and roll—already a synthesis of three blues styles— together with the "deep blues" of Robert Johnson and other early bluesmen and forging it into a powerful new sound. Four decades later, a mellower Bob Dylan takes much the same approach in "Someday Baby," except that he goes back further in time and stays there stylistically. This retrospective approach is "modern" mainly in the musicians' mastery of musical styles that date back more than half a century, and the unique qualities that Dylan brings to the music at this point in his career.

19–2b Alicia Keys

The opening track on Alicia Keys's second album *The Diary of Alicia Keys* (2003) is entitled **"Harlem's Nocturne."** The title is a play on a famous swing-era instrumental song entitled "Harlem Nocturne" that was composed and arranged for Ray Noble's fine big band. The song became a jazz standard: for generations, it has been a showcase for saxophonists, including Harry Haller of the Viscounts, whose recording of the song entered the charts twice, in 1959 and 1966.

The title "Harlem Nocturne" is in turn a play on the understanding of "nocturne" in classical music. A nocturne is night music, an instrumental composition that somehow suggests night. Most nocturnes are compositions for solo piano. The best-known nocturnes are those composed by the Polish composer Frédéric Chopin (1810–1849). The genre remained popular in classical music through the early twentieth century.

If one were to play the opening of Keys's "Harlem's Nocturne" for classical music aficionados unfamiliar with her music and ask them to identify the composer, they might well suggest someone like the late Romantic French composer Gabriel Fauré. The "drop it!" would quickly break the spell.

In beginning in this way, Keys further establishes the breathtaking breadth of her mastery: someone who is skilled enough to compose works that sound like classical music from the nineteenth-century (like the Chopin that she studied and performed growing up) and perform them idiomatically and expressively, then suddenly switch gears to sound like someone brought in around 1968 to record at Stax Records in Memphis, Tennessee or Fame Studio in Muscle Shoals, Alabama.

Alicia Keys (born 1981, Alicia Cook) was precocious. Raised in the "Hell's Kitchen" section of Manhattan, which is directly west of Times Square, Carnegie Hall and center of the entertainment industry, she had easy access to high-level instruction in voice, piano, and dance. At twelve, she matriculated in the Professional Performing Arts School, located not far from her home. Around the time she graduated at sixteen at the top of her class, she had a recording contract with Columbia records and a song ("Dah Dee Dah (Sexy Thing)") that she wrote and recorded used on the soundtrack to the film *Men in Black*.

Songs in A Minor (2001), her first studio album, soared to the top of the *Billboard 200* chart the week it was released. Keys, the album, and "**Fallin'**," the first single from the album, won five Grammy Awards the following year. In 2003, she released her second album, the eagerly anticipated release *The Diary of Alicia Keys* (2003). Among the tracks on the album was another award-winning song, "If I Ain't Got You."

The song begins with a piano prelude: simple, artfully performed broken chords over which Keys begins to vocalize wordlessly. After a brief pause, Keys begins to sing the verse in a low register, supporting her vocal line with an occasional chord or two. The only steady rhythm is the tapping on a closed hi-hat; the taps divide each slow beat into three equal parts. The song builds slowly but inexorably through a long bridge to a peak during the chorus, as Keys sings the title phrase several times. During the second statement of the melody, horns join in, playing sustained chords. The broken chords of the prelude return at the end, this time supported by bass and drums. Retrospectively, we discover that the chords of the prelude also serve as the harmony supporting the chorus of the song. The song ends as it began, with Keys playing almost alone—a few chords, then a filigree figure that rises, then dissolves.

Except for the piano playing that frames the heart of the song, Keys has channeled one branch of the slow soul music of the sixties. It's exemplified definitively in Aretha Franklin's recordings of "**Dr. Feelgood**" and the Carole King song "**(You Make Me Feel Like) A Natural Woman**." This approach in turn goes back another decade to Ray Charles, in songs like "**Drown In My Own Tears**." In this and several other of his hit songs from the late fifties, Charles had scandalized some members of the black community by secularizing gospel style and infusing it with the subject matter and the intense feeling of the blues.

Gospel music influenced much early rock-era black music, from doo-wop through Motown and soul. However, there is no branch of black popular music with a more obvious connection to black gospel than slow, soulful songs, of which "If I Ain't Got You" is a contemporary example. The connection begins with the underlying rhythm, which moves at an extremely slow tempo. We can gauge the role of tempo in helping to define the style by comparing it to other slow styles in rock-era music. There's slow-blues slow (e.g., Muddy Waters's "Hoochie Coochie Man" @ 75 BPM); rock-ballad slow (e.g., The Beatles' "Something" @ 66 BPM); and slow doo-wop slow (The Flamingos' "I Only Have Eyes For You" @ 59 BPM). And then there's black gospel slow (Thomas A. Dorsey's "Old Ship of Zion" @ 40 BPM and Alicia Keys's "If I Ain't Got You" @ 42 BPM).

The slow tempo and distinctive triplet division of the beat make the connection with black gospel immediate, because no other popular style features a rhythm like this. Perhaps more than any other musical feature, this rhythmic approach connects Keys's song directly to the precedents cited above, and indirectly to a particular style of black gospel. It complements the passion, richness, and range of her singing, as well as the instrumental setting.

Because she evokes sixties slow soul so faithfully, the classical-style piano passages stand out because they contrast so sharply with the rest of the song and because they are so unexpected. Their inclusion has been a successful strategy in much of her music; it works especially well here.

Keys's soulful singing and piano playing have remained at the center of her musical approach, even as she has explored more contemporary trends, as a solo artist and in collaborations with musicians as diverse as Usher and Angelique Kidjo.

19–2c The Tedeschi Trucks Band

It's not often that a rock band also serves as a matchmaker; the Tedeschi Trucks Band (or TTB, as they identify themselves on their website) is a rare exception. The band takes its name from the two principals, the wife/husband team of singer/guitarist Susan Tedeschi (b. 1970) and guitarist Derek Trucks (b. 1979). They met in 1999, when Tedeschi and her band were on tour with the Allman Brothers, which included Trucks. For several years after they married in 2001, they maintained separate professional lives: each toured and recorded with their own band. Finally, in 2007, they merged the two bands into one that they originally called Soul Stew Revival. In 2010, they rebooted as the Tedeschi Trucks Band and released their first album *Revelator* the following year. The album won the Grammy Award for Best Blues Album in 2012.

The band has also maintained a heavy touring schedule. In a 2016 interview, Tedeschi described how the family-like atmosphere of their band has spilled over to their audiences.

> "One cool thing I think over the past few years of us having a band together is it's brought our fans together too, like his fans and my fans, a lot of 'em have even hooked up and gotten married! We have people who say like, 'I was your fan, and my husband was Derek's fan, and we met at your shows.' So in a way, it's really cool, like we can bring people together."

What brought Tedeschi and Trucks together was the blues and the rock-era music with a deep connection to the blues. Trucks is the nephew of Butch Trucks, a drummer with the Allman Brothers throughout their 45-year career. Derek Trucks joined the band in 1999 and remained with the group until they disbanded in 2014. He grew up listening to Eric Clapton (he's named after Clapton's pseudonym with the Dominos) and master slide guitarist Elmore James. He got his first guitar when he was nine and was sitting in with the Allman Brothers within a year. He would go on to record and tour with Clapton; his performances at Clapton's Crossroads festival were sensations.

Trucks grew up in Jacksonville, Florida, where his family has roots, and where Southern rock took root. His wife and coleader Susan Tedeschi grew up southeast of Boston in an Italian family ("tedeschi" means "German" in Italian). Her father was a fan of country blues singers such as Lightning Hopkins. Drawn to black music, she listened to her father's blues recordings and sang in a black gospel choir. After graduating from Boston's Berklee College of Music, she gradually built her career and built up her skills as a blues guitarist.

Not surprisingly, she and her future husband found common ground musically. More surprisingly, they have been able to parlay that into a mutually respectful professional relationship, with a big band (bassist, keyboardist, two drummers, two guitars, three backup singers [including former Trucks Band lead singer Mike Mattison] and three horn players), all of whom seem to get along like family. Their sound is a soulful stew that draws on the blues, soul, and the blues-influenced rock of the late sixties and early seventies, with Tedeschi singing with the deep feeling and heightened inflection of singers like Janis Joplin and Bonnie Raitt. We hear these qualities in "**Come See About Me**," a track from *Revelator*.

"Come See About Me" begins with the drummers creating a loose-jointed sixteen-beat rhythm, over which Trucks plays a short slide solo, before he and Tedeschi play an extended line that is the instrumental signature of the track. Tedeschi moans (to borrow Hank Williams Sr.'s word) the man-trouble lyric. Her singing evokes the heartfelt no-frills delivery of generations of blues singers. Particularly since the formation of TTB, she has become an exemplar of contemporary blues singing.

Truck's slide guitar playing is an ideal complement to Tedeschi's singing. Trucks plays with vocal-like inflection, with a fast, intense vibrato. In his occasional responses to Tedeschi's singing and especially in solo work, Trucks explores the full range of the instrument: in the studio recording, he is mainly in the higher register, but in the live recording from Atlanta shown below, he ventures into the low register. The striking differences between the two solos offers evidence of his exceptional skill as an improviser. Trucks is a serious student of jazz: the couple's children are named Charles, for the masterful saxophonist Charlie Parker, and Sophia Naima; Sophia's middle name is a the title of a song by saxophonist John Coltrane. Trucks's study of jazz, blues, and rock has enabled him to develop a unique approach that synergistically blends elements of all three genres into a transcendent personal style. He's learned from masters in all three, and has transformed what he's learned into something unique.

The success of groups like the Tedeschi Trucks Band evidence the continued vitality of music that draws on the blues, and the soul and rock that the blues helped shape. They are among the current generation of musicians who help keep these traditions alive.

19-2d First-Generation Rock in the Twenty-First Century

The music of Bob Dylan, Alicia Keys, and the Tedeschi Trucks Band bring the past into the present. The artists come from different generations, and explore different musical territory. However, their music shares three features that make them more than simply an attempt to work in an earlier style.

- *The artists truly understand the styles in which they are working.* By 2006, Dylan had lived with the music he drew from for more than half a century. Trucks was playing with the Allman Brothers as a teenager, and Tedeschi immersed herself in black music early on. In an interview, Peter Edge, the vice president of A&R at J Records, Alicia Keys's label, concurred with the observation that she is "a self-contained and sincere R&B artist" by comparing her in this regard to Stevie Wonder.
- *They and the musicians working with them are masterful.* Dylan surrounded himself with excellent musicians whose support showcases his unique interpretation of this blues standard. Keys is comfortable as both a singer and pianist fluent in classical and gospel-style R&B piano playing. Tedeschi continues the line of women who can sing the blues with passion, and Trucks is a peerless master of slide guitar.

- *Each has a distinctive ability.* For Dylan, it's the lyrics; for Keys it's her facility as a pianist and her ability to change styles; for TTB, it's Trucks's ability to construct powerful, expressive solos in the moment.

Collectively, they demonstrate that musicians of all generations can create vital new music in timeless styles.

Their music, the timeless music of bands like AC/DC, the continuing popularity of classic rock, the secure market share of country music, and the emergence of new acts working in older styles—"roots" rock, early R&B, rockabilly—demonstrate the appeal of the enduring values of first-generation rock-era music. Music that was good when it came out 40 or 50 years ago is still good, and, as numerous surveys have verified, it still attracts a large audience. So does music that continues to explore that musical territory.

CHAPTER 20

ALTERNATIVES IN THE TWENTY-FIRST CENTURY

Learning Objectives:

1) Explain how Green Day successfully incorporated both pop and punk genres into their style.

2) Recall the individual characteristics of exemplary "diva" singers in the early 2000s.

3) Discuss the defining stylistic components used in Eminem's rap music.

4) Summarize Angélique Kidjo's contributions to Afropop.

5) Give examples of key cross-cultural synthesized genres that gained popularity in the 1990s.

6) Clarify the musical terms: "Active Rock," "Mainstream Rock," and "Modern Rock."

Chapter Introduction

In December 2009, *Billboard* magazine published a list that they dubbed "Artists of the Decade." They explained how they chose the twenty acts that made their list in this way:

> "They strutted, they rocked and they grooved on the charts all decade; these are the 20 music stars with the best performance on the Billboard 200 albums chart and the Hot 100 over the last ten years."

Bookending the artists of the decade list were Eminem at No. 1 and Christina Aguilera at No. 20. Rounding out the top five were Usher, Nelly, Beyoncé, and Alicia Keys. The only rock act in the Top 10 was Nickelback at No. 7. The only alternative rock act in the Top 20 was Linkin Park at No. 19.

Flash back to a similar list for the seventies—Joel Whitburn's chart-based "artists of the seventies" list. Rock acts from Elton John (at No. 1) to George Harrison (at No. 20) dominate the list. A comparison of the two lists highlights the extent to which the commercial center of gravity in the music industry has shifted away from rock toward R&B, rap, and pop. A focus only on commercial success fails to capture the breadth of musical activity in rock-era music, here and around the world.

Experience an interactive version of this era in ⋮ MINDTAP

The music that has developed from rock is now a global musical language, and a platform for meaningful social and cultural expression. And it fails to capture the activity of those acts who choose to explore creative paths that delight critics but do not attract broad support.

In this chapter, we discuss twenty-first century music that samples music based on second-generation rock-era genres that has been commercially, culturally, and/or critically significant. We begin with the pop punk of Green Day.

20-1 Pop Punk

Of all the challenges facing punk bands, perhaps the most complex was creating a viable fusion of punk and pop. As we have noted in previous chapters, punk reshaped rock and pop during the eighties and early nineties. However, punk was a reaction against rock and pop; in attitude and musical substance, it was in direct opposition to mainstream music. As a result, the difficulty for punk was reconciling punk values with a pop sensibility. The danger was that the David and Goliath opposition of pop and the rock music establishment would morph into Jonah and the whale.

Pop punk caught on in the mid-nineties, principally on the strength of albums and tours by bands such as Green Day, the Offspring, and Rancid. Other bands, such as Weezer and blink-182, followed in their wake. Its rise can be understood as both a product of and reaction against grunge. Grunge brought the hard edge of alternative music into the mainstream, thus laying the foundation for a more aggressive tone in mainstream music. At the same time, those who were not ready for a steady diet of Nirvana-style doom and gloom welcomed music that blended punk's edge with a more upbeat tone.

No band has done this more successfully than Green Day: guitarist/vocalist Billie Jo Armstrong (b. 1972), bassist Mike Dirnt (born Michael Pritchard, 1972) and drummer Tré Cool (born Frank Wright, 1972). The group, which has its roots in the East Bay region of northern California, was precocious: Armstrong and Dirnt played their first gig in 1988 as Sweet Children; Green Day, with drummer John Kiffmeyer, released their first record and completed their first nationwide tour in 1990. In 1991, Tré Cool replaced Kiffmeyer. Three years later, the group signed a contract with Reprise records and released *Dookie*, which put them and pop punk in the mainstream consciousness. Their career since that time has been a steady ascent. Their 2004 album *American Idiot*, which won a Grammy as Best Rock Album in 2005, reached the top of the charts in both the United States and the United Kingdom, and received favorable reviews from the mainstream press. We sample their fusion of punk and pop in "**Wake Me Up When September Ends**," one of the tracks from the album. (The album and the video of the song include the unofficial fourth member of the band, guitarist Jason White [b. 1973], who has toured with the band since 1999.)

Certainly since they signed a contract with a major label, Green Day has been castigated by the alternative and punk diehards for selling out. The discontent surfaced with *Dookie* and resurfaced strongly with *American Idiot*. One component of their discontent was the extraordinary success of the album; the album has already sold well over 10,000,000 units worldwide, including 1,000,000 digital downloads. But those who feel that the band has put aside the attitude and atmosphere of punk in order to embrace pop will find plenty of ammunition in "Wake Me Up When September Ends."

The lyric of the song is personal, not political. It alludes to Armstrong's pain as he recalls the death of his father, who died in the September when Armstrong was ten. More generally, it is a bittersweet lament over the loss of innocence.

(Interestingly, the video for the song completely recontextualizes the lyric: it depicts the relationship of a young couple who are torn apart when the man enlists in the military and is sent to Iraq.)

Musically, the song has more in common with the Everly Brothers' **"All I Have To Do Is Dream"** than any punk or alternative song on the playlist. The tempo is slow, and the tone is nostalgic, although the objects of nostalgia are distinctly different. In both, a tuneful melody is the dominant element—in "Wake Me Up When September Ends," even in the restatement of the melody, in which the accompaniment is fleshed out with pounding punk power chords and drumbeats. Further, both the development of the opening phrase of the melody from a simple riff and the use of AABA form turn back the clock even further: this is the most characteristic melodic style and form in the Tin Pan Alley songs of the twenties and thirties. Finally, the delicate bell-like sounds that complement Armstrong's acoustic guitar during the opening are far removed from punk's characteristic sound world. By contrast, the punk elements seem to be an overlay: they are certainly not essential to the message of the song or its identity, which is all but complete after a full statement of the melody.

Those who value the song and the album—and there are many—can point out that accusing Green Day of selling out because they incorporated pop elements is simply a matter of putting theory before practice. The more appropriate issue is whether lyric and music work together to convey a consistent musical message. From this perspective, the pop elements are more relevant to the lyric than punk.

20-2 The Divas: Female Pop Stars after 1995

Diva is the feminine form of the Latin word for God or God-like; it shares a common etymology with *divine*. *Diva* came into English through Italian, where it identifies a female opera singer performing a leading role. More recently, it has come to refer to female pop singing stars, and even more generally, to any woman with star quality (and too often the attitude seems to be part of the baggage).

20-2a The Emergence of the Divas

In 1998, VH1 sponsored its inaugural Divas concert, an all-star event presented to raise funds for the station's "Save the Music" foundation. The concert brought together two rock-era queens—Aretha Franklin (the queen of soul) and Gloria Estefan (the queen of Latin pop)—and three rising stars: Mariah Carey, Céline Dion, and Shania Twain. The Divas concert series ran for six more years; the last concert took place in 2004. The format remained much the same: bring together established stars and new talent; younger invitees included Christina Aguilera, Mary J. Blige, Faith Hill, Jewel, Beyoncé, Brandy, Shakira, and Jessica Simpson.

These stars and other young female performers, such as Alicia Keys, Jennifer Lopez, and Britney Spears, formed a new generation of pop singers. Their numbers show Madonna's enormous impact; it is clear that her unprecedented commercial success paved the way for their entry into the music business. Not surprisingly, in light of this connection, image has been as important as sound. Most look as good as they sing, and all are portrayed as glamorous on album covers and in the media. A few—for example, Britney Spears, Jennifer Lopez—enjoy a tabloid-driven celebrity apart from their music.

The diva label was not simply show-business hype: for the most part, they are skilled singers with pleasant, accessible voices and, in some cases, distinctive, even unique, vocal abilities. For example, Mariah Carey's vocal range is more than twice that of a typical pop singer (her songs have often included extensive reminders of this fact), and the fluency of Christina Aguilera's melismatic singing deserves comparison with not only great black singers like Aretha but also opera singers.

They are a diverse group: Shania Twain and Céline Dion are Canadian. Twain took the name Shania, an Ojibwa word, to affirm her connection with Native Americans: her stepfather is a full-blooded member of the nation. Dion is from French-speaking Canada. Shakira is Colombian. Jennifer Lopez is a child of Puerto Rican parents. Christina Aguilera's father is from Ecuador. Beyoncé, Mary J. Blige, and Brandy are black; Mariah Carey has white, black, and Latino blood. Several gravitated toward pop from their "home" styles: Twain and Hill began as country singers; Dion's first songs were in French; Alicia Keys, Beyoncé, and Mary J. Blige have strong R&B roots.

Their common ground extends beyond gender, appearance, success, and on-stage compatibility. They and their producers have incorporated the defining elements of eighties/nineties pop into their music. Their music may retain features of their home style—Jennifer Lopez singing in Spanish, rapper Jay-Z on a Beyoncé track, steel guitar in a Faith Hill song. Still, the use of rich textures with synthesized instruments and active rhythms, in support of a tuneful melody that sets a lyric about love, brings much of their music into the pop middle ground. Their chart success evidences the same.

It is fitting that Aretha was one of the five artists invited to perform at the first Divas concert. Clearly, she was the dominant musical personality, although she only sang with others, and she has been the dominant influence on the vocal style of many of the younger divas—black, white, or Latina. Indeed, the prevailing vocal style of these performers might be described as Aretha-lite.

Her influence is evident in the singers' diction, which has something of the intonation and cadence of black speech; in the vocal quality, typically a more restrained echo of her soulful sound; and in the forms of expressive nuance, especially the use of melisma. Each has personalized her style to some degree, but most share a connection to the more soulful black vocal style of the sixties and beyond, which Aretha's singing epitomizes. The young divas may have modeled their image and performance style after Madonna, but their musical and vocal conception derives most directly from Aretha and her peers. We hear evidence of both influence and individuality in Christina Aguilera's hit, "What a Girl Wants."

Christina Aguilera: "What a Girl Wants"

If *American Bandstand* was required after-school viewing for teens in the late fifties, then the *Mickey Mouse Club* was the must-watch show for their younger siblings. Both shows aired on ABC every afternoon. The *Mickey Mouse Club* was one of Walt Disney Productions' first excursions into television programming. The show featured two older men guiding a group of perky kids through an hour of kids' news, singing, dancing, cartoons, and stories. All sported the mouse-eared beanies that were as required an accessory for pre-teens as coonskin caps had been a few years previously (the Davy Crockett fad) and that a single white sequined glove would be for Michael Jackson fans in the early eighties. The show ran from 1955 to 1959, when Disney elected to cancel it.

In 1989, thirty years after its initial cancellation, the Disney Corporation revived the show for a second time. (The first attempt, which went on the air in 1977, was a failure.) This time the show aired on the Disney Channel, a premium cable channel that commenced in 1983. This would prove to be the longest-running version of the show; *MMC*, as it was called, would air for seven seasons. It would also help launch the careers of three top pop acts: the male vocal group 'N Sync and two pop divas, Britney Spears and Christina Aguilera.

By the time Christina Aguilera (b. 1980) joined the *Mickey Mouse Club* in 1992, she had been an active performer for half of her life. By six, she was performing in talent shows around Pittsburgh, where she grew up; she competed on *Star Search* at nine. Aguilera's star rose quickly. In 1998, she was chosen to sing **"Reflection"** for the animated Disney feature *Mulan*; this led to the release of her self-titled first album, which quickly went to the top of the album charts in 1999; so did "Genie in a Bottle" and **"What a Girl Wants"**—the top two singles from the album.

"What a Girl Wants" puts a contemporary sheen on the well-established rock-era black pop style even as it showcases Aguilera's considerable vocal ability. The lyrics impart a postfeminist flavor to a discussion of love: Aguilera asks her significant other to give her some space as she looks around (but never touches). That she asks for it and that he assents to her request show that, in song at least, relationships should offer equal opportunity to both parties.

The story unfolds in typical fashion: a series of verses build smoothly to a catchy chorus with a can't-miss hook. The melody unfolds in smooth undulations, and at a pace that allows the words to be easily understood; Aguilera saves most of her vocal acrobatics for interludes and obbligato flights during the chorus.

Although the song is based on the familiar verse/chorus model, "What a Girl Wants" is anything but formulaic. From the introduction that features just Aguilera and percussion sounds through the pseudo-classical synthesizer interlude through the chorus that never really ends (to suggest that Aguilera's looking-but-not-touching will not stop anytime soon), the song evidences the considerable skills of songwriter-producer Guy Roche, who co-wrote the song with Shelley Peiken. Both have supplied numerous hits for Aguilera and other leading pop acts.

Roche created a rich setting for Aguilera's singing: it combines backup vocals plus synthesized percussive and pitched sounds, with subtle colors added via conventional instruments: the strummed acoustic guitar gives warmth to the largely synthesized accompaniment.

The rhythms of "What a Girl Wants" belong to the new century; they show the influence of post-Motown black pop and dance music. From the pop of the eighties, it takes the largely implicit beat keeping and highly syncopated patterns; its especially active rhythms show the influence of dance music. The basic tempo of the song, which we sense from the alternation of bass note and backbeat, is quite slow: about 75 beats per minute, or just over half the speed of a disco track or rock song. In the verse, both Aguilera's vocal and the strummed guitar move at sixteen-beat speed. The dance music influence becomes most evident in the rhythms that move twice this fast: that is, eight times as fast as the beat. These especially animated rhythms include synthesizer noodles, percussion bursts, and most spectacularly, Aguilera's flawless melismas, which are the contemporary pop counterpart to not only the melismatic flourishes of Aretha Franklin, Patti LaBelle, and other top black singers but also the florid embellishments heard in operatic arias for sopranos. (Especially in these moments, Aguilera earns her diva status.)

The stylized melismas are one dimension of Aguilera's black-influenced vocal style. Her delivery of the verse sounds black, or at least beige; it is quite different in inflection and intonation from her everyday speech, as heard in television interviews, for example. The basic quality is rich and resonant, although not as gritty as Aretha or Tina Turner. The inflection of the vocal line—for instance, the occasional bluesy bent note—also betrays black influence.

Especially when considered in the context of the pop music landscape at the turn of the century, Aguilera's vocal sound and style seem not so much a case of Aguilera deliberately trying to sound black as singing in the prevailing popular style. Pop singing, like so many other aspects of the style, evidences the profound influence and the continuing evolution of the black pop tradition that took shape in the early sixties. By the end of the century, it was so thoroughly assimilated that the music of black, Latino, and white pop performers represented a smooth stylistic continuum, rather than several distinct styles.

The infusion of dance rhythms into pop virtually demands movement on video and in live performance. With Michael Jackson as the quintessential role model, elaborate choreography became the norm in music videos; the video of "What a Girl Wants" is typical in this respect. This sets up a curious dissonance between the song's subject and its presentation. The lyrics read like an intimate conversation. If they had been set to music in the sixties or seventies, the song would probably have been a slow rock ballad. Although there are brief scenes where Aguilera lies in the lap of her video heartthrob, the bulk of the video features her dancing with her crew.

The dissonance becomes clear if we think of singing in popular music as a more urgent and compelling form of speech. The great women singers, from Bessie Smith and Billie Holiday through Aretha Franklin and Tina Turner, conveyed their feelings mainly through their voices. They stood and sang their songs; vigorous movement wasn't necessary to get the message across. However, the conventions of pop and music videos virtually preclude such a presentation; there has to be activity, especially when the rhythms of the song all but require it. The song is effective in spite of the conflict between the message of the lyrics and the musical setting, rather than because of it.

Aguilera and the numerous other young divas were a commanding presence in pop music at the end of the twentieth century and the beginning of the twenty-first century. They joined an earlier generation of stars that included Whitney Houston and Janet and La Toya Jackson. No group of pop performers was more frequently heard or was more in the public eye. They reaped the fruit of the efforts of Madonna and the many other women who worked to break down the gender barrier in popular music. Their success evidenced the fact that the pop music world was a level playing field with respect to race and gender.

20-3 Eminem and the Mainstreaming of Rap

A quick glance at Eminem's record sales might lead one to think history was simply repeating itself: white musicians co-opt a black music and popularize it without really understanding the style. It was a recurring pattern in the twentieth century, most notoriously in the fifties, when pop singers tried to cover rhythm-and-blues songs. The reality in this case is far more complex.

There is no doubt about Eminem's commercial success. He is among the most successful artists of the 2000s. All of his studio albums have gone multiplatinum, and all but the first peaked at the top of the album charts. He has had numerous chart-topping singles, including **"Lose Yourself"** and **"Love the Way You Lie."**

However, Eminem (born Marshall Mathers, 1972) has paid his dues along the way. As a teen, he participated in battle raps with black rappers and eventually earned the respect of African-American hip-hop audiences. Early in his career, he teamed with black rapper Royce da 5′9″ to form Soul Intent. His mentor has been

Dr. Dre, who has provided the musical context for his raps. And he could easily have been a child of the ghetto: raised by a single mom; moving around constantly; dropping out of school; devastated by an uncle who committed suicide; fathering a child out of wedlock; dealing with substance abuse issues; trying to hold together a tumultuous relationship with his longtime partner, Kimberly Scott, whom he met in 1989, married in 1999, divorced in 2001, remarried and divorced again in 2006; fending off lawsuits; and picking public spats with other celebrities. As with other rappers, his life has spilled over into his art. Among the numerous lawsuits that have been filed against him are those by his mother and ex-wife, who have sued him for defamation of character. Many of his songs, including "Love the Way You Lie," are or could easily be autobiographical.

Eminem recorded "Love the Way You Lie" for his 2010 album *Recovery*. Both the album and the single quickly went to the top of the charts. In this track, he partnered with R&B star Rihanna; she sang the chorus, and his raps provided the verse. (Interestingly, she recorded another version of the song with sung verse and chorus and with a rap by Eminem interpolated.) The track exemplifies the synergy that can result when rap and song are combined. Rihanna's sung chorus, which opens the track and is repeated throughout, is the hook that anchors the track in listeners' ears. The unvarying repetition serves at least two purposes: it lodges the hook more deeply even as it underscores the main theme of the track, and it doesn't deflect attention away from the rap by introducing variety. The four-chord accompaniment that is also recycled under both chorus and rap helps glue the two together.

Eminem's rap is musical Everclear—the 190-proof kind. It is an intense, condensed account of a tumultuous relationship. The juxtaposition of sung and rapped content highlights the power of rap: words sung to music typically take much longer to deliver, and even when they are delivered rapidly, the musical setting can attenuate the impact of the words. The high pitch of Eminem's delivery energizes the violent contrasts in his rap, which in turn resonates with the violence in the relationship. His vivid images flash by (in words and also in the video) like a film on fast forward. The track and the video are a gripping four-and-a-half–minute reality show.

Eminem's overwhelming commercial success, critical acclaim, and his widespread acceptance within the music industry and by black and white audiences evidence his almost unique position in contemporary musical life: he is a highly skilled performer in an almost exclusively black genre, who happens to be white.

In the twenty-first century, rap—in all of its manifestations and combinations—is an enduring and significant part of the rock-era musical world. The numerous rap/R&B syntheses—and rap/rock hybrids such as rapcore, rap rock, and rap metal, even hick-hop!—offer further evidence of its strong presence in popular music.

20–4 Electronica as Popular Music: Moby

In a 1993 review, Jon Pareles, the contemporary popular music critic of the *New York Times*, wrote:

> If techno music is going to make the leap from dance clubs to the pop charts, its starkly propulsive dance rhythms are going to need melodies, identifiable stars or both. Moby, a one-man band from New York City, could be the techno performer whose showmanship carries him to a wider audience without turning techno tracks into pop songs.

Nine years later, Moby made the front covers of *Spin, Wired,* and the *New York Times Magazine.* In the United States, Moby (born Richard Melville Hall, 1965—he took his professional name from the famous novel *Moby Dick,* by Herman Melville, a distant relation) has put a face on electronica, in part by bringing his music closer to a mainstream pop style. This of course has provoked cries of outrage from hardcore clubbers who feel that he's selling out. Nevertheless, the genre has significantly broadened its audience base.

Moby began his professional career in 1982, playing guitar in a punk band called the Vatican Commandos; he left a year later. By 1989, he had redirected his energies to electronic music. Over the next decade, he attracted a loyal following, first in Great Britain, then in the United States, among dance club audiences as a recording artist and DJ. His first hit was **"Go,"** a single from his 1993 album *The Story So Far.* His breakthrough came in 1999, with the release of the album *Play.* Although sales started slowly, by 2002 the album had sold over ten million units, earning it diamond album certification. Several singles, including **"South Side,"** also charted. More tellingly, every one of the eighteen tracks on the album has been licensed for commercials, films, and soundtracks. With this album, electronica, as represented by Moby's music, found mainstream success.

Moby originally recorded "South Side" with Gwen Stefani (b. 1969), the vocalist with No Doubt, a Jamaican-influenced alternative band. The version that featured her did not appear on the first release of the album. However, the single version and the reissue of the album did include her. That she was present, and a key component of the song, indicates a significant difference between "South Side" and "Nude Photo." "South Side" assimilates the electronic elements into a traditional rock song format: the song has a beginning and an end; an instrumental introduction; a (rap-inspired spoken) verse; a sung chorus with a can't-miss hook; and a vintage-style guitar solo. In this format, the song is clearly directed toward radio airplay, instead of being confined to use within a club. Indeed, the song reached No. 3 on *Billboard's* Modern Rock Tracks and No. 14 on their Hot 100 chart.

The electronic elements—including the rhythm track, the orchestral strings-inspired sound cushion under the chorus, and numerous other subtle effects—are merged with rock and rap elements to create a new fusion for the turn of the millennium. However, the song follows a time-honored pattern in popular music that we first observed in the music for the minstrel show: create a new sound by assimilating outsider styles (fiddle music/ techno) into the prevailing style.

It is clear that "South Side" owes much of its success to the incorporation of rock and rap elements. Historically, when a new sound emerges, audiences have first embraced versions of it that contain familiar elements: the cover versions of R&B songs in the fifties are a noteworthy example. However, it is also clear that by incorporating these familiar elements into "South Side," Moby has abandoned the esthetic of techno, as exemplified in tracks such as "Nude Photo." It is a song, not a dance track. Whether this is good or bad—or neither—depends on your point of view. Those who preferred their techno "pure" would be turned off by the song (and many of Moby's longtime fans felt betrayed by his move to the mainstream). Those who were not ready to take their electronica straight welcomed the more familiar features.

Moby's *Play* has been a rare exception; the large family of electronica styles commands a relatively small market share. Nevertheless, its influence on popular music has been profound. Rap, pop, rock, world music—there is hardly a contemporary sound that does not show at least some influence of the technology and tools of dance music.

20–5 Afropop and the Growth of World Music

All along the upper west coast of Africa, from Senegal to Zaire, native popular musics have flourished. Each country has its own popular style; indeed, many "national" styles actually emerge from a people within a country, such as the Wolof in Senegal. Nigeria is home to *juju* and <u>Afrobeat</u>; Ghana has highlife. *Makossa* is a popular local dance music in Cameroon; so is *soukous* in Zaire. *Gbegbe* grew up alongside other African popular styles in the Ivory Coast; *mbalax* is native to Senegal and the Gambia.

Some styles are updated versions of older popular styles. Highlife, for example, dates back to mid-century but was modernized with the addition of electric guitars and other changes. Other styles are transformations of traditional music in the seventies, Nigerian musicians created *gbegbe* to give their traditional music a modern sound.

National styles have moved freely from country to country. *Juju* has flourished in Ghana and Sierra Leone, as well as Nigeria. Not surprisingly, perhaps, the colonial language has had some effect on the dissemination of a style. Highlife is more popular in English-speaking countries; *soukous* more popular in French-speaking nations. But cross-fertilization transcends tribal, national, and linguistic barriers. In Africa and within the expatriate communities in Europe and the United States, musicians listen to and learn from each other. As a result, there are common elements in much West African music. Some of them distinguish it not only from US/UK rock-era music but also Afrocentric Caribbean styles.

We hear the fruits of an African/international fusion in a track featuring two of Africa's musical ambassadors.

20–5a The Sound of Afropop

In 1991, Senegalese singer Youssou N'Dour (b. 1959) was appointed a Goodwill Ambassador for the United Nations Children's Fund (UNICEF). Eleven years later, Angélique Kidjo (b. 1960), a native of Benin, also became a UNICEF Goodwill Ambassador. Senegal and Benin are former French colonies in sub-Saharan Africa. Senegal is along the west coast: Dakar, the capital city and N'Dour's hometown, is the westernmost city on the African continent. Benin is a small country directly west of Nigeria and southeast of Senegal.

Kidjo and N'Dour are the best-known African female and male singers, respectively. They have earned widespread critical acclaim: both have won Grammys, and the *New York Times* labeled N'Dour "one of the world's greatest singers." Both have been extraordinarily active on behalf of causes that they believe to be important: Kidjo for education and human rights—she founded the Batonga foundation to provide young African girls with upper-level education to prepare them for leadership positions; and N'Dour for technology and health—N'Dour helped organize the 2006 Africa Live: The Roll Back Malaria Concert, which was given in Dakar.

Kidjo moved to Paris in 1983, where she obtained work as a backup vocalist. By 1989, she had a recording contract and a career in Europe. Within a few years, she had become the best-known African female vocalist since Miriam Makeba. N'Dour's international career also took off in the eighties after Peter Gabriel recruited him for his first WOMAD concert.

In 2005, N'Dour's *Egypt* won a Grammy for Best Contemporary World Music Album; three years later, Kidjo received the same honor for *Djin Djin*. For Kidjo, *Djin Djin* was a conscious effort to return to her roots, to recapture and integrate into her music the rhythms and sounds of her home country. She had grown up listening to native musicians and rock, funk, and pop from abroad; the album is an expression of that rich heritage. The album features an impressive list of guest artists, including Peter Gabriel, Alicia Keys, saxophonist Branford Marsalis, Josh Groban, and Carlos Santana. Among the most popular tracks on the album is "**Ae Ae**"

"Ae Ae" comes in two versions. The versions are identical except for the vocals. In the second version, N'Dour joins Kijdo and improvises a vocal obbligato over an otherwise instrumental interlude. "Ae Ae" features three of the most common features of African/international fusions: the extensive and prominent use of traditional African instruments; complete western rhythm sections, typically laying down a sixteen-beat rhythm; and melody and harmony that put a distinctively African spin on the major scales and three basic chords of European tonal harmony. In addition to a large array of unpitched percussion instruments, "Ae Ae" uses a *balafon*, a xylophone-like instrument, and a *kora*, a harp-lute made from a calabash. Both play moving lines behind the vocal throughout the song.

The rhythm section on "Ae Ae" includes drum set, electric bass, guitars, and organ, in addition to the African percussion instruments. The musicians lay down a vibrant groove based on the ubiquitous sixteen-beat rhythm, with an active bass line and a dense, percussive texture. The particular timbre of the electric guitar on this recording is distinctive to much West African music, and the African instruments, both pitched and unpitched, color the sound to give it a specifically African flavor. Still, it is a version of the international groove so popular around the turn of the century.

The approach to melody and harmony represent a common feature of pop styles throughout West Africa: an adaptation of European tonality in which melodies are constructed entirely from the seven notes of diatonic scales (rather than pentatonic scales) and harmony consists of progressions built from two or three chords that cycle with little or no change throughout the song. In "Ae Ae," there are three progressions, all built from I, IV, and V: one for the solo verse, the second for the bridge, and the third for the chorus.

This Afropop approach to melody and harmony has more in common with the hymns and other religious music brought to Africa by missionaries than with western popular music. The choral singing heard on this recording also highlights this European connection.

Weaving through the buoyant rhythms are the voices of Kidjo and N'Dour. Kidjo's lyric is part commentary on the plight of Africans who emigrate to Europe to escape the poverty, poor health, and political turmoil in Africa, and part exhortation to Africans to become self-sufficient. In this respect, the song continues the practice among members of the African diaspora (Kidjo now lives in New York) of sending a powerful message over a compelling groove. As Kidjo said in the video about *Djin Djin,* she wants to "entertain each other but learn at the same time."

In "Ae Ae," as in much of the music by African artists who have enjoyed international success, there is something of the atmosphere of a family reunion. It is not so much a coming together of people as of styles and cultures—music from the mother continent meeting up with its offspring in the Americas. What Africa had sent to the Americas via the slave trade came back to Africa transmuted but still compatible, so that they could be easily blended. A second wave of African music, mixed from traditional sounds and their evolutionary mutations among the diaspora, has found a welcome audience in America and around the world.

20-6 Ethno-Techno and a Cross-Cultural Synthesis

The music of Afro Celt Sound System is the product of two remarkable fusions: first, the fusion of Celtic music with the music of west Africa, and second, the fusion of these traditional musics with cutting edge techno.

Afro Celt Sound System was the inspiration of Simon Emmerson, a Grammy-nominated producer, guitarist, and programmer. The idea of combining African and Celtic music had taken root several years earlier, and in his work on Senegalese vocalist Baaba Maal's first album, he recruited an Irish musician for one of the tracks. In 1995, he brought together a diverse group of musicians—Celtic musicians from Ireland and Brittany, including multi-instrumentalist James McNally and Breton harpist Myrdhin; West African musicians such as Masamba Diop, a master of the talking drum; and contemporary musicians/programmers like Martin Russell for an appearance at the 1995 WOMAD festival and a recording session.

McNally, who has worked with many leading contemporary acts, including U2, the Pogues, Sinead O'Connor, and Peter Gabriel, described the approach of AfroCelts like this: "[W]e try to cross-pollinate and also use electronica to allow people to actually think about their heritage and their culture as something that's not of the past, but still very important and still evolving." We hear one dimension of this cross-pollination in "**Whirl-Y-Reel 1**," a track from *Sound Magic*.

"Whirly-Y-Reel 1" (there is a "Whirl-Y-Reel 2" on the disc) is a fascinating, joyous fusion of old and new, man and machine, African and Celtic. An electronic dance track runs through the entire song. Other instruments join in and drop out. There are Celtic harp/talking drum jams, pipe and whistle duets that sound centuries old and as new as today, a variety of percussion sounds—some synthetic, others computer generated. What's always present is the great groove.

It is truly a sign of the times that an imaginative producer like Emmerson would combine these two traditions and use electronically generated rhythms as the glue that bonds everything together, and that the group would succeed. Throughout this book, we have traced the American offspring of these two traditions: Celtic music shaped the music of the minstrel show, then old time music and country; African music shaped blues, jazz, R&B and so much more. What American society had kept apart for so much of its history comes together in recordings like these. Musically, at least, the integration is seamless.

20-7 "Modern Rock" in the Twenty-First Century

"Modern rock" is a radio format that typically focuses its programming mainly around rock from the eighties to the present. It emerged as a format in the mid-eighties as an outlet for alternative bands. *Billboard* began tracking radio airplay in this form in 1988. It became a more viable platform in the early nineties, in the wake of the crossover success of Nirvana's *Nevermind*. A 1996 decision that enabled communications companies to buy more than one station in a market had two consequences that worked at cross purposes. On the one hand, companies wanted to offer diverse formats in the same market, so that stations owned by the same company weren't in competition with each other. On the other hand, the cost of owning a station grew astronomically, so that station managers had to create playlists that attracted listeners beyond the more adventurous members of the target audience of males whose ages range between 18 and 34. To broaden their audiences, station playlists often went beyond what was generally considered alternative, or switched to an "Active Rock" format, which mixes modern rock and classic rock tracks, or "Mainstream Rock," which generally includes more hard rock and heavy metal than modern rock.

Throughout the new century, the rock radio marketplace has remained fluid, in both format and playlist. As of June 2017, *Billboard* offers ten Rock Charts for albums and singles, including three for what once was modern rock: "Alternative Songs," "Alternative Albums," and "Adult Alternative Songs."

We will use the term "modern rock" here to refer to a branch of second-generation rock-era music. Some of it derives most directly from punk and new wave; other tracks owe more to electronica. However, all of the albums from which the tracks in the table below were drawn delighted at least some critics: all of the albums were highly ranked in various "best of the decade/half decade" lists in publications like *Rolling Stone*, *Spin*, and *NME*. Below you'll find a ten-track playlist with thumbnails sketches of each track.

Cat Power: **Cherokee** (2000)	Transparent but not routine punkish rock beat. Multiple mostly repetitive lines, including acoustic piano, under vocal. Gradual thickening and more active drums toward end of each statement of form. Extensive repetition in vocal lines (chorus has a chorus). Lines simple but layers produce rich fabric of sound. Stylized rock rhythm throughout.
The Strokes: **The Modern Age** (2001)	Punk-inspired drums and syncopated guitar chords set up Velvet Underground-like proto-punk texture and rhythm. Sustained prominently under the vocal. Verse = wall of sound underneath vocal; slow oscillation between two chords; bridge = two different (and unusual) chords; no chorus with melodic hook; abrupt, bizarre ending.
The White Stripes: **Seven Nation Army** (2003)	Repetitious bass riff joined by thumping bass drum beat, snare drum backbeat; provides accompaniment for almost monotonal vocal. Guitar adds harmonized version of riff, which runs throughout the song; guitar riff effectively the chorus. Rock beat implied throughout, but heard explicitly only just before guitar joins riff.
The Killers: **Mr. Brightside** (2004)	High guitar pattern (broken chord) at rock-beat speed; joined by double-time drums; bass joins in with reinforcement of rock rhythmic layer on repeated notes. Punk-like rock beat through bridge and chorus; shimmering texture with high guitar, low bass. New harmony, thickened texture in bridge and chorus, both of which are long.
M.I.A.: **Paper Planes** (2007)	Basic rock beat in drums; horn-like synths support vocal with repeated pattern. Frequent changes of texture: increase in density, and simple sixteen-beat rhythm, then new riff-like lines; intermittent vocal line over synth parts, other part in and out. Discrete blocks of sound under vocal sharply define formal sections.

(Continued)

MGMT: **Kids** (2007)	Synth melodic line over heavy beat/backbeat alternation. Other parts added, along with rock beat. Synth bass and drums main accompanying parts under vocal; intro line above vocal returns; sections defined by addition/subtraction of synth and percussion parts. Long instrumental interlude between statements. Dominant synth line remains unchanged throughout.
Grimes: **Oblivion** (2012)	Simple texture for the first half: bouncy, distinctive bass line at rock beat speed and percussive backbeat support two reverbed, wispy vocal lines; one is wordless. At midpoint, other parts—piano-like synth, more percussion, etc.—augment basic texture; constantly varying—add/subtract parts, but oscillation between two chords unvarying. Second statement begins with bass outlining.
Arctic Monkeys: **Do I Wanna Know?** (2013)	Trademark long guitar/bass line over beat/backbeat percussion. After slightly varied bridge (more instruments), guitar/bass line becomes vocal line as well; serves as chorus when voices reinforce the line. Beginning of second statement of form: bass outlines lines other parts drop out. They return shortly. Guitar/bass line dominant throughout; more prominent than verse vocals. Strong beat and backbeat; implied rock beat.
Vampire Weekend: **Diane Young** (2013)	Multiple texture layers: evocative of 1950s rock and roll in vocal style, basic rock beat drums with occasional double-time breaks, but also sustained synth sounds and irregular synth percussion; frequent changes in density, with surf-guitar style descending lines, sudden contrast.
St. Vincent: **Digital Witness** (2014)	Horn-style synth line, simple rock beat with strong beat and backbeat underneath vocal; abrupt change 1: wall of synth sound, and simple sixteen-beat rhythm in drums. Abrupt change 2: buzzing bass, rock beat and vocals. Denser texture on subsequent statements of form. Synth line repeats with variation in texture.

Although the tracks encompass a wide range of music, they share certain musical features and approaches. Most pervasive is a direct, often punk-influenced approach to rhythm. Most tracks feature a strong beat and/or backbeat; several layer on the rock rhythmic layer in the drum sounds and in repeated bass notes and guitar chords. Occasional sixteen-beat rhythms remain basic. Throughout there is typically little syncopation. The tracks divide almost evenly between basic rock-band instrumentation and synth-generated sounds; in either case, patterns that take time to unfold are repeated through long blocks of sound, or even the entire track. As a rule, variety comes from changes in texture rather than melody. These textural shifts range from abrupt contrasts of blocks of sound to the gradual addition or subtraction of lines. In most cases, the dominant instrumental parts dominate not only more subtle instrumental strands, but also the vocal line.

Like the Green Day song, these ten tracks derive in varying degrees from punk. Philosophically, they come from opposite ends. The Green Day song homogenizes punk by incorporating pop elements, moving it toward a more mainstream approach. In these tracks, we can sense each of the acts trying to define a distinctive musical personality. They use punk and new wave principles as a launching pad for further exploration into the expressive possibilities of the genre.

So it should not be too surprising that critics rated these albums highly because each of the acts has cultivated an expanded sound palette. They may start from basic rock-band instrumentation or electronic analogs, but in either case, their quest for new sounds distinguishes this music from both mainstream rock and earlier alternative. The tracks are bands on a sound spectrum that has characterized some of the most adventurous music of the twenty-first century. The difference between these tracks and those in the following chapter are a matter of degree, not method.

20-8 Rock's Second Generation in the Twenty-First Century

The two bodies of music surveyed in this chapter highlight the lack of alignment between commercial success and creative innovation. The best-selling music of the early twenty-first century that grew out of second-generation rock-era styles included music that moved outside styles—punk, rap, even electronica—toward the center by incorporating more mainstream elements: sung sections in rap and even electronica, less aggressive punk. The albums by Green Day, Christina Aguilera, Eminem, and even Moby had multi-platinum sales in the United States. By contrast, only the Killers album was certified multi-platinum in the United States, and half of the albums did not reach the 500,000 units needed for gold certification.

This dissonance between innovation and commercial success provides compelling evidence that there will be no sequel to the rock revolution of the sixties, where an innovative new sound transformed popular music. The continuing enthusiasm for country music and classic rock and its contemporary counterparts reinforce this evidence. However, the explorations into the innovative use of sound in post-punk music are part of a larger wave of innovation that has brought sound into the forefront as the element that most distinguishes twenty-first century popular music from the music of the previous century. We explore this concept in greater detail in the next chapter .

CHAPTER 21

THE SOUND WORLD OF TWENTY-FIRST CENTURY POPULAR MUSIC

Learning Objectives:

1) List the three features of a sound when presented in combination with other sounds.

2) Comment on the methods used to bring a particular sound to the forefront of a performance.

3) Clarify how melodic "rappification" is executed.

4) Discuss what is meant by a "timeless" form.

5) Define the musical genre: **industrial rock**.

6) Describe the multifaceted attempts to create a twenty-first century sound.

Chapter Introduction

The composer and philosopher John Cage (1912–1992) was the great sound explorer of the twentieth century. No one did more to expand the range of what could be considered "acceptable" sound in a work of music. Many of his peers and critics, even those aligned with the mid century avant-garde, found his music provocative at best and not music at worst. Others found it inspirational. Among the latter were important and innovative rock and electronic musicians: Lennon and McCartney, Frank Zappa, Brian Eno (a seminal figure in ambient music and the sound sculptor for U2's mature sound), Sonic Youth, Richard James (dba Aphex Twin), and Radiohead.

Cage's most famous composition is *4'33"*. To perform it, one or more musicians sit at or with their instrument(s), and move pages of the music at particular time intervals to indicate the move to a new section. After four minutes and thirty-three seconds have passed, the performer signals that the piece has concluded. The premiere of the work took place in an open-air setting in Woodstock, New York, during the summer of 1952, seventeen years before the famous festival. Because there are no conventional musical sounds produced during the performance, *4'33"* has been dubbed Cage's "silent piece." But that nickname misses the point of the work that absolute silence is impossible, and that there is music in the sounds around us.

Experience an interactive version of this era in **MINDTAP**

Cage died in 1992. Had he lived through the end of the decade, he might well have been intrigued and perhaps gratified by the diverse ways in which his ideas and works had shaped the more adventurous popular music of that decade. Perhaps he would have enjoyed the numerous marriages between high- and low-tech sounds and the innovative ways in which sound exploration has stretched the boundaries of popular music.

21-1 Sound Parameters

In the broadest sense of the term, sound is what we hear. In the more limited connotation used in this account, sound refers more specifically to three parameters of these sounds: the resources used to produce the sound, how loud they are, and how they combine. Resources include voices, conventional instruments, digitally generated sounds, samples, and everyday "found" sounds. But a simple resources list—vocals, guitars, bass, drums—may be no more than an outline. Increasingly, we have been more interested in *how* musicians sing, play their instruments, or create sounds digitally, and to what extent they define or individualize the sounds they produce, either through modification of a conventional instrument, or by discovering new sounds.

The overall volume level of a recorded or live performance (or presenting a recording in performance, as DJs do) is the most obvious feature of the music, particularly when it's extremely loud or soft. More subtle, and typically much more interesting, is the relative volume levels of the various parts: which are in the forefront and which are in the background.

When we hear sounds in combination, we want to notice three additional features of sound. One is how many parts there are. The second is the density of the sound—how they are distributed across the audible spectrum: are they close together in pitch or far apart? The third is the ranges (or registers) in which they lie (high, middle, low).

This list of sound attributes is long and necessarily somewhat complex, because the innovative and creative approaches to sound in the nineties (even more than in previous decades) are the antithesis of the garage-band esthetic. This music largely belongs to digital artists, engineers, and producers. It is often music of considerable richness, with many skillfully mixed layers of sound. The innovations have included all of these aspects of sound.

21-1a The Expanding Sound World of the Nineties

New sounds and sound combinations have been part of American popular music since its inception: the core instruments of the minstrel show were unusual, heterogeneous, and largely unprecedented. Sound was a crucial element in the revolutions of the twenties and sixties. However, in defining the music of an era, sound was secondary: aggressive guitars, bass, and drums distinguished the core rock style from sub-styles that were hybrids of rock and established traditions, such as folk rock, soft rock, and country rock. Rhythm, by contrast, played the primary role in linking all of this music and distinguishing it from the music of the previous generation.

However, by the nineties sound had become the primary source of innovation in popular music. Creative musicians employed two complementary strategies: expanding and diversifying sounds and sound combinations, and minimizing musical interest in the other musical elements—melody, harmony, rhythm, and form. Together, these strategies brought sound to the forefront as a differentiating element to an unprecedented degree. They were most obvious in electronica and rap, but they also surfaced, often to a lesser extent, in other music, especially alternative rock.

Widely-used methods for bringing sound to the forefront included:

- An expanded range of timbres, mainly through electronically generated and manipulated sounds, but also occasionally through "found" sounds of various kinds, as well as instruments not typically associated with pre-nineties rock, R&B, country, and pop
- Abrupt, often jarring, contrasts in the various parameters of sound: volume, register, density, and timbre
- Unusual sound combinations, including those avoid or substantially modify genre-specific sound choices
- Sonic "makeup": delicate background sounds that enhance more prominent layers

None of these methods was unprecedented; one can find pre-1990 instances of all of them. What was different was the extent to which they were used, either singly or (more often) in combination with others and with the de-emphasis of other musical elements.

Nineties musicians used specific approaches to the other elements that reduced traditional sources of interest and variety, which in turn focused more attention on the sonic qualities. The most radical was simply to not include them, and there are critically acclaimed tracks without a steady and inviting beat, or something approaching a "singable" melody, chords of any kind, or a form that coalesces into a perceptible pattern. And there were also less radical but still innovative approaches to the other elements. Among widely used were these:

- Rhythmic "signatures": extensive repetition of a distinctive rhythmic pattern that are related to but different from basic "number" beats. These signature rhythms would typically last through long stretches or even the entire length of a track. Often the rhythmic signatures are produced electronically, with a sound that is analogous but different from a conventional drum kit. This helps focus attention on the sound of the rhythm.
- Chord cycles: the continuous repetition of a sequence of two, three or four chords. Typically, these chord sequences effectively form a harmonic loop that repeats extensively: at least through a long section—even the entire track.
- Melodic "rappification": not only interpolating or overlaying rap into an otherwise sung track, but also creating sung sections with fast streams of notes in a conversational rhythm and/or a narrow range, with little melodic interest. As with the other elements, this kind of melody is showcased sonically, with electronically modified vocal sounds or distinctive instrumental sounds.
- "Timeless" form: the repetitive rhythms and the absence or repetition of harmony and melody tend to eliminate or reduce (in frequency and prominence) the milestones that mark off sections in a track. In the most extreme realizations of this approach it's almost as if a track has neither beginning nor end (which is how it's experienced when mixed by a DJ).

These strategies appeared more frequently in electronica and rap than alternative, and typically in a more extreme form. Still, the sound-oriented music of the decade employed at least some of these strategies, as we can hear in a sampling of critically acclaimed music from the nineties. The order of the tracks reflects the extent to which these strategies appear. Aphex Twin's "**#3**" is almost completely about sound; "1979" and "Smell Like Teen Spirit" show rock acts gravitating toward the approach to sound that took shape in the nineties.

Aphex Twin: #3	Distinctive electronic sounds, repetitive harmony, no melody and beat-speed rhythms, little change throughout
Chemical Brothers: **Dig Your Own Hole**	Range of distinctive electronic sounds, including some that sound more like everyday noises rather than conventional musical sounds; rhythmic signature from repeated riff and drum-like percussion pattern; no harmony; little in the way of melody beyond the riff; layers come and go
Basement Jaxx: **Rendez-Vu**	sci-fi–like electronic sounds mixed with Spanish-sounding acoustic guitar; four-chord cycle throughout almost all of the track; sections comprised of multiple layers, including several high-register synth sounds; vocals mainly repeated riffs in a narrow range; drums w/brushes sound playing double-time shuffle rhythm;
Björk: **Human Behavior**	"Empty" sound: voice, military-style snare drum, low register timpani playing repeated pattern, occasional high chord and clusters of high synth sounds. No harmony
Nine Inch Nails: **I Do Not Want This**	Drumlike sounds = rhythmic signature instead of number beat; no harmony, although piano-like riff implies two chords; wide array of electronic sounds, including layers of high register synthesized sounds periodically appearing in background
Nas: **Life's a Bitch**	Sustained high-register synth note; repeated signature rhythm; two-chord cycle throughout; no melody; surprising jazz trumpet at end; open-ended form
Tupac: **California Love**	Broad array of extra percussion, non-pitched sounds: shaker, whistle, etc.; two-chord cycle with distinctive rhythm throughout song; electronic modification of sung sections
Radiohead: **Paranoid Android**	Abrupt and dramatic contrasts in volume between sections, high synth sounds; rich fabric of sound, with several percussion layers;
Smashing Pumpkins: **1979**	Repeated two-chord cycle through much of the song; unusual guitar sound
Nirvana: **Smells Like Teen Spirit**	Four-chord cycle; abrupt contrasts in volume

We have discussed four of these tracks in previous chapters; we focus on two more next.

21-2 Industrial Rock

The industrial rock movement in rock has its roots in two avant-garde trends in classical music: *musique concrète* (the assembling of musical compositions from prerecorded sounds) and electronic music. In the seventies, industrial pioneers such as Throbbing Gristle melded electronic and concrete sounds and noises with percussion sounds and used it as a backdrop for provocative lyrics that explored subjects, such as deviant sexual practices, widely regarded as taboo. Within a decade, adventurous bands had begun to incorporate industrial sounds into other genres, most notably heavy metal and rock.

Among the most creative minds fusing industrial music with rock has been Trent Reznor (b. 1965). Reznor, who studied computer engineering at Allegheny College before dropping out and moving to Cleveland, found work as a handyman at Right Track Studio and received permission to record his own music when the studio was not in use. This solitary work was a prelude to the rest of his career: several demos from his time at Right Track appeared on **Pretty Hate Machine**, his first Nine Inch Nails album.

Nine Inch Nails came into being in 1988, if only in Reznor's head. The name of the group was a seemingly whimsical choice. As Reznor acknowledged in a 1994 interview, Nine Inch Nails was chosen for its appearance—it was easily abbreviated and the reverse *N* made a striking visual image; Reznor claimed it had no literal meaning. Nine Inch Nails has had a schizophrenic existence: in the studio, the "band" is Reznor and his equipment; on tour, it is a working band that Reznor assembles for that purpose. In a 2002 interview with rock journalist Anthony de Curtis, Reznor contrasted his meticulous production in the studio with what he called the "chaotic" experience of performing his music live. It is in the studio that Reznor crafted his distinctive fusion of industrial, punk, and heavy metal. We sample it through "I Do Not Want This," a track from **The Downward Spiral** (1994), his third complete album as Nine Inch Nails.

A common complaint about the music of Nine Inch Nails by "pure" industrial acts and their fans was that Reznor had diluted the impact of industrial rock by shoehorning it into conventional pop songs. If we listen to "I Do Not Want This" reductively, we can hear how the various sections coalesce into the familiar verse/chorus form: there is an instrumental introduction, two verse-like sections, and a two-part chorus, which is repeated. What seems like an instrumental outro transforms into an extended interlude that leads to the shattering climax.

However, if we look at this familiar form not as a mold but as a point of departure, we can hear how Reznor has crafted the form to portray a person perpetually on the edge, and one who occasionally loses it. From the start, Reznor blends industrial and conventional sounds: initially, the mix pairs an electronically generated percussion sound in a distinctive rhythm with a lonely, discordant piano riff that would have sounded completely at home in the atonal music of the early twentieth century. The vocal part—more than spoken, less than sung—enters over this bleak backdrop. The second segment of the verse abruptly shifts to a new, more complex texture, with wordless singing, whispered text, and several layers of electronic percussion sounds. The piano riff returns at the beginning of the chorus, as Reznor sings, "I Do Not Want This" in a quavery voice that sounds on the verge of hysteria, as well as preserving the wordless vocal of the previous section. More electronic sounds, including an insistent repeated note in a low register, produced on a synthesizer, ramp up the tension.

It all boils over in the second part of the chorus, where Reznoz screams, "Don't you tell me how I feel" over heavily distorted power chords played in an irregularly accented sixteen-beat rhythm. The second pass through the form features consistently more activity, as if the protagonist of the lyric is inside a pressure cooker and someone has turned up the heat.

By using industrial sounds and the heavy distortion of heavy metal, and contrasting it with the fragile piano figure, Reznor seems to convey in music as well as words and voice the alienation of the individual in contemporary culture. The juxtaposition of the relentless and impersonal industrial sounds with the vocal parts and piano riff suggest that the distress conveyed in the lyric derives at least in part from the essential impersonality of technology.

The sense of alienation created by technology has been a familiar theme throughout the twentieth century. Its repeated refrains include not only its impersonality, but also its potential for evil—even though the Big Brother world depicted in George Orwell's *1984* has yet to materialize—and the increasingly rapid pace of its evolution. Precisely because the industrial elements are so prominent and persistent in "I Do Not Want This," and because the contrast between those sounds (and the distorted power chords) and the piano figure and vocal sounds is so jarring, it is hard *not* to create a causal relationship between those sounds and the distress projected in the lyric and its spoken/sung/chanted/shouted delivery.

This connection between technology and alienation is reinforced by the contrast in sound world between "I Do Not Want This" and the other tracks on *The Downward Spiral*. By incorporating industrial elements into his music and mixing them with more conventional instruments, Reznor has expanded his sound palette enormously. Not surprisingly, he creates a sound world that is as distinctive as the lyric for each track on his albums. This is one of the most striking and appealing features of his music, especially his later releases.

The Downward Spiral did for Reznor and industrial alternative what *Nevermind* did for Nirvana and grunge. The album peaked at No. 2 on the *Billboard* Top 200 chart and eventually went multiplatinum. Critics continued to laud it: it eventually made top-album lists by *Rolling Stone* and *Q*.

Reznor has continued to develop his technological skills in step with the rapid developments in music-related computer technology, and to share them with those who enjoy his music, sometimes in unusual ways. He has begun sharing multitrack sessions via his website; these have been available in various file formats. Fans can download the file, open it in the application of their choice, and remix it as they choose. In this endeavor, he joins other music/technology pioneers such as Todd Rundgren, whose 1995 album *The Individualist* was among the first to be released via the Internet and an early enhanced CD.

21-3 Radiohead and the New Art Rock of the Nineties

Like the original members of the Red Hot Chili Peppers, the members of Radiohead all went to the same high school: Abingdon School, a private school outside of Oxford. Drummer Phil Selway (b. 1967), guitarist Ed O'Brien (b. 1968), guitarist-vocalist Thom Yorke (b. 1968), bassist Colin Greenwood (b. 1969), and multi-instrumentalist Jonny Greenwood (b. 1971)—Colin's younger brother—formed the band On A Friday in 1986. They went to different universities but continued to practice together over vacations during their college years and came together again as Radiohead in 1992.

Their first album made it quite clear that the group would find their own direction. The album name **Pablo Honey** came from a bit by the Jerky Boys, a comedy group whose CDs consist of irritatingly funny phone calls. "Creep," the single that got them noticed, is very much in the spirit of the times: it is Buddy Holly, deeply depressed. Musically, however, it does little to predict the group's future.

The alienation that marked Radiohead's early work becomes even more apparent in subsequent albums. This may be evident before the first sound: The booklet that comes with **OK Computer** (1997) contains the lyrics displayed almost randomly amid collage-like images. Both words and images are hard to decode. **Kid A** (2000) is even more frugal with content: there are simply fragments of images and no lyrics. It is as if the group is challenging its audience: we have something of value to say to you, but you have to work hard to discover what it is. This attitude extends to their songs, as we hear in "Paranoid Android," from *OK Computer*.

"Paranoid Android" was a boundary-stretching single: this is apparent on even the first hearing, because the song is almost six-and-a-half minutes long, more than double the length of a typical single. The lyrics are at once unremittingly depressing and incoherent. We have the impression of someone (human or android) holding his head and screaming "I can't stand this any more" as he goes mad.

The song is profoundly disturbing, not because the music is as dark as the lyrics, but because it is often so beautiful. It begins with a pan-Latin sound: intricate guitar figuration outlining exotic harmony, plus the shaker associated with Brazilian music and the claves of Cuban music, then a higher-pitched classical guitarlike line. There is no bass yet; the music floats. Yorke delivers the lyric slowly and in measured fashion, which directs our attention more to the haunting, plaintive quality of his voice. The refrain of this part has only two syllables: "what's then"; because there are only two words, our attention goes even more to the sound of his voice. A beautiful halo of sound surrounds it, as bass and a high synthesizer part enrich the texture. All this seems to resonate with the melancholy that is so much a part of Latin culture. Radiohead seems to have captured its essence in this part of the song, although they apply it to a quite different end.

A long transition to a new section begins with a guitar riff set against the Latin percussion. The riff appears on two levels and in two forms. The first statement lines up with four-beat measures. The higher-pitched restatement has a beat removed (four beats + three). The sense of imbalance that the foreshortened riff creates helps set up the next vocal section, which has no apparent connection to the previous section. We get a spark of distortion, then another statement of the riff with full-bore distortion. It gains in power because of the contrast with the two previous sections. After a brief guitar solo, we get a sustained chord, then a slower section with wordless vocal harmonies. Yorke sings over these simple but beautiful harmonies. Little by little, other layers are added; by the time the guitar riff interrupts again, the sonority is rich with vocal parts and sustained stringlike synthesizer sounds. The reprise of the guitar riff is strictly instrumental; with its abrupt ending, it seems to signal a descent into madness.

The facts of the song—its sprawling length; the three distinct sections, plus the reprise of the second section; the strong contrast in character within and between sections; the deliberate delivery of the lyrics—are there. The reading of it is necessarily subjective. I have offered one response to "Paranoid Android"; your response might be quite different.

The more significant point is that the conflicts and discontinuities within the words, within the music, and between the words and music demand that listeners engage with the song in more than a casual way. In particular, the music is complex and rich enough—even though it is also quite accessible—to admit multiple levels of meaning. Not since the Beatles' demise has a group blended accessibility, challenge, sound imagination, and sound variety so artfully. This is rock aspiring to significance.

21–3a Alienation and Fragmentation

The two songs discussed here in more depth create different sound worlds with different resources. "I Do Not Want This" mixes conventional piano and distorted guitar with industrial sounds. "Paranoid Android" adds beautiful synthesized sounds and Latin percussion to the core rock band. These varied sound worlds in turn reflect the different tone and content of the lyrics.

Despite these differences, the songs have two common elements that place them in the nineties. One is the sense of alienation that the lyrics project. In both there is palpable tension between the outside world and the world inside the protagonist's head. The other is a musical feature: the sudden and jarring contrasts that typify much forward-looking music of the nineties. In both tracks, the abrupt shifts from soft to loud seem to suggest a sudden loss of control: flying into a violent rage because the person can't stand it anymore. These shifts magnify the message of the words; as used here, they provide the most consistent and powerful expression of the alienation depicted in the lyrics.

The strong sectional contrasts—sometimes to the point of discontinuity—describe a formal approach that is precisely the opposite of that used in more conventional rock songs. There the refrain establishes the mood of the songs; the function of the verses is to amplify and explain that overall mood. Here, the various sections create their own moods; we are violently whipped from one to the next. This kind of sonic fragmentation within a song is common in recent alternative music, in part because of the critical and commercial success of Nirvana, Nine Inch Nails, and Radiohead.

This small sampling of nineties music hints at the extent to which the increasing prominence of sound helped define a new musical generation. Not surprisingly, it's most evident in the electronic-based genres, but the presence of some of these strategies in alternative rock helped distinguish this music from eighties rock. These strategies would help define a twenty-first century sound in a range of commercially and critically important music.

21–3b Toward A Twenty-First Century Sound

With *Kid A* (2000), their fourth studio album, Radiohead welcomed the new millennium with a comprehensive and artistic answer to the question, "What is a twenty-first century sound?" The album was a significant new direction for the group, and it confounded audiences expecting the band to continue along the exploratory path of their previous album *OK Computer*. That album had established their reputation as arguably the most adventurous and artistically significant rock band of the nineties. Many critics and fans looked forward with keen anticipation to their next release, which they hoped would chart future directions in rock.

During the long interval between albums, Radiohead had collectively agreed that they needed a different direction—Yorke would comment in an interview just before the release of *Kid A* that he felt that rock had "run its course." Following Yorke's lead, the band absorbed a range of styles: electronic artists, most notably Björk and Aphex Twin, hip-hop artists like Blackalicious, mid twentieth century avant-garde jazz and electronic sources. They assembled their new album over a three-year period, after considerable trial and error and numerous false starts. The end product was something that few if any expected.

Kid A was a rock album only in the sense that it is music released by a rock band—in principle much like the cutting-edge music of Dylan and the Beatles in the mid-sixties. The familiar conventions of first- or second-generation rock—the rhythms, instruments, forms—are largely absent. Instead there are broad and varied tapestries of sound inspired by the music that the band had been studying—and sampling.

This new twenty-first century sound is apparent from the outset. The opening track, **"Everything In Its Right Place"** begins with a repeated keyboard pattern that seems to hang in time—there is no steady timekeeping underneath—which is embedded in a cloud of electronic and electronically processed sounds. Yorke's vocal line is minimalistic, often focusing on a single pitch. Sonically, the track is a grand arch, cresting in the middle through the addition of numerous parts, often in different rhythms, or with no regular rhythm at all, and receding to the end as the parts fade out.

What makes the track so novel—and so compelling—is that its expressive weight is almost exclusively in sound: the novelty of the timbres and the mixing of them. Both the vocal line and keyboard part are extremely repetitious: shifts from one pattern to the next occur infrequently. It is the variations in timbre, volume, and density that give the music its shape and its appeal.

By demonstrating its expressive potential, Radiohead affirmed the validity of sound as a primary source of musical interest. What made this album so radical and so confusing to many critics and fans was the decisive break with or transmutation of virtually all rock conventions. The innovation was not so much in what they did—there were precedents for everything, but more how all-in they went in their search for a new direction and the artistry with which they realized their conception. Their approach built on the complementary strategies—highlight sound elements; minimize musical interest in the other elements—that they helped pioneer during the nineties. These strategies became the key elements in a twenty-first century approach to sound, though seldom to the extent heard in *Kid A*.

21-4 Mainstreaming Sound in the Twenty-First Century

The sound-centric innovations of the nineties found more widespread application in the new century. Increasingly, it was found in music that climbed its way to the upper rungs of the charts and onto "best of" lists, which was not the case at the end of the previous century.

What's striking about the development of a twenty-first century approach to sound is how its innovations turn twentieth century practice on its head. Throughout the twentieth century, the path to innovation was to coalesce around a new set of conventions: new beats, sounds, melody building. Even though the revolutionary rock of the sixties was far more eclectic and assimilative than pre-rock pop, there were still common musical conventions. These conventions linked a wide and disparate body of new music and distinguished it from the established styles of the fifties.

In particular, rock-defining rhythms are like the beef in a hamburger: one can dress it up with exotic cheeses, rolls, and sauces, or simply slap it in a bun with some American cheese, but it's not a hamburger without the beef. By contrast, the post-nineties approach to sound and its role was much more like a buffet: a virtually infinite smorgasbord of sounds and sound combinations, from which artists could choose any sounds that suited their concept for a particular track.

There is nothing in this approach comparable to the number beats. As we'll encounter in the music below, this approach is defined not only by what's included but also what's *not* included.

We offer thumbnail sketches of widely varied instances of this approach in a broad range of music: hip-hop, R&B, pop, alternative. All of the tracks feature commercially successful and/or critically acclaimed acts whose music sounds as if it is from this century.

Linkin Park: **In The End** (2000)	Two speeds simultaneously: rap + drums; slow vocal line. Repeated chord progressions; opening sound combination: piano, synth cello, electronic noise; piano loop throughout.
Arcade Fire: **Rebellion (Lies)** 2004	Repetitive, narrow-ranged melody, two long-term chord cycles, separation between loud low bass and loud high piano, varying string textures behind prominent instruments and voices.
Beyoncé: **Halo** 2008	Classically-inspired piano intro and interlude; patter-like vocal line, composite rhythmic signature; progression from "empty" sound in verse—mainly voice, bass, percussion— to dense, multilayered chorus with backup vocal echos and string "halo"
Coldplay: **Viva La Vida** (2008)	String band replaces rock band as core instruments; other unusual instrumental sounds: for example timpani, church bell, choir. Chord cycles through much of track. String pattern = rhythmic signature.
Lady Gaga: **Bad Romance** (2009)	Array of electronic sounds, from buzzing bass through high white noise; different sound palette for verse, bridge, chorus. Abrupt and striking contrasts between sections. Chord cycles in chorus; no harmony in verse. Richly layered, especially in chorus
Bon Iver: **Holocene** (2011)	Rhythmic signature in guitar accompaniment, enhanced with drums later in track; complex, slow moving, slightly varying chord cycle; melody made up of short phrase floats on accompaniment, low register saved for emphasis; gradual buildup through track; subtle background sounds throughout
Adele: **Turning Tables** (2011)	Just piano and strings accompaniment to vocal; distinctive chord cycle and accompaniment pattern; sharp contrasts between sections, and dramatic use of silence
Kanye West: **On Sight** (2013)	Rhythmic signature played by synth sounds composite; abrupt contrasts through samples; no harmony under rap, instead repeated riff-like patterns
James Blake: **Retrograde** (2013)	Minimalist beginning: voice, piano, then basic beat/ backbeat. Electronic siren-like sounds, low-end bass line reinforcement in middle; thickening toward end of siren sounds, then abrupt halt.

(Continued)

Taylor Swift: **Blank Space** (2014)	Electronic soundscape intro, accompaniment for chatty verse (no harmony at beginning). Rhythmic signature when percussion ends. Sustained sounds outline four-chord cycle in chorus; numerous background sounds flesh out sound behind Swift.
Drake, et al.: **One Dance** (2016)	Jarring interaction between calypso-like rhythm in percussion and offbeat piano chords; electronic sounds, more electronic sounds behind Drake's vocal; several background vocal sounds, constant addition and subtraction of electronic sound fragments; abrupt end.

Despite their obvious differences, these tracks share a common focus on making sound prominent and distinctive. They differ widely in the degree to which they commit to a break from the past, and the individual ways in which they realize their sound conception.

For example, **Arcade Fire's "Rebellion (Lies)"** traces its lineage back at least to the sixties, in the proto-punk of the Velvet Underground's song **"I'm Waiting for the Man**." What gives the track a more contemporary sound are its sound features: the special string instrument effects, and the gradual scaling up of volume and density from verse through chorus. These give the song a shape despite the relentless punk-influenced rhythm and repetitive melodic fragments.

By contrast, Adele gives **"Turning Tables"** a fresh sound mainly through subtraction: no bass, guitar, drums, or electronics. Instead, there are just piano and symphonic strings behind her voice. In these sound choices, the song has more in common with classical song from the nineteenth century than it does with rock or pop from the nineties.

There is no one element of the strategy that predominates. The closest to a universal might well be the "sonic makeup": more than ever before, popular music belongs to producers and electronic artists, and tech companies have brought sophisticated software to the marketplace at far more affordable price points.

21-5 Sound, Comfort Music, and the Balance Among Melody, Rhythm, and Sound

All of the twenty-first century music mentioned in this unit has attracted a large and supportive audience that finds it appealing, and much of it is beautiful in innovative, even unprecedented, ways. So it's worth pondering why this sound-centric music hasn't become the dominant music of this time, in the way that the fox-trot song did in the twenties and thirties, or the way rock did in the sixties and seventies.

Our access to an almost unlimited amount of music has played a role in diffusing listeners' preferences. The ease with which we can choose among millions of recordings was unimaginable before the digital age. So our tastes are not constrained by the relatively limited availability of music on the radio and in record stores, as they were during the modern and rock revolutions.

There are also music-related reasons that help account for the absence of a new dominant style. First, the nature of sound-related innovation encouraged individuality, not adherence to a set of conventions. Second, sound elements do not engage us physically the way melody or rhythm do. There's no aspect of sound comparable to singing along during the chorus or moving in time with the beat. Third, the most popular music of the modern and rock revolutions pulled listeners in and kept them there through across-the-board access and appeal: not only because of new sounds and a new beat, but also because of catchy riff-based melodies and formal milestones that helped listeners navigate through a song. So it would seem that for a significant percentage of listeners, the stylized rhythms and suppressed melodic and harmonic interest of much twenty-first century popular music render the music less appealing than earlier music, where sound, rhythm, and especially melody (and the lyrics that are sung to it) are more in balance.

In the mid-2010s, the audience for sixties and seventies music is far greater and more diverse than the audience for twenties and thirties music during the sixties and seventies. Some of this has to do with the quality and accessibility of modern-era music during the early rock era. The recordings of the twenties and thirties were inferior and originally available in outdated formats—when "albums" really were albums of 78 rpm discs—and there was little financial incentive to reissue them, because older styles and artists were no longer fashionable. By contrast, established acts from the last century routinely outdraw twenty-first century artists on concert tours. Their music, even remastered reissues, continues to sell well and attract listeners on streaming services. Today there is nothing approaching the pressure that established artists felt during the rock revolution to update their sound—pressure so intense that it drove Frank Sinatra into a brief retirement.

Considerable evidence suggests that we live in a transformative time. The current generation is the first in over a century where the music of earlier generations remains as vital a part of our musical life as the most current music. This vitality is more than an exercise in nostalgia: younger artists continue to breathe new life into traditional styles, on their own or even in collaboration with those whom they listened to for inspiration. Today's listeners have the best of both worlds: they can pick and choose from contemporary offerings according to their taste and easily revisit high quality versions of music from an earlier time. It's an unprecedented and unmixed blessing.

Point/Counterpoint: Is the Rock Era Over?

To return to Thom Yorke's comment about rock having "run its course," here's the context of that exchange, as recorded in 2000 in an interview with Andrew Smith in The Guardian. It was published the day before the release of *Kid A*:

Smith: Do you have any sympathy with the idea that rock has run its course and there's nothing left to do but trot out the tired clichés?

Yorke: Oh yeah, absolutely. Totally. I 100 percent agree with it.

Smith: But Radiohead are regarded as one of the few groups capable of taking it anywhere new.

Yorke: God help us if we are. The thing I have a problem with is the fact that so much of what people—of what journalists—term rock music now is really not based on the music itself, but based on the lifestyle that goes with it. It's like a lifestyle choice . . . That doesn't mean that people should stop using drums and guitars, but why stand up and say, "I'm a rock star—in ten years time I'm going to get f*cked up on smack . . ." The mythology around it has run its course and is stale and uncreative now, and it has been destroying the people who've been trying to make the music.

I worry about that in the context of the album we've just done, as well. I absolutely want no part in any suggestions that our decision to use some electronic instruments is some kind of lifestyle choice. It's not. You use the instrument to help you get across a certain thing that you want to get across. That's all.

In the course of this account, we have provided content that justifies answering the question, "Is the rock era over?" with both a "no" and a "yes." Which answer one chooses depends largely on perspective.

From a commercial perspective, the answer is unquestionably "no." Classic rock is the dominant radio format. Both new releases and reissues of music by classic rock acts continue to sell well, and their tours continue to attract large audiences.

Moreover, subsequent generations of musicians working within this musical tradition are finding new things to say, as we noted in our discussion of Alicia Keys and the Tedeschi Trucks Band.

Finally, there has not been a revolutionary new music that has emerged to supplant rock as the dominant style. Instead, rock-era music has continued to evolve away from the core rock style that coalesced during the sixties to the point that the stylistic connection between AC/DC's "Rock and Roll Train" and Drake's "One Dance" is not obvious if we simply hear the tracks one after the other, without the intervening evolutionary steps.

However, from a music-historical perspective, the answer is effectively "yes." The rock revolution overthrew the established order in popular music. The break with the past was sudden and decisive. Almost overnight, rock became commercially and culturally dominant, and prerock genres turned however reluctantly to rock in order to become relevant.

But rock was also the continuation of an evolutionary process that began in the first part of the twentieth century and that had its first revolution in the twenties. The surest guide to the beginning, development, and end of this process is its rhythmic foundation. As we noted on numerous occasions, the "number" beats have been the most prevalent style feature of a musical generation. Almost all of the songs of the 1910s and 1920s were supported with the two-beat rhythm of the foxtrot. In the latter half of the thirties, swing brought four-beat rhythms into the mainstream, and set up the opposition of swing and sweet. The eight-beat rhythm of rock took shape in the fifties and reached maturity in the late sixties. Disco brought sixteen-beat rhythms into the mainstream; the interplay between eight- and sixteen-beat rhythms has continued from the eighties to the present. The common thread and consistent reference point in this evolutionary process has been the backbeat, which we began to hear in recordings from the twenties and which is still present in much of today's music. More than any other musical feature, the number beats linked the popular music of almost all of the twentieth century, and articulated four generations of popular music.

This evolutionary process came to an end in the nineties. Its logical continuation, a 32-beat (!) rhythm, is not practical even at moderate dance tempos. Most rock-era musicians have continued to use the established rhythms, but the more forward-looking musicians were exploring nongeneric alternatives, as we highlighted in the last two chapters.

When this evolutionary process finally "ran its course," musicians like Yorke looked elsewhere for new inspiration. He and others found it in sound, but sound has been a differentiating, rather than a unifying, feature. So we are still waiting for a different direction. The rock revolution occurred 40 years after the modern revolution of the twenties. Fifty years after the rock revolution, we are still waiting for a revolutionary new music that will cement rock's status as a classic music.

However, the most compelling reason involved the music itself. During the course of the twentieth century, popular music went from music in which melody was dominant to styles in which rhythm was dominant. At the turn of the previous century, the most popular songs were waltz songs like "Take Me Out to the Ball Game," where the melody was the most prominent and distinctive feature. The new dance music of the teens and twenties and its integration into popular song began the shift toward more rhythmically engaging music, not only with the bouncy two-beat rhythm of the fox trot but also with melodies built from syncopated riffs. Each successive stage of this evolution was defined principally by a more active rhythmic foundation: the four-beat rhythm of swing in the late thirties and forties, the eight-beat rhythm of rock in the sixties, and the sixteen-beat rhythms that mainstreamed in the seventies and eighties. At the same time, the rhythmic elements of melody became more prominent: riffs repeated syncopated patterns rather developing into more melodically varied parts. In addition, percussive sounds became more prominent, especially during the latter half of the century; eventually even the voice became a percussion instrument with rap.

By the nineties, this large-scale evolutionary shift had reached an end point. The pendulum had swung completely from melody to rhythm, as heard in the two important new trends of the eighties, techno and rap. A 32-beat rhythm was theoretically possible but functionally impractical. It was apparent to creative minds that further innovation required a new direction altogether. It was found in sound.

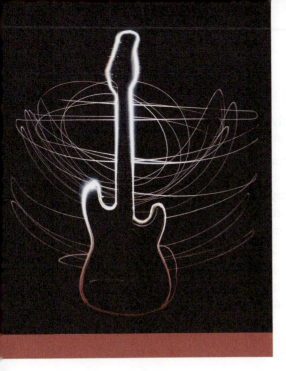

GLOSSARY

A

accents   A musical event that stands out from its neighbors because of a change in one or more musical elements. The most common sources of accent are intensity (the event is louder), duration (longer), density (the event contains more parts), or pitch (higher or lower).

acoustic recording   An early recording process in which sound vibrations were transferred directly to the recording medium (cylinder or disc) by means of a large horn or cone. In 1925 it was replaced by electric recording.

Afropop   A fusion of West African and pop music.

album-oriented radio   A type of FM radio format that emphasized a restricted playlist.

alternative   A term to describe a family of rock-related, punk-inspired styles that began in the early eighties and continues into the twenty-first century.

amplifier   A piece of equipment that can increase the strength of an electric signal.

arpeggios   A chord whose pitches are performed one after the other instead of simultaneously. Also called broken chord.

art rock   A rock substyle that sought to elevate rock from teen entertainment to artistic statement, often by drawing on or reworking classical compositions (e.g., Emerson, Lake, and Palmer's version of Mussorgsky's Pictures at an Exhibition). Art rock was often distinguished by the use of electronic effects and mood music-like textures far removed from the propulsive rhythms of early rock.

B

backbeat   A percussive accent occurring regularly on the second beat of beat pairs: 1 2 1 2 or 1 2 3 4.

beat   (1) The rhythmic quality of a piece of music that invites a physical response ("that song has a good beat"). (2) The (usually) regular marking of time at walking/dancing/moving speed (usually between 72 and 144 beats per minute). (3) The rhythmic foundation of a style or substyle, distinguished by the consistent use of regular rhythms and rhythmic patterns: a two-beat, a rock beat, a shuffle beat.

big band   Swing-era or swing-style music performed by a big band.

blackface   Minstrel show practice in which white and (later) black performers applied burnt cork to darken their complexion.

bluegrass   An updated version of country's old-time string band music. Bluegrass developed in the late 1940s under the guidance of mandolinist Bill Monroe.

bop   A jazz style that developed in the 1940s, characterized by fast tempos, irregular streams of notes, and considerable rhythmic conflict.

bossa nova   A samba-based, jazz-influenced Brazilian popular-song style that became popular in the United States in the early 1960s.

break dancing   A vigorous dance form associated with hip-hop music and culture.

British invasion   An influx of British bands in the early 60s whose styles borrowed from American pop, rock and roll, rhythm and blues, and early blues and who, in turn, were to have a profound influence in the emergence of rock.

C

call-and-response   A rapid exchange, usually of riffs, between two different timbres: solo voice and guitar; solo voice and choir; or saxophones and trumpets.

Charleston   The most popular of the vigorous new dances of the early 1920s.

chord progression   A sequence of chords. Many of the chord progressions in popular music follow well-used patterns, such as the chord progressions for "Heart and Soul" and "La Bamba."

chords   A group of pitches considered as a single unit. The notes of a chord may be played simultaneously, or they may be played in a series as an arpeggio.

chorus   (1) A large singing group. (2) In verse/chorus and rock songs, that part of a song in which both melody and lyrics are repeated. (3) In blues and Tin Pan Alley songs, one statement of the melody.

classic blues   The popular blues style of the 1920s, which typically featured a woman singing the blues (e.g., Bessie Smith) accompanied by one or more jazz musicians.

clave rhythm   The characteristic rhythm of Afro-Cuban music. It can be represented as: //X x x X x x X x // x x x X x X x x x //. The x's indicate an eight-beat rhythm; X's are accented notes. To create a reverse clave rhythm, switch the two measures.

concept album   A rock-era album which represented a unified artistic vision rather than a compilation of a group or individual's songs.

country blues   A family of African American folk blues styles that flourished in the rural South. Country blues differs from commercial blues mainly in its accompanying instrument-usually acoustic guitar-and its tendency toward less regular forms.

country music   A music genre which emerged out of the commercialization, broadcasting, and recording of southern folk music.

country rock   Music combining a strong honky-tonk two-beat with a clear, simple rock rhythm.

cover version   Recording of a song by an act other than the first to record it

deconstruction   Construction of a song out of several components, which can be digitally modified, added to, and otherwise manipulated to create other versions of the song.

D

deep blues   Early acoustic blues originating from the Missis-sippi and surrounding areas.

disco   A dance music that rose to popularity in the mid seventies. Disco songs typically had a relentless beat; a complex rhythmic texture, usually with a 16-beat rhythm; and rich orchestration, typically an augmented rhythm section with horns and strings.

doo-wop   A pop-oriented R&B genre that typically featured remakes of popular standards or pop-style originals sung by black vocal groups. Doo-wop died out in the early 1960s with the rise of the girl groups and Motown.

E

eight-beat rhythm   A rhythmic template in which the fastest rhythmic layer moves twice the speed of the beat: two times per beat! four beats = 8-beat rhythm. Also called a "rock beat" because it is the most common rhythmic foundation in early rock and punk.

electronica   The umbrella term for a large and varied family of musical styles: house, techno, trance, ambient, jungle, drum & bass, industrial dance, and many more.

F

folk music   Music made by a group of people (e.g., Cajuns, Navahos, or whites from rural Appalachia), mostly without formal musical training, primarily for their own amusement or for the amusement of others in the group. Within the group, folk music is transmitted orally. Within the popular tradition, folk music has also referred to folksongs sung by commercial musicians (e.g., the Kingston Trio) or music with elements of folk style (e.g., the folk rock of the late 1960s).

form   The organization of a musical work in time.

fox-trot   A popular social dance of the 1920s and 30s that introduced a clearly black beat into mainstream culture.

funk   An R&B-derived style that developed in the 1970s, primarily under the guidance of George Clinton. It is character-ized mainly by dense textures (bands may include eight or more musicians) and complex, often sixteen-beat rhythms.

G

gangsta rap   A form of rap which emerged in the late 80s and expressed the violence of inner-city life.

genre   Stylistic category.

glam rock   A rock style of the early 1970s in which theatrical elements—makeup, outlandish dress—were prominent. David Bowie, in his various incarnations, is considered by many to be the major figure in glam rock.

gospel   A family of religious music styles: there is white and black gospel music. Black gospel music has had the more pro-found influence on popular music by far. Created around 1930 by Thomas Dorsey and others, gospel has influenced popular singing, especially rhythm and blues, since the early 1950s.

grunge   A style of rock music which emerged in the late 80s which fused punk disaffection with the power and distortion of heavy metal.

H

harmonics   Sound created on a stringed instrument by depressing the string only partway at certain points, creating higher-pitched sounds with a distinctive ring

harmony   Chords and the study of chord progressions.

headbanging   An high-energy, violent dance which evolved around heavy metal.

heavy metal   A hard rock style that developed in the early 1970s, featuring often ear-splitting volume; heavy use of distortion; simplified chord progressions and melodies; lyrics that reflect adolescent, often male preoccupations; and elaborate stage shows.

hip-hop   A term used to describe the African American culture from which rap emerged. Its artistic expressions include not only rap but also break dancing and graffiti.

hokum   An upbeat blues style that emerged between the first and second world wars.

house music   An early techno style based originally in Chicago; it was a low-budget continuation of disco.

improvisation   The act of creating music spontaneously rather than performing a previously learned song the same way every time. Improvisation is one of the key elements in jazz. It gives musicians the opportunity to express inspirations and react to situations; requires virtuosity, melodic inventiveness, personal-ity, and the ability to swing.

I

inflection   Moment-to-moment changes in dynamic level. Aretha Franklin sings in a highly inflected style.

instrumentation   Literally, the instruments chosen to perform a particular score; broadly, the instrumental and vocal accompaniment for a recording.

interpolation   The insertion of a song into a musical comedy for which it was not written. Interpolation was common in the early years of musical comedy, when producers would insert a song into a show simply because it was a hit.

J

jazz   A group of popular related styles primarily for listening. Jazz is usually distinguished from the other popular music of an era by greater rhythmic freedom (more syncopation and/or less insistent beat keeping), extensive improvisation, and more adventurous harmony. There are two families of jazz styles: those based on a four-beat rhythm and those based on a rock or 16-beat rhythm.

jump band   In the late 1940s, a small band—rhythm section plus a few horns that played a rhythm-and-blues style influenced by big-band swing and electric blues. Saxophonist/ vocalist Louis Jordan was a key performer in this style.

L

loops   A short sound file that can be repeated or combined with other loops to create a background for a song.

M

mainstream   Prevailing styles.

majors   Major record labels.

mambo   First twentieth-century Latin dance fads to develop on American soil; it merged authentic Afro-Cuban *son* with big-band horns and riffs

march   Music composed in regularly accented, usually duple meter that is appropriate to accompany marching; a composition in the style of march music.

measure   A consistent grouping of beats. A waltz has measures containing three beats; a march has measures with two beats. Also called bar.

medley   A group of songs connected by musical interludes.

melody   The most musically interesting part of a musical texture. The melody is typically distinguished from other parts by the interest and individuality of its contour and rhythm.

mento   The Jamaican popular music of the early 1950s.

microphones   A device that converts sound waves into an electric signal. The microphone has been in use in popular music since the 1920s.

minstrel-show   A form of stage entertainment distinguished by cruel parodies of African Americans. Minstrelsy was popular from the early 1840s to the end of the nineteenth century.

mix   A series of songs or dance tracks seamlessly connected by a disc jockey.

modal harmony   Chords built from modal scales, rather than major and minor scales. Modal scales are common in British folk music.

Motown   A set of stylistic features heard in sixties Motown recordings: melodic saturation, a good mellow beat, a broad spectrum of sound and a predictable format.

MTV   A cable network which began broadcasting music videos in 1981.

multitrack recording   The process of recording each part of a performance separately, then mixing them into a complete performance. The Beatles, along with their producer George Martin, were among the first to take full advantage of multi-track recording techniques.

musique concrète   Music created by using prerecorded sounds.

N

New Orleans jazz   Style of jazz performance based on the early bands that performed in and around New Orleans; revived in the late 1940s, it is based on collective improvisa-tion and quick tempos. The front-line instruments usually include cornet or trumpet, clarinet, and trombone, with a rhythm section usually including banjo, tuba, and sometimes piano. Also called Dixieland jazz.

new wave   The "back to basics" movement within rock beginning in the late 1970s, featuring simplified instrumentation and basic chords and melodies. An early new wave band was the Talking Heads.

no wave   Post-punk substyle, characterized by the music of Sonic Youth.

O

obbligato   A second melody playing under the main melody.

overdubbing   The process of recording an additional part onto an existing recording.

P

Payola   The practice of record companies' bribing disk jokeys to secure airplay for their records.

Philadelphia sound   An early 70s style which revised, expanded upon, and modernized the Motown sound.

pitch   The relative highness or lowness of a musical sound, determined by the frequency with which it vibrates.

popular music   Music that appeals to a mass audience, is intended to have wide appeal, and has a sound and a style distinct from classical or folk music.

psychedelic rock   A rock substyle defined not by a musical feature but simply by the music's ability to evoke or enhance the drug experience.

punk   A rock style that emerged in the late 1970s characterized musically by relatively simple instrumentation, rhythms, and production. The Ramones and the Sex Pistols were among the best-known punk bands.

Q

queercore   A movement which reacted against mainstream gay and lesbian views and musically centered around punk and industrial rock.

R

race records   A term that came into use in the early 1920s to describe recordings by African American artists intended for sale primarily in the African American community.

ragtime   A popular style at the turn of the twentieth century that mixed European forms, harmony, and textures with African-inspired syncopation. Ragtime began as a piano music, but soon the term was applied to any music—song and dance as well as piano music—that had some syncopation.

rap   A musical style of the 1980s and beyond characterized by a rhymed text spoken in a heightened voice over a repetitive, mostly rhythmic accompaniment.

rave   A huge dance party conducted in a large space: outdoors, an abandoned warehouse, or even a large club. Ecstasy and other "designer" drugs were very much part of the scene; they suppressed the need to eat or sleep.

reggae   The most widely known Jamaican popular music, it has a distinctive, intoxicating rhythm. It emerged around 1970 in the music of Jimmy Cliff, Bob Marley, and others.

Revue   A type of stage entertainment popular in the first third of the century. Revues were topical; they often lampooned prominent public figures. They had a flimsy plot, designed to link—however loosely—a series of songs, dance numbers, and comedy routines.

rhythm and blues   A term used since the mid forties to describe African American popular styles, especially those influenced by blues and/or dance music.

rhythm section   The part of a musical group that supplies the rhythmic and harmonic foundation of a performance. Usually includes at least one chord instrument (guitar, piano, or key-board), a bass instrument, and a percussion instrument (typically the drum set).

rhythm   The time dimension of music. The cumulative result of musical events as they happen over time.

riff   A short (two to seven pitches), rhythmically interesting melodic idea.

riot grrrl   A 90s militant feminist movement which supported post-punk bands.

rock beat   Eight evenly spaced sounds per measure (or two per beat) over a strong backbeat.

Rock steady   Ska's evolution in the latter half of the sixties, in which musicians added a backbeat layer over the afterbeats.

rockabilly   According to Carl Perkins, a country take on rhythm and blues, performed mainly by white Southerners, that combined elements of country music with rock and roll. Rockabilly was most popular in the mid fifties.

S

samples   A small sound file. There are two basic kinds of samples in common use. One is the recorded sound of a voice or group of voices, an instrument (such as a grand piano) or group of instruments (a violin section), or some other sound. This sound can then be activated through another device. The other main kind of sampling involves lifting short excerpts from existing recordings to use in a new recording, much like a visual artist will use found objects to create a collage or assemblage. It has been a staple of rap background tracks since the technology became available in the mid eighties.

singer-songwriters   A term that came into use around 1970 to describe songwriters who performed their own music. The music of singer-songwriters was generally characterized by an emphasis on melody, a folk-like accompaniment, and a relatively low dynamic level.

sixteen-beat rhythm   A rhythmic template in which the fastest rhythmic layer moves four times the speed of the beat: 4 times per beat 3 4 beats 5 16-beat rhythm. First popularized in disco and funk, it has been the most widely used style beat since the early eighties.

ska   The dominant Jamaican popular music through the first part of the 1960s. The most distinctive feature of ska is a strong after -beat: a strong, crisp chunk on the latter part of each beat.

soul   A term used widely in the 1960s by both white and black Americans to describe popular music by African Americans, particularly music, like that of James Brown, marginally influenced by pop or white rock styles.

standard   A song that remains popular well after its initial appearance; songs that live on in recordings, films, and live performances.

style   The set of those common features found in the music of a time, place, culture, or individual.

Surf music   A regional rock from California notable for high-register close harmony vocals and innovative guitar effects.

swing   Rhythmic play over a four-beat rhythm

syncopations   Accents that come between the beats of a regular rhythm, rather than with them.

synthesizers   A family of electronic instruments in which sounds are produced electronically, either by generating a waveform within the machine or by digitally recording acoustic sounds (e.g., the tones of a piano). Most, but not all, synthesizers are operated by a keyboard.

T

techno   Post-disco dance music in which most or all of the sounds are electronically generated.

tempo   The speed of the beat.

textures   The relationship of the parts in a musical performance.

thumb-brush   An early country guitar style in which the performer plays the melody on the lower strings and, between melody notes, brushes the chords on the upper strings. It was first popularized by Maybelle Carter.

timbre   The distinctive tone quality of a voice or an instrument.

Tin Pan Alley A nickname for a section of East 28th Street in New York City, where many music publishers had their offices. Also, the styles of the songs created in the first half of the century for these publishers: a Tin Pan Alley song refers to songs by Irving Berlin, George Gershwin, and their contemporaries.

toasting The practice developed by Jamaican disc jockeys of delivering a steady stream of patter. Much of it was topical, even personal: they would pick out, and sometimes pick on, people in the crowd that had gathered around. Toasting is a direct forerunner of rap: both initially featured topical, humorous commentary over pre-existing music.

trio One of the two main sections of a march, in a different key.

triplet Rhythmic pattern that divides each beat into three equal parts

twelve-bar blues The most widely used form for one chorus of a blues song. It is defined principally by its chord progression, which features I, IV, and V in a consistent pattern over twelve bars: I(1), I(3) / IV(5), I(7) / V(9), I(11). The 12- bar blues form is used in both vocal and instrumental songs. In sung 12- bar blues songs, the typical lyric is a rhymed couplet, with the first line repeated.

two-beat The division of the measure into two primary beats or accents; the rhythmic basis of the fox trot and other early syncopated instrumental styles.

U

unison Two performers playing the same pitch.

V

verse/chorus The most popular song form of the late nineteenth century. The verse tells a story in several stages (this section is strophic, i.e., different words are set to the same melody), whereas the chorus, which comes at the end of each verse, repeats both words and melody to reinforce the main message of the song. In early verse/chorus songs, the chorus was often sung by a small group, usually a quartet.

vibrato Subtle alteration of the pitch of a note.

W

western swing A swing style of country music which emerged in the Southwest in the 1930s.

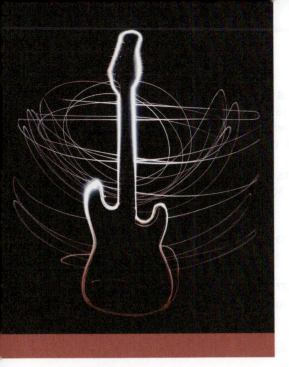

INDEX